13th International Conference on Computational Semantics (IWCS 2019)

Long Papers

Gothenburg, Sweden
23-27 May 2019

ISBN: 978-1-5108-8760-2

IWCS 2019

**Proceedings of the 13th International Conference on
Computational Semantics - Long Papers**

23–27 May, 2019
University of Gothenburg
Gothenburg, Sweden

Introduction

Welcome to the 13th edition of the International Conference on Computational Semantics (IWCS 2019) in Gothenburg. The aim of IWCS is to bring together researchers interested in any aspects of the annotation, representation and computation of meaning in natural language, whether this is from a lexical or structural semantic perspective. It embraces both symbolic and machine learning approaches to computational semantics, and everything in between. This is reflected in the themes of the sessions which take place over full 3 days. The programme starts with formal and grammatical approaches to the representation and computation of meaning, interaction of these approaches with distributional approaches, explore the issues related to entailment, semantic relations and frames, and unsupervised learning of word embeddings and semantic representations, including those that involve information from other modalities such as images. Overall, the papers capture a good overview of different angles from which the computational approach to natural language semantics can be studied.

The talks of our three keynote speakers also reflect these themes. The work of Mehrnoosh Sadrzadeh focuses on combination categorial grammars with word- and sentence embeddings for disambiguation of sentences with VP ellipsis. The work of Ellie Pavlick focuses on the evaluation of the state-of-the art data-driven models of language for what they "understand" in terms of inference and what is their internal structure. Finally, the work of Raffaella Bernardi focuses on conversational agents that learn grounded language in visual information through interactions with other agents. We are delighted they have accepted our invitation and we are looking forward to their talks. We include the abstract of their talks in this volume.

In total, we accepted 25 long papers (51% of submissions), 10 short papers (44% of submissions) and 7 student papers (54% of submissions) following the recommendations of our peer reviewers. Each paper was reviewed by three experts. We are extremely grateful to the Programme Committee members for their detailed and helpful reviews. The long and student papers will be presented either as talks or posters, while short papers will be presented as posters. Overall, there are 7 sessions of talks and 2 poster sessions (introduced by short lighting talks) which we organised according to the progression of the themes over 3 days, starting each day with a keynote talk. The sessions are organised in a way to allow plenty of time in between to allow participants to initiate discussions over a Swedish *fika*.

To encourage a broader participation of students we organised a student track where the papers have undergone the same quality review as long papers but at the same time the reviewers were instructed to provide comments that are beneficial to their authors to develop their work. To this end we also awarded a Best Student Paper Award.

The conference is preceded by 5 workshops on semantic annotation, meaning relations, types and frames, vector semantics and dialogue, and on interactions between natural language processing and theoretical computer science. In addition to the workshops, this year there is also a shared task on semantic parsing. The workshops and the shared task will take place over the two days preceding the conference.

There will be two social events. A reception which is sponsored by the City of Gothenburg will be opened by the Lord Mayor of Gothenburg and will take place on the evening of the second day of the workshops and before the main conference. A conference dinner will take place in Liseberg Amusement Park where participants will also get a chance to try some of their attractions.

IWCS 2019 has received general financial support (covering over a half of the costs) from the Centre for Linguistics Theory and Studies in Probability (CLASP) which in turn is financed by a grant from the

Swedish Research Council (VR project 2014-39) and University of Gothenburg. CLASP also hosts the event. We are also grateful to the Masters Programme in Language Technology (MLT) at the University of Gothenburg, Talkamatic AB and the City of Gothenburg for their financial support.

We very much hope that you will have an enjoyable and inspiring time!

Simon Dobnik, Stergios Chatzikyriakidis, and Vera Demberg

Gothenburg & Saarbrücken

May 2019

Organisers:

Local Chairs: Stergios Chatzikyriakidis and Simon Dobnik
Program Chairs: Stergios Chatzikyriakidis, Vera Demberg, and Simon Dobnik
Workshops Chair: Asad Sayeed
Student Track Chairs: Vlad Maraev and Chatrine Qwaider
Sponsorships Chair: Staffan Larsson

Program Committee:

Lasha Abzianidze, Laura Aina, Maxime Amblard, Krasimir Angelov, Emily M. Bender, Raffaella Bernardi, Jean-Philippe Bernardy , Rasmus Blanck, Gemma Boleda, Alessandro Bondielli, Lars Borin, Johan Bos, Ellen Breitholtz, Harry Bunt, Aljoscha Burchardt, Nicoletta Calzolari, Emmanuele Chersoni, Philipp Cimiano, Stephen Clark, Robin Cooper, Philippe de Groote, Vera Demberg, Simon Dobnik, Devdatt Dubhashi, Katrin Erk, Arash Eshghi, Raquel Fernández, Jonathan Ginzburg, Matthew Gotham, Eleni Gregoromichelaki, Justyna Grudzinska, Gözde Gül Şahin, Iryna Gurevych , Dag Haug, Aurelie Herbelot, Julian Hough, Christine Howes, Elisabetta Jezek, Richard Johansson, Alexandre Kabbach, Lauri Karttunen, Ruth Kempson, Mathieu Lafourcade, Gabriella Lapesa, Shalom Lappin, Staffan Larsson, Gianluca Lebani, Kiyong Lee, Alessandro Lenci, Martha Lewis, Maria Liakata, Sharid Loáiciga, Zhaohui Luo, Moritz Maria, Aleksandre Maskharashvili, Stephen Mcgregor, Louise McNally, Bruno Mery, Mehdi Mirzapour, Richard Moot, Alessandro Moschitti, Larry Moss, Diarmuid O Seaghdha, Sebastian Pado, Ludovica Pannitto, Ivandre Paraboni, Lucia C. Passaro, Sandro Pezzelle, Manfred Pinkal, Paul Piwek, Massimo Poesio, Sylvain Pogodalla, Christopher Potts, Stephen Pulman, Matthew Purver, James Pustejovsky, Alessandro Raganato, Giulia Rambelli, Allan Ramsay, Aarne Ranta, Christian Retoré, Martin Riedl, Roland Roller, Mehrnoosh Sadrzadeh, Asad Sayeed, Tatjana Scheffler, Sabine Schulte Im Walde, Marco S. G. Senaldi, Manfred Stede, Matthew Stone, Allan Third, Kees Van Deemter, Eva Maria Vecchi, Carl Vogel, Ivan Vulić, Bonnie Webber, Roberto Zamparelli

Invited Speakers:

Mehrnoosh Sadrzadeh, Queen Mary, University of London
Ellie Pavlick, Brown University
Raffaella Bernardi, University of Trento

Invited Talks

Mehrnoosh Sadrzadeh: Ellipsis in Compositional Distributional Semantics

Ellipsis is a natural language phenomenon where part of a sentence is missing and its information must be recovered from its surrounding context, as in "Cats chase dogs and so do foxes.". Formal semantics offers different methods for resolving ellipsis and recovering the missing information, but the problem has not been considered for distributional semantics, where words have vector embeddings and combinations thereof provide embeddings for sentences. In elliptical sentences these combinations go beyond linear as copying of elided information is necessary. I will talk about recent results in our NAACL 2019 paper, joint with G. Wijnholds, where we develop different models for embedding VP-elliptical sentences using modal sub-exponential categorial grammars. We extend existing verb disambiguation and sentence similarity datasets to ones containing elliptical phrases and evaluate our models on these datasets for a variety of linear and non-linear combinations. Our results show that indeed resolving ellipsis improves the performance of vectors and tensors on these tasks and it also sheds some light on disambiguating their sloppy and strict readings.

Ellie Pavlick: What Should Constitute Natural Language "understanding"?

Natural language processing has become indisputably good over the past few years. We can perform retrieval and question answering with purported super-human accuracy, and can generate full documents of text that seem good enough to pass the Turing test. In light of these successes, it is tempting to attribute the empirical performance to a deeper "understanding" of language that the models have acquired. Measuring natural language "understanding", however, is itself an unsolved research problem. In this talk, I will discuss recent work which attempts to illuminate what it is that state-of-the-art models of language are capturing. I will describe approaches which evaluate the models' inferential behaviour, as well as approaches which rely on inspecting the models' internal structure directly. I will conclude with results on human's linguistic inferences, which highlight the challenges involved with developing prescriptivist language tasks for evaluating computational models.

Raffaella Bernardi: Beyond Task Success: A Closer Look at Jointly Learning to See, Ask, and GuessWhat

The development of conversational agents that ground language into visual information is a challenging problem that requires the integration of dialogue management skills with multimodal understanding. Recently, visual dialogue settings have entered the scene of the Machine Learning and Computer Vision communities thanks to the construction of visually grounded human-human dialogue datasets against which Neural Network models (NNs) have been challenged. I will present our work on GuessWhat?! in which two NN agents interact to each other so that one of the two (the Questioner), by asking questions to the other (the Answerer), can guess which object the Answerer has in mind among all the entities in a given image (GuessWhat?!). I will present our Questioner model: it encodes both visual and textual inputs, produces a multimodal representation, generates natural language questions, understands the Answerers' responses and guesses the object. I will compare our model's dialogues with models that exploit much more complex learning paradigms, like Reinforcement Learning, showing that more complex machine learning methods do not necessarily correspond to better dialogue quality or even better quantitative performance. The talk is based on work available at `https://vista-unitn-uva.github.io/`.

Table of Contents

Projecting Temporal Properties, Events and Actions

Tim Fernando
Trinity College Dublin
Tim.Fernando@tcd.ie

Abstract

Temporal notions based on a finite set A of properties are represented in strings, on which projections are defined that vary the granularity A. The structure of properties in A is elaborated to describe statives, events and actions, subject to a distinction in meaning (advocated by Levin and Rappaport Hovav) between what the lexicon prescribes and what a context of use supplies. The projections proposed are deployed as labels for records and record types amenable to finite-state methods.

1 Introduction

Reflecting on years of work on discourse semantics, Hans Kamp writes

> when we interpret a piece of discourse — or a single sentence in the context in which it is being used — we build something like a model of the episode or situation described; and an important part of that model are its event structure, and the time structure that can be derived from that event structure by means of Russell's construction (Kamp, 2013, page 13).

The event structure Kamp has in mind is "made up of those comparatively few events that figure in this discourse" (page 9). Let us put aside for the moment how to extract from a discourse D the set E_D of events that figure in D, and observe that if the set E_D is finite (as typically happens in practice), so is the linear order returned by the Russell construction for time (details in section 2 below). This is in sharp contrast to the continuum $\mathbb{R}$, with which "real" time is commonly identified (Kamp and Reyle, 1993), or to any unbounded linear order supporting the temporal interval structure defined in Allen and Ferguson (1994), where a different perspective on events is adopted.

> We take the position that events are primarily linguistic or cognitive in nature. That is, the world does not really contain events. Rather, events are the way by which agents classify certain useful and relevant patterns of change (Allen and Ferguson, 1994, page 533).

Allen and Ferguson specify temporal structure *before* introducing events (or, for that matter, properties and actions), reversing the conceptual priority events enjoy over time in the Russell construction mentioned by Kamp. Without embracing this reversal, the present paper builds on elements of Allen and Ferguson (1994) and other works to construct time from not only events, but also properties and actions. The aim is to find a temporal ontology of finite strings that is not *too big* (which $\mathbb{R}$ or any infinite linear order arguably is) and not *too small* (which the linear order from Russell's construction can be, depending on the event structure it is fed as input). Insisting on temporal structure that is *just right* is reminiscent of Goldilocks, and perhaps more germanely, the *Goldilocks effect* observed in Kidd et al. (2012) as the tendency of human infants to look away from events that are overly simple or overly complex. Whether or not any useful link can be forged between that work and the present paper, I am not able to say. But I do claim that the notions of projections brought out below provide helpful handles on granularity, especially when granularity is varied.

That granularity is given, in the simplest case, by a finite set A of properties, expressing in section 2 events, as conceived in the Russell construction. More sophisticated pictures of events are considered and "relevant patterns of change" captured through an explicit account of action and incremental change in section 3. Strings and languages are presented in section 4 as records and record types labeled with projections, bringing out certain affinities with *Type Theory with Records* (Cooper and Ginzburg, 2015).

2　Strings from properties and changes

Leibniz's law, decreeing that any difference $x \neq y$ be discernible via some property, can be expressed in monadic second-order logic (MSO, e.g. Libkin (2010)) as the implication

$$x \neq y \;\supset\; (\exists P)\neg(P(x) \equiv P(y)) \tag{LL}$$

with $\neg(P(x) \equiv P(y))$ asserting P separates x from y. A special case of inequality $\neq$ is the successor relation S that specifies a notion of step. We link that step to a set $\{P_a\}_{a \in A}$ of properties P_a named with a finite set A (conflating the property P_a with its name $a \in A$ when convenient), and adopt the abbreviation $x \equiv_A y$ for the conjunction expressing the inseparabilty in A of x and y

$$x \equiv_A y \;:=\; \bigwedge_{a \in A} (P_a(x) \equiv P_a(y)).$$

Two substitutions in (LL), S for $\neq$, and the negation of $x \equiv_A y$ for its consequent, turn (LL) into

$$xSy \;\supset\; x \not\equiv_A y \tag{LL$_A$}$$

(pronounced "S-steps require change$_A$"). If we represent x by its A-*profile*

$$A[x] \;:=\; \{a \in A \mid P_a(x)\}$$

specifying the properties in A that hold of x, we can can study S-chains

$$x_1 S x_2 \text{ and } x_2 S x_3 \text{ and } \cdots \text{ and } x_{n-1} S x_n$$

through strings $A[x_1]A[x_2]\cdots A[x_n]$ of subsets of A. In model-theoretic terms, this suggests construing a string $s = \alpha_1 \cdots \alpha_n$ of subsets α_i of A as the model

$$\mathrm{Mod}(s) \;:=\; \langle [n], S_n, \{[\![P_a]\!]_s\}_{a \in A}\rangle$$

with domain/universe

$$[n] := \{1, \ldots, n\}$$

of string positions, interpreting S as the successor relation

$$S_n \;:=\; \{(i, i+1) \mid i \in [n-1]\}$$

$+1$ on $[n]$, and P_a as the set

$$[\![P_a]\!]_{\alpha_1 \cdots \alpha_n} \;:=\; \{i \in [n] \mid a \in \alpha_i\}$$

of positions in s where a occurs (for each $a \in A$). For example, the string $\boxed{}\,\boxed{a}\,\boxed{a,a'}\,\boxed{a'}\,\boxed{}$ of length 5 (with string symbols drawn as boxes) corresponds to the model with universe $[5] = \{1,2,3,4,5\}$, interpreting P_a as $\{2,3\}$ and $P_{a'}$ as $\{3,4\}$. (Note $\boxed{}$ is the empty set $\emptyset$ *qua* string of length 1, not to be confused with the null string of length 0 or the empty language.) The *vocabulary of s, $voc(s)$,* is the smallest set A' such that s is a string of subsets of A'

$$voc(\alpha_1 \cdots \alpha_n) \;=\; \bigcup_{i=1}^{n} \alpha_i$$

(making, for example, $\{a, a'\}$ the vocabulary of $\boxed{}\,\boxed{a}\,\boxed{a,a'}\,\boxed{a'}\,\boxed{}$).

Rather than fixing A once and for all, we let A vary, keeping it finite for bounded granularity (restricting our attention to finite strings of finite sets). If $A = \emptyset$, then $x \equiv_A y$, which is to say, the strings that satisfy (LL$_\emptyset$) are exactly those of length 1 (or 0, if we allow a model with empty universe). Evidently, the space of models of (LL$_A$) increases as we enlarge A. Given a string s of sets that may or not be subsets of A, we define the *A-reduct of s* to be the string obtained by intersecting s componentwise with A

$$\rho_A(\alpha_1 \cdots \alpha_n) := (\alpha_1 \cap A) \cdots (\alpha_n \cap A)$$

(Fernando, 2016). For instance, the $\{a\}$-reduct of the string $\boxed{\;|\,a\,|\,a, a'\,|\,a'\,|\;}$ is

$$\rho_{\{a\}}\big(\boxed{\;|\,a\,|\,a, a'\,|\,a'\,|\;}\big) \;=\; \boxed{\;|\,a\,|\,a\,|\;\;}.$$

Whereas $\boxed{\;|\,a\,|\,a, a'\,|\,a'\,|\;}$ satisfies (LL$_{\{a,a'\}}$), its $\{a\}$-reduct satisfies neither (LL$_{\{a,a'\}}$) nor (LL$_{\{a\}}$). The problem is that $\boxed{\;|\,a\,|\,a\,|\;\;}$ stutters. In general, a *stutter of* a string $\alpha_1 \cdots \alpha_n$ is a position $i \in [n-1]$ such that $\alpha_i = \alpha_{i+1}$. $\boxed{\;|\,a\,|\,a\,|\;\;}$ has two stutters, 2 and 4. It is easy to see that a string s is stutterless iff it satisfies (LL$_{voc(s)}$). The consequent $x \not\equiv_A y$ of (LL$_A$) is equivalent to the disjunction

$$\bigvee_{a \in A} ((\neg P_a(x) \wedge P_a(y)) \vee (P_a(x) \wedge \neg P_a(y)))$$

where each $a \in A$ can separate x from y in one of two ways, corresponding to a's left and right borders, $l(a)$ and $r(a)$, respectively. We introduce predicates $P_{l(a)}$ saying: P_a is false but S-after true

$$P_{l(a)}(x) \;\equiv\; \neg P_a(x) \wedge (\exists y)(xSy \wedge P_a(y)) \tag{1}$$

and $P_{r(a)}$ saying: P_a is true but not S-after

$$P_{r(a)}(x) \;\equiv\; P_a(x) \wedge \neg(\exists y)(xSy \wedge P_a(y)). \tag{2}$$

Then $x \not\equiv_A y$ is equivalent under xSy to $\bigvee_{a \in A}(P_{l(a)}(x) \vee P_{r(a)}(x)))$

$$xSy \;\supset\; (x \not\equiv_A y \;\equiv\; \bigvee_{a \in A}(P_{l(a)}(x) \vee P_{r(a)}(x))).$$

Hence, (LL$_A$) is equivalent to

$$(\exists y)(xSy) \;\supset\; \bigvee_{a \in A}(P_{l(a)}(x) \vee P_{r(a)}(x)) \tag{3}$$

assuming (1), (2), and

$$xSy \wedge xSz \supset y = z. \tag{4}$$

(4) expresses the determinism of S, which is built into strings. As for (1) and (2), let $A_\bullet$ be the set of borders in A

$$A_\bullet \;:=\; \{l(a) \mid a \in A\} \cup \{r(a) \mid a \in A\}$$

and define the *border translation $b(s)$ of* a string $\alpha_1 \cdots \alpha_n$ to be the string $\beta_1 \cdots \beta_n$ of subsets of $voc(s)_\bullet$ specified by (1) and (2)

$$\beta_i \;:=\; \{l(a) \mid a \in \alpha_{i+1} - \alpha_i\} \cup \{r(a) \mid a \in \alpha_i - \alpha_{i+1}\} \text{ for } i < n \tag{5}$$
$$\beta_n \;:=\; \{r(a) \mid a \in \alpha_n\}$$

(Fernando, 2018). For example,

$$b\big(\boxed{\;|\,a, a'\,|\,a'\,|\;}\big) = \boxed{\;|\,l(a), l(a')\,|\,r(a)\,|\,r(a')\,|\;}.$$

In general, (5) says that for a non-final position i,

$$\beta_i \neq \square \;\iff\; (\alpha_{i+1} - \alpha_i) \cup (\alpha_i - \alpha_{i+1}) \neq \square$$
$$\iff\; \alpha_{i+1} \neq \alpha_i.$$

That is, s is stutterless iff $b(s)$ is $\square$-lite, where by definition, a string $\alpha_1 \cdots \alpha_n$ is *$\square$-lite* if for each $i \in [n-1]$, α_i is not $\square$. For the record, we have

Proposition 1. *For any sets A and X, and for any string $s \in (2^X)^*$, the following are equivalent.*

(i) $Mod(s)$ satisfies (LL_A)

(ii) $\rho_A(s)$ is stutterless

(iii) $Mod(b(\rho_A(s)))$ satisfies (3)

(iv) the $A_\bullet$-reduct of $b(s)$ is $\square$-lite.

Implicit in Proposition 1 are two notions of string compression,

$$s\alpha\alpha s' \;\rightsquigarrow\; s\alpha s' \tag{6}$$

for strings over the alphabet 2^A to satisfy (LL_A), and

$$s\square s' \;\rightsquigarrow\; ss' \qquad \text{for } s' \neq \epsilon \tag{7}$$

for strings over the alphabet $2^{A_\bullet}$ to satisfy the border translation (3) of (LL_A). Destuttering (6) is implemented fully by *block compression bc*

$$bc^{-1}\alpha_1 \cdots \alpha_n \;=\; \alpha_1^+ \cdots \alpha_n^+ \qquad \text{for stutterless } \alpha_1 \cdots \alpha_n$$

while $\square$-removal $d_\square$ implements (7) with*out* the proviso $s' \neq \epsilon$

$$d_\square^{-1}\alpha_1 \cdots \alpha_n \;=\; \square^* \alpha_1 \square^* \cdots \square^* \alpha_n \square^* \qquad \text{for } \square\text{-less } \alpha_1 \cdots \alpha_n$$

where a $\square$-*less* string is a string of non-empty sets. In Durand and Schwer (2008), $\square$-less strings are called *S-words* ("S for Set"), and the *S-projection over A of s* defined to be $d_\square(\rho_A(s))$. To make room for *bc* and link up with Allen and Ferguson (1994) and the Russell construction mentioned in the Introduction, let us agree that, given strings s and s' of sets,

(i) s *bc-projects to s'* if the $voc(s')$-reduct of s without stutters is s'

$$bc(\rho_{voc(s')}(s)) = s'$$

(ii) s $\square$-*projects to s'* if the $voc(s')$-reduct of s without any $\square$ is s'

$$d_\square(\rho_{voc(s')}(s)) = s'$$

(iii) an *s-period* is an $a \in voc(s)$ such that s *bc*-projects to $\boxed{\;}\boxed{a}\boxed{\;}$.

The occurrences of $\square$ to the left and right in $\boxed{\;}\boxed{a}\boxed{\;}$ represent the left and right bounds on a period in Allen and Ferguson (1994). As with intervals, periods a and a' can be related by exactly one element of the set

$$\mathcal{AR} \;:=\; \{\text{b, bi, o, oi, m, mi, d, di, s, si, f, fi, e}\}$$

of Allen relations (Allen, 1983). Each $R \in \mathcal{AR}$ is pictured as a stutterless string $\mathfrak{s}_{aRa'}$ in Table 1 so that for any string s of sets, and all distinct a, a',

$$a \text{ and } a' \text{ are both } s\text{-periods} \;\iff\; (\exists R \in \mathcal{AR}) \; s \text{ } bc\text{-projects to } \square\mathfrak{s}_{aRa'}\square .$$

Table 1. Allen relations as stutterless strings

R	$\mathfrak{s}_{aRa'}$	R^{-1}	$\mathfrak{s}_{aR^{-1}a'}$	R	$\mathfrak{s}_{aRa'}$	R^{-1}	$\mathfrak{s}_{aR^{-1}a'}$
b	$\boxed{a}\;\boxed{a'}$	bi	$\boxed{a'}\;\boxed{a}$	d	$\boxed{a'}\,\boxed{a,a'}\,\boxed{a'}$	di	$\boxed{a}\,\boxed{a,a'}\,\boxed{a}$
o	$\boxed{a}\,\boxed{a,a'}\,\boxed{a'}$	oi	$\boxed{a'}\,\boxed{a,a'}\,\boxed{a}$	s	$\boxed{a,a'}\,\boxed{a'}$	si	$\boxed{a,a'}\,\boxed{a}$
m	$\boxed{a}\,\boxed{a'}$	mi	$\boxed{a'}\,\boxed{a}$	f	$\boxed{a'}\,\boxed{a,a'}$	fi	$\boxed{a}\,\boxed{a,a'}$
e	$\boxed{a,a'}$						

Let us call a string s an *A-timeline* if s is stutterless and every $a \in A$ is an s-period. For $a \neq a'$, the $\{a, a'\}$-timelines are exactly the strings $\Box \mathfrak{s}_{aRa'} \Box$, for $R \in \mathcal{AR}$. How do these $\{a, a'\}$-timelines compare to the linear orders obtained by the Russell construction on event structures over $\{a, a'\}$?

Without entering into all the details of the event structure $\langle A, \prec, \bigcirc \rangle$ on which the Russell construction is applied, suffice it to say we can derive $\mathfrak{s}_{a \text{ m } a'}$ from $a \prec a'$, $\mathfrak{s}_{a \text{ mi } a'}$ from $a' \prec a$, and $\mathfrak{s}_{a \text{ e } a'}$ from $a \bigcirc a'$, while every other string $\mathfrak{s}_{aRa'}$ is ruled out by the following fact about a linear order $<$ obtained via Russell

($\dagger$) the instants related by $<$ are certain subsets of A, no two of which are related by $\subseteq$.

For example, for $A = \{a, a'\}$, $<$ cannot describe $\mathfrak{s}_{a \text{ o } a'} = \boxed{a}\,\boxed{a, a'}\,\boxed{a'}$ since $\boxed{a} \subseteq \boxed{a, a'}$. But can we not get around the antichain condition ($\dagger$) by fleshing $\mathfrak{s}_{a \text{ o } a'}$ out as

$$\boxed{a, \text{pre}(a')}\,\boxed{a, a'}\,\boxed{\text{post}(a), a'}$$

and similarly for all other strings $\mathfrak{s}_{aRa'}$? In general, the idea would be for any set A and string s of sets, to form the *A-closure of s*, $cl_A(s)$, by setting $cl_A(\alpha_1 \cdots \alpha_n)$ to $\beta_1 \cdots \beta_n$ where

$$\beta_i := \alpha_i \cup \{\text{pre}(a) \mid a \in (A - \alpha_i) \cap \bigcup_{k=i+1}^{n} \alpha_k\} \cup \{\text{post}(a) \mid a \in (A - \alpha_i) \cap \bigcup_{k=1}^{i-1} \alpha_k\}$$

adding two negations, $\text{pre}(a)$ and $\text{post}(a)$, for every $a \in A$ (familiar in the A-series of McTaggart (1908) as past and future). The difficulty with $cl_A(s)$ is that if a is an s-period, then neither $\text{pre}(a)$ nor $\text{post}(a)$ can be a $cl_A(s)$-period, as

$$\textit{bc}(\rho_{\{\text{pre}(a)\}}(cl_A(s))) = \boxed{\text{pre}(a)\ \ } \quad \text{and} \quad \textit{bc}(\rho_{\{\text{post}(a)\}}(cl_A(s))) = \boxed{\ \ \text{post}(a)}.$$

To cover $\text{pre}(a)$ and $\text{post}(a)$, infinitely many periods are assumed in Allen and Ferguson (1994), each bounded to the left and right.

An alternative is to drop the bounds on periods, and work with *semi-intervals* (Freksa, 1992). Or rather than introducing $\text{pre}(a)$ and $\text{post}(a)$ through the A-closure $cl_A(s)$, we might apply the border translation $b(s)$ for left and right borders $l(a)$ and $r(a)$ that capture moments of change (as opposed to instants, under the Russell construction, of pairwise overlapping events). Table 2 records $\Box$-less strings $b(\Box \mathfrak{s}_{aRa'})$, depicting how R orders $l(a), l(a'), r(a), r(a')$. For example, $\boxed{l(a)}\,\boxed{r(a)}\,\boxed{l(a')}\,\boxed{r(a')}$ depicts b's ordering $l(a) < r(a) < l(a') < r(a')$ while $\boxed{l(a), l(a')}\,\boxed{r(a), r(a')}$ depicts e's ordering $l(a) = l(a') < r(a) = r(a')$.

Table 2. Allen relations as $\Box$-less strings, after Durand and Schwer (2008)

R	$b(\Box \mathfrak{s}_{aRa'})$				R^{-1}	$b(\Box \mathfrak{s}_{aR^{-1}a'})$			
b	$l(a)$	$r(a)$	$l(a')$	$r(a')$	bi	$l(a')$	$r(a')$	$l(a)$	$r(a)$
d	$l(a')$	$l(a)$	$r(a)$	$r(a')$	di	$l(a)$	$l(a')$	$r(a')$	$r(a)$
o	$l(a)$	$l(a')$	$r(a)$	$r(a')$	oi	$l(a')$	$l(a)$	$r(a')$	$r(a)$
m	$l(a)$	$r(a), l(a')$		$r(a')$	mi	$l(a')$	$r(a'), l(a)$		$r(a)$
s	$l(a), l(a')$		$r(a)$	$r(a')$	si	$l(a), l(a')$		$r(a')$	$r(a)$
f	$l(a')$	$l(a)$	$r(a), r(a')$		fi	$l(a)$	$l(a')$	$r(a), r(a')$	
e	$l(a), l(a')$		$r(a), r(a')$		e				

Table 2 with $l(a)$ and $r(a)$ replaced both by a, and $l(a')$ and $r(a')$ replaced both by a' leads to Figure 4 in (Durand and Schwer, 2008, page 3288). These replacements simplify, for example, $b(\Box \mathfrak{s}_{a \text{ b } a'})$ to

$$\boxed{a}\,\boxed{a}\,\boxed{a'}\,\boxed{a'}$$

with the first occurrence of a understood as a's left border, and the second as a's right. Insofar as these simplifications suffice to represent Allen relations in strings, MSO is overkill. The "relevant patterns of change" associated with events in Allen and Ferguson (1994) are, however, another matter, or so the next section argues, pointing to action and activity left out of $l(a)$ and $r(a)$.

3   Border action and activity

Box-removal $d_\square$ implements the Aristotelian slogan *no time without change* under the assumption that

(B)   all predicates appearing in a box (string symbol) express change.

While (B) holds for the strings in Table 2, it fails for those in Table 1, the approriate compression in which is destuttering bc, or *be* cumulative. By definition, a predicate P on intervals is *cumulative* if whenever an interval i meets (abuts) an interval i' for the combined interval $i \sqcup i'$,

$$P(i) \text{ and } P(i') \implies P(i \sqcup i').$$

The converse

$$P(i \sqcup i') \implies P(i) \text{ and } P(i') \qquad \text{whenever } i \text{ meets } i'$$

is the defining condition for *divisive* predicates P. Cumulativity and divisiveness combine for the condition (H) for *homogeneity*

(H)   for all intervals i and i' whose union $i \cup i'$ is an interval,

$$P(i \cup i') \iff P(i) \text{ and } P(i').$$

If $d_\square$ assumes (B), bc assumes strings are built from homogeneous predicates. Stative predicates are commonly assumed to be homogeneous, as in the well-known aspect hypothesis from Dowty (1979) claiming

> the different aspectual properties of the various kinds of verbs can be explained by postulating a single homogeneous class of predicates — stative predicates — plus three or four sentential operators or connectives. (page 71)

Developing Dowty's aspect hypothesis in terms of strings arguably runs counter to assumption (B) above. Many non-statives are given by *result verbs* that center around some prescribed post-state, as opposed to some *manner* of change (Levin and Rappaport Hovav, 2013, for example). It is natural to identify that post-state with the *consequent state* in Moens and Steedman (1988), where the Aristotle-Ryle-Kenny-Vendler verb classification (Dowty, 1979) is reworked according to Table 3.

Table 3. Moens and Steedman (1988)'s reconstruction of ARKV, annotated with strings

	atomic	extended		
+conseq	culmination (achievement)	culminated process (accomplishment)		
a	$\boxed{\text{pre}(a)\mid a}$	$\boxed{\text{pre}(a), \text{ap}(f)\mid \text{pre}(a), \text{ap}(f), \text{ef}(f)\mid \text{ef}(f), a}$		
−conseq	point (semelfactive)	process (activity)		
f	$\boxed{\text{ap}(f)\mid \text{ef}(f)}$	$\boxed{\text{ap}(f)\mid \text{ap}(f), \text{ef}(f)\mid \text{ef}(f)}$		

Table 3 formulates the culmination resulting in consequent state a as the string $\boxed{\text{pre}(a)\mid a}$, which is associated with the left border $l(a)$ by the border translation b and closure cl_A from the previous section. Line (1) in that section implies

$$\neg P_a(x) \wedge (\exists y)(xSy \wedge P_a(y)) \supset P_{l(a)}(x) \tag{8}$$

which can be read as a law of *inertia* (Dowty, 1986) saying pre(a) persists (forward) unless a *force* is applied, $l(a)$. If we associate a result verb with a force, it is not surprising that a force f should represent a *manner verb* lacking a lexically prescribed post-state (Levin and Rappaport Hovav, 2013), marked $-$conseq in Table 3 (with f below). The point (semelfactive) string $\boxed{\text{ap}(f)\mid \text{ef}(f)}$ is built from two properties, ap(f) saying f is applied, and ef(f) representing a contextually supplied effect of that application. We are borrowing here a basic distinction drawn in Levin and Rappaport Hovav (2013) between the meaning of a verb that is lexically specified (before the verb is used) and the meaning inferred from a specific context of use. When ef(f) is a, it is tempting to reduce ap(f) to $l(a)$, except that the lexical/contextual distinction tells us to resist that reduction. Whereas the contextually supplied effect of a manner verb may vary with the use of the verb, the lexically prescribed post-state of a result verb does not. Moreover, while a point (semelfactive) can apply successively (for a process/activity), the implication

$$P_{l(a)}(x) \supset \neg P_a(x)$$

(saying $l(a)$ cannot co-exist with a in the same box) blocks successive culminations.

How is it possible that ap(f) and ef(f) can be boxed together, as in the rightmost column in Table 3 (when pre(a) and a cannot)? An instructive example, given by incremental change tracked by a scale $\prec$ on a set D of degrees, is a force $\uparrow D$ for a $\prec$-increase, with the effect at y

$$P_{\text{ef}(\uparrow D)}(y) \; \approx \; (\exists d \in D)\, P_d(y) \wedge (\exists x S y)(\exists d' \prec d) P_{d'}(x)\,. \tag{9}$$

Unfortunately, the right side of $\approx$ in (9) quantifies over d and d', which appear as subscripts in $P_d(y)$ and $P_{d'}(x)$, not as arguments y and x. Working instead with any finite subset $D_\circ$ of D (which may well be infinite), we turn (9) into the MSO formula

$$P_{\text{ef}(\uparrow D)}(y) \; \equiv \; \bigvee_{d \in D_\circ} P_{\succ d}(y) \wedge (\exists x)(x S y \wedge P_{\approx d}(x)) \tag{10}$$

built with predicates $P_{\approx d}$ approximating D by $D_\circ$. Given $D_\circ$, (10) says the $D_\circ$-degree at y is greater than the $D_\circ$-degree d at the S-predecessor x of y. Now, whereas $l(a)$ and $r(a)$ cannot co-occur

$$P_{l(a)}(x) \supset \neg P_{r(a)}(x),$$

we should look out for an opposing force $\downarrow D$ before leaping from ap$(\uparrow D)$ to ef$(\uparrow D)$

$$P_{\text{ap}(\uparrow D)}(x) \wedge x S y \wedge \neg P_{\text{ap}(\downarrow D)}(x) \; \supset \; P_{\text{ef}(\uparrow D)}(y). \tag{11}$$

If we unwind the disjunction characterizing ef$(\uparrow D)$ in (10), (11) gives

$$P_{\approx d}(x) \wedge P_{\text{ap}(\uparrow D)}(x) \wedge x S y \wedge \neg P_{\text{ap}(\downarrow D)}(x) \; \supset \; P_{\succ d}(y) \qquad (d \in D_0). \tag{12}$$

To allow $P_{\succ d}(x)$ in place of $P_{\approx d}(x)$ in (12), we modify (10) slightly to

$$P_{\text{ef}(\uparrow D)}(y) \; \equiv \; \bigvee_{d \in D_\circ} P_{\succ d}(y) \wedge (\exists x)(x S y \wedge (P_{\succ d}(x) \vee P_{\approx d}(x))) \tag{13}$$

which means $\uparrow D$ may have the effect not of change but rather preservation (of $P_{\succ d}$). Pressure to change $P_{\succ d}$ comes from $\downarrow D$, for which we have $\downarrow$-counterparts to (11)

$$P_{\text{ap}(\downarrow D)}(x) \wedge x S y \wedge \neg P_{\text{ap}(\uparrow D)}(x) \; \supset \; P_{\text{ef}(\downarrow D)}(y) \tag{14}$$

and to (13)

$$P_{\text{ef}(\downarrow D)}(y) \; \equiv \; \bigvee_{d \in D_\circ} P_{\prec d}(y) \wedge (\exists x)(x S y \wedge (P_{\prec d}(x) \vee P_{\approx d}(x))).$$

The implications (11) and (14) reveal shortcomings that the borders $l(a)$ and $r(a)$ have as pictures of transitions associated with events. The account of inertia from the half of line (1) expressed by (8) is unproblematic enough: change requires force. But the other half of (1), the converse of (8), misrepresents how complicated determining the effects of forces can be. Incrementality (the possibility of more than two degrees) opens the door to competition, necessitating the "no-intervention" provisos, $\neg P_{\mathrm{ap}(\downarrow D)}(x)$ and $\neg P_{\mathrm{ap}(\uparrow D)}(x)$, in the antecedents of (11) and of (14). In Allen and Ferguson (1994), thwarted forces lead to a predicate $Try(f, t)$ that takes an *action* (or force) term f and time period t, corresponding above to $P_{\mathrm{ap}(f)}(t)$.[1]

Whether we refer to f as a force or an action, what are we to make of the property $\mathrm{ap}(f)$? As far as the point (semelfactive) entry $\boxed{\mathrm{ap}(f) \mid \mathrm{ef}(f)}$ in Table 3 is concerned, $\mathrm{ap}(f)$ is clearly non-stative — i.e., subject to $\Box$-removal, as opposed to destuttering $d_\Box$. But turning to a force f given by incremental change, our revision (13) of (10) has the effect beyond (12) of adding (via (11)) the implications

$$P_{\succ d}(x) \wedge P_{\mathrm{ap}(\uparrow D)}(x) \wedge xSy \wedge \neg P_{\mathrm{ap}(\downarrow D)}(x) \supset P_{\succ d}(y) \qquad (d \in D_0).$$

Conservative forces that guard against change are left out of $l(a)$,[2] along with incrementality and competition. If $\uparrow D$ can have the effect of *not* changing $P_{\succ d}$, what becomes of the assumption (B) above behind box-removal $d_\Box$? In Moens and Steedman (1988), the difference between a state and a process (activity)

$$\boxed{\mathrm{ap}(f) \mid \mathrm{ap}(f), \mathrm{ef}(f) \mid \mathrm{ef}(f)} \qquad (15)$$

is blurred by a *progressive state*. Arguably, that progressive state pertains to the second box $\boxed{\mathrm{ap}(f), \mathrm{ef}(f)}$ in (15), perhaps with $\mathrm{ap}(f)$ replaced by a stative variant, $\mathrm{ap}_s(f)$. Aspectual type shifts are commonly associated with reconstruals, and rather than attempt to resolve the aspectual character of $\mathrm{ap}(f)$ definitively, suffice it to repeat Levin and Rappaport Hovav (2013)'s claim that context is required to spell out the effect $\mathrm{ef}(f)$ of a manner verb f. That wrinkle is a sign of, in Robin Cooper's words, "semantics in flux," challenging a legacy from Montague (1974)

> the impression of natural languages as being regimented with meanings determined once and for all by an interpretation (Cooper, 2012, page 271).

This impression is congenial with Allen and Ferguson (1994)'s avowed position that temporal structure is prior to properties, events and actions — a position open to dispute (harking back to Russell).

4 Projections within records and record types

Semantic flux is an important motivation for Type Theory with Records (TTR), against which it is instructive to understand the present paper's

Main Claim   *Temporal notions such as those in Allen and Ferguson (1994) and Moens and Steedman (1988) can be represented in strings structured by MSO and finitary projections, on which we can reason through finite-state methods.*

The promise of finite-state methods (mentioned in the Main Claim) rests on (i) a classic theorem due to Büchi, Elgot and Trakhtenbrot (Libkin, 2010) mapping MSO-sentences to finite automata checking satisfaction (and back), and (ii) the computability by finite-state transducers of the projections proposed. These projections operate between finite sets A and A', composing $f \in \{bc, d_\Box, id\}$ (where id is the identity function) with ρ_A for the function $f_{A,A'} = \rho_A; f : (2^{A'})^* \to (2^A)^*$ mapping a string s of subsets of A' to the string $f(\rho_A(s))$ of subsets of A that f returns when fed the A-reduct $\rho_A(s)$ of s.

Proposition 2.   *Given any set Θ, let $Fin(\Theta)$ be the set of finite subsets of Θ. For $f \in \{bc, d_\Box, id\}$, the family $\{f_{A,A'} : (2^{A'})^* \to (2^A)^*\}_{A,A' \in Fin(\Theta)}$ is a projective system — i.e., $f_{A,A}$ is the identity on $(2^A)^*$ and $f_{A,A''}$ is the composition $f_{A',A''}; f_{A;A'}$ for all $A \subseteq A' \subseteq A'' \in Fin(\Theta)$.*

---

[1] Talk of "forces" complements inertia, while "action" is in the title of Davidson (1967) and is likened in Allen and Ferguson (1994) to a *program* (quite natural to *apply*). Programs in *Dynamic Logic* (Harel et al., 2000) underly yet another approach to verb semantics (Naumann, 2001; Pustejovsky and Moszkowicz, 2011), relations with which I hope to take up elsewhere.

[2] A force that resists change is old hat to readers familiar with, for instance, Talmy (1988).

Recall from section 2 the introduction of strings and the projections ρ_A, bc and $d_\square$ through a bounded form of Leibniz's law in MSO (linking stutterless and $\square$-less strings according to Proposition 1). MSO properties are restricted to unary predicates over string positions, compelling us in section 3 to sidestep the formula

$$(\exists d \in D)\, P_d(y) \wedge (\exists x S y)(\exists d' \prec d) P_{d'}(x) \tag{16}$$

(in (9)) saying the D-degree at y is greater than at its predecessor. Logical hygiene around $P_a(x)$ dictates separating the temporal entities over which the property-argument x ranges from the bits incorporated into the property-index a. Among the latter bits are degrees d in $P_{\succ d}$ and $P_{\approx d}$, as well as actions/forces f in $P_{\mathrm{ap}(f)}$ and $P_{\mathrm{ef}(f)}$. That said, any finite $\prec$-chain

$$d_1 \prec d_2 \prec \cdots \prec d_n \quad \text{in } D$$

yields an approximation of (16) as the finite disjunction

$$\bigvee_{i=1}^{n} P_{>i}(y) \wedge (\exists x)(x S y \wedge P_i(x)) \tag{17}$$

much as time is sampled in section 2 by a string s, with string positions populating the MSO-model $\mathrm{Mod}(s)$.[3] A basic flaw, however, in (17) is that the indices $> i$ and i (appearing as subscripts in $P_{>i}$ and P_i) leave out the attribute that is being graded. That is, the degree d in P_d ought properly to be fleshed out as an attribute-value pair (ℓ, v) with a grade or value v that a force $\uparrow D$ can raise (and $\downarrow D$ lower). The letter ℓ for attribute can also be understood as a ℓabel in a record $\{\langle \ell_i, v_i\rangle\}_{i\in[k]}$ or record-type $\{\langle \ell_i, T_i\rangle\}_{i\in[k]}$. In the remainder of this paper, we decompose strings that capture changes in $\{P_a\}_{a\in A}$ in terms of records and record types with labels equal to subsets of A, approaching MSO (under the projections above) bottom-up and perhaps even probabilistically.

Given a finite set A, and $f \in \{bc, d_\square, id\}$, an (A, f)-*string* is a string s over the alphabet 2^A such that $f(s) = s$ (meaning s is stutterless for $f = bc$, or s is $\square$-less for $f = d_\square$). An (A, f)-*record* is a record $\{\langle \ell_i, v_i\rangle\}_{i\in[k]}$ such that each label ℓ_i is a subset of A, and each v_i is an (ℓ_i, f)-string. We can decompose a string s over 2^A into its $\{a\}$-reducts for the (A, id)-record $\{\langle \{a\}, \rho_{\{a\}}(s)\rangle\}_{a\in A}$, from which we can reconstruct s by componentwise union $\&_\circ$ of strings of the same length

$$\alpha_1 \cdots \alpha_n \; \&_\circ \; \alpha'_1 \cdots \alpha'_n \; := \; (\alpha_1 \cup \alpha'_1) \cdots (\alpha_n \cup \alpha'_n)$$

by repeatedly appealing to

$$\rho_{A_1 \cup A_2}(s) \; = \; \rho_{A_1}(s) \;\&_\circ\; \rho_{A_2}(s)\,. \tag{18}$$

For $f = bc$ or $d_\square$, however, (18) will not do,[4] assuming the (A, f)-record $\{\langle \ell_i, v_i\rangle\}_{i\in[k]}$ is understood as describing the set $\mathcal{L}(\{\langle \ell_i, v_i\rangle\}_{i\in[k]})$ of (A, f)-strings that f-project to each v_i

$$\mathcal{L}(\{\langle \ell_i, v_i\rangle\}_{i\in[k]}) \; := \; \{f(s) \mid s \in (2^A)^* \text{ and } (\forall i \in [k])\, f(\rho_{\ell_i}(s)) = v_i\}.$$

Under this assumption, the (A, bc)-record $\{\langle \{a\}, \boxed{\ }\boxed{a}\boxed{\ }\rangle\}_{a\in A}$ describes the set of A-timelines (as defined in section 2). To specify an Allen relation R between a and a', we form the label $\{a, a'\}$ and pair it with the string $\square s_a R a' \square$ from Table 1. But what if say, we know only that the Allen relation between a and a' is either meet, m, or before, b? Then we should pair the label $\ell = \{a, a'\}$ with the set

$$\{\,\boxed{\ }\boxed{a}\boxed{a'}\boxed{\ }\,,\; \boxed{\ }\boxed{a}\boxed{\ }\boxed{a'}\boxed{\ }\,\}$$

of $(bc, \{a, a'\})$-strings picturing a m a' and a b a'. Mildly generalizing the notions above, let us agree

---

[3] In terms familiar from, for example, Grenon and Smith (2004), strings that structure occurrents/perdurants along temporal S-steps may arise from strings that structure continuants/endurants along a $\prec$-scale. See also Jackendoff (1996).

[4] While any finite string is too short to serve as a timeline, it can be extended indefinitely through inverse limits relative to the composition of ρ_A with bc or $d_\square$. MSO under these projections has a formulation, spelled out in Fernando (2016), as an *institution* in the sense of Goguen and Burstall (1992). So too does a finite-state fragment of TTR (Fernando, 2017), although how to relate these institutions category-theoretically remains (as far as I know) to be worked out.

(i) an (A, f)-*record type* is a record type $\{\langle \ell_i, T_i\rangle\}_{i\in[k]}$ such that each label ℓ_i is a subset of A, and each T_i is a set of (ℓ_i, f)-strings

(ii) the *language described by* an (A, f)-record type $\{\langle \ell_i, T_i\rangle\}_{i\in[k]}$ is the set $\mathcal{L}(\{\langle \ell_i, T_i\rangle\}_{i\in[k]})$ of (A, f)-strings that for each $i \in [k]$, f-project to some string in T_i

$$\mathcal{L}(\{\langle \ell_i, T_i\rangle\}_{i\in[k]}) \ := \ \{f(s) \mid s \in (2^A)^* \text{ and } (\forall i \in [k])\ f(\rho_{\ell_i}(s)) \in T_i\}.$$

Different (A, f)-record types can describe the same language, as illustrated by the $[k+1]$-timelines in

$$\mathcal{L}(\{\langle \{i\}, \boxed{\ \ \boxed{i}\ \ }\rangle\}_{i\in[k+1]}) \ = \ \mathcal{L}(\{\langle \{i, i+1\}, L_i\rangle\}_{i\in[k]}) \tag{19}$$

where $k \geq 1$ and L_i is the set of 13 strings, $\square \mathfrak{s}_{iRi+1}\square$, one per Allen relation R

$$L_i \ = \ \{\square \mathfrak{s}_{iRi+1}\square \mid R \in \mathcal{AR}\}.$$

What is gained by complicating the $([k+1], \textit{bc})$-record type on the left side of (19) to that to its right? Labels with two intervals (such as i and $i+1$) allow us to represent information updates that eliminate strings from L_i. Indeed, this is the basis of interval networks which operate around a transitivity table (Allen, 1983, Figure 4) that specifies for every pair (R_1, R_2) of Allen relations, the set $t(R_1, R_2)$ of Allen relations R such that under some $\{1, 2, 3\}$-timeline, $1R_1 2$, $2R_2 3$ and $1R3$

$$t(R_1, R_2) \ = \ \{R \in \mathcal{AR} \mid \text{there is a } \{1, 2, 3\}\text{-timeline that } \textit{bc}\text{-projects to}$$
$$\square \mathfrak{s}_{1R_1 2}\square \text{ and } \square \mathfrak{s}_{2R_2 3}\square \text{ and } \square \mathfrak{s}_{1R3}\square\}.$$

For example, $t(\text{m},\text{m}) = \{\text{b}\}$ since $\boxed{\ \boxed{1}\boxed{2}\boxed{3}\ }$ is the one string in the language described by

$$\{\langle \{1, 2\}, \boxed{\ \boxed{1}\boxed{2}\ }\rangle, \langle \{2, 3\}, \boxed{\ \boxed{2}\boxed{3}\ }\rangle\}$$

whereas $t(\text{m},\text{d}) = \{\text{o},\text{d},\text{s}\}$ means exactly three strings belong to the language described by

$$\{\langle \{1, 2\}, \boxed{\ \boxed{1}\boxed{2}\ }\rangle, \langle \{2, 3\}, \boxed{\ \boxed{3}\boxed{2, 3}\boxed{3}\ }\rangle\}$$

(where $\mathfrak{s}_{a\,d\,a'} = \boxed{a'}\boxed{a, a'}\boxed{a'}$). The challenge, in general, is, given a set L of (A, f)-strings, to describe L through an (A, f)-record type $\{\langle \ell_i, T_i\rangle\}_{i\in[k]}$ such that, if possible,

(†) no two labels in the set $\{\ell_i\}_{i\in[k]}$ are $\subseteq$-comparable   (minimizing redundancy)

(‡) each T_i is a singleton $\{v_i\}$ (minimizing branching).

The antichain condition (†) on labels mirrors one for Russell instants in section 2, and can be satisfied by keeping only the labels that are $\subseteq$-maximal. (‡) can be a more difficult, if not impossible, demand (Woods and Fernando, 2018). A measure of non-determinism being unavoidable, L may serve as a sample space on which to define a probability mass function (Fernando and Vogel, 2019). The strings in L are finite, and hold no mysteries. To make this point forcefully, I close on an aspirational note, brazenly quoting the physicist John Archibald Wheeler on *it from bit*

> every *it* – every particle, every field of force, even the space-time continuum itself – derives its function, its meaning, its very existence entirely – even if in some contexts indirectly – from the apparatus-elicited answers to yes-or-no questions, binary choices, bits. *It from bit* symbolizes the idea that every item of the physical world has at bottom – a very deep bottom, in most instances – an immaterial source and explanation; that which we call reality arises in the last analysis from the posing of yes-no questions and the registering of equipment-evoked responses; in short, that all things physical are information-theoretic in origin and that this is a participatory universe (Wheeler, 1990, page 5).

Here, *it* is the value/string v_i (or type/language T_i), linked by ℓ_i in records (or record types), and based (at a shallow bottom) on "yes-no questions" P_a, the responses to which are registered by the apparatus of MSO in S-steps.

Acknowledgments

My thanks to three anonymous referees for their comments. This research is supported by Science Foundation Ireland (SFI) through the CNGL Programme (Grant 12/CE/I2267) in the ADAPT Centre, `https://www.adaptcentre.ie`. The ADAPT Centre for Digital Content Technology is funded under the SFI Research Centres Programme (Grant 13/RC/2106) and is co-funded under the European Regional Development Fund.

References

Allen, J. (1983). Maintaining knowledge about temporal intervals. *Communications of the ACM 26*(11), 832–843.

Allen, J. and G. Ferguson (1994). Actions and events in interval temporal logic. *Journal of Logic and Computation 4*(5), 531–579.

Cooper, R. (2012). Type theory and semantics in flux. In *Philosophy of Linguistics*, pp. 271–323. Handbook of Philosophy of Science, Volume 14, Elsevier.

Cooper, R. and J. Ginzburg (2015). TTR for natural language semantics. In S. Lappin and C. Fox (Eds.), *Handbook of Contemporary Semantic Theory* (Second ed.)., pp. 375–407. Wiley-Blackwell.

Davidson, D. (1967). The logical form of action sentences. In N. Rescher (Ed.), *The Logic of Decision and Action*, pp. 81–95. University of Pittsburgh Press.

Dowty, D. (1979). *Word Meaning and Montague Grammar*. Reidel, Dordrecht.

Dowty, D. (1986). The effects of aspectual class on the temporal structure of discourse: semantics or pragmatics? *Linguistics and Philosophy 9*(1), 37–61.

Durand, I. and S. Schwer (2008). A tool for reasoning about qualitative temporal information: the theory of S-languages with a Lisp implementation. *Journal of Universal Computer Science 14*(20), 3282–3306.

Fernando, T. (2016). On regular languages over power sets. *Journal of Language Modelling 4*(1), 29–56.

Fernando, T. (2017). Intensions, types and finite-state truthmaking. In S. Chatzikyriakidis and Z. Luo (Eds.), *Modern Perspectives in Type-Theoretical Semantics*, pp. 223–243. Springer.

Fernando, T. (2018). Intervals and events with and without points. In *Proceedings of the Symposium on Logic and Algorithms in Computational Linguistics 2018*, pp. 34–46. Stockholm University DiVA Portal for digital publications.

Fernando, T. and C. Vogel (2019). Prior probabilities of Allen interval relations over finite orders. In *Proc 11th International Conference on Agents and Artificial Intelligence (ICAART 2019), Special Session on Natural Language Processing in AI*. Prague.

Freksa, C. (1992). Temporal reasoning based on semi-intervals. *Artificial Intelligence 54*, 199–227.

Goguen, J. and R. Burstall (1992). Institutions: abstract model theory for specification and programming. *Journal of the ACM 39*(1), 95–146.

Grenon, P. and B. Smith (2004). SNAP and SPAN: Towards dynamic spatial ontology. *Spatial Cognition and Computation 4*(1), 69–103.

Harel, D., D. Kozen, and J. Tiuryn (2000). *Dynamic Logic*. MIT Press.

Jackendoff, R. (1996). The proper treatment of measuring out, telicity, and perhaps even quantification in English. *Natural Language and Linguistic Theory 14*(2), 305–354.

Kamp, H. (2013). The time of my life. https://lucian.uchicago.edu/blogs/elucidations/files/2013/08/Kamp_TheTimeOfMyLife.pdf.

Kamp, H. and U. Reyle (1993). *From Discourse to Logic*. Kluwer.

Kidd, C., S. Piantadosi, and R. Aslin (2012). The Goldilocks effect: Human infants allocate attention to visual sequences that are neither too simple nor too complex. *PLoS ONE 7*(5), 1–8.

Levin, B. and M. Rappaport Hovav (2013). Lexicalized meaning and manner/result complementarity. In B. Arsenijević, B. Gehrke, and R. Marín (Eds.), *Subatomic Semantics of Event Predicates*, pp. 49–70. Springer.

Libkin, L. (2010). *Elements of Finite Model Theory*. Springer.

McTaggart, J. (1908). The unreality of time. *Mind 17*, 457– 73.

Moens, M. and M. Steedman (1988). Temporal ontology and temporal reference. *Computational Linguistics 14*(2), 15– 28.

Montague, R. (1974). *Formal Philosophy*. Yale University Press.

Naumann, R. (2001). Aspects of changes: a dynamic event semantics. *Journal of Semantics 18*, 27–81.

Pustejovsky, J. and J. Moszkowicz (2011). The qualitative spatial dynamics of motion in language. *Spatial Cognition and Computation 11*(1), 15–44.

Talmy, L. (1988). Force dynamics in language and cognition. *Cognitive Science 12*(1), 49 – 100.

Wheeler, J. (1990). Information, physics, quantum: The search for links. In W. Zurek (Ed.), *Complexity, Entropy and the Physics of Information*, pp. 3–28. Addison-Wesley.

Woods, D. and T. Fernando (2018). Improving string processing for temporal relations. *Proc. 14th Joint ACL-ISO Workshop on Interoperable Semantic Annotation (ISA-2018)*, 76–86.

A Type-coherent, Expressive Representation as an Initial Step to Language Understanding

Gene Louis Kim and Lenhart Schubert
Department of Computer Science, University of Rochester
{gkim21,schubert}@cs.rochester.edu

Abstract

A growing interest in tasks involving language understanding by the NLP community has led to the need for effective semantic parsing and inference. Modern NLP systems use semantic representations that do not quite fulfill the nuanced needs for language understanding: adequately modeling language semantics, enabling general inferences, and being accurately recoverable. This document describes underspecified logical forms (ULF) for Episodic Logic (EL), which is an initial form for a semantic representation that balances these needs. ULFs fully resolve the semantic type structure while leaving issues such as quantifier scope, word sense, and anaphora unresolved; they provide a starting point for further resolution into EL, and enable certain structural inferences without further resolution. This document also presents preliminary results of creating a hand-annotated corpus of ULFs for the purpose of training a precise ULF parser, showing a three-person pairwise interannotator agreement of 0.88 on confident annotations. We hypothesize that a divide-and-conquer approach to semantic parsing starting with derivation of ULFs will lead to semantic analyses that do justice to subtle aspects of linguistic meaning, and will enable construction of more accurate semantic parsers.

1 Introduction

Episodic Logic (EL) is a semantic representation extending FOL, designed to closely match the expressivity and surface form of natural language and to enable deductive inference, uncertain inference, and NLog-like inference (Morbini and Schubert, 2009; Schubert and Hwang, 2000; Schubert, 2014). Kim and Schubert (2016) developed a system that transforms annotated WordNet glosses into EL axioms which were competitive with state-of-the-art lexical inference systems while achieving greater expressivity. While EL is representationally appropriate for language understanding, the current EL parser is too unreliable for general text: The phrase structures produced by the underlying Treebank parser leave many ambiguities in the semantic type structure, which are disambiguated incorrectly by the hand-coded compositional rules; moreover, errors in the phrase structures can further disrupt the resulting logical forms (LFs). Kim and Schubert (2016) discuss the limitations of the existing parser as a starting point for logically interpreting glosses of WordNet verb entries. In order to build a better EL parser, it seems natural to take advantage of recent advances in corpus-based parsing techniques.

This document describes a type-coherent initial LF, or *unscoped logical forms* (ULF), for EL which captures the predicate-argument structure in the EL semantic types and is the first critical step in fully-resolved semantic interpretation of sentences. Montague's profoundly influential work (Montague, 1973) demonstrates that systematic assignments of appropriate semantic types to words and phrases allows us to view language as akin to formal logic, with meanings determined compositionally from syntactic structures. This view of language directly supports inferences, at least to the extent that we can resolve – or are prepared to tolerate – ambiguity, context-dependence, and indexicality, towards which semantic types are agnostic. ULF takes a minimal step across the syntax-semantics interface by doing exactly this – selecting the semantic types of words within EL. Thus ULFs are amenable to corpus-construction and statistical parsing using techniques similar to those used for syntax, and they enable generation of context-dependent structural inferences. The nature of these inferences is discussed in more detail in Section 3.4.

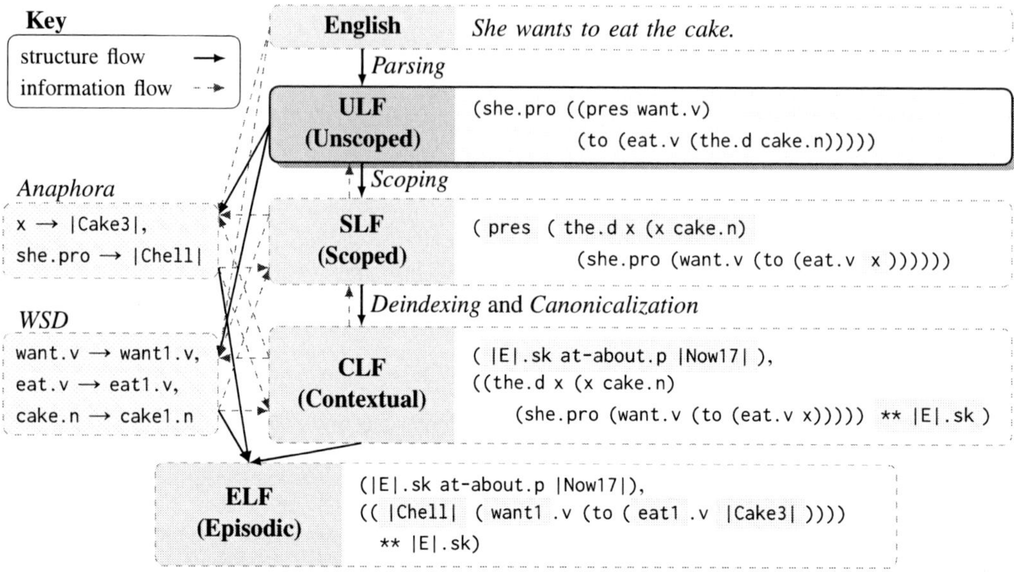

Figure 1: The semantic interpretation process, with the ULF step in the fore. Structurally dependent steps in the interpretation process are connected by solid black arrows and structurally independent information flow is represented with dashed blue arrows. The components that changed from the previous structural step are highlighted in yellow. Backward information arrows indicate that arriving at the optimal choice at a particular step may depend on "later" – or structurally dependent – steps.

Our working hypothesis in designing ULF is that a divide-and-conquer approach starting with preliminary surface-like LFs is a practical way to generate fully resolved interpretations of natural language in EL. Figure 1 shows a diagram of our divide-and-conquer approach, which is elaborated upon in Section 3.3. We also outline a framework for quickly and reliably collecting ULF annotations for a corpus in a multi-pronged approach. Our evaluation of the annotation framework shows that we achieve annotation speeds and agreement comparable to those for the *abstract meaning representation* (AMR) project, which has successfully built a large enough corpus to drive research into corpus-based parsing (Banarescu et al., 2013). Further resources relating to this project, including a more in-depth description of ULFs, the annotation guidelines, and related code are available from the project website http://cs.rochester.edu/u/gkim21/ulf/.

2 Episodic Logic

EL is a semantic representation that extends FOL to more closely match the expressivity of natural languages. It echoes both the surface form of language, and more crucially, the semantic types that are found in all languages. Some semantic theorists view the fact that noun phrases denoting both concrete and abstract entities can appear as predicate arguments (*Aristotle, everyone, the fact that there is water on Mars*) as grounds for treating all noun phrases as being of higher types (e.g., second-order predicates). EL instead uses a small number of reification operators to map predicate and sentence intensions to individuals. As a result, quantification remains first-order (but allows quantified phrases such as *most people who smoke*, or *hardly any errors*). Another distinctive feature of EL is that it treats the relation between sentences and episodes (including events, situations, and processes) as a *characterizing* relation, written '**'. This coincides with the Davidsonian treatment of events as extra variables of predicates (Davidson, 1967) when we restrict ourselves to positive, atomic predications. However, '**' also allows for logically complex characterizations of episodes, such as *not eating anything all day*, or *each superpower menacing the other with its nuclear arsenal* (Schubert, 2000).

EL defines a hierarchical ontology over the domain of individuals, $\mathcal{D}$. $\mathcal{D}$ includes simple individuals, e.g. *John*, possible situations, $\mathcal{S}$, possible worlds, $\mathcal{W} \subset \mathcal{S}$, various numerical types, propositions, $\mathcal{P}$, and kinds, $\mathcal{K}$, as well as others that are not important for the purposes of this document. A complete description of the ontology is provided by Schubert and Hwang (2000). The types of some predicates are further restricted by these categories. For example, the predicate `claim.v` – as in *"I claim that grass is red."* – has the type $\mathcal{P} \to (\mathcal{D} \to (\mathcal{S} \to \mathbf{2}))$, since its first argument is a proposition and the second argument is a simple individual (in the semantics of EL the agent argument is supplied last, though it precedes the predicate in the surface syntax).

The semantic types in EL are defined by recursive functions over individuals, $\mathcal{D}$, and truth values, $\{0,1\}$, written as $\mathbf{2}$. Semantic values of predicates applied to their surface arguments can yield a value in $\mathbf{2}$ at a given (possible) situation, or be *undefined* there (indicating irrelevance of the predication in the given situation). Most predicates in EL are of type $\mathcal{D}^n \to (\mathcal{S} \to \mathbf{2})$ (where $\mathcal{D}^2 \to \mathbf{2}$ abbreviates $\mathcal{D} \to (\mathcal{D} \to \mathbf{2})$, $\mathcal{D}^3 \to \mathbf{2}$ abbreviates $\mathcal{D} \to (\mathcal{D} \to (\mathcal{D} \to \mathbf{2}))$, and so on). That is, they are first-order intensional predicates.[1] Monadic predicates play a particularly important role in EL as well as ULF, and we will abbreviate their type $\mathcal{D} \to (\mathcal{S} \to \mathbf{2})$ as $\mathcal{N}$. In EL syntax, square brackets indicate infixed operators (i.e. $[\tau_n \, \pi \, \tau_1 \, ... \, \tau_{n-1}]$ where π is the operator) and parentheses indicate prefixed operators (i.e. $(\pi \, \tau_1 \, ... \, \tau_n)$ where π is the operator). Predicative formulas such as `[|Aristotle| famous.a]` or `[|Romeo| love.v |Juliet|]` are regarded as temporal and must be evaluated with respect to a situation via an episode-relating operator (e.g. '**') to supply the episode and thus produce an atemporal formula.

There are also a limited number of type-shifting operators in EL to map between some of these types. The kind operator, 'k', shifts a monadic predicate into a kind, $(\mathcal{D} \to (\mathcal{S} \to \mathbf{2})) \to \mathcal{K}$, and the operator , 'that', forms propositions from sentence intensions, $(\mathcal{S} \to \mathbf{2}) \to \mathcal{P}$. *"that grass is red"*, a segment of an earlier example, is formulated as `(that [(k grass.n) red.a])` in EL, uses both of these operators.

3 Unscoped logical form

ULFs are type-coherent initial LFs which provide a stepping stone to capturing full sentential EL meanings. They enable interesting classes of structural inferences that are of broader scope than those enabled by Natural Logic (NLog) (Sánchez Valencia, 1995), and unlike NLog inferences do not depend on prior knowledge of the propositions to be confirmed or refuted. ULF captures the full predicate argument structure of EL while leaving word sense, scope, and anaphora unresolved. Therefore, ULFs can be analyzed using the formal EL type system while taking the scopal ambiguities into account. There is not enough space here to exhaustively discuss how ULF handles various phenomena, so the discussion will be restricted to the broad framework of ULF and the most crucial aspects of the semantics. Please refer to `http://cs.rochester.edu/u/gkim21/ulf/` for complete information on ULF.

3.1 ULF Syntax

All atoms in ULF, with the exception of certain logical functions and syntactic macros, are marked with an atomic syntactic type. The atomic syntactic types are written with suffixed tags: `.v`, `.n`, `.a`, `.p`, `.pro`, `.d`, `.aux-v`, `.aux-s`, `.adv-a`, `.adv-e`, `.adv-s`, `.adv-f`, `.cc`, `.ps`, `.pq`, `.mod-n`, or `.mod-a`, except for names, which use wrapped bars, e.g. `|John|`. These are intended to echo the part-of-speech origins of the constituents, such as *verb, noun, adjective, preposition, pronoun, determiner,* etc., respectively; some of them contain further specifications as relevant to their entailments, e.g., `.adv-e` for locative or temporal adverbs (implying properties of events). The distinctions among predicates of sorts `.v`, `.n`, `.a`, `.p`, corresponding to English parts of speech, are often suppressed in other LFs for language, but are semantically important. For example, *"Bob danced"* can refer to a brief episode while *"Jill was a dancer"* generally cannot (and may suggest Jill is no longer alive); this is related to the fact that verbal predicates are typically "stage-level" (episodic) while nominal predicates are generally "individual-level" (enduring). Whereas in EL the bracket type specifies whether prefix or infix notation is being used, in ULF this distinction is inferred from the semantic types of the constituents and only parentheses are used.

---

[1] Some predicates allow for a monadic predicate complement such as *look* in *"They look happy"*.

> (1) *Could you dial for me?*
>   `(((pres could.aux-v) you.pro (dial.v {ref1}.pro (adv-a (for.p me.pro)))) ?)`
> (2) *If I were you I would be able to succeed.*
>   `((if.ps (i.pro ((cf were.v) (= you.pro)))))`
>   `(i.pro ((cf will.aux-s) (be.v (able.a (to succeed.v)))))))`
> (3) *Flowers are weak creatures*
>   `((k (plur flower.n)) ((pres be.v) (weak.a (plur creature.n))))`
> (4) *Very few people still debate the fact that the earth is heating up*
>   `(((fquan (very.mod-a few.a)) (plur person.n))`
>   `(still.adv-s (debate.v`
>   `(the.d (n+preds fact.n (= (that ((the.d |Earth|.n)`
>   `((pres prog) heat_up.v))))))))))`

Figure 2: Example sentences with corresponding raw ULF annotations. Examples (1) and (2) are from the Tatoeba database, (3) is from *The Little Prince*, and (4) is from the Web. Strictly speaking, weak.a in (3) is actually missing a type-shifting operator mod-n, a simplification discussed in Section 4.

Atoms that are implicit in the sentence or elided and thus supplied by the annotator are wrapped in curly brackets, such as {ref}.pro in example (1) of Figure 2.

For practical purposes we distinguish *raw ULF* from *postprocessed ULF*. In raw ULF we allow certain argument-taking constituents to be dislocated from their "proper" place, so as to adhere more closely to linguistic surface structure and thereby facilitate annotation. For example, sentence-level operators (of type adv-s) appearing mid-sentence may be left "floating" (e.g., (|Alice| certainly.adv-s ((pres know.v) |Bob|))), since they can be automatically lifted to the sentence-level; and verb-level adverbs (of type adv-a) can be interleaved with arguments (e.g., ((past speak.v) sternly.adv-a (to.p-arg |Bob|))), even though semantically they operate on the whole verb phrase. Kim and Schubert (2017) presented this method of dislocated annotation for sentence-level operators. In postprocessed ULF, we can understand all atoms and subexpressions of well-formed formulas (wffs) as being one of the following ULF constituent types (modulo some following remarks):

entity, predicate, determiner, monadic predicate modifier, sentence, sentence modifier,
connective, lambda abstract, or one of a limited number of type-shifting operators,

where the predicates and operators that act on predicates are subcategorized by whether the predicate is derived from a noun, verb, adjective, or preposition. These constituent types uniquely map to particular semantic types, i.e., are aliases for the formal types. Clausal constituents are combined according to their bracketing and semantic types.

A qualification of the above general claim is that unscoped tense operators, determiners, and coordinators remain in their surface position even in postprocessed ULF. For example, in (|Bob| ((pres own.v) (a.d dog.n))), pres is actually an unscoped sentence-level operator (which, in conversion to EL, is deindexed to yield a characterization of an episode by the sentence, and a temporal predication about that episode). We also retain coordinated expressions such as ((in.p |Rome|) and.cc happy.a), where this will ultimately lead to a sentential conjunction in EL. Similarly, (a.d dog.n) is kept in argument position as if it were of semantic type $\mathcal{D}$ (thus, as if the determiner were of semantic type $\mathcal{N} \to \mathcal{D}$).[2] Such unscoped constituents do not disrupt type coherence, because the possible conversions to type-coherent EL are well-defined.

Finally, both raw ULFs and postprocessed ULFs can contain macros. For example, the macro operator n+preds is used for postmodified nominal predicates such as (n+preds dog.n (on.p (a.d leash.n))) – see also example (4) in Figure 2; this avoids immediate introduction of a λ-abstracted conjunction of predicates, simplifying the annotation task. Appendix C discusses macros further, including their formal definitions. Section 4 will ground the high-level discussions in this and the following section with a concrete discussion of modifiers.

---

[2]The actual semantic type of determiners in EL, after lambda-abstraction of the restrictor and matrix formula, is $\mathcal{N} \to (\mathcal{N} \to (S \to 2))$. See Appendix A for full details.

3.2 ULF Type Structure

The type-shifting operators mentioned in the previous section are crucial for type coherence in ULFs. In example (1) the phrase *"for me"* is coded as (adv-a (for.p me.pro)), rather than simply (for.p me.pro) because it is functioning as a *predicate modifier*, semantically operating on the verbal predicate (dial.v {ref1}.pro) (*dial a certain thing*). Let $\mathcal{N}_{ADJ}$, $\mathcal{N}_N$, and $\mathcal{N}_V$ be the sortal refinements of the monadic predicate type $\mathcal{N}$ corresponding to adjectives, nouns, and verbs, respectively. (adv-a (for.p me.pro)) has type $\mathcal{N}_V \rightarrow \mathcal{N}_V$. Without the adv-a operator the prepositional phrase is just a 1-place predicate. Its use as a predicate is apparent in contexts like *"This puppy is for me"*. Note that semantically the 1-place predicate (for.p me.pro) is formed by applying the 2-place predicate for.p to the (individual-denoting) term me.pro. If we apply (for.p me.pro) to another argument, such as |Snoopy| (the name of a puppy), we obtain a sentence intension.[3] So semantically, adv-a is a *type-shifting operator* of type $\mathcal{N} \rightarrow (\mathcal{N}_V \rightarrow \mathcal{N}_V)$.

This brings up the issue of *intensionality*, which is preserved in ULF. Example (2) is a counterfactual conditional, and the consequent clause *"I would be able to succeed"* is not evaluated in the actual world, but in a possible world where the (patently false) antecedent is imagined to be true. ULF captures this with the 'cf' operator in place of the tense and the EL formulas derived from it are evaluated with respect to *possible situations (episodes)*, whose maxima are possible worlds. The type of 'cf' is $(S \rightarrow 2) \rightarrow (S \rightarrow 2)$ after operator scoping to the sentence-level, but like tense operators is kept with the verb in raw ULF, essentially functioning as a predicate-level identity function, $(\lambda X.X)$, there.

'to' in (2), 'k' in (3), and 'that' in (4) are all operators that reify different semantic categories, shifting them to abstract individuals. 'to' (synonym: ka) shifts a verbal predicate to a *kind (type) of action or attribute*, $\mathcal{N}_V \rightarrow \mathcal{K}_A$; 'k' shifts a nominal predicate to a *kind* of thing, $\mathcal{N}_N \rightarrow \mathcal{K}$ (so the subject in example (3) is the abstract kind, *flowers*, whose instances consist of sets of flowers); and 'that' produces a reified *proposition*, $(S \rightarrow 2) \rightarrow \mathcal{P}$ (again an abstract individual) from a sentence meaning. Using these type shifts, EL and ULF are able to maintain a simple, classical view of predication, while allowing greater expressivity than the most widely employed LFs.

3.3 Role of ULF in Comprehensive Semantic Interpretation

ULFs are underspecified, but their surface-like form and the type structure they encode make them well-suited to reducing underspecification by using well-established linguistic principles and exploiting the distributional properties of language. Figure 1 shows the interpretation process for EL formulas and the role of ULFs in providing the first step into it. Due to the structural dependencies between the components in the interpretation process, the optimal choice at any given component depends on the overall coherence of the final interpretation; hence the backward arrows in the figure. Word sense disambiguation (WSD) and anaphora have no structural dependencies in the interpretation process so they are separated from and fully connected to the post-ULF components. These resolutions are depicted in the last step in the figure.

WSD & Anaphora: While (weak.a (plur creature.n)) in example (3) does not specify which of the dozen WordNet senses of *weak* or three senses of *creature* is intended here, the type structure is perfectly clear: A predicate modifier is being applied to a nominal predicate. ULF also does not assume unique adicity of word-derived predicates such as run.v, since such predicates can have intransitive, simple transitive and other variants, but the adicity of a predicate in ULF is always clear from its structural context – we know that it has all its arguments in place when an argument (the "subject") is placed on its left, as in English.

Linguistic constraints (e.g. *binding constraints*) exist for coreference resolution. For example, in *"John said that he was robbed"*, *he* can refer to *John*; but this is not possible in *"He said that John was robbed"*, because in the latter, *he* C-commands *John*, i.e., in the phrase structure of the sentence, it is a sibling of an ancestor of *John*. ULF preserves this structure, allowing use of such constraints. While ULF

---

[3] (for.p me.pro) has type $\mathcal{D} \rightarrow (S \rightarrow 2)$ and |Snoopy| has type $\mathcal{D}$, so (|Snoopy| (for.p me.pro)) has a type that resolves to $S \rightarrow 2$ (i.e. a sentence intension).

constrains the word senses and coreferences through adicity and syntactic structure, WSD and anaphora resolution should not be applied to isolated sentences since word sense patterns and coreference chains often span multiple sentences.

Scoping: Unscoped constituents (determiners, tense operators, and coordinators) can generally "float" to more than one possible position. Following a view of scope ambiguity developed by Schubert and Pelletier (1982) elaborated by Hurum and Schubert (1986), these constituents always float to pre-sentential positions, and determiner phrases leave behind a variable that is then bound at the sentential level. The accessible positions are constrained by linguistic restrictions, such as *scope island* constraints in subordinate clauses (Ruys and Winter, 2010). Beyond this, many factors influence preferred scoping possibilities, with surface form playing a prominent role (Manshadi et al., 2013). The proximity of ULF to surface syntax enables the use of these constraints.

Deindexing and Canonicalization: Much of the past work relating to EL has been concerned with the principles of *deindexing* (Hwang, 1992; Hwang and Schubert, 1994; Schubert and Hwang, 2000). Deindexing corresponds to the introduction of event variables for explicitly characterizing the sentence it is linked to via the '**' operator (this variable becomes |E|.sk in Figure 1 after Skolemization). Hwang and Schubert's approach to tense-aspect processing, constructing *tense trees* for temporally relating event variables, is only possible if the LF being processed reflects the original clausal structure – as ULF indeed does. Canonicalization is the mapping of an LF into "minimal", distinct propositions, with top-level Skolemization. The CLF step in Figure 1 contains two separate formulas as a result of this process.

Episodic Logical Forms (ELF): When episodes have been made explicit and all anaphoric and word ambiguities are resolved the result is a set of *episodic logical forms*. These can be used in the EPILOG inference engine for reasoning that combines linguistic semantic content with world knowledge.[4] A variety of complex EPILOG inferences are reported by Schubert (2013), and Morbini and Schubert (2011) give examples of self-aware metareasoning. EPILOG also reasoned about snippets from the Little Red Riding Hood story, for example using knowledge about the world and goal-oriented behavior to understand why the presence of nearby woodcutters prevented the wolf from attacking Little Red Riding Hood when he first saw her (Hwang, 1992; Schubert and Hwang, 2000).

3.4 Inference with ULFs

An important insight of NLog research is that language can be used directly for inference, requiring only phrase structure analysis and upward/downward entailment marking (polarity) of phrasal contexts. This means that NLog inferences are *situated* inferences, i.e., their meaning is just as dependent on the utterance setting and discourse state as the linguistic "input" that drives them. This insight carries over to ULFs, and provides a separate justification for computing ULFs, apart from their utility in the process of deriving EL interpretations from language. The semantic type structure encoded by ULFs provides a more reliable and general basis for situated inference than mere phrase structure. Here, briefly, are some kinds of inferences we can expect ULFs to support with minimal additional knowledge due to their structural nature:

- *NLog inferences based on generalizations/specializations.* For example, *"Every NATO member sent troops to Afghanistan"*, together with the knowledge that France is a NATO member and that Afghanistan is a country entails that *France sent troops to Afghanistan* and that *France sent troops to a country*.

- *Inferences based on implicatives.* For example, *"She managed to quit smoking"* entails that *She quit smoking* (and the negation of the premise leads to the opposite conclusion). Inferences of this sort have been demonstrated for headlines using ELFs by Stratos et al. (2011).

- *Inferences based on attitudinal and communicative verbs.* For example, *"John denounced Bill as a charlatan"* entails that *John probably believes that Bill is a charlatan*, that *John asserted to his*

---

[4]EPILOG is competitive against state-of-the-art FOL theorem provers (Morbini and Schubert, 2009).

listeners (or readers) that Bill is a charlatan, and that *John wanted his listeners (or readers) to believe that Bill is a charlatan*. These inferences would be hard to capture within NLog, since they are partially probabilistic, require structural elaboration, and depend on constituent types.

- *Inferences based on counterfactuals.* For example, *"If I were rich, I would pay off your debt"* and *"I wish I were rich"* both implicate that *the speaker is not rich*. This depends on recognition of the counterfactual form, which is distinguished in ULF.

- *Inferences from questions and requests.* For example, *"When are you getting married?"* enables the inferences that the addressee will get married (in the foreseeable future), that the questioner wants to know the expected date of the event, and that the addressee probably knows the answer and will supply it. Similarly an apparent request such as *"Could you close the door?"* implies that the speaker wants the addressee to close the door, and expects that he or she will do so.

4 Predicate and Sentence Modification in Depth

Here we ground the general description of ULF given so far with an in-depth discussion of how ULF handles modification. This is done with the purpose of demonstrating how the core syntax of ULF, its syntactic looseness, and semantic types fit together in practice. EL semantic types represent *predicate modifiers* as functions from *monadic* intensional predicates to *monadic* intensional predicates, i.e., $\mathcal{N} \rightarrow \mathcal{N}$, which enables handling of intersective, subsective, and intensional modifiers such as in the examples

```
((mod-n wooden.a) shoe.n), ((mod-n ice.n) pick.n), (fake.mod-n ruby.n),
((mod-a worldly.a) wise.a), (very.mod-a fit.a), (slyly.adv-a grin.v).
```

Modifier extensions .mod-n, and .mod-a respectively reflect the linguistic categories of noun-premodifying (attributive) adjectives and adjective-premodifying adverbs; correspondingly, operators mod-n, and mod-a type-shift prenominal predicates to modifiers applicable to predicates of sorts .n and .a respectively. Modifier extension .adv-a reflects the linguistic category of VP adverbials, and operator adv-a creates such modifiers from predicates. Thus, *"walk with Bob"* is represented in raw and postprocessed ULF respectively as

```
(walk.v (adv-a (with.p |Bob|))) and ((adv-a (with.p |Bob|)) walk.v).
```

Adverbial modifiers of the sort .adv-a intuitively modify actions, experiences, or attributes, as distinct from events. Thus *"He lifted the child easily"* refers to an action that was easy for the agent, rather than to an easy event. Actions, experiences, and attributes in EL are individuals comprised of agent-episode pairs, and this allows modifiers of the sort .adv-a to express a constraint on both the agent and the episode it characterizes. As such, actions are not explicitly represented in ULF but rather derived during deindexing when event variables are introduced.

A formula or nonatomic verbal predicate in ULF may contain sentential modifiers of type $(S \rightarrow 2) \rightarrow (S \rightarrow 2)$: .adv-s, .adv-e, and .adv-f. Again there are type-shifting operators that create these sorts of modifiers from monadic predicates. Ones of the sort .adv-s are usually modal (and thus opaque), e.g.,

```
perhaps.adv-s, (adv-s (without.p (a.d doubt.n)));
```

However, negation is transparent in the usual sense – the truth value of a negated sentence depends only of the truth value of the unnegated sentence. Modifiers of sort .adv-e are transparent, typically implying temporal or locative constraints, e.g.,

```
today.adv-e, (adv-e (during.p (the.d drought.n))), (adv-e (in.p |Rome|));
```

these constraints are ultimately cashed out as predications about episodes characterized by the sentence being modified. (This is also true for the past and pres tense operators.) Similarly any modifier of sort .adv-f is transparent and implies the existence of a multi-episode (characterized by the sentence as a whole) whose temporally disjoint parts each have the same characterization (Hwang and Schubert, 1994); e.g.,

```
regularly.adv-f, (adv-f (at.p (three.d (plur time.n))));
```

The earlier *walk with Bob* example shows how in ULF the operator and operand can be inferred from the constituent types. Consider the types for play.v and (adv-a (with.p (the.d dog.n))). Since they have types $\mathcal{N}_V$ and $\mathcal{N}_V \rightarrow \mathcal{N}_V$, respectively, we can be certain that `(adv-a (with.p (the.d dog.n)))` is the operator while `play.v` is the operand.

In practice, we're able to drop the `mod-a`, `mod-n`, and `nnp` type-shifters during annotation since we can post-process them with the appropriate type-shifter to make the composition valid. We assume in these cases that the prefixed predicate is intended as the operator, which reflects a common pattern in English. Thus, "burning hot melting pot" would be hand annotated as

```
((burning.a hot.a) (melting.n pot.n))
```

which would be post-processed to

```
((mod-n ((mod-a burning.a) hot.a)) ((mod-n melting.n) pot.n))
```

While the prefixed predicate modification allows us to formally model non-intersective modification, there are modification patterns in English that force an intersective interpretation, e.g., post-nominal modification and appositives, and we annotate them accordingly. *"The buildings in the city"* is annotated

```
(the.d (n+preds (plur building.n) (in.p (the.d city.n))))
```

which is equivalent (via the n+preds macro) to

```
(the.d (λx ((x (plur building.n)) and.cc (x (in.p (the.d city.n)))))).
```

5 Annotating a ULF Corpus

The syntactic relaxations in ULF and the annotation environment work hand-in-hand to enable quick and consistent annotations. ULF syntax relaxations are designed to: (1) Preserve surface word order and (2) Make the annotations match linguistic intuitions more closely. As a result, annotating a sentence with its ULF interpretation boils down to marking the words with their semantic types, bracketing the sentence according to the operator-operand relations, then introducing macros and logical operators as necessary to make the ULF type-consistent. The annotation environment is designed to assist in this process by improving the readability of long ULFs and catching mistakes that are easy to miss. The environment is shared across annotators with certainty marking so that more experienced annotators can correct and give feedback to trainees. This streamlines the training process and minimizes the mistakes entering into the corpus. Here are the core annotator features.[5]

1. **Syntax and bracket highlighting.** Highlights the cursor location and the closing bracket, unmatched brackets and quotes, operator keywords, and badly placed operators.

2. **Sanity checker.** Alerts the annotator to invalid type compositions and suggests corrections for common mistakes.

3. **Certainty marking.** Annotators can mark whether they are certain of an annotation's correctness so that partial progress can be made while preserving the integrity of the corpus.

4. **Sentence-specific comments.** Annotators can record their thoughts on partially complete annotations so that others can pick up where they left off.

The ULF type system makes it possible to build a robust sanity checker for the annotator. The type system severely restricts the space of valid ULF formulas and usually when an annotator makes an error in annotation, it leads to a type inconsistency.

6 Experimental Results and Current Progress

We ran a timing study and an interannotator agreement (IA) study to quantify the efficacy of the presented annotation framework. We timed 80 annotations of the Tatoeba dataset and found the average annotation speed to be 8 min/sent with 4 min/sent among the two experts and 11 min/sent among the three trainees that participated. AMRs reportedly took on average 10 min/sent (Hermjakob, 2013). In the IA study five

---

[5]The annotator can be accessed from the ULF project website and a screenshot of it is in Appendix D.

annotators each annotated between 18 and 23 sentences from the same set of 23 sentences, marking their certainty of the annotations as they normally would. The sentences were sampled from the four datasets listed in Table 1. The mean and standard deviation of sentence length were 15.3 words and 10.8 words, respectively.

We computed a similarity score between two annotations using *EL-smatch* (Kim and Schubert, 2016), a generalization of *smatch* (Cai and Knight, 2013) which handles non-atomic operators. The document-level EL-smatch score between all annotated sentence pairs was 0.70. When we restricted the analysis to just annotations that were marked *certain*, the agreement rose to 0.78. The complete pairwise scores are shown in Table 2. Notice that annotators 1, 2, and 3 had very high agreement with each other. If we restrict the agreement to just those three annotators, the full and certain-subset scores are 0.79 and 0.88, respectively. Out of all the annotations, less than a third were marked as uncertain or incomplete. AMR annotations reportedly have annotator vs consensus IA of 0.83 for newswire and 0.79 for web text (Tsialos, 2015).

This study also demonstrates that the certainty marking indeed reflects the quality of the annotation, thus performing the role we intended. Also, based on the high agreement between annotators 1, 2, and 3, we can conclude that consistent ULF annotations across multiple annotators is possible. However, the lower scores of annotators 4 and 5, even in annotations marked as certain, indicates room for improvement in the annotation guidelines and training of some annotators.

Table 1: Current sentence annotation counts broken down by dataset and certainty. DG and PG are the Discourse Graphbank and Project Gutenberg, respectively. The *Old* column annotations are from before we added the certainty feature.

	Cert.	*Unc.*	*Inc.*	*Old*	*All*
Tatoeba	533	66	24	396	1019
DG	102	37	4	0	143
UIUC QC	179	50	0	0	229
PG	113	59	17	0	189
Total	**927**	212	45	396	1580

Table 2: Pairwise IA scores, where the left score is over all annotations and the right score is only over annotations marked as certain.

	2	3	4	5
1	0.80/0.88	0.79/0.89	0.69/0.77	0.63/0.75
2	-	0.77/0.86	0.72/0.77	0.62/0.75
3	-	-	0.69/0.75	0.63/0.73
4	-	-	-	0.62/0.71

We have so far collected 927 certain annotations and have 1,580 in total. The full annotation breakdown is in Table 1. We started with the English portion of the Tatoeba dataset (https://tatoeba.org/eng/), a crowd-sourced translation dataset. This source tends to have shorter sentences, but they are more varied in topic and form. We then added text from Project Gutenberg (http://gutenberg.org), the UIUC Question Classification dataset (Li and Roth, 2002), and the Discourse Graphbank (Wolf, 2005). Preliminary parsing experiments on a small dataset (900 sentences) show promising results and we expect to be able to build an accurate parser with a moderately-sized dataset and representation-specific engineering (Kim, 2019).

7   Related Work

A notable development in general representations of semantic content has been the design of AMR (Banarescu et al., 2013) followed by numerous research studies on generating AMR from English and on using it for downstream tasks. AMR is intended as a kind of intuitive normal form for the relational context of English sentences in order to assist in machine translation. Given this goal, AMR deliberately neglected issues such as articles, tense, the distinction between real and hypothetical entities, and non-intersective modification. In the context of inference, this risks making false conclusions such as that a *"big ant"* is bigger than a *"small elephant"*.

Still, this development was an inspiration to us in terms of both the quest for broad coverage and methods of learning and evaluating semantic parsers. There has also been much activity in developing semantic parsers that derive logical representations, raising the possibility of making inferences with those representations (Artzi et al., 2015; Artzi and Zettlemoyer, 2013; Howard et al., 2014; Kate and

Mooney, 2006; Konstas et al., 2017; Kwiatkowski et al., 2011; Liang et al., 2011; Poon, 2013; Popescu et al., 2004; Tellex et al., 2011). The techniques and formalisms employed are interesting (e.g., learning of CCG grammars that generate λ-calculus expressions), but the targeted tasks have generally been question-answering in domains consisting of numerous monadic and dyadic ground facts ("triples"), or simple robotic or human action descriptions.[6]

Noteworthy examples of formal logic-based approaches, not targeting specific applications are Bos' (2008) and Draiccio et al.'s (2013), whose hand-built semantic parsers respectively generate FOL formulas and OWL-DL expressions. But these representations preclude generalized quantifiers, modification, reification, attitudes, etc. Manshadi and Allen (2012) presented an intuitive graphical representation, like AMR, but allowing for modals, generalized quantifiers, etc., and not attempting to canonicalize meanings in the way AMR does. The difference from ULF is that it focuses on binary structural relations such as *restrictor*, *body*, or *modifier* between semantic components, rather than operator-operand type structure. It is not directly intended for inference, but readily lends itself to incremental disambiguation. We are not aware of any work on inference generation of the type ULFs targets, based on these projects.

A couple of yet-unmentioned but notable semantic annotation projects are the Groningen Meaning Bank (Bos et al., 2017), with discourse representation structure (DRS) annotations (Kamp, 1981) and the Redwoods treebank (Flickinger et al., 2012; Oepen et al., 2002) with Minimal Recursion Semantics (MRS) (Copestake et al., 2005) annotations. DRSs have the same representational limitations as Bos' (2008) system. MRS is descriptively powerful and linguistically motivated, with significant resources including a hand-built grammar, multiple parsers, and a large annotated dataset (Bub et al., 1997; Callmeier, 2001). Given that MRS and Manshadi and Allen's graphical representation are object-language agnostic, meta-level semantic representations, inference systems cannot be built directly for them based on model-theoretic notions of interpretation, truth, satisfaction, and entailment. However, the lack of an object-language leaves open the possibility of forming a correspondence between these representations and ULF that fully respects both formalisms. Finally, the use of unscoped LFs in a rule-to-rule framework was first introduced by Schubert and Pelletier (1982) and a similar approach to scope ambiguity was taken by the Core Language Engine (Alshawi and van Eijck, 1989).

8   Conclusion & Future Work

ULF, the underspecified initial representation for EL described in this document, captures a subset of the semantic information of EL that allows it to be annotated reliably, participate in the complete resolution to EL, and form the basis for structural inferences that are important for language understanding tasks. We will continue this work by expanding the corpus of ULF annotations and training a statistical parser over that corpus. Automatic ULF parses could then be used as the backbone for a complete EL parser or as the core representation for NLP tasks that require sentence-level formal semantic information or structural inferences.

9   Acknowledgements

We would like to thank Burkay Donderici, Benjamin Kane, Lane Lawley, Tianyi Ma, Graeme McGuire, Muskaan Mendriatta, Akihiro Minami, Georgiy Platonov, Sophie Sackstein, and Siddharth Vashishta for raising thoughtful questions in the development of this work. We are grateful to the anonymous reviewers for their helpful feedback. This work was supported by DARPA CwC subcontract W911NF-15-1-0542.

---

[6]For example, Ross et al. (2018) develop a CCG-based semantic parser for action annotations in videos, representing sentences in an approximate way—neglecting determiners and treating all entity references as variables.

References

Alshawi, H. and J. van Eijck (1989, June). Logical forms in the core language engine. In *Proceedings of the 27th Annual Meeting of the Association for Computational Linguistics*, Vancouver, British Columbia, Canada, pp. 25–32. Association for Computational Linguistics.

Artzi, Y., K. Lee, and L. Zettlemoyer (2015, September). Broad-coverage CCG semantic parsing with AMR. In *Proceedings of the 2015 Conference on Empirical Methods in Natural Language Processing*, Lisbon, Portugal, pp. 1699–1710. Association for Computational Linguistics.

Artzi, Y. and L. Zettlemoyer (2013). Weakly supervised learning of semantic parsers for mapping instructions to actions. *Transactions of the Association for Computational Linguistics 1*(1), 49–62.

Banarescu, L., C. Bonial, S. Cai, M. Georgescu, K. Griffitt, U. Hermjakob, K. Knight, P. Koehn, M. Palmer, and N. Schneider (2013, August). Abstract Meaning Representation for sembanking. In *Proceedings of the 7th Linguistic Annotation Workshop and Interoperability with Discourse*, Sofia, Bulgaria, pp. 178–186. Association for Computational Linguistics.

Barwise, J. and R. Cooper (1981). Generalized quantifiers and natural language. In *Philosophy, language, and artificial intelligence*, pp. 241–301. Springer.

Bos, J. (2008). Wide-coverage semantic analysis with Boxer. In *Proceedings of the 2008 Conference on Semantics in Text Processing*, STEP '08, Stroudsburg, PA, USA, pp. 277–286. Association for Computational Linguistics.

Bos, J., V. Basile, K. Evang, N. Venhuizen, and J. Bjerva (2017). The Groningen Meaning Bank. In N. Ide and J. Pustejovsky (Eds.), *Handbook of Linguistic Annotation*, Volume 2, pp. 463–496. Springer.

Bub, T., W. Wahlster, and A. Waibel (1997, Apr). Verbmobil: the combination of deep and shallow processing for spontaneous speech translation. In *1997 IEEE International Conference on Acoustics, Speech, and Signal Processing*, Volume 1, pp. 71–74 vol.1.

Cai, S. and K. Knight (2013, August). Smatch: an evaluation metric for semantic feature structures. In *Proceedings of the 51st Annual Meeting of the Association for Computational Linguistics (Volume 2: Short Papers)*, Sofia, Bulgaria, pp. 748–752. Association for Computational Linguistics.

Callmeier, U. (2001). Efficient parsing with large-scale unification grammars. Master's thesis, Universität des Saarlandes, Saarbrücken, Germany.

Copestake, A., D. Flickinger, C. Pollard, and I. A. Sag (2005). Minimal Recursion Semantics: An introduction. *Research on Language and Computation 3*(2), 281–332.

Davidson, D. (1967). The logical form of action sentences. In N. Rescher (Ed.), *The Logic of Decision and Action*. University of Pittsburgh Press.

Draicchio, F., A. Gangemi, V. Presutti, and A. Nuzzolese (2013). FRED: From natural language text to rdf and owl in one click. In *P. Cimiano et al. (eds.), ESWC 2013*, pp. 263–267. Springer.

Flickinger, D., Y. Zhang, and V. Kordoni (2012). DeepBank: A dynamically annotated treebank of the wall street journal. In *Proceedings of the Eleventh International Workshop on Treebanks and Linguistic Theories*, pp. 85–96. EdiÃğÃțes Colibri.

Hermjakob, U. (2013). AMR Editor: A tool to build abstract meaning representations.

Howard, T. M., S. Tellex, and N. Roy (2014). A natural language planner interface for mobile manipulators. In *2014 IEEE International Conference on Robotics and Automation (ICRA)*, pp. 6652–6659.

Hurum, S. and L. Schubert (1986, May). Two types of quantifier scoping. In *Proc. 6th Can. Conf. on Artificial Intelligence (AI-86)*, Montreal, Canada, pp. 19–43.

Hwang, C. and L. Schubert (1993). Episodic Logic: A situational logic for natural language processing. In P. Aczel, D. Israel, Y. Katagiri, and S. Peters (Eds.), *Situation Theory and its Applications 3 (STA-3)*, pp. 307–452. CSLI.

Hwang, C. H. (1992). *A logical approach to narrative understanding*. Ph. D. thesis, University of Alberta.

Hwang, C. H. and L. K. Schubert (1994). Interpreting tense, aspect and time adverbials: A compositional, unified approach. In *Proceedings of the First International Conference on Temporal Logic*, ICTL '94, London, UK, pp. 238–264. Springer-Verlag.

Kamp, H. (1981). A theory of truth and semantic representation. In J. A. G. Groenendijk, T. M. V. Janssen, and M. B. J. Stokhof (Eds.), *Formal Methods in the Study of Language*, Volume 1, pp. 277–322. Amsterdam: Mathematisch Centrum.

Kate, R. J. and R. J. Mooney (2006, July). Using string-kernels for learning semantic parsers. In *Proceedings of the 21st International Conference on Computational Linguistics and 44th Annual Meeting of the Association for Computational Linguistics*, Sydney, Australia, pp. 913–920. Association for Computational Linguistics.

Kim, G. and L. Schubert (2016, August). High-fidelity lexical axiom construction from verb glosses. In *Proceedings of the Fifth Joint Conference on Lexical and Computational Semantics*, Berlin, Germany, pp. 34–44. Association for Computational Linguistics.

Kim, G. and L. Schubert (2017, April). Intension, attitude, and tense annotation in a high-fidelity semantic representation. In *Proceedings of the Workshop Computational Semantics Beyond Events and Roles*, Valencia, Spain, pp. 10–15. Association for Computational Linguistics.

Kim, G. L. (2019). Towards parsing unscoped episodic logical forms with a cache transition parser. In *the Poster Abstracts of the Proceedings of the 32nd International Conference of the Florida Artificial Intelligence Research Society*.

Konstas, I., S. Iyer, M. Yatskar, Y. Choi, and L. Zettlemoyer (2017, July). Neural AMR: Sequence-to-sequence models for parsing and generation. In *Proceedings of the 55th Annual Meeting of the Association for Computational Linguistics (Volume 1: Long Papers)*, Vancouver, Canada, pp. 146–157. Association for Computational Linguistics.

Kwiatkowski, T., L. Zettlemoyer, S. Goldwater, and M. Steedman (2011, July). Lexical generalization in CCG grammar induction for semantic parsing. In *Proceedings of the 2011 Conference on Empirical Methods in Natural Language Processing*, Edinburgh, Scotland, UK., pp. 1512–1523. Association for Computational Linguistics.

Li, X. and D. Roth (2002). Learning question classifiers. In *Proceedings of the 19th International Conference on Computational Linguistics - Volume 1*, COLING '02, Stroudsburg, PA, USA, pp. 1–7. Association for Computational Linguistics.

Liang, P., M. Jordan, and D. Klein (2011, June). Learning dependency-based compositional semantics. In *Proceedings of the 49th Annual Meeting of the Association for Computational Linguistics: Human Language Technologies*, Portland, Oregon, USA, pp. 590–599. Association for Computational Linguistics.

Manshadi, M. and J. Allen (2012, May). A universal representation for shallow and deep semantics. In *Joint ISA-7 Workshop on Interoperable Semantic Annotation SRSL-3 Workshop on Semantic Representation for Spoken Language I2MRT Workshop on Multimodal Resources and Tools*, pp. 52.

Manshadi, M., D. Gildea, and J. Allen (2013, August). Plurality, negation, and quantification:towards comprehensive quantifier scope disambiguation. In *Proceedings of the 51st Annual Meeting of the Association for Computational Linguistics (Volume 1: Long Papers)*, Sofia, Bulgaria, pp. 64–72. Association for Computational Linguistics.

Montague, R. (1973). The proper treatment of quantification in ordinary English. In K. J. J. Hintikka, J. Moravcsic, and P. Suppes (Eds.), *Approaches to Natural Language: Proceedings of the 1970 Stanford Workshop on Grammar and Semantics*, pp. 221–242. Dordrecht: Reidel.

Morbini, F. and L. Schubert (2009, June). Evaluation of Epilog: A reasoner for Episodic Logic. In *Proceedings of the Ninth International Symposium on Logical Formalizations of Commonsense Reasoning*, Toronto, Canada.

Morbini, F. and L. Schubert (2011, January). Metareasoning as an Integral Part of Commonsense and Autocognitive Reasoning. In M. T. Cox and A. Raja (Eds.), *Metareasoning: Thinking about thinking*. MIT Press.

Oepen, S., K. Toutanova, S. Shieber, C. Manning, D. Flickinger, and T. Brants (2002). The LinGo Redwoods Treebank: Motivation and preliminary applications. In *Proceedings of the 19th International Conference on Computational Linguistics - Volume 2*, COLING '02, Stroudsburg, PA, USA, pp. 1–5. Association for Computational Linguistics.

Poon, H. (2013, August). Grounded unsupervised semantic parsing. In *Proceedings of the 51st Annual Meeting of the Association for Computational Linguistics (Volume 1: Long Papers)*, Sofia, Bulgaria, pp. 933–943. Association for Computational Linguistics.

Popescu, A.-M., A. Armanasu, O. Etzioni, D. Ko, and A. Yates (2004). Modern natural language interfaces to databases: Composing statistical parsing with semantic tractability. In *Proceedings of the 20th International Conference on Computational Linguistics*, COLING '04, Stroudsburg, PA, USA. Association for Computational Linguistics.

Ross, C., A. Barbu, Y. Berzak, B. Myanganbayar, and B. Katz (2018, October 31 - November 4). Grounding language acquisition by training semantic parsers using captioned videos. In *Proceedings of the 2018 Conference on Empirical Methods in Natural Language Processing (EMNLP)*, Brussels, Belgium, pp. 2647–2656.

Ruys, E. and Y. Winter (2010). Quantifier scope in formal linguistics. In D. M. Gabbay and F. Guenthner (Eds.), *Handbook of Philosophical Logic*, pp. 159–225. Springer, Dortrecht.

Sánchez Valencia, V. (1995). Natural logic: parsing driven inference. *Linguistic Analysis 25*, 258–285.

Schubert, L. (2013). NLog-like inference and commonsense reasoning. In A. Zaenen, V. de Paiva, and C. Condoravdi (Eds.), *Perspectives on Semantic Representations for Textual Inference, special issue of Linguistic Issues in Language Technology (LiLT 9)*, Volume 9, pp. 1–26.

Schubert, L. (2014, June). From treebank parses to Episodic Logic and commonsense inference. In *Proceedings of the ACL 2014 Workshop on Semantic Parsing*, Baltimore, MD, pp. 55–60. Association for Computational Linguistics.

Schubert, L. and F. Pelletier (1982). From English to logic: Context-free computation of 'conventional' logical translations. *Am. J. of Computational Linguistics 8 [now Computational Linguistics] 8*, 26–44.

Schubert, L. K. (2000). The situations we talk about. In J. Minker (Ed.), *Logic-based Artificial Intelligence*, pp. 407–439. Norwell, MA, USA: Kluwer Academic Publishers.

Schubert, L. K. and C. H. Hwang (2000). Episodic Logic meets Little Red Riding Hood: A comprehensive natural representation for language understanding. In L. M. Iwańska and S. C. Shapiro (Eds.), *Natural Language Processing and Knowledge Representation*, pp. 111–174. Cambridge, MA, USA: MIT Press.

Stratos, K., L. K. Schubert, and J. Gordon (2011). Episodic Logic: Natural Logic + reasoning. In *Proceedings of the International Conference on Knowledge Engineering and Ontology Development (KEOD)*.

Tellex, S., T. Kollar, S. Dickerson, M. Walter, A. Banerjee, S. Teller, and N. Roy (2011). Understanding natural language commands for robotic navigation and mobile manipulation. In *AAAI Conference on Artificial Intelligence*.

Tsialos, A. (2015, March). Abstract meaning representation for sembanking. Available at www.inf.ed.ac.uk/teaching/courses/tnlp/2014/Aristeidis.pdf, accessed December 8, 2018.

Wolf, F. (2005). *Coherence in natural language : data structures and applications*. Ph. D. thesis, Massachusetts Institute of Technology, Dept. of Brain and Cognitive Sciences.

A   Quantifier Semantics

Noun phrases can occur in any position here an individual variable or constant can occur, and in postprocessing are replaced by bound variables. Therefore the *positional* types of noun phrases are individuals, $\mathcal{D}$. Therefore, we can treat determiners such as every.d in ULF as if they were of type $(\mathcal{N} \to \mathcal{D}$, i.e. a function from a predicate to an individual. For example consider the ULF formula ((every.d dog.n) (pres run.v)). (every.d dog.n) seems to be able to occur in any place that |John| and they.pro can occur.

((every.d dog.n) (pres run.v)),   (i.pro ((pres like.v) (every.d dog.n))),

(|John| (pres run.v)),   (i.pro ((pres like.v) |John|)),

(they.pro (pres run.v));   (i.pro ((pres like.v) they.pro));

Semantically we consider they.pro and them.pro to be the same, as they only differ in syntactic position. Then since dog.n (and any other argument of a determiner) is a monadic predicate, we can infer that the *positional* type of determiners is $\mathcal{N} \to \mathbf{2}$. This will be transformed after scoping into a formula of the form $(\delta v : \phi \ \psi)$, where δ is the determiner, and ϕ and ψ correspond to the formulas resulting from substituting the scoped variable into the restrictor and matrix predicates, respectively. These formulas are interpreted in EL via satisfaction conditions over the quantified variable and two formulas (a restrictor formula and the nuclear scope), e.g., for an sentence such as *"Most car crashes are due to driver error"*,

$$(\text{most } v : \phi \ \psi)^{\mathcal{M} \, \mathcal{U}} = 1 \text{ iff}$$

$$\text{for most } d \in \mathcal{D} \text{ for which } \phi^{\mathcal{M} \, \mathcal{U}_{v:d}} = 1, \psi^{\mathcal{M} \, \mathcal{U}_{v:d}} = 1$$

where $\mathcal{M}$ is the model, $\mathcal{U}$ is the variable assignment function, and $\mathcal{U}_{v:d}$ is the same as $\mathcal{U}$ except that its value for variable v is d. When this formula is evaluated with respect to an episode, it corresponds to a formula of the form

$$[(\text{several } v : \phi \ \psi) ** \eta],$$

where '$**$' is the operator relating a sentence to the episode it *characterizes* (describes as a whole), which is discussed in Section 2. $(\delta v : \phi \ \psi)$ can equivalently be rewritten as $(\delta \ (\lambda v \ \phi) \ (\lambda v \ \psi))$ and we can define δ as a second-order intensional predicate of type $\mathcal{N} \to \mathcal{N} \to S \to \mathbf{2}$ similar to the approach used in generalized quantifier theory (Barwise and Cooper, 1981).

B   Episodic Operators

'$**$', '$*$', and '$@$' are *episodic* operators, which relate formulas to episode variables in Episodic Logic. They do not appear in ULFs since ULFs do not have explicit episode variables. However, these operators are foundational to Episodic Logic semantics in handling event structure and intensional semantics. All formulas in EL must be evaluated with respect to one of these operators to obtain a truth value since sentence intensions in EL have the type $S \rightarrow \mathbf{2}$.

- '**' - the *characterizing* operator

  '**' relates an episode variable to a formula that *characterizes* it. In other word, the formula describes the episode as a whole, or the nature of the episode, rather than a tangential part or a temporal segment of it. This, however, does not mean that the characterizing formula must describe *every* detail of the episode. It can in fact be quite abstract. For instance, *"John had a car accident"* and *"John hit some black ice and his car skidded into a tree"* might characterize the same event. As such, for most news stories the headline and the first sentence of the article are likely to both characterize the same event even though the headline is much shorter. Formally,

$$[\phi ** \eta]^{\mathcal{M}\mathcal{U}} = 1 \text{ iff } \phi^{\mathcal{M}\mathcal{U}}(\eta^{\mathcal{M}\mathcal{U}}) = 1;$$

$$[(\text{not } \phi) ** \eta]^{\mathcal{M}\mathcal{U}} = 1 \text{ iff } \phi^{\mathcal{M}\mathcal{U}}(\eta^{\mathcal{M}\mathcal{U}}) = 0.$$

  The semantic type of ϕ is $S \rightarrow \mathbf{2}$ (a sentence intension) and the semantic type of η is S, a situation. Therefore, η characterizes ϕ just in the case that the interpretation of ϕ with respect to the model $\mathcal{M}$ and variable assignment function $\mathcal{U}$ evaluated over the interpretation of η with respect to $\mathcal{M}$ and $\mathcal{U}$ is true.

- '*' - the *truth* operator

  '*' relates an episode variable to a formula that is *true* in that episode. This is a weaker operator than '**' in that a formula that is '*'-related can be a just a segment or an incidental aspect of the episode to be true. Therefore, $[\phi ** \eta]$ entails $[\phi * \eta]$, but not the other way. Therefore, *"There was black ice on the road"* and *"John was driving"* could both be '*'-related to the episode characterized by the example given in for the '**' operator. Formally,

$$[\phi * \eta]^{\mathcal{M}\mathcal{U}} = 1 \text{ iff there is an episode } s \sqsubseteq \eta^{\mathcal{M}\mathcal{U}} \text{ such that } \phi^{\mathcal{M}\mathcal{U}}(s) = 1.$$

  Where $\sqsubseteq$ is an episode part-of relation. It's formal definition is given by Hwang and Schubert (1993). Intuitively we can think of $s \sqsubseteq \eta$ to mean that s is a subepisode of η.

- '@' - the *concurrent* operator

  '@' relates an episode variable to a formula characterizes another episode that runs concurrent with it. So this operator can be rewritten in the following way. $[\phi @ \eta]$ entails and is entailed by (some e : $[e$ same-time $\eta] [\phi ** e]$). Formally, @ us defined as

$$[\phi @ \eta]^{\mathcal{M}\mathcal{U}} = 1 \text{ iff there is an episode } s \in S \text{ with } time(s) = time(\eta^{\mathcal{M}\mathcal{U}}) \text{ such that } \phi^{\mathcal{M}\mathcal{U}}(s) = 1.$$

C   More About Macros

ULF macros are different syntactic rewriting operators to reduce the annotator burden of encoding complex, but regular, semantic structures or avoid unnecessary word reordering. Table 3 lists the definitions and simple examples of the basic ULF macros. The sub macro is the *substitution* macro which performs a simple substitution of its first argument into the position of *h within the second argument. This is used for topicalization, such as *"Swiftly, the fox ran away"*, which topicalizes *"Swiftly"* from the sentence *"The fox swiftly ran away"*. The rep macro is the *replace* operator and the exact same as sub with the arguments swapped and using *p instead of *h as the placeholder variable. This is used for rightward-displaced clauses, such as, *"A man answered the door with a white beard"*, in which *with a white beard* is really displaced from the expected post-nominal position, i.e *"A man with a white beard ..."*.

Table 3: List of basic rewriting macros in ULF. $=_m$ is the macro defining operator.

Name	*Definitions*	*Example*
sub	(sub C S[*h]) $=_m$ S[*h←C]	(sub A (B *h)) $=_m$ (B A)
rep	(rep S[*p] C) $=_m$ S[*p←C]	(rep (A *p) B) $=_m$ (A B)

n+preds	(n+preds N P$_1$ ... P$_n$) $=_m$
	    (λx ((x N) and.cc (x P$_1$) ... (x P$_n$)))
		(n+preds dog.n red.a) $=_m$
		    (λx ((x dog.n) and.cc (x red.a)))

np+preds	(np+preds NP P$_1$ ... P$_n$) $=_m$
	    (the.d (λx ((x = NP) and.cc
	       (x P$_1$) ... (x P$_n$))))
		(np+preds he.pro red.a) $=_m$
		    (the.d (λx ((x = he.pro) and.cc
		       (x red.a))))

's	((NP 's) N) $=_m$ (the.d ((poss-by NP) N))	((|John| 's) dog.n) $=_m$ (the.d ((poss-by |John|) dog.n))

Next, n+preds and np+preds are macros for handling post-nominal modification. n+preds modifies a noun and returns a noun, whereas np+preds modifies an entity and returns a modified entity. Intuitively, np+preds handles non-restrictive modifiers, whereas n+preds handles restrictive modifiers. This makes sense since the modifying predicates in n+preds are added before the determiner, thus introduced into the restrictor of the quantification.

The 's macro is for handling possession using an appended marker to the possessor just as is done in English (e.g. "John's dog"). Formally, this maps to a pre-modifying possession relation. So *"John's dog"* is hand-annotated as ((|John| 's) dog.n), which expands out to (the.d ((poss-by |John|) dog.n)). poss-by is a binary predicate relating two entities, semantic type $\mathcal{D} \rightarrow (\mathcal{D} \rightarrow (\mathcal{S} \rightarrow 2))$. so (poss-by |John|) resolves to semantic type of a predicate, $\mathcal{N}$. Notice that this is a predicate-noun pair so as discussed in Section 4 the mod-n type-shifter is automatically introduced, resulting in (the.d ((mod-n (poss-by |John|)) dog.n)).

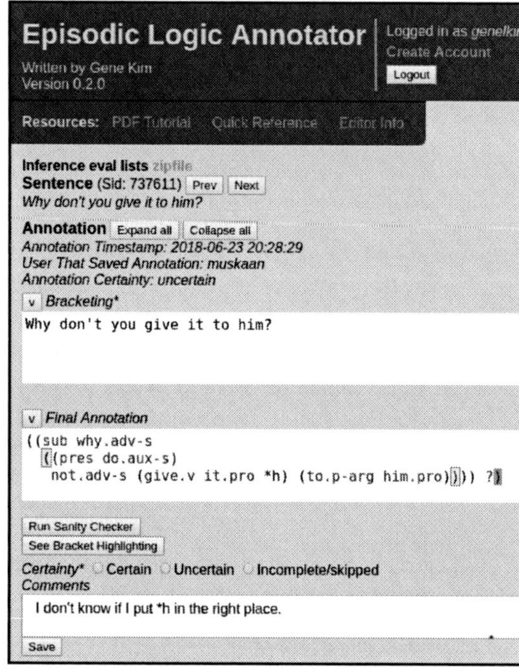

Figure 3: Current ULF annotator state with example annotation process.

D Additional Annotator Info

Here we reiterate the annotator features as described in Section 5 with reference to an image of it in Figure 3.

1. **Syntax and bracket highlighting.** Highlights the cursor location and the closing bracket, unmatched brackets and quotes, operator keywords, and badly placed operators. The "Final Annotation" window in Figure 3 shows the cursor matching bracket in yellow-green highlighting, an unmatched bracket in red, the sub macro in purple, and sentence-level operators in blue.

2. **Sanity checker.** Alerts the annotator to invalid type compositions and suggests corrections for common mistakes.

3. **Certainty marking.** Annotators can mark whether they are certain of an annotation's correctness so that partial progress can be made while preserving the integrity of the corpus. The bottom of

Figure 3 shows radio buttons for selecting the certainty of the annotation.

4. **Sentence-specific comments.** Annotators can record their thoughts on partially complete annotations so that others can pick up where they left off. The bottom-most window in view in Figure 3 is the sentence-specific comment window. These comments are viewable by all annotators when accessing this sentence.

E Additional Grounding Examples

Here are a couple of additional sections that ground the high-level ULF background in concrete examples.

E.1 More Resources on Predicate Modifiers

A type of modification not covered in the main document is entity-predicate modification. The type shifter from an individual to a nominal predicate modifier is named nnp and has semantic type, $\mathcal{D} \to (\mathcal{N}_N \to \mathcal{N}_N)$. It is for indicating premodification of a common noun by a proper noun; e.g.,

```
((nnp |Seattle|) skyline.n).
```
All of the operators discussed in Section 4 and here are listed alongside a ULF example, and its semantic type in Table 4.

Table 4: Predicate and sentence modifier forming operators in ULF along with examples and their semantic types.

Name	Example	Semantic Type
mod-a	`((mod-a worldly.a) wise.a)`	$\mathcal{N} \to (\mathcal{N}_{ADJ} \to \mathcal{N}_{ADJ})$
mod-n	`((mod-n (very.mod-n happy.a)) dog.n)`	$\mathcal{N} \to (\mathcal{N}_N \to \mathcal{N}_N)$
adv-a	`(play.v (adv-a (with.p (a.d dog.n))))`	$\mathcal{N} \to (\mathcal{N}_V \to \mathcal{N}_V)$
nnp	`((nnp |Seattle|) skyline.n)`	$\mathcal{D} \to (\mathcal{N}_N \to \mathcal{N}_N)$
adv-s	`(show_up.v (adv-s (to.p (my.d surprise.n))))`	$(S \to 2) \to (S \to 2)$
adv-e	`(eat.v (adv-e (at.p (a.d cafe.n))))`	$(S \to 2) \to (S \to 2)$
adv-f	`(run.v (adv-f (very.mod-a often.a)))`	$(S \to 2) \to (S \to 2)$

Ultimately in EL, adv-a, adv-e, and adv-f will be reconstrued as predications over actions and events via meaning postulate inferences. Agent-episode pairs that intuitively represent actions, experiences, or attributes are distinct from events. For example, *"He fell painfully"* refers to a painful experience rather than to a painful event and *"He excels intellectually"* refers an intellectual attribute rather than to an intellectual event or situation. .adv-a type modifiers constrain both the agent and the episode in the pair. No sharp or exhaustive classification of such pairs into actions, experiences, and attributes is presupposed by this – the point is just to make available the subject of sentences in working out entailments of VP-modification. Since actions are formed by pairing an agent with an event variable, they are not explicitly represented in ULF. The meaning postulate inferences on .adv-a type modifiers would infer from (he.pro (play.v (adv-a (with.p (a.d dog.n))))) the following deindexed ULF [[[he.pro play.v] ** E1.sk] and.cc [(pair he.pro E1.sk) (with.p (a.d dog.n))]]. The meaning postulate inference of .adv-e type modifiers to predications over events is also straightforward. The ULF formula (she.pro (eat.v (adv-e (at.p (a.d cafe.n))))) leads to the deindexed, inferenced formula [[[she.pro eat.v] ** E1.sk] and.cc [(pair she.pro E1.sk) (at.p (a.d cafe.n))]].

E.2 Topicalization & Relative Clauses in ULF

The sub macro was introduced to reduce the amount of lexical reordering by annotators when annotating sentences with syntactic movement such as topicalization. sub takes two constituents, the second of which must contain the symbol *h. When the operator is evaluated the first argument is inserted into the position of *h in the second argument. *"Swiftly, the fox ran away"* for example would be annotated as (in raw ULF form)

```
(sub swiftly.adv-a ((the.d fox.n) ((past run.v) away.adv-a *h)))
```

and when the sub macro is evaluated, becomes

```
((the.d fox.n) ((past run.v) away.adv-a swiftly.adv-a)).
```

For relative clauses we introduce one extra post-processed element which is the relativizer, annotated with a .rel extension. *"The coffee that you drank"* is annotated in raw ULF with macros as

```
(the.d (n+preds coffee.n (sub that.rel (you.pro ((past drink.v) *h)))))
```

During post-processing, the embedded sentence in which the .rel variable lies is λ-abstracted and the lambda variable replaces the .rel variable. Post-processing that.rel leads to

```
(the.d (n+preds coffee.n (λx (sub x (you.pro ((past drink.v) *h))))))
```

Now if we evaluate both n+preds and sub, and perform one lambda reduction we get

```
(the.d (λy ((y coffee.n) and.cc (you.pro ((past drink.v) y)))))
```

which is exactly the meaning that is expected that is expected from the relative clause. That is, *"The coffee that you drank"* is a coffee ((y coffee.n)) and is something that you drank ((you.pro ((past drink.v) y))).

A semantic annotation scheme for quantification

Harry Bunt
Department of Cognitive Science and Artificial Intelligence
Tilburg University, The Netherlands
`harry.bunt@uvt.nl`

Abstract

This paper describes in brief an annotation scheme called 'QuantML' which was proposed last December to the International Organisation for Standardisation (ISO) as a starting point for developing a standard for interoperable rooted in the theory of generalised quantifiers, neo-Davidsonian semantics, and DRT, covers a wide range of aspects of quantification. The scheme consists of (1) an abstract syntax which defines 'annotation structures' as triples and other set-theoretic constructs; (b) a compositional semantics of annotation structures; (3) an XML representation of annotation structures.

1 Introduction

Quantification is widespread in spoken and written language; it can be found in nearly every sentence, since it occurs whenever a predicate is applied to one or more argument sets (rather than single arguments). This commonly happens in two of the linguistically most prominent units: clauses and noun phrases. In clauses it happens when a verb is combined with sets of arguments, as in *"Last year the American car manufacturers produced more than 12 million vehicles"*. In noun phrases it happens when a head noun is subject to modification, as in *"I'm carrying some heavy books"*.

A widely held view is that the quantifiers of natural language are not determiners like *"some"* and *"all"*, in spite of their superficial similarity with the quantifiers of formal logic, but rather noun phrases, like *"more than 12 million vehicles"* and *"some heavy books"*. Other types of quantifiers can also be found, such as adverbs for temporal or spatial quantification (*"always"*, *"nowhere"*, *"sometimes"*), but these are of minor importance compared to noun phrases. Hobbs and Shieber (1987) have argued that the sentence *"Some representatives of every department in most companies saw a few samples of every product"*, containing five noun phrases, has 42 readings, corresponding to equally many linguistically valid alternative scopings of the five quantifiers (of the120 mathematically possible permutations). Bunt and Muskens (1999) show that, when other ambiguity types are taken into account, such as those of a quantification's distributivity, the number of possible readings of an ordinary written sentence may run into the thousands.

Quantification is the main source of structural ambiguity in natural langue; therefore applications of natural language processing for which semantic information is important, such as information extraction, and question answering, need effective ways of interpreting quantification expressions. This calls for a flexible and interoperable way of indicating aspects of quantification.

This paper presents an annotation scheme, called 'QuantML', where a range of aspects of natural language quantification are captured by a relatively small number of features, distributed over the components of annotation structures in a way that allows a compositional semantic interpretation. The QuantML scheme is based on a number of preliminary studies including Bunt (2017), Bunt et al. (2018), and Bunt (2018), and has recently been accepted as the basis for developing Part 12 of the ISO Semantic annotation framework (ISO 24617).

2 Related work

ISO standard 24617-1 for the annotation of time and events, commonly known as 'ISO-TimeML', has certain provisions for dealing with time-related quantification. For example, the temporal quantifier *"daily"* is represented as follows, where "P1D" stands for "period of one day":

(1) <TIMEX3 xml:id="t5" target="#token0" type="SET" value="P1D" quant="EVERY"/>

In ISO-TimeML @quant is one of the attributes of temporal entities, used to indicate that the entity is involved in a quantification. The limitations of this approach for annotating temporal quantification have been discussed by Bunt & Pustejovsky (2010).

ISO-Space (ISO 24617-7) uses the @quant attribute as well, applying it to spatial entities, and in addition uses the attribute @scopes to specify a scoping relation. The following example, taken from ISO 24617-7:2014, illustrates this:

(2) a. There's a lamp$_{se1}$ on$_{ss1}$ every desk$_{se2}$.

    b. <spatialEntity id="se1" target=""#token2" pred="lamp" form="nom" countable="true" quant="1" scopes="∅"/>
    <spatialEntity id="se2" target="#token5" pred="desk" form="nom" countable="true" quant="every" scopes="#se1"/>
    <spatialSignal id="ss1" target="#token3" type="dirTop" />
    <qsLink id="qsl1" relType="EC" figure="#se1" ground="#se2" trigger="#ss1"/>
    <oLink id="ol1" relType="above" figure="#se1" ground="#se2" trigger="#ss1" frameType="intrinsic" referencePt="#se2" projective="false" />

From a semantic point of view, this use of the @scopes attribute is not very satisfactory since the relative scoping of quantifications over different sets of entities is not a local property of one of these quantifications; therefore an annotation such as (2) does not have a compositional semantics.

The Parallel Meaning Bank (PMB, Abzianidze et al., 2017), building upon the Groningen Meaning Bank (GMB, Bos et al., 2017), is a corpus of semantically annotated sentences and texts in English, German, Dutch and Italian in raw and tokenised format with formal meaning representations. The PMB aims to provide fine-grained meaning representations in DRT for the most likely interpretation of a sentence, with a minimal use of underspecification. The GMB and the PMB are very useful resources for semantic study, but this work is somewhat different from the usual kind of annotation work, where semantic features are associated with small stretches of text or speech.

3 Granularity in quantification annotation

3.1 Ambiguity and lack of specificity

The multiplicity of possible readings of quantifications forms a challenge for language understanding systems, but hardly for humans, who are mostly not aware of the ambiguities. Human annotators who are not trained linguists or logicians likewise tend not to see all the possible readings of quantifications. Automatic annotation processes run into the same problems as language understanding systems, having a lack of general world knowledge and situation-specific context information. Both for manual and for automatic annotation it is therefore of practical importance to not be forced to make more specific choices than the available information and skills justify. On the other hand, it should of course be possible for a skilled annotator to make precise annotations if sufficiently detailed information is available. A useful annotation scheme should thus allow specifications with varying degrees of granularity.

The ambiguity challenge that quantification poses for automatic language understanding has led to the development of underspecification techniques in computational semantics, in particular for under-specified representation of quantifier scope (e.g. Alshawi, 1992; Bos, 1995; Reyle, 1993, Willis & Manandhar, 2001). In the same vein, QuantML allows the annotation of quantifier scope to be underspecified by making the specification of scope relations between a pair of quantifiers optional.

Scope is not the only source of quantifier ambiguity; ambiguities in the distributivity and individuation of quantifiers make the ambiguity problem even more dramatic than has generally been assumed in the literature, due to issues concerning precision and individuation which are considered next.

3.2 Precision and distributivity

Ambiguity in natural language quantification is mostly considered in terms of the number of logically precise interpretations. But natural language expressions are sometimes not meant to be interpreted with logical precision. This is in particular the case for quantifier distributivity. Consider the following example:

(3) The men carried all the boxes upstairs.

In the event(s) described by this sentence it is not necessarily the case that all the carrying was done either collectively or individually; the sentence could for instance describe a set of events in which the men collectively carried the heaviest boxes, and individually the lighter ones. This means that the distributivity of the quantification over the set of men is neither collective nor individual (and the same is true for the quantification over the boxes); the term 'unspecific' has been introduced for this distributivity (Bunt, 1985). This interpretation can be represented in second-order predicate logic as shown in (4), where following Kamp & Reyle (1993)[1] the notation X^* is used to designate the set consisting of the members and subsets of X, and moreover the subscript notation P_0 to designate the characteristic predicate of the reference domain of a quantifier,[2] which is a contextually determined part of the quantifier's source domain (as determined by an NP head), characterized by the predicate P.

(4) $\forall x$ [box$_0$(x) $\rightarrow$ $\exists y$ $\exists e$ [man$_0$*(y) $\wedge$ carry-up(e) $\wedge$ agent(e,y) $\wedge$ $\exists z$ [box$_0$*(z) $\wedge$ [x=z $\vee$ x$\in$z] $\wedge$ theme(e,z)]]]

This representation says that for every box in a given reference domain there is a carry-event in which a contextually distinguished man or group of men carried it upstairs or carried a set of boxes upstairs that contains it.

A quantification with unspecific distributivity has both individual and collective participation as special cases, so 'unspecific' could be used to avoid having to choose a more specific distributivity. In the case of (3), 'unspecific' is the correct distributivity to assign. In cases where it is difficult to decide on the distributivity, 'unspecific' could be useful as a coarse-grained default value in annotations.[3]

3.3 Individuation

The 'individuation' of a quantification is another source of ambiguity, as illustrated in (5):

(5) a. I see no chicken in the garden.
    b. I see no chicken in the stew.

The count/mass distinction is often characterized semantically in terms of 'individuation': *"To learn 'apple' ... we must learn how much counts as an apple. (...) Such terms possess built-in modes (...) of dividing their reference (..) Consider 'shoe', 'pair of shoes', and 'footwear': (...) two of the them divide their reference differently, and the third not at all."* (Quine, 1960). In other words, count nouns have a domain of reference made up of individuals, while that of a mass noun is made up of entities (often called 'quantities') with mereological part-whole relations.

---

[1] Kampl & Reyle 1983, Section 4.2.2

[2] Also known as 'context set', Westerståhl, 1985.

[3] See also Schwertel, 2005 for a discussion of vagueness and lack of specificity in quantification.

Quantifiers expressed by an NP with a count head noun may be ambiguous in a different way, as illustrated by (6a). This sentence could for example describe a series of events where last Monday Mario had a pizza, on Wednesday he had another pizza plus a few slices, and on Friday he had the slices remaining from Wednesday. Pizzas are a domain where it is common to consider parts of individuals, like in many domains related to food and drink. For other domains this may be less common, but in principle every physical object has parts, and many abstract objects as well. When interpreting an NP that describes domain involvement or domain size in terms of a non-integer number of individuals, this is clearly necessary. The interpretation of sentence (6a) as describing a set of events in which Mario has eaten some pieces of pizza, adding up to a total of three pizzas, can be represented by (6b), where P^+ designates the property of being a part of an individual that has the property P,[4] and Σ designates the joining together of parts of an individual.[5]

(6) a. Mario had three pizzas last week.

 b. $\exists Y \, (\forall y \, (y \in Y \rightarrow (\text{pizza}^+(y) \wedge \exists e \, (\text{eat}(e) \wedge \text{agent}(e, \text{Mario}) \wedge \text{theme}(e, y)))) \wedge |\Sigma Y|^{pizza}=3)$

In model-theoretic semantics it is commonly assumed that individuals are atomic concepts, but for examples like the above we must assume an ontology where individuals have parts (in the mereological sense). This part-whole relation has the same logical properties as the corresponding relation for mass nouns.[6] A quantification where parts of individuals should be taken into account will be said to have the individuation *"count/parts"*.

Individuation and distributivity are distinct aspects of quantification; elements from a domain with count/parts individuation can for example participate collectively in a quantification, as in the report from a weight-lifting contest that *"Tarzani lifted 27.5 pizzas"* (see (15) below), if Tarzani lifted a pile of 25 whole pizzas topped by a short stack of five pizza halves.

4   Methodology

4.1   Theoretical background

The theory of generalized quantifiers (GQT) has been successful in describing and understanding many aspects of natural language quantification. Together with neo-Davidsonian event semantics and Discourse Representation Theory (DRT), GQT forms the theoretical basis of the approach to quantification annotation taken in this paper.

GQT exploits the fact that quantification in natural language differs from that in formal logic in that logical quantifiers like "for all x" and "there exists an x" range over all the individual objects in a given universe of discourse, whereas quantifying expressions in natural language like *"all the students"*, *"an essay"*, *"some coffee"*, indicate a restricted domain that the quantification applies to GQT therefore views noun phrases as the quantifiers of natural language (rather than determiners) (Barwise and Cooper, 1981; see e.g. also van Benthem and ter Meulen, 1985 and Szabolcsi, 2010). This view generalizes to natural language quantifiers like *"two books"*, *"less than three weeks"*, *"thirty tons of peanut butter"*. Semantically, generalized quantifiers are viewed as expressing properties of sets of individuals; for example, the quantifier *"more than three essays"* is interpreted as the property of being a set that contains more than three essays.

---

[4]Formally, $P^+(x) \leftrightarrow \exists y \, (P(y) \wedge x \sqsubseteq y)$.

[5]Expressing the size of a collection of pizza-parts in terms of number of pizzas assumes (1) a way of measuring the size of pizzas and pizza-parts, and (2) a standard size. The notation $|..|^D$ designates such a measure function for the domain D. Note that, for example, eight quarters of three different pizzas together have a size of 2 pizzas, even though it may not be possible to physically join the parts to form two well-formed pizzas. The mereological sum 'Σ' in (6b) is used to avoid counting the size of overlapping parts more than once.

[6]The most important properties are: (1) a part of a part of an individual is again a part of that individual: $(x \sqsubseteq a \wedge y \sqsubseteq x) \rightarrow y \sqsubseteq a$; (2) the mereological sum of parts of an individual is another part of that individual: $(x \sqsubseteq a \wedge y \sqsubseteq a) \rightarrow \Sigma(x,y) \sqsubseteq a$; (3) every object is part of itself: $x \sqsubseteq x$. See Bunt (1985) for a detailed discussion of the logic of mereological part-whole relations, including a discussion of Lesniewski's mereology and Leonard & Goodman's 'calculus of individuals'.

Davidson (1967) proposed to treat events as individual objects, facilitating the semantic interpretation of adverbs, like *"quickly"*, *"passionately"*, and adverbial quantifying expressions such as *"everywhere"*, *"never"* and *"at least three times"*. Following Parsons (1990), this event-based semantics can be expressed in semantic representations by means of one-place predicates applied to existentially quantified event variables, and two-place predicates to indicate the semantic roles of the participants in an event. This 'neo-Davidsonian' approach has been adopted in the ISO annotation standards 24617-1 (Time and events), 24617-4 (Semantic roles), 24617-7 (Spatial information), and 24617-8 (Discourse relations). Champollion (2015) has shown that GQT and neo-Davidsonian semantics can be combined successfully. Still, natural language quantification is a semantically extremely complex set of phenomena, and especcially the interpretation of plural noun phrases presents certain theoretical challenges for GQT (see e.g. Schwertel, 2005), some of which have been successfully been approached in DRT (Kamp and Reyle, 1993), which has other limitations. Luckily, providing a semantics for quantification *annotations* is less challenging than providing a semantics for natural language expressions involving quantifications.

Several of the ISO semantic annotation standards use DRT's Discourse Representation Structures (DRSs) for defining a semantics of annotation structures. QuantML follows suit, combining ideas from GQT, neo-Davidsonian semantics, and DRSs in the semantics of its annotation structures.

4.2 Annotation scheme architecture

The annotation scheme outlined in this paper has been designed according to the ISO principles of semantic annotation (ISO standard 24617-6). This means that the scheme has a three-part definition consisting of (1) an abstract syntax that specifies the possible *annotation structures* at a conceptual level as set-theoretical constructs, such as pairs and triples of concepts; (2) a semantics that specifies the meaning of the annotation structures defined by the abstract syntax; (3) a concrete syntax, that specifies a representation format for annotation structures using XML expressions. Defining the semantics at the level of the abstract syntax puts the focus of an annotation standard at the conceptual level, rather than that of representation formats. Alternative representation formats may be defined with guaranteed interoperability (Bunt et al., 2018). Annotators (human or automatic) deal with concrete representations only, but they can rely on the existence of an underlying abstract syntax and semantics.

Example (7) shows the QuantML annotation structure (in a slightly simplified form), XML representation, and semantics for the collectdive reading of a simple sentence. Besides the usual box notation of DRT also a string notation will be used, which is shown in (7e). Capital variables are used to designate non-empty sets.

(7) a. Two thousand students protested

  Markables: m1 = Two thousand students; m2 = students; m3 = protested

 b. QuantML annotation structure:

  $\langle\,\langle m3, \langle protest\rangle\rangle, \{\langle m1, \langle student, \lambda z.|z|= 2000, indef\,\rangle\rangle\}, agent, collective\rangle, \{\}\rangle$

 c. Annotation representation:

```
<entity xml:id="x1" target="#m1" pred="student" involvement="2000"/>
<entity xml:id="e1" target="#m3" pred="protest"/>
<participantLink event="#e1" participant="#x1" semRole="agent" distr="collective"/>
```

 d. Semantics:

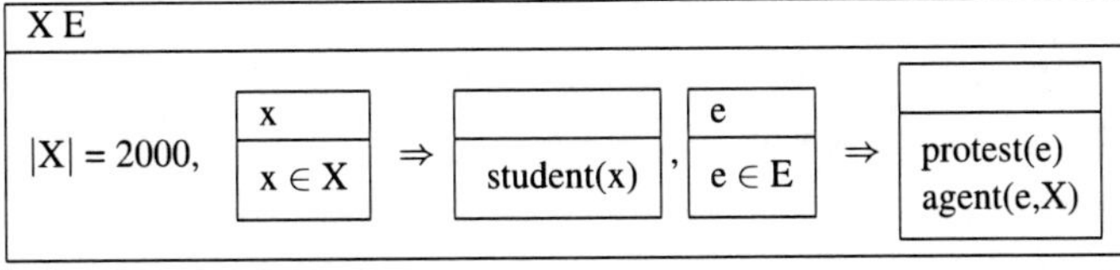

 e. $[X, E \mid |X|{=}2000, [x \in X \rightarrow student(x)], [e \in E \rightarrow [\,protest(e), agent(e,X)]]]$

It may be noted that the annotation semantics in (7d,e) is structurally the same as the DRS that Kamp and Reyle propose for the collective reading of the sentence *"Three lawyers hired a new secretary"* (Kamp and Reyle 1993, p. 327). For the individual reading of the sentence (7a), where the students act in individual protest-events (e.g. writing personal letters of protest), the annotation structure and its XML representation would both have 'individual' instead of 'collective' (and narrow event scope, by default), and the DRS interpretation would be as in (8):

(8) $[X, E \mid |X|=2000, [x \in X \rightarrow \text{student}(x)], [e \in E \rightarrow \text{protest}(e)], [x \in X \rightarrow [e \mid e \in E, \text{agent}(e,x)]]]$

Note also that the discourse referent X in these DRSs stands for the set of entities that participate in the protest events, which corresponds to the set of entities (or the property) that in a classical linguistic analysis is denoted by the VP. The DRS thus has a condition of the form $[x \in X \rightarrow ...\theta(e,x)]$ for the individual reading and a condition with $\theta(e,X)$ for the collective reading. The two conditions $|X|=2000$, $[x \in X \rightarrow \text{student}(x)]$ together reflect the GQT interpretation of the subject NP.

5   QuantML specification

5.1   Abstract syntax

The structures defined by the abstract syntax are n-tuples of elements that are either basic concepts, taken from a store called the 'conceptual inventory', or, recursively, such n-tuples. Two types of structure are distinguished: entity structures and link structures. An entity structure contains semantic information about a segment of primary data and is formally a pair $\langle m, s \rangle$ consisting of a markable, which refers to a segment of primary data, and certain semantic information. A link structure contains information about the way two or more segments of primary data are semantically related.

QuantML conceptual inventory:

- unary predicates that characterize source domains (such as 'book', 'student', and 'water) or event domains (such as 'lift', 'carry', 'drink'), or that correspond to adjectives or to prepositions;
- binary predicates that correspond to semantic roles (agent, theme, instrument,...); for this purpose, the semantic roles defined in ISO 24617-4 (Semantic roles) are used;
- numerical predicates for specifying reference domain involvement, reference domain size, the size of certain parts of a reference domain, or the number of repetitions or frequency of recurrence in event structures;
- predicates for specifying proportional reference domain involvement, such as 'all', 'some', 'most';
- parameters for specifying definiteness: 'definite' and 'indefinite'; domain individuation: 'count', 'mass', and 'count/parts'; and distributivity: 'collective', 'individual', 'homogeneous', 'group', 'unspecific';
- basic units of measurement, such as 'meter', 'kilogram', 'litre', and the operators 'division' and 'multiplication' for forming complex units;
- the polarity values 'positive' and 'negative';
- parameters for specifying event scope: 'wide' and 'narrow', and for specifying whether scope inversion occurs: 'inverse' or 'linear' (default value).
- ordering relations for specifying the relative scopes of quantifiers over sets of participants: 'wider', 'equal', 'dual', and 'unscoped'.

QuantML has three kinds of entity structures: (1) for events; (2) for participants; (3) for restrictions on sets of participants. A quantified set of participants is characterized by the following properties:

1. the source domain, from which the participants are drawn;
2. the reference domain, typically a subset of the source domain;
3. the individuation of the reference domain;
4. the quantitative (absolute or proportional) involvement of the reference domain;
5. the size of the reference domain, or of groups, subsets, or parts of the reference domain involved in the quantified predication (optional).

The entity structure $\langle m, s \rangle$ for a set of participants thus contains a triple s = $\langle \langle D, v \rangle, q, d \rangle$ with D = characteristic domain predicate, v = individuation, q = reference domain involvement, and d = definiteness, with possibly an additional size specification. The domain component is more complex when the restrictor of an NP contains one or more head noun modifiers and/or multiple, conjoined heads (see Bunt 2018 for details).

Entity structures for sets of events are simpler than those for participants; they contain just a predicate that characterizes a domain of events, and if applicable the cardinality of a set of repeated events or the frequency of recurring events.

Two kinds of link structure are defined: participation structures, which link participants to events, and scope link structures. Participation structures specify (1) a set of events; (2) a set of participants; (3) a semantic role; (4) the distributivity of the participation; (5) the relative scope of the event quantification. Scope link structures specify the relative scope of two participant entity structures.

Annotation structures for quantification are associated mostly with clauses and their constituent NPs and verbs. The annotation structure for a clause is a quadruple consisting of an event structure, a set of participant structures, a set of participation link structures, and a (possibly empty) set of scope link structures. In a complete clause annotation structure all participant entity structures are linked to the verb's event entity structure, and all the relative scopes of all participant entity structures are specified.

5.2   Concrete syntax

A concrete syntax is specified here in the form of an XML representation of annotation structures. For each type of entity structure, defined by the abstract syntax, a corresponding XML element is defined; each of these elements has an attribute @xml:id whose value is a unique identifier, and an attribute @target, whose value anchors the annotation in the primary data, having a markable as value (or a sequence of markables). In addition, these elements have the following attributes:

<entity>: @domain, @involvement, @definiteness and @size (optional);

<event>: @pred (event type), @number (optional), and @frequency (optional);

<qDomain>: @source (with multiple values in the case of a conjunctive head) and @restrictions;

<sourceDomain>: @pred, @individuation;

<adjMod>: @pred, @distr, and @restrictions (optional);

<nnMod>: @pred, @distr, and @restrictions (optional);

<ppMod>: @pRel, @pEntity, @distr, @linking;

<relClause>: @semRole, @clause, @distr, @linking;

<amount>: @num, @unit;

<complexUnit>: @unit1, @operation, @unit2.

For each of the two types of link structure defined by the abstract syntax, an XML element is defined:

<participantLink> with the attributes @event, @participant, @semRole, @distr, @evScope (default value: narrow) and @polarity (default value: positive);

<scopeLink> with the attributes @arg1, @arg2, @scopeRel.

5.3   Semantics

The QuantML semantics specifies a recursive interpretation function I_Q that translates annotation structures into DRSs in a compositional way: the interpretation of an annotation structure is obtained by combining the interpretations of its component entity structures and participation link structures, in a way that is determined by scope link structures (if any). A full specification of the QuantML semantics would go beyond the scope of this paper; the reader is referred to Bunt (2018, Appendix C). Here we outline the overall approach and present some interesting parts of the definition of I_Q.

The QuantML interpretation function translates every participant entity structure, event entity structure, and participation link structure into a DRS and combines these. Consider the example in (7). The entity structures for *"Two thousand students"*, and *"protested"* are translated into the DRSs shown in (10). For the participant entity structure this is achieved by applying an instance of clause (9a) in the I_Q definition, which interprets entity structures with source domain D, individuation v, involvement q, and definiteness *indef*. The interpretation q' of domain involvement specification q is defined in (9b-c), and that of the domain specification in (9d-e).

(9) a. $I_Q(\langle m1, \langle\langle\langle m2, D\rangle, v\rangle, q, \mathit{indef}\rangle\rangle\rangle) = [\, X \mid q'(X), [x \in X \to D'(x)]\,]$

    b. $q' = I_Q(q) \circ F_Q(v)$

    c. $F_Q(v)$: $F_Q(count) = \lambda X.|X|$; $F_Q(mass) = F_Q(count/parts) = \lambda X.|\Sigma X|$

    d. $D' = I_Q(\langle D, v\rangle)$

    e. $I_Q(\langle D, v\rangle)$: $I_Q(\langle D, count\rangle) = I_Q(\langle D, mass\rangle) = I_Q(D)$; $I_Q(\langle D, count/parts\rangle) = I_Q(D)^+$

(10) a. $I_Q(\langle m1, \langle\langle\langle m2, student\rangle, count\rangle, \lambda z.|z| = 2000, indef\,\rangle\rangle\rangle) = [\, X \mid |X|=2000, [x \in X \to student(x)]\,]$

    b. $I_Q(\langle m3, \langle protest\rangle\rangle) = [\, E \mid [\, e \in E \to protest(e)]\,]$

The DRS in (10a) says that there exists a set with the property of containing two thousand students, reflecting the GQT approach to NP interpretation. The DRS in (10b) together with (12) illustrates the adoption of neo-Davidsonian event semantics.

The participation link structure has in this example the form $\langle \varepsilon_E, \{\varepsilon_{Pl}\}, R, d, \sigma\rangle$, where ε_E and ε_{Pl} are the participant and event entity structures that are linked in the Agent role (R = Agent), with d = collective, and σ (event scope) = narrow. The semantic interpretation of such a structure is defined as follows, where '$\cup$' designates the familiar merge operation for DRSs:

(11) $I_Q\langle \varepsilon_E, \{\varepsilon_{Pl}\}, R, d, \sigma\rangle = I_Q\langle \varepsilon_{Pl}\rangle \cup (I_Q\langle \varepsilon_E\rangle \cup I_Q(R, d, \sigma))$

Triples like $\langle\, R, d, \sigma\rangle$ are interpreted as shown in (12):

(12) a. $I_Q(R, \text{individual}, \text{narrow}) = [\, X, E \mid x \in X \to [\, e \mid E \in E, agent(e, x) \,]\,]$

    b. $I_Q(R, \text{individual}, \text{wide}) = [\, X, E \mid x \in X \to [\, e \mid E \in E, agent(e, x) \,]\,]$

    c. $I_Q(R, \text{collective}, \sigma) = [\, X, E \mid x \in X \to [\, e \mid E \in E, R(e, X) \,]\,]$

Applying rule (11) to the right-hand sides of (10) and (12c), with the values for R, d and σ substituted, gives the desired result shown in (7d,e):

$[X, E \mid |X|=2000, [x \in X \to student(x)], [e \in E \to [\, protest(e), agent(e,X)]]]$

The annotation structures defined by the QuantML abstract syntax can be deeply nested, since participation link structures contain the entity structures that they link; see the argument of the I_Q function in (11). (Their XML representations, by contrast, are 'flat', which is more convenient for their practical use.) A participant entity structure inside a link structure can itself have a complex structure, for instance due to the head noun of an NP being modified by a quantifying relative clause. In a well-formed annotation structure for a clause that contains only a single NP, like (7), such a link structure contains all the semantic information. The only scoping in such cases is between the NP quantifier and the verb viewed as an event quantifier (which is useful for examples like *"All passengers died in the crash"* and *"Mary wants to buy an inexpensive coat"*, cf. Szabolcsi, 2010). For clauses with multiple NPs the additional information about their relative scopes is taken into account in the I_Q function by applying 'scoped merge' operations to their interpretations, and where appropriate inversion operations in order to obtain the interpretations of 'inversely linked' quantified head noun modification by a PP or a relative clause (Barker, 2014). The reader is referred to Bunt (2018) for details.

6   Using QuantML

This section illustrates the use of QuantML with a few examples. The first example concerns two quantifications with unspecific distributivity and an NP head with adjectival modification.

(13) a. Two young men carried all the boxes upstairs.

Markables: m1=Two young men, m2=young, m3=young men, m4=men, m5=carried upstairs, m6=all the boxes, m7=boxes

b. QuantML annotation structure:

$\langle \langle$m5, $\langle$cary-upstairs$\rangle\rangle$, $\{\langle$m1, $\langle\langle\langle$m4,man$\rangle$,$\langle$m2,young$\rangle\rangle$, $\lambda z.|z| = 2, indef\rangle\rangle$, $\langle$m6, $\langle\langle$m7,box$_0\rangle$, $all, def\rangle\rangle\}$,
$\{\langle\langle$m5,$\langle$carry-upstairs$\rangle\rangle$,$\{\langle$m1,$\langle\langle\langle$m4,man$\rangle$,$\langle$m2,young$\rangle\rangle$,$\lambda z.|z|= 2, indef\rangle\}$, agent, *unspecific, narrow*$\rangle$,
$\langle\langle$m5,$\langle$carry-upstairs$\rangle\rangle$,$\{\langle$m6,$\langle\langle$m7, box$_0\rangle$, *all,def*$\rangle\}$, theme, *unspecific, narrow*$\rangle\}$, $\{\}\rangle$

c. Annotation representation:

```
<entity xml:id="x1" target="#m1" domain="#x2" involvement="2" definiteness="indef"/>
<qDomain xml:id="x2" target="#m3" source="#x3" restrs="#r1"/>
<sourceDomain xml:id="x3" target="#m4" individuation="count" pred="man"/>
<adjMod xml:id="r1" target="#m2" distr="individual" pred="young"/>
<event xml:id="e1" target="#m5" pred="carry-up"/>
<entity xml:id="x4" target="#m6" domain="#x5" involvement="all" definiteness+"def"/>
<sourceDomain xml:id="x5" target="#m7" individuation="count" pred="box"/>
<participantLink event="#e1" participant="#x1" semRole="agent" distr="unspecific"
    eventScope="narrow"/>
<participantLink event="#e1" participant="#x1" semRole="agent" distr="unspecific"
    eventScope="narrow"/>
<scopeLink arg1="#x4" arg2="#x1" scopeRel="wider"/>
```

d. Semantics:
[X, Y, E | e $\in$ E $\rightarrow$ carry-up(e), x $\in$ X $\rightarrow$ [man$_0$(x), young(x)], |X|=2, y $\in$ Y $\leftrightarrow$ box$_0$(y), x $\in$ man* $\rightarrow$ [y, e | e $\in$ E, y $\in$ Y*, agent(e,x), theme(e,y)], y $\in$ box$_0$* $\rightarrow$ [x, e | e $\in$ E, x $\in$ X, agent(e,x), theme(e,y)]]

The next example illustrates the annotation and interpretation of a cumulative quantification with a mass NP. The cumulativity means that none of the two NP quantifiers outscopes the other; this is annotated as their scopes being equal.

(14) a. The girls ate most of the chocolate.

Markables: m1=The girls, m2=girls. m3=ate, m4=most of the chocolate, m5=chocolate

b. QuantML annotation structure:

$\langle \langle$m3, $\langle$eat$\rangle\rangle$, $\{\langle$m1, $\langle$girl, *all, def*$\rangle\rangle\}$, $\{\langle$m4, $\langle$chocolate, *most,def*$\rangle\rangle\}$,
$\{\langle$m3, $\langle$eat$\rangle\rangle$, $\{\langle$m1, $\langle$girl, *all, def* $\rangle\rangle\}$, agent, unspecific, narrow$\rangle$,
$\langle$m3, $\langle$eat$\rangle\rangle$, $\{\langle$m4, $\langle$chocolate$_0$, *most, def* $\rangle\rangle\}$, theme, unspecific, narrow$\rangle\}$, $\{\}\rangle$

c. Annotation representation:

```
<entity xml:id="x1" target="#m1" domain="#x2" involvement="all" definiteness="def"/>
<sourceDomain xml:id="x2" target="#m2" individuation="count" pred="girl"/>
<entity xml:id="x3" target="#m4" domain="#x4" involvement="most" definiteness="def"/>
<sourceDomain xml:id="x4" target="#m5" individuation="mass" pred="chocolate"/>
<event xml:id="e1" target="#m3" pred="eat"/>
<participantLink event="#e1" participant="#x1" semRole="agent" distr="individual"
    eventScope="narrow"/>
<participantLink event="#e1" participant="#x3" semRole="patient" distr="individual"
    eventScope="narrow"/>
<scopeLink arg1="#x1" arg2="#x3" scopeRel="equal"/>
```

d. Semantics:

Interpretation of the entity structure for *"most of the chocolate"*:

$I_Q(\varepsilon_{P2}) = [\,X \mid |\Sigma(X)| \geq |\Sigma(\text{chocolate}_0)|/2,\ x \in X \rightarrow \text{chocolate}_0(x)\,]$.

Interpretation of the annotation structure for the sentence:

$I_Q(< \varepsilon_E,\ \{\varepsilon_{P1}, \varepsilon_{P2}\},\ \{L_{P1}, L_{P2}\}\ \{\text{sc}1\}>) = I_Q(L\varepsilon_E, \varepsilon_{P1}) \cup^= I_Q(L(\varepsilon_E, \varepsilon_{P2})) =$
$[\,X\ Y\ E \mid x \in X \leftrightarrow \text{girl}_0(x),\ y \in Y \rightarrow \text{chocolate}(y),\ |\Sigma(Y)| \geq |\Sigma(\text{chocolate}_0)|/2,\ e \in E \rightarrow \text{eat}(e),$
$\qquad x \in X \rightarrow [\,e\ y \mid e \in E,\ y \in Y,\ \text{agent}(e,x),\ \text{theme}(e,y)\,]$
$\qquad y \in Y \rightarrow [\,e\ x \mid e \in E,\ x \in X,\ \text{agent}(e,x),\ \text{theme}(e,y)\,]\,]$

In words, this DRS says that there is a set Y of quantities of chocolate that together make up all the contextually distinguished chocolate (referred to as *"the chocolate"*), and a set of eat-events such that each of the girls in the set (X) of contextually distinguished girls (*"the girls"*) ate some of the quantities of chocolate, and each of the quantities of chocolate was eaten by one of those girls.

The third example concerns a proper name and a quantification with "count/parts" individuation and collective (!) distributivity.

(15) a. Tarzani lifted twenty-seven-and-a-half pizzas.

        Markables: m1=Tarzani, m2=lifted. m3=twenty-seven-and-a-half pizzas, m4=pizzas

    b. QuantML annotation structure:

$\langle\ \langle m2, \langle \text{lift} \rangle \rangle,\ \{\langle m1, \langle\langle \text{tarzani, count} \rangle\ \textit{all, def,}\ 1 \rangle\rangle\},\ \langle m3, \langle\langle \text{pizza, count/parts} \rangle,\ \langle 27.5, \text{pizza} \rangle,\ \textit{indef}\,\rangle\rangle\},$
$\{\langle m2, \langle \text{lift} \rangle \rangle,\ \{\langle m1, \langle\langle \text{tarzani,}\ \textit{all, def,}\ 1\ \rangle\rangle\},\ \text{agent, individual, narrow}\rangle,$
$\langle m2, \langle \text{lift} \rangle \rangle,\ \{\langle m3, \langle\langle \text{pizza, count/parts} \rangle,\ \langle 27.5, \text{pizza} \rangle,\ \textit{indef}\,\rangle\rangle\},\ \text{theme, collective, narrow}\rangle\},\ \{\}\rangle$

    c. Annotation representation:

```
<entity xml:id="x1" target="#m1" domain="#x2" involvement="all" definiteness="de" size="1"/>
<sourceDomain xml:id="x2" target="#m1" individuation="count" pred="tarzani"/>
<event xml:id="e1" target="#m2" pred="lift"/>
<entity xml:id=x3" target=#m3 domain=#x4 involvement=27.5 definiteness=indef/>
<sourceDomain xml:id="x4" target="#m4" individuation="count/parts" pred="pizza"/>
<participantLink event="#e1" participant="#x1" semRole=agent" distr="individual" eventScope="wide"/>
<participantLink event="#e1" participant="#x3" semRole="theme" distr="collective" eventScope="wide"/>
<scopeLink arg1="#x1" arg2="#x3" scopeRel="wider"/>
```

    d. Semantics:

$[\,E \mid e \in E \rightarrow \text{lift}(e),\ e \in E \rightarrow [\,Y \mid y \in Y \rightarrow \text{pizza}^+(y),\ |\Sigma Y|^{pizza}=27.5,\ \text{agent}(e,\text{tarzani}_0),\ \text{theme}(e,Y)]\,]$

7   Conclusions and Further Work

The QuantML annotation scheme was recently proposed to the International Organisation for Standardisation for developing into part 12 of the ISO Semantic Annotation Framework, and was accepted as such in March 2019 (ISO, 2019a). The QuantML scheme is rooted in the theory of generalized quantifiers, neo-Davidsonian event semantics, and DRT, and is methodologically shaped after the ISO principles of semantic annotation (ISO standard 24617-6). Different from these semantic theories, the proposed annotation scheme has a number of provisions for leaving aspects of quantification unspecified, on the one hand intended to reflect the vagueness and ambiguity that natural language quantifications may have, and on the other hand to allow annotators to make annotations with varying degrees of granularity.

The current proposal still has several loose ends, e.g. related to modality and polarity and to intensional contexts. It is also fair to say that, where GQT and DRT do not provide adequate solutions for all the complexities of quantification in natural language, currently no annotation scheme can be expected to do much better.

The next important thing after or while further elaborating the proposed annotation scheme, is to apply it in annotation projects and see to what extent it may need to be adapted in order to be optimally useful for language technology applications and for empirically-based semantic investigations.

References

Abzianidze, L., J. Bjerva, K. Evang, H. Haagsma, R. van Noord, P. Ludmann, D.-D. Nguyen, and J. Bos (2017). The Parallel Meaning Bank: Towards a multilingual corpus of translations annotated with compositional meaning representations. In *Proceedings of the 15th Conference of the European Chapter of the Association for Computational Linguistics: Volume 2, Short Papers*, Valencia, Spain, pp. 242–247. Association for Computational Linguistics.

Alshawi, H. (1992). *The Core Language Engine*. Cambridge, Mass.: MIT Press.

Barker, C. (2014). Scope. In S. Lappin and C. Fox (Eds.), *The Handbook of Contemporary Semantic Theory*, pp. 40–76. John Wiley.

Barwise, J. and R. Cooper (1981). Generalized quantifiers and natural language. *Linguistics and Philosophy 4*, 159–219.

Benthem, J. v. and A. ter Meulen (1985). *Generalized Quantifiers in Natural Language*. Dordrectht: Foris.

Bos, J. (1995). Predicate logic unplugged. In *Proceedings 10th Amsterdam Colloquium*, Amsterdam, pp. 133–142. ILLC.

Bos, J., V. Basile, K. Evang, N. Venhuizen, and J. Bjerva (2017). The Groningen Meaning Bank. In N. Ide and J. Pustejovsky (Eds.), *Handbook of Linguistic Annotation*, pp. 463–496. Berlin: Springer.

Bunt, H. (1985). *Mass Terms and Model-Theoretic Semantics*. Cambridge University Press.

Bunt, H. (2017). Towards interoperable annotation of quantification. In *Proceedings ISA-13, Thirteenth International Workshop on Interoperable Semantic Annotation*, Montpellier, France.

Bunt, H. (2018). *Semantic Annotation of Quantification in Natural Language*. TiCC Technical Report 2018-15. Tilburg Center for Cognition and Communication, Tilburg University.

Bunt, H. and R. Muskens (1999). Computational Semantics. In H. Bunt and R. Muskens (Eds.), *Computing Meaning, Vol. 1*, pp. 1–32. Dordrecht: Kluwer Academic Publishers.

Bunt, H., V. Petukhova, A. Malchanau, A. Fang, and K. Wijnhoven (2018). The DialogBank: Dialogues with interoperable annotations. *Language Resources and Evaluation 2018*.

Bunt, H. and J. Pustejovsky (2010). Annotating temporal and event quantification. In *Proceedings ISA-5, Fifth International Workshop on Interoperable Semantic Annotation*, pp. 15–22. City University of Hong Kong.

Bunt, H., J. Pustejovsky, and K. Lee (2018a). Towards an ISO Standar for the Annotation of Quantification. In *Proceedings of the 11th International Conference on Language Resources and Evaluation (LREC 2018)*, Miyazaki, Japan.

Bunt, H., J. Pustejovsky, and K. Lee (2018b). Towards an ISO Standard for the Annotation of Quantification. In *Proceedings 11th International Conference on Language Resources and Evaluation (LREC 2018)*, Myazaki, Japan. ELRA.

Champollion, L. (2015). The interaction of compositional semantics and event semantics. *Linguistics and Philosophy 38 (1)*, 31–66.

Davidson, D. (1967). The Logical Form of Action Sentences. In N. Resher (Ed.), *The Logic of Decision and Action*, pp. 81–95. Pittsburgh: The University of Pittsburgh Press.

Hobbs, J. and S. Shieber (2004). An algorithm for generating quantifier scopings. *Computational Linguistics 13*(1-2), 47–63.

ISO (2012). *ISO 24617-1: 2012, Language Resource Management - Semantic Annotation Framework (SemAF) - Part 1: Time and events*. Geneva: International Organisation for Standardisation ISO.

ISO (2014a). *ISO 24617-4: 2014, Language Resource Management - Semantic Annotation Framework (SemAF) - Part 4: Semantic roles*. Geneva: International Organisation for Standardisation ISO.

ISO (2014b). *ISO 24617-7: 2014, Language Resource Management - Semantic Annotation Framework (SemAF) - Part 7: Spatial information*. Geneva: International Organisation for Standardisation ISO.

ISO (2015). *ISO 24617-6:2015, Language Resource Management - Semantic Annotation Framework (SemAF) - Part 6: Principles of semantic annotation*. Geneva: International Organisation for Standardisation ISO.

ISO (2016). *ISO 24617-8:2016, Language Resource Management - Semantic Annotation Framework (SemAF) - Part 8: Semantic relations in discourse, Core annotation scheme (DR-Core)*. Geneva: International Organisation for Standardisation ISO.

Kamp, H. and U. Reyle (1993). *From Discourse to Logic*. Dordrecht: Kluwer Academic Publishers.

Parsons, T. (1990). *Events in the Semantics of English: A Study in Subatomic Semantics*. Cambridge, MA: MIT Press.

Pustejovsky, J., H. Bunt, and K. Lee (2010). ISO-TimeML. In *Proceedings of LREC 2010*, Malta. ELDA, Paris.

Pustejovsky, J., H. Bunt, and A. Zaenen (2017). Designing annotation schemes: From theory to model. In N. Ide and J. Pustejovsky (Eds.), *Handbook of Linguistic Annotation*, pp. 21–72. Berlin: Springer.

Quine, W. (1960). *Word and Object*. Cambridge, Mass.: MIT Press.

Schwertel, U. (2005). *Plural Semantics for Natural Language Understanding - A Computational Proof-Theoretic Approach*. Ph.D. Thesis, University of Zurich.

Szabolcsi, A. (2010). *Quantification*. Cambridge (UK): Cambridge University Press.

Westerståhl, D. (1985). Determiners and context sets. In J. van Benthem and A. ter Meulen (Eds.), *Generalized Quantifiers in Natural Language*, pp. 45–71. Dordrecht: Foris.

Willis, A. and S. Manandhar (2001). The availability of partial scopings in an underspecified semantic representation. In *Computing Meaning, Vol. 2*, pp. 129–145. Dordrecht: Springer.

Re-Ranking Words to Improve Interpretability of Automatically Generated Topics

Areej Alokaili[1,2], **Nikolaos Aletras**[1] and **Mark Stevenson**[1]
[1]University of Sheffield, United Kingdom
[2]King Saud University, Saudi Arabia
{areej.okaili,n.aletras,mark.stevenson}@sheffield.ac.uk

Abstract

Topics models, such as LDA, are widely used in Natural Language Processing. Making their output interpretable is an important area of research with applications to areas such as the enhancement of exploratory search interfaces and the development of interpretable machine learning models. Conventionally, topics are represented by their n most probable words, however, these representations are often difficult for humans to interpret. This paper explores the re-ranking of topic words to generate more interpretable topic representations. A range of approaches are compared and evaluated in two experiments. The first uses crowdworkers to associate topics represented by different word rankings with related documents. The second experiment is an automatic approach based on a document retrieval task applied on multiple domains. Results in both experiments demonstrate that re-ranking words improves topic interpretability and that the most effective re-ranking schemes were those which combine information about the importance of words both within topics and their relative frequency in the entire corpus. In addition, close correlation between the results of the two evaluation approaches suggests that the automatic method proposed here could be used to evaluate re-ranking methods without the need for human judgements.

1 Introduction

Probabilistic topic modelling (Blei, 2012) is a widely used approach in Natural Language Processing (Boyd-Graber et al., 2017) with applications to areas such as enhancing exploratory search interfaces (Chaney and Blei, 2012; Aletras et al., 2014; Smith et al., 2017; Aletras et al., 2017) and developing interpretable machine learning models (Paul, 2016). A topic model, e.g. Latent Dirichlet Allocation (LDA) (Blei et al., 2003) learns a low-dimensional representation of documents as a mixture of latent variables called topics. Topics are multinomial distributions over a predefined vocabulary of words.

Traditionally, topics have been represented by lists of the topic's n most probable words, however it is not always straightforward to interpret them due to noisy or domain specific data, spurious word co-occurrences and highly-frequent/low-informative words assigned with high probability (Chang et al., 2009).

Improving the interpretability of topic models is an important area of research. A range of approaches have been developed including computing topic coherence (Newman et al., 2010; Mimno et al., 2011; Aletras and Stevenson, 2013a; Lau et al., 2014), determining optimal topic cardinality (Lau and Baldwin, 2016), labelling topics text and/or images (Lau et al., 2011; Aletras and Stevenson, 2014, 2013b; Aletras and Mittal, 2017; Sorodoc et al., 2017) and corpus pre-processing (Schofield et al., 2017). However, methods for re-ranking topic words to improve topic interpretability have not been systematically evaluated yet. We hypothesise that some words relevant to a particular topic have not been assigned with a high probability due to data sparseness or low frequency in the training corpus. Our goal is to identify these words and re-rank the list representing the topic to make it more comprehensible. Table 1 shows topics represented by the 30 most probable words. Words displayed in bold font are more general (less informative, e.g. with high document frequency) while the remaining words are more likely to represent

Table 1: Examples of topics represented by 30 most probable words from New York Times. Less informative words are shown in **bold**.

Topic
space museum **years** history science earth mission **could** art shuttle universe flight **people theory world** radar crew **site** pincus plane **three** scientists **day century** pilot exhibit **back anniversary** landing **project**
percent million market company stock **billion sales** bank shares **price business** investors **money** share **companies rates** fund **interest rate quarter prices** investment funds financial amp analysts **growth industry york** banks
film **even** movie **world** stars **man much little story good way** star **best** show **see well seems** american **people love** hollywood director **big ever rating though great seem** production **makes**
officials agency office report department investigation government **former** federal **charges secret information card** cia law agents security **documents case** investigators **official** fraud intelligence illegal **commission service** police **cards** enforcement attorney

a coherent thematic subject. For example in the second topic, relevant words (e.g. investment, fund) have been assigned with lower probability compared to less informative words (e.g. percent, million). As a result, these words will not appear in the top 10 words.

This paper compares several word ranking methods and evaluate them using two approaches. The first approach is based on a crowdsourcing task in which participants are provided with a document and a list of topics then asked to identify the correct one, i.e. the topic that is most closely associated with the document. Topics are represented by word lists ranked using different methods. The effectiveness of the re-ranking approaches is evaluated by computing the accuracy of the participants on identifying the correct topic. The second evaluation approach is based on an information retrieval (IR) task and does not rely on human judgements. The re-ranked words are used to form a query and retrieve a set of documents from the collection. The effectiveness of the word re-ranking is then evaluated in terms of how well it can retrieve documents in the collection related to the topic. Results show that re-ranking topic words improves performance in both experiments.

The paper makes the following contributions. It highlights the problem of re-ranking topic words and demonstrates that it can improve topic interpretability. It introduces the first systematic evaluation of topic word re-ranking methods using two approaches: one based on crowdsourcing and another based on an IR task. The latter evaluation is an automated approach and does not rely on human judgments. Experiments demonstrate strong agreement between the results produced by these approaches which indicates that the IR-based approach could be used as an automated evaluation method in future studies. The paper also compares multiple approaches to word re-ranking and concludes that the most effective ones are those which combine information about the importance of words within topics and their relative frequency across the entire corpus. Code used in the experiments described in this paper can be downloaded from `https://github.com/areejokaili/topic_reranking`.

2 Background

The standard approach to representing topics has been to show the top n words with the highest probability given the topic, e.g. (Blei and Lafferty, 2009a,b). However, these words may not be the ones that are most informative about the topic and a range of approaches to re-ranking them has been proposed in the literature.

Blei and Lafferty (2009a) proposed a re-ranking method inspired by the tf-idf word weighting which includes two types of information: firstly, the probability of a word given a topic of interest and, secondly, the same probability normalised by the average probability across all topics. The intuition behind this approach is that good words for representing a topic will be those which have both high probability for a given topic and low probability across all topics. Blei and Lafferty (2009a) did not describe any empirical evaluation of the effectiveness of their approach.

Other word re-ranking methods have also combined information about the overall probability of a word and its relative probability in one topic compared to others. Chuang et al. (2012) describe a word re-ranking method applied within a topic model visualisation system. Their approach combines information about the word's overall probability within the corpus and its distinctiveness for a particular topic which is computed as the Kullback-Leibler divergence between the distribution of topics given the word and the distribution of topics. Sievert and Shirley (2014) also combine both types of information within a topic visualisation system. Bischof and Airoldi (2012) developed an approach for hierarchical topic models which balances information about the word frequency in a topic and the exclusivity of that word to that topic relative to a set of similar topics within the hierarchy.

Others have proposed approaches that only take into account the relative probability of each word in a topic compared to the others. Song et al. (2009) introduced a word ranking method based on normalising the probability of a word in a topic with the sum of the probabilities of that word across all topics. They evaluated their method against two other methods, the topic model's default ranking and the approach proposed by Blei and Lafferty (2009a), and found that it performed better than either. A similar method was proposed by Taddy (2012) who used the ratio of the probability of a word given a topic and the word's probability across the entire document collection.

Recently, Xing and Paul (2018) proposed to use information gathered while fitting the topic model. They made use of topic parameters from posterior samples generated during Gibbs sampling and re-weighted words based on their variability. Words with high uncertainty (i.e. their probabilities fluctuate relatively highly) are less likely to be representative of the topic than those with more stable probability estimates.

Topic re-ranking has also been explored within the context of measuring topic quality (Gollapalli and Li, 2018). A main claim of that work is that word importance should not only depend on its probability within a topic but also on its association with relevant neighbour words in the corpus. This information is incorporated by constructing topic-specific graphs capturing neighborhood words in a corpus. The PageRank (Brin and Page, 1998) algorithm is used to assign word importance scores based on centrality and then re-rank words based on their importance. The top n words with the highest PageRank values are used to compute the topics quality.

A common characteristic of previous work on topic word re-ranking is that it has been carried out within the context of an application of topic models (e.g. topic visualisation) and approaches have been evaluated in terms of these applications, if at all. The fact that word re-ranking methods have been considered in previous studies demonstrates their importance. The lack of direct and systematic evaluation is addressed in this work.

3 Word Re-ranking Methods

This paper explores a range of methods for word re-ranking based around the main approaches that have been applied to the problem (see Section 2). Let $\hat{\varphi}_{w,t}$ be the probability of a word w given a topic t produced by a topic model, e.g. LDA.[1] The following methods are used to re-rank topic words.

Original LDA Ranking (R_{Orig}) The most obvious and commonly used method for ranking words associated with a topic is to use $\hat{\varphi}_{w,t}$ to score each word, i.e. $score_{w,t} = \hat{\varphi}_{w,t}$. The ranking generated by this scoring function is equivalent to choosing the n most probable words for the topic and is referred to as R_{Orig}.

Normalised LDA Ranking (R_{Norm}) The first re-ranking method is a simple extension of R_{Orig} that represents approaches that normalise the probability of a word given a particular topic by the sum of probabilities for that word across all topics (Song et al., 2009; Taddy, 2012). This measure is computed as:

---

[1] We use the topic-word posterior distribution of LDA, but re-ranking can be applied to any topic model that estimates probabilities for words given topics.

$$score_{w,t} = \frac{\hat{\varphi}_{w,t}}{\sum_{j=1}^{T} \hat{\varphi}_{w,j}} \tag{1}$$

where T denotes the number of topics in the model. This approach scales the importance of words based on their overall occurrence within all topics in the model and downweights those that occur frequently.

Tf-idf Ranking ($R_{\mathbf{TFIDF}}$) The second re-ranking method was proposed by Blei and Lafferty (2009a) and represents methods that combine information about the probability of a word in a single topic with information about its probability across all topics (Bischof and Airoldi, 2012; Chuang et al., 2012; Sievert and Shirley, 2014). Blei and Lafferty re-rank each word as:

$$score_{w,t} = \hat{\varphi}_{w,t} \; log \frac{\hat{\varphi}_{w,t}}{\left(\prod_{j=1}^{T} \hat{\varphi}_{w,j}\right)^{\frac{1}{T}}} \tag{2}$$

Inverse Document Frequency (IDF) Ranking ($R_{\mathbf{IDF}}$) The final word re-ranking method explored in this paper is a variant on the previous method that takes account of a word's distribution across documents rather than topics. This method has not been explored in previous literature. In this approach each word is weighted by the Inverse Document Frequency (IDF) score across the corpus used to train the topic model:

$$score_{w,t} = \hat{\varphi}_{w,t} \; log \frac{|D|}{|D_w|} \tag{3}$$

where D is the entire document collection and D_w the documents within D containing the word w.

To better understand the effect of re-ranking words, consider the various representations of two topics shown in Table 2. The first row for each topic represents the baseline rank produced by topic model (R_{Orig}), while the other rows show the topic after re-ranking using Equations 1, 2 and 3, respectively. The bold words included in the original ranking (R_{Orig}) are down weighted and removed by at least two methods. Underlined words are those weighted higher by a re-ranking method and included in the topic representation.

Table 2: Examples of topic representations produced using various ranking approaches. Words in the R_{Orig} representation that were removed by at least two methods are shown in **bold**. Words that are ranked higher by the other approaches and included in the topic representation are shown underlined.

Method	Topic
R_{Orig}	space museum **years** history science earth mission **could** art shuttle
R_{Norm}	pincus abrams downey gettysburg particles sims emery landers lillian alamo
R_{TFIDF}	museum space earth shuttle pincus science universe radar exhibit art
R_{IDF}	museum space pincus science earth shuttle universe radar history mission
R_{Orig}	film **even** movie **world** stars **man much little story good**
R_{Norm}	vampire que winchell tomei westin swain marisa laughlin faye beatty
R_{TFIDF}	film movie stars vampire rating spielberg hollywood star characters actors
R_{IDF}	film movie stars vampire rating star spielberg even hollywood story

4 Experiment 1: Human Evaluation of Topic Interpretability

The first experiment compares the effectiveness of different topic representations (i.e. word re-rankings) by asking humans to choose the correct topic for a given document. We hypothesize that humans would be able to find the correct topic more easily when the representation is more interpretable.

4.1 Dataset and Preprocessing

We randomly sampled approximately 33,000 news articles from the New York Times included in the English GigaWord corpus fifth edition.[2] Documents were tokenized and stopwords removed. Words occurring in fewer than five or more than half of the documents were also removed to control for rare and common words. The size of the resulting vocabulary is approximately 52,000 words.

4.2 Topic Generation

Topics were generated using LDA's implementation in Gensim[3] fitted with online variational Bayes (Hoffman et al., 2010). The most important tuning parameter for LDA models is the number of topics and it was set to 50 after experimenting with varying number of topics optimised for coherence. To assess the quality of the resulting LDA models, topic coherence was computed[4] using: (1) C_V (Röder et al., 2015); (2) C_{UCI} (Newman et al., 2010); and (3) C_{NPMI} (Bouma, 2009).

4.3 Crowdsourcing Task

A job was created on the Figure Eight[5] crowdsourcing platform (previously known as CrowdFlower) in which participants were presented with ten micro-tasks per page[6]. Each micro-task consists of a text followed by six topics represented by a list of n words selected using one of the re-ranking methods presented in Section 3. Participants were asked to select the topic that was most closely associated with the text.

Micro-tasks were created using 48 New York Times articles (see Section 4.1). The correct answer is the topic with the highest probability given the article and incorrect answers (i.e. distractors) are five topics with low probabilities. The probability of the correct topic was at least 0.6 and the probability of the five distractors lower than 0.3.[7] Each article micro-tasks were created using each of the four ranking methods (Section 3) generated from topics created using three cardinalities (5, 10, 20). Five assessments were obtained for each micro-task and consequently 60 judgments were obtained for each document.[8]

Figure 1 shows an example of the micro-task presented to participants were they are asked to choose one of the topics. Participants are first provided with a brief description and an example to help them understand the task, followed by a quiz of ten micro-tasks to ensure their reliability and to eliminate random answers (Kazai, 2011). Participants who fail to answer seven out of ten micro-tasks correctly are eliminated from the job. If they qualify and proceed, a further quality micro-task is added per page and they need to maintain an accuracy of responses above 70%. To ensure non-redundant results, participants were always shown questions using the same topic word re-ranking method and the same number of words per topic. Also, participants can only answer a single page of 10 micro-tasks.

---

[2]https://catalog.ldc.upenn.edu/LDC2011T07
[3]https://radimrehurek.com/gensim
[4]The implementations available in Gensim were used.
[5]https://www.figure-eight.com/
[6]One of the ten micro-tasks on each page is reserved for quality assessment.
[7]Alternative values for these parameters were explored but it was found that lowering the probability of the correct answer and/or raising the probability of the distractors made the task too difficult.
[8]4 (ranking methods) $\times$ 3 (cardinalities) $\times$ 5 (judgments per document)

"ground controllers grew increasingly worried Thursday about a malfunctioning navigational unit aboard the shuttle Columbia as the ship's busy crew packed for Friday's trip home. The trouble with one of the shuttle's three Inertial Measurement Units, or IMUs, began days ago, but erratic readings from the device have worsened, said Jeff Bantle, National Aeronautics and Space Administration entry flight director. Bantle informed the seven-member crew that additional degradation could alter the shuttle's landing plan if there is also poor weather at the Kennedy Space Center in Florida. The shuttle is scheduled to land at Kennedy on Friday at 6:47 a.m. EDT. ``We have brought up Edwards Air Force Base just in case,'' said Bantle, referring to NASA's alternative landing site in California. Three IMUs are not needed for landing, however, and flight controllers were confident Thursday that the spacecraft would land as scheduled. An IMU that had been powered down to preserve energy was brought into operation Thursday as a backup, Bantle said. IMUs are important because they send data to an on-flight computer about the shuttle's position relative to the Earth. Spikes "

water	city	space	players	race	medical
river	police	museum	baseball	cup	hospital
fish	york	years	owners	day	doctors
boat	mayor	history	league	racing	patients
sea	street	science	strike	old	treatment
beer	people	earth	season	run	doctor
ship	officials	mission	union	back	hospitals
fishing	officers	could	cap	horse	health
lake	giuliani	art	salary	mile	medicine
boats	fire	shuttle	labor	three	patient
A	B	C	D	E	F

Figure 1: Example of the crowdsourcing micro-task interface.

4.4 Results and Discussion

Results for R_{Orig}, R_{Norm}, R_{TFIDF} and R_{IDF} when topics are represented by the 5, 10 and 20 highest scoring words are shown in Table 3. *Accuracy* represents the percentage of questions for which participants were able to identify the correct topic (i.e. topic with the highest probability given the document). *Time/page* is the mean time taken for participants to complete a page of 10 questions. *Coherence* is the average coherence of the topics, computed using NPMI (Aletras and Stevenson, 2013a)[9].

Table 3: Results of experiment comparing re-ranking methods in which crowdsourcing participants were asked to associate topic representations with documents. Topics are represented with their top 5, 10 or 20 probable words.

#words		Ranking Methods			
		R_{Orig}	R_{Norm}	R_{TFIDF}	R_{IDF}
5	Accuracy (%)	64	55	70	**73**
	Time/page	11:46	13:13	13:00	11:28
	Coherence (NPMI)	0.092	0.035	0.112	0.100
10	Accuracy (%)	67	48	**76**	70
	Time/page	12:40	15:23	12:15	12:31
	Coherence (NPMI)	0.072	0.038	0.091	0.084
20	Accuracy (%)	69	64	**74**	72
	Time/page	14:18	14:30	11:47	11:13
	Coherence (NPMI)	0.050	0.029	0.071	0.062

Results show a variation in performance which indicates that re-ranking words affects individual's ability to interpret topics. Performance when the words are ranked using R_{TFIDF} and R_{IDF} outperform the default ranking (R_{Orig}). Performance when words are ranked using R_{Norm} is considerably lower than their word re-ranking methods, both in terms of accuracy and time taken to complete the task.

These results show that the improvement obtained by using R_{TFIDF} and R_{IDF} is consistent when the number of words in the representation is varied. Results using R_{Orig} improve as the number of words

---

[9]The implementation provided by `https://github.com/jhlau/topic_interpretability` was used.

increases but never achieve the same performance as the re-ranking methods (except R_{Norm}), even when 20 words are included. This demonstrates that choosing the most appropriate words to represent a topic is more useful than simply increasing the number of words shown to the user. In fact, increasing the number of words shown for the default ranking appears to come at the cost of slowing down the time taken for a user to interpret the topic. The same increase in task completion time is not observed for R_{TFIDF} and R_{IDF} and this may be down to the fact that more useful words appear earlier in the ranking, allowing participants to interpret the topic more quickly.

The R_{TFIDF} and R_{IDF} approaches both combine information about the word's importance within an individual topic and across the entire document collection which results into more effective rankings than R_{Orig}. On the other hand, R_{Norm} only considers the relative importance of a word across topics and it would be possible for a word with a relatively low probability given the topic to be ranked highly if that word also had low probability across all the other topics.

Our results contrast with those reported by Song et al. (2009) who concluded that R_{Norm} was more effective for word re-ranking than R_{Orig} and R_{TFIDF} (see Section 3). However, their evaluation methodology used a single annotator per-task and asked them to judge whether words included within topic representations were important or not. Our approach measures a participants ability to interpret topic representations more directly and makes use of multiple annotations. The low results for R_{Norm} suggest that crowdworkers were simply unable to interpret many of the topics and, in those cases, their judgments about which words are important are unlikely to be reliable.

Overall R_{TFIDF} appears to be the most effective of the re-ranking approaches evaluated. This method achieves the best performance for 10 and 20 words, although not as well as R_{IDF} for 5 words.

5 Experiment 2: Automatic Evaluation of Topic Interpretability via Document Retrieval

In this second experiment, we automate the evaluation of the different topic representations obtained by re-ranking the topic words. The automated evaluation is based on an IR task in which the re-ranked topic words are used to form a query and retrieve documents relevant to the topic. The motivation behind this approach is that the most effective re-rankings are the ones that can retrieve documents related to the topic, while ineffective re-rankings will not be able to distinguish these from other documents in the collection. This evaluation method does not rely on human judgments, unlike the crowdsourcing approach presented in the previous section.

5.1 Evaluation Pipeline

The evaluation approach assumes that given a document collection in which each document is mapped to a label (or labels) indicating its topic. We refer to these labels as *gold standard topics* (to distinguish them from the automatically generated topics created by the topic model).

First, a set of automatically generated topics are created by running a topic model over a document collection. For each gold standard topic, a set of all documents labelled with that topic is created. The document-topic distribution created by the topic model is then used to identify the most probable automatically generated topic within that set of documents. This is achieved by summing the document-topic distributions and choosing the automatically generated topic with the highest value. A query is then created by selecting the re-ranked top n words from that automatically generated topic and use it to retrieve a set of documents from the collection. The set of retrieved documents is then compared against the set of all documents labelled with the gold standard label.

5.2 Datasets

Evaluation was carried out using datasets representing documents from a wide range of domains: news articles, scientific literature and online reviews.

Table 4: Datasets statistics.

Dataset	Documents	Distinct Words
NYT Annotated	39,218	60,339
MEDLINE	23,640	18,571
Amazon	40,000	24,943

5.2.1 New York Times

A subset of the NYT annotated dataset[10] consisting of approximately approximately 39,000 articles was used for this experiment[11]. This collection contains news articles from the *New York Times* labelled with 1,746 topics which we use as gold standard labels. These labels, which we refer to as NYT_topics, belong to a controlled set of topic categories and have been manually verified by NYTimes.com production staff. Each article has at least one NYT_topic, and articles are organised into a topic hierarchy. Examples of NYT_topics include:

- *Top/Features/Travel/Guides/Destinations/North America/United States*

- *Top/News/New York and Region*

- *Top/News/Technology*

The hierarchy into which the topics are organised is quite deep in some places and consequently we truncated each topic to the top most four levels of the hierarchy to control the number of topics. For example, the topic *Top/Features/Travel/Guides/ Destinations/North America/United States* is truncated to *Top/Features/Travel/Guides*. This produces a total of 132 truncated NYT_topics. The number of articles associated with each of the 132 NYT_topics ranges from 1 to 18,489. To avoid NYT_topics that are associated with small numbers of documents, we used the 50 NYT_topics that are associated with the most documents which resulted in NYT_topic that are each associated with at least 560 documents.

5.2.2 MEDLINE

MEDLINE contains abstracts of more than 25 million scientific publications in medicine and related fields. These abstracts are labelled with *Medical Subject Headings* (MeSH) codes which index publications into a hierarchy structure. Each publication is associated with a set of MeSH codes to describe the content of the publication.

The 50 most frequently used MeSH codes with the most publications from a subset of MEDLINE containing publications from 2017. This set of code are referred to as *MeSH_topics*.

5.2.3 Amazon Product Reviews

The Amazon Product Reviews dataset (McAuley et al., 2015)[12] contains reviews of products purchased from the Amazon website. Reviews are organized into 24 top-level categories each of which is divided into subcategories. The number of subcategories ranges from 1 to 1961. We chose eight main categories (*Cell Phones and Accessories, Electronics, Movies and TV, Musical Instrument, Office Products, Pet Supplies, Tools and Home Improvement and Automotive*) and extracted the 10 sub-categories with the most reviews from each which yielded 76 distinct sub-categories. This set of categories is referred to as *AMZ_topics*. 5,000 product reviews are extracted from each main category and reviews must belong to at least one category from the 50 most frequent in the AMZ_topics, resulting in a total of 40,000 reviews.

---

[10]https://catalog.ldc.upenn.edu/LDC2008T19

[11]Note that this is a different dataset to the one used for experiment 1 and contains the gold standard topics required for this evaluation

[12]http://jmcauley.ucsd.edu/data/amazon

Table 5: Results of experiment in which top 5, 10 and 20 ranked words are used to form query.

#Words	R_{Orig}	R_{Norm}	R_{TFIDF}	R_{IDF}
		Ranking Method		
New York Times Dataset				
5	0.0945	0.0463	**0.1363**	0.1187
10	0.1161	0.0608	**0.1417**	0.1291
20	0.1256	0.0721	**0.1392**	0.1321
Medline Dataset				
5	0.1420	0.0202	**0.1738**	0.1578
10	0.1518	0.0289	**0.1612**	0.1575
20	0.1498	0.0372	**0.1662**	0.1642
Amazon Product Reviews Dataset				
5	0.0231	0.0202	0.0208	**0.0244**
10	0.0195	0.0154	**0.0244**	0.0236
20	0.0258	0.0137	**0.0279**	0.0266

5.3 Experimental Settings

Each of the datasets was indexed using Apache Lucene.[13] The same preprocessing steps used in Experiment 1 were applied to the datasets and the statistics of the datasets are shown in Table 4.

For each dataset, LDA was used to generate topics and the number of topics for each dataset was set based on optimising for coherence which yielded 35 for NYT, 45 for MEDLINE and 35 for Amazon. The automatically generated topic that was most closely associated with each of the gold topics (i.e. 50 NYT_topics, 50 MeSH_topics and 50 AMZ_topics) were identified by applying the process outlined above in Section 5.1. The top 5, 10 and 20 words from this topic is used to form a query which is submitted to Lucene. The BM25 retrieval model (Robertson, 2004) was used to measure the similarity between the document to a given query. The documents retrieved by applying these queries are compared against the entire set of documents labelled with the dataset topics (i.e. NYT_topic, MeSH_topics, or AMZ_topics) by computing Mean Average Precision (MAP)[14] which is commonly used as a single metric to summarise IR system performance.

5.4 Results and Discussion

Queries were created using the top 5, 10, and 20 topic words using the R_{Orig}, R_{Norm}, R_{TFIDF}, and R_{IDF} re-rankings and applied to each of the three datasets (Section 5.2). Results are shown in Table 5.

Re-ranking words using R_{TFIDF} and R_{IDF} consistently enhances retrieval performance compared to the default ranking (R_{Orig}). R_{TFIDF} produces the best results in the majority of configurations, the exception being when 5 words are used with the Amazon corpus where R_{IDF} outperforms the other re-ranking methods. Re-ranking using R_{Norm} is less effective than all the other rankings, including the default ranking. The relative performance of the four approaches is generally stable when the number of words used to form the query is varied and across the three datasets representing very different genres of text that were used in this experiment.

These results demonstrate that topic word re-ranking can produce words which are more effective for discriminating documents describing a particular topic from those which do not. The pattern of results is very similar to the crowdsourcing experiments suggesting that the re-rankings preferred by human subjects are those which are also useful within applications such as document retrieval.

---

[13] http://lucene.apache.org/

[14] MAP is computed using the *trec_eval* tool: http://trec.nist.gov/trec_eval/

6 Evaluating Topic Representations

This paper presented two novel methods for the evaluation of topic representations: a crowdsourcing experiment that relied on human judgments (Section 4) and an automated evaluation based on an IR task (Section 5). Although there are some differences between results using the two methods, the relative performance of the re-ranking methods explored in this paper are very similar. The correlations between results of the crowdsourcing experiment and IR evaluations are statistically significant for all three datasets (Pearson's r varies between 0.81 and 0.90, $p < 0.05$). This suggests that the automated evaluation approach presented in Section 5 is a useful tool for assessing the effectiveness of methods for word re-ranking with the advantage that results can be obtained more rapidly than methods that require human judgments. However, human judgments are recommended when performance is similar and automated evaluation should not be relied upon to make fine-grained distinctions between approaches, as is common for some tasks (e.g. Machine Translation (Papineni et al., 2002)).

7 Conclusion

We presented a study on word re-ranking methods designed to improve topic interpretability. Four methods were presented and assessed through two experiments. In the first experiment, participants on a crowdsourcing platform were asked to associate documents with related topics. In the second experiment, automated evaluation was based on a document retrieval task.

Re-ranking the topic words was found to improve the interpretability of topics and therefore should be used as a post-processing step to improve topic representation. The most effective re-ranking schemes were those which combined information about the importance of words both within topics and their relative frequency in the entire corpus, thereby ensuring that less informative words are not used.

References

Aletras, N., T. Baldwin, J. Lau, and M. Stevenson (2014). Representing Topics Labels for Exploring Digital Libraries. In *Proceedings of the 14th ACM/IEEE-CS Joint Conference on Digital Libraries (JCDL '14)*, pp. 239–248.

Aletras, N., T. Baldwin, J. H. Lau, and M. Stevenson (2017). Evaluating Topic Representations for Exploring Document Collections. *Journal of the Association for Information Science and Technology 68*(1), 154–167.

Aletras, N. and A. Mittal (2017). Labeling Topics with Images using Neural Networks. In *European Conference on Information Retrieval (ECIR '17)*, pp. 500–505.

Aletras, N. and M. Stevenson (2013a). Evaluating Topic Coherence using Distributional Semantics. In *Proceedings of the 10th international conference on Computational Semantics (IWCS '13)*, Volume 13, , Potsdam, Germany, pp. 13–22.

Aletras, N. and M. Stevenson (2013b). Representing Topics Using Images. In *Proceedings of the 2013 Conference of the North American Chapter of the Association for Computational Linguistics: Human Language Technologies (NAACL HLT '13)*, pp. 158–167.

Aletras, N. and M. Stevenson (2014). Labelling Topics using Unsupervised Graph-based Methods. In *Proceedings of the 52nd Annual Meeting of the Association for Computational Linguistics (ACL '14)*, pp. 631–636.

Bischof, J. and E. Airoldi (2012). Summarizing Topical Content with Word Frequency and Exclusivity. In *Proceedings of the 29 th International Conference on Machine Learning (ICML '12)*, pp. 201–208.

Blei, D. (2012). Probabilistic topic models. *Communications of the ACM 4*(55), 77–84.

Blei, D. and J. Lafferty (2009a). Topic Models. *Text mining: classification, clustering, and applications 10*(71), 34.

Blei, D. and J. Lafferty (2009b). Visualizing Topics with Multi-Word Expressions. *arXiv preprint arXiv:0907.1013.*

Blei, D., A. Ng, and M. Jordan (2003). Latent Dirichlet Allocation. *Journal of machine Learning research 3*, 993–1022.

Bouma, G. (2009). Normalized (Pointwise) Mutual Information in Collocation Extraction. In *In Proceedings of the International Conference of the German Society for Computational Linguistics and Language Technology (GSCL 09)*, pp. 31–40.

Boyd-Graber, J., Y. Hu Google, and D. Mimno (2017). Applications of Topic Models. *Foundations and Trends R in Information Retrieval 11*(2-3), 143–296.

Brin, S. and L. Page (1998, 4). The Anatomy of a Large-scale Hypertextual Web search engine. *Computer Networks and ISDN Systems 30*(1-7), 107–117.

Chaney, A. and D. Blei (2012). Visualizing Topic Models. In *Proceedings of the 6th International AAAI Conference Weblogs and Social Media (AAAI ICWSM '12)*, pp. 419–422.

Chang, J., J. Boyd-Graber, S. Gerrish, C. Wang, and D. Blei (2009). Reading Tea Leaves: How Humans Interpret Topic Models. In *Proceedings of the 22nd International Conference on Neural Information Processing Systems (NIPS '09)*, pp. 288–296.

Chuang, J., C. Manning, and J. Heer (2012). Termite: Visualization Techniques for Assessing Textual Topic Models. In *Proceeding of the International Working Conference on Advanced Visual Interfaces (AVI '12)*, pp. 74–77.

Gollapalli, S. and X.-l. Li (2018). Using PageRank for Characterizing Topic Quality in LDA. In *Proceedings of the ACM SIGIR International Conference on the Theory of Information Retrieval (ICTIR '18)*, pp. 115–122.

Hoffman, M., F. Bach, and D. Blei (2010). Online Learning for Latent Dirichlet Allocation. In *Proceedings of the 23rd Advances in Neural Information Processing Systems (NIPS '10)*, pp. 856–864.

Kazai, G. (2011). In Search of Quality in Crowdsourcing for Search Engine Evaluation. In *Proceedings of the 33rd European Conference on Advances in Information Retrieval (ECIR '11)*, pp. 165–176.

Lau, J. and T. Baldwin (2016). The Sensitivity of Topic Coherence Evaluation to Topic Cardinality. In *Proceedings of the 15th Annual Conference of the North American Chapter of the Association for Computational Linguistics: Human Language Technologies (NAACL-HLT '16)*, pp. 483–487.

Lau, J., K. Grieser, D. Newman, and T. Baldwin (2011). Automatic Labelling of Topic Models. In *Proceedings of the 49th Annual Meeting of the Association for Computational Linguistics: Human Language Technologies (ACL HLT '11)*, pp. 1536–1545.

Lau, J., D. Newman, and T. Baldwin (2014). Machine Reading Tea Leaves: Automatically Evaluating Topic Coherence and Topic Model Quality. In *Proceedings of the 14th Conference of the European Chapter of the Association for Computational Linguistics (EACL '14)*, pp. 530–539.

McAuley, J., C. Targett, Q. Shi, and A. van den Hengel (2015). Image-Based Recommendations on Styles and Substitutes. In *Proceedings of the 38th International ACM SIGIR Conference on Research and Development in Information Retrieval (SIGIR '15)*, pp. 43–52.

Mimno, D., H. Wallach, E. Talley, M. Leenders, and A. Mccallum (2011). Optimizing Semantic Coherence in Topic Models. In *Proceedings of the Conference on Empirical Methods in Natural Language Processing (EMNLP '11)*, pp. 262–272.

Newman, D., H. Lau, K. Grieser, and T. Baldwin (2010). Automatic Evaluation of Topic Coherence. In *Proceedings of Human Language Technologies: The 11th Annual Conference of the North American Chapter of the Association for Computational Linguistics (NAACL HLT10)*, pp. 100–108.

Papineni, K., S. Roukos, T. Ward, and W.-J. Zhu (2002). BLEU: A Method for Automatic Evaluation of Machine Translation. In *Proceedings of the 40th Annual Meeting on Association for Computational Linguistics (ACL '02)*, pp. 311–318.

Paul, M. (2016). Interpretable Machine Learning: Lessons from Topic Modeling. In *CHI Workshop on Human-Centered Machine Learning*.

Robertson, S. (2004, 10). Understanding Inverse Document Frequency: on Theoretical Arguments for IDF. *Journal of Documentation 60*(5), 503–520.

Röder, M., A. Both, and A. Hinneburg (2015). Exploring the Space of Topic Coherence Measures. In *Proceedings of the eight ACM International Conference on Web Search and Data Mining (WSDM '15)*, pp. 399–408. ACM.

Schofield, A., M. Magnusson, and D. Mimno (2017). Pulling Out the Stops: Rethinking Stopword Removal for Topic Models. In *Proceedings of the 15th Conference of the European Chapter of the Association for Computational Linguistics (EACL '17)*, Volume 2, pp. 432–436.

Sievert, C. and K. Shirley (2014). LDAvis: A Method for Visualizing and Interpreting Topics. In *Preceedings of the Workshop on Interactive Learning Visualization, and Interfaces*, pp. 63–70.

Smith, A., T. Lee, F. Poursabzi-Sangdeh, J. Boyd-Graber, N. Elmqvist, and L. Findlater (2017). Evaluating Visual Representations for Topic Understanding and Their Effects on Manually Generated Topic Labels. *Transactions of the Association for Computational Linguistics 5*, 1–15.

Song, Y., S. Pan, S. Liu, M. Zhou, and W. Qian (2009). Topic and Keyword Re-ranking for LDA-based Topic Modeling. In *Proceedings of the 18th ACM Conference on Information and Knowledge Management (CIKM '09)*, pp. 1757–1760.

Sorodoc, I., J. H. Lau, N. Aletras, and T. Baldwin (2017). Multimodal Topic Labelling. In *Proceedings of the 15th Conference of the European Chapter of the Association for Computational Linguistics (EACL '17)*, pp. 701–706.

Taddy, M. (2012). On Estimation and Selection for Topic Models. In *Proceedings of the 15th International Conference on Artificial Intelligence and Statistics (AISTATS '12)*, pp. 1184–1193.

Xing, L. and M. J. Paul (2018). Diagnosing and Improving Topic Models by Analyzing Posterior Variability. In *Proceedings of the Advancement of Artificial Intelligence (AAAI '18)*, pp. 6005–6012.

An Improved Approach for Semantic Graph Composition with CCG

Austin Blodgett   Nathan Schneider
Georgetown University, Department of Linguistics
{ajb341, nathan.schneider}@georgetown.edu

Abstract

This paper builds on previous work using Combinatory Categorial Grammar (CCG) to derive a transparent syntax-semantics interface for Abstract Meaning Representation (AMR) parsing. We define new semantics for the CCG combinators that is better suited to deriving AMR graphs. In particular, we define relation-wise alternatives for the application and composition combinators: these require that the two constituents being combined overlap in one AMR relation. We also provide a new semantics for type raising, which is necessary for certain constructions. Using these mechanisms, we suggest an analysis of eventive nouns, which present a challenge for deriving AMR graphs. Our theoretical analysis will facilitate future work on robust and transparent AMR parsing using CCG.

1   Introduction

At the heart of semantic parsing are two goals: the disambiguation of linguistic forms that can have multiple meanings, and the normalization of morphological and syntactic variation. Among many techniques for semantic parsing, one profitable direction exploits computational linguistic grammar formalisms that make explicit the correspondence between the linguistic form of a sentence and the semantics (e.g., broad-coverage logical forms, or database queries in a domain-specific query language). In particular, English semantic parsers using Combinatory Categorial Grammar (CCG; Steedman, 2000) have been quite successful thanks to the CCGBank resource (Hockenmaier and Steedman, 2007; Honnibal et al., 2010) and the broad-coverage statistical parsing models trained on it (e.g., Clark and Curran, 2004; Lewis et al., 2016; Clark et al., 2018).

The CCG formalism assumes that all language-specific grammatical information is stored in a lexicon: each word in the lexicon is associated with a structured syntactic **category** and a semantic form, such that the compositional potentials of the category and the semantics are isomorphic. A small universal set of **combinators** are responsible for assembling constituents into a full syntactic derivation; each combinator operates on adjacent constituents with appropriate categories to produce a new constituent and its compositional semantics, subject to constraints. A full grammar thus allows well-formed sentences to be transduced into semantic structures. The categories and combinators cooperate to license productive syntactic constructions like control and wh-questions, requiring the correct word order and producing the correct semantic dependencies. For example, consider the sentence "Who did John seem to forget to invite to attend?": the correct logical form—in propositional logic, something like $seem(forget(John_i, invite(John_i, who_j, attend(who_j))))$—is nontrivial, requiring a precise account of several constructions that conspire to produce long-range dependencies.

Whereas CCG traditionally uses some version of lambda calculus for its semantics, there has also been initial work using CCG to build parsers for Abstract Meaning Representation (AMR; Banarescu et al., 2013), a standard with which a large "sembank" of English sentences[1] has been manually annotated.[2] To

---

[1] See https://amr.isi.edu/download.html

[2] As originally defined, AMR is English-specific. However, a companion annotation standard, corpus, and parsers exist for Chinese (Xue et al., 2014; Li et al., 2016; Wang et al., 2018), and initial investigations have been made toward adapting AMR to several other languages (Xue et al., 2014; Migueles-Abraira et al., 2018; Anchiêta and Pardo, 2018).

date, dozens of publications[3] have used the corpus to train and evaluate semantic parsers—most using graph-based or transition-based parsing methods (e.g., Flanigan et al., 2014; Wang et al., 2016; Lyu and Titov, 2018) to transform the sentence string or syntactic parse into a semantic graph via a learned statistical model, without any explicit characterization of the syntax-semantics interface. There is good reason to apply CCG to the AMR parsing task: apart from transparency of the syntax-semantics interface, state-of-the-art AMR parsers are known to be weak at reentrancy (e.g., Lyu and Titov, 2018), which presumably can be partially attributed to syntactic reentrancy in control constructions, for example. Prior work applying CCG to AMR parsing has begun to address this, but some of the important mechanisms that make CCG a linguistically powerful and robust theory have yet to be incorporated into these approaches.

In this paper, we build on a core insight of previous work (e.g., Artzi et al., 2015; Beschke and Menzel, 2018) that AMR fragments can be directly represented as the semantics of CCG lexical entries. With appropriate definitions of the lexical items and combinatorial rules of CCG, the compositionality of CCG gives a derivation of a full AMR "for free". In other words, AMR parsing can be reduced to CCG parsing (plus some additional semantic disambiguation and postprocessing). On a practical level, this should allow us to take advantage of existing CCG datasets and parsing methods for AMR parsing. In addition, explicitly storing AMR fragments in the CCG lexicon would provide a level of interpretability not seen in most statistical AMR parsers: the transparent syntax-semantics interface would decouple errors in the grammar from errors in the parsing model.

As a prerequisite for building a CCG-based AMR parser, or inducing a broad-coverage grammar (CCG lexicon) from data, we consider in this paper the formal mechanisms that would be necessary to derive AMRs with linguistic robustness. In particular, we address a variety of challenging syntactic phenomena with respect to AMR, showing the semantic fragments, associated syntactic categories, and combinators that will facilitate parsing of constructions including control, wh-questions, relative clauses, case marking, nonconstituent coordination, eventive nouns, and light verbs. In so doing, we offer new semantics of combinators for semantic graphs beyond the proposals of previous work.

After an overview of related work (§2),[4] we introduce our formalism for AMR graph semantics in CCG (§3). §4 gives example derivations for well-known linguistic phenomena including control, complex coordination, and eventive nouns. §5 discusses some implications of our approach.

2   Related Work

AMR formalizes sentence meaning via a graph structure. The AMR for an English sentence is a directed acyclic graph that abstracts away from morphological and syntactic details such as word order, voice, definiteness, and morphology, focusing instead on lexical semantic predicates, roles, and relations. Semantic predicate-argument structures are based on the PropBank frame lexicon (Kingsbury and Palmer, 2002) and its frame-specific core argument roles (named *ARG0*, *ARG1*, etc.). AMR supplements these with its own inventory of noncore relations like :time and :purpose, and some specialized frames for the semantics of comparison, for example. Named entities are typed and linked to Wikipedia pages; dates and other values are normalized. Edges in the graph correspond to roles/relations, and nodes to predicate or non-predicate "concepts", which are lemmatized. Reentrancy is used for within-sentence coreference.

A limited amount of prior research has combined CCG and AMR. Artzi et al. (2015) and Misra and Artzi (2016) develop an AMR parser using CCG by reformulating AMR graphs as logical forms in lambda calculus. We opt here for an approach similar to that of Beschke and Menzel (2018), where AMR subgraphs with free variables are treated as the semantics in the CCG lexicon. This requires definitions of the combinators that operate directly on AMR subgraphs rather than lambda calculus expressions.

Beschke and Menzel (2018) situate their formalization within the literature on graph grammars. They formulate their approach in terms of the HR algebra (Courcelle and Engelfriet, 2012), which Koller (2015) had applied to AMR graphs (but not with CCG). In this formalism, graph fragments called s-graphs are assembled to derive full graphs. S-graphs are equivalent to the AMR subgraphs described in this paper.

---

[3]`https://nert-nlp.github.io/AMR-Bibliography/` is a categorized list of publications about or using AMR.
[4]Due to space constraints, we assume the reader is familiar with the basics of both CCG and AMR.

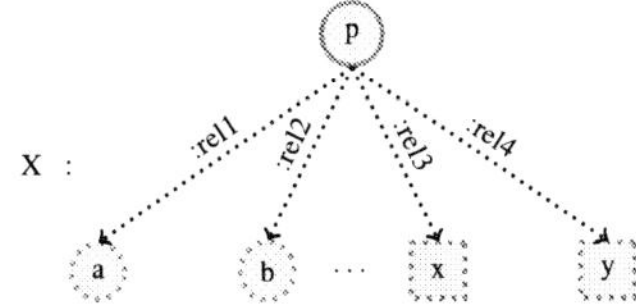

Figure 1: Basic shape of AMR subgraph: Free variables (square, blue) are represented with *x, y, z*, etc. AMR nodes (round, red) are represented with *a, b, c*, etc. Dots indicate that part of the graph may be present or not.

In particular, Beschke and Menzel define the semantics of CCG combinators in terms of HR-algebraic operations on s-graphs. They discuss a small set of combinators from Lewis and Steedman (2014) that includes forward and backward application and forward, backward, crossed, and generalized variants of composition. We introduce equivalent semantics for application and composition (§3.2), avoiding the conceptually heavy notation and formalism from the HR algebra. They also specify Conjunction and Identity combinators, which we adapt slightly to suit our needs, and a Punctuation combinator. More significantly, they treat unary operators such as type raising to have no effect on the semantics, whereas we will take another route for type raising (§3.4), and will introduce new, *relation-wise* versions of application and composition (§3.3). Finally, whereas Beschke and Menzel devote most of their paper to a lexicon induction algorithm and experiments, we focus on the linguistic motivation for our definition of the combinators, and leave the development of suitable lexicon induction techniques to future work.

A related graph formalism called *hyperedge replacement grammar* is also used in the AMR parsing literature (Jones et al., 2012; Chiang et al., 2013; Peng et al., 2015; Peng and Gildea, 2016; Björklund et al., 2016; Groschwitz et al., 2018). Hyperedge replacement grammars (Rozenberg, 1997) are a formal way of combining subgraphs to derive a larger graph, based on an extension of Context Free Grammars to graphs instead of strings. Readers may assume that the graph formalism described in this paper is a simplified hyperedge replacement grammar which only allows hyperedges of rank 1.

3   Graph Semantics

AMR is designed to represent semantics at the sentence level. For CCG lexical entries and combinators to parse AMR semantics, we need to formalize how AMR subgraphs can represent the semantics of individual words, and how combinators combine subgraphs to derive a full AMR. This section will formalize AMR subgraph semantics and CCG combinators for *function application, composition*, and *type raising*. Additionally, we propose new *relation-wise* variants of application and composition which are unique to graph semantics.

Each AMR subgraph contains nodes and edges from the resulting AMR as well as some nodes which correspond to free variables. The basic shape of an AMR subgraph appears in figure 1. Formally, an AMR subgraph is a tuple $\langle G, R, FV \rangle$, where G is a connected, labeled, directed acyclic graph; R is the root node in G; and FV is an ordered list of the nodes of G which are free and must be substituted by the end of the derivation. Though not shown in figure 1, the root of an AMR subgraph may be a free variable. Intuitively, a subgraph with at least one free variable corresponds to a function, and a subgraph with no free variables corresponds to a constant.

Textual notation. Taking inspiration from the PENMAN notation used for AMR, we use the notation (a :rel1 ($\boxed{2}$:rel2 $\boxed{1}$)) to denote an AMR subgraph rooted at a constant a, with a :rel1 edge to a free variable, $\boxed{2}$, which in turn has a child free variable, $\boxed{1}$.

Table 1 shows the formulation of graph semantics for all the combinators described below. The formulas are schematic with attention paid to the resulting order of free variables, which semantically distinguishes application from composition. Another combinator in CCG, crossing composition, has the same semantics as regular composition. Semantics for the substitution combinator is left to future work.

3.1   Syntax-Semantics Isomorphism

A core property of CCG is that it provides transparency in the syntax-semantics interface: both syntactic categories and semantic forms are defined as functions permitting a compositional derivation of the

combinator	function (left/right)	arg. (right/left)	result	FV ordering
Binary				
Application	$\ldots_1$ $\boxed{1}$ $\ldots_2$	a $\ldots_3$	$\ldots_1$ a $\ldots_2$ $\ldots_3$	$\boxed{2},\ldots,\boxed{\mathbf{1}},\ldots$
Composition (B, B^2)	$\ldots_1$ $\boxed{1}$ $\ldots_2$	a $\ldots_3$	$\ldots_1$ a $\ldots_2$ $\ldots_3$	$\boxed{\mathbf{1}},\ldots,\boxed{2},\ldots$
Relation-wise Application (R)	$\ldots_1$ $\boxed{1}$:rel$_x$ b $\ldots_2$	a :rel$_x$ $\boxed{\mathbf{1}}$ $\ldots_3$	$\ldots_1$ a :rel$_x$ b $\ldots_2$ $\ldots_3$	$\boxed{2},\ldots,\boxed{\mathbf{2}},\ldots$
Relation-wise Composition (RB)	$\ldots_1$ $\boxed{1}$:rel$_x$ b $\ldots_2$	a :rel$_x$ $\boxed{\mathbf{2}}$ $\ldots_3$	$\ldots_1$ a :rel$_x$ b $\ldots_2$ $\ldots_3$	$\boxed{\mathbf{1}},\boxed{\mathbf{3}},\ldots,\boxed{2},\ldots$
...Second-order (RB^2)	$\ldots_1$ $\boxed{1}$:rel$_x$ b $\ldots_2$	a :rel$_x$ $\boxed{\mathbf{3}}$ $\ldots_3$	$\ldots_1$ a :rel$_x$ b $\ldots_2$ $\ldots_3$	$\boxed{\mathbf{1}},\boxed{\mathbf{2}},\boxed{\mathbf{4}},\ldots,\boxed{2},\ldots$
Unary				
Type Raising (T)	a $\ldots_1$		$\boxed{1}$:? a $\ldots_1$	$\boxed{1},\boxed{\mathbf{1}},\ldots$
N-ary ($\leq$1 FV per operand)				
Conjunction (&)	x	a $\ldots_1$, b $\ldots_2,\ldots$	x :op1 a $\ldots_1$:op2 b $\ldots_2\ldots$	$\boxed{1}$

Table 1: Formal semantic rules for AMR combinators. Boxed numbers stand for free variables (FVs) in the semantics of each of the constituents being combined: $\boxed{1}$ stands for the lowest indexed FV in the function (head) constituent, and $\boxed{\mathbf{1}}$ for the lowest indexed FV in the argument constituent, if any. Ellipses $\ldots_n$ denote optional dominating structure (if preceding) and optional dominated structure (if following). Any FVs in these optional structures are preserved in the result, in the order given in the last column. For relation-wise combinators, the function constituent's relation may also be **:?**. Crossing composition (B$_\times$) and its variants behave semantically like their non-crossing counterparts. Not shown: exceptions to application and composition for the identity function (ID), discussed in §4.

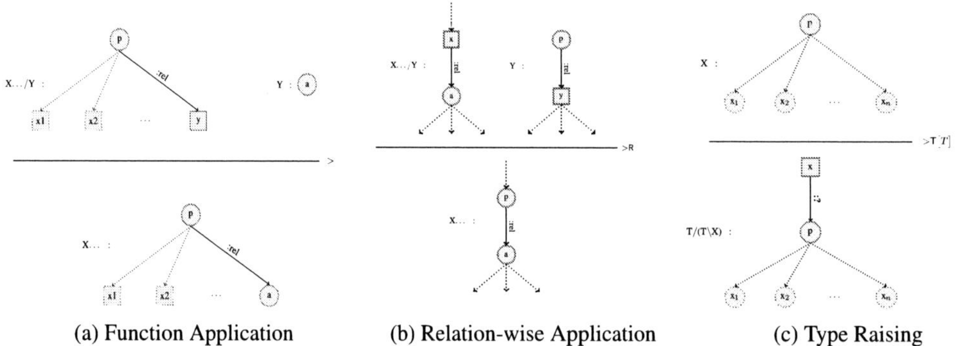

(a) Function Application (b) Relation-wise Application (c) Type Raising

Figure 2: Combinators illustrated in terms of semantic graph structure. The semantics of composition differs from application only in ordering of free variables (not shown).

sentence. The syntactic category determines which constituents may be constructed and in what word order. In the semantics, the word order (direction of the slashes) is irrelevant, but the functional structure— the arity and the order in which arguments are to be applied—must match in order for the semantics to remain well-formed as the sentence is derived based on the syntactic categories and combinatorial rules.

In other words, the functional structure of the category must be isomorphic to the functional structure of the semantics. For example, a hypothetical CCG category V\W/X/(Y/Z) would naturally correspond to a ternary function whose first argument, Y/Z, is itself a unary function.

This brings us to the following principle:

Principle of Functional Isomorphism. The semantics of a word or constituent cannot have higher arity than the CCG category calls for, and every functional category must take at least one semantic argument. For instance, a word or constituent with category PP/NP must have exactly 1 semantic argument; and the VP adjunct category (S\NP)\(S\NP) a.k.a. S\NP\(S\NP) can be interpreted as having 1 or 2 semantic arguments.

Without proving it formally, we remark that this helps ensure that syntactic well-formedness according to the categories will guarantee semantic well-formedness, with no attempt to apply something that is not expecting any arguments, and no free variables remaining in the semantics at the end of a sentence derivation. (An edge case where this guarantee might not hold is noted in fn. 6.)

3.2 Function Application and Composition

In **Function Application** of AMR subgraphs, a free variable (blue) can be filled by the root of another AMR subgraph. The case of right function application is shown in figure 2a. Function application can only substitute the first free variable in FV corresponding to the rightmost syntactic argument.

While application and composition always differ syntactically, from a graph semantics point of view, composition turns out to be the same as function application, where the root of one subgraph is substituted for a free variable in another subgraph. The difference between application and composition is captured in the resulting order of free variables. In the case of composition, the argument's free variables are placed first on the free variable stack followed by the function's free variables. This allows free variables in the AMR subgraph to consistently match syntactic arguments in the CCG category. This is a difference between composition in this work and in Beschke and Menzel's (2018) work, where the semantics of application and composition is the same.

3.3 Relation-wise Application and Composition

When deriving a constituent, there are situations where it is desirable to have a semantic edge that is shared between the two constituents being combined. For example, we specify the following lexical entry for the control verb "decide", indexing arguments in the category with subscripts for clarity: $S_b \backslash NP_2 / (S_{to} \backslash NP)_1$: decide-01 :ARG0 ② :ARG1 (① **:ARG0** ②). Unlike a simple verb, "decide" selects for an embedded clause and controls its subject, coindexing it with the matrix subject. This is indicated in the semantics with the bolded :ARG0 edge, which needs to unify with the :ARG0 edge of the embedded predicate. Thus the constituent "you decide to eat yesterday" in figure 7 is formed by merging the :ARG0 edge expected by "decide" and the :ARG0 edge expected by "eat" so that they may later be filled by the same node, you. Note that the number of semantic free variables respects the functional structure of the category (§3.1). To facilitate this, we define novel **relation-wise** variants of the application and composition combinators that expect an edge in common (call it the **shared edge**). Apart from control, relation-wise combinators are also useful for derivations with type raising and various interesting syntactic constructions.

The schematic graph structures serving as inputs and outputs for relation-wise combinators are shown in figure 2b, and the full definition is given in table 1. Notably, the function constituent has its lowest-indexed free variable at the *source* of the shared edge, and the argument constituent has a free variable at the *target* of the shared edge (the variable's index depending on the kind of application or composition). In the result, each free variable unifies with the node or variable at the same side of the edge in the other constituent. Other material attached to the shared edge in either constituent will be preserved in the result.

The regular vs. relation-wise distinction applies only to the *semantics*; syntactically, relation-wise application (composition) is just like regular application (composition). During parsing, relation-wise combinators apply if and only if the two constituents being combined share a common relation with the appropriate free variables; otherwise, the non–relation-wise version of the combinator is used.

Relation-wise Composition (RB) differs from **Relation-wise Application** (R) in the index of the argument's free variable being unified and in the resulting order of free variables. Just as regular composition can be used to adjust the order that constituents are normally combined and "save an argument for later", relation-wise composition does this with respect to a common edge. Examples of both relation-wise and non–relation-wise composition appear in figure 7.

3.4 Type Raising

In CCG, **Type Raising** (T) converts an argument into a function. For example, the nominative case of the pronoun "I" can be coded in the syntactic category by making it a function that expects a verb phrase on the right and returns a sentence, thus preventing "I" from serving as an object. For our framework to support type raising, we need an appropriate semantic conversion that respects the functional structure of the category—thus, the type-raised semantics must take an argument. However, as type raising can be applied to different types of arguments, we do not know a priori which relation label to produce.

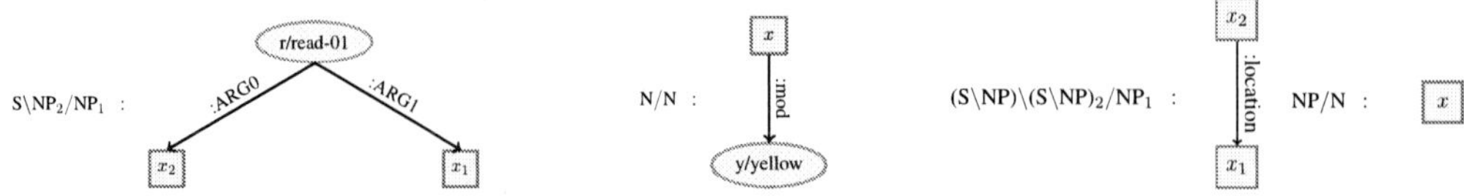

(a) "read"; (r/read-01 :ARG0 ② :ARG1 ①) (b) "yellow"; (① :mod y/yellow) (c) "at"; (② :location ①) (d) "the"; ID

Figure 3: Linguistic examples as AMR subgraphs: (a) transitive verb, (b) adjective, (c) preposition (in VP adjunct), (d) determiner (identity semantics).

Therefore, we introduce the notion of an **underspecified edge**, denoted **:?**. The type-raised structure has a free variable at the source of the underspecified edge, with the original subgraph at the target, as shown in figure 2c. For example, see "John" and "Mary" in figure 5, where type raising is necessary to support subject+verb constituents for coordination. The type-raised constituent must eventually be the input to a relation-wise combinator, which will specify the label on the edge.

Note that in this strategy of representing type raising, the isomorphism between functions in semantics and syntactic category is maintained. This fits with CCG's philosophy of a transparent syntax-semantics interface (§3.1). By contrast, Beschke and Menzel's (2018) strategy was to leave the result of type raising semantically unchanged, creating a mismatch between the syntax and the semantics.

4   Linguistic Examples

This section explains the use of the combinators discussed in §3 for particular linguistic constructions.

Transitive and Intransitive Verbs. Figure 3a shows the semantics for a transitive verb. Since "read" has more than one semantic argument, the order of free variables matters: ①, the first free variable, must correspond to NP_1, the rightmost syntactic argument in the category.

Adjectives. Figure 3b shows the semantics for an adjective. Note that, unlike in the examples above, the root of this subgraph is a free variable, since the root of this subgraph is what will be filled in. Ordinary adverbs have similar semantics.

Prepositional Phrases (Adjunct). Figure 3c shows semantics for the locative preposition "at". To derive a prepositional phrase, assume available constituents "at": (② :location ①) and "the library": (l/library), which may be combined by application.

Null Semantics: Articles, etc. Some linguistic features, including tense and definite/indefinite articles, are not represented in AMR. For CCG derivations to deal with these elements, there will need to be a semantic representation which allows them to be "syntactic sugar", affecting the syntactic category but adding nothing to the semantics in the derivation. We call this the **identity function**, following Beschke and Menzel (2018), and notate it as ID. More precisely, if a constituent a has ID as its semantics, then a, when combined with another constituent b via application or composition (either as the function or as the argument), will produce b's semantics for the resulting constituent.

Figure 4 shows the use of application (and identity application) combinators to derive a simple sentence. Figure 5 demonstrates type raising, relation-wise composition, and conjunction as tools to derive a sentence with complex coordination.

Passives, Control, and Wh-questions. Figures 6 and 7 show CCG derivations with AMR semantics for three well-known linguistic phenomena in English: passives, control, and wh-questions. In a passive

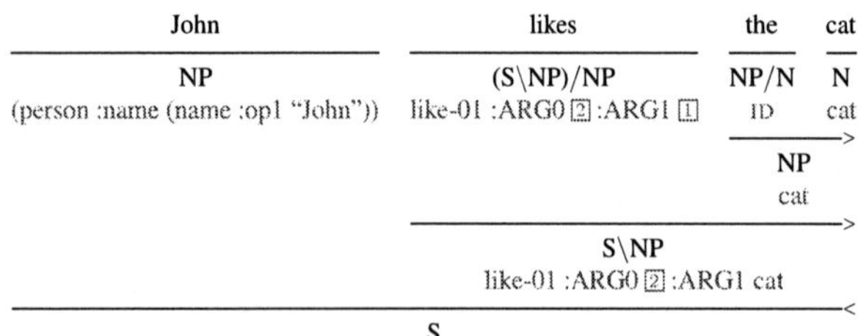

Figure 4: **application and identity**: "John likes the cat"

	John	likes	and	Mary	hates	cats
	NP	(S\NP)/NP	Conj	NP	(S\NP)/NP	NP
	(person :name (name :op1 "John"))	like-01 :ARG0 ② :ARG1 ①	and	(person … "Mary")	hate-01 :ARG0 ② :ARG1 ①	cat

> ──── >T [s]
> S/(S\NP)
> ① :? (person … "John")
> ──── >RB
> S/NP
> like-01 :ARG0 (person … "John") :ARG1 ①

> ──── >T [s]
> S/(S\NP)
> ① :? (person … "Mary")
> ──── >RB
> S/NP
> hate-01 :ARG0 (person … "Mary") :ARG1 ①

> ──── &
> S/NP
> and :op1 (like-01 :ARG0 (person … "John") :ARG1 ①) :op2 (hate-01 :ARG0 (person … "Mary") :ARG1 ①)

> ──── >
> S
> a/and :op1 (l/like-01 :ARG0 (p/person :name (n/name :op1 "John")) :ARG1 c/cat)
> :op2 (h/hate-01 :ARG0 (p2/person :name (n2/name :op1 "Mary")) :ARG1 c)

Figure 5: **complex coordination and type raising**: "John likes and Mary hates cats"

	John	was	eaten	by	bears
	NP	(S\NP)/(S_{pass}\NP)	S_{pass}\NP	(S\NP)\(S\NP)/NP	NP
	(person :name (name :op1 "John"))	ID	(eat-01 :ARG1 ①)	② :ARG0 ①	bear

> ──── >
> S\NP
> (eat-01 :ARG1 ①)

> S\NP
> (S\NP)\(S\NP)
> ② :ARG0 bear

> ──── <
> S\NP
> (eat-01 :ARG0 bear :ARG1 ①)

> ──── <
> S
> (eat-01 :ARG0 bear :ARG1 (person :name (name :op1 "John")))

Figure 6: **passive**: "John was eaten by bears"

construction, a semantically core argument may be added by a syntactically optional adjunct phrase as in figure 6. Note that in this semantic representation, only syntactically required arguments are represented in a predicate's semantics, and so the passive verb *eaten* does not include an :ARG0 edge.

Figure 7 shows both control and wh-question formation. Control is an important problem for graph semantics as it requires representing the subject (here *you*) as the agent of two predicates (see §3.3). Wh-questions are another complex and difficult phenomenon that is handled by CCG derivation. Additionally, figure 7 gives examples of both types of composition: relation-wise and non–relation-wise.

4.1 Inverse Core Roles and Relative Clauses

AMR provides notation for *inverse roles* that reverse the usual ordering of a relation. These are indicated with the -of suffix: (a :rel-of b) is equivalent to (b :rel a). This ensures that the graph can be constructed with a single root, and provides a convenient mechanism for expressing derived nominals and relative clauses. For instance, the noun phrases "teacher" and "a person who teaches" both receive the AMR (person :ARG0-of teach-01). If the subject matter is expressed, that is slotted into the :ARG1 of teach-01. This can be handled by treating "teachers" as a predicate of sorts, as seen in the derivation below.

	math	teachers
	N	NP\N
	math	person :ARG0-of (teach-01 :ARG1 ①)

> ──── <
> NP
> person :ARG0-of (teach-01 :ARG1 math)

	people	who	teach	math
	NP	NP\NP/(S\NP)	S\NP/NP	NP
	person	② :ARG0-of ①	teach-01 :ARG0 ② :ARG1 ①	math

> ──── >
> S\NP
> teach-01 **:ARG0** ② :ARG1 math

> ──── >R
> NP\NP
> ② **:ARG0-of** teach-01 :ARG1 math

> ──── <
> NP
> person :ARG0-of (teach-01 :ARG1 math)

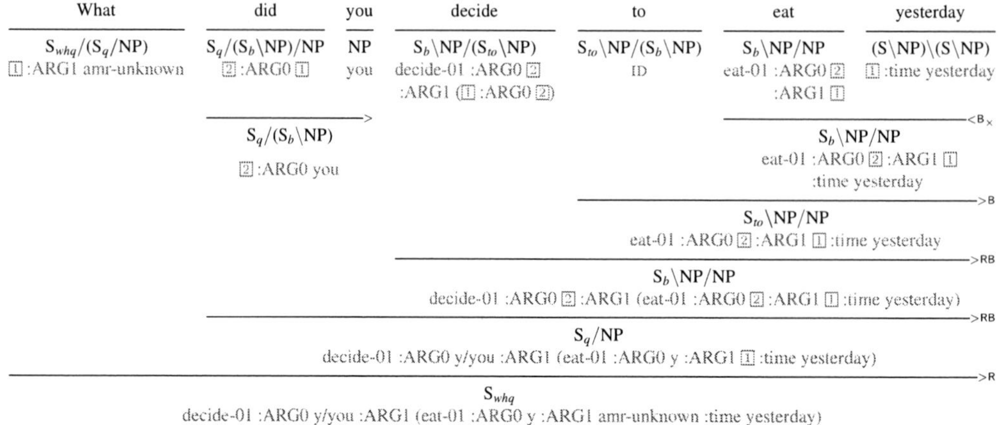

Figure 7: **wh-question and control, relation-wise and non–relation-wise composition**: "What did you decide to eat yesterday?" $B_\times$ stands for *crossing composition*, which has the same semantics as composition.

Also illustrated is the relative clause paraphrase, "people who teach math". Here, the relativizer "who" needs to fill the appropriate role of the verbal predicate with its noun head "people". An inverse role is produced so that person, rather than teach-01, will be the root of the resulting subgraph. The relation-wise application combinator must therefore be aware of inverses: it must match the :ARG0-of with the :ARG0 edge in the operand and effectively merge the two relations. Alternatively, the phrase could be parsed by first relation-wise composing "who" with "teach", which requires similar handling of the inverse role, and then attaching "math" by application.

4.2 Eventive Nouns and PP Complements

This section will describe an approach to the semantics of eventive nouns like "decision", and in the process will illustrate our treatment of prepositional phrase complements (as opposed to adjuncts: beginning of §4), which in CCG are traditionally given the category PP.

In English, many eventive nouns can be linked to semantic arguments via prepositional phrases, possessives, and light verb constructions, as shown in table 2. AMR uses a canonical form with a predicate (typically based on a verbal paraphrase), treating *John decided*, *John's decision*, and *John made a/his decision* as semantically equivalent. Despite some work on integrating event nominals and multiword expressions into CCG (Constable and Curran, 2009; Honnibal et al., 2010; de Lhoneux, 2014), we are not aware of any CCG analyses of **light verb constructions**, which have been studied computationally in other frameworks (e.g., Baldwin and Kim, 2010; Bonial et al., 2014; Ramisch et al., 2018), that gives them semantics equivalent to a content verb paraphrase. We offer such an analysis based on three principles:

1. The event frame is in the semantics of the eventive noun or verb.
2. For any syntactic argument of a noun or verb, the corresponding edge (and free variable) is in the semantics of the noun or verb.
3. Any function word (light verb, *'s*, preposition, or infinitival *to*) that links the eventive noun to its semantic argument has an associated edge (and free variables) in its semantics.

Note that when a verb or noun takes a PP complement, principles 2 and 3 force both the verb or noun and the preposition to hold the same edge in their semantics. This is compatible with relation-wise combinators as described in §3.3. The result is a nice analysis where both the eventive noun or verb and its complement preposition signal *patientness*.

With this analysis, the associated light verbs given in table 2 ("make", "pay", etc.) as well as possessive *'s* take the semantics ① :ARG0 ②, and associated prepositions take the semantics ② :ARG1 ①. In other words, for each eventive noun, either a special light verb or a possessive contributes the agentive semantic

light verb construction	possessive form	AMR predicate
make a **decision** [about/on]	my **decision** [about/on]	decide-01
pay **attention** [to]	my **attention** [to]	attend-02
make an **attempt** [to]	my **attempt** [to]	attempt-01
take a **nap**	my **nap**	nap-01
take a **picture** [of]	— ("my picture" is not eventive)	photograph-01 *(suggested)*

Table 2: English eventive nouns shown with a light verb or possessive; words in square brackets mark additional semantic arguments. (In the AMR corpus, "take pictures" is actually treated superficially with take-01 :ARG1 picture, but we suggest photograph-01 instead.)

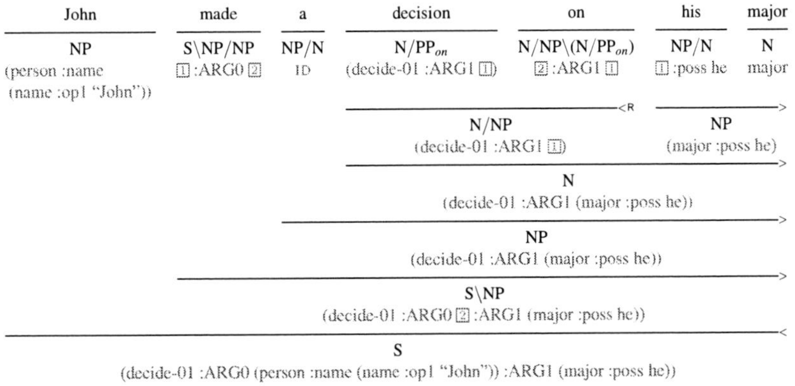

Figure 8: **light verb construction**: "John made a decision on his major"

relation—and (if present) a special preposition or infinitive *to* may contribute the patient semantic relation—thus allowing derivation of the same AMR regardless of form.

Figure 8 shows the derivation for "decision" in its light verb construction form. The preposition "on" redundantly represents the :ARG1 edge, and is merged with "decision" by relation-wise application.[5] The light verb "made" specifies the :ARG0 edge.

5   Discussion

Unlike many semantic formalisms, AMR does not specify a 'compositional story': annotations do not include any sort of syntactic derivation, or even gold alignments between semantic units and words in the sentence. This presents a challenge for AMR parsing, which in practice relies on various forms of automatic or latent alignments (see Szubert et al., 2018). Above, we have presented an analysis that lays the foundation for a linguistically principled treatment of CCG-to-AMR parsing that meets a variety of challenges in the syntax-semantics interface, and does so in a transparent way so that parsing errors can be diagnosed. We believe the approach is reasonably intuitive, flowing naturally from CCG syntax, AMR semantics, and the notion of free variables in subgraphs, without the additional need for complicated lambda calculus notation or a highly general graph grammar formalism.

To realize this vision in practice, an approach is needed to build a CCG parser enriched with graph semantics for deriving AMRs. We anticipate that existing CCG parsing frameworks can be adapted—for example, by developing an alignment algorithm to induce the semantics for lexical entries from the AMR corpus, and running an off-the-shelf parser like EasySRL (Lewis et al., 2015) at training and test time for the syntactic side of the derivation. This approach would take advantage of the fact that our analysis assumes the ordinary CCG syntax for obtaining the compositional structure of the derivation. The only additional steps would be a) disambiguating the semantics of lexical entries in the derivation, and b) applying the semantics of the combinators as specified in table 1. For each use of application or

---

[5]The category $N/NP\backslash(N/PP_{on})$ for "on" is suggested by Mark Steedman's analysis of English prepositions as particles (personal communication) and also maintains the Principle of Functional Isomorphism of §3.1.

composition, the semantic parser would check whether the conditions for relation-wise combination hold, and otherwise apply the ordinary version of the combinator.[6]

Because AMRs are annotated by humans for raw sentences, rather than on top of a syntactic parse, we cannot expect a parser to elegantly handle the full construction of all AMRs according to compositional rules. Several components of AMR parsing are not part of CCG parsing and will have to be performed as postprocessing steps. These components include named entity recognition, time expression parsing, coreference resolution, and wikification, all of which need to be performed after (or before) CCG parsing. Additionally, there is a risk that a CCG lexicon may 'overgenerate', producing invalid parses, and additional checking—either in the combinators, or as postprocessing or reranking—may be warranted.

We are aware of certain phenomena where the approach described above would be unable to fully match the conventions of AMR in the CCG-derived semantics. The analysis presented for **coordination** (with the conjunction combinator: see figure 5) would address only one of the ways it can be expressed in AMR, with a concept like and or or and operands. In other cases, coordinated modifiers are treated as sister relations in the AMR, with no explicit concept for the conjunction. Even when the conjunction is explicit in the AMR, it may be placed at a different level in the gold and CCG-derived AMRs: e.g., when two purpose adjuncts are coordinated, the derivation will result in semantic conjunction over the predicate rather than a conjunction under the :purpose relation. In sentences where a semantic predicate is **duplicated** in the AMR with different participants, e.g. due to right node raising, a copy mechanism would be needed to avoid spurious reentrancy. The treatment of **modal auxiliaries** as above the main event predicate in the AMR will be problematic for the CCG derivation when there is a preposed adjunct (as in "*Tomorrow*, John may eat rice") because the modifier will semantically attach under the root of the semantics of the rest of the clause (possible-01 from "may") rather than the main event predicate eat-01. Full derivations for these problem cases, as well as examples of purpose clauses, raising, and subject and object control, are given in appendix A. We will explore whether such limitations can be addressed via postprocessing of the parse, or whether additional expressive power in the combinators is necessary.

Finally, as pointed out by Bender et al. (2015), AMR annotations sometimes go beyond the compositional 'sentence meaning' and incorporate elements of 'speaker meaning', though an empirical study of AMR data found the rate of noncompositional structures to be relatively low (Szubert et al., 2018). Beschke and Menzel (2018) give interesting examples of AMR fragments that would be difficult to derive compositionally, e.g., "settled on Indianapolis for its board meeting", where the AMR attaches Indianapolis as the location of the meeting and the meeting as the thing that was settled on (reflecting the inference *settle on* LOCATION *for* ACTIVITY $\Rightarrow$ *settle on* [ACTIVITY *at* LOCATION]).

6   Conclusion

We have given the linguistic motivation for a particular method of deriving AMR semantic graphs using CCG. Our specification of AMR subgraphs and CCG combinators ensures a tight correspondence between syntax and semantics, which we have illustrated for a variety of linguistic constructions (including light verb construction semantics, which to the best of our knowledge has not previously been explored for CCG). Future empirical work can make use of this framework to induce CCG lexicons for AMR parsing.

---

[6]We have considered an alternative analysis where underspecified :? edges would be used not only for type raising, but for all case-marked pronouns, prepositions marking syntactic arguments, and other constructions where a word's syntactic category involves an argument to a separate predicate. Thus, only the predicate would be allowed to specify semantic roles for its syntactic arguments. Relation-wise combinators would then require that the shared edge would be underspecified in the function constituent. The rationale would be that this avoids redundant specification of core roles like :ARG0 and :ARG1 in the lexical entries—e.g. in figure 7, the :ARG1 for "What", the :ARG0 for "did", and the second :ARG0 for "decide" would all be replaced with :?. After all, constructions like wh-questions, control, and case target syntactic relations (subject/object), which are merely *correlated* with semantic roles. And as pointed out by a reviewer, under the current approach, a wrong choice of semantic role for a cased pronoun's semantics could result in the use of a regular combinator rather than a relation-wise combinator, leaving a free variable in the predicate unsatisfied and essentially breaking the syntax-semantics isomorphism. An argument in favor of the current policy is that prepositions can contain information about roles to a certain extent, and redundant specification of semantic roles may actually be helpful when confronted with a noisy parser and lexicon. We leave this open as an empirical question for parsing research.

Acknowledgments

We want to thank Paul Portner, Adam Lopez, members of the NERT lab at Georgetown, and anonymous reviewers for their helpful feedback on this research, as well as Matthew Honnibal, Siva Reddy, and Mark Steedman for early discussions about light verbs in CCG.

References

Anchiêta, R. T. and T. A. S. Pardo (2018, May). Towards AMR-BR: A SemBank for Brazilian Portuguese language. In N. Calzolari, K. Choukri, C. Cieri, T. Declerck, S. Goggi, K. Hasida, H. Isahara, B. Maegaard, J. Mariani, H. Mazo, A. Moreno, J. Odijk, S. Piperidis, and T. Tokunaga (Eds.), *Proc. of LREC*, Miyazaki, Japan, pp. 974–979.

Artzi, Y., K. Lee, and L. Zettlemoyer (2015, September). Broad-coverage CCG semantic parsing with AMR. In *Proc. of EMNLP*, Lisbon, Portugal, pp. 1699–1710.

Baldwin, T. and S. N. Kim (2010). Multiword expressions. In N. Indurkhya and F. J. Damerau (Eds.), *Handbook of Natural Language Processing, Second Edition*, pp. 267–292. Boca Raton, FL: CRC Press, Taylor and Francis Group.

Banarescu, L., C. Bonial, S. Cai, M. Georgescu, K. Griffitt, U. Hermjakob, K. Knight, P. Koehn, M. Palmer, and N. Schneider (2013, August). Abstract Meaning Representation for sembanking. In *Proc. of the 7th Linguistic Annotation Workshop and Interoperability with Discourse*, Sofia, Bulgaria, pp. 178–186.

Bender, E. M., D. Flickinger, S. Oepen, W. Packard, and A. Copestake (2015, April). Layers of interpretation: on grammar and compositionality. In *Proc. of IWCS*, London, UK, pp. 239–249.

Beschke, S. and W. Menzel (2018, June). Graph Algebraic Combinatory Categorial Grammar. In *Proc. of *SEM*, New Orleans, Louisiana, pp. 54–64.

Björklund, H., F. Drewes, and P. Ericson (2016). Between a rock and a hard place – Uniform parsing for hyperedge replacement DAG grammars. In A. Dediu, J. Janoušek, C. Martín-Vide, and B. Truthe (Eds.), *Language and Automata Theory and Applications*, Lecture Notes in Computer Science, pp. 521–532.

Bonial, C., M. Green, J. Preciado, and M. Palmer (2014, April). An approach to 'take' multi-word expressions. In *Proc. of the 10th Workshop on Multiword Expressions*, Gothenburg, Sweden, pp. 94–98.

Chiang, D., J. Andreas, D. Bauer, K. M. Hermann, B. Jones, and K. Knight (2013, August). Parsing graphs with hyperedge replacement grammars. In *Proc. of ACL*, Sofia, Bulgaria, pp. 924–932.

Clark, K., M. Luong, C. D. Manning, and Q. Le (2018, November). Semi-supervised sequence modeling with cross-view training. In *Proc. of EMNLP*, Brussels, Belgium, pp. 1914–1925.

Clark, S. and J. R. Curran (2004, July). Parsing the WSJ using CCG and log-linear models. In *Proc. of ACL*, Barcelona, Spain, pp. 103–110.

Constable, J. and J. Curran (2009). Integrating verb-particle constructions into CCG parsing. In *Proc. of the Australasian Language Technology Association Workshop 2009*, Sydney, Australia, pp. 114–118.

Courcelle, B. and J. Engelfriet (2012, June). *Graph Structure and Monadic Second-Order Logic: A Language-Theoretic Approach*. Cambridge University Press.

de Lhoneux, M. (2014, August). CCG parsing and multiword expressions. http://arxiv.org/abs/1505.04420.

Flanigan, J., S. Thomson, J. Carbonell, C. Dyer, and N. A. Smith (2014, June). A discriminative graph-based parser for the Abstract Meaning Representation. In *Proc. of ACL*, Baltimore, Maryland, USA, pp. 1426–1436.

Groschwitz, J., M. Lindemann, M. Fowlie, M. Johnson, and A. Koller (2018, July). AMR dependency parsing with a typed semantic algebra. In *Proc. of ACL*, Melbourne, Australia, pp. 1831–1841.

Hockenmaier, J. and M. Steedman (2007, August). CCGbank: A corpus of CCG derivations and dependency structures extracted from the Penn Treebank. *Computational Linguistics 33*(3), 355–396.

Honnibal, M., J. R. Curran, and J. Bos (2010, July). Rebanking CCGbank for improved NP interpretation. In *Proc. of ACL*, Uppsala, Sweden, pp. 207–215.

Jones, B., J. Andreas, D. Bauer, K. M. Hermann, and K. Knight (2012, December). Semantics-based machine translation with hyperedge replacement grammars. In *Proc. of COLING 2012*, Mumbai, India, pp. 1359–1376.

Kingsbury, P. and M. Palmer (2002, May). From TreeBank to PropBank. In *Proc. of LREC*, Las Palmas, Canary Islands, pp. 1989–1993.

Koller, A. (2015, April). Semantic construction with graph grammars. In *Proc. of IWCS*, London, UK, pp. 228–238.

Lewis, M., L. He, and L. Zettlemoyer (2015, September). Joint A* CCG parsing and semantic role labelling. In *Proc. of EMNLP*, Lisbon, Portugal, pp. 1444–1454.

Lewis, M., K. Lee, and L. Zettlemoyer (2016, June). LSTM CCG Parsing. In *Proc. of NAACL-HLT*, San Diego, California, USA, pp. 221–231.

Lewis, M. and M. Steedman (2014, October). A* CCG parsing with a supertag-factored model. In *Proc. of EMNLP*, Doha, Qatar, pp. 990–1000.

Li, B., Y. Wen, L. Bu, W. Qu, and N. Xue (2016, August). Annotating The Little Prince with Chinese AMRs. In *Proc. of LAW X – the 10th Linguistic Annotation Workshop*, Berlin, Germany, pp. 7–15.

Lyu, C. and I. Titov (2018, July). AMR parsing as graph prediction with latent alignment. In *Proc. of ACL*, Melbourne, Australia, pp. 397–407.

Migueles-Abraira, N., R. Agerri, and A. D. d. Ilarraza (2018, May). Annotating Abstract Meaning Representations for Spanish. In N. Calzolari, K. Choukri, C. Cieri, T. Declerck, S. Goggi, K. Hasida, H. Isahara, B. Maegaard, J. Mariani, H. Mazo, A. Moreno, J. Odijk, S. Piperidis, and T. Tokunaga (Eds.), *Proc. of LREC*, Miyazaki, Japan, pp. 3074–3078.

Misra, D. K. and Y. Artzi (2016, November). Neural shift-reduce CCG semantic parsing. In *Proc. of EMNLP*, Austin, Texas, pp. 1775–1786.

Peng, X. and D. Gildea (2016, June). UofR at SemEval-2016 Task 8: Learning Synchronous Hyperedge Replacement Grammar for AMR parsing. In *Proc. of SemEval*, San Diego, California, USA, pp. 1185–1189.

Peng, X., L. Song, and D. Gildea (2015, July). A Synchronous Hyperedge Replacement Grammar based approach for AMR parsing. In *Proc. of CoNLL*, Beijing, China, pp. 32–41.

Ramisch, C., S. R. Cordeiro, A. Savary, V. Vincze, V. Barbu Mititelu, A. Bhatia, M. Buljan, M. Candito, P. Gantar, V. Giouli, T. Güngör, A. Hawwari, U. Iñurrieta, J. Kovalevskaitė, S. Krek, T. Lichte, C. Liebeskind, J. Monti, C. Parra Escartín, B. QasemiZadeh, R. Ramisch, N. Schneider, I. Stoyanova, A. Vaidya, and A. Walsh (2018, August). Edition 1.1 of the PARSEME Shared Task on Automatic

Identification of Verbal Multiword Expressions. In *Proc. of the Joint Workshop on Linguistic Annotation, Multiword Expressions and Constructions (LAW-MWE-CxG-2018)*, Santa Fe, New Mexico, USA, pp. 222–240.

Rozenberg, G. (1997). *Handbook of Graph Grammars and Comp.*, Volume 1. World scientific.

Steedman, M. (2000). *The Syntatic Process*. Cambridge, MA: MIT Press.

Szubert, I., A. Lopez, and N. Schneider (2018, June). A structured syntax-semantics interface for English-AMR alignment. In *Proc. of NAACL-HLT*, New Orleans, Louisiana, pp. 1169–1180.

Wang, C., B. Li, and N. Xue (2018, June). Transition-based Chinese AMR parsing. In *Proc. of NAACL-HLT*, New Orleans, Louisiana, pp. 247–252.

Wang, C., S. Pradhan, X. Pan, H. Ji, and N. Xue (2016, June). CAMR at SemEval-2016 Task 8: An extended transition-based AMR parser. In *Proc. of SemEval*, San Diego, California, USA, pp. 1173–1178.

Xue, N., O. Bojar, J. Hajič, M. Palmer, Z. Urešová, and X. Zhang (2014, May). Not an interlingua, but close: comparison of English AMRs to Chinese and Czech. In N. Calzolari, K. Choukri, T. Declerck, H. Loftsson, B. Maegaard, J. Mariani, A. Moreno, J. Odijk, and S. Piperidis (Eds.), *Proc. of LREC*, Reykjavík, Iceland, pp. 1765–1772.

A   Additional Derivations

Below are full derivations illustrating raising, subject control, object control, an object control wh-question, a modal auxiliary with preposed VP adjunct, a purpose clause, coordinated purpose clauses, and right node raising with a shared main verb.

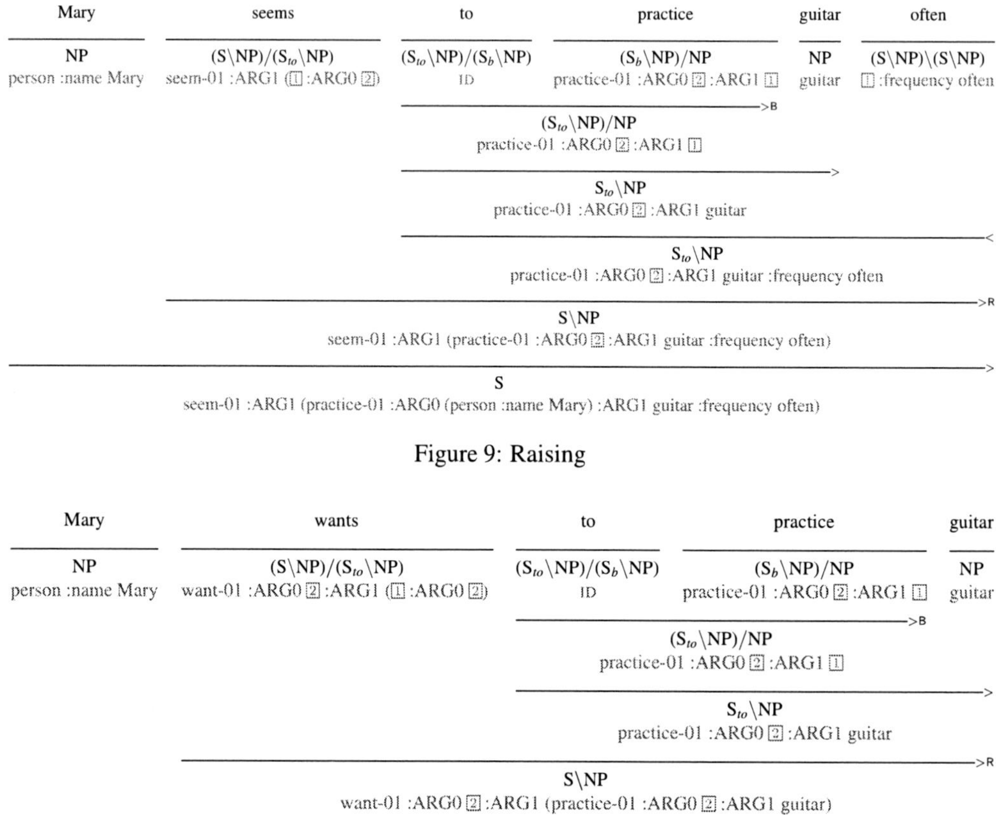

Figure 9: Raising

Mary	wants	to	practice	guitar
NP	$(S\backslash NP)/(S_{to}\backslash NP)$	$(S_{to}\backslash NP)/(S_b\backslash NP)$	$(S_b\backslash NP)/NP$	NP
person :name Mary	want-01 :ARG0 ② :ARG1 (① :ARG0 ②)	ID	practice-01 :ARG0 ② :ARG1 ①	guitar

$(S_{to}\backslash NP)/NP$ >B
practice-01 :ARG0 ② :ARG1 ①

$S_{to}\backslash NP$ >
practice-01 :ARG0 ② :ARG1 guitar

$S\backslash NP$ >R
want-01 :ARG0 ② :ARG1 (practice-01 :ARG0 ② :ARG1 guitar)

S   >
w/want-01 :ARG0 (p/person :name Mary) :ARG1 (p2/practice-01 :ARG0 p :ARG1 g/guitar)

Figure 10: Subject control

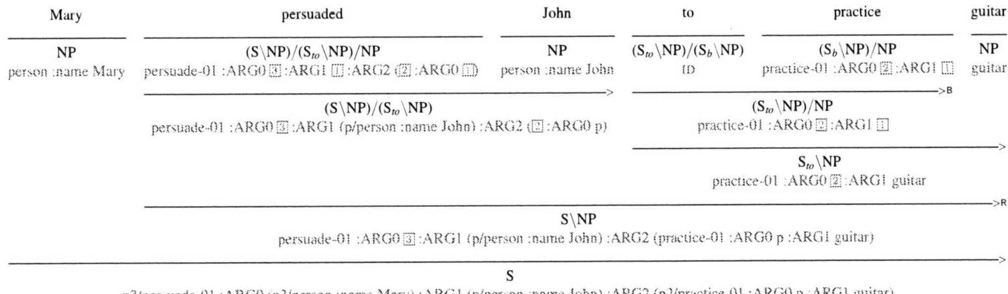

Figure 11: Object control. Note that the PropBank predicate persuade-01 specifies :ARG0 for the persuader, :ARG1 for the persuadee, and :ARG2 for the impelled action.

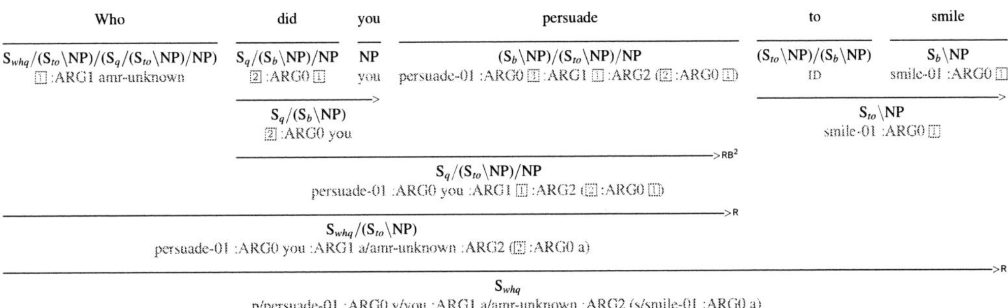

Figure 12: Object control wh-question: "Who did you persuade to smile?" (example suggested by a reviewer)

Tomorrow	John	may	eat	rice
S/S	NP	$(S{\backslash}NP)/(S_b{\backslash}NP)$	$(S_b{\backslash}NP)/NP$	NP
[1] :time tomorrow	person :name John	possible-01 :ARG1 [1]	eat-01 :ARG0 [2] :ARG1 [1]	rice

$$\text{>B}$$

$(S{\backslash}NP)/NP$
possible-01 :ARG1 (eat-01 :ARG0 [2] :ARG1 [1])

$$\text{>}$$

$S{\backslash}NP$
possible-01 :ARG1 (eat-01 :ARG0 [2] :ARG1 rice)

$$\text{<}$$

S
possible-01 :ARG1 (eat-01 :ARG0 (person :name John) :ARG1 rice)

S
possible-01 :ARG1 (eat-01 :ARG0 (person :name John) :ARG1 rice) **:time** tomorrow

CORRECT: possible-01 :ARG1 (eat-01 :ARG0 (person :name John) :ARG1 rice **:time** tomorrow)

Figure 13: Modal auxiliary with preposed adjunct: "Tomorrow, John may eat rice". In the derived AMR, the temporal modifier is placed incorrectly under the modal predicate rather than the main event predicate.

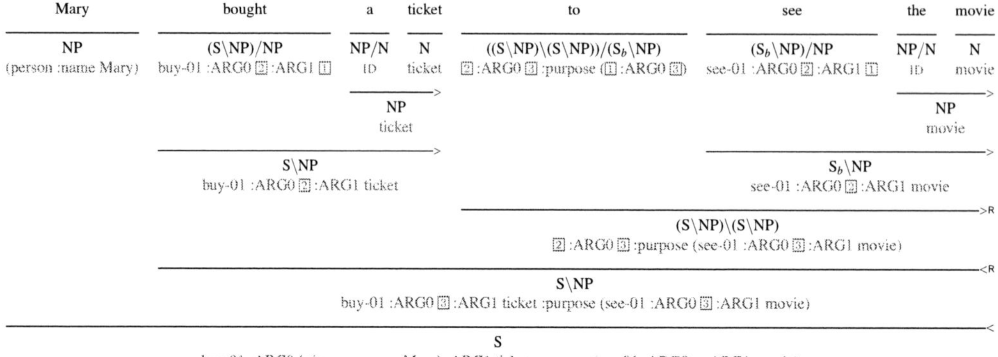

Figure 14: *to*-purpose

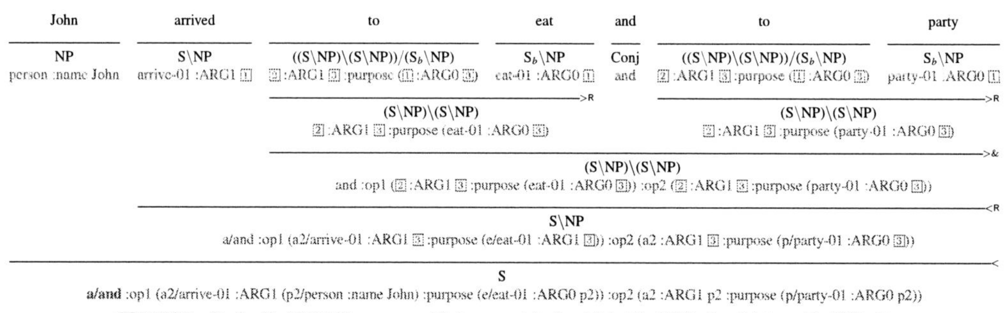

Figure 15: Coordinated purpose clauses: "John arrived to eat and to party". Note that the PropBank predicate arrive-01 has no :ARG0; its subject is :ARG1. The lexical semantics for infinitive purpose *to* is chosen accordingly. However, the placement in the derived AMR of the semantic conjunction and is incorrect.

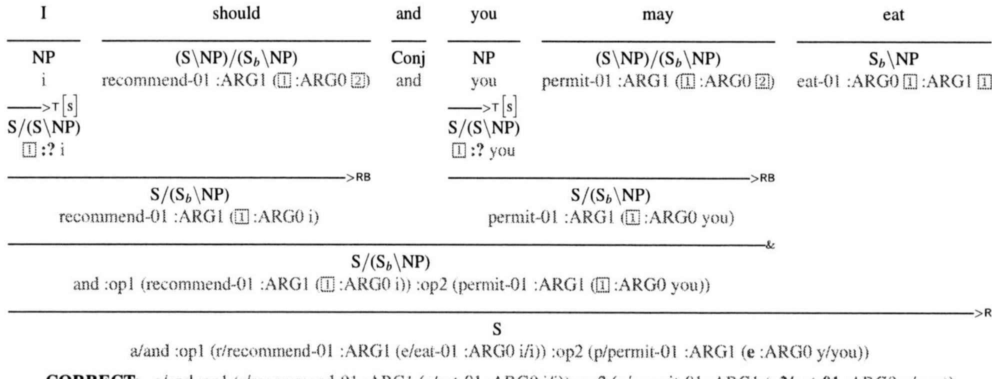

Figure 16: Right node raising with shared main verb: "I should and you may eat". The derived AMR has a reentrancy for the eat-01 predicate where there should be a separate copy of the predicate.

A Semantic Ontology of Danish Adjectives

Eckhard Bick

Institute of Language and Communication
University of Southern Denmark
eckhard.bick@mail.dk

Abstract

This paper presents a semantic annotation scheme for Danish adjectives, focusing both on prototypical semantic content and semantic collocational restrictions on an adjective's head noun. The core type set comprises about 110 categories ordered in a shallow hierarchy with 14 primary and 25 secondary umbrella categories. In addition, domain information and binary sentiment tags are provided, as well as VerbNet-derived frames and semantic roles for those adjectives governing arguments. The scheme has been almost fully implemented on the lexicon of the Danish VISL parser, DanGram, containing 14,000 adjectives. We discuss the annotation scheme and its applicational perspectives, and present a statistical breakdown and coverage evaluation for three Danish reference corpora.

1   Introduction

This paper describes a multi-dimensional semantic classification system for Danish adjectives. The system has been implemented for a fairly unabridged computational lexicon, with 14,000 adjectival lemmas, and is intended for use with Danish NLP tools in general, and machine translation and semantic correctness grading of generated Danish sentences in particular.

Lexical resources about the semantics of adjectives are much harder to come by than corresponding dictionaries for nouns and verbs, not least in the context of less-resourced languages like Danish. Nouns allow the construction of ontologies based on hyponym-hyperonym relations (e.g. Princeton WordNet, Fellbaum 1998 for English, and DanNet, Pedersen et al. 2009, for Danish), and verbs can be classified using argument relations and restrictions (e.g. FrameNet, Baker et al. 1998 and Ruppenhofer 2010, for English). However, both methods are less ideal for adjectives - only a small set of adjectives takes arguments, hyponym-hyperonym relations are problematic, and traditional WordNet synonym clusters and antonym relations do not constitute a true classification system. One way out is using noun classification as a proxy and linking adjectives to nouns or verbs:

(a) property nouns denoting the property that the adjective describes, e.g. linking "hot", "tepid", "cool", "cold", "ice-cold" etc. to the noun "temperature", a method that works well for antonymy and scale adjectives. Thus, EuroWordNet (Vossen 1998) uses a "near synonymy" relation across word classes, e.g. "obese/obesity", "infamous/infamy".

(b) derivational base: A large percentage of adjectives are morphologically derived from nouns or verbs using suffixes, e.g. *"V-lig"* (V-able), *"N-lig"* (N-like), *"N-fuld"* (being full of s.th.), *"N-løs"* (not having s.th.). In addition, many Danish adjectives are morphologically past or present participles and can thus be linked to a verbal base (*"V-et"* - V-ed, *"V-ende"* - V-ing).

(c) nominal heads: Adjectves can be classified according to their prototypical head houn, using categories like "animal adjective" (*"tame"* - tame, *"vild"* - wild, *"glubsk"* - voracious) or "food adjectives" (*"bagt"* - baked, *"fersk"* - fresh, *"lækker"* - tasty).

However, (c) lumps semantically very different adjectives together (e.g. states, quality, source, purpos etc. for the food category), and neither (a) nor (b) is, on its own, applicable to the entire adjective lexicon, and morphological/derivational links, in particular, are slippery ground, as meaning can change over time, and become less transparent. Thus, *"huslig"* ("housely") does not mean "house-like" (the literal meaning), but rather "house-related" (tasks) or a human psychological trait of "housewife-ness". Also, sometimes the adjective is primary in a derivation relation, as in *"tapper" > "tapper-hed"* (brave > braven-ess), risking a sparceness of information, if the corresponding noun is simply classified as "property" exactly because its core is really adjectival.

GermaNet (Hamp & Feldweg, 1997) addresses the problems with (a) and (b) by establishing a separate semantic class hierarchy[1] for adjectives, with 16 classes at level 1 and 78 classes at level 2, with relations like *"green" > colour > perception* or *"short" > dimension > spatial*. Transparent denominal and deverbal derivations is classified as "pertainyms". For Danish, Nimb & Pedersen (2012) suggest the use of thesaurus data to build a type (c) classification by harvesting "property_of" relations between adjectives and typical collocate classes (e.g. person, thing, feeling, food). However, the authors mention the need for validation, and the current public version of DanNet[2] does not contain a "property_of" feature.

2   Existing resources

DanNet (and its dictionary precursor STO[3]) is one of two large sets of lexical resources used in Danish language technology. However, it only contains about 3,000 adjectives, with a flat 12-category ontology, and while there is information about hyperonym relations to either other adjectives or nouns, 23% are linked directly to the top node "property" or "property:physical" without any real classificational information. The other resource is the lexicon of the Danish VISL parser, DanGram (Bick 2001), containing 103,000 non-name lemma entries, of which about 14,000 are adjectives. The lexicon specifies syntactic word-order information for 11,400 of these, comprising obligatory predicative or attributive use, and so-called "modificational zones" (ordering in case of multiple prenominal adjectives).

<pred> predicative use only: *alene (alone), beliggende (situated), slut (finished)*

<att> attributive use only: *al (all), aldersmæssig (age-related), aldrende (becoming older)*

<mod1> (specificational): <u>*bestemte*</u> alvorlige organiske sygdomme (*certain* serious organic diseases)

<mod2> (descriptional): bestemte <u>*alvorlige*</u> organiske sygdomme (certain *serious* organic diseases)

<mod3> (classificational): bestemte alvorlige <u>*organiske*</u> sygdomme (certain serious *organic* diseases)

<jj>, ad-adjectival, adjectives that modify other adjectives

On top of these syntactic tags, the adjective lexicon also contains some semantic tags. However, while DanGram's noun ontology[4] and Danish FrameNet (Bick 2011) have been used in numerous NLP projects (treebanks, CALL, MT etc.), so far no corresponding semantic system for adjectives has been published. Our current work strives to review, systematize and document existing semantic tags, and to introduce and implement a completely new ontology, more akin to the GermaNet system, where each category in addition to its semantic feature values also should allow the prediction of the semantic class of its typical head noun.

---

[1]   http://www.sfs.uni-tuebingen.de/GermaNet/adjectives.shtml (accessed 14 January 2019)

[2]   version 2.2 (https://cst.ku.dk/projekter/dannet/)

[3]   a Danish "word database" with 68,000 entries and morphological, syntactic and semantic information: https://cst.ku.dk/sto_ordbase/

[4]   http://visl.sdu.dk/semantic_prototypes_overview.pdf

3   Category scheme

In our proposed system, the primary semantic tags used for adjectives have the form <j....> and are combinatorially restricted feature prototypes, meaning that they specify a feature type of a certain semantic head (noun) class. For instance, <jshape> modifies concrete objects, and <jpsych> (psychological feature) combines with human heads (<H...>), but also actions (<act>) and semiotic products (<sem>).

There are 110-120 tags in all[5], most of which can be lumped in 14 or - with subclasses - 25 umbrella classes, most of them linked to prototypical head types. For instance, all tags within the *people* groups imply [+hum] (human), <jappro> (appropriateness) and <jbehave> combine with actions [+act], and <jsem> is about features of works of art, plans, laws or speeches [+sem]. For some category definitions and examples, see table 3.

- **people**: <jpsych> (feelings), <janat> (body features), <jage>, <jstate-h>, <jsick>, <jclo-h> (clothedness), <jappear> (appearance)
- **effecting**: <jaff> (affection), <jeff> (effecting), <jaff-h> (affected), <jimp> (important),
- **quality**: <jqual> (quality), <jpower>, <jskill>, <jappro> (appropriate), <jlike> (liked), <jreg> (regulated)
- **properties**:
  - *inherent*: <jprop>, <jtype>, <jbuild> (building), <jornam> (ornamental)
  - *+measure*: <jsize>, <jweight>, <jtemp> (temperature), <jspeed>,
  - *-measure*: <jshape>, <jsurf> (surface), <jsub> (composition), <jmat> (material), <jchem> (chemical), <jcol> (color), <jlight>
  - *state*: <jstate>, <jdam> (damage), <jnormal>, <jres> (result),
  - *sensed properties*: <jpercep> (perception)
- **quantity**: <jquant> (quantity), <jdegree>, <jcont> (content), <jsetop> (set operation), <jmanner-q>
- **identity**: <jident> (identity), <jauth> (authentic), <jcomp> (comparison), <jname>
- **cognitive**:
  - *thought*: <jcog> (cognitive), <jideo> (ideological), <jlike-h> (liking), <jmeta>
  - *speech*: <jcom> (communication), <jling> (language)
  - *epistemiological*: <jfact> (fact, true, likely), <jfame>
  - *semiotic* [+sem]: <jsem>, <jgenre>, <jdomain>, <jstruct> (structure)
- **event**: <jevent>, <jprocess>, <jchance>, <jchange>, <jcause>, <jsit> (situation)
- **doing**: <jact> (action), <juse>, <jhand> (handled), <jmove>, <jmanner>, <jbehave>, <jmethod>, <jres> (resulting), <jcrea> (created), <jlink>, <jtarget>
- **culture**:
  - *food*: <jfood>
  - *society*: <jsoc> (social), <jpol> (politics), <jinst> (institution), <jrel> (religious), <jprof> (professional), <jright> (entitled)
  - *domain jargon*: <jtech> (technical), <jjur> (law), <jmed> (medicine)

---

[5]   This number of categories was deemed a reasonable level of granularity for empirical reasons. For practical purposes (parsing and corpus annotation), having too many increases the error rate in automatic tagging and risk introducing nuances that border on vagueness and often cannot be reliably distinguished by human annotators either. Too few categories, on the other hand, will mean a generalisation and abstraction level that misses out on many interesting semantic distinctions and is too course for contextual disambiguation tasks.

○ *cultural products*: <jV> (vehicles), <jVwater> (ships), <jclo> (clothing features)

○ *money*: <jmon> (money), <jmon-h>, <jposs> (owned), <jposs-h> (owning), <jval>(value)

- **nature**: <jbio>, <jA> (animals), <jB> (plants), <jL> (place feature), <jwea> (weather)
- **auxiliary**: <jbe>, <jcan> (possible), <jmust>, <jmay> (allowed), <jwill> (ready to)
- **space**: <jnat> (nationality), <jgeo> (geography), <jloc> (location), <jdir> (direction), <jori> (origin), <jpos> (position)
- **time**: <jtime>, <jord> (order), <jper> (period)

Sentiment and polarity markers

A number of feature types exhibit a plus/minus polarity, for instance <jtemp> (temperature: hot/cold), <jlike> (*liked* or *disliked*), <jappro> (*appropriate* or *inappropriate*). This polarity is resolved by means of <Q+> and <Q-> tags that are primarily meant as sentiment analysis tags, but will also double in almost all cases as polarity distinctors. "-h" marks a separate subclass for human heads, e.g. <poss> ("owned") and <poss-h> ("owning"). Where necessary, other, more specific, non-standard semantic head types can be added by means of a <H:...> tag, e.g. <H:furn> for "polstret" (padded).

4   Frames for adjectives

A small, but important, proportion[6] of Danish adjectives can take valency-governed arguments, almost all in the form of prepositional phrases (pp's). In these cases it is possible to say that the adjective is the core constituent of a predication, much like verbs or de-verbal nouns. We classify these constructions using an equivalent verbnet frame, and both frame and argument structure are provided in the adjective lexicon.

1. forelsket i *(in love with)* - FN:**like**/head§COG/i§TH   [cognizer - theme]

2. bange for *(afraid of)* - FN:**emote_obj**/for§CAU/head§EXP   [cause - experiencer]

3. benovet over *(embarrassed about)* - FN:**affect_exp**/head§EXP/over§CAU

4. beslægtet med *(related to)* - FN:**relate**/med§COM/head§TH   [theme - co-argument]

5. blind for *(ignorant of)* - FN:**neglect**/for§TH/head§AG   [agent - theme]

6. dygtig til *(good at)* - FN:**can**/head§AG/til§ACT'icl   [agent - action]

7. sur på *(angry at)* FN:**emote**/head§EXP/på§CAU'H   [experiencer - cause]
   sur over at *(angry because)* FN:**emote**/head§EXP/over§ACT'fcl [experience - action]

8. ond mod *(mean against)* - <FN:**affect_exp**/head§AG/mod§EXP'H>   [agent - experiencer]

9. afhængig af - FN:**depend**/head§EXP'H/head§SOA'act/head§BEN/af§CAU
   person hooked on s.th. - FN:depend/**head§EXP'H**/head§SOA'act/head§BEN/af§CAU
   action depending on s.th. - FN:depend/head§EXP'H/**head§SOA'act**/head§BEN/af§CAU
   city relying on tourism - FN:depend/head§EXP'H/head§SOA'act/**head§BEN**/af§CAU

Each noun frame entry (FN) lists first the corresponding verb frame and then a slash-separated list of possible semantic role arguments[7] (marked §) with their slot filler conditions (1-9). We distinguish

---

[6]   Currently, about 300 adjectives have been assigned frame-carrying valencies. As for verbs and nouns, structural complexity correlates with token frequency, so frame-capable adjectives are overrepresented in running text, with a token ratio higher than their type ratio.

between primary conditions and secondary, optional subconditions (present in 6-9). Primary conditions are placed before the role concerned, secondary condition after it. The former are syntactic slot conditions (either 'head' or a bound preposition lexeme), the latter are categorial conditions concerning semantic class (e.g. 'H'=human, 'act'=action), or form conditions such as 'icl' (non-finite clause, 6) or 'fcl' (finite clause, 7).

In the Danish data, adjectives only rarely have two completely different frames. More common are cases where there is some variation within the same frame, with different prepositions (7) or different semantic slot fillers (9) corresponding to different semantic roles. In these cases it is optional, whether frames are duplicated (7) or fused by appending argument variants (9).

5 Coverage statistics

In order to evaluate coverage, we tagged a Danish reference corpus consisting of DSL's period corpora, Korpus90, Korpus2000 and Korpus2010 (Asmussen 2015), covering modern post-war Danish up to the 90s and the years around 2000 and 2010, respectively. The first corpus has a broad genre and period scope, including some spoken data. The second is dominated by news and magazine texts and the third includes online material of various types. Together, the three corpora can be said to provide a fair cross-section of modern Danish.

Based on DanGram's morphological disambiguation, and a POS error rate under 1%, the corpus set contained 5.6 million adjective tokens distributed across 27,280 adjective types. In this count, hapaxes were ignored - inspection showed them to be mostly spelling errors and ad hoc foreign loan words. In about 1% of adjective tokens (37% of types), the parser had to use live compounding analysis[8]. Table 1 shows adjectival coverage percentages for both semantic class tagging (j-tags) and domain tagging (D-tags), first for all words, then separately for live compound analysis.

Tag type	% tokens	% types
semantic class tags (j-tags)	99.24	85.10
domain tags (D-tags)	95.64	73.89
j-tags / compounds	93.96	93.40
D-tags / compounds	75.99	76.82

Table 1: Corpus overage (all words)

As can be seen from the percentages, general running text coverage is very good (99.4%), but due to obvious Zipf-curve effects type coverage is considerably lower (85.1%). Live compounds have a worse token coverage, but better type coverage. Though surprising at first glance, this can be explained by the fact that the class-controlling second parts of compounds are dominated by relatively few, well-know suffixes and participles, leading to a good type-coverage. At the same time, because the individual compounds are all rare compared to ordinary adjectives, there is no pronounced positive effect of counting tokens rather than types.

If (a) purely heuristic (i.e. non-compound) analyses, (b) lexicon-registered erroneous forms and (c) foreign words are excluded (about 1,800 types or 11,500 tokens), coverage increases, as could be expected.

---

[7] The Danish FrameNet foresees about 35 argument-capable roles and an additional 15 satellite roles

[8] These are cases, where a word was unknown in the sense, that it could not be reduced to a lemma or a compound found in the lexicon, but where the parser was able to come up with a likely compound analysis of its own at run time.

Tag type	% tokens	% types
semantic class tags (j-tags)	99.39	90.53
domain tags (D-tags)	95.82	78.78
j-tags / compounds	95.12	94.47
D-tags / compounds	77.01	77.75

Table 2: Corpus overage (recognized words and compounds only)

Table 3 contains a breakdown of the 22 statistically most important tag types by frequency (covering 80% of tokens and 52% of types), providing definitions and examples. For sense discrimination and other NLP tasks, it is an advantage that the category distribution curve is relatively even, with small differences between neighbouring frequencies, and even the top category below the 10% mark in token terms. By comparison, DanNet contains not only fewer items, but also exhibits a much steeper frequency curve, indicating less discriminatory power. Thus, when looking at type frequencies, our system "peaks" at 6%, with a spread over several, very different categories, while DanNet links 34% of adjective types to just "Property", and equally 34% to the hyperonym "beskaffenhed" (type). Even when classes and hyperonyms are combined, 23% are linked to combinations of Property/Property:physical and "beskaffenhed".

Tag	definition	% tokens	% types	examples
<jsize>	size	9.51	1.36	kæmpestor, lav, bred
<jqual>	quality	7.8	2.96	god, dårlig, ringe, pæn, smuk
<jnat>	nation, region, town	7.49	**5.81**	afghansk, chilensk, aarhusiansk
<jtime>	time	5.62	1.52	tyveårs, fortsat, sen, sjælden
<jstate>	state, non-human	4.69	2.04	frisk, åben, lukket, vakkelvorn
<jcog>	cognition	4.25	**3.19**	gennemtænkt, klar, enkel
<jquant>	quantity	4.2	0.74	halv, hel, rigelig, samlet
<jpsych>	psychological, feeling	3.79	**5.45**	vred, varmhjertet, arbejdsom
<jimp>	importance, impact	3.48	1.63	(u)vigtig, nødvendig, afgørende
<jage>	age	3.17	1.94	alderældst, attenårig, ung
<jord>	order (successive)	2.57	0.24	efterfølgende, gradvis, sidste
<jident>	identity	2.53	1.67	konkret, samme, selveste
<jsoc>	social	2.5	1.71	offentlig, privat, fri, uafhængig
<jappro>	appropriate	2.45	1.22	(u)egnet, rigtig, forkert, farlig
<jpol>	politics	2.11	1.56	sprogpolitisk, blokfri, autonom
<jnormal>	normal	2.09	0.56	almindelig, særlig, elementær
<jcol>	colour	2.04	3.8	grøn, lyseblå, ternet, tigerstribet
<jmanner>	manner	1.97	3.02	klodset, uorganiseret, mesterlig
<jfact>	fact, truth, probability	1.95	0.96	sand, korrekt, sikker, (u)mulig
<jdegree>	degree	1.92	1.29	gennemført, ekstrem, drastisk
<jbehave>	behaviour	1.86	3.27	anmassende, barbarisk, barnlig
<jtype>	type (underspecified)	1.67	**6.19**	-mæssig, kvindelig, -betonet
		79.66	52.13	

Table 3: Semantic class distribution

Some of the categories in table 3 have a much higher type/token ration than others, indicating a larger lexical spread, and more work for the lexicographer per annotated token. This is true not only for the underspecified "type" category, but also for people's geographical provenance (<jnat>), cognition adjectives (<jcog>) and states-of-mind (<jpsych>).

6   Applications

The DanGram parser is used in a number of ongoing research projects, where improving adjective annotation might have an impact.

Greenlandic machine translation

Since Greenlandic linguistic tradition, based on morphological clues, does not recognize the existence of adjectives in the language, it is a non-trivial task to match Danish adjectives to Greenlandic lexical items. Often, the Greenlandic "adjective candidate" can translate into either a noun or an adjective in Danish. With a semantic-combinatorial classification of Danish adjectives, it might be easier to decide whether a word matches the semantics of a potential head noun, and hence should be treated as an adjective, or not.

Sentence grading

One interesting area within Intelligent Computer-Aided Language Learning (ICALL) is the automatic generation of exercises, and the grading of possible solutions. For instance, an ICALL system can generate sentences or question-answer pairs based on known vocabulary. If this is done solely based on syntactic slots, however, a large proportion of the suggested sentences will be meaningless. Thus, when using an adjective, it has to match the semantic type of its syntactic slot, normally defined by a noun. "Red ideas" and "angry houses" should be weeded out, while slight or metaphorical mismatches ("angry machines" or "red elephants", if recognized as such, might even contribute to making an exercise interesting and fun.

Sentiment analysis for hate speech

Hate speech research has lately drawn considerable public and political interest, as well as funding. Both in terms of technology (extracting and recognizing hate speech from online data) and linguistics, it is useful to be able to perform semantic annotation, and looking at what kind of adjectives are used in connection with hate speech target objects (immigrants, Muslims, Jews) is one way of decoding the linguistics of hate speech. Both sentiment analysis and adjective semantics are interesting in this regard, and to the best of our knowledge, no complete sentiment mark-up has ever been published for Danish adjectives.

7   Conclusions and outlook

We have presented a full-fledged lexico-semantic annotation scheme for adjectives and shown that the implemented Danish version can achieve 99% token coverage and 90% type coverage, while exhibiting a shallow frequency distribution curve with a high discriminatory potential.

It will be interesting to see if ongoing NLP work in the area of machine translation, semantic sentence grading and hate speech recognition can be made to profit from an improved lexical base for adjective annotation.

8   Acknowledgments

I would like to thank my colleague Anders Hougaard, now an associate professor at my university, for his valuable work on the semantic and syntactic classification of Danish adjectives during the early stage of the VISL project[9] in the late 90s. The domain tags mentioned in this paper are to a large degree motivated by and based on his contributions.

---

[9]   http://visl.sdu.dk, a cross language grammar initiative at SDU with both an NLP and a teaching perspective

References

Asmussen, Jørg. *Corpus Resources & Documentation*. Det Danske Sprog- og Litteraturselskab, (http://korpus.dsl.dk, last updated 2018)

Baker, Collin F., J.Fillmore, J. Charles, and John B. Lowe. "The Berkeley FrameNet project." In *Proceedings of the COLING-ACL*. Montreal, Canada, 1998

Bick, Eckhard. "A FrameNet for Danish." In *Proceedings of NODALIDA 2011, May 11-13, Riga, Latvia*. NEALT Proceedings Series, Vol. 11, pp. 34-41. Tartu: Tartu University Library, 2011.

Bick, Eckhard. "En Constraint Grammar Parser for Dansk." In *8. Møde om Udforskningen af Dansk Sprog, 12.-13. oktober 2000*, ed. Peter Widell & Mette Kunøe, pp. 40-50, Århus University, 2001.

Fellbaum, Christiane, ed. "WordNet: An Electronic Lexical Database." *Language, Speech and Communications*. Cambridge, Massachusetts: MIT Press, 1998

Hamp, Birgit, and Helmut Feldweg. "GermaNet - a Lexical-Semantic Net for German." In *Proceedings of the ACL workshop Automatic Information Extraction and Building of Lexical Semantic Resources for NLP Applications,* Madrid, 1997.

Nimb, Sanni, and Bolette S. Pedersen. "Towards a richer wordnet representation of properties – exploiting semantic and thematic information from thesauri." In *LREC 2012 Proceedings*. Istanbul, Turkey, 2012

Pedersen, Bolette S., Sanni Nimb, Jørg Asmussen, Nicolai H. Sørensen, Lars Trap-Jensen, and Henrik Lorentzen. "DanNet – the challenge of compiling a WordNet for Danish by reusing a monolingual dictionary." *Lang Resources & Evaluation* 43, 269–299, 2009.

Vossen, Piek, ed. *EuroWordNet: A Multilingual Database with Lexical Semantics Networks.* Dordrecht: Kluwer Academic Publishers, 1998

Ruppenhofer, Josef, Michael Ellsworth, Miriam R. L. Petruck, Christopher R. Johnson, and Jan Scheffczyk. *FrameNet II: Extended Theory and Practice.* 2010 (http://framenet.icsi.berkeley.edu/ index.php?option=com_wrapper&Itemid=126)

Towards a compositional analysis of German light verb constructions (LVCs) combining Lexicalized Tree Adjoining Grammar (LTAG) with frame semantics

Jens Fleischhauer   Thomas Gamerschlag   Laura Kallmeyer   Simon Petitjean
Heinrich Heine University Düsseldorf, Germany
{fleischhauer,gamer,kallmeyer,petitjean}@phil.hhu.de

Abstract

Complex predicates formed of a semantically 'light' verbal head and a noun which contributes the major part of the meaning are frequently referred to as 'light verb constructions' (LVCs). In the paper, we present a case study of LVCs with the German posture verb *stehen* 'stand'. In our account, we model the syntactic as well as semantic composition of such LVCs by combining *Lexicalized Tree Adjoining Grammar* (LTAG) with frames. Starting from the analysis of the literal uses of posture verbs, we show how the meaning components of the literal uses are systematically exploited in the interpretation of *stehen*-LVCs. The paper constitutes an important step towards a compositional and computational analysis of LVCs. We show that LTAG allows us to separate constructional from lexical meaning components and that frames enable elegant generalizations over event types and related constraints.

1   Light verb constructions

Light verb constructions (LVCs) are complex predicates consisting of – at least – two lexical elements forming a joint predication. The grammatical head of the construction is a semantically light verb which does not express the same predicational content as it does in its non-light ('heavy') uses. Rather, the predicational content is mainly contributed by a nominal element which is either realized within an NP or as a PP as illustrated by the German examples in (1-a) and (1-b), respectively.

(1)   a.   *ein Bad nehmen*   b.   *unter Beobachtung stehen*
           'to take a bath'   'to be under surveillance'

In its light use as in (1-a) the verb *nehmen* 'take' does not express a change of possession as it does in its heavy use: *ein Bad nehmen* 'take a bath' does not denote an event in which an individual is taking possession of a bath. Instead, the LVC in (1-a) denotes an event of bathing with the meaning mainly contributed by the noun *Bad* 'bath'. Likewise *unter Beobachtung stehen* in (1-b) does not refer to a situation in which someone exhibits the particular posture specified by *stehen* 'stand' in its heavy use but rather means that someone is the undergoer of the activity expressed by the eventive noun *Beobachtung* 'surveillance'. As illustrated by the examples, the nominal element used in an LVC is characteristically an eventive noun which determines the event denoted by the LVC as a whole. In this regard, Butt and Geuder (2001) state that light verbs make a (often just subtle) semantic contribution to the predication and are not able to denote full-fledged events of their own (in contrast to their heavy pendants).

Various authors (e.g. Fleischer 1997; Fellbaum et al. 2006) consider LVCs as idioms since constructions of this type often have a conventionalized interpretation and especially the light verb cannot be interpreted literally. In their discussion of idioms, Nunberg et al. (1994) argue that idiomaticity does not contradict semantic compositionality. The authors distinguish between 'idiomatic expressions' (e.g. *kick the bucket*) on the one hand and 'idiomatically combining expressions' on the other hand. Idiomatically combining expressions (ICEs) are semantically compositional and most LVCs fall into that class. After having identified the probable figurative meaning of the different components of an ICEs, its meaning can be build up compositionally. Such a compositional view is supported by the observation that ICEs come in families (e.g. Sag et al. 2002; see Gibbs and Nayak 1989; Nunberg et al. 1994; Fleischhauer and Neisani 2019 for further evidence supporting a compositional analysis of ICEs). Light Verb Constructions belonging to the same family instantiate the same interpretational pattern. For example, the LVCs in (2) which instantiate the pattern *vor* (lit. 'in front of') + NP + *stehen* 'stand' all have the same 'prospective' interpretation and can be paraphrased as 'be close to the change of state expressed by NP'.

(2)   *vor dem Ruin stehen* 'to face ruin', *vor dem Kollaps stehen* 'to be at the brink of collapse', *vor der Explosion stehen* 'to be before the explosion/to be ready to explode', *vor der Vollendung stehen* 'to near completion', *vor dem Abschluss stehen* 'to near completion/to be before the end', *vor dem Untergang stehen* 'to be on the brink of decline', *vor der Fertigstellung stehen* 'to near completion'

The existence of families such as the one in (2) shows that the individual LVCs are not interpreted idiosyncratically but rather on the base of systematic interpretational patterns. In line with this, Nunberg et al. (1994) argue that the existence of such families would be surprising, if the members of the families were not built compositionally.

As a consequence of assuming compositionality, LVCs show a mismatch between syntactic and semantic composition: syntactically, the light verb is the head of the construction and realizes the nominal element as its complement whereas the nominal element is the semantic head contributing the major part of the meaning.

The semantic composition of light verb constructions has only rarely been adressed explicitly in the semantics literature. Noteable exceptions come from work on the composition of event structure (e.g. Karimi 1997; Folli et al. 2005; Pantcheva 2009) and from Butt and Geuder (2001). The work on event structure usually neglects lexical semantics and therefore only covers a part of the meaning of light verb constructions. The current paper aims at filling this gap by presenting a case study on the semantic composition of German LVCs of the 'prospective family' presented in (2).

2   Case study: LVCs with *stehen* ('stand')

German *stehen* 'stand' is basically a verb expressing the posture of its theme argument. In addition, it also allows for the specification of the theme's location by means of a spatial PP as in (3). The sentence in (3) has the interpretation that the subject referent *Peter* is in an upright posture and is located at a place denoted by *vor dem Haus* 'in front of the house'. The spatial preposition locates the referent of its external argument within a neighboring region of a reference object (cf. Wunderlich and Herweg 1991; Kaufmann 1995 among others). In the case of *vor*, the referent of the internal argument (Peter) is located in a spatial region in front of the reference object (the house). Following Talmy (1972) among others, we refer to the reference object as 'ground'.

(3)   *Peter steht vor dem Haus.* 'Peter is standing in front of the house.'

In (3), *stehen* 'stand' is used as a heavy verb. A light use of *stehen* is shown in (4). Its meaning is that the boiler is close to explosion but not that the boiler is spatially located in a preregion of the explosion event. Such a literal interpretation does not make sense since the event does not denote a location with respect to which an object can be located.

(4)   *Der Kessel steht vor der Explosion.* 'The boiler is close to explosion.'

The interpretation of (4) is that the boiler is in a state anterior to an explosion event. Such an interpretation is called 'prospective' in the aspectual literature (e.g. Comrie 1976, 64). This particular kind of light verb construction is one way of expressing prospective aspect in German although it is not a grammaticalized aspect construction. The prospective interpretation only arises with eventive nouns denoting a change of state such as *Explosion* 'explosion' or *Vollendung* 'completion'. Crucially, the meaning of the LVC in (4) is not that the boiler will definitely explode. Prospective aspect is weaker than the future tense and only expresses that if the boiler remains in its current state, this will possibly result in an explosion.

The LVC exploits the ability of the preposition to refer to both location in space and time relative to a spatial entity or an event. It is important to note that the preposition does not depend on the co-occurrence of a light verb (LV) such as *stehen* 'stand' to be able to express the fact that the event denoted by its internal argument is about to take place. This is clearly shown by the fact that a *vor*-PP can also be used attributively in this reading as illustrated by (5).

(5)   *Ein Kessel kurz vor der Explosion ist eine große Gefahr.*
      'A boiler close to explosion is a great danger.'

As in the LVC in (4), the PP in (5) conveys the meaning that the event referred to by the PP-internal NP is close albeit not inevitable in spite of the absence of an LV. The LV therefore is not required for establishing this particular reading and can be regarded as more or less copula-like, selected in order to license a PP parallel to its heavy use. Another aspect central to the analysis of LVCs of the *vor* + NP + *stehen*–type is the selection of the subject argument in dependence of the argument structure of the PP-internal NP: Since the noun *Explosion* 'explosion' refers to an event with only a single participant undergoing the change of state referred to by the NP, it is exactly this argument which is selected as an argument to be realized as the subject of the LVC. However, if the PP-internal NP comes with a more complex argument structure as in (6), the LVC exhibits some flexibility in regard to subject choice:

(6)   a.   *Die Gemeinde steht kurz vor der Fertigstellung der Umgehungsstraße.*
            'The local community is about to complete the bypass.'
    b.   *Die Umgehungsstraße steht kurz vor der Fertigstellung durch die Gemeinde.*
            'The bypass is about to be completed by the local community.'

In (6) the eventive noun *Fertigstellung* 'completion' derives from the transitive verb *fertigstellen* 'to complete' via *ung*–nominalization (see e.g. Ehrich and Rapp 2000 on *ung*–nominalization in German). As shown by the contrast between (6-a) and (b), either the actor or the theme argument of the underlying verb can be realized as subject of the LVC while the remaining argument is realized as a genitive NP as in (6-a) or via a *durch*-PP as in (b) depending on its semantic role (theme vs. actor).

Given the observations illustrated above, a proper analysis of LVCs of the type *vor* + NP + *stehen* has to account for at least (i) the way the meaning of the construction is derived compositionally given the meaning of the parts outside this construction and (ii) the selection of the subject argument on the base of the argument structure of the PP-internal NP.

3   The framework: LTAG and frames

3.1   Frame semantics

Frames emerged as a representation format of conceptual and lexical knowledge (Fillmore, 1982; Barsalou, 1992; Löbner, 2014). They are commonly presented as semantic graphs with labeled nodes and edges, as in Fig. 1, where nodes correspond to entities (individuals, events, . . .) and edges to (functional or non-functional) relations between these entities. In Fig. 1 all relations except *part-of* are meant to be functional. This representation offers a fine-grained decomposition of meaning and should not be confused with the FrameNet frames, although the former can help to capture the structural relations of the latter (cf. Osswald and Van Valin, 2014).

Frames can be formalized as extended typed feature structures (Petersen, 2007; Kallmeyer and Osswald, 2013; Lichte and Petitjean, 2015), involving a finite set of types *loc_state, house, person, . . .*, a finite set of attributes (partial functions from frame nodes to frame nodes) THEME, GROUND, LOCATION, . . . and a finite set of (non-functional) relations, for instance *part-of* (which is a one to many mapping). Frame nodes are typed where we assume that a node can have more than one type (see the *loc_state* ∧

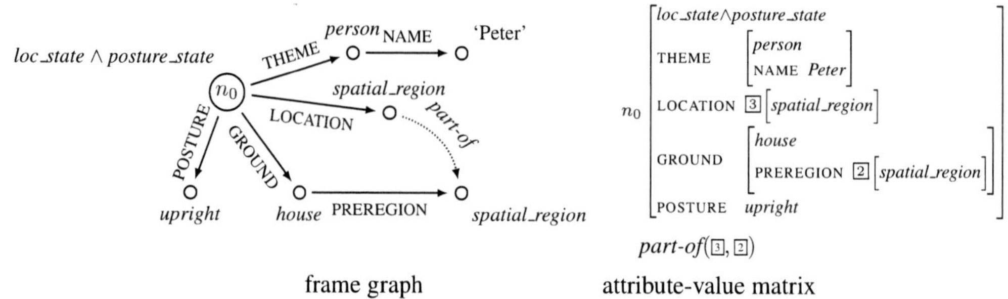

frame graph   attribute-value matrix

Figure 1: Frame for (3) *Peter steht vor dem Haus* ('Peter is standing in front of the house')

posture_state node in Fig. 1). We assume some of the frame nodes to be accessible via unique labels, in Fig. 1 for instance the label n_0 uniquely points to the *loc_state* $\wedge$ *posture_state* node of the frame. As mentioned above, frame nodes can be connected via functional attributes or via non-functional relations. We require however that every node in a frame is reachable from some labeled node via an attribute path, i.e., via a sequence of functional attributes.[1]

Besides concrete frames, there is a frame signature that constrains the general form of semantic frames. Within this signature, we allow to define subtype relations (e.g., every *loc_state* is a *state*), type incompatibilities (e.g., nothing can be of type *state* and *person* at the same time), requirements for the existence of attributes for nodes of certain types (e.g., a *state* always has a THEME) etc. We will see more examples below.

3.2 Lexicalized Tree Adjoining Grammars with frames

For syntactic modeling and syntactic composition, we choose *Lexicalized Tree Adjoining Grammar* (LTAG Joshi and Schabes, 1997; Abeillé and Rambow, 2000). A LTAG consists of a finite set of *elementary trees*. Larger trees can be derived via the composition operations *substitution* (replacing a leaf with a new tree) and *adjunction* (replacing an internal node with a new tree). An adjoining tree has a unique non-terminal leaf that is its *foot node* (marked with an asterisk). When adjoining such a tree to some node v, in the resulting tree, the subtree with root v from the old tree ends up below the foot node.

In order to capture syntactic generalizations, the non-terminal node labels are enriched with feature structures (Vijay-Shanker and Joshi, 1988). Each node has a top and a bottom feature structure (except substitution nodes, which have only a top). Nodes in the same elementary tree can share features. Substitutions and adjunctions trigger unifications: In a substitution step, the top of the root of the new tree unifies with the top of the substitution node. In an adjunction step, the top of the root of the adjoining tree unifies with the top of the adjunction site and the bottom of the foot of the adjoining tree unifies with the bottom of the adjunction site. Furthermore, in the final derived tree, top and bottom must unify in all nodes.

For the syntax-semantics interface, we pair LTAG elementary trees with semantic representations, in our case frames (Kallmeyer and Osswald, 2013). Syntactic nodes are enriched with (untyped) interface features such as I(NDIVIDUAL) and E(VENT) that contribute labels of nodes in the related semantic frame. Upon substitution and adjunction, the unification of interface features triggers the identification of frame node labels and, consequently, the unification of the linked semantic frames.

An example (involving only substitution) is given in Fig. 2. The three substitutions lead to $\boxed{1} = \boxed{7}$ (which unifies the frame contributed by *Peter* with the THEME of the *loc_state*), $\boxed{0} = \boxed{4}$ (which unifies the posture *loc_state* frame introduced by *steht* with the frame contributed by *vor*, thereby also unifying the GROUND of the former with the GROUND of the latter), $\boxed{2} = \boxed{3}$ (which unifies the LOCATION of the *loc_state* with the first element of the *part-of* relation) and $\boxed{5} = \boxed{8}$ (which unifies the *house* frame with the value of the GROUND feature, whose PREREGION value is the second element of the *part-of* relation).

---

[1]This condition is important for restricting the computational complexity of unification, i.e, of merging two frames.

82

As a result, we obtain the frame from Fig. 1.

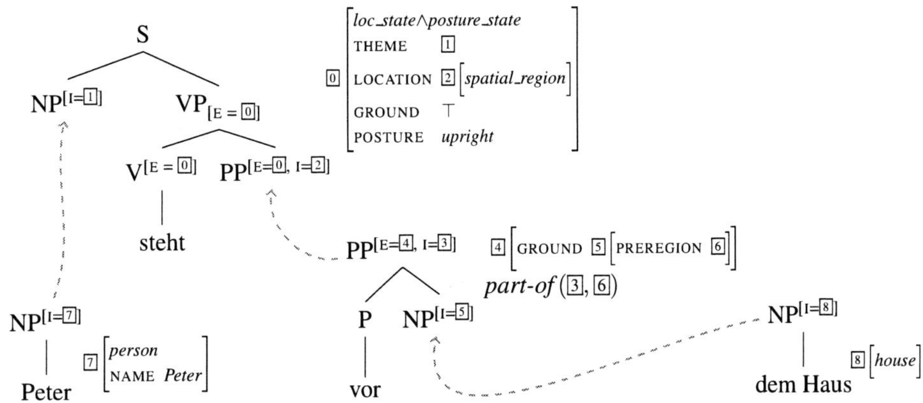

Figure 2: LTAG-frame derivation for (3), leading to the frame from Fig. 1

Generalizations over elementary tree frame pairs and constraints over frame types are captured in the so-called metagrammar in form of a principled and factorized description of syntactic and semantic building blocks. We will use this in the next sections when developing our analysis of LVCs with *stehen*.

There has been only very little work on computational implementations of LVCs so far that take both syntax and semantics into consideration. Vaidya et al. (2014) propose an LTAG analysis for certain LVCs in Hindi but, in contrast to our paper, do not deal with semantics. Their syntactic analysis is such that the light verb adjoins into the noun, i.e., the noun spans the entire subcategorization frame. This requires separate and largely unrelated analyses for the literal uses and the light verb uses of verbs such as *stehen*. Our analysis is more factorized and thereby more unified, and it establishes links between the subject NP and semantic arguments of the embedded event NP via appropriate frame unifications.

4   The analysis

In the following, we develop an analysis of LVCs of the type *stehen* + *vor* + NP, combined with an analysis of the literal use of *stehen* as in Fig. 1. The goal is to factorize into the contributions of literal and non-literal *stehen*, the contributions of the respective constructions (LVC with PP versus *loc_state* NP-V-PP), the contribution of the NP embedded in the PP within the LVC, and the contribution of the preposition *vor*. We will see, that the use of LTAG allows us to separate lexical contributions from constructional ones (the latter are paired with unanchored trees), and the use of frames, in particular of the type hierarchy, allows for elegant generalizations, specifically, for a uniform meaning of *vor*.

4.1   Literal *stehen* versus LVC *stehen* + *vor* + NP

As a first step towards decomposing (3) *Peter steht vor dem Haus* ('Peter is standing in front of the house') and (4) *Der Kessel steht vor der Explosion* ('The boiler is close to explosion') into form-meaning components, we assume that there are different constructions for the literal (3) and the LVC case (4). The former construction, *n0Vpploc* is characterized as requiring a THEME NP and a LOCATION PP and it describes a *loc_state* involving a theme, a location and a ground. It can, for instance, be anchored by *stehen* ('stand'), *wohnen* ('live'), *liegen* ('lie'), etc. The latter, *n0Vpplvc*, is more general, it describes a state (determined by the PP) and the subject NP contributes the THEME of that state. Fig. 3 shows the two constructions. The diamond marks the position of the lexical anchor.

Concerning the lexical anchor *stehen*, we assume that we have two different lexical entries, for the literal and the LVC reading respectively. In the literal case, the frame type is *posture_state* and we have

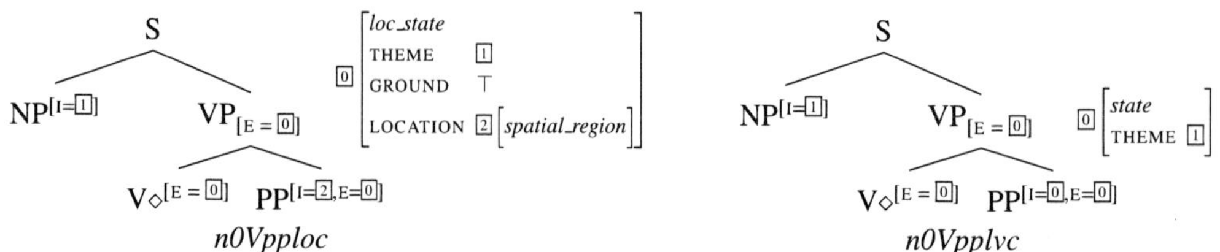

Figure 3: The two unanchored constructions

an attribute POSTURE = *upright* while in the LV case, the lexical entry only specifies the type as *state*.[2] The relation between the two readings is captured within our factorization of lexical entries. The literal reading extends the light verb reading by further restricting its type and adding the POSTURE attribute.

On an abstract level, the preposition *vor* expresses the same relation either between the LOCATION of the *loc_state* and the object denoted by the NP embedded in the PP or between the *state* itself and the event denoted by the PP-internal NP. In both cases, it means that the former is part of some PREREGION of the latter where PREREGION is to be understood in a very general way, not limited to spatial regions but including also prestates of events.[3] Along these lines, we define both *spatial_region* and *state* as incompatible subtypes of *region*, expressed in general frame constraints that are part of the type hierarchy:

(7)   a.   *spatial_region* $\rightarrow$ *region*   b.   *state* $\rightarrow$ *region*   c.   *state* $\wedge$ *spatial_region* $\rightarrow$ $\perp$

These constraints are taken to be universal quantifications over frame nodes, i.e., (7-a) is short for $\forall x[spatial\_region(x) \rightarrow region(x)]$.

With these additional constraints, we can characterize the meaning contribution of *vor* as follows: *vor* establishes a relation *part-of* between the frame node contributed as I feature at the PP node (Peter's location or the state denoted by the light verb) and a GROUND (the house or the explosion) with respect to which the former is positioned. More precisely, it expresses that the location (resp. the state in the LVC case) is part of the PREREGION of the GROUND. Fig. 4

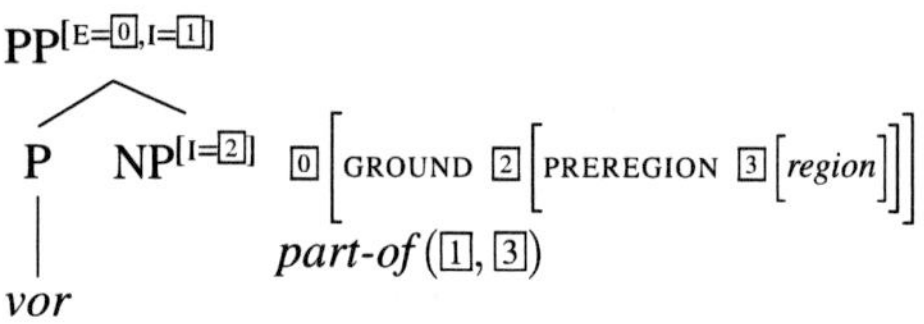

Figure 4: Anchored tree for the preposition *vor*.

gives the corresponding elementary tree with its frame. When combining this with the *loc_state* construction, the interface feature I at the PP node provides the location, while in the LVC construction, it has the same value as the E feature, i.e., it provides the overall state. The relation *part-of* is defined between elements of type *region* with the additional constraint that the elements must have the same type (this excludes for instance a *part-of* relation between elements of the incompatible types *spatial_region* and *state*). We furthermore assume a general frame constraint stating that in a case where *part-of* relates two states, they must have identical THEME values.

The embedded NP provides an object coming with a certain topological structure in the literal meaning and an event in the LVC case. More concretely, *house* is of the more general type *building*, which comes with an INREGION, an ATREGION and also a PREREGION that can be addressed via corresponding prepositions. The values of these attributes are of type *spatial_region*. We assume constraints as in (8). (ATTR : *type* in some node x is short for $\exists y[\text{ATTR}(x,y) \wedge type(y)]$.) With these constraints, the lexical entry of *Haus* can be restricted to giving the type *house*. The effect of the constraints will lead to the form meaning pair on the left of Fig. 5.

---

[2]We might actually need a second literal reading without a POSTURE specification for sentences as *Die Wolken stehen vor der Sonne* ('The clouds are in front of the sun').

[3]We consider this abstract conception of PREREGION as allowing for (temporal) states as well as spatial regions as directly reflecting the metaphorical relation between the literal spatial reading of the preposition and the figurative temporal interpretation. Consequently, our analysis takes up ideas of conceptual metaphors such as "time is space" (Lakoff and Johnson, 1980) while it also offers a concrete formal treatment of such figurative processes.

(8) a. *house → building*
  b. *building* → INREGION : *spatial_region*
  c. *building* → ATREGION : *spatial_region*
  d. *building* → PREREGION : *spatial_region*

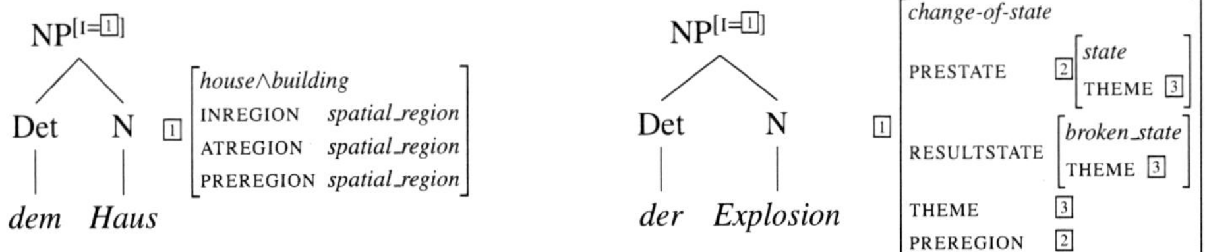

Figure 5: Anchored elementary trees for the NPs embedded in the PP in (3) and (4)

Explosion, in contrast, denotes an event of type *change-of-state* with a RESULTSTATE of type *broken_state*. Furthermore, we assume the general constraints in (9) and (10) stating that a *change-of-state* has a PRESTATE, and a RESULTSTATE, all of them having as THEME the THEME of the overall change of state. ($\triangleq$ stands for path equality, i.e., structure sharing: ATTR1 $\triangleq$ ATTR2 in some node x corresponds to $\exists y[\text{ATTR1}(x, y) \wedge \text{ATTR2}(x, y)]$.) Note that although we assume that a change of state always comes with a PRESTATE, this PRESTATE is not part of the event structure encoded by an eventive noun such as *Explosion*. This is evident if one looks at the referents of event nouns which are subject to polysemy but never include a PREREGION as a potential referent (see Kawaletz and Plag 2015 for a frame account of the polysemy of event nominalizations). Likewise, although a spatial object has some (possibly variable) PREREGION, this region is not a part of it. Therefore, PRESTATE has to be differentiated from some event internal INITIAL STATE which precedes the RESULT STATE and in which the result does not hold yet. Since the phenomena we account for do not require reference to the INITIAL STATE of a *change-of-state frame*, INITIAL STATE is not represented in the *change-of-state frame* for the sake of simplicity. Furthermore, the PRESTATE is also the PREREGION of the event. Combining these constraints with the lexical entry for *Explosion* yields the elementary tree frame pair on the right of Fig. 5.

(9) a. *change-of-state* → PRESTATE : *state*
  b. *change-of-state* → RESULTSTATE : *state*

(10) a. *change-of-state* → THEME $\triangleq$ PRESTATE : THEME
  b. *change-of-state* → THEME $\triangleq$ RESULTSTATE : THEME
  c. *change-of-state* → PREREGION $\triangleq$ PRESTATE

For the literal case (3), we have already seen in Fig. 2 how the form meaning fragments are put together. Fig. 6 shows the LTAG derivation for (4). The syntactic composition triggers unifications between 1 and 7, between 0, 3 and 4, and between 5 and 8. Furthermore, the constraints on *part-of* relations lead to a unification of 1 and 11, the THEME attributes of the two states that are related.

The resulting frame is given in Fig. 7. According to this frame, the boiler is in a state that is part of the prestate of its explosion.[4]

A combination of a *vor*-PP embedding a *change-of-state* NP with the literal *loc_state* construction is excluded because it would lead to a *part-of* relation between a *spatial_region* and a *state*, two types that

---

[4]Note that the temporal structure of the explosion event in relation to its prestate is only implicit in this frame. The prestate stands in a *precedes* relation to the change of state, which in turn stands in an *overlap* relation to the result state. In other words, the state represented in Fig.7 is such that the explosion has not happened yet. Furthermore, we assume that the fact that a prestate holds does not necessarily entail the event itself, i.e., is compatible with a situation where the event never happens. Note, however, that this is only implicit since the frame semantics used here does not distinguish between instantiated frames and frames that are rather frame types. In future work, we will explore ways to explicitly include uninstantiated frames (in other words complex frame types) along the lines of Balogh and Osswald (2017), which is close to what we find in *Type Theory with Records* (TTR, Cooper 2012).

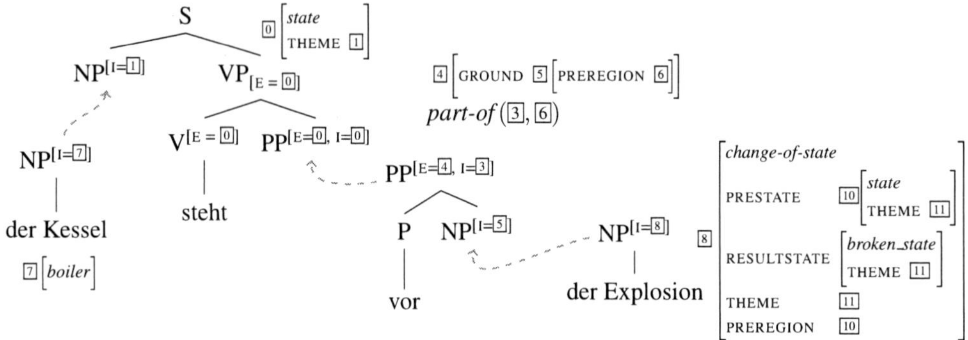

Figure 6: LTAG-frame derivation for (4)

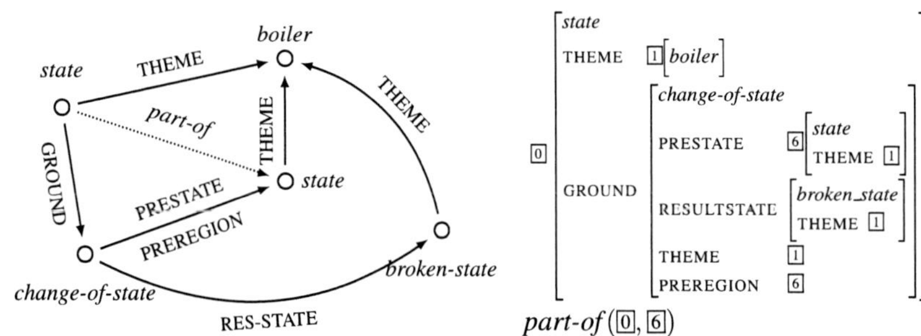

Figure 7: Frame for (4)

are not unifiable.[5] For the same reason, the combination of the LVC construction with a PP embedding a *building* NP is ruled out.

4.2 LVCs with an NP event that has actor and undergoer

Now let us turn to LVCs involving *stehen* and a *vor*-PP with a noun that denotes an accomplishment involving an actor and a theme. An example was *Fertigstellung* ('completion') in (6), repeated below:

(11) a. *Die Gemeinde steht kurz vor der Fertigstellung der Umgehungsstraße.*
          'The local community is about to complete the bypass.'
      b. *Die Umgehungsstraße steht kurz vor der Fertigstellung durch die Gemeinde.*
          'The bypass is about to be completed by the local community.'

The additional complication, compared to *vor der Explosion stehen* is that both the actor or the theme of the event denoted by the noun embedded in the PP can be realized as the subject NP of the LVC. Depending which argument is realized as the subject, the interpretation varies slightly. The LVC makes a predication about the local community in (11-a) whereas it predicates about the bypass in (11-b). This results in a more active-like reading for (11-a), as the actor is the subject of the complex predicate, and in a more passive-like reading for (11-b). However, the prestate remains unspecified apart from being a prestate of a particular event and as such being affected by it. We leave it for future research to explore potential semantic asymmetries between realization variants of the type illustrated in (11).

---

[5]A reviewer remarks that this restriction is too strong. However, apparent counterexamples involving the literal meaning of *stehen* with a PP-internal noun referring to a change of state involve some kind of coercion such that the event is shifted to the place where it takes place. For instance, in a sentence such as *Die Ingenieure standen direkt vor der Explosion* 'The engineers were standing right in front of the explosion' *vor der Explosion* is interpreted as 'in front of the place where the explosion happened'.

We pursue a similar analysis as in the case of a *change-of-state*, namely that the LVC *stehen vor NP* indicates that the subject is in a prestate of the NP event. The notion of prestate is, however, less fixed in the case of *Fertigstellung* since both actor and theme can be the theme of the prestate, depending on the structure of the NP. Roughly, if the NP event has an active-like interpretation (N + genitive NP denoting the theme), the prestate refers to the actor as in (11-a) and if it has a passive-like reading (N + *durch*-PP

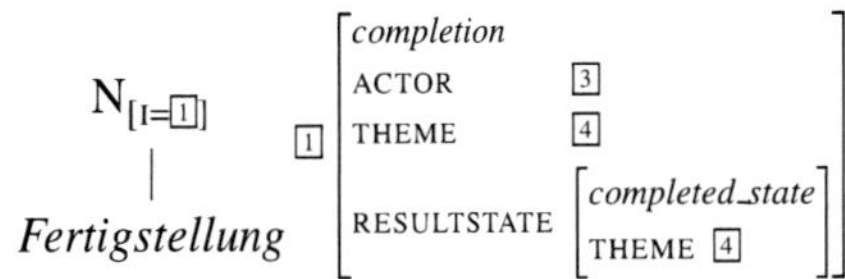

Figure 8: Lexical meaning of *Fertigstellung* ('completion')

denoting the actor), the prestate refers to the theme as in (11-b). In other words, there are different constructions that come with different specifications of the THEME of the PRESTATE. The (simplified) lexical meaning contribution of *Fertigstellung* is given in Fig. 8.[6]

This can then anchor either of the two constructions (unanchored trees) in Fig. 9. Nn_{gen} represents

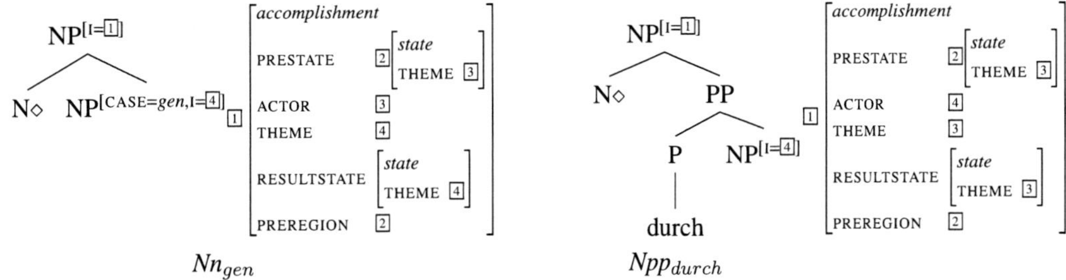

Figure 9: Unanchored elementary trees for accomplishment denoting nouns

an NP with a genitive argument slot that contributes the theme while the actor is not realized. In this case, the theme of the prestate is the actor. In the second construction, Npp_{durch}, a PP with preposition *durch* realizes the actor inside the NP while the theme is missing. In this case, the prestate of the event concerns the theme. Combining the respective anchored trees with the trees for the LVC construction yields the two desired readings.

Semantically ill-formed sentences such as (12) can then be excluded by type constraints for semantic roles. An actor has to be capable of volition, which is not the case for objects such as bypass. Therefore, the bypass cannot be the actor of completion.

(12) *#die Umgehungsstraße steht vor der Fertigstellung der Planung*
      'the bypass is close to finishing the planning'

4.3 Implementation

In order to check the theoretical analyses presented in the previous sections, we created a toy grammar consisting of the pairs of LTAG trees and frames appearing in our examples.[7] The grammar was developed using XMG-2 (Petitjean et al., 2016), a grammar engineering tool based on the notion of metagrammar. In this framework, developing a grammar consists in writing a compact and factorized description, called the metagrammar. This linguistic resource, consisting of reusable abstractions described using logic and constraints, is compiled with XMG-2 to obtain the non-factorized grammar. Such a grammar can be used for parsing, thereby allowing to check that automatic semantic analyses are consistent with the ones that we presented. To do so, we used the parser TuLiPA for LTAG and semantic frames (Arps

---

[6]We ignore here the fact that *Fertigstellung* is derived from the verb *fertigstellen* via *-ung* nominalization and that this also should be modeled in a principled way within the syntax-semantics interface. For possible analyses of such phenomena using frames see for instance Andreou and Petitjean (2017).

[7]Our implementation and the instructions to experiment with it are available online:
`https://github.com/spetitjean/XMG-2/tree/master/MetaGrammars/synframe/LVC`.

and Petitjean, 2018), giving as parameters the toy grammar and its type hierarchy. TuLiPA was able to compute the expected derivations for all the examples.

5 Conclusion and future work

In this paper, we develop a compositional analysis of the semantics of German LVCs involving the posture verb *stehen* ('stand') and a *vor*-PP. The chosen framework combines LTAG with frames, which comes with constructionist elements (LTAG) and with the possibility to formulate general semantic constraints via frame types and constraints on the type hierarchy. This allows us to propose an analysis that has the following features: It separates the meaning contribution of the light verb from the form-meaning contribution of the different constructions (literal location-state versus LVC-*vor*-PP construction). Furthermore, it assumes a single uniform tree-frame pair for the preposition *vor*, which establishes a part-of relation between a region (the location in the literal case and the state in the LVC case) and the preregion of the frame of the PP-internal NP (the spatial region in front of an object in the literal case and the prestate of an event in the LVC case). Unifications triggered by syntactic composition lead to a further specification of the type of region/preregion and part-of relation. Moreover, our analysis also distinguishes different constructions for eventive nouns, depending on the NP-internal syntactic realization of their arguments. This allows for a construction-specific specification of the participant of a prestate of the event, which leads to the possibility to identify the theme of the state denoted by the light verb either with the actor or the theme of the PP-internal event, depending on the structure of the NP.

Even though this paper covers only a few cases of LVCs, it shows clearly that the combination of a constructionist syntactic approach with frame semantics yields elegant means of generalization and allows for a large degree of decomposition and factorization concerning the various form-meaning pairs.

As a next step, the analysis presented within the current paper should be extended to cover further families of *stehen*-LVCs. There exist further families using the same preposition (13), as well as LVCs using different prepositions (e.g. *außer* 'without' or *zu* 'to'). The LVCs in (13) at first sight seem to be instances of the pattern discussed above. However, they do not have a prospective interpretation, rather they express that the subject is confronted with a certain task or question. Two particularly interesting questions are: first, what is the semantic contribution of the LV and second, how is the preposition interpreted. Especially with respect to the P element, it is clear that it cannot have the same interpretation as in the prospective-family discussed in this paper.

(13)   *vor einer Frage stehen* 'to be faced with a question', *vor einer Aufgabe stehen* 'to be confronted with a task', *vor dem Problem stehen* 'to be confronted with a problem'

The compositional analysis presented within the current paper is somewhat incomplete, as we ignored the semantic contribution of the article. Contrary to e.g. Leiss (2000), it seems reasonable to claim that the article has a semantic function since its use is not fixed (14). To yield a compositional analysis of the entirely LVC, the contribution of the article needs to be integrated as well.

(14)   a.   *Die Fabrik steht vor der Explosion.* 'The factory is close to explosion.'
        b.   *Die Fabrik steht vor einer erneuten Explosion.* 'The factory is close to explosion again.'

The current paper presents a promising first step in the compositional analysis of LVCs, which will be extended along the lines sketched above.

Acknowlededgments

We would like to thank three anonymous reviewers for their valuable comments that contributed to improving the paper. The work presented in this article was partially funded by the German Science Foundation (DFG) as part of CRC 991 and by the European Research Council (ERC grant TreeGraSP).

References

Abeillé, A. and O. Rambow (2000). Tree Adjoining Grammar: An Overview. In A. Abeillé and O. Rambow (Eds.), *Tree Adjoining Grammars: Formalisms, Linguistic Analyses and Processing*, pp. 1–68. Stanford, CA: CSLI Publications.

Andreou, M. and S. Petitjean (2017). Describing derivational polysemy with XMG. In I. Eshkol and J.-Y. Antoine (Eds.), *Actes de TALN 2017, 24e Conférence sur le Traitement Automatique des Langues Naturelles*, Volume 2, pp. 94–101.

Arps, D. and S. Petitjean (2018). A parser for LTAG and frame semantics. In *Proceedings of LREC 2018*, pp. 2223–2229.

Balogh, K. and R. Osswald (2017). A frame-based analysis of verbal particles in Hungarian. Manuscript.

Barsalou, L. W. (1992). Frames, concepts, and conceptual fields. In A. Lehrer and E. F. Kittay (Eds.), *Frames, Fields, and Contrasts*, New Essays in Semantic and Lexical Organization, Chapter 1, pp. 21–74. Hillsdale, New Jersey: Lawrence Erlbaum Associates.

Butt, M. and W. Geuder (2001). On the (Semi)Lexical Status of Light Verbs. In N. Corver and H. van Riemsdijk (Eds.), *Semilexical Categories: On the content of function words and the function of content words*, pp. 323–370. Berlin: Mouton.

Comrie, B. (1976). *Aspect*. Cambridge: Cambridge University Press.

Cooper, R. (2012). Type theory and semantics in flux. In R. Kempson, N. Asher, and T. Fernando (Eds.), *Philosophy of Linguistics Handbook of the Philosophy of Science*, pp. 271–323. Elsevier BV.

Ehrich, V. and I. Rapp (2000). Sortale Bedeutung und Argumentstruktur: *ung*-Nominalisierungen im deutschen. *Zeitschrift für Sprachwissenschaft 19.2*, 245–303.

Fellbaum, C., A. Geyken, A. Herold, F. Koerner, and G. Neumann (2006). Corpus-based studies of German idioms and light verbs. *International Journal of Lexicography 19 (4)*, 349–360.

Fillmore, C. J. (1982). Frame semantics. In *Linguistics in the Morning Calm*, pp. 111–137. Seoul: Hanshin Publishing Co.

Fleischer, W. (1997). *Phraseologie der deutschen Gegenwartssprache* (2. Edition ed.). Tübingen: Niemeyer.

Fleischhauer, J. and M. Neisani (2019). Adverbial and attributive modification of persian separable light verb constructions. *Journal of Linguistics*, 1–41.

Folli, R., H. Harley, and S. Karimi (2005). Determinants of event type in Persian complex predicates. *Lingua 115*, 1365–1401.

Gibbs, R. W. and N. P. Nayak (1989). Psycholinguistic studies on the syntactic behavior of idioms. *Cognitive Psychology 21*, 100–138.

Joshi, A. K. and Y. Schabes (1997). Tree-adjoining grammars. In G. Rozenberg and A. Salomaa (Eds.), *Handbook of Formal Languages. Vol. 3: Beyond Words*, pp. 69–123. Berlin: Springer.

Kallmeyer, L. and R. Osswald (2013). Syntax-driven semantic frame composition in Lexicalized Tree Adjoining Grammar. *Journal of Language Modelling 1*, 267–330.

Karimi, S. (1997). Persian complex verbs: Idiomatic or compositional. *Lexicology 3(2)*, 273–318.

Kaufmann, I. (1995). *Konzeptuelle Grundlagen semantischer Dekompositionsstrukturen: Die Kombinatorik lokaler Verben und prädikativer Komplemente*. Tübingen: Niemeyer.

Kawaletz, L. and I. Plag (2015). Predicting the semantics of english nominalizations: A frame-based analysis of -ment suffixation. In P. S. . L. K. L. Bauer (Ed.), *Semantics of Complex Words*, pp. 289–319. Dordrecht: Springer.

Lakoff, G. and M. Johnson (1980). *Metaphors we live by*. Chicago: University of Chicago Press.

Leiss, E. (2000). *Artikel und Aspekt*. Berlin/New York: Walter de Gruyter.

Lichte, T. and S. Petitjean (2015). Implementing semantic frames as typed feature structures with XMG. *Journal of Language Modelling 3*(1), 185–228.

Löbner, S. (2014). Evidence for frames from human language. In T. Gamerschlag, D. Gerland, R. Osswald, and W. Petersen (Eds.), *Frames and Concept Types. Applications in Language and Philosophy*, Volume 94 of *Studies in Linguistics and Philosophy*, pp. 23–67. Dordrecht: Springer.

Nunberg, G., I. A. Sag, and T. Wasow (1994). Idioms. *Language 70*(3), 491–538.

Osswald, R. and R. D. Van Valin (2014). FrameNet, frame structure, and the syntax-semantics interface. In T. Gamerschlag, D. Gerland, R. Osswald, and W. Petersen (Eds.), *Frames and Concept Types. Applications in Language and Philosophy*, Volume 94 of *Studies in Linguistics and Philosophy*, pp. 125–156. Dordrecht: Springer.

Pantcheva, M. (2009). First Phase Syntax of Persian Complex Predicates: Argument Structure and Telicity. *JSAL 2*(1), 53–72.

Petersen, W. (2007). Representation of concepts as frames. *The Baltic International Yearbook of Cognition, Logic and Communication 2*, 151–170.

Petitjean, S., D. Duchier, and Y. Parmentier (2016). XMG2: Describing description languages. In M. Amblard, P. de Groote, S. Pogodalla, and C. Retoré (Eds.), *Proceedings of Logical Aspects of Computational Linguistics (LACL) 2016, Nancy, December 2016*, Number 10054 in Lecture Notes in Computer Science, Berlin, pp. 255–272. Springer.

Sag, I., T. Baldwin, F. Bond, A. Copestake, and D. Flickinger (2002). Multiword Expressions: A Pain in the Neck for NLP. In A. Gelbukh (Ed.), *Computational linguistics and intelligent text processing*, pp. 1–15. Berlin: Springer.

Talmy, L. (1972). *Semantic Structures in English and Atsugewi*. Ph. D. thesis, University of California, Berkeley.

Vaidya, A., O. Rambow, and A. Palmer (2014). Light verb constructions with 'do' and 'be' in Hindi: A TAG analysis. In *Proceedings of the Workshop on Lexical and Grammatical Resources for Language Processing, Coling 2014*, pp. 127–136.

Vijay-Shanker, K. and A. K. Joshi (1988). Feature structures based tree adjoining grammar. In *Proceedings of COLING*, Budapest, pp. 714–719.

Wunderlich, D. and M. Herweg (1991). Lokale & Direktionale. In A. von Stechow and D. Wunderlich (Eds.), *Semantik – Ein internationales Handbuch zeitgenössischer Forschung*, pp. 758–785. Berlin/New York: de Gruyter.

Words are Vectors, Dependencies are Matrices: Learning Word Embeddings from Dependency Graphs

Paula Czarnowska, Guy Emerson and Ann Copestake
Department of Computer Science and Technology
University of Cambridge
{pjc211, gete2, aac10}@cam.ac.uk

Abstract

Distributional Semantic Models (DSMs) construct vector representations of word meanings based on their contexts. Typically, the contexts of a word are defined as its closest neighbours, but they can also be retrieved from its syntactic dependency relations. In this work, we propose a new dependency-based DSM. The novelty of our model lies in associating an independent meaning representation, a matrix, with each dependency-label. This allows it to capture specifics of the relations between words and contexts, leading to good performance on both intrinsic and extrinsic evaluation tasks. In addition to that, our model has an inherent ability to represent dependency chains as products of matrices which provides a straightforward way of handling further contexts of a word.

1 Introduction

Within computational linguistics, most research on word-meaning has been focusing on developing Distributional Semantic Models (DSMs), based on the hypothesis that a word's sense can be inferred from the contexts it appears in (Harris, 1954). DSMs associate each word with a vector (a.k.a. *word embedding*) that encodes information about its co-occurrence with other words in the vocabulary. In recent work, the most popular DSMs learn the embeddings using neural-network architectures. In particular, the Skip-gram model of Mikolov et al. (2013) has gained a lot of traction due to its efficiency and high quality representations. Skip-gram embeddings are trained with an objective that forces them to be similar to the vectors of their words' contexts. The latter, *context-word* vectors, are a separate parameter of the model jointly learned along with the main *target-word* vectors. Like most DSMs, Mikolov et al. (2013)'s model derives contexts of a word from a pre-defined window of words that surround it.

An alternative way of defining contexts in Skip-gram was explored by Levy and Goldberg (2014), who altered the model to accept contexts coming from a different vocabulary to that of the target-words. The contexts were retrieved from targets' syntactic dependency relations and were a concatenation of the word linked to the target and the dependency-label. Each context type was associated with an independent vector representation. In contrast to Skip-gram, which captures *relatedness*[1], Levy and Goldberg (2014)'s embeddings exhibited a more intuitive notion of similarity. For example, the former regards the vector for *abba*, a popular Swedish pop group, as close to that for *agnetha* – a name of the group's member, while the latter considers it close to the vectors for other pop group names. But Levy and Goldberg (2014)'s method of constructing contexts prevented their model from directly capturing how dependency types affect relations between target and context-words, as the labels were not associated with independent representations. At the same time it intensifies the problems associated with data sparsity due to the large and fine-grained context-vocabulary.

In this work, we address the shortcomings of Levy and Goldberg (2014)'s approach by introducing the *dependency-matrix model* – a DSM which associates meaning with each type of dependency. Instead

---

[1]Turney (2012) refers to relatedness as *domain similarity* and highlights its differences from *function similarity* that quantifies the degree to which words share similar functional roles.

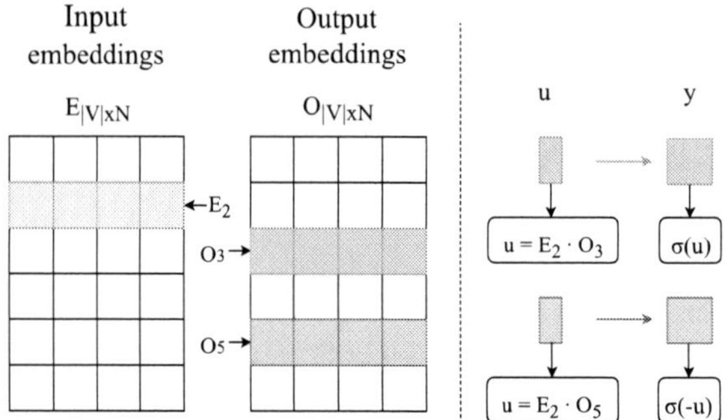

Figure 1: A graphical representation of Skip-gram displaying its parameters (left) and how $P(C = 1|V_2, V_3)$ and $1 - P(C = 1|V_2, V_5)$ are calculated for the real and a negative context, respectively. N is the embedding dimensionality.

of simply appending the labels to context-words, they are promoted to a separate parameter of the model. They become matrices, acting as linear maps on the context-word vectors and trained alongside the embeddings. We hypothesised that this approach will lead to higher-quality representations, as it allows the model to capture important interactions between all three: labels, contexts and targets, while diminishing the data sparsity problem at the same time.

2   Background

2.1   The Skip-gram Model

We now give a short formal overview of the Skip-gram model, since we will build on this to specify our dependency-matrix model in Section 3.

Skip-gram was based on the feed-forward neural probabilistic language model of Bengio et al. (2003). It is trained to predict the context-words of a given target-word, where the contexts are the immediate neighbours of the latter and are retrieved using a window of an arbitrary size n (by capturing n words to the left of the target and n words to its right). During training the model is exposed to vast amounts of training data pairs (V_t, V_c), where V is the vocabulary and $t, c \in \{1, ..., |V|\}$ are indices of a target-word and one of its contexts. The objective of negative-sampling Skip-gram, as introduced by Mikolov et al. (2013), is to differentiate between the correct training examples retrieved from the corpus and the incorrect, randomly generated pairs. For each correct example the model draws m negative ones, with m being a hyperparameter. These incorrect samples hold the same V_t as the original, while their V_c is drawn from an arbitrary noise distribution. Mikolov et al. (2013) recommend setting the noise distribution to the unigram distribution raised to the power 0.75 and we used this setting in this work.

Following Goldberg and Levy (2014), let D be the set of all correct pairs, D' denote a set of all negatively sampled $|D| \times m$ pairs and $P(C = 1|V_t, V_c)$ be the probability of (V_t, V_c) being a correct pair, originating from the corpus. The last is calculated using the sigmoid function:

$$\sigma(u) = \frac{1}{1 + e^{-u}} \tag{1}$$

$$\text{where } u = E_t \cdot O_c$$

Here, $E \in \mathbb{R}^{|V| \times N}$ stands for an *input-embedding* matrix, holding representations of target-words and $O \in \mathbb{R}^{|V| \times N}$ stands for the *output-embedding* matrix, holding context representations (see Figure 1). Given this setting, the negative-sampling objective is defined as maximising

$$\sum_{(V_t, V_c) \in D} \log \sigma(u) + \sum_{(V_t, V_c) \in D'} \log \sigma(-u) \tag{2}$$

The model is trained using stochastic gradient ascent, with the learning rate changing throughout the training process and being proportional to the number of remaining training examples.

2.2 Dependency-based Embeddings

Since word meaning is closely related to syntactic behaviour, a feasible alternative to the window-method is to extract the contexts from the word's syntactic relations. This can be achieved by constructing the context vocabulary V^C through pairing all word types with labels of relations they can participate in. For instance, among the contexts composed from *dog* would be *dog/nsubj* and *dog/dobj*. Alternatively, one can keep the vocabulary unchanged and adjust the context selection method to disregard the labels and only pick words in relation with the target. The first approach was taken in some of the earliest works incorporating syntactic information into the count-based DSMs. Grefenstette (1994) used V^C that consists of tokens such as *subject-of-talk* and his vectors held binary values denoting whether the target-word has co-occurred with the contexts in V^C. This approach was later extended by Lin (1998) who replaced the binary values with frequency counts. Even more methods for incorporating syntactic information were introduced in the general frameworks of Padó and Lapata (2007)'s and Baroni and Lenci (2010). Baroni and Lenci (2010) represented corpus-extracted frequencies of (word, link, word) tuples as a third order tensor and, through its matricisation, generated various matrix-arrangements of the data. In particular, as an alternative to the standard *word by (link, word)* matrix, the framework allows the focus to be placed on links (which can be dependencies) and represent them in terms of the words they connect through a *link by (word, word)* matrix.

More recently, Levy and Goldberg (2014) modified Skip-gram to use contexts of the form *context-word's form/label*. The context-word can be either the head or a modifier of the target, with the first role causing the dependency to be marked as *inverse*. For example, if we take the sentence '*I like rain*':

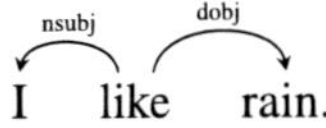

for *rain* we obtain *like/dobj*$^{-1}$ context, marked with $^{-1}$ to reflect the relation's inverse nature.

One weaker side of this model is that it does not directly capture how the dependency type affects the relation between the head and the dependent. For instance, during training it does not recognise that the *nsubj* dependency in both sentences

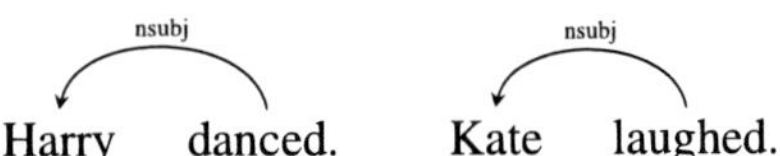

is in fact a relation of the very same type and cannot make use of the available subjecthood information – a good indicator of words' agentivity or animacy. In fact, it does not provide any mechanisms for indicating that the contexts *danced/nsubj*$^{-1}$ and *laughed/nsubj*$^{-1}$ have anything in common, apart from the fact that they will likely be contexts of similar words. Naturally, the latter is strongly informative in its own right, but associating meaning with specific types of dependencies could further improve the model's performance. One benefit of such a solution is the increased informativeness of rare context-words in cases when they appear in common relations.

Another disadvantage of Levy and Goldberg (2014)'s context creation is that it intensifies data sparsity issues. Many of the fine-grained contexts are likely to be relatively uncommon, and thus less informative. The rarest are excluded from V^C, which potentially leads to the loss of relevant information. In particular, this problem applies to when the model is trained on smaller corpora. The model's extensive V^C also means it cannot be extended to handle chains of dependencies, as it would be infeasible to additionally incorporate further contexts, such as *I/dobj*$^{-1}$*/nsubj*. This limits the model to using a small number of contexts per target, since a word typically participates in few relations.

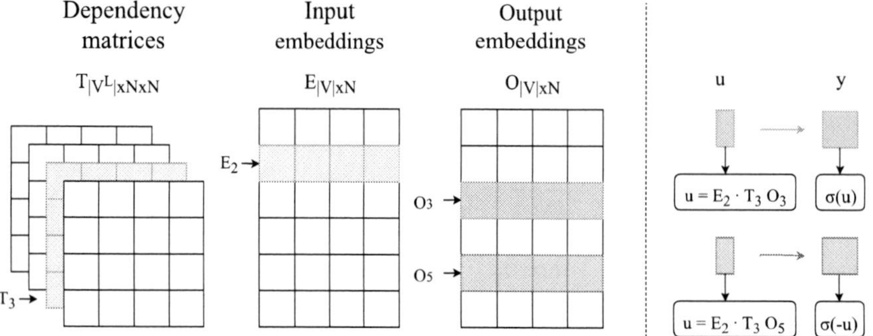

Figure 2: A representation of our model displaying its parameters (left) and how $P(C = 1|V_2, V_3, V_3^L)$ and $1 - P(C = 1|V_2, V_5, V_3^L)$ are calculated for real and negative contexts, respectively.

3   Dependency-matrix model

In the *dependency-matrix* (DM) model each type of dependency is associated with its own meaning representation – a matrix, which embodies the characteristics of words it typically links. The target and context-words are as in the original Skip-gram, drawn from the same vocabulary and represented as vectors of equal dimensions. The difference lies in how we define u from Eq. 1. It is no longer the dot product of target and context-word vectors, but the dot product of the target-word vector and the *context-vector*, with the latter being the result of multiplying the *context dependency-matrix* by the *context-word vector*, where the dependency-matrix is a representation of the relation linking the target to its context. An important feature of the model is its inherent ability to represent chains of dependency relations – it can be easily extended to handle contexts coming from further dependencies of the target by multiplying the context-word vector by a number of matrices, as further explained in Section 4.2.

The dependency-matrices modify meanings captured in the context-word vectors. In this behaviour, they are similar to representations of relational words, such as verbs or adjectives, in Compositional Semantic Models based on tensor products. For instance, Baroni and Zamparelli (2010) represent adjectives as matrices that enhance information encoded in the noun vectors with adjective-specific characteristics. Another example is the model of Paperno et al. (2014) in which each relational word is associated with a vector encoding its core meaning and a number of matrices – one for each argument the word takes. The matrices act as linear maps on the corresponding arguments' vectors, altering those depending on the role they play with respect to the predicate. At its core, this role corresponds to the type of dependency linking these words. This is closely aligned with the approach taken in this work, with the main difference lying in the granularity of representations.

3.1   Training

The model's training objective closely resembles that of Skip-gram (Eq. 2).

$$\sum_{(V_t, V_c, V_d^L) \in D} \log \sigma(u) + \sum_{(V_t, V_c, V_d^L) \in D'} \log \sigma(-u) \tag{3}$$

As before, D is a set of all positive training examples and D' consists of those negatively sampled. The model is trained on triples (V_t, V_c, V_d^L), where V^L is the label vocabulary and d is an index to the label of the relation between V_t and V_c. Given that in the DM model the final context representations are products of two independent components: word-form vectors and dependency-matrices, we redefine u as

$$u = E_t \cdot T_d O_c \tag{4}$$

where $T \in \mathbb{R}^{|V^L| \times N \times N}$ is a third order tensor holding the matrices, while E and O, as before, hold the input and output-embeddings (see Figure 2).[2]

The following table gives an example of training triples obtained for the sentence *'I like rain'*. Note that, as in Levy and Goldberg (2014), we create two training examples for each dependency relation.

target (V_t)	context-word (V_c)	label (V_d^L)
I	like	$nsubj^{-1}$
like	I	$nsubj$
like	rain	$dobj$
rain	like	$dobj^{-1}$

It is important to note here that the incorporation of V_d^L does not influence the negative-sampling procedure. For each positive example the system samples m triples, which all share the same V_t and V_d^L as the original – the labels are not sampled.

4   Evaluation

We compared the performance of our model to that of Skip-gram (SG), Levy and Goldberg (2014)'s model (LG) and Skip-gram for which the contexts are retrieved from the target's syntactic relations but the labels are disregarded (SGdep). Our primary evaluation involved a number of standard word similarity datasets, as well as the RELPRON dataset (Rimell et al., 2016). In addition, we tested our model's performance on the task of differentiating between similarity and relatedness relations and evaluated it qualitatively, by manually inspecting the types of captured similarities. We also conduct experiments on three extrinsic tasks: dependency-parsing, chunking and part-of-speech tagging. Previous findings have shown the dependency embeddings are well suited for these tasks (Bansal et al., 2014; Melamud et al., 2016) so our primary objective here was to compare the performance of DM to that of LG.

All models were trained on the WikiWoods corpus (Flickinger et al., 2010), which contains a 2008 Wikipedia snapshot, counting approximately 1.3M articles. Throughout this work we used Universal Dependencies (Nivre et al., 2016; Schuster and Manning, 2016) with all training examples for the dependency models generated from WikiWoods parsed with the Stanford Neural Network Dependency parser (Chen and Manning, 2014). Because words typically participate in only a few relations, the number of training data instances obtained from the parses was a third of the number obtained for Skip-gram.

We tuned the embedding dimensionality for all tasks and the number of negative samples for RELPRON and word similarity. For the extrinsic tasks we experimented with dimensions 50, 100 and 200, while for RELPRON and word similarity we experimented with setting m to 5, 10 and 15, and considered dimensions of 50, 100, 200 and 300. In the case of word similarity we based the hyperparameter choice on the SimLex-999 results, as the similarity datasets do not provide standard development sets. In all training conditions we removed all tokens in the target and context vocabularies with frequencies less than 100. For Skip-gram, we used the dynamic window of size $n = 5$.

Following the original word2vec tool[3], we sampled the initial values of the input-embeddings from a uniform distribution over the range (-0.5, 0.5) and divided them by the embedding dimensionality. We initialised the output-embeddings with zeros and dependency-matrices as identity matrices. The models were trained in an online fashion using stochastic gradient updates, with the learning rate initially set to 0.025 and linearly decreased during training, based on the number of remaining training examples. All of the models shared the same code-base, to ensure reliable comparison.

---

[2]One can also view T_d as a bilinear map combining the elements of the input and the output-embedding vector spaces.
[3]https://code.google.com/archive/p/word2vec/

	DM	LG	SG	SGdep
SimLex-999	**0.423**	0.414	0.398	0.411
RW	**0.361**	0.324	0.285	0.323
SimVerb-3500	**0.301**	0.257	0.242	0.259
WS353 (sim)	**0.751**	0.730	0.732	0.742
WS353 (rel)	0.457	0.441	**0.532**	0.46
MEN	0.679	0.613	**0.728**	0.688

Table 1: Word similarity evaluation results, the values are Spearman's correlation coefficients.

4.1 Word Similarity Datasets

Word similarity evaluation is one of the most common methods of testing vector space semantic models. The similarity datasets consist of word-pairs associated with human-assigned similarity scores. The task is to measure how well the model's scores, obtained using the learned embeddings, correlate with the gold-standard. After the scores are computed for each pair, typically using the cosine similarity measure, the pairs are ranked by these values. This ranking is then compared to the gold-standard ranking using Spearman's rank correlation coefficient.

The datasets used for this evaluation included Agirre et al. (2009)'s relatedness and similarity splits of WordSim353 (WS353) (Finkelstein et al., 2001), MEN (Bruni et al., 2014) which consists of 3000 similar and related pairs, the Rare Word (RW) collection (Luong et al., 2013), incorporating 2034 pairs of infrequent and morphologically complex words, SimLex-999 (Hill et al., 2016) consisting of 999 similar word pairs and SimVerb-3500 (Gerz et al., 2016) which includes 3500 similar verb-only pairs.

The models performed best using 300 dimensional embeddings and 20 negative samples (apart from SG, which performed best with 15 samples). As reported in Table 1, DM outperformed LG on all benchmarks and SGdep on all *similarity* datasets. The latter demonstrates that the labels are a valuable information source and our model's superiority over LG should not be attributed solely to decreasing data sparsity. Despite being trained on three times less training examples than SG, DM and SGdep managed to beat SG on all datasets but MEN and WS353 (rel). Importantly, both of these datasets measure relatedness rather than similarity.

4.2 RELPRON

RELPRON was introduced by Rimell et al. (2016) as an evaluation dataset for semantic composition. It consists of term-property pairs, with each term matched to up to ten properties. Each property takes the form of a hypernym of the term, modified by a simple relative clause. For example, the term *dog* has the property *mammal that people walk*. The full dataset consists of 1087 properties and 138 terms, with a test set of 569 properties and 73 terms and a development set of 518 properties and 65 terms. The task is to determine matching properties for all terms. This is framed as an information retrieval task – for each term the properties are ranked according to their similarity to that term and the matching properties should have the highest ranks. The correctness of the rankings is assessed using Mean Average Precision (MAP). An alternative task is to determine the correct term for each property. Here, the evaluation measure becomes Mean Reciprocal Rank (MRR), as each property has only one matching term.

In RELPRON evaluation we sought to investigate the utility of the dependency context representations for semantic composition. Since each property contains the term's hypernym, it is easy to determine the relations between the term and the words in the property. For both MAP and MRR rankings, we constructed a vector for each property, and then used cosine similarity between term vectors and property vectors. We experimented with two approaches to constructing property vectors, both based on weighted vector addition, which Rimell et al. (2016) showed to perform well as a composition method, despite its simplicity. The first, *simple-sum* (SS), is the sum of the words' input-embeddings. The second, *enhanced-sum* (ES), makes use of the dependency structure.

	DM	LG	SG	SGdep
Development set				
MAP (SS)	0.390	0.354	**0.451**	0.418
MAP (ES)	0.472	0.426	0.485	**0.497**
MRR (SS)	0.525	0.489	**0.567**	0.523
MRR (ES)	0.612	0.592	**0.614**	0.587
Test set				
MAP (SS)	0.324	0.292	**0.436**	0.371
MAP (ES)	0.400	0.315	**0.475**	0.439
MRR (SS)	0.465	0.444	**0.549**	0.501
MRR (ES)	0.557	0.509	**0.574**	0.543

Table 2: Results of MAP and MRR evaluation on the test and development sets of RELPRON.

Simple-sum composition

Simple-sum composes a property representation by summing the input-embeddings of the agent a, verb v and patient p in a phrase[4]. The final similarity metric is the cosine between the resulting vector and the term's input-embedding:

$$cos(E_t,\ E_a + E_v + E_p)$$

Enhanced-sum composition

The motivation behind the enhanced-sum formula is to compose semantic representations of phrases based on a dependency graph, with a focus on one specific word – in this case, the head noun, which is the term's hypernym.

There are two ways that we can view the head noun: as a target word, or as a context. Viewing the head noun as a target word, the verb acts as a context, and the other noun acts as a *further* context. To represent the phrase, we therefore want to sum the head noun's input embedding, the verb's context embedding, and the other noun's further context embedding. This composed vector should be close to the term's input embedding.

Viewing the head noun as a context, the verb acts as the target word, and the other noun also acts as a context. To represent the phrase, we therefore want to sum the head noun's context embedding, the verb's input embedding, and the other noun's context embedding. This composed vector should be close to the term's context embedding.

Because of these two ways that we can view the head noun, in all of the following formulae, there are two cosines. The exact formulae differ across the models, as each model represents contexts differently. For the dependency models, the formulae also depend on the semantic role of the head noun (agent or patient), as it determines which dependency-matrices are used. Below, we present the formulae for the case where the hypernym is the agent, as in *fuel: material that supplies energy*. The case where the hypernym is the patient is analogous, but with different labels for the dependencies.

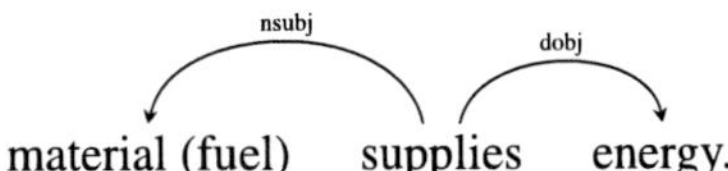

---

[4]We ignore the relative pronoun in the property representation as its contribution to semantics in RELPRON is indicating semantic dependencies between content words. In fact, in many relative clauses, there is a semantically equivalent 'bare relative' (Sag, 1997). E.g. 'mammal that people walk' has meaning equivalent to 'mammal people walk'. In addition, adding a vector for "that" would result in applying exactly the same semantic shift to every property and would not affect their ranking.

For Skip-gram and SGdep, the dependency labels are not used. There is no way to represent a further context (a path of multiple dependencies) except as a normal context, so the enhanced-sum uses the following (note O_p for the further context p):

$$cos(E_t, \ E_a + O_v + O_p)$$
$$+ \ cos(O_t, \ O_a + E_v + O_p)$$

For LG, the context word and dependency are combined. There is no way to represent a further context. Unlike for Skip-gram, it would be problematic to use $O_{p/dobj}$, because the head noun would never have been observed with a *dobj* context during training. We instead use the input embedding E_p:

$$cos(E_t, \ E_a + O_{v/nsubj^{-1}} + E_p)$$
$$+ \ cos(O_{t/nsubj}, \ O_{a/nsubj} + E_v + O_{p/dobj})$$

For DM, we have a principled way to represent the further context, through the multiplication of two dependency matrices. The input embedding E_p is mapped by $T^T_{dobj^{-1}}$ to the output embedding space, and then mapped by $T_{nsubj^{-1}}$ to the input embedding space.[5] This composition method (multiplying dependency matrices, and summing over words) can be applied to any possible dependency graph:

$$cos(E_t, \ E_a + T_{nsubj^{-1}}O_v + T_{nsubj^{-1}}T^T_{dobj^{-1}}E_p)$$
$$+ \ cos(T_{nsubj}O_t, \ T_{nsubj}O_a + E_v + T_{dobj}O_p)$$

For RELPRON evaluation, DM and SGdep performed best using 300 dimensional embeddings and *m*, the number of negative samples, set to 20. SG used 300 dimensions and *m=15*, while LG 200 dimensions and *m=5*. The results in Table 2 demonstrate that the DM model is once again superior to LG, outperforming the latter on both MAP and MRR evaluation. Overall, Skip-gram is the best performing model. As discussed by Emerson and Copestake (2017), models capturing relatedness can perform well on RELPRON, as they directly recognise the association between the term and the other argument of the verb (*fuel* and *energy* from the previous example).

All models benefit from ES, which proves our proposed composition method is viable. Notably, the enriched similarity metric is particularly beneficial for DM, which experiences the highest performance increase: on the development set DM's MAP (ES) and MRR (ES) scores are competitive to that of SG. This demonstrates the information encoded in DM's dependency-enhanced contexts is valuable for this task and the proposed representations of further contexts work well. Training the model on longer dependency paths could further increase its performance, but we leave this for future work.

The general performance drop on the test set, also observed by Emerson and Copestake (2017) and Rimell et al. (2016), could be attributed to a number of factors, including the test set being $\sim$10% larger than the development set and containing more *generic* properties, ranked highly by many terms. For example, in DM evaluation it contained 26 properties which appeared in the top 15 ranking of 7 or more terms (out of 73). In comparison, the development set had only 9 such properties.

4.3 Similarity vs Relatedness

To test the model's ability to distinguish between *similarity* and *relatedness* relations we evaluated it on the task of ranking similar word-pairs above related ones. For this evaluation, following Levy and Goldberg (2014), we incorporated WS353 and Chiarello et al. (1990)'s dataset that Turney (2012) used for differentiating between functional and domain similarities. For both datasets we plotted precision-recall curves based on the rankings and calculated the AUC values. In the case of WS353, we disregarded the pairs that appear in both similarity and relatedness splits, which constituted the majority of pairs with scores equal or lower than 5 (out of 10). Figure 3 demonstrates that all dependency models are superior to SG on this task and there is not much difference in their performance.

---

[5]More precisely, the model is trained to maximise $E_p \cdot T_{dobj^{-1}}O_v$, so we expect $T^T_{dobj^{-1}}E_p$ to be close to O_v. The model is also trained to maximise $E_a \cdot T_{nsubj^{-1}}O_v$, so we expect $T_{nsubj^{-1}}O_v$ to be close to E_a. Combining these two results, we expect $T_{nsubj^{-1}}T^T_{dobj^{-1}}E_p$ to be close to E_a.

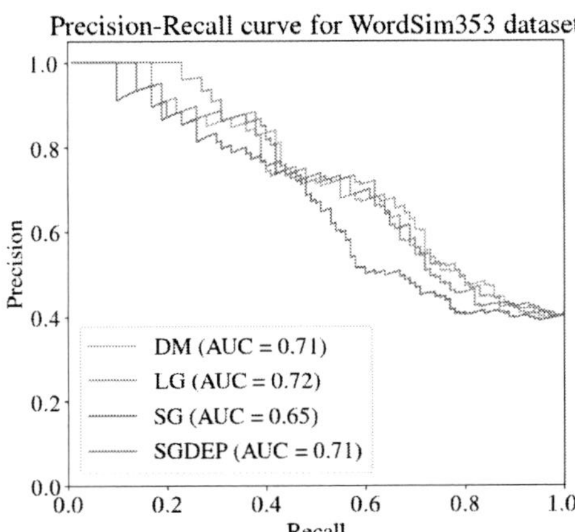
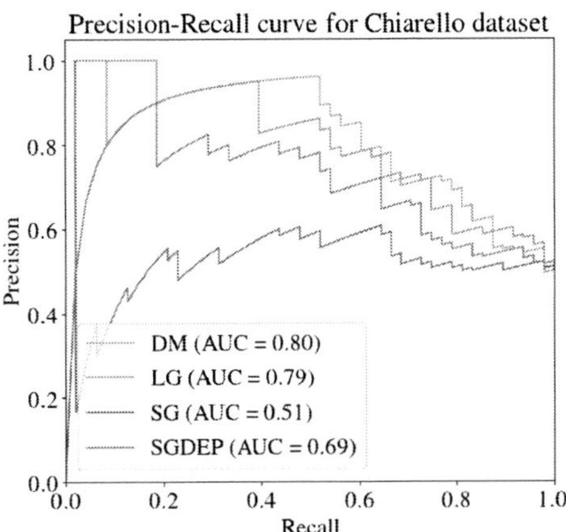

Figure 3: Precision-recall curves showing the results on ranking similar pairs above the related ones.

	DM	LG	SG	SGdep
dolphin	whale, shark, sailfish, porpoise	porpoise, giraffe, seahorse, orca	bottlenose, tursiops, stenella, delphis	whale, seahorse, shark, porpoise
voldemort	hordak, soth, sidious, ganondorf	saruman, darkseid, hordak, melkor	dumbledore, horcrux, hagrid, dementors	melkor, xykon, hordak, ganondorf
abba	sizzla, tvxq, mecano, cascada	roxette, a-ha, t.a.t.u., n.w.a.	agnetha, fältskog, lyngstad, eban	roxette, a-ha, n.w.a, tider
cycling	swimming, skiing, speedskating, motorcycling	bicycling, biking, yachting, wakeboarding	bicycling, cyclo-cross, bicycle, biking	biking, motorcycling, luge, snowboarding

Table 3: Examples of word similarities learned by the models.

4.4 Qualitative Evaluation

To inspect the types of similarities captured by the models we made a selection of four words from the vocabulary and analysed their closest neighbours according to each model. The examples presented in Table 3 confirm Levy and Goldberg (2014)'s findings, with SG capturing both similarity and relatedness and the dependency models demonstrating a bias towards similarity. Good examples of that are the neighbours of *abba* or *voldemort*. For the first SG selected words such as *agnetha* or *lyngstad* – the names of members of the Swedish pop group ABBA. The dependency models, on the other hand, associated *abba* with other music bands, such as A-ha, Roxette or Sizzla. For *voldemort*, a villain from the Harry Potter series, the dependency models considered other fictional villains as most similar, while SG returned mostly names of characters from the books.

4.5 Dependency Parsing

In this experiment we used the input-embeddings of DM, LG and SG to initialise word representations of the Stanford Neural Network Dependency parser (Chen and Manning, 2014). The parser was trained and tested on the English Penn Treebank; sections 2–21 of WSJ were used for training, section 22 for development, while section 23 was reserved for testing. We trained the model for 20000 iterations using the default hyperparameters[6]. The embeddings were fine-tuned to the task during training. In addition to initialising the parser with input-embeddings, for the DM model using 50 dimensions we experimented with concatenations of the input and output-embeddings. We refer to this setting as DMio. Note that this could not be done for LG, as it only provides a single representation for each word.

DM and SG performed best with 100 dimensions, while LG used 50. Table 4 presents the results

---

[6]https://nlp.stanford.edu/software/nndep.shtml

	DM	LG	SG	DMio
Dependency Parsing				
UAS	**91.49**	91.40	91.33	**92.01**
LAS	**90.02**	89.99	89.82	**90.66**
POS Tagging (accuracy)				
tuned	95.58	**95.69**	95.53	**95.69**
fixed	95.25	**95.28**	94.30	94.71
Chunking (accuracy)				
tuned	92.66	**93.11**	92.68	92.84
fixed	**92.45**	92.06	92.28	**92.57**

Table 4: Results of the dependency parsing, part-of-speech tagging and chunking evaluation.

achieved by the models measured with the unlabeled (UAS) and labeled attachment scores (LAS). Although all models performed well on this task, DM proved to be the best input-embedding initialisation. DMio performed overall best, demonstrating that utilising information encoded in the output-embeddings can be more beneficial than simply increasing the dimensionality of the embeddings.

4.6   Part-of-speech Tagging

For the POS tagging we made use of the publicly available word embedding evaluation framework, *VecEval* (Nayak et al., 2016). VecEval's word-labelling model resembles the one introduced by Collobert et al. (2011). First, it constructs the representation of the token's context by concatenating embeddings of the surrounding words and then passes it through two neural network layers, followed by a softmax classifier. We trained and tested this model using the same WSJ splits used for the dependency parsing task. We initialised the model with the embeddings of DM, LG and SG and experimented with two settings: one that allows fine-tuning the embeddings to the task through backpropagation (*tuned*) and one that keeps the embeddings fixed (*fixed*). For POS tagging DM and SG performed best with the same embedding dimensions as for the dependency parsing, while best LG model used 100 dimensions. Table 4 demonstrates that in the *tuned* setting all models achieve comparable performance, while in the *fixed* setting, both dependency models outperform SG, with LG reaching overall best performance.

4.7   Chunking

We evaluated SG, DM and LG on the chunking CoNLL'00 shared task (Tjong Kim Sang and Buchholz, 2000), which uses WSJ sections 15–18 for training and section 20 for testing. Similar to POS tagging, we employed the *VecEval*'s model based on that of Collobert et al. (2011) and experimented with *fixed* and *tuned* settings. The best performing models followed the same hyperparameter setting as for POS tagging. The results presented in Table 4 show that in the *tuned* setting LG reaches the best performance, while in the *fixed* setting, which allows us to investigate information inherently present in the embeddings, DM outperforms the other models.

5   Conclusion

We introduced the dependency-matrix model (DM) – a novel Skip-gram-based DSM that represents words' contexts as products of dependency-label matrices and context-word vectors, both of which are independent parameters of the model. Such handling of the labels allows DM to fully exploit the information encoded in the word-context relations and provides a straightforward way to handle further contexts of a word by representing chains of dependencies as products of matrices – one for each dependency in a chain. Our model proved to be superior or on par with Levy and Goldberg (2014)'s model, an alternative DSM incorporating the labels, across all evaluation benchmarks. It was also the overall best performing model on word similarity and dependency parsing evaluation.

References

Agirre, E., E. Alfonseca, K. Hall, J. Kravalova, M. Pas, and A. Soroa (2009). A study on similarity and relatedness using distributional and WordNet-based approaches. *Human Language Technologies: The 2009 Annual Conference of the North American Chapter of the ACL* (June), 19–27.

Bansal, M., K. Gimpel, and K. Livescu (2014). Tailoring continuous word representations for dependency parsing. In *Proceedings of the 52nd Annual Meeting of the Association for Computational Linguistics (Volume 2: Short Papers)*, pp. 809–815. Association for Computational Linguistics.

Baroni, M. and A. Lenci (2010). Distributional memory: A general framework for corpus-based semantics. *Computational Linguistics 36*(4), 673–721.

Baroni, M. and R. Zamparelli (2010). Nouns are vectors, adjectives are matrices: Representing adjective-noun constructions in semantic space. In *Proceedings of the 2010 Conference on Empirical Methods in Natural Language Processing*, pp. 1183–1193. Association for Computational Linguistics.

Bengio, Y., R. Ducharme, P. Vincent, and C. Jauvin (2003). A neural probabilistic language model. *Journal of machine learning research 3*(Feb), 1137–1155.

Bruni, E., N.-K. Tran, and M. Baroni (2014). Multimodal distributional semantics. *Journal of Artificial Intelligence Research 49*, 1–47.

Chen, D. and C. D. Manning (2014). A fast and accurate dependency parser using neural networks. In *Proceedings of the 2014 Con- ference on Empirical Methods in Natural Lan- guage Processing (EMNLP)*, pp. 740–750.

Chiarello, C., C. Burgess, L. Richards, and A. Pollock (1990). Semantic and associative priming in the cerebral hemispheres: Some words do, some words don't... sometimes, some places. *Brain and language 38*(1), 75–104.

Collobert, R., J. Weston, L. Bottou, M. Karlen, K. Kavukcuoglu, and P. Kuksa (2011). Natural language processing (almost) from scratch. *Journal of Machine Learning Research 12*(Aug), 2493–2537.

Emerson, G. and A. Copestake (2017). Semantic composition via probabilistic model theory. In *Proceedings of the 12th International Conference on Computational Semantics (IWCS)*.

Finkelstein, L., E. Gabrilovich, Y. Matias, E. Rivlin, Z. Solan, G. Wolfman, and E. Ruppin (2001). Placing search in context: The concept revisited. In *Proceedings of the 10th international conference on World Wide Web*, pp. 406–414. ACM.

Flickinger, D., S. Oepen, and G. Ytrestøl (2010). WikiWoods: Syntacto-semantic annotation for English Wikipedia. *7th International Conference on Language Resources and Evaluation*.

Gerz, D., I. Vulić, F. Hill, R. Reichart, and A. Korhonen (2016). SimVerb-3500: A large-scale evaluation set of verb similarity. In *EMNLP*.

Goldberg, Y. and O. Levy (2014). word2vec explained: Deriving Mikolov et al.'s negative-sampling word-embedding method. *arXiv preprint arXiv:1402.3722*.

Grefenstette, G. (1994). *Explorations in Automatic Thesaurus Discovery*. Norwell, MA, USA: Kluwer Academic Publishers.

Harris, Z. S. (1954). Distributional structure. *Word 10*(2-3), 146–162.

Hill, F., R. Reichart, and A. Korhonen (2016). Simlex-999: Evaluating semantic models with (genuine) similarity estimation. *Computational Linguistics*.

Levy, O. and Y. Goldberg (2014). Dependency-based word embeddings. In *Proceedings of the 52nd Annual Meeting of the Association for Computational Linguistics*, Volume 2, pp. 302–308.

Lin, D. (1998). Automatic retrieval and clustering of similar words. In *Proceedings of the 17th international conference on Computational linguistics-Volume 2*, pp. 768–774. Association for Computational Linguistics.

Luong, T., R. Socher, and C. D. Manning (2013). Better word representations with recursive neural networks for morphology. In *CoNLL*, pp. 104–113.

Melamud, O., D. McClosky, S. V. Patwardhan, and M. Bansal (2016). The role of context types and dimensionality in learning word embeddings. In *HLT-NAACL*.

Mikolov, T., K. Chen, G. Corrado, and J. Dean (2013). Efficient estimation of word representations in vector space. *ICLR Workshop*.

Mikolov, T., I. Sutskever, K. Chen, G. S. Corrado, and J. Dean (2013). Distributed representations of words and phrases and their compositionality. pp. 3111–3119.

Nayak, N., G. Angeli, and C. D. Manning (2016). Evaluating word embeddings using a representative suite of practical tasks. In *Proceedings of the 1st Workshop on Evaluating Vector-Space Representations for NLP*, pp. 19–23.

Nivre, J., M.-C. de Marneffe, F. Ginter, Y. Goldberg, J. Hajic, C. D. Manning, R. McDonald, S. Petrov, S. Pyysalo, N. Silveira, R. Tsarfaty, and D. Zeman (2016). Universal dependencies v1: A multilingual treebank collection. In *Proceedings of the Tenth International Conference on Language Resources and Evaluation (LREC 2016)*. European Language Resources Association (ELRA).

Padó, S. and M. Lapata (2007). Dependency-based construction of semantic space models. *Computational Linguistics 33*(2), 161–199.

Paperno, D., N. The Pham, and M. Baroni (2014). A practical and linguistically-motivated approach to compositional distributional semantics. In *Proceedings of the 52nd Annual Meeting of the Association for Computational Linguistics*, pp. 90–99. Association for Computational Linguistics.

Rimell, L., J. Maillard, T. Polajnar, and S. Clark (2016). RELPRON: A relative clause evaluation data set for compositional distributional semantics. *Computational Linguistics 42*(4), 661–701.

Sag, I. A. (1997). English relative clause constructions. *Journal of linguistics 33*(2), 431–483.

Schuster, S. and C. D. Manning (2016). Enhanced English universal dependencies: An improved representation for natural language understanding tasks.

Tjong Kim Sang, E. F. and S. Buchholz (2000). Introduction to the conll-2000 shared task: Chunking. In *Proceedings of the 2Nd Workshop on Learning Language in Logic and the 4th Conference on Computational Natural Language Learning - Volume 7*, ConLL '00, pp. 127–132. Association for Computational Linguistics.

Turney, P. D. (2012). Domain and function: A dual-space model of semantic relations and compositions. *Journal of Artificial Intelligence Research 44*, 533–585.

Temporal and Aspectual Entailment

Thomas Kober
University of Edinburgh
tkober@inf.ed.ac.uk

Sander Bijl de Vroe
University of Edinburgh
sbdv@ed.ac.uk

Mark Steedman
University of Edinburgh
steedman@inf.ed.ac.uk

Abstract

Inferences regarding *Jane's arrival in London* from predications such as *Jane is going to London* or *Jane has gone to London* depend on *tense* and *aspect* of the predications. Tense determines the temporal location of the predication in the past, present or future of the time of utterance. The aspectual auxiliaries on the other hand specify the internal constituency of the event, i.e. whether the event of *going to London* is completed and whether its consequences hold at that time or not.

While tense and aspect are among the most important factors for determining natural language inference, there has been very little work to show whether modern NLP models capture these semantic concepts. In this paper we propose a novel entailment dataset and analyse the ability of a range of recently proposed NLP models to perform inference on temporal predications. We show that the models encode a substantial amount of morphosyntactic information relating to tense and aspect, but fail to model inferences that require reasoning with these semantic properties.

1 Introduction

Tense and aspect are two of the main contributors to the semantics of a proposition, describing the temporal location of a predication and its internal constituency, thereby considerably influencing the entailment relations it licenses. For example, while *arrive in LOC* $\models$ *be in LOC* is generally considered a valid entailment rule, the case is complicated when different tenses and aspectual auxiliaries[1] of a given verb are considered as sentences (1) and (2) illustrate.

(1) Jane *has arrived* in London.

$\models$ Jane *is* in London now.

(2) Jane *will arrive* in London.

$\not\models$ Jane *is* in London now.

Understanding the difference between an event that has happened and whose consequences hold at the present moment, and an event that is currently happening or will happen in the future, is crucial for answering questions such as *Where is Jane?* or *Is Jane in London now?* Inferring the consequences of events is important for understanding the relation between entities in the world. For example, if we read that *Lady Catherine has bought Longbourn estate*, the inference that the acquisition is *completed*, and that the resulting consequence is that Lady Catherine now *owns* Longbourn estate, is paramount for keeping knowledge bases up-to-date.

In this paper we propose a novel entailment dataset that requires models to correctly determine the internal and external temporal structure of predications when performing natural language inference. To the best of our knowledge, this is the first dataset that is primarily focused on assessing natural language inference between temporally and aspectually modified predications.

---

[1]For brevity we will refer to predications with different tenses and aspectual auxiliaries as *temporal predications*.

As a first evaluation on our new dataset we compare to what extent five distributional embedding models, word2vec (Mikolov et al., 2013), Anchored Packed Trees (Weir et al., 2016), fastText (Bojanowski et al., 2017), ELMo (Peters et al., 2018), and BERT (Devlin et al., 2018), and two bi-directional LSTM (biLSTM) encoders, pre-trained on SNLI (Bowman et al., 2015) and DNC (Poliak et al., 2018), respectively, are able to perform natural language inference on temporal predications. In our evaluation, we refrain from fine-tuning any of the models as our goal is to assess to what extent tense and aspect are captured in these models *per se*. As a pre-requisite diagnostic task for natural language inference between temporal predications we analysed whether the models encode the morphosyntax of tense and aspect and found that they capture a considerable amount of morphosyntactic information in their respective embedding spaces. However, neither of the models outperforms a majority class baseline on our proposed dataset due to their reliance on contextual similarity for performing inference, suggesting that models based on distributional semantics struggle with the more latent nature of tense and aspect. Our contributions in this paper are as follows:

- We assess the extent to which the models in our evaluation encode information about the agreement between an inflected verb and its aspectual auxiliary, and whether a translation operation between different tenses can be learnt from the embedding spaces.

- We propose a novel entailment dataset that requires models to perform inference with temporal predications, and evaluate the five embedding models and two pre-trained biLSTM encoders.

- We analyse the performance of the models and show that their reliance on contextual similarity is problematic for correctly modelling natural language inference governed by tense and aspect.

2 Tense, Aspect and Entailment

Tense is a grammatical category which is encoded in the morphology of the verb in English (e.g. past *loved* vs. non-past *loves*). It establishes a point of reference that allows the temporal organisation of events in a discourse. In English, tense interacts with aspectual auxiliaries such as the verbs *be* or *have* that influence the internal constituency of a predication, and determine whether an event is completed or ongoing. Tense and aspect therefore control the internal and external temporal structure of an event and govern the inferences that a predication licenses (Reichenbach, 1947; Dahl, 1985; Steedman, 1997). There is evidence that such morphology is represented in distributional embeddings (Mitchell and Steedman, 2015; Vylomova et al., 2016). In this paper we are concerned with perfect and progressive aspect, but do not focus on any other types of aspect such as the *Aktionsart* of a predication (Vendler, 1957), which we leave to future work.

2.1 The Interaction between Temporality and Entailment

Perfect aspect (typically) describes events as a completed whole, and licenses inferences regarding the consequences of that event. The use of different tenses and aspects for past events influences their relevance to the present moment and thereby their entailment behaviour. For example, the consequences of an event in the present perfect hold at the time of utterance, whereas events in the simple past or the past perfect do not (Comrie, 1985; Moens and Steedman, 1988; Depraetere, 1998; Katz, 2003). This is shown in sentences (3) and (4), where only sentence (3) licenses the inference of Elizabeth being in Meryton *now*.

(3) Elizabeth *has gone* to Meryton.

   $\models$ Elizabeth *is* in Meryton now.

(4) Elizabeth *went / had gone* to Meryton.

   $\not\models$ Elizabeth *is* in Meryton now.

This property can be explained through a Reichenbachian view of the present perfect, where the point of reference coincides with the point of speech, thereby indicating its current relevance (Reichenbach,

1947). On the other hand, events in the past simple or the past perfect license inferences for consequent states in the past, as sentence (5) shows.

(5) Elizabeth *went* / *had gone* to Meryton.

$\models$ Elizabeth *was* in Meryton.

(6) Mary *is going* to Netherfield now.

$\not\models$ Mary *has arrived* / *is* in Netherfield.

Progressive aspect describes ongoing events and therefore does not license inferences regarding their consequences as sentence (6) shows. It furthermore gives rise to the imperfective paradox (Dowty, 1979), which only seems to license inferences for non-culminated processes (Moens and Steedman, 1988), as sentences (7) and (8) show.

(7) Catherine *was walking* in the woods.

$\models$ Catherine *walked* in the woods.

(8) Jane *was reaching* London.

$\not\models$ Jane *reached* / *was in* London.

The modal future introduces an event whose realisation is uncertain, therefore any inferences about its outcome are only licensed if common-sense knowledge suggests that this is almost always the course of events as sentence (9) shows.

(9) Charles *will meet* with Jane.

$\models$ Charles *will see* Jane.

The correct treatment of tense and aspect in a predication is crucial for inferring the consequences it licenses, which is important for answering questions about a given paragraph, or creating and updating knowledge bases.

3 Models

We analyse five distributional embedding models and two pre-trained biLSTM sentence encoders for their ability to perform inference on temporal predications. Our choice of models is motivated by the observation that modelling entailment between temporal predications requires a bespoke representation of the inflected verb in the context of the given aspectual auxiliary and its arguments.

word2vec. We evaluate the ability of `word2vec` representations for performing inference with temporal predications. Contextualisation[2] can be achieved by averaging two word vectors, which has been shown to be a strong baseline for a range of problems (Iyyer et al., 2015; Wieting et al., 2016). Notably, adding or averaging word vectors approximates the intersection of their feature spaces (Tian et al., 2017).

APTs. Anchored Packed Trees are a recently proposed vector space model that take distributional composition to be a process of lexeme contextualisation. APTs are based on a higher-order dependency-typed structure that gives rise to a weighted, directed and labelled graph. Contextualisation is achieved through distributional composition, which requires aligning two lexemes according to their syntactic relation, and then merging the aligned representations. APTs are the only count-based (i.e. non-neural) model in our evaluation.

fastText. The `fastText` model represents each word as a sum of bag-of-character n-grams, thereby making better use of subword information and therefore — potentially — providing a better mechanism for encoding morphosyntactic relations. Contextualisation is achieved through averaging the respective word vectors in a phrase.

ELMo. ELMo is based on a deep bidirectional LSTM language model that creates multiple layers of representations for every token. Contextualised representations are obtained from the internal states of the LSTMs, where Peters et al. (2018) showed that lower levels of the architecture capture syntactic characteristics, and higher-levels capture semantic characteristics of words.

---

[2]We refer to expressing the meaning of a word in its context as *contextualisation*.

BERT. BERT uses multi-headed bi-directional self-attention and is based on the Transformer architecture (Vaswani et al., 2017). Devlin et al. (2018) observed that sequential language model architectures are limited by the unidirectionality of the models. Therefore they proposed a novel training objective that jointly conditions on left and right context in all layers. They showed that their training regime results in substantial gains over serial language model-based architectures on numerous NLP tasks.

Pre-trained biLSTM. For our new entailment dataset, we pre-trained two bi-directional LSTM (Hochreiter and Schmidhuber, 1997) sentence encoders on SNLI (Bowman et al., 2015) and DNC (Poliak et al., 2018), representing two recently released large-scale entailment datasets. Our choice of biLSTMs was motivated by their strong performance in recent studies (Balazs et al., 2017; Conneau et al., 2017).

`Word2vec`, APTs and `fastText` follow the *one representation per word* paradigm (Kober et al., 2017), where every lexeme is represented by one vector, and contextualisation is typically achieved through distributional composition. ELMo, BERT and the pre-trained biLSTMs, on the other hand ,create context-sensitive representations on the token level. This results in different representations for the same word, depending on its current context.

4 Experiments

We created two experiments to assess the extent of morphosyntactic information relating to tense and aspect that is encoded in the respective embedding spaces. Subsequently we propose a novel entailment dataset and evaluate the capability of the embedding models and the pre-trained biLSTMs to perform inference on temporal predications. All our resources are available from `https://github.com/tttthomasssss/iwcs2019`.

4.1 Auxiliary-Verb Agreement

The first experiment evaluates whether the models are able to capture the agreement between an inflected verb and its corresponding aspectual auxiliary. For example, the models should be able to determine that *will visit* represents a correct combination whereas *will visiting* does not. We consider capturing the morphosyntactic interplay between an inflected verb and its aspectual auxiliary a pre-requisite for adequately modelling the semantics of tense and aspect.

We cast the problem as a classification task with the goal of distinguishing correct auxiliary-verb pairs from incorrect ones with a diagnostic classifier. This methodology is similar to the approach of Linzen et al. (2016) who assessed the ability of LSTMs to learn number agreement in English subject-verb phrases. For the dataset, we extracted verbs from the One Billion Word Benchmark (OBWB) (Chelba et al., 2013) where each inflected verb form occurred at least 50 times. We then paired the inflected verb forms with their corresponding auxiliaries to form positive pairs, and subsequently paired each of the different inflected verb forms with all incorrect auxiliaries to build the negative pairs. We filtered the negative pairs for plausible combinations such as *is eaten* by removing valid passive constructions and any invalid combination that occurred at least 5 times in the OBWB corpus. The final dataset consists of almost $36k$ auxiliary-verb combinations with a positive : negative class distribution of 38 : 62.

4.2 Translation Operation

In the second experiment we assess whether it is possible to learn a translation operation between different tenses in the embedding space. We consider learning a translation operation in two ways: firstly a simple vector offset on the basis of the averaged difference between inflected verbs with their auxiliaries and their respective lemmas. Secondly, we train a feedforward neural network to project the infinitive representation of a verb to one of its inflected forms. The goal for both approaches is then to generate an unseen inflected verb form from a given unseen lemma.

The averaged offset translation is shown in Equation 1, where the offset o_t is calculated on the basis of a set of seed verbs S of size n, and vector representations x_t and x_ℓ of the inflected form, or contextualised form if the tense requires an auxiliary, and lemma form of the verb x, respectively. At prediction time, we are trying to create x'_t by adding the offset o_t to the lemma x'_ℓ (where $x' \notin S$). Equation 2 shows the setup where we use a neural network to learn a translation matrix from infinitive forms to inflected forms, where f is a tense-specific neural network with a single hidden layer, that takes an unseen lemma representation x'_ℓ as input and generates an inflected form x'_t, and where Θ_t represent the learnable parameters of the network.

$$o_t = \frac{1}{n} \sum_{x \in S} x_t - x_\ell \qquad (1) \qquad\qquad x'_t = f(x'_\ell; \Theta_t) \qquad (2)$$

We subsequently evaluate whether the correctly inflected verb is in the nearest neighbour list of the generated verb. The inflected verb generation setup is inspired by Bolukbasi et al. (2016) and Shoemark et al. (2017), who used a similar method in their respective works. For the dataset, we extracted verbs from the OBWB corpus where each inflected verb form occurred at least 50 times, resulting in $\approx 2.8k$ verbs per tense.

4.3 Entailment with Temporal Predications

Lastly, we propose **TEA** — the Temporal Entailment Assessment dataset. **TEA** contains pairs of short sentences with the same argument structure that differ in tense and aspect of the main verb, and follows a binary label annotation scheme (*entailment* vs. *non-entailment*). Example sentences from **TEA** are shown in Table 1. The absence and infeasibility of creating a lexical resource for consequent state

John *is visiting* London.	$\models$	John *has arrived* in London.
John *will visit* London.	$\not\models$	John *has arrived* in London.
John *is visiting* London.	$\not\models$	John *has left* London.
John *is visiting* London.	$\models$	John *will leave* London.
George *has acquired* the house.	$\models$	George *owns* the house.
George *is acquiring* the house.	$\not\models$	George *owns* the house.

Table 1: Examples from **TEA**.

inference patterns creates the necessity for NLP systems to learn these rules from data. With **TEA**, we cast the problem of determining when a new consequent state is licensed by an event as a natural language inference task, thereby providing a first evaluation set for modern NLP models.

Data Collection. We sampled candidate pairs from the before-after category of VerbOcean (Chklovski and Pantel, 2004), the WordNet verb entailment graph (Fellbaum, 1998), the entailment datasets of Weisman et al. (2012) and Vulić et al. (2017), and the relation inference dataset of Levy and Dagan (2016). Subsequently, we manually filtered the list, and discarded candidate verb pairs without any temporal relation to each other. For each pair we chose nouns as arguments to form full sentences. The arguments further served the purpose of reducing ambiguity and avoiding habitual readings.

TEA covers entailments between an all-by-all combination of the present simple, present progressive, present perfect, past simple, past progressive, past perfect and the modal future, covering perfect and progressive aspect. The dataset contains 11138 sentence pairs with a class distribution of 22 : 78 (entailment : non-entailment). More detailed dataset statistics are presented in Appendix A.

Data Annotation. We interpreted entailment as common-sense inference (Dagan et al., 2006), and considered a positive entailment relation between two temporal predications if a human annotator would decide that sentence 2 is *most likely* true given sentence 1. We decided against a crowdsourced annotation of **TEA** as our aim was to maximise the consistency of fine-grained entailment decisions. Therefore, **TEA** was labelled by two annotators[3], where the first round of annotation resulted in just under 20% disagreement across the whole dataset. The relatively high level of disagreement suggests that even for annotators who (more or less) know what they are looking for, assessing whether an entailment holds between two temporal predications is a very challenging task.

---

[3]The first and second author of this paper.

Disagreements in **TEA** were resolved on a case-by-case basis and all sentence pairs with an initial disagreement have been resolved and included in the dataset. We found that with temporality involved, suddenly *everything* appeared to become uncertain. Hence we approached the disagreement resolution by first discussing which of several possible readings is the strongest, and whether that reading is sufficiently more likely than any other possible reading. Subsequently we discussed whether the strong reading is above the *almost always true* threshold.

Often, disagreements resulted from different assumptions regarding the ordering of the events' nuclei. For example, even if we accept that *buys* entails *chooses*, *will buy* does not necessarily entail *will choose*. The reason is that this pair is ambiguous between two readings, a "has-just-chosen-and-now-will-buy" reading on one hand, and a "will-choose-and-then-will-buy" reading on the other, which seem to be equally likely in the absence of any further context[4].

Even when ordering was clear, however, disagreements could arise over beliefs of when an utterance becomes licensed. Saying *will graduate*, for example, can be considered reasonable at any time, or only once *graduation* is sufficiently imminent and likely. In the latter case, *is studying* can be considered sufficiently likely to be an entailment, while in the former case the entailment is less clear[5]. Overall, world knowledge and intuition played into disagreements heavily, causing cases to fall just above or below the common-sense inference threshold depending on the annotator.

We identified a possible annotation artefact in **TEA** due to our decision to annotate the dataset sequentially rather than randomly. While this greatly reduced the cognitive load, we were confronted with possible contradictions between different tenses of entailed predicates (for example, a single event cannot happen in the past *and* the future). This initially led to more conservative annotations, since some pairs when viewed independently can sound very plausible. We tried to factor out this source of bias when resolving the disagreements, and are confident that the annotations in **TEA** are robust.

An interesting avenue for future work would be adding temporal adverbials to further reduce ambiguity for annotators — and to analyse whether models can handle them correctly. The addition of temporal adverbials might alleviate the temporal ordering ambiguity, as for example reading *will buy in 5 years* might help us conclude the ordering with *will choose*, since *choosing* is probably near *buying*.

5   Results and Analysis

For our experiments we used the publicly available versions of each embedding model. For the evaluation on **TEA**, we trained two biLSTMs on SNLI and DNC in addition to the embedding models, achieving 83% and 88% accuracy on the SNLI and DNC development sets, respectively. Appendix B lists further details for all models.

5.1   Auxiliary-Verb Agreement

For assessing whether the auxiliary-verb agreement can be detected with a diagnostic classifier, we built a binary classification task, using stratified J-K-fold cross-validation (Moss et al., 2018) and report averaged accuracy. We used the scikit-learn (Pedregosa et al., 2011) logistic regression classifier with default hyperparameter settings.

The results in Table 2 show that the representations of APTs and BERT are specific enough for a linear classifier to distinguish plausible from implausible combinations. The reason for the strong performance of APTs stems from its sparsity — plausible auxiliary-verb combinations result in representations with numerous non-zero entries, whereas implausible combinations rarely contain more than a handful of non-zero elements. While `word2vec` and `fastText` seem to capture the morphosyntactic relation between an auxiliary and an inflected verb to some extent, their performance is substantially worse than APTs and BERT. Somewhat surprisingly, the results for ELMo are worse than the majority class baseline for all auxiliaries. One possible reason for the comparatively weak performance of `word2vec`,

---

[4] In this case we decided that if *will buy* is true, the choosing didn't happen yet, so *will buy* $\models$ *will choose*.

[5] We decided *will graduate* $\models$ *is studying*.

Auxiliary	word2vec	APT	fastText	ELMo	BERT	Majority Class
is	0.65 (+/- 0.02)	0.88 (+/- 0.01)	0.67 (+/- 0.02)	0.52 (+/- 0.01)	**0.90** (+/- 0.01)	0.53
will	0.48 (+/- 0.01)	**0.94** (+/- 0.01)	0.58 (+/- 0.01)	0.63 (+/- 0.01)	0.89 (+/- 0.01)	0.67
has	0.84 (+/- 0.01)	**0.94** (+/- 0.00)	0.77 (+/- 0.01)	0.63 (+/- 0.01)	0.91 (+/- 0.01)	0.66
had	0.84 (+/- 0.01)	**0.95** (+/- 0.00)	0.78 (+/- 0.01)	0.62 (+/- 0.01)	0.93 (+/- 0.01)	0.66
was	0.72 (+/- 0.02)	0.86 (+/- 0.01)	0.74 (+/- 0.02)	0.52 (+/- 0.01)	**0.92** (+/- 0.01)	0.53
Average	0.71 (+/- 0.01)	**0.92** (+/- 0.00)	0.71 (+/- 0.01)	0.59 (+/- 0.00)	0.91 (+/- 0.00)	0.61

Table 2: Auxiliary-verb agreeement results. Results are averaged accuracies with standard deviations in brackets.

fastText and especially ELMo in comparison to BERT is the latter's more global training objective that does not rely on sequential input. For ELMo, we also tried running it with full sentence contexts for all auxiliary-verb combinations, which, however, did not lead to improved performance (results omitted).

5.2 Translation Operation

For obtaining an averaged vector offset, we randomly sampled a seed set of verb types from our dataset to learn an offset vector, and subsequently aimed to predict the inflected form for all remaining verb types in the dataset. We sampled 10 different seed sets of size 10 for our experiments[6].

For learning a translation operation with a neural network we used a simple feedforward architecture with a single hidden layer and a tanh activation function, using Adam with a learning rate of 0.01 to optimise the mean squared error between the generated inflected verb and the true inflected verb. Due to the neural network requiring more training data than the averaged vector offset approach, we evaluated the model using 10-fold cross-validation. For APTs we projected the explicit co-occurrence space down to 100 dimensions using SVD before feeding the representations to the neural network.

Performance for both approaches is reported in terms of *Mean Reciprocal Rank (MRR)*, averaged over the 10 randomly sampled seed sets and the 10 cross-validation folds, for the averaged offset vector and neural network approaches, respectively. For calculating MRR, the query space for retrieving an inflected verb, given its lemma and the computed translation operation, is based on all contextualised auxiliary-verb combinations, and all inflected forms of all verbs.

Creating translation operations in embedding space is primarily a word-type level task and thus potentially puts BERT and ELMo at a disadvantage as they produce representations on the token level. This is reflected in Figure 1, where both ELMo and BERT perform poorly in comparison to word2vec and fastText. APTs also exhibit weak performance on this task, with this time the sparsity of its high-dimensional representations being disadvantageous. Interestingly, performance generally dropped — except for word2vec — when moving from the simple vector offset approach to a neural network based translation operation, providing evidence that the morphosyntax of tense and aspect is well represented as a linear offset in the embedding space. One of the main reasons for the poor performance of ELMo

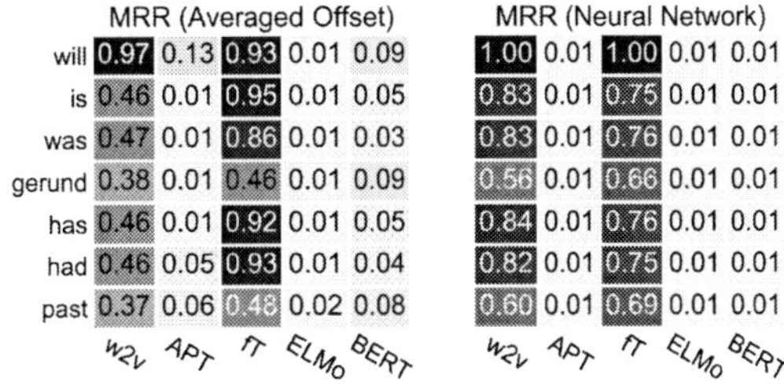

Figure 1: Translation operation results based on averaged MRR.

and BERT was that the obtained offset vectors and learnt translation matrices varied substantially across runs. Figure 2 shows the average cosine similarities (left) and average Euclidean distances (middle) between the computed offset vectors for each subtask across all 10 runs. Figure 2 furthermore shows the average Frobenius distances (right) between the learnt neural network translation matrices across all 10 folds. Figure 2 mirrors the general performance trend in Figure 1, with vector offsets obtained

---

[6]In preliminary experiments we found that a seed set of 5-10 verbs is sufficient.

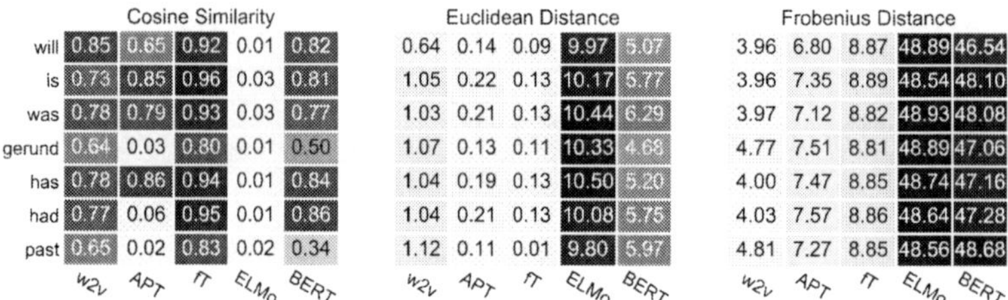

Figure 2: Average cosine similarities and Euclidean distances of averaged offset vectors and Frobenius distances of the learnt neural network weight matrices.

from `word2vec` and `fastText` having high average cosine similarity and low average Euclidean distance. Furthermore, the lower average Frobenius distance for `word2vec` is reflected in its improved performance in comparison to `fastText` whose translation matrices exhibit a larger average Frobenius distance. For ELMo in particular, the offset vectors and translation matrices differ considerably across experimental runs. The large average Frobenius distances for ELMo and BERT also suggest that the neural network struggled to find a good minimum during learning.

5.3 Entailment with Temporal Predications

The results in this section so far have shown that morphosyntactic information relating to tense and aspect is encoded in the different embedding spaces. In the following we use **TEA** to analyse whether these models are able to use that information for natural language inference. As our goal is to assess to what extent tense and aspect are captured by the models, we refrain from fine-tuning them on **TEA**.

For evaluation we measure precision and recall over varying thresholds and report performance in terms of average precision[7]. **TEA** can also serve as an additional evaluation set for sentence encoder models trained on large-scale natural language inference datasets such as SNLI or DNC, which themselves include very little temporal information in their respective test sets. We therefore additionally cast **TEA** as a binary classification task, and report accuracy and macro-averaged F1-score for the two pre-trained biLSTM models.

Table 3 shows the average precision scores for the models and the accuracy and F1-scores for the two pre-trained biLSTMs in comparison to a majority class baseline and a baseline predicting the majority class per tense pair. We used cosine as similarity measure for the embedding models and the softmax prediction scores for the biLSTMs. For APTs, we also tried the asymmetric inclusion score BInc (Szpektor and Dagan, 2008), however found cosine working better. We furthermore experimented with distributional inference (Kober et al., 2016), and found a small positive impact on recall but a slightly larger negative dip in precision, which overall led to slightly lower average precision scores. The results show

Model	Avg. Precision	Accuracy	F1-Score
word2vec	0.31	-	-
APT	0.28	-	-
fastText	0.30	-	-
ELMo	0.21	-	-
BERT	0.27	-	-
biLSTM-DNC	0.22	0.58	0.49
biLSTM-SNLI	0.21	0.51	0.47
Maj. class	0.22	0.78	0.44
Maj. class / tense pair	**0.35**	**0.80**	**0.66**

Table 3: **TEA** results. All model results are significantly worse at the $p < 0.01$ level w.r.t. the majority class / tense pair baseline, using a randomised bootstrap test (Efron and Tibshirani, 1994).

that neither of the models are able to outperform the majority class / tense baseline. This highlights that despite the use of short and simple sentences in the dataset, the latent nature of tense and aspect make **TEA** a very challenging problem.

---

[7] Also known as the area under the precision-recall curve.

In order to analyse the causes for the low performance across models, we calculated the false positive and false negative rates for different similarity threshold ranges for each of the models. Figure 3 shows that even for high thresholds, the neural embedding models frequently predict entailment when there isn't one, thereby producing a high rate of false positives (highlighted at the top of Figure 3). Conversely, a sparse model such as APTs, fails to predict entailment when there actually is one, resulting in a high rate of false negatives (highlighted at the bottom of Figure 3). Our results show that natural language

	w2v	APT	fT	BERT	ELMo	DNC	SNLI
FP -]1.00, 0.75]	0.16	0.00	0.40	0.11	0.01	0.18	0.28
FP -]0.75, 0.50]	0.72	0.00	0.78	0.52	0.05	0.26	0.42
FP -]0.50, 0.25]	0.78	0.01	0.78	0.65	0.28	0.32	0.51
FP -]0.25, 0.00]	0.78	0.06	0.78	0.66	0.50	0.43	0.63
FN -]1.00, 0.75]	0.15	0.22	0.09	0.18	0.21	0.17	0.15
FN -]0.75, 0.50]	0.01	0.22	0.00	0.06	0.20	0.14	0.11
FN -]0.50, 0.25]	0.00	0.21	0.00	0.03	0.14	0.13	0.08
FN -]0.25, 0.00]	0.00	0.18	0.00	0.03	0.08	0.10	0.04

Figure 3: False Positive (FP) and False Negative (FN) rates.

inference on temporal predications is a challenging problem, especially for distributional semantic approaches. One reason is that these models are primarily governed by contextual similarity which is a bad proxy for inference in the case of a dataset such as **TEA**. For example, if *Jane has arrived in London*, then she *was going to London* at some earlier point, but it is not the case that she currently *is going to London*. Furthermore, when she *has arrived in London*, she *is visiting London* at the moment, and *will leave* again at some point in the future.

The predications in the short narrative above are very diverse in terms of tense and aspect, however the main verbs — or even the predications as a whole — typically have high distributional similarity, which inevitably leads to numerous false entailment decisions as reflected in Figure 3.

In the following we briefly analyse the impact of distributional similarity and investigate to what extent the similarity scores between two predications change when tense and aspect influence the entailment. Table 4 shows that the cosine similarity between temporally and aspectually modified predications is typically higher than for their respective lemmas. This further indicates that many false positives of the neural network based models in our results are due to high distributional similarity scores between predications. For APTs the cosine scores — even when normalised — are generally very low due to their sparsity and high dimensionality, highlighting their bias towards false negatives. However, Table 4

Predication Pair	w2v	APT	fT	ELMo	BERT	DNC	SNLI
visit ⊨ leave	0.36	0.09	0.53	0.59	0.69	0.69	0.28
is visiting ⊨ will leave	0.57	0.02	0.60	0.60	**0.77**	0.26	**0.26**
is visiting ⊭ has left	0.58	0.03	0.71	0.65	0.72	0.32	0.20
visit ⊨ arrive	0.45	0.07	0.55	0.49	0.71	0.58	0.45
is visiting ⊨ has arrived	**0.62**	**0.04**	**0.69**	**0.51**	**0.84**	0.25	**0.51**
is visiting ⊭ will arrive	0.57	0.01	0.60	0.50	0.81	0.32	0.25
win ⊨ play	0.52	0.14	0.54	0.59	0.73	0.39	0.32
has won ⊨ has played	**0.75**	**0.25**	**0.88**	**0.60**	**0.85**	**0.55**	0.23
has won ⊭ will play	0.60	0.11	0.64	0.55	0.78	0.31	0.36

Table 4: Similarity scores between the example predicates. DNC and SNLI refer to the two biLSTMs pre-trained on DNC and SNLI, respectively.

also shows that in most cases the distributional similarity between an entailed pair is higher than for a non-entailed pair (boldfaced in Table 4). This indicates that the embedding models do appear to capture *some* of the semantics of tense and aspect in their respective contextualised representations. However, their high distributional similarity overwhelms any finer distinction that the models might have extracted.

While our analysis indicates that the embedding models are able to extract knowledge about tense and aspect, the signal is not strong enough to reliably perform inference. A potential avenue for future work would therefore be the development of models that are able to better represent tense and aspect, while not being primarily governed by distributional similarity.

6 Related Work

Most previous work on inference between verbs was concerned with extracting inference rules from raw text (Lin and Pantel, 2001; Szpektor et al., 2004, 2007; Hashimoto et al., 2009; Melamud et al., 2013). As a next step, Berant et al. (2010) and Hosseini et al. (2018) leverage these rules to build entailment graphs for modelling natural language inference. However in both cases the entailment graphs are built on the basis of *verb lemmas* and do not take tense and aspect into account. One example of using tense for inference is Pavlick and Callison-Burch (2016), who leverage implicative verbs to determine that *managed to solve X* $\models$ *X is solved*. Our proposed dataset **TEA** fills a gap in the natural language inference evaluation repertoire by focusing on temporal and aspectual entailment. Recent years saw the release of a number of large-scale datasets, such as SNLI (Bowman et al., 2015), MNLI (Williams et al., 2017) or DNC (Poliak et al., 2018), but neither of these datasets focuses on, or includes a substantial proportion of, inference examples between temporal predications.

    TEA is related to work on causality (Mirza et al., 2014; Mirza and Tonelli, 2014), however our dataset has been created from scratch rather than derived from TimeBank (Pustejovsky et al., 2003), as for example explicit *buys* $\models$ *owns* relations are rarely encountered in the same paragraph or connected by explicit causal links. Therefore, **TEA** captures many consequent state inferences that are missing from previous datasets. The most closely related task to **TEA** is the relation inference dataset of Levy and Dagan (2016), which however, contains only very few examples where temporality is a governing factor.

7 Future Work

In future work we plan to leverage tense- and aspect-based information for constructing temporal entailment graphs (Lewis and Steedman, 2014), where nodes represent tensed predicates (e.g. *has visited*), and edges represent entailment relations. Temporal entailment graphs, together with knowledge about the *completedness* or *current relevance* of an event, can be applied to procedural reasoning, such as tracking the state of entities through text, similar to recent work of Bosselut et al. (2017), and Henaff et al. (2017). We furthermore plan to focus on other types of aspect such as *Aktionsart*.

8 Conclusion

In this paper we highlighted that tense and aspect are two of the most important factors for performing natural language inference. We introduced a novel entailment dataset, **TEA**, that contains pairs of short sentences and focuses on entailment relations between temporally and aspectually modified verbs. We showed that distributional embedding models capture a considerable amount of the morphosyntactic information relating to tense and aspect in their embedding spaces. However, neither the embedding models, nor two pre-trained biLSTMs, were able to outperform a simple rule-based baseline on **TEA**, primarily due to their reliance on contextual similarity for inference. In this sense, tense and aspect semantically resemble logical operators like negation rather than distributional components. The challenge will be to combine logical operator semantics with distributional representations of content words.

Acknowledgements

We thank Javad Hosseini, Paola Merlo and Nate Chambers for valuable discussions and comments on this work. We also thank our anonymous reviewers for their helpful feedback which led to a substantially improved paper. This research was supported in part by ERC Advanced Fellowship GA 742137 SEMANTAX, a Google faculty award, a Bloomberg L.P. Gift award, and a University of Edinburgh/Huawei Technologies award to Mark Steedman.

References

Balazs, J., E. Marrese-Taylor, P. Loyola, and Y. Matsuo (2017). Refining raw sentence representations for textual entailment recognition via attention. In *Proceedings of the 2nd Workshop on Evaluating Vector Space Representations for NLP*, pp. 51–55. Association for Computational Linguistics.

Berant, J., I. Dagan, and J. Goldberger (2010, July). Global learning of focused entailment graphs. In *Proceedings of the 48th Annual Meeting of the Association for Computational Linguistics*, Uppsala, Sweden, pp. 1220–1229. Association for Computational Linguistics.

Bojanowski, P., E. Grave, A. Joulin, and T. Mikolov (2017). Enriching word vectors with subword information. *Transactions of the Association for Computational Linguistics 5*, 135–146.

Bolukbasi, T., K.-W. Chang, J. Zou, V. Saligrama, and A. Kalai (2016). Man is to computer programmer as woman is to homemaker? debiasing word embeddings. In *Proceedings of the 30th International Conference on Neural Information Processing Systems*, NIPS'16, USA, pp. 4356–4364. Curran Associates Inc.

Bosselut, A., O. Levy, A. Holtzman, C. Ennis, D. Fox, and Y. Choi (2017). Simulating action dynamics with neural process networks. In *In Proceedings of ICLR*.

Bowman, S. R., G. Angeli, C. Potts, and C. D. Manning (2015, September). A large annotated corpus for learning natural language inference. In *Proceedings of the 2015 Conference on Empirical Methods in Natural Language Processing*, Lisbon, Portugal, pp. 632–642. Association for Computational Linguistics.

Chelba, C., T. Mikolov, M. Schuster, Q. Ge, T. Brants, P. Koehn, and T. Robinson (2013). One billion word benchmark for measuring progress in statistical language modeling. Technical report, Google.

Chklovski, T. and P. Pantel (2004, July). Verbocean: Mining the web for fine-grained semantic verb relations. In D. Lin and D. Wu (Eds.), *Proceedings of EMNLP 2004*, Barcelona, Spain, pp. 33–40. Association for Computational Linguistics.

Comrie, B. (1985). *Tense*. Cambridge Textbooks in Linguistics. Cambridge University Press.

Conneau, A., D. Kiela, H. Schwenk, L. Barrault, and A. Bordes (2017, September). Supervised learning of universal sentence representations from natural language inference data. In *Proceedings of the 2017 Conference on Empirical Methods in Natural Language Processing*, Copenhagen, Denmark, pp. 681–691. Association for Computational Linguistics.

Dagan, I., O. Glickman, and B. Magnini (2006). The pascal recognising textual entailment challenge. In J. Quiñonero-Candela, I. Dagan, B. Magnini, and F. d'Alché Buc (Eds.), *Machine Learning Challenges. Evaluating Predictive Uncertainty, Visual Object Classification, and Recognising Tectual Entailment*, Berlin, Heidelberg, pp. 177–190. Springer Berlin Heidelberg.

Dahl, Ö. (1985). *Tense and Aspect Systems*. Blackwell Publishing Ltd.

Depraetere, I. (1998). On the resultative character of present perfect sentences. *Journal of Pragmatics 29*(5), 597 – 613.

Devlin, J., M.-W. Chang, K. Lee, and K. Toutanova (2018, October). BERT: Pre-training of Deep Bidirectional Transformers for Language Understanding. *ArXiv e-prints*.

Dowty, D. (1979). *Word Meaning and Montague Grammar*. Holland: Dordrecht.

Efron, B. and R. Tibshirani (1994). *An Introduction to the Bootstrap*. CRC press.

Fellbaum, C. (1998). *WordNet: An Electronic Lexical Database*. Bradford Books.

Gardner, M., J. Grus, M. Neumann, O. Tafjord, P. Dasigi, N. F. Liu, M. Peters, M. Schmitz, and L. S. Zettlemoyer (2017). Allennlp: A deep semantic natural language processing platform.

Hashimoto, C., K. Torisawa, K. Kuroda, S. De Saeger, M. Murata, and J. Kazama (2009, August). Large-scale verb entailment acquisition from the Web. In *Proceedings of the 2009 Conference on Empirical Methods in Natural Language Processing*, Singapore, pp. 1172–1181. Association for Computational Linguistics.

Henaff, M., J. Weston, A. Szlam, A. Bordes, and Y. LeCun (2017). Tracking the world state with recurrent entity networks. In *In Proceedings of ICLR*.

Hochreiter, S. and J. Schmidhuber (1997, nov). Long short-term memory. *Neural Computation 9*(8), 1735–1780.

Hosseini, M. J., N. Chambers, S. Reddy, X. R. Holt, S. B. Cohen, M. Johnson, and M. Steedman (2018). Learning typed entailment graphs with global soft constraints. *Transactions of the Association for Computational Linguistics 6*, 703–717.

Iyyer, M., V. Manjunatha, J. Boyd-Graber, and H. Daumé III (2015, July). Deep unordered composition rivals syntactic methods for text classification. In *Proceedings of the 53rd Annual Meeting of the Association for Computational Linguistics and the 7th International Joint Conference on Natural Language Processing (Volume 1: Long Papers)*, Beijing, China, pp. 1681–1691. Association for Computational Linguistics.

Katz, G. (2003). On the stativity of the english perfect. In *Perfect explorations*. de Gruyter, The Hague.

Kingma, D. P. and J. Ba (2014). Adam: A method for stochastic optimization. *CoRR abs/1412.6980*.

Kober, T. (2018). *Inferring Unobserved Co-occurrence Events in Anchored Packed Trees*. Ph. D. thesis, University of Sussex.

Kober, T., J. Weeds, J. Reffin, and D. Weir (2016, November). Improving sparse word representations with distributional inference for semantic composition. In *Proceedings of the 2016 Conference on Empirical Methods in Natural Language Processing*, Austin, Texas, pp. 1691–1702.

Kober, T., J. Weeds, J. Reffin, and D. Weir (2017, July). Improving semantic composition with offset inference. In *Proceedings of the 55th Annual Meeting of the Association for Computational Linguistics (Volume 2: Short Papers)*, Vancouver, Canada, pp. 433–440. Association for Computational Linguistics.

Kober, T., J. Weeds, J. Wilkie, J. Reffin, and D. Weir (2017, April). One representation per word - does it make sense for composition? In *Proceedings of the 1st Workshop on Sense, Concept and Entity Representations and their Applications*, Valencia, Spain, pp. 79–90.

Levy, O. and I. Dagan (2016, August). Annotating relation inference in context via question answering. In *Proceedings of the 54th Annual Meeting of the Association for Computational Linguistics (Volume 2: Short Papers)*, Berlin, Germany, pp. 249–255. Association for Computational Linguistics.

Lewis, M. and M. Steedman (2014, June). Combining formal and distributional models of temporal and intensional semantics. In *Proceedings of the ACL 2014 Workshop on Semantic Parsing*, Baltimore, MD, pp. 28–32. Association for Computational Linguistics.

Lin, D. and P. Pantel (2001, aug 26–29). DIRT — discovery of inference rules from text. In F. Provost and R. Srikant (Eds.), *Proceedings of the Seventh ACM SIGKDD International Conference on Knowledge Discovery and Data Mining (KDD-01)*, New York, pp. 323–328. ACM Press.

Linzen, T., E. Dupoux, and Y. Goldberg (2016). Assessing the ability of lstms to learn syntax-sensitive dependencies. *Transactions of the Association for Computational Linguistics 4*, 521–535.

Melamud, O., J. Berant, I. Dagan, J. Goldberger, and I. Szpektor (2013, August). A two level model for context sensitive inference rules. In *Proceedings of the 51st Annual Meeting of the Association for Computational Linguistics (Volume 1: Long Papers)*, Sofia, Bulgaria, pp. 1331–1340. Association for Computational Linguistics.

Mikolov, T., E. Grave, P. Bojanowski, C. Puhrsch, and A. Joulin (2018). Advances in pre-training distributed word representations. In *Proceedings of the International Conference on Language Resources and Evaluation (LREC 2018)*.

Mikolov, T., I. Sutskever, K. Chen, G. S. Corrado, and J. Dean (2013). Distributed representations of words and phrases and their compositionality. In C. Burges, L. Bottou, M. Welling, Z. Ghahramani, and K. Weinberger (Eds.), *Advances in Neural Information Processing Systems 26*, pp. 3111–3119. Curran Associates, Inc.

Mirza, P., R. Sprugnoli, S. Tonelli, and M. Speranza (2014). Annotating causality in the tempeval-3 corpus. In *Proceedings of the EACL 2014 Workshop on Computational Approaches to Causality in Language (CAtoCL)*, pp. 10–19. Association for Computational Linguistics.

Mirza, P. and S. Tonelli (2014). An analysis of causality between events and its relation to temporal information. In *Proceedings of COLING 2014, the 25th International Conference on Computational Linguistics: Technical Papers*, pp. 2097–2106. Dublin City University and Association for Computational Linguistics.

Mitchell, J. and M. Steedman (2015). Orthogonality of syntax and semantics within distributional spaces. In *Proceedings of the 53rd Annual Meeting of the Association for Computational Linguistics and the 7th International Joint Conference on Natural Language Processing (Volume 1: Long Papers)*, pp. 1301–1310. Association for Computational Linguistics.

Moens, M. and M. Steedman (1988). Temporal ontology and temporal reference. *Computational Linguistics 14*(2), 15–28.

Moss, H., D. Leslie, and P. Rayson (2018). Using j-k-fold cross validation to reduce variance when tuning nlp models. In *Proceedings of the 27th International Conference on Computational Linguistics*, pp. 2978–2989. Association for Computational Linguistics.

Paszke, A., S. Gross, S. Chintala, G. Chanan, E. Yang, Z. DeVito, Z. Lin, A. Desmaison, L. Antiga, and A. Lerer (2017). Automatic differentiation in pytorch. In *NIPS-W*.

Pavlick, E. and C. Callison-Burch (2016, November). Tense manages to predict implicative behavior in verbs. In *Proceedings of the 2016 Conference on Empirical Methods in Natural Language Processing*, Austin, Texas, pp. 2225–2229. Association for Computational Linguistics.

Pedregosa, F., G. Varoquaux, A. Gramfort, V. Michel, B. Thirion, O. Grisel, M. Blondel, P. Prettenhofer, R. Weiss, V. Dubourg, J. Vanderplas, A. Passos, D. Cournapeau, M. Brucher, M. Perrot, and E. Duchesnay (2011, November). Scikit-learn: Machine learning in python. *Journal of Machine Learning Research 12*, 2825–2830.

Peters, M., M. Neumann, M. Iyyer, M. Gardner, C. Clark, K. Lee, and L. Zettlemoyer (2018). Deep contextualized word representations. In *Proceedings of the 2018 Conference of the North American Chapter of the Association for Computational Linguistics: Human Language Technologies, Volume 1 (Long Papers)*, pp. 2227–2237. Association for Computational Linguistics.

Poliak, A., A. Haldar, R. Rudinger, J. E. Hu, E. Pavlick, A. S. White, and B. Van Durme (2018). Collecting diverse natural language inference problems for sentence representation evaluation. In *Proceedings of the 2018 Conference on Empirical Methods in Natural Language Processing*, pp. 67–81. Association for Computational Linguistics.

Pustejovsky, J., P. Hanks, R. Sauri, A. See, R. Gaizauskas, A. Setzer, D. Radev, B. Sundheim, D. Day, L. Ferro, and M. Lazo (2003, March). The TIMEBANK corpus. In *Proceedings of Corpus Linguistics 2003*, Lancaster, pp. 647–656.

Reichenbach, H. (1947). *Elements of Symbolic Logic*. London: Macmillan.

Shoemark, P., J. Kirby, and S. Goldwater (2017). Topic and audience effects on distinctively scottish vocabulary usage in twitter data. In *Proceedings of the Workshop on Stylistic Variation*, pp. 59–68. Association for Computational Linguistics.

Srivastava, N., G. Hinton, A. Krizhevsky, I. Sutskever, and R. Salakhutdinov (2014). Dropout: A simple way to prevent neural networks from overfitting. *Journal of Machine Learning Research 15*, 1929–1958.

Steedman, M. (1997). Temporality. In J. van Benthem and A. ter Meulen (Eds.), *Handbook of Logic and Language*, pp. 895–938. Amsterdam: North-Holland.

Szpektor, I. and I. Dagan (2008, August). Learning entailment rules for unary templates. In *Proceedings of the 22nd International Conference on Computational Linguistics (Coling 2008)*, Manchester, UK, pp. 849–856. Coling 2008 Organizing Committee.

Szpektor, I., E. Shnarch, and I. Dagan (2007, June). Instance-based evaluation of entailment rule acquisition. In *Proceedings of the 45th Annual Meeting of the Association of Computational Linguistics*, Prague, Czech Republic, pp. 456–463. Association for Computational Linguistics.

Szpektor, I., H. Tanev, I. Dagan, and B. Coppola (2004, July). Scaling web-based acquisition of entailment relations. In D. Lin and D. Wu (Eds.), *Proceedings of EMNLP 2004*, Barcelona, Spain, pp. 41–48. Association for Computational Linguistics.

Tian, R., N. Okazaki, and K. Inui (2017). The mechanism of additive composition. *Machine Learning 106*(7), 1083–1130.

Vaswani, A., N. Shazeer, N. Parmar, J. Uszkoreit, L. Jones, A. N. Gomez, L. u. Kaiser, and I. Polosukhin (2017). Attention is all you need. In I. Guyon, U. V. Luxburg, S. Bengio, H. Wallach, R. Fergus, S. Vishwanathan, and R. Garnett (Eds.), *Advances in Neural Information Processing Systems 30*, pp. 5998–6008. Curran Associates, Inc.

Vendler, Z. (1957). Verbs and times. *Linguistics in Philosophy*, 97–121.

Vulić, I., D. Gerz, D. Kiela, F. Hill, and A. Korhonen (2017). Hyperlex: A large-scale evaluation of graded lexical entailment. *Computational Linguistics 43*(4), 781–835.

Vulić, I. and N. Mrkšić (2018). Specialising word vectors for lexical entailment. In *Proceedings of the 2018 Conference of the North American Chapter of the Association for Computational Linguistics: Human Language Technologies, Volume 1 (Long Papers)*, pp. 1134–1145. Association for Computational Linguistics.

Vylomova, E., L. Rimell, T. Cohn, and T. Baldwin (2016). Take and took, gaggle and goose, book and read: Evaluating the utility of vector differences for lexical relation learning. In *Proceedings of the 54th Annual Meeting of the Association for Computational Linguistics (Volume 1: Long Papers)*, pp. 1671–1682. Association for Computational Linguistics.

Weir, D., J. Weeds, J. Reffin, and T. Kober (2016, December). Aligning packed dependency trees: a theory of composition for distributional semantics. *Computational Linguistics, special issue on Formal Distributional Semantics 42*(4), 727–761.

Weisman, H., J. Berant, I. Szpektor, and I. Dagan (2012). Learning verb inference rules from linguistically-motivated evidence. In *Proceedings of the 2012 Joint Conference on Empirical Methods in Natural Language Processing and Computational Natural Language Learning*, pp. 194–204. Association for Computational Linguistics.

Wieting, J., M. Bansal, K. Gimpel, and K. Livescu (2016). Towards universal paraphrastic sentence embeddings. In *Proceedings of the International Conference on Learning Representations*.

Williams, A., N. Nangia, and S. R. Bowman (2017). A broad-coverage challenge corpus for sentence understanding through inference. *ArXiv e-prints*.

A Supplemental Material

A.1 Dataset Details

Table 5 shows a detailed overview of the number of examples per tense and aspect pair, as well as their class distribution.

Category	Num. Examples	Class distribution (*entailment : non-entailment*)
Present progressive - Present progressive	188	33 : 67
Present progressive - Past progressive	188	23 : 77
Present progressive - Present perfect	213	20 : 80
Present progressive - Past perfect	213	12 : 88
Present progressive - Future simple	216	28 : 72
Present progressive - Present simple	216	27 : 73
Present progressive - Past simple	216	26 : 74
Past progressive - Present progressive	188	0 : 100
Past progressive - Past progressive	188	55 : 45
Past progressive - Present perfect	213	7 : 93
Past progressive - Past perfect	213	46 : 54
Past progressive - Future simple	216	1 : 99
Past progressive - Present simple	216	0 : 100
Past progressive - Past simple	216	49 : 51
Present perfect - Present progressive	213	12 : 88
Present perfect - Past progressive	213	44 : 56
Present perfect - Present perfect	240	26 : 74
Present perfect - Past perfect	240	26 : 74
Present perfect - Future simple	243	16 : 84
Present perfect - Present simple	243	17 : 83
Present perfect - Past simple	243	42 : 58
Past perfect - Present progressive	213	0 : 100
Past perfect - Past progressive	213	58 : 42
Past perfect - Present perfect	240	3 : 97
Past perfect - Past perfect	240	59 : 41
Past perfect - Future simple	243	0 : 100
Past perfect - Present simple	243	0 : 100
Past perfect - Past simple	243	58 : 42
Future simple - Present progressive	216	3 : 97
Future simple - Past progressive	216	1 : 99
Future simple - Present perfect	243	1 : 99
Future simple - Past perfect	243	1 : 99
Future simple - Future simple	246	47 : 53
Future simple - Present simple	246	2 : 98
Future simple - Past simple	246	1 : 99
Present simple - Present progressive	216	21 : 79
Present simple - Past progressive	216	29 : 71
Present simple - Present perfect	243	15 : 85
Present simple - Past perfect	243	17 : 83
Present simple - Future simple	246	19 : 81
Present simple - Present simple	246	29 : 71
Present simple - Past simple	246	26 : 74
Past simple - Present progressive	216	0 : 100
Past simple - Past progressive	216	55 : 45
Past simple - Present perfect	243	5 : 95
Past simple - Past perfect	243	54 : 46
Past simple - Future simple	246	0 : 100
Past simple - Present simple	246	1 : 99
Past simple - Past simple	246	56 : 44
Progressive - Progressive	3464	20 : 80
Progressive - Perfect	2748	18 : 82
Perfect - Progressive	2748	16 : 84
Perfect - Perfect	2178	37 : 63
TOTAL	11138	22 : 78

Table 5: Detailed statistics of **TEA**.

B Supplemental Material

B.1 Model Details

word2vec. We used the 300-dimensional vectors trained on GoogleNews, available from `https://code.google.com/archive/p/word2vec/`.

APTs. We used order 2 APTs trained on Gigaword, with PPMI weighting and no negative SPPMI shift which were used in Kober (2018). As composition function we used *composition by intersection* which has previously been shown to work well for modelling the similarity of short phrases (Kober et al., 2016, 2017).

fastText. We used the 300-dimensional pre-trained vectors with subword information trained on Wikipedia (Mikolov et al., 2018).

ELMo. We are using the pre-trained model released by Peters et al. (2018) and accessible via the AllenNLP toolkit (Gardner et al., 2017).

BERT. We are using the BERT-big model released by Devlin et al. (2018) and available from `https://github.com/google-research/bert`.

Pre-trained biLSTM. We are using a bi-directional LSTM (Hochreiter and Schmidhuber, 1997) with max pooling, but without an attention layer. We follow Balazs et al. (2017) in aggregating the embedded and pooled premise and hypothesis representations before passing them to a single fully connected layer, with a relu activation function and a dropout (Srivastava et al., 2014) probability of 0.3. The model is optimised with Adam (Kingma and Ba, 2014) using a learning rate of 0.01. The model is implemented in PyTorch (Paszke et al., 2017). Table 6 lists the accuracies on the SNLI and DNC development and test sets for our model.

Dataset	Dev Accuracy	Test Accuracy
SNLI	0.83	0.82
DNC	0.88	0.87

Table 6: Accuracies on the development and test sets for the pre-trained biLSTMs on SNLI and DNC, respectively.

Don't Blame Distributional Semantics if it can't do Entailment

Matthijs Westera   Gemma Boleda

Universitat Pompeu Fabra, Barcelona, Spain

{firstname.lastname}@upf.edu

Abstract

Distributional semantics has had enormous empirical success in Computational Linguistics and Cognitive Science in modeling various semantic phenomena, such as semantic similarity, and distributional models are widely used in state-of-the-art Natural Language Processing systems. However, the theoretical status of distributional semantics within a broader theory of language and cognition is still unclear: What does distributional semantics model? Can it be, on its own, a fully adequate model of the meanings of linguistic expressions? The standard answer is that distributional semantics is not fully adequate in this regard, because it falls short on some of the central aspects of *formal* semantic approaches: truth conditions, entailment, reference, and certain aspects of compositionality. We argue that this standard answer rests on a misconception: These aspects do not belong in a theory of expression meaning, they are instead aspects of *speaker* meaning, i.e., communicative intentions in a particular context. In a slogan: words do not refer, speakers do. Clearing this up enables us to argue that distributional semantics on its own is an adequate model of expression meaning. Our proposal sheds light on the role of distributional semantics in a broader theory of language and cognition, its relationship to formal semantics, and its place in computational models.

Keywords: distributional semantics, expression meaning, formal semantics, speaker meaning, truth conditions, entailment, reference, compositionality, context

1   Introduction

Distributional semantics has emerged as a promising model of certain 'conceptual' aspects of linguistic meaning (e.g., Landauer and Dumais 1997; Turney and Pantel 2010; Baroni and Lenci 2010; Lenci 2018) and as an indispensable component of applications in Natural Language Processing (e.g., reference resolution, machine translation, image captioning; especially since Mikolov et al. 2013). Yet its theoretical status within a general theory of meaning and of language and cognition more generally is not clear (e.g., Lenci 2008; Erk 2010; Boleda and Herbelot 2016; Lenci 2018). In particular, it is not clear whether distributional semantics can be understood as an actual model of expression meaning – what Lenci (2008) calls the 'strong' view of distributional semantics – or merely as a model of something that *correlates* with expression meaning in certain partial ways – the 'weak' view. In this paper we aim to resolve, in favor of the 'strong' view, the question of what exactly distributional semantics models, what its role should be in an overall theory of language and cognition, and how its contribution to state of the art applications can be understood. We do so in part by clarifying its frequently discussed but still obscure relation to formal semantics.

Our proposal relies crucially on the distinction between what linguistic *expressions* mean outside of any particular context, and what *speakers* mean by them in a particular context of utterance. Here, we term the former **expression meaning** and the latter **speaker meaning**.[1] At least since Grice 1968 this distinction is generally acknowledged to be crucial to account for how humans communicate via

---

[1] English inconveniently conflates what speakers do and what expressions do in a single verb "to mean". In other languages the two types of 'meaning' go by different names, e.g., in Dutch, sentences 'betekenen' (mean, lit. 'be-sign' or 'signify') while speakers 'bedoelen' (mean, lit. 'be-goal').

language. Nevertheless, the two notions are sometimes confused, and we will point out a particularly widespread confusion in this paper. Consider an example, one which will recur throughout this paper:

(1)   The red cat is chasing a mouse.

The expression "the red cat" in this sentence can be used to refer to a cat with red hair (which is actually orangish in color) or to a cat painted red; "a mouse" to the animal or to the computer device; and in the right sort of context the whole sentence can be used to describe, for instance, a red car driving behind a motorbike. It is uncontroversial that the same expression can be used to communicate very different speaker meanings in different contexts. At the same time, it is likewise uncontroversial that not *anything goes*: what a speaker can reasonably mean by an expression in a given context – with the aim of being understood by an addressee – is constrained by its (relatively) context-invariant expression meaning. An important, long-standing question in linguistics and philosophy is what type of object could play the role of expression meaning, i.e., as a context-invariant common denominator of widely varying usages.

There exist two predominant candidates for a model of expression meaning: distributional semantics and formal semantics. **Distributional semantics** assigns to each expression, or at least each word, a high-dimensional, numerical vector, one which represents an abstraction over occurrences of the expression in some suitable dataset, i.e., its *distribution* in the dataset. **Formal semantics** assigns to each expression, typically via an intermediate, logical language, an interpretation in terms of reference to entities in the world, their properties and relations, and ultimately truth values of whole sentences.[2] To illustrate the two approaches, simplistically (and without intending to commit to any particular formal semantic analysis or (compositional) distributional semantics – see Section 5):

(2)   The red cat is chasing a mouse.
       Formal semantics: $\iota x(\text{RED}(x) \wedge \text{CAT}(x) \wedge \exists y(\text{MOUSE}(y) \wedge \text{CHASE}(x, y)))$
       Distributional semantics: $\nearrow \searrow \swarrow \rightarrow \downarrow \nearrow \leftarrow$ (i.e., a vector for each word)

Distributional and formal semantics are often regarded as two models of expression meaning that have *complementary strengths and weaknesses* and that, accordingly, must somehow be combined for a more complete model of expression meaning (e.g., Beltagy et al. 2013; Erk 2013; Baroni et al. 2014; Asher et al. 2016; Boleda and Herbelot 2016). For instance, in these works the vectors of distributional semantics are regarded as capturing lexical or conceptual aspects of meaning but not, or insufficiently so, truth conditions, reference, entailment and compositionality – and vice versa for formal semantics.[3]

Contrary to this common perspective, we argue that distributional semantics on its own can in fact be a fully satisfactory model of expression meaning, i.e., the 'strong' view of distributional semantics in Lenci 2008. Crucially, we will do so *not* by trying to show that distributional semantics can do all the things formal semantics does – we think it clearly cannot, at least not on its own – but by explaining that a semantics *should not* do all those things. In fact, formal semantics is mistaken about its job description, a mistake that we trace back, following a long strand in both philosophical and psycholinguistic literature, to a failure to properly distinguish speaker meaning and expression meaning. By clearing this up we aim to contribute to a firmer theoretical understanding of distributional semantics, of its role in an overall theory of communication, and of its employment in current models in NLP.

2   What we mean by distributional semantics

By distributional semantics we mean, in this paper, a broad family of models that assign (context-invariant) numerical vector representations to words, which are computed as abstractions over occur-

---

[2]Our formulation covers only the predominant, model-theoretic (or truth-conditional, referential) type of formal semantics, not, e.g., proof-theoretic semantics. We concentrate on this for reasons of space, but our proposal applies more generally.

[3]To clarify: when it is said that distributional semantics falls short, this pertains to distributional semantics on its own, i.e., a set of word vectors, combined perhaps with some basic algebraic operations or, at most, a simple classifier. By contrast, when distributional semantics is incorporated in a larger model (see section 2) the resulting system as a whole can be very successful.

rences of words in contexts. Implementations of distributional semantics vary, primarily, in the notion of context and in the abstraction mechanism used. A **context** for a word is typically a text in which it occurs, such as a document, sentence or a set of neighboring words, but it can also contain images (e.g., Feng and Lapata 2010; Silberer et al. 2017) or audio (e.g., Lopopolo and Miltenburg 2015) – in principle any place where one may encounter a word could be used. Because of how distributional models work, words that appear in similar contexts end up being assigned similar representations. At present, all models need large amounts of data to compute high-quality representations. The closer these data resemble our experience as language learners, the more distributional semantics is expected to be able in principle to generate accurate representations of – as we will argue – expression meaning.

As for the **abstraction mechanism** used, Baroni et al. (2014) distinguish between classic "count-based" methods, which work with co-occurrence statistics between words and contexts, and "prediction-based" methods, which instead apply machine learning techniques (artificial neural networks) to induce representations based on a prediction task, typically predicting the context given a word. For instance, the Skip-Gram model of Mikolov et al. (2013) would, applied to example (1), try to predict the words "the", "red", "is", "chasing", etc. from the presence of the word "cat" (more precisely, it would try to make these context words more likely than randomly sampled words, like "democracy" or "smear"). By training a neural network on such a task, over a large number of words in context, the first layer of the network comes to represent words as vectors, usually called *word embeddings* in the neural network literature. These word embeddings contain information about the words that the network has found useful for the prediction task.

In both count-based and prediction-based methods, the resulting vector representations encode abstractions over the distributions of words in the dataset, with the crucial property that words that appear in similar contexts are assigned similar vector representations.[4] Our arguments in this paper apply to both kinds of methods for distributional semantics.

Word embeddings emerge not just from models that are expressly designed to yield word representations (such as Mikolov et al. 2013). Rather, any neural network model that takes words as input, trained on whatever task, must 'embed' these words in order to process them – hence any such model will result in word embeddings (e.g., Collobert and Weston 2008). Neural network models for language are trained for instance on language modeling (e.g., word prediction; Mikolov et al. 2010; Peters et al. 2018) or Machine Translation (Bahdanau et al., 2015). As long as the data on which these models are trained consist of word-context pairs, the resulting word embeddings qualify, for present purposes, as implementations of distributional semantics, and our proposal in the current paper applies also to them. Of course some implementations within this broad family may be better than others, and the type of task used is one parameter to be explored: It is expected that the more the task requires a human-like understanding of language, the better the resulting word embeddings will represent – as we will argue – the meanings of words. But our arguments concern the theoretical underpinnings of the distributional semantics framework more broadly rather than specific instantiations of it.

Lastly, some implementations of distributional semantics impose biases, during training, for obtaining word vectors that are more useful for a given task. For instance, to obtain word vectors useful for predicting lexical entailment (e.g., that being a cat entails being an animal), Vulić and Mrkšić (2017) impose a bias for keeping the vectors of supposed hypernyms, like "cat" and "animal", close together (more precisely: in the same direction from the origin but with different magnitudes). This kind of approach presupposes, incorrectly as we will argue, that distributional semantics *should* account for entailment. It results in word vectors that are more useful for a particular task, but the model will be worse as a model of expression meaning. We will return to this type of approach in section 3.2.

---

[4]Both methods also share the characteristic that the dimensions of the high-dimensional space are automatically induced, and hence not directly interpretable (this is the main way in which they are different from traditional semantic features; see Boleda and Erk 2015). As a consequence, much work exploring distributional semantic models has relied not on the dimensions themselves but on geometric relations between words, in particular the notion of similarity (e.g., measured by cosine; as an anonymous reviewer notes, such technical notions of similarity need not completely align with semantic similarity in a more intuitive sense).

3 Distributional semantics as a model of expression meaning

We present two theoretical reasons why distributional semantics is attractive as a model of expression meaning, before arguing in section 4 that it can also be sufficient.

3.1 Reason 1: Meaning from use; abstraction and parsimony

We take it to be uncontroversial that what expressions mean is to be explained at least in part in terms of how they are used by speakers of the relevant linguistic community (e.g., Wittgenstein 1953; Grice 1968).[5] A similar view has motivated work on distributional semantics (e.g., Lenci 2008; also at its conception, e.g., Harris 1954). For instance, what the word "cat" means is to be explained at least in part in terms of the fact that speakers have used it to refer to cats, to describe things that resemble cats, to insult people in certain ways, and so on. Note that the usages of words generally resist systematic categorization into definable senses, and attempts to characterize word meaning by sense enumeration generally fail (e.g., Kilgarriff 1997; Hanks 2000; Erk 2010; cf. Pustejovsky 1995).

A minimal, parsimonious way of explaining the meaning of an expression in terms of its uses is to say simply that **the meaning of an expression is an abstraction over its uses**. Such abstractions are, of course, exactly what distributional semantics delivers, and the view that it corresponds to expression meaning is what Lenci (2008) calls the 'strong' view of distributional semantics. Distributional semantics is especially parsimonious because it relies on (mostly) domain-independent mechanisms for abstraction (e.g., principal components analysis; neural networks). Of course not all implementations are equally adequate, or equally parsimonious; there are considerable differences both in the abstraction mechanism relied upon and in the dataset used (see section 2). But the family as a whole, defined by the core tenet of associating with each word an abstraction over its use, is highly suitable in principle for modeling expression meaning. This makes the 'strong' view of distributional semantics attractive.

An alternative to the 'strong' view is what Lenci (2008) calls the 'weak' view: that an abstraction over use may be *part* of what determines expression meaning, but that more is needed. This view underlies for instance the common assumption that a more complete model of expression meaning would require integrating distributional and formal semantics (e.g., Beltagy et al. 2013; Erk 2013; Baroni et al. 2014; Asher et al. 2016; Boleda and Herbelot 2016). But in section 4 we argue that the notions of formal semantic, like reference, truth conditions and entailment, do not belong at the level of expression meaning in the first place, and, accordingly, that distributional semantics can be sufficient as a model of expression meaning. Theoretical parsimony dictates that we opt for the least presumptive approach compatible with the empirical facts, i.e., with what a theory of expression meaning should account for.

Some authors equate the meaning of an expression not with an abstraction over all uses, but only *stereotypical* uses: what an expression means would be what a stereotypical speaker in a stereotypical context means by it (e.g., Schiffer 1972; Bennett 1976; Soames et al. 2002). This approach is appealing because it does justice to native speaker's intuitions about expression meaning, which are known to reflect stereotypical speaker meaning (see Section 4). However, several authors have pointed out that stereotypical speaker meaning is ultimately not an adequate notion of expression meaning (e.g., Bach 2002; Recanati 2004). To see just one reason why, consider the following arbitrary example:

(3)   Jack and Jill got married.

A stereotypical use of this expression would convey the speaker meaning that Jack and Jill got married *to each other*. But this cannot be the (context-invariant) meaning of the expression "Jack and Jill got married", or else the following additions would be redundant and contradictory, respectively:[6]

---

[5]For compatibility with a more cognitive, single-agent perspective of language, such as *I-language* in the work of Chomsky (e.g., 1986), this could be restricted to the uses of a word as experienced by a single agent when learning the language.

[6]An anonymous reviewer rightly points out that this presupposes that notions like redundancy and contradiction apply to expression meanings. We think they don't (see Section 4), at least not in their strictly logical senses, but they would if expression meaning were to be construed as stereotypical speaker meaning, which is the position we are criticizing here.

(4)   Jack and Jill got married *to each other*.

(5)   Jack and Jill got married *to their respective childhood friends*.

Hence the stereotypical speaker meaning of (3) cannot be its expression meaning. For many more examples and discussion see Bach 2002. Another challenge for defining expression meaning as stereotypical speaker meaning is that of having to define "stereotypical". It cannot be defined simply as the most frequent type, because that presupposes that uses can be categorized into clearly delineated, countable types. Moreover, an 'empty' context is a context too, and not the most stereotypical one.

Summing up: what an expression means depends on how speakers use it, but the uses of an expression more generally resist systematic categorization into enumerable senses, and selecting a stereotypical use isn't adequate either. Equating expression meaning with an abstraction over all uses, as the 'strong' view of distributional semantics has it, is more adequate, and particularly attractive for reasons of parsimony.

3.2   Reason 2: Distributional semantics as a model of concepts

Another reason why distributional semantics is attractive as a model of expression meaning is the following. As mentioned in section 1, distributional semantics is often regarded as a model of 'conceptual' aspects of meaning (e.g., Landauer and Dumais 1997; Baroni and Lenci 2010; Boleda and Herbelot 2016). This view seems to be motivated in part empirically: distributional semantics is successful at what are intuitively conceptual tasks, like modeling word similarity, priming and analogy. Moreover, it aligns with the widespread view in philosophy and developmental psychology that abstraction over instances is a main mechanism of concept formation (e.g., the influential work of Jean Piaget). Let us explain why concepts, and in particular those modeled by distributional semantics (because there is some confusion about their nature), would be suitable representatives of expression meaning.

It is sometimes assumed that the word vector for "cat" should model the concept CAT (we discuss some work that makes this assumption below). This may be a 'true enough' approximation for practical applications, but theoretically it is, strictly speaking, on the wrong track. This is because the word vector for "cat" does not model the concept CAT – that would be an abstraction over occurrences of *actual cats*, after all. Instead, the word vector for "cat" is an abstraction over occurrences of *the word*, not the animal, hence it would model the concept of *the word* "cat", say, THEWORDCAT. The extralinguistic concept CAT and the linguistic concept THEWORDCAT are very different. The concept CAT encodes knowledge about cats having fur, four legs, the tendency to meow, etc.; the concept THEWORDCAT instead encodes knowledge that the word "cat" is a common noun, that it rhymes with "bat" and "hat", how speakers have used it or tend to use it, that the word doesn't belong to a particular register, and so on.[7]

Our distinction between THEWORDCAT and CAT, or between linguistic and extralinguistic concepts, is not new, and word vectors are known to capture the more linguistic kind of information, and to be (at best) only a proxy for the extralinguistic concepts they are typically used to denote by a speaker (e.g., Miller and Charles 1991). But it appears to be sometimes overlooked. For instance, the assumption that the word vector for "cat" would (or should) model the extralinguistic concept CAT is made in work using distributional semantics to model entailment, e.g., that being a cat entails being an animal (e.g., Geffet and Dagan 2005; Roller et al. 2014; Vulić and Mrkšić 2017). But clearly the entailment relation holds between the extralinguistic concepts CAT and ANIMAL – being a cat entails being an animal – *not* between the linguistic concepts THEWORDCAT and THEWORDANIMAL actually modeled by distributional semantics: being the word "cat" does not entail (in fact, it excludes) being the word "animal". Hence these approaches are, strictly speaking, theoretically misguided – although their conflation of linguistic and extralinguistic concepts may be a defensible simplification for practical purposes.

There have been many proposals to integrate formal and distributional semantics (e.g., Beltagy et al. 2013; Erk 2013; Baroni et al. 2014; Asher et al. 2016), and a similar confusion exists in at least some of them (Asher et al., 2016; McNally and Boleda, 2017). We are unable within the scope of the cur-

---

[7]To clarify: the difference persists even if the notion of context in distributional semantics is enriched to include, say, pictures of cats, or even actual cats. The distributions it models would still be distributions *of words*, not of things like cats.

rent paper to do justice to the technical sophistication of these approaches, but for present purposes, impressionistically, the type of integration they pursue can be pictured as follows:

(6)   The red cat is chasing a mouse.
       Formal semantics: $\iota x(\text{RED}(x) \wedge \text{CAT}(x) \wedge \exists y(\text{MOUSE}(y) \wedge \text{CHASE}(x,y)))$
       Distributional semantics: $\nearrow \searrow \swarrow \rightarrow \downarrow \nearrow \leftarrow$ (i.e., a vector for each word)
       Possible integration: $\iota x(\searrow(x) \wedge \swarrow(x) \wedge \exists y(\leftarrow(y) \wedge \downarrow(x,y)))$ (very simplistically)

Again, this may be a 'true enough' approximation, but it is theoretically on the wrong track. The atomic constants in formal semantics are normally understood (e.g., Frege 1892 and basically anywhere since) to denote the extralinguistic kind of concept, i.e., CAT and not THEWORDCAT. Put differently, entity x in example (6) should be entailed to be a cat, not to be the word "cat". This means that the distributional semantic word vectors are, strictly speaking, out of place in a formal semantic skeleton like in (6).[8]

In short, distributional semantics models linguistic concepts like THEWORDCAT, not extralinguistic concepts like CAT. But this is not a shortcoming; it makes distributional semantics more adequate, rather than less adequate, as a model of expression meaning, for the following reason. A prominent strand in the literature on concepts conceives of concepts as *abilities* (e.g., Dummett 1993; Bennett and Hacker 2008; for discussion see Margolis and Laurence 2014). For instance, possessing the concept CAT amounts to having the ability to recognize cats, discriminate them from non-cats, and draw certain inferences about cats. The concept CAT is, then, the starting point for *interpreting* an object as a cat and draw inferences from it. It follows that the concept THEWORDCAT is the starting point for interpreting a word as the word "cat" and drawing inferences from it, notably, inferences about what a speaker in a particular context may use it for: for instance, to refer to a particular cat.[9] Thus, **the view of distributional semantics as a model of concepts, but crucially concepts *of words*, establishes word vectors as a necessary starting point for interpreting a word.** This is exactly the explanatory job assigned to expression meaning: a context-invariant starting point for interpretation. Not coincidentally, for neural networks that take words as input, distributional semantics resides in the first layer of weights (see Section 2).

Summing up, this section presented two reasons why distributional semantics is attractive as a model of expression meaning. The next section considers whether it could also be *sufficient*.

4   Limits of distributional semantics: words don't refer, speakers do.

In many ways the standard for what a theory of expression meaning ought to do has been set by formal semantics. Consider again our simplistic comparison of distributional semantics and formal semantics:

(7)   The red cat is chasing a mouse.
       Formal semantics: $\iota x(\text{RED}(x) \wedge \text{CAT}(x) \wedge \exists y(\text{MOUSE}(y) \wedge \text{CHASE}(x,y)))$
       Distributional semantics: $\nearrow \searrow \swarrow \rightarrow \downarrow \nearrow \leftarrow$ (i.e., a vector for each word)

The logical formulae into which formal semantics translates this example are assigned precise interpretations in (a model of) the outside world. For instance, RED would denote the set of all red things, CAT

---

[8] The mathematical techniques of the aforementioned approaches do not depend for their validity on the exact nature of the vectors. We hope that these techniques can be used to represent not expression meaning but speaker meaning (see section 4), provided we use vector representations of the distribution of actual cats, instead of the word "cat".

[9] This is because how a speaker may use a word is constrained by how speakers have used it in the past – a trait of linguistic convention. Since the concept THEWORDCAT reflects uses of "cat" in the past, among which are referential uses, it constrains (hence warrants inferences about) what it may be used by a given speaker to refer to. (To clarify: this does not imply that the actual or potential referents of a word are actually part of its meaning – see Section 4.) The same holds for the distributional semantic word vector for "cat", although instantiations of distributional semantics may differ in how much referentially relevant information they encode. Presumably, more information of this sort is encoded when reference is prominent in the original data, for instance when a distributional semantic model is trained on referential expressions grounded in images (Kazemzadeh et al., 2014); otherwise such information needs to be induced from patterns in the text alone (like any other semantic information in text-only distributional semantics).

the set of all cat-like things, CHASE a set of pairs where one chases the other, the variable x would be bound to a particular entity in the world, etc., and the logical connectives can have their usual truth-conditional interpretation.[10] In this way formal semantics accounts for reference to things in the world and it accounts for truth values (which is what sentences refer to; Frege 1892). Moreover, referents and truth values across possible worlds/situations in turn determine truth conditions, and thereby entailments – because one sentence entails another if whenever the former is true the latter is true as well.[11] By contrast, distributional semantics on its own (cf. footnote 3) struggles with these aspects (Boleda and Herbelot 2016; see also the work discussed in section 3.2 on entailment), which has motivated afore-mentioned attempts to integrate formal and distributional semantics (e.g., Beltagy et al. 2013; Erk 2013; Baroni et al. 2014; Asher et al. 2016; Boleda and Herbelot 2016). Put simply, distributional semantics struggles because there are no entities or truth values in distributional space to refer to. Nevertheless, we think that this isn't a shortcoming of distributional semantics; **we argue that a theory of expression meaning *shouldn't* model these aspects**.[12]

We think that these referential notions on which formal semantics has focused are best understood to reside at the level of speaker meaning, not expression meaning. In a nutshell, **our position is that words don't refer, speakers do** (e.g., Strawson 1950) – and analogously for truth conditions and entailment. The fact that speakers often refer *by means of* linguistic expressions doesn't entail that these expressions must in themselves, out of context, have a determinate reference, or even be capable of referring (or capable of entailing, of providing information, of being true or false). Parsimony (again) suggests that we do not assume the latter: To explain why a speaker can use, e.g., the expression "cat" to refer to a cat, it is sufficient that, in the relevant community, that is how the expression is often used. It is theoretically superfluous to assume in addition that the expression "cat" itself refers to cats.

Now, most work in formal semantics would acknowledge that "cat" out of context doesn't refer to cats, and that its use in a particular context to refer to cats must be explained on the basis of a less determinate, more underspecified notion of expression meaning. More generally, expressions are well-known to underdetermine speaker meaning (e.g., Bach 1994; Recanati 2004), as basically any example can illustrate (e.g., (1) "red cat" and (3) "got married"). However, this alone does not imply that the notions of formal semantics are inadequate for characterizing expression meaning; in principle one could try to define, in formal semantics, the referential potential of "cat" in a way that is compatible with its use to refer to cats, to cat-like things, etcetera. And one could define the expression meaning of "Jack and Jill got married" in a way that is compatible with them marrying each other and with each marrying someone else.[13] What is problematic for a formal semantic approach is that the *ways* in which expressions underdetermine speaker meaning are not clearly delineated and enumerable, and that there is no symbolically definable common core among all uses.[14] This argument was made for instance by Wittgenstein (1953), who notes that the uses of an expression (his example was "game") are tied together

---

[10]In fact, the common reliance on an intermediate formal, logical language is not what defines formal semantics; what matters is that it treats natural language itself as a formal language (Montague, 1970), by compositionally assigning precise interpretations to it – and this can be done directly, or indirectly via translation to a logical language as in our example.

[11]There are serious shortcomings to the formal semantics approach, some of which we discuss below, but others which aren't relevant for present purposes. An important criticism that we won't discuss is that the way in which formal semantics assigns interpretations to natural language relies crucially on the manual labor of hard-working semanticists, which does not scale up.

[12]Truth conditions, entailments and reference are just three sides of the same central, referential tenet of formal semantics, and what we will say about reference in what follows will apply to truth conditions and entailment, and vice versa. An anonymous reviewer draws our attention also to the logical notions of satisfiability and validity, i.e., possible vs. necessary truth. Our proposal applies to these notions too, regardless of whether they are understood in terms of quantification over possible ways the world may be, or in terms of quantification over possible interpretations.

[13]For instance, an anonymous reviewer notes that richer logical formalisms such as dependent type theory are well-suited for integrating contextual information into symbolic representations.

[14]Similarly, Bach (2005, among others) has criticized the common approach in formal semantics of incorporating, in definitions of expression meaning, 'slots' where supposed context-sensitive material is to be plugged in. The meaning of a scalar adjective like "big", for instance, would contain a slot for 'standard of comparison' to be filled by context in order to explain why the same thing may be described as "big" in one context but not in another (e.g., Kennedy 2007). Bach (2005) notes that this type of approach does not generalize to all the ways in which expression meaning underdetermines speaker meaning; the meaning of each expression would essentially end up being a big empty slot, to be magically filled by context.

not by definition but by family resemblance. More recent iterations of this argument can be found in criticisms of the "classical", definitional view of concepts (e.g., Rosch and Mervis 1975; Fodor et al. 1980; Margolis and Laurence 2014), and in criticisms of sense enumeration approaches to word meaning (e.g., Kilgarriff 1997; Hanks 2000; Erk 2010; cf. Pustejovsky 1995), which we already mentioned briefly before: it is unclear what constitutes a word sense, and no enumeration of senses covers all uses.

The only truly common core among all uses of any given expression is that they are all, indeed, uses of the same expression. Hence, if expression meaning is to serve its purpose as a common core among all uses, i.e., as a context-invariant starting point of semantic/pragmatic explanations, then it must reflect all uses. As we argued in section 3, distributional semantics, conceived of as a model of expression meaning (i.e., the 'strong' view of Lenci 2008), embraces exactly this fact. This makes the representations of distributional semantics, but not those of formal semantics, suitable for characterizing expression meaning. By contrast, (largely) discrete notions like reference, truth and entailment are useful, at best, at the level of *speaker* meaning – recall that our position is that words don't refer, speakers do (Strawson, 1950).[15] That is, one can fruitfully conceive of a particular speaker, in some individuated context, as intending to refer to discrete things, communicating a certain determinate piece of information that can be true or false, entailing certain things and not others. This still involves considerable abstraction, as any symbolic model of a cognitive system would (Marr, 1982); e.g., speaker intentions may not always be as determinate as a symbolic model presupposes. But the amount of abstraction required, in particular the kind of determinacy of content that a symbolic model presupposes, is not as problematic in the case of speaker meaning as for expression meaning. The reason is that a model of speaker meaning needs to cover only a single usage, by a particular speaker situated in a particular context; a model of expression meaning, by contrast, needs to cover countless interactions, across many different contexts, of a whole community of speakers. The symbolic representations of formal semantics are ill-suited for the latter.

Despite the foregoing considerations being prominent in the literature, formal semantics has continued to assume that referents, truth conditions, etc., are core aspects of expression meaning. The main reason for this is the traditional centrality of supposedly 'semantic' intuitions in formal semantics (Bach, 2002), either as the main source of data or as the object of investigation ('semantic competence', for criticism see Stokhof 2011). In particular, formal semantics has attached great importance to intuitions about truth conditions (e.g., "semantics with no treatment of truth conditions is not semantics", Lewis 1972:169), a tenet going back to its roots in formal logic (e.g., Montague 1970 and the earlier work of Frege, Tarski, among others). Clearly, if expressions on their own do not even *have* truth conditions, as we have argued, these supposedly semantic intuitions cannot genuinely be about expression meaning. And that is indeed what many authors have pointed out. Strawson (1950); Grice (1975); Bach (2002), among others, have argued that **what seem to be intuitions about the meaning of an expression are really about what a stereotypical speaker would mean by it** – or at least they are heavily influenced by it. Again example (3) serves as an illustration here: intuitively "marry" means "marry each other", but to assume that this is therefore its expression meaning would be inadequate (as we discussed in section 3.1). But we want to stress that this is not just an occasional trap set by particular kinds of examples; just being a bit more careful doesn't cut it. It is the foundational intuition that expressions can even *have* truth conditions that is already inaccurate. Our intuitions are *fundamentally* not attuned to expression meaning, because expression meaning is not normally what matters to us; it is only an instrument for conveying speaker meaning, and, much like the way we string phonemes together to form words, it plays this role largely or entirely without our conscious awareness. The same point has been made in the more psycholinguistic literature (Schwarz, 1996), occasionally in the formal semantics/pragmatics literature (Kadmon and Roberts, 1986), and there is increasing acknowledgment of this also in experimental pragmatics, in particular of the fact that participants in experiments imagine stereotypical contexts (e.g., Westera and Brasoveanu 2014; Degen and Tanenhaus 2015; Poortman 2017).

Summing up, the standard that formal semantics has set for what a theory of expression meaning

---

[15]We are not discussing another long-standing criticism of formal semantics, namely that referring (and asserting something that can be true or false) is not all that speakers do with language (e.g., Austin 1975; Searle 1969). We do not claim that formal semantics would be *sufficient* as a model of speaker meaning; only that its notions are more adequate there than at the level of expression meaning.

ought to account for, and which makes distributional semantics appear to fall short, turns out to be misguided. Reference, truth conditions and entailment belong at the level of speaker meaning, not expression meaning. It entails that distributional semantics on its own need not account for these aspects, either theoretically or computationally; it should only provide an adequate starting point. Interestingly, this corresponds exactly to its role in current neural network models, on tasks that involve identifying aspects of speaker meaning. Consider the task of visual reference resolution (e.g., Plummer et al. 2015), where the inputs are a linguistic description plus an image and the task is to identify the intended referent in the image. A typical neural network model would achieve this by first activating word embeddings (a form of distributional semantics; Section 2) and then combining and transforming these together with a representation of the image into a representation of the intended referent – speaker meaning.

5   Compositionality

Language is compositional in the sense that what a larger, composite expression means is determined (in large part) by what its components mean and the way they are put together. Compositionality is sometimes mentioned as a strength of formal semantics and as an area where distributional semantics falls short (a.o. Beltagy et al., 2013). But in fact both approaches have shown strengths and weaknesses regarding compositionality (see Boleda and Herbelot 2016 for an overview). To illustrate, consider again:

(8)   The red cat is chasing a mouse.

In this context the adjective "red" is used by the speaker to mean something closer to ORANGE (because the "red hair" of cats is typically orange), unlike its occurrence in, say, "red paint". Distributional semantics works quite well for this type of effect in the composition of content words (e.g., Baroni et al. 2014; McNally and Boleda 2017), an area where formal semantics, which tends to leave the basic concepts unanalyzed, has struggled (despite efforts such as Pustejovsky 1995). Classic compositional distributional semantics, in which distributional representations are combined with some externally specified algorithm (which can be as simple as addition), also works reasonably well for short sentences, as measured for instance on sentence similarity (e.g., Mitchell and Lapata 2010; Grefenstette et al. 2013; Marelli et al. 2014). But for longer expressions distributional semantics on its own falls short (cf. our clarification of "on its own" in footnote 3), and this is part of what has inspired aforementioned works on integrating formal and distributional semantics (e.g., Coecke et al. 2011; Grefenstette and Sadrzadeh 2011; Beltagy et al. 2013; Erk 2013; Baroni et al. 2014; Asher et al. 2016).

However, that distributional semantics falls short of accounting for full-fledged compositionality does not mean that it cannot be a sufficient model of expression meaning. For that, it should be established first that compositionality wholly resides at the level of expression meaning – and it is not clear that it does. Let us take a closer look at the main theoretical argument for compositionality, the argument from *productivity*.[16] According to this argument, compositionality is necessary to explain how a competent speaker can understand the meaning of a composite expression that they have never before encountered. However, in appealing to a person's supposed understanding of the meaning of an expression, this argument is subject to the revision proposed in Section 4: it reflects speaker meaning, not expression meaning. More correctly phrased, then, the type of data motivating the productivity argument is that a person who has never encountered a speaker uttering a certain composite expression, is nevertheless able to understand *what some (actual or hypothetical) speaker would mean by it*. And this leaves undetermined where compositionality should reside: at the level of expression meaning, speaker meaning, or both.

To illustrate, consider again example (8), "The red cat is chasing a mouse". A speaker of English who has never encountered this sentence will nevertheless understand what a stereotypical speaker would mean by it (or will come up with a set of interpretations) – this is an instance of productivity. One explanation for this would be that the person can compositionally compute an expression meaning for the

---

[16]To clarify: the issue here is not whether *distributed* representations can be composed, but whether *distributional* representations – i.e., abstractions over distributions of use – can and should be composed. Sophisticated approaches exist for composing *distributed* representations (notably the tensor product approach of Smolensky 1990).

whole sentence, and from there infer what a speaker would mean by it. This places the burden of compositionality entirely on the notion of expression meaning. An alternative would be to say that the person first infers speaker meanings for each word (say, the concept CAT for "cat"),[17] and then composes these to obtain a speaker meaning of the full sentence. This would place the burden of compositionality entirely on the notion of speaker meaning (cf. the notion of *resultant procedure* in Grice 1968; see Borge 2009 for a philosophical argument for compositionality residing at the speaker meaning level). The two alternatives are opposite extremes of a spectrum; and note that the first is what formal semantics proclaims, yet the second is what formal semantics does, given that the notions it composes in fact reside at the level of speaker meaning (e.g., concepts like CAT as opposed to THEWORDCAT; and the end product of composition in formal semantics is typically a truth value). There is also a middle way: The person could in principle compositionally compute expression meanings for certain intermediate constituents (say, "the red cat", "a mouse" and "chases"), then infer speaker meanings for these constituents (say, a particular cat, an unknown mouse, and a chasing event), and only *then* continue to compose these to obtain a speaker meaning for the whole sentence. This kind of middle way requires that a model of expression meaning (distributional semantics) accounts for some degree of compositionality (say, the direct combination of content words), with a model of speaker meaning (say, formal semantics) carrying the rest of the burden. The proposal in McNally and Boleda (2017) is a version of this position.

The foregoing shows that the productivity argument for compositionality falls short as an argument for compositionality *of expression meanings*; that is, **compositionality may well reside in part, or even entirely, at the level of speaker meaning**. We will not at present try to settle the issue of where compositionality resides – though we favor a view according to which compositionality is multi-faceted and doesn't necessarily reside exclusively at one level.[18] What matters for the purposes of this paper is that the requirement imposed by formal semantics, that a theory of expression meaning should account for full-fledged compositionality, turns out to be unjustified.

6 Outlook

We presented two strong reasons why distributional semantics is attractive as a model of expression meaning, i.e., in favor of the 'strong' view of Lenci 2008: The parsimony of regarding expression meaning as an abstraction over use; and the understanding of these abstractions as concepts and, thereby, as a necessary starting point for interpretation. Moreover, although distributional semantics struggles with matters like reference, truth conditions and entailment, we argued that a theory of expression meaning *should not* account for these aspects: words don't refer, speakers do (and likewise for truth conditions and entailments). The referential approach to expression meaning of formal semantics is based on misinterpreting intuitions about stereotypical speaker meaning as being about expression meaning. The same misinterpretation has led to the common view that a theory of expression meaning should be compositional, whereas in fact compositionality may reside wholly or in part (and does reside, in formal semantics) at the level of speaker meaning. Clearing this up reveals that distributional semantics is the more adequate approach to expression meaning. In between our mostly theoretical arguments for this position, we have shown how a consistent interpretation of distributional semantics as a model of expression meaning sheds new light on certain applications: e.g., distributional semantic approaches to entailment and attempts at integrating distributional and formal semantics.

---

[17]We discuss this here as a hypothetical possibility; to assume that individual words of an utterance can be assigned speaker meanings may not be a feasible approach in general.

[18]The empirical picture is undecisive in this regard: just because distributional semantics appears to be able to handle certain aspects of compositionality, that doesn't mean it should. After all, word vectors like "cat" have been quite successfully used as a proxy for extra-linguistic concepts like CAT, even though as we explained this is strictly speaking a misuse (conflating CAT and THEWORDCAT; see section 3.2). Perhaps the moderate success of distributional semantics on for instance adjective-noun composition like "red cat" reflects the fact that the extra-linguistic concepts RED and CAT compose (speaker meaning), even if the linguistic concepts THEWORDRED and THEWORDCAT don't (expression meaning).

Acknowledgments

We are grateful to the anonymous reviewers for their valuable comments. This project has received funding from the European Research Council (ERC) under the European Union's Horizon 2020 research and innovation programme (grant agreement No 715154), and from the Spanish Ramón y Cajal programme (grant RYC-2015-18907). This paper reflects the authors' view only, and the EU is not responsible for any use that may be made of the information it contains.

References

Asher, N., T. Van de Cruys, A. Bride, and M. Abrusán (2016). Integrating type theory and distributional semantics: a case study on adjective–noun compositions. *Computational Linguistics 42*(4), 703–725.

Austin, J. L. (1975). *How to do things with words*, Volume 88. Oxford university press.

Bach, K. (1994). Conversational impliciture. *Mind and Language 9*, 124–62.

Bach, K. (2002). Seemingly semantic intuitions. In J. Campbell, M. O'Rourke, and D. Shier (Eds.), *Meaning and Truth*. New York: Seven Bridges Press.

Bach, K. (2005). Context ex machina. *Semantics versus pragmatics 1544*.

Bahdanau, D., K. Cho, and Y. Bengio (2015). Neural machine translation by jointly learning to align and translate. In *Proceedings of ICLR Conference Track*, San Diego, CA.

Baroni, M., R. Bernardi, and R. Zamparelli (2014). Frege in space: A program of compositional distributional semantics. *LiLT (Linguistic Issues in Language Technology) 9*.

Baroni, M., G. Dinu, and G. Kruszewski (2014). Don't count, predict! a systematic comparison of context-counting vs. context-predicting semantic vectors. In *Proceedings of the 52nd Annual Meeting of the Association for Computational Linguistics (Volume 1: Long Papers)*, Volume 1, pp. 238–247.

Baroni, M. and A. Lenci (2010). Distributional memory: A general framework for corpus-based semantics. *Computational Linguistics 36*(4), 673–721.

Beltagy, I., C. Chau, G. Boleda, D. Garrette, K. Erk, and R. Mooney (2013). Montague meets markov: Deep semantics with probabilistic logical form. In *Second Joint Conference on Lexical and Computational Semantics (* SEM), Volume 1: Proceedings of the Main Conference and the Shared Task: Semantic Textual Similarity*, Volume 1, pp. 11–21.

Bennett, J. (1976). *Linguistic Behavior*. Cambridge University Press.

Bennett, M. R. and P. M. S. Hacker (2008). *History of cognitive neuroscience*. John Wiley & Sons.

Boleda, G. and K. Erk (2015). Distributional semantic features as semantic primitives–or not. In *AAAI Spring Symposium on Knowledge Representation and Reasoning, Stanford University, USA*.

Boleda, G. and A. Herbelot (2016). Formal distributional semantics: Introduction to the special issue. *Computational Linguistics 42*(4), 619–635.

Borge, S. (2009). Intentions and compositionality. *SATS 10*(1), 100–106.

Chomsky, N. (1986). *Knowledge of language: Its nature, origin, and use*. Praeger.

Coecke, B., M. Sadrzadeh, and S. Clark (2011). Mathematical Foundations for a Compositional Distributional Model of Meaning. *Linguistic Analysis: A Festschrift for Joachim Lambek 36*(1–4), 345–384.

Collobert, R. and J. Weston (2008). A unified architecture for natural language processing: Deep neural networks with multitask learning. In *Proceedings of the 25th international conference on Machine learning*, pp. 160–167. ACM.

Degen, J. and M. K. Tanenhaus (2015). Processing scalar implicature: A constraint-based approach. *Cognitive science 39*(4), 667–710.

Dummett, M. (1993). *The seas of language*. Oxford University Press.

Erk, K. (2010). What is word meaning, really?:(and how can distributional models help us describe it?). In *Proceedings of the 2010 workshop on geometrical models of natural language semantics*, pp. 17–26. Association for Computational Linguistics.

Erk, K. (2013). Towards a semantics for distributional representations. In *Proceedings of the 10th International Conference on Computational Semantics (IWCS 2013)–Long Papers*, pp. 95–106.

Feng, Y. and M. Lapata (2010). Visual information in semantic representation. In *Human Language Technologies: The 2010 Annual Conference of the North American Chapter of the Association for Computational Linguistics*, pp. 91–99. Association for Computational Linguistics.

Fodor, J. A., M. F. Garrett, E. C. Walker, and C. H. Parkes (1980). Against definitions. *Cognition 8*(3), 263–367.

Frege, G. (1892). Über sinn und bedeutung. *Zeitschrift für Philosophie und philosophische Kritik 100*(1), 25–50.

Geffet, M. and I. Dagan (2005). The distributional inclusion hypotheses and lexical entailment. In *Proceedings of the 43rd Annual Meeting on Association for Computational Linguistics*, pp. 107–114. Association for Computational Linguistics.

Grefenstette, E., G. Dinu, Y.-Z. Zhang, M. Sadrzadeh, and M. Baroni (2013). Multi-Step Regression Learning for Compositional Distributional Semantics. In *Proceedings of IWCS 2013 (10th International Conference on Computational Semantics)*, East Stroudsburg PA, pp. 131–142. ACL.

Grefenstette, E. and M. Sadrzadeh (2011). Experimental support for a categorical compositional distributional model of meaning. In *Proceedings of the Conference on Empirical Methods in Natural Language Processing (EMNLP '11)*, pp. 1394–1404.

Grice, H. P. (1968). Utterer's meaning, sentence-meaning, and word-meaning. In *Philosophy, Language, and Artificial Intelligence*, pp. 49–66. Springer.

Grice, H. P. (1975). Logic and conversation. In P. Cole and J. Morgan (Eds.), *Syntax and Semantics*, Volume 3, pp. 41–58.

Hanks, P. (2000). Do word meanings exist? *Computers and the Humanities 34*(1-2), 205–215.

Harris, Z. S. (1954). Distributional structure. *Word 10*(2-3), 146–162.

Kadmon, N. and C. Roberts (1986). Prosody and scope: The role of discourse structure. In *CLS 22: Proceedings of the Parasession on Pragmatics and Grammatical Theory*, pp. 16–18. Chicago Linguistic Society.

Kazemzadeh, S., V. Ordonez, M. Matten, and T. L. Berg (2014). Referit game: Referring to objects in photographs of natural scenes. In *EMNLP*.

Kennedy, C. (2007). Vagueness and grammar: The semantics of relative and absolute gradable adjectives. *Linguistics and philosophy 30*(1), 1–45.

Kilgarriff, A. (1997). I don't believe in word senses. *Computers and the Humanities 31*(2), 91–113.

Landauer, T. K. and S. T. Dumais (1997). A solution to plato's problem: The latent semantic analysis theory of acquisition, induction, and representation of knowledge. *Psychological review 104*(2), 211.

Lenci, A. (2008). Distributional semantics in linguistic and cognitive research. *Italian journal of linguistics 20*(1), 1–31.

Lenci, A. (2018). Distributional models of word meaning. *Annual review of Linguistics 4*, 151–171.

Lewis, D. (1972). General semantics. In *Semantics of natural language*, pp. 169–218. Springer.

Lopopolo, A. and E. Miltenburg (2015). Sound-based distributional models. In *Proceedings of the 11th International Conference on Computational Semantics*, pp. 70–75.

Marelli, M., S. Menini, M. Baroni, L. Bentivogli, R. Bernardi, R. Zamparelli, et al. (2014). A sick cure for the evaluation of compositional distributional semantic models. In *LREC*, pp. 216–223.

Margolis, E. and S. Laurence (2014). Concepts. In E. N. Zalta (Ed.), *The Stanford Encyclopedia of Philosophy* (Spring 2014 ed.). Metaphysics Research Lab, Stanford University.

Marr, D. C. (1982). *Vision: a Computational Investigation into the Human Representation and Processing of Visual Information*. San Francisco: Freeman & Co.

McNally, L. and G. Boleda (2017). Conceptual versus referential affordance in concept composition. In *Compositionality and concepts in linguistics and psychology*, pp. 245–267. Springer.

Mikolov, T., M. Karafiát, L. Burget, J. Černockỳ, and S. Khudanpur (2010). Recurrent neural network based language model. In *Eleventh annual conference of the international speech communication association*.

Mikolov, T., I. Sutskever, K. Chen, G. S. Corrado, and J. Dean (2013). Distributed representations of words and phrases and their compositionality. In *Advances in neural information processing systems*, pp. 3111–3119.

Mikolov, T., W.-t. Yih, and G. Zweig (2013). Linguistic regularities in continuous space word representations. In *Proceedings of the 2013 Conference of the North American Chapter of the Association for Computational Linguistics: Human Language Technologies*, pp. 746–751.

Miller, G. A. and W. G. Charles (1991). Contextual correlates of semantic similarity. *Language and cognitive processes 6*(1), 1–28.

Mitchell, J. and M. Lapata (2010). Composition in distributional models of semantics. *Cognitive science 34*(8), 1388–1429.

Montague, R. (1970). Universal grammar. *Theoria 36*(3), 373–398.

Peters, M. E., M. Neumann, M. Iyyer, M. Gardner, C. Clark, K. Lee, and L. Zettlemoyer (2018). Deep contextualized word representations. In *Proc. of NAACL*.

Plummer, B. A., L. Wang, C. M. Cervantes, J. C. Caicedo, J. Hockenmaier, and S. Lazebnik (2015). Flickr30k entities: Collecting region-to-phrase correspondences for richer image-to-sentence models. In *Proceedings of the IEEE international conference on computer vision*, pp. 2641–2649.

Poortman, E. B. (2017). Concept typicality and the interpretation of plural predicate conjunction. In *Compositionality and concepts in linguistics and psychology*, pp. 139–162. Springer.

Pustejovsky, J. (1995). *The generative lexicon*. MIT press.

Recanati, F. (2004). *Literal meaning*. Cambridge University Press.

Roller, S., K. Erk, and G. Boleda (2014). Inclusive yet selective: Supervised distributional hypernymy detection. In *Proceedings of COLING 2014, the 25th International Conference on Computational Linguistics: Technical Papers*, pp. 1025–1036.

Rosch, E. and C. B. Mervis (1975). Family resemblances: Studies in the internal structure of categories. *Cognitive psychology 7*(4), 573–605.

Schiffer, S. (1972). *Meaning*. Oxford: Oxford University Press.

Schwarz, N. (1996). *Cognition and Communication: Judgmental Biases, Research Methods and the Logic of Conversation*. Hillsdale, NJ: Erlbaum.

Searle, J. R. (1969). *Speech acts: An essay in the philosophy of language*, Volume 626. Cambridge university press.

Silberer, C., V. Ferrari, and M. Lapata (2017). Visually grounded meaning representations. *IEEE transactions on pattern analysis and machine intelligence 39*(11), 2284–2297.

Smolensky, P. (1990). Tensor product variable binding and the representation of symbolic structures in connectionist systems. *Artificial intelligence 46*(1-2), 159–216.

Soames, S. et al. (2002). *Beyond rigidity: The unfinished semantic agenda of naming and necessity*. Oxford University Press on Demand.

Stokhof, M. (2011). Intuitions and competence in formal semantics. In B. P. andM Glanzberg and J. Skilters (Eds.), *Formal Semantics and Pragmatics*, Number 6 in Baltic International Yearbook of Cognition, Logic and Communication, pp. 1–23. New Prairie Press.

Strawson, P. F. (1950). On referring. *Mind 59*(235), 320–344.

Turney, P. D. and P. Pantel (2010). From frequency to meaning: Vector space models of semantics. *Journal of artificial intelligence research 37*, 141–188.

Vulić, I. and N. Mrkšić (2017). Specialising word vectors for lexical entailment. In *NAACL 2018*.

Westera, M. and A. Brasoveanu (2014). Ignorance in context: The interaction of modified numerals and quds. In S. D. Todd Snider and M. Weigand (Eds.), *Semantics and Linguistic Theory (SALT) 24*, pp. 414–431.

Wittgenstein, L. (1953). *Philosophical Investigations*. Oxford: Blackwell. Edited by G.E.M. Anscombe (trans.) and R. Rhees.

Ambiguity in Explicit Discourse Connectives

Bonnie Webber
University of Edinburgh
bonnie.webber@ed.ac.uk

Rashmi Prasad
Interactions LLC.
rprasad@interactions.com

Alan Lee
University of Pennsylvania
aleewk@seas.upenn.edu

Abstract

Discourse connectives are known to be subject to both *usage* and *sense* ambiguity, as has already been discussed in the literature. But discourse connectives are no different from other linguistic expressions in being subject to other types of ambiguity as well. Four are illustrated and discussed here.

1 Introduction

Discourse connectives, like other linguistic expressions, are subject to ambiguity. Two types of ambiguity — *usage ambiguity*, whether or not a given token is serving as a discourse connective in its context, and *sense ambiguity*, what discourse relation(s) a given token is signalling — were the subject of a study by Pitler and Nenkova (2009), who showed how syntactic features could help resolve them both.

But discourse connectives are no different from other linguistic expressions in being subject to other types of ambiguity as well. Four of them are discussed here, as a way of encouraging researchers to determine whether existing disambiguation methods suffice to handle them or whether the methods need to be extended. Ignoring the full range of ambiguity of discourse connectives can lead to discourse relations being mis-labelled both manually (during annotation) and automatically (during discourse parsing).

As background to presenting these ambiguities, Section 2 briefly reviews the original Penn Discourse TreeBank (the PDTB-2), the findings of Pitler and Nenkova (2009), and how the recently released PDTB-3 extends and, in some cases corrects, annotation in the PDTB-2. We then turn to four additional types of discourse connective ambiguity that have been discussed in the context of other linguistic forms. Section 3 discusses *part-of-speech ambiguity*, which can affect how a given token functions as a discourse connective. Section 4 discusses *multi-word ambiguity*, where a sequence of tokens can be ambiguous between a sequence of separate elements and a single *multi-word* discourse connective. Section 5 discusses a *scope ambiguity* that affects the sense of discourse connectives. Finally, Section 6 discusses *semantic role ambiguity* involving the arguments of certain CONCESSION relations.

2 Background

2.1 PDTB-2

The Penn Discourse Treebank (Prasad et al., 2008) was created as the largest public repository of annotated discourse relations (over 43K), including over 18.4K signalled by explicit discourse connectives (coordinating or subordinating conjunctions, or discourse adverbials). All relations in the corpus are labelled with either one or two senses from a three-level sense hierarchy, whose top level comprised four non-terminal senses: EXPANSION, COMPARISON, CONTINGENCY and TEMPORAL. Most discourse relations were labelled with terminal senses, except where annotators were unable to decide and backed off to a level-2 (or in some cases, a top-level) sense. Discourse relations consisted of two arguments labelled *Arg1* and **Arg2**, with each relation anchored by either an explicit discourse connective or adjacency. In the latter case, annotators inserted one or more *implicit connectives* that signalled the sense(s) they inferred to hold between the arguments. The approach in the PDTB-2 is agnostic about any higher-level discourse structure, and as such, made no attempt to build a tree or graph structure of relations over the text as a whole. The size and availability of the PDTB-2 spawned the field of *shallow discourse parsing*, as in the 2015 and 2016 CoNLL shared tasks (Xue et al., 2015, 2016), as well as the development of similar resources for other languages, including Chinese, Hindi, and Turkish. An in-depth discussion of the PDTB-2 can be found in (Prasad et al., 2014).

2.2 Pitler & Nenkova (2009)

Pitler and Nenkova (2009) showed how syntactic features could be used in disambiguating both *usage ambiguity* and *sense ambiguity*. To understand these types of ambiguity, consider the word *since*. Ex. 1 illustrates its non-discourse usage, where *since* is simply a temporal preposition. Both Ex. 2 and Ex. 3 illustrate discourse usages and also the *sense ambiguity* of *since*, signalling a purely temporal relation in Ex. 2 and a purely causal relation in Ex. 3.

(1) She has been up since 5am.

(2) There have been over 100 mergers since the most recent wave of friendly takeovers ended.

(3) It was a far safer deal since the company has a healthier cash flow.

Using data in the PDTB-2, Pitler and Nenkova (2009) showed that *usage ambiguity* can be resolved with high accuracy, as can *sense ambiguity* with respect to the four top-level sense classes (cf. Section 2.1). (N.B. They took multi-labelled tokens to be classified correctly if at least one of the senses was correctly identified.) They showed how high accuracy could be achieved in both disambiguation tasks by using both the token itself and its syntactic features in classification. Features included the syntactic category of the node dominating all and only the token itself, the category of its immediate parent, and the categories of its siblings. When they added interactions between connectives and syntactic features, and interactions between the features themselves, accuracy increased over 10 points and f-score, nearly 20 points.

Since Pitler & Nenkova's results are not incompatible with other types of discourse connective ambiguity, their work is a good jumping off point for experimenting with the additional types of discourse connective ambiguity we discuss here.

2.3 PDTB-3

The PDTB-3[1] contains ∼12.5K more intra-sentential relations (i.e., ones that lie wholly within the projection of a top-level S-node) and ∼1K more inter-sentential relations than the PDTB-2 (Webber et al., 2019). New senses have been added to the sense hierarchy (Table 1) and used for annotating new tokens, as well as for re-annotating existing tokens.

Newly annotated intra-sentential relations include ones between the conjuncts of conjoined verb phrases and conjoined clauses; ones between free or headed adjuncts and the clauses they adjoin to; ones associated with subordinators such as *in order*, prepositions such as *with*, *for*, and *in*; and ones between infinitival clauses (or other subordinating structures) and their matrix clause. New annotation also includes explicitly marked question-response pairs, and lexico-syntactic constructions that are *unambiguous* signals of particular discourse relations, such as the *so*-construction, signalling RESULT (Ex. 4), the *too*-construction, signalling NEGATIVE-RESULT (Ex. 5), and *auxiliary inversion*, signalling a CONDITIONAL relation (Ex. 6).[2]

---

[1] https://catalog.ldc.upenn.edu/LDC2019T05

[2] Discourse relations in the paper are formatted with *Arg1* indicated in italics and **Arg2** in bold, with the discourse connnective (explicit or implicit) or alternative lexicalization underlined.

Level-1	Level-2	Level-3
TEMPORAL	SYNCHRONOUS	–
	ASYNCHRONOUS	[PRECEDENCE,SUCCESSION]
CONTINGENCY	CAUSE	REASON
		RESULT
		NEGRESULT
	CAUSE+BELIEF	REASON+BELIEF
		RESULT+BELIEF
	CAUSE+SPEECHACT	REASON+SPEECHACT
		RESULT+SPEECHACT
	CONDITION	[ARG1,ARG2]-AS-COND
	CONDITION+SPEECHACT	–
	NEGATIVE-CONDITION	[ARG1,ARG2]-AS-NEGCOND
	NEGATIVE-CONDITION+SPEECHACT	–
	PURPOSE	[ARG1,ARG2]-AS-GOAL
COMPARISON	CONCESSION	[ARG1,ARG2]-AS-DENIER
	CONCESSION+SPEECHACT	ARG2-AS-DENIER+SPEECHACT
	CONTRAST	–
	SIMILARITY	–
EXPANSION	CONJUNCTION	–
	DISJUNCTION	–
	EQUIVALENCE	–
	EXCEPTION	[ARG1,ARG2]-AS-EXCPT
	INSTANTIATION	[ARG1,ARG2]-AS-INSTANCE
	LEVEL-OF-DETAIL	[ARG1,ARG2]-AS-DETAIL
	MANNER	[ARG1,ARG2]-AS-MANNER
	SUBSTITUTION	[ARG1,ARG2]-AS-SUBST

Table 1: PDTB-3 Sense Hierarchy. Only asymmetric senses extend to Level-3.

(4) *The fit is so good*, **we see this as a time of opportunity**. [wsj_0317]

(5) *Things have gone too far* **for the government to stop them now** [wsj_2454]

(6) *…but would have climbed 0.6%*, **had it not been for the storm** [wsj_0573]

Differences in how discourse relations are annotated in the PDTB-2 and the PDTB-3 reflect (1) changes and/or additions to the sense hierarchy; (2) different criteria for choosing one sense label over another; and (3) rigorous attention to *semantic consistency* (Hollenstein et al., 2016), checking that similar tokens have been annotated in a similar way, thereby reducing annotation noise and improving what can be induced from the corpus.

Note that additions to the sense hierarchy have introduced new *sense ambiguities* that weren't present in the PDTB-2. A case in point is the discourse adverbial *as well*, all of whose tokens were sense-annotated EXPANSION.CONJUNCTION in the PDTB-2 (cf. Ex. 7 and Ex. 8). With the new sense COMPARISON.SIMILARITY, *as well* is now ambiguous between conveying EXPANSION.CONJUNCTION, which Ex. 7 is still taken to do, and COMPARISON.SIMILARITY, which Ex. 8 was re-annotated as.

(7) There is speculation that property/casualty firms will sell even more munis *as they scramble to raise cash to pay claims related to Hurricane Hugo and the Northern California earthquake.* **Fundamental factors are at work** as well. [wsj_0671]

(8) *"They continue to pay their bills and will do so,"* says Ms. Sanger. "We're confident **we'll be paying our bills for spring merchandise** as well." [wsj_1002]

The PDTB-3 records the *provenance* of each token. This shows that, of the ∼53600 tokens annotated in the PDTB-3, ∼57% are unchanged from the PDTB-2, ∼19% (∼9900 tokens) have been changed in some way from their earlier annotation, and the remaining 24% are new to the PDTB-3. Provenance allows us to compare the use of new senses in annotating new tokens and in re-annotating existing tokens. For example, the new sense COMPARISON.SIMILARITY was used in annotating 135 new tokens and in re-annotating 68 tokens, of which 41 were associated with explicit connectives. Of the 41, 18 involved the discourse adverbial *similarly*; 10, the subordinating conjunction *as if*; while the rest involved tokens of *as, as though, as well, much as, just as meanwhile* and *while*. While *similarly* thus unambiguously signals COMPARISON.SIMILARITY, for these other connectives, the new sense has meant a new ambiguity. These additional sense ambiguities argue for re-applying Pitler & Nenkova's analysis to the PDTB-3.

3 Part-of-Speech Ambiguity

Part-of-Speech (PoS) affects how three items function as discourse connectives: *since*, *before*, and *however*. *Since* is ambiguous between a subordinating conjunction (PoS=IN), as in Ex. 9, and an adverbial (PoS=RB), as in Ex. 10.

(9) *However,* since **Eastern first filed for Chapter 11 protection March 9**, *it has consistently promised to pay creditors 100 cents on the dollar.* [wsj_0475]

(10) His company, Misa Manufacturing Inc., *was forced to seek protection from creditors under federal bankruptcy law in 1987* **and has** since **been liquidated**. [wsj_1830]

This ambiguity also affects the sense of *since*. As a subordinating conjunction, *since* signals either REASON or (temporal) SUCCESSION (cf. Ex 9), while as a discourse adverbial, its temporal sense is the reverse — PRECEDENCE (cf. Ex. 10).

The same holds for *before*, which is also ambiguous between a subordinating conjunction (PoS=IN) and an adverbial (PoS=RB). As a subordinating conjunction, it conveys PRECEDENCE (cf. Ex. 11), while as a discourse adverbial, it conveys the reverse —SUCCESSION (cf. Ex. 12).

(11) They said they wanted *to wait for the outcome of any government investigation* before **deciding what to do**. [wsj_0357]

(12) *The Japanese are in the early stage right now,"* said Thomas Kenney, …. "Before, **they were interested in hard assets and they saw magazines as soft**. [wsj_1650]

Finally, *however* is ambiguous between a simple adverbial (PoS=RB) and a *WH-Adverb* subordinator (Pos=WRB). The latter is shown in Ex. 13.

(13) *The 1987 crash was "a false alarm* however **you view it**," says University of Chicago economist Victor Zarnowitz. [wsj_2397]

As a simple discourse adverbial, the most common sense of *however* is COMPARISON.CONCESSION.ARG2-AS-DENIER. As a subordinator, the most common sense of *however* is the reverse, COMPARISON.CONCESSION.ARG1-AS-DENIER.[3]

As for resolving these ambiguities, reliable disambiguation of their *usage* as discourse connectives only requires correct PoS-tagging to disambiguate how they are functioning as discourse connectives.

4 Multi-word Expression Ambiguity

Another ambiguity arises when a multi-word sequence can be analyzed either as a sequence of separate elements or as a single multi-word connective. Four sequences (*but then*, *only to*, *or otherwise* and *but also*) are ambiguous in this way.

Take *but then*: It can be interpreted as as a sequence of connectives, with *but* conveying COMPARISON.CONTRAST or COMPARISON.CONCESSION.ARG2-AS-DENIER and *then* conveying TEMPORAL.ASYNCHRONOUS.PRECEDENCE, as in

(14) Small businesses say a recent trend is like a dream come true: more-affordable rates for employee-health insurance, initially at least. But then they wake up to a nightmare. [wsj_0518]

Alternatively, it can be interpreted as a single multi-word connective that expresses COMPARISON.CONCESSION.ARG2-AS-DENIER, as in

(15) *To many, it was a ceremony more befitting a king than a rural judge seated in the isolated foothills of the southern Allegheny Mountains.* But then **Judge O'Kicki often behaved like a man who would be king – and, some say, an arrogant and abusive one**. [wsj_0267]

---

[3] CONCESSION is annotated when a causal relation expected on the basis of one argument is cancelled or denied by the situation described in the other.

(N.B. The CONCESSION label corresponds to a paraphrase with *even though* – e.g. "Even though it was a ceremony more befitting a king than a rural judge seated in the isolated foothills of the southern Allegheny Mountains, Judge O'Kicki often behaved like a man who would be king ...". Multi-word *but then* also implies that "you shouldn't be surprised at this because", but this is not something that was annotated in the PDTB-3.)

Another ambiguous sequence is *only to*. On the one hand, *only* can be interpreted as modifying *to*, as it does in *only because*, *only when*, etc., indicating that Arg2 is the only thing in the given relation with Arg1, cf.

(16) *Tax-exempt airport and street-corner solicitations were intended* **only to provide start-up funds**. [wsj_0282]

On the other hand, *only to* can be interpreted as a single multi-word connective conveying that Arg2 is a surprising, unexpected situation that follows Arg1, as in

(17) *Two former secretaries told the grand jury they were summoned to the judge's chambers on separate occasions to take dictation*, only to **find the judge in his bikini underwear**. [wsj_0267]

This is indicated by *only to* being labelled both PRECEDENCE and CONCESSION.ARG2-AS-DENIER.

A third ambiguous sequence is *or otherwise*. It can be analyzed as two separate connectives, with *otherwise* expressing CONTINGENCY.NEGATIVE-CONDITION.ARG1-AS-NEGCOND, as in Example 18 (paraphrasable as "if you don't stay in the center of the path, you might trip and fall."), or as a single multi-word connective, with *or otherwise* conveying that the disjuncts are mutually exclusive **and** that their union covers the full sct, as in Example 19.

(18) *Walk down the center of the path*, or otherwise, **you might trip and fall**.

(19) A new Maryland law frees store owners of liability if a customer *trips* or otherwise **gets hurt** on the way to the restroom. [wsj_1270]

The final ambiguous sequence that we note here, *but also* (or in some cases, just the word *but*), sometimes appears as part of the paired connective *not only ... but also* (cf. Ex. 20), usually sense-annotated as CONJUNCTION.

(20) Market participants say *investors are* not only *licking their wounds following the turbulence last week*, but they have also **been made nervous by two events in West Germany**. [wsj_1187]

Alternatively, the sequence can be analyzed as two distinct connectives — *but*, signalling CONTRAST or CONCESSION.ARG2-AS-DENIER, and *also*, signalling CONJUNCTION. This is how they have been labelled in wsj_0044 (Ex. 21).

(21) a. Editorials in the Greenville newspaper *allowed that Mrs. Yeargin was wrong*, but **also said the case showed how testing was being overused**. [wsj_0044]

b. Editorials in the Greenville newspaper *allowed that Mrs. Yeargin was wrong*, **but** also **said the case showed how testing was being overused**. [wsj_0044]

As with both usage and sense ambiguity, it would be useful to determine whether syntactic features might help distinguish whether a particular multi-word span should be analyzed as a single connective or separate elements.

5   Scope Ambiguity

Scope was only an issue in the PDTB-2 with respect to attribution, where a verb of attribution such as *say* or *think* might be superficially negated, while having the negation actually work to reverse the polarity of the attributed argument or relation (The PDTB Research Group, 2008). But scope is also a source of ambiguity in the PDTB-3, where it can affect the sense of *to-clause* constructions.

Absent modality or negation, a *to-clause* construction has a simple sense ambiguity. The *to-clause* can be **Arg2** of either a CONTINGENCY.PURPOSE.ARG2-AS-GOAL relation (Ex. 22), or of a CONTINGENCY.CAUSE.RESULT relation (Ex. 23).

(22) The Galileo project started in 1977, and *a number of project veterans were on hand* **to watch the launch**. [wsj_1817]

(23) *Georgia Gulf stock rose $1.75 a share yesterday* **to close at $51.25 a share**. [wsj_0080]

(By definition, PURPOSE requires a volitional agent, and generally can be paraphrased by inserting *in order*, while with RESULT, inserting *therefore* leads to a more appropriate paraphrase.)

However, in the context of a modal (e.g., *need, have to, must, require.* etc.) or future tense (or present tense used as future), an additional ambiguity appears, whose disambiguation depends on whether the scope of the modal or future tense includes just *Arg1* or both arguments. Specifically, if the scope includes just *Arg1*, annotators have taken the sense as being conditional (ARG2-AS-COND), because while the situation specified in the *to-clause* (**Arg2**) might be the agent's purpose, there is no assertion that it is so. This can be seen in the use of *if* as an appropriate paraphrase, as in Ex. 24–25

(24) *Banks need a competitive edge* **to sell their products**. [wsj_0238]
paraphrase: Banks need a competitive edge <u>if</u> they are to sell their products.

(25) He said *the index would have to be in the low 40% range for several months* **to be considered a forecast of recession**. [wsj_0036]
paraphrase: He said the index would have to be in the low 40% range for several months <u>if</u> it is to be considered a forecast of recession.

In contrast, if the modal or future operator seems best interpreted as scoping both arguments, as in

(26) The two companies have been discussing a transaction *under which Fresenius would buy Delmed stock for cash* **to bring its beneficial ownership to between 70% and 80% of Delmed's fully diluted common stock**. [wsj_1066]
paraphrase: … under which it **would** be the case that Fresenius buys Delmed stock for cash to bring its beneficial ownership to …

then we are back to the original sense ambiguity between PURPOSE.ARG2-AS-GOAL and RESULT.

This same CONDITIONAL sense ambiguity also arises when there is negation or a question in *Arg1*, because its scope is again ambiguous between being just over *Arg1* or over both arguments. This can be manually disambiguated by seeing whether *if* can be appropriately inserted in a positive paraphrase of *Arg1* (in the case of negation) or a non-question paraphrase of *Arg1* (in a question context). If so, scope only extends over *Arg1*, and the sense is CONDITION.ARG2-AS-COND, as in

(27) … which, unlike utilities, aren't regulated *and therefore don't need government approval* **to construct new plants**. [wsj_0560]
paraphrase: … and therefore they need government approval <u>if</u> they are to construct new plants

In the case of the question in Ex. 28,

(28) *Do you really need this much money* **to put up these investments**? [wsj_0629]

"You really need this much money if you are to put up these investments" was not considered an appropriate non-question paraphrase of the original: The question was taken to scope both arguments. As such, one is back to the original sense ambiguity of *to-clause* constructions between PURPOSE.ARG2-AS-GOAL and RESULT. Since here, an appropriate paraphrase involves *in order* — "You really need this much money in order to put up these investments" — PURPOSE.ARG2-AS-GOAL was taken to be an appropriate sense label. In all, of over 1600 relations whose **Arg2** was a *to-clause* construction, about 9% were sense-labelled CONDITION.ARG2-AS-COND.

While scope cannot be disambiguated by purely syntactic means, disambiguating these cases may require methods that go beyond the purely syntax-based approach of Pitler and Nenkova (2009).

6   Semantic Role Ambiguity

In English, *semantic role ambiguity* has mainly been discussed in the context of "garden path" sentences (Konstas et al., 2014), where in

(29) a. The horse raced past the barn ...

    b. The man served the potatoes ...

there is an ambiguity as to whether *the horse* (*the man*) is in the agent role of main verb *raced* (*served*) or the patient role of *raced* (*served*) as head of a reduced relative clause. Where listeners consistently make the wrong choice, it is considered a "garden path" sentence.

A few verbs in English such as *shame* demonstrate *semantic role ambiguity* even without considering reduced relative clauses. As shown in Ex. 30, even after processing the direct object of *shame* (i.e., *me*), there is still an ambiguity as to who plays the role of shamer and who, the shamee.

(30) My son shamed me ...
    a. into giving some of our cookies to the other children.
    paraphrase: My son made me feel ashamed of myself (causing me to do something)
    b. by keeping all the cookies for himself.
    paraphrase: My son made me feel ashamed of him (by keeping the cookies for himself)

With discourse connectives, four subordinating conjunctions that can signal a CONCESSION relation — *although*, *though*, *even though*, and *while* — show a similar ambiguity when they head a postposed subordinate clause. The ambiguity here is which clause raises the causal inference and which denies it. It is an ambiguity that does not appear with preposed subordinate clauses.

More specifically, we noted in Section 2.3 that some senses are asymmetric, meaning that the relation is directional. To capture this directionality, each asymmetric relation has two Level-3 senses, in one of which *Arg1* plays the specified role, while in the other case, **Arg2** does so (cf. Table 1).

In general, an explicit connective that signals an asymmetric sense does so unambiguously. For example, when *otherwise* signals exception, the exception is *Arg1* (EXPANSION.EXCEPTION.ARG1-AS-EXCPT), as in Ex. 31. In contrast, when *except* signals exception, the exception is **Arg2** (EXPANSION.EXCEPTION.ARG2-AS-EXCPT), as in Ex. 32.

(31) *Twenty-five years ago the poet Richard Wilbur modernized this 17th-century comedy merely by avoiding "the zounds sort of thing," as he wrote in his introduction.* <u>Otherwise,</u> **the scene remained Celimene's house in 1666.** [wsj_0936]

(32) *Boston Co. officials declined to comment on Moody's action on the unit's financial performance this year* <u>except</u> **to deny a published report that outside accountants had discovered evidence of significant accounting errors in the first three quarters' results.**

While CONCESSION relations are asymmetric, the subordinating conjunctions *although, though, even though* and *while* are not always unambiguous signals. That is, when they head a preposed subordinate clause (402 tokens in the PDTB-3), they were taken as unambiguously signalling the relation COMPARISON.CONCESSION.ARG1-AS-DENIER, where the matrix clause (*Arg1*) denies the causal inference raised by the subordinate clause, **Arg2**, as in Ex. 33.

(33) The documents also said *that* <u>although</u> **the 64-year-old Mr. Cray has been working on the project for more than six years,** *the Cray-3 machine is at least another year away from a fully operational prototype.* [wsj_0018]

However, when postposed with respect to its matrix clause, there is an ambiguity as to whether the matrix clause (*Arg1*) plays the role of denying the causal inference raised in **Arg2**, as in Ex. 34, or whether the subordinate clause (**Arg2**) plays the role of denying the causal inference raised in *Arg1*, as in Ex. 35.

(34) The company's research suggests *that its name recognition among most consumers remains unusually low,* <u>although (CONCESSION.ARG1-AS-DENIER)]</u> **its array of brands – including Maxwell House coffee, Jell-O, Cheez Whiz, and Miller beer – blanket supermarket shelves.** [wsj_0326]

(35) *Unemployment still is officially recorded at 16.5%, the highest rate in Europe,* <u>although (CONCESSION.ARG2-AS-DENIER)</u> **actual joblessness may be lower**. [wsj_0456]

In the PDTB-3, there are 324 tokens of postposed CONCESSION relations with one of these four connectives. Of these, 260 have been labelled CONCESSION.ARG1-AS-DENIER, as with comparable preposed subordinate clauses, while the remaining 64 have been labelled CONCESSION.ARG2-AS-DENIER. The only differences between the four connectives is their relative frequency with which they appear in post-position and the degree of ambiguity when they do.

Conn	total labelled CONCESSION	Proportion in post-position	ARG1-AS-DENIER	ARG2-AS-DENIER
even though	95	0.74	44	26
though	219	0.60	7	125
although	311	0.37	11	103
while	237	0.03	2	6

While further analysis should identify features that will help disambiguate the sense of post-posed CONCESSIVES, it is nevertheless worth establishing that semantic role ambiguity is not limited to verbs.

7   Conclusion

We hope to have shown that discourse connectives are no different from other linguistic expressions in being subject to many types of ambiguity. Besides *usage ambiguity* and *sense ambiguity* (Pitler and Nenkova, 2009), we hope to have shown that discourse connectives are subject to ambiguities associated with *parts-of-speech, multi-word expressions, scope* and *semantic roles*. We hope this will now encourage researchers to explore whether existing disambiguation methods suffice to handle this larger range of discourse connective ambiguities or whether such methods need to be extended.

References

Hollenstein, N., N. Schneider, and B. Webber (2016). Inconsistency detection in semantic annotation. In *Proceedings, Language Resources and Evaluation Conference (LREC 2016)*, Potoroz, Slovenia.

Konstas, I., F. Keller, V. Demberg, and M. Lapata (2014). Incremental semantic role labeling with tree adjoining grammar. In *Proceedings, Empirical Methods in Natural Language Processing*.

Pitler, E. and A. Nenkova (2009). Using syntax to disambiguate explicit discourse connectives in text. In *ACL-IJCNLP '09: Proceedings of the 47th Meeting of the Association for Computational Linguistics and the 4th International Joint Conference on Natural Language Processing*.

Prasad, R., N. Dinesh, A. Lee, E. Miltsakaki, L. Robaldo, A. Joshi, and B. Webber (2008). The Penn Discourse TreeBank 2.0. In *Proceedings, 6th International Conference on Language Resources and Evaluation*, Marrakech, Morocco.

Prasad, R., B. Webber, and A. Joshi (2014). Reflections on the Penn Discourse Treebank, comparable corpora and complementary annotation. *Computational Linguistics 40(4)*, 921–950.

The PDTB Research Group (2008). The Penn Discourse TreeBank 2.0 Annotation Manual. Available at http://www.seas.upenn.edu/~pdtb/, or as part of the download of LDC2008T05.

Webber, B., R. Prasad, A. Lee, and A. Joshi (2019). The Penn Discourse Treebank 3.0 Annotation Manual. Technical report, University of Pennsylvania. Available at https://catalog.ldc.upenn.edu/docs/LDC2019T05/PDTB3-Annotation-Manual.pdf.

Xue, N., H. T. Ng, S. Pradhan, R. Prasad, C. Bryant, and A. Rutherford (2015). The CoNLL-2015 shared task on shallow discourse parsing. In *Proc 19th Conference on Computational Natural Language Learning – Shared Task*, Beijing, pp. 1–16.

Xue, N., H. T. Ng, S. Pradhan, A. Rutherford, B. Webber, C. Wang, and H. Wang (2016). CoNLL 2016 shared task on multilingual shallow discourse parsing. In *Proc 20th Conference on Computational Natural Language Learning – Shared Task*, Berlin, pp. 1–19.

Aligning Open IE Relations and KB Relations using a Siamese Network Based on Word Embedding

Rifki Afina Putri
School of Computing, KAIST
rifkiaputri@kaist.ac.kr

Giwon Hong
School of Computing, KAIST
gch02518@kaist.ac.kr

Sung-Hyon Myaeng
School of Computing, KAIST
myaeng@kaist.ac.kr

Abstract

Open Information Extraction (Open IE) aims at generating entity-relation-entity triples from a large amount of text, aiming at capturing key semantics of the text. Given a triple, the relation expresses the type of semantic relation between the entities. Although relations from an Open IE system are more extensible than those used in a traditional Information Extraction system and a Knowledge Base (KB) such as Knowledge Graphs, the former lacks in semantics; an Open IE relation is simply a sequence of words, whereas a KB relation has a predefined meaning. As a way to provide a meaning to an Open IE relation, we attempt to align it with one of the predefined set of relations used in a KB. Our approach is to use a Siamese network that compares two sequences of word embeddings representing an Open IE relation and a predefined KB relation. In order to make the approach practical, we automatically generate a training dataset using a distant supervision approach instead of relying on a hand-labeled dataset. Our experiment shows that the proposed method can capture the relational semantics better than the recent approaches.

1 Introduction

Open Information Extraction (Open IE) aims at extracting key information from a large amount of text into a structured format, commonly in the form of triples, *(subject entity, relation, object entity)*, where the relation denotes the type of a semantic relation between the entities. As opposed to the traditional Information Extraction that generates triples over a predefined relation set, Open IE can extract all possible relations without having to be restricted to a predefined set of relations. However, a relation from an Open IE system is merely a sequence of words coming from the sentence containing the entities, resulting in ambiguous and semantically redundant relations. For example, Open IE may extract *"died in"* and *"location of death"* as two distinct relations although they should be treated as semantically equal and expressed (or canonicalized) with a single relation type.

In order to address this problem, some methods have been proposed to canonicalize Open IE relations (Yates and Etzioni, 2009; Galárraga et al., 2014; Vashishth et al., 2018). Given that they rely on a clustering method, however, they tend to suffer from over-generalization. For example, the latest canonicalization method called CESI (Vashishth et al., 2018) would put *"is brother of," "is son of," "is main villain of,"* and *"was professor of"* into the same relation cluster. While these relation phrases have a common pattern (to be + noun + of) and expresses that the subject entity has a certain role, the overarching relational category is too general to be useful.

Besides Open IE, Knowledge Base (KB) systems such as DBpedia, Freebase, and Wikidata, also store general facts in a triple format. Different from Open IE, the relations in a KB are already classified into distinct semantic categories. Although KB relations are better defined semantically than Open IE relations, they are limited in terms of quantity and coverage. Dutta et al. (2015) attempted to mitigate the weaknesses of the two approaches by aligning the relations of Open IE triples to those in DBpedia, thereby adding semantics to Open IE triples. While useful, their approach is primarily based on the frequency of triples without explicitly taking into account the relational semantics.

In this paper, we propose a new model using a Siamese network for aligning relations from Open IE to those from KB (i.e. relation alignment task) for the purpose of providing more semantics to Open IE relations, which are to be used for question answering as in TriviaQA (Joshi et al., 2017). The Siamese network, a form of a neural network, takes two sequences of word embeddings representing an Open IE relation and a KB relation and compares them. The network is trained to learn the semantic similarities between an Open IE relational phrase and a KB relation type name that are considered identical in their meanings. By utilizing word embeddings as the input of the network and encode relational descriptions, we can incorporate their semantics information without an extra process of extracting linguistic features from the training data. In order to mitigate the problem of manually constructing training data, i.e. pairs of an Open IE relational phrase and a KB relation type name, we propose a distant supervision method that does not require manual annotations. Our contributions in this paper are:

- We propose a novel method of applying a Siamese network for the relation alignment task. To the best of our knowledge, our model is the first attempt that incorporates the semantic information of the textual descriptions of relations, specifically for the relation alignment task.

- We propose to automatically generate a training dataset using a distant supervision approach so that we avoid manual creation of training data, which can be prohibitive, thereby making the proposed approach practical.

- We experimentally confirm that our model better captures relational semantics than the clustering and the statistical rule-based approaches with a significant margin. We also analyze different variations of the Siamese network to provide insights about the relation alignment task.

2   Related Work

Open IE Canonicalization. Yates and Etzioni (2009) proposed a simple probabilistic method for identifying Open IE triples which has a similar meaning. They calculated similarity between two relation phrases and clustered them with a greedy agglomerative clustering method. Although their model works well in finding synonyms for relation phrases, it still suffers from the polysemy problem. Galárraga et al. (2014) canonicalized relation phrases by employing a rule mining algorithm called AMIE (Galárraga et al., 2013) to mine the relationship rules between relation phrases and clustered the relation phrases based on the generated rules. Recently, Vashishth et al. (2018) improved Dutta's model by using relation embeddings and side information as the features for the clustering method. They canonicalized the Open IE relations by clustering the embedding. Our task is different from their task since we focus on adding more semantics to the Open IE relations by aligning them to the KB relations.

Instead of relying on only one Open IE systems, Bovi et al. (2015) proposed a method called KB-Unify to integrate the triples from different Open IE systems into a single repository. Our work differs from their work since we attempt to align the Open IE and KB relations. Our task is mostly similar to the alignment task presented by Dutta et al. (2015), which was introduced in Section 1. They aimed to bring the benefits of Open IE and KB by mapping the Open IE triples to existing KB triples (DBpedia) by using a statistical rule-based approach. While their result seems promising, it only relies on frequency of the triples without considering semantics. Besides, it suffers from an efficiency problem arising from frequency calculation.

Word Sense Alignment. Gurevych et al. (2016) define Word Sense Alignment as linking senses or concepts that has an identical meaning from multiple Lexical Knowledge Bases (LKB). There has been a lot of work with various goals such as aligning WordNet, Cyc, and VerbNet for building knowledge representation (Crouch and King, 2005), aligning FrameNet, VerbNet, and WordNet for semantic parsing (Shi and Mihalcea, 2005), and building large-scale LKB alignments (Matuschek, 2015; Gurevych et al., 2012; Navigli and Ponzetto, 2012). Although this task is conceptually similar with our relation alignment task, we focus on aligning the relation meaning of Open IE and KB, not word sense in general.

Relation Extraction using Distant Supervision. There are many works that used distant supervision method to generate the dataset for relation extraction task such as Mintz et al. (2009) and Riedel et al. (2010). Sorokin and Gurevych (2017) proposed a LSTM-based neural network to extract relation using another relation in the same sentence as a contextual information and utilized Wikidata to construct the dataset. Even though we also use Wikidata in our dataset generation method, however, we aim to align the Open IE relations to the extracted relations in Wikidata.

3 Model Description

3.1 Task Description

Let $\mathbf{x}_{OIE}$ be an Open IE triple and $\mathbf{x}_{KB}$ be a KB triple. Given $\mathbf{x}_{OIE}$ and $\mathbf{x}_{KB}$ as the input, the goal is to determine whether the relation in $\mathbf{x}_{OIE}$ can be aligned to (i.e. expressed with) that of $\mathbf{x}_{KB}$. If they can be aligned, the model will give 0 ("semantically same") as the output, or 1 ("not semantically same" or "semantically different") otherwise. For example, given (**English**, *are language of*, **England**) as the Open IE triple and (**English**, *official language*, **England**) as the KB triple, we want to determine whether the relation *are language of* is semantically close enough to and hence can be replaced by the KB relation *official language*. Given the task, our proposed model essentially gives the distance of the Open IE and KB relations based on the weights learned for the network so that it predicts whether the pair is semantically same or not.

3.2 A Siamese Network for Relation Alignment

The concept of a Siamese network was introduced by Bromley et al. (1993) and typically used for measuring the similarity of two inputs. It consists of two identical sub-networks that extract the features from two inputs, respectively. Then the distance from the two sub-network outputs is calculated to determine the input similarity. Note that the two sub-networks will have been learned at the training stage in such a way that the distance between the semantically identical inputs is minimized. The overall model architecture is in Figure 1.

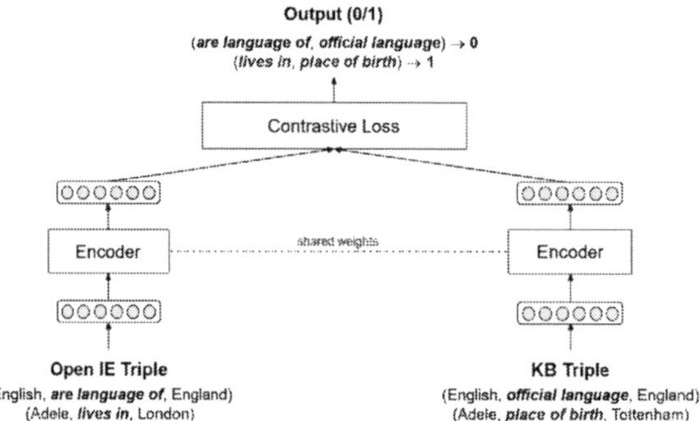

Figure 1: General architecture of the proposed model including the input and output example. The *blue* text represents positive example and the *red* text represents negative example.

In the proposed network, the first and second sub-networks attempt to capture the features from the Open IE and the KB relations, respectively. The embeddings of the input words on each sub-network are encoded to produce a new vector. Note that the encoders share the same weights. For training, we use a contrastive loss function. The details of the model are described in the following sub-section.

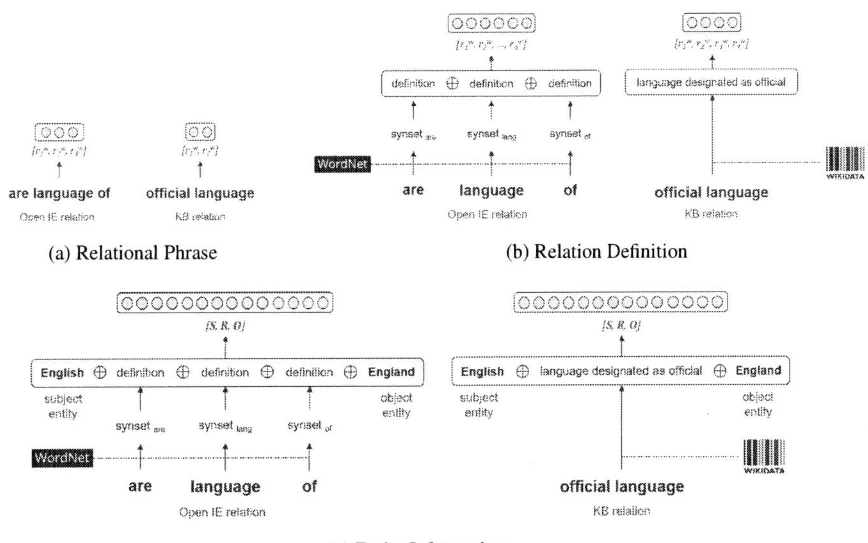

Figure 2: The illustration of input representation.

3.2.1 Input Representation

Before an input is fed into the encoder, each word in the input is converted into a fixed size n-dimensional word embedding. Given that relation phrases from Open IE and names (from a KB) can be too short to carry enough semantics, we also utilize relation definitions and entity information when input representations are computed. Therefore, we have three input representations as follows:

- **Relational Phrase.** For a relational phrase input (Figure 2a), each word w is transformed into real-valued vector $r^w \in \mathbb{R}^d$ where d is the dimension of the word embedding. For the encoding of the entire phrase, we concatenate the word vectors for the phrase to generate a phrase embedding, $\mathbf{x} = [r_1^w, r_2^w, ..., r_n^w]$, where n is the number of words in the phrase.

- **Relation Definition.** For a relation definition input (Figure 2b), we utilize WordNet to obtain an Open IE relation phrase definition and Wikidata for additional relation description of each KB relation. For an Open IE relation, we transform each word in the relation phrase into WordNet synset using the Lesk algorithm[1]. The definition of each synset is then obtained from the WordNet dictionary. For a KB relation, we utilize Wikidata API[2] to get its description that serves as the definition. Finally, the input representation is formed by concatenating of the word vectors in the definition text, i.e., $\mathbf{x} = [r_1^w, r_2^w, ..., r_n^w]$ where n is the number of words in the definition.

- **Entity Information.** Besides relation information, we consider entity information as an additional feature in our model (Figure 2c). The entity information is construed as the context surrounding the relation and hence providing the semantics of the relation. The subject and the object entity phrases are concatenated to the relation phrase or definition, i.e., $\mathbf{x} = [\mathbf{S}, \mathbf{R}, \mathbf{O}]$ where $\mathbf{S} = [s_1^w, s_2^w, ..., s_t^w]$, $\mathbf{R} = [r_1^w, r_2^w, ..., r_u^w]$, $\mathbf{O} = [o_1^w, o_2^w, ..., o_v^w]$; t and v denotes the number of words in the subject and object entities, respectively, and u denotes the number of words in the relation phrase.

---

[1] https://www.nltk.org/_modules/nltk/wsd.html
[2] https://query.wikidata.org

3.2.2 Encoder

After we have the input representations for Open IE and KB relations, the next step is to feed them to the encoder. Considering the past success of CNN in extracting appropriate features for relation extraction from a sequence of words (Nguyen and Grishman, 2015), we opt for two encoders as follows:

- **Convolutional Neural Network (CNN).** CNN has three main parts: convolution, max-pooling, and fully-connected linear layers. In the convolution layer, we aim to extract the local features from the given input text. By extracting local features, we can create a subject, a relation, and an object representation similar to n-gram features. The max-pooling layer selects the most important features contained in the phrase. The output from the max-pooling layer is fed to a feed-forward fully-connected linear layer. Finally, its output is used as our final relation representation.

- **Piecewise Convolutional Neural Network (PCNN).** In PCNN, which was first introduced by Zeng et al. (2015), the original max-pooling layer is modified into piecewise max-pooling. We apply a max operation over a segment of the phrase so that the model can extract the important features without losing the information coming from the subject entity, the relation, and the object entity, separately. Finally, similar to the CNN encoder, the output from the feed-forward linear layer is used as the final relation representation.

3.3 Contrastive Loss Function

For learning, we apply a contrastive loss function defined as the sum of the loss of positive examples (semantically same relations) and the loss of negative examples (semantically different relations). More formally, the loss function is defined as:

$$L = (1 - Y)D^2 + Y(max(0, m - D))^2; m > 0 \tag{1}$$

$$D = |\mathbf{x'}_{OIE} - \mathbf{x'}_{KB}| \tag{2}$$

where Y and D denote the label of the input pairs (0 for semantically same, 1 for semantically different) and the euclidean distance between the Open IE and the KB relation vectors (i.e. the output from the encoder explained in the previous section) respectively, with m being a margin. Note that the first term of Equation 1 is used for positive examples and the second term for negative examples. When training, we want to make the distance of the positive pairs smaller and the distance of the negative pairs inside the margin larger.

4 Dataset Generation using Distant Supervision

The distant supervision method for the task of relation extraction was first introduced by Mintz et al. (2009). It assumes that any sentence containing an entity pair participating in a triple of a known KB is likely to contain a relevant expression of the relation of the triple. As a result, it becomes possible to construct positive training instances for the relation in the triple by taking the expressions between the occurrences of the two entities. The collection of textual expressions can be used as revealing the target relation. By adopting this approach, we can obtain the sentences containing the target relation in KB and use them to extract Open IE triples with the relation. Once the Open IE triples are generated, we apply some rules to annotate them as positive or negative automatically so that we obtain training data for the KB relations used in collection the Open IE triples. The training data generation steps are as follows:

1. Select the top 200 most frequent relations[3] in the KB and collect the KB triples containing one of the relations. We utilize Wikidata (Vrandečić and Krötzsch, 2014) as our KB.

---

[3] As of October, 2018

2. Crawl the sentences for each triple using the distant supervision method. In other words, we pick the sentences containing the two entities of the triple. In order to reduce ambiguities associated with the occurrences of the entities, we retrieve sentences from the Wikipedia page of each entity.

3. Apply Open IE to each sentence to extract Open IE triples. In this paper, we use the existing Stanford Open IE system (Angeli et al., 2015).

4. Align Open IE and KB triples. The triples *sharing the same entity pair* are labeled as *semantically same* or *positive* (0). But if *one of the entities* is *different*, it labeled as *different* or *negative* (1).

5. From the previous step, we will get a small amount of positive examples but a high number of negative examples. To handle the data imbalance problem, we add more positive examples by swapping a pair of alignments when the other sides of the two alignments share the same relation but with different entities. For example, when we have positive examples as follows:

$$(\textbf{Inn}, \textit{country}, \textbf{Switzerland}), (\textbf{Inn}, \textit{is river in}, \textbf{Switzerland}), 0$$
$$(\textbf{Villavicencio}, \textit{country}, \textbf{Colombia}), (\textbf{Villavicencio}, \textit{is city in}, \textbf{Colombia}), 0$$

we generate two additional positive examples by swapping the right hand side triples as follows:

$$(\textbf{Inn}, \textit{country}, \textbf{Switzerland}), (\textbf{Villavicencio}, \textit{is city in}, \textbf{Colombia}), 0$$
$$(\textbf{Villavicencio}, \textit{country}, \textbf{Colombia}), (\textbf{Inn}, \textit{is river in}, \textbf{Switzerland}), 0$$

5 Experiments

The goal of our experiments are two-fold: the first is to examine the influence of different input representations and encoder variations of our model in capturing the semantics of the relations of the Open IE and the KB and the second is to compare our model against the existing approaches for aligning Open IE and KB relations. The existing approaches that serve as the baselines are:

- **CESI** (Vashishth et al., 2018): For this model, we adjust the clustering result so that it can be compared with our model for the evaluation tasks to be described below. If two relations are in the same cluster, then they are labeled as semantically same; otherwise different.

- **Dutta et al.** (2014): This model uses a statistical rule-based approach for aligning relations. It calculates a confidence score of every possible Open IE relations mapping to a KB relations based on occurrence statistics of the particular mapping. If the mapping has a higher confidence than the threshold determined by linear regression, it is labeled as semantically same; otherwise different. Because the code has not been shared by the authors, we implemented their method on our own.

Besides the above baselines, we also apply our alignment rule (denotes as **rule-based** in Table 2) used in the dataset generation process (see Section 4) for predicting the label, i.e., the triples sharing the same entity pair are labeled as semantically same; otherwise different. Note that this case is used as a reference point in explaining the performance of the proposed method and the other baselines. It also can be used to measure the quality of the distant supervision dataset.

Since there is no standard evaluation suit available for the relation alignment task, we provide three evaluations to reveal different aspects of the proposed model and compensate for the limitations of each.

1. **Internal Evaluation with Automatically Generated Dataset.** The goal is to examine different variations of the proposed model using automatically generated test data of a large quantity. It is internal because we only compare different variations of the proposed model, not against other methods. We split our automatically generated dataset into training, validation, and testing datasets (see Table 1 for details).

- **CNN_no_def**: This version uses CNN as the encoder and relational phrases and relation names (no definitions) as the input representation for both Open IE and KB relations.

- **CNN_def**: This is the same as CNN_no_def except that relation definitions are added.

- **CNN_def_ent**: This version is the same as CNN_def except that entity information is added.

- **PCNN_no_def_ent**: This version uses PCNN as the encoder and relational phrases and relation names for Open IE and KB relations as the input, respectively, as well entity information.

- **PCNN_def_ent**: This is the same as PCNN_no_def_ent except relation definitions are added.

Set	# triples	# sentences	# alignments		
			Positive	Negative	Total
Training	86,178	102,863	430,364	430,364	860,728
Validation	34,726	42,874	184,621	184,621	369,242
Testing	32,309	39,477	168,257	168,257	336,514

Table 1: Statistics of our dataset generated by the distant supervision method.

Since we use a large number of sentences and triples extracted thereof, this evaluation allows us to test different variations for all the relations exhaustively.

2. **Manual Evaluation.** This evaluation is intended to overcome a drawback of the internal evaluation, which relies on the assumption that the gold standard generated by distant supervision is always correct. Another limitation is that it does not include external evaluation. Therefore, in this evaluation, we use a manually annotated test data set and use it as the gold standard to make the evaluation more reliable and compare the performance of the proposed model with the two existing approaches mentioned above.[4] An added value is that we can indirectly examine the reliability of the internal evaluation method by comparing the relative ordering of the variations. To build the dataset, we randomly sampled 400 alignments from the distant supervision testing data. The dataset has all unique entity pairs and it covers 90 unique KB relations. For each pair of relations, one from Open IE and the other from KB, we asked three annotators to decide whether the relations were semantically same or not, resulting in 258 "same" and 142 "different" relation pairs. The inter-judge agreement was 81.88% in Fleiss' Kappa.

3. **Qualitative Analysis.** The goal is to examine the strengths and weaknesses of the proposed model by looking at different lexico-syntactic complexities of the relational phrase patterns, relative to the two baselines. We chose a smaller sample of the alignment result than the above "manual evaluation", including ten semantically same relation pairs and five semantically different ones. For the semantically same relation pairs, we divide the set into two categories: lexical similarity vs difference. Lexical similarity means the relations share at least one similar word, for example *"died in"* and *"place of death"* relations. Lexical difference means the relational phrases do not share a lexically similar word at all, for example *"'s son is"* and *"child"* relations.

For the evaluation metric, we use precision (P), recall (R), F1, and accuracy (Acc) scores.

$$P = \frac{T_P}{T_P + F_P} \qquad R = \frac{T_P}{T_P + F_N} \qquad F1 = 2 \cdot \frac{P \times R}{P + R} \qquad Acc = \frac{n_{correct}}{n_{total}} \qquad (3)$$

where T_P denotes the number of true positives, F_P the number of false positives, F_N the number of false negatives, $n_{correct}$ the number of correct predictions, and n_{total} the number of total testing data. Note that the score presented in this paper is the best score over multiple runs.

In the training process, we applied the filter height of 1 and 2 with 100 feature maps for the convolutional layer. For the input, we used pre-trained fastText (Bojanowski et al., 2017) with 300 dimension size and update the weight of the word embeddings. For learning, we applied a stochastic gradient descent algorithm using Adam optimizer (Kinga and Adam, 2015) with 0.001 as the learning rate. The

---

[4]The dataset and code are available at: `https://github.com/rifkiaputri/rel-aligner`

batch with size was 128. Also, we employed dropout in the feed-forward linear layer with a probability of 0.5. For the loss function, we set the margin m as 2.

6 Result and Discussion

6.1 Internal Evaluation

The relative performance differences among the five versions are summarized in Figure 3a. In addition to the ordering of the five variations, the difference between CNN and PCNN encoders is most notable. Detailed analyses are as follows.

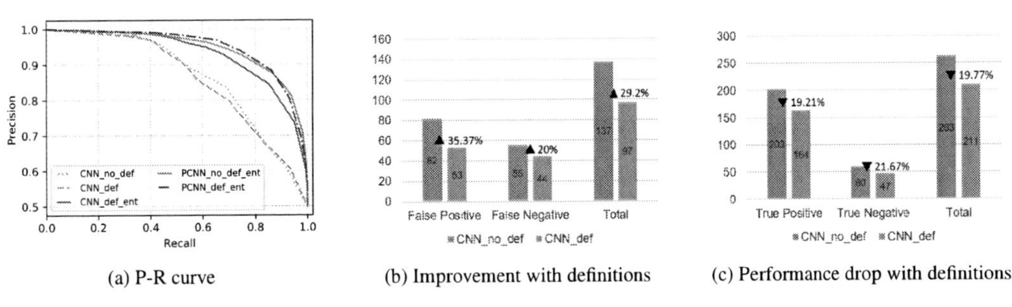

<table>
<tr><td>(a) P-R curve</td><td>(b) Improvement with definitions</td><td>(c) Performance drop with definitions</td></tr>
</table>

Figure 3: Internal evaluation result.

Relational Phrase vs. Relation Definition. While our intuition was that the additional information obtainable from the relation definitions would help compensate for the lack of semantics in a short relation phrases and names, it turns out that the overall gain shown in Figure 3a is not as significant as our expectation. A further analysis shows, however, that definitions help reduce incorrect predictions as in Figure 3b. Out of 137 errors (82 false positives and 55 false negatives) made by CNN_no_def, 40 were predicted correctly by including definitions (CNN_def), resulting in 29.2% improvement. On the other hand, out of 263 correct prediction in CNN_no_def (203 true positives and 60 true negatives), 52 were predicted incorrectly in CNN_def, resulting in 19.77% drop. This suggests that adding definition has potential to enrich the semantics; more sophisticated approaches are left for future research.

Impact of entity information. We observe that the performance of CNN_def_ent is significantly higher than that of the CNN_def model. From this result, we can conclude that adding entity information contributes to predicting the similarity between two relations. It suggests that entity information provides the context with which relation phrases and names can be aligned more accurately. It is consistent with the result in Zeng et al. (2015) that also shows the importance of including entities in relation classification.

CNN vs. PCNN. Compared to the performance CNN_def_ent, PCNN_def_ent is clearly better, strongly suggesting that for the relation alignment task, the PCNN encoder is better than CNN, regardless of whether relation definitions are used. A rational explanation for this result is that we lose important information when we apply max-pooling to the entire input representation including entities and relational phrases in CNN. Note that in PCNN, piecewise max-pooling allows the model to extract major features from three different segments of the representation (i.e. subject entity, relation, and object entity). Therefore, this result confirms that the piecewise max-pooling helps in preserving more meaningful features resulting from the convolutional layer for the relation alignment task.

6.2 Manual Evaluation

For more reliable evaluation of the proposed model, we compared it against the baselines using the 400 gold standards labeled by human. The summary result for predicting the semantically same and different

Model	Semantically Same			Semantically Different			Overall
	P	R	F1	P	R	F1	Acc
Dutta	0.740	0.496	0.594	0.427	0.683	0.526	56.25%
CESI	**1.000**	0.066	0.124	0.371	**1.000**	0.541	39.75%
Rule-based	*0.645*	*1.000*	*0.784*	*0.000*	*0.000*	*0.000*	*64.50%*
CNN_no_def	0.742	0.547	0.629	0.443	0.655	**0.528**	58.50%
CNN_def	0.726	0.678	0.701	0.478	0.535	0.505	62.75%
CNN_def_ent	0.659	0.891	0.758	0.451	0.162	0.238	63.25%
PCNN_no_def_ent	0.678	0.880	0.766	0.523	0.239	0.329	65.25%
PCNN_def_ent	0.669	**0.922**	**0.775**	**0.545**	0.169	0.258	**65.50%**

Table 2: Manual evaluation result.

relation pairs in Table 2 clearly shows the proposed model (CNN and PCNN) outperforms the baselines, CESI and Dutta, in predicting the semantically same pairs. Although CESI has the highest precision score, it has the lowest recall among all models variations due to the bias of predicting most of the data as semantically different. While it is possible to apply a different threshold in forming clusters for different precision and recall pairs, the low F1 value precludes its moderate performance for relation alignment. Compared to CESI models, Dutta's model shows better performance, especially in recall and F1 scores for predicting semantically same pairs. Based on this result, it is obvious that using a simple probabilistic rule-based approach is better than using the clustering approach for the relation alignment task. However, it is much worse than our model variations, with a high number of false negatives, resulting in the low recall and F1 scores.

The scores of the *rule-based* model in Table 2 is provided as a reference point of our proposed models. Since the rule-based model predicts the label using the alignment rules in our distant supervision dataset generation, a pair (one from Open IE and the other from KB) sharing the same entities in respective triples is judged to be semantically same by this model. That is, all the 400 pairs are predicted to be semantically same. From the alignment task perspective, it gives 100% recall for the semantically same case (all of the 258 "same" pairs are predicted correctly) and 0% recall for semantically different case. Since all the 142 "different" pairs are predicted as "same", the overall accuracy score is 64.5%. It shows that the training process is still needed since we cannot only rely on the alignment rules in our dataset generation. Moreover, since the *rule-based* model predictions are made with the distant supervision rule, we can also infer the quality of our distant supervision dataset based on the scores of the model (64.5% alignments are correctly labeled by distant supervision). Note that the low F1 score for predicting semantically different pairs in the proposed model is attributed to the high number of false negatives in the dataset. However, it still has the highest overall accuracy score compared to the two baselines.

6.3   Qualitative Analysis

We selected a sample of the alignment result and examined the label of each model to obtain insights about success and failure cases. As in Table 3, the variations of the proposed model tend to perform very well in predicting positive examples. For negative examples (labeled as "semantically different" in Table 3), almost no model predicts the alignment label perfectly, with an exception of the CESI model. Note that CESI has the tendency of predicting most alignments as semantically different, generating many false negatives. The "correct" decisions made for the semantically different pairs are likely to be attributed to this tendency.

Furthermore, the proposed model appears to make correct predictions for a pair where the relation expressions are lexically different but semantically same, as in ⟨'s son is, child⟩, ⟨'s serial is, notable work⟩, and ⟨was first married to, spouse⟩. However, CESI and Dutta's fail to predict them correctly because they are difficult to be predicted the models using symbolic representation of words. This result indicates that distributed representation of words as in embeddings has a clear advantage in dealing with semantics even when radically different words are used in relation phrases. For semantically and lexically similar relational phrase pairs such as ⟨died in, place of death⟩, ⟨died of, cause of death⟩, and ⟨was filmed in, filming location⟩, almost all models predict the alignment correctly, except CESI, again

Open IE Relation	KB Relation	Dutta	CESI	CNN			PCNN		Gold
				no_def	def	def_ent	no_def_ent	def_ent	
Semantically same - lexically similar									
died in	place of death	0	1	0	0	0	0	0	0
died of	cause of death	0	1	0	0	0	0	0	0
founding member of	member of	1	0	0	0	0	0	0	0
was filmed in	filming location	0	1	0	0	0	0	0	0
permanent capital of	capital of	1	0	0	0	0	0	0	0
Semantically same - lexically different									
' son is	child	1	1	0	0	0	0	0	0
's serial is	notable work	1	1	0	0	0	0	0	0
was first married to	spouse	1	1	0	0	0	0	0	0
is main villain of	present in work	0	1	0	1	0	0	0	0
first aired with	original language of work	1	1	1	1	0	0	0	0
Semantically different									
was born in	place of death	0	1	0	0	0	0	0	1
have won	nominated for	1	1	0	0	0	0	0	1
began trip to	place of death	1	1	1	0	1	1	0	1
was born in	work location	0	1	0	0	0	0	0	1
leave	father	1	1	1	1	1	1	1	1

Table 3: Alignment results of some Open IE and KB relations.

due to its tendency of judging pairs as semantically different. In another example, ⟨*founding member of, member of*⟩ and ⟨*permanent capital of, capital of*⟩, Dutta's model makes an incorrect prediction which attributed to the fact that the model relies heavily on the frequency of the training instance and that the frequency of the pairs is low.

Note that most models fail to correctly predict the cases where the pairs look similar but are in fact semantically different as in ⟨*was born in, place of death*⟩. We argue that this is caused by the existence of noisy instances in our training dataset. As explained in Section 4, when we automatically labeled the dataset with distant supervision, it assumed that the triples sharing the same subject and object entities would have a semantically same label. Obviously, this assumption does not always hold. Out of 4,274 examples of ⟨*was born in, place of death*⟩ pair in the training set, around 96% of the instances are labeled as semantically same because the triples share the same entities. In other words, the false positive problem is due to the distance supervision used for constructing training instances.

7 Conclusion and Future Works

In this paper, we present a Siamese network for aligning the relations of Open IE (Stanford Open IE) and relations of KB (Wikidata). As a way to overcome the difficulty of acquiring a large number of training instances, we built an extensive amount of training dataset using the distant supervision method which does not require manual annotation. In the experiments, we first confirm that using word embedding as the input of Siamese network is effective in extracting the semantics information compared to the probabilistic rule-based model and the clustering-based model. Adding a textual definition and entity information as the additional feature may also help to reduce the false positive and false negative errors that occur when we only use short relational phrases input.

Despite the superiority of the performance over the baselines, the dataset resulting from the distant supervision method still suffers from noises, i.e., incorrectly labeled alignment instances. The model variations presented in this paper have not been able to handle this problem, which we leave for future work. Another thing to consider is the number of KB relations. In this paper, we covered the top-200 most frequent relations over a total of more than 1000 relations in Wikidata. Even though we can include all the relations, the number of triples and sentence examples of the last relation is not as much as those of the first relation. Future work will have to investigate on how to handle the imbalance number of relation instances and increase the number of KB relations that are aligned through it.

Finally, relation alignment can be useful for several downstream tasks such as KB completion and question answering. In KB completion, we can combine the Open IE and KB relations by aligning semantically same relations to the existing KB and adding new relations from Open IE, which are not semantically the same as any of the KB relations. In question answering task, less ambiguous triples resulting from the alignment process can be also used for question answering systems.

Acknowledgement

This work was supported by the Institute of Information & Communications Technology Planning & Evaluation (IITP) grant funded by the Korea government (MSIT) (No. 2013-0-00179, Development of Core Technology for Context-aware Deep-Symbolic Hybrid Learning and Construction of Language Resources) and Next-Generation Information Computing Development Program through the National Research Foundation of Korea (NRF) funded by the Ministry of Science, ICT (2017M3C4A7065962).

References

Angeli, G., M. J. J. Premkumar, and C. D. Manning (2015). Leveraging linguistic structure for open domain information extraction. In *Proceedings of the 53rd Annual Meeting of the Association for Computational Linguistics and the 7th International Joint Conference on Natural Language Processing (Volume 1: Long Papers)*, Volume 1, pp. 344–354.

Bojanowski, P., E. Grave, A. Joulin, and T. Mikolov (2017). Enriching word vectors with subword information. *Transactions of the Association for Computational Linguistics 5*, 135–146.

Bovi, C. D., L. E. Anke, and R. Navigli (2015). Knowledge base unification via sense embeddings and disambiguation. In *EMNLP*, pp. 726–736. The Association for Computational Linguistics.

Bromley, J., I. Guyon, Y. LeCun, E. Säckinger, and R. Shah (1993). Signature verification using a "siamese" time delay neural network. In *Proceedings of the 6th International Conference on Neural Information Processing Systems*, NIPS'93, San Francisco, CA, USA, pp. 737–744. Morgan Kaufmann Publishers Inc.

Crouch, D. and T. H. King (2005). Unifying lexical resources. In *Proceedings of the Interdisciplinary Workshop on the Identification and Representation of Verb Features and Verb Classes*, pp. 32–37.

Dutta, A., C. Meilicke, and H. Stuckenschmidt (2014). Semantifying triples from open information extraction systems. In U. Endriss and J. Leite (Eds.), *STAIRS*, Volume 264 of *Frontiers in Artificial Intelligence and Applications*, pp. 111–120. IOS Press.

Dutta, A., C. Meilicke, and H. Stuckenschmidt (2015). Enriching structured knowledge with open information. In *Proceedings of the 24th International Conference on World Wide Web*, WWW '15, Republic and Canton of Geneva, Switzerland, pp. 267–277. International World Wide Web Conferences Steering Committee.

Galárraga, L., G. Heitz, K. Murphy, and F. M. Suchanek (2014). Canonicalizing open knowledge bases. In *Proceedings of the 23rd ACM International Conference on Conference on Information and Knowledge Management*, CIKM '14, New York, NY, USA, pp. 1679–1688. ACM.

Galárraga, L. A., C. Teflioudi, K. Hose, and F. Suchanek (2013). Amie: Association rule mining under incomplete evidence in ontological knowledge bases. In *Proceedings of the 22Nd International Conference on World Wide Web*, WWW '13, New York, NY, USA, pp. 413–422. ACM.

Gurevych, I., J. Eckle-Kohler, S. Hartmann, M. Matuschek, C. M. Meyer, and C. Wirth (2012). Uby: A large-scale unified lexical-semantic resource based on lmf. In *Proceedings of the 13th Conference of the European Chapter of the Association for Computational Linguistics*, pp. 580–590. Association for Computational Linguistics.

Gurevych, I., J. Eckle-Kohler, and M. Matuschek (2016). *Linked Lexical Knowledge Bases: Foundations and Applications*. Morgan & Claypool Publishers.

Joshi, M., E. Choi, D. S. Weld, and L. Zettlemoyer (2017). Triviaqa: A large scale distantly supervised challenge dataset for reading comprehension. *arXiv preprint arXiv:1705.03551*.

Kinga, D. and J. B. Adam (2015). A method for stochastic optimization. In *International Conference on Learning Representations (ICLR)*, Volume 5.

Matuschek, M. (2015). *Word sense alignment of lexical resources*. Ph. D. thesis, Technische Universität.

Mintz, M., S. Bills, R. Snow, and D. Jurafsky (2009). Distant supervision for relation extraction without labeled data. In *Proceedings of the Joint Conference of the 47th Annual Meeting of the ACL and the 4th International Joint Conference on Natural Language Processing of the AFNLP: Volume 2 - Volume 2*, ACL '09, Stroudsburg, PA, USA, pp. 1003–1011. Association for Computational Linguistics.

Navigli, R. and S. P. Ponzetto (2012). Babelnet: The automatic construction, evaluation and application of a wide-coverage multilingual semantic network. *Artificial Intelligence 193*, 217–250.

Nguyen, T. H. and R. Grishman (2015). Relation extraction: Perspective from convolutional neural networks. In *Proceedings of the 1st Workshop on Vector Space Modeling for Natural Language Processing*, pp. 39–48.

Riedel, S., L. Yao, and A. McCallum (2010). Modeling relations and their mentions without labeled text. In *Joint European Conference on Machine Learning and Knowledge Discovery in Databases*, pp. 148–163. Springer.

Shi, L. and R. Mihalcea (2005). Putting pieces together: Combining framenet, verbnet and wordnet for robust semantic parsing. In *International conference on intelligent text processing and computational linguistics*, pp. 100–111. Springer.

Sorokin, D. and I. Gurevych (2017). Context-aware representations for knowledge base relation extraction. In *Proceedings of the 2017 Conference on Empirical Methods in Natural Language Processing*, pp. 1784–1789.

Vashishth, S., P. Jain, and P. Talukdar (2018). Cesi: Canonicalizing open knowledge bases using embeddings and side information. In *Proceedings of the 2018 World Wide Web Conference*, WWW '18, Republic and Canton of Geneva, Switzerland, pp. 1317–1327. International World Wide Web Conferences Steering Committee.

Vrandečić, D. and M. Krötzsch (2014, September). Wikidata: A free collaborative knowledgebase. *Commun. ACM 57*(10), 78–85.

Yates, A. and O. Etzioni (2009, March). Unsupervised methods for determining object and relation synonyms on the web. *J. Artif. Int. Res. 34*(1), 255–296.

Zeng, D., K. Liu, Y. Chen, and J. Zhao (2015). Distant supervision for relation extraction via piecewise convolutional neural networks. In *Proceedings of the 2015 Conference on Empirical Methods in Natural Language Processing*, pp. 1753–1762.

Language-Agnostic Model for Aspect-Based Sentiment Analysis

Md Shad Akhtar[†], Abhishek Kumar[†], Asif Ekbal[†], Chris Biemann[⋆] and Pushpak Bhattacharyya[†]
[†]*Department of CSE, Indian Institute of Technology Patna*
{shad.pcs15,abhishek.ee14,asif,pb}@iitp.ac.in
[⋆]*Universität Hamburg, Germany*
biemann@informatik.uni-hamburg.de

Abstract

In this paper, we propose a language-agnostic deep neural network architecture for aspect-based sentiment analysis. The proposed approach is based on Bidirectional Long Short-Term Memory (Bi-LSTM) network, which is further assisted with extra hand-crafted features. We define three different architectures for the successful combination of word embeddings and hand-crafted features. We evaluate the proposed approach for six languages (i.e. *English, Spanish, French, Dutch, German* and *Hindi*) and two problems (i.e. *aspect term extraction* and *aspect sentiment classification*). Experiments show that the proposed model attains state-of-the-art performance in most of the settings.

1   Introduction

Sentiment analysis (Pang and Lee, 2008) is often target-centric. In aspect-based sentiment analysis (ABSA), we aim to identify the polarity of expressed sentiments towards a feature or aspect. These features or aspects are usually explicitly mentioned in the text. Also, a sentence may contain more than one aspect terms, and the task is to assign separate sentiments to each of them, e.g. in *"The **food** was great! But **service** was below par."* there are two aspects (*'food'* and *'service'*), and the expressed sentiment towards *food* and *service* are *positive* and *negative*, respectively. Such analysis offers fine-grained information to a user or an organization who seeks users opinion towards any specific entity. For example, based on the users' feedback, an individual can draw a general perception about the specific attribute or aspect of a product or service, and he/she can make an informed decision about the product or service under observation. Similarly, an organization can utilize the feedback to refine its product/service or to take a decision in the business model.

Aspect-based sentiment analysis (Pontiki et al., 2014, 2016) has two subproblems at its core, i.e., aspect term identification (or opinion target extraction) and aspect sentiment classification. Given a text, aspect term identification task aims to find the boundaries of all the aspect terms present in the text, whereas aspect sentiment classification task classifies each of these identified aspect terms into one of the predefined sentiment classes (e.g., *positive, negative, neutral* etc.). A sentence may contain any number of aspect terms or no aspect term at all. The terms 'aspect term' and 'opinion target' are often used interchangeably and refer to the same span of text.

Motivation and Contribution

A survey of the literature for ABSA suggests a number of works for different languages (Kumar et al., 2016; Brun et al., 2016; Çetin et al., 2016). Although the reported performance for these works are good, they usually suffer in handling the language diversity, i.e., the systems that reported state-of-the-art performance for one language typically do not work well for the other languages. The unavailability of such a generic system motivates us to build a language-agnostic model for aspect based sentiment analysis. We propose a generic deep neural network architecture that handles the language divergence to a great extent. Our model is based on Bidirectional Long Short-Term Memory (Bi-LSTM) network

(Graves et al., 2005) that also utilizes extra hand-crafted features. We evaluate our proposed approach for four European (i.e., *Spanish, French, Dutch & German*), one Indian (i.e., *Hindi*) and English languages. The contributions of our work are *three-fold*: a) we propose an efficient and generic neural network architecture that works across multiple languages; b) we utilize a small set of handcrafted features (one each for aspect extraction and aspect classification) for the training and evaluation; and c) we provide the new state-of-the-art performance for two problems of ABSA across six different languages.

Rest of the paper is organized as follows: In Section 2, we present the literature survey. The proposed methodology has been discussed in detail in Section 3. In Section 4, we furnished experimental results and provided the necessary analysis. Finally, we conclude in Section 5.

2   Related Works

Sentiment analysis is a well-studied problem of natural language processing for English language (Turney, 2002; Pang et al., 2002, 2005; Pang and Lee, 2008; Jagtap and Pawar, 2013; Kim and Hovy, 2006). However, in recent times, researchers have focused on various extensions of sentiment analysis, e.g., aspect based sentiment analysis (Pontiki et al., 2014; Kiritchenko et al., 2014; Akhtar et al., 2016), multi-lingual sentiment analysis (Balamurali et al., 2012; Mishra et al., 2017; Brun et al., 2016; Kumar et al., 2016), multi-modal sentiment analysis (Poria et al., 2017; Zadeh et al., 2018; Ghosal et al., 2018), sentiment analysis in Twitter (Ghosh et al., 2015; Mohammad et al., 2013) etc.

For ABSA, System GTI (Alvarez-López et al., 2016) used a Support Vector Machine (SVM) and Conditional Random Field (CRF) based approach for aspect extraction and sentiment classification, respectively. They used language-dependent features like lemmas and Part-of-Speech (PoS) tags to achieve the state-of-the-art score for aspect extraction in Spanish. IIT-TUDA (Kumar et al., 2016) also used a number of hand-crafted features like character n-grams, dependency relations, prefix and suffix for SVM and CRF. They achieved comparable performance for *Spanish, French & Dutch*. System XRCE (Brun et al., 2016) used a feedback ensemble network that obtained the best performance for aspect classification on the French dataset. System TGB (Çetin et al., 2016) used a Logistic Regression based model to address the aspect sentiment classification and reported to achieve the best score on Dutch dataset. Mishra et al. (2017) used a Bi-LSTM based model, whereas Naderalvojoud et al. (2017) adopted a deep recurrent neural network model for the German dataset. Akhtar et al. (2016) developed an aspect based sentiment analysis datasets for Hindi. They employed CRF and SVM for aspect term extraction and aspect sentiment classification, respectively. For aspect based sentiment analysis in English, Kiritchenko et al. (2014) reported the best performance in SemEval-2014 shared task on ABSA (Pontiki et al., 2014).

There have been few attempts at injecting handcrafted features into the neural network architecture for enhancing the overall performance (Akhtar et al., 2016; Araque et al., 2017) of sentiment analysis. Akhtar et al. (2016) combined CNN representation and optimized features for learning a Support Vector Machine. Authors in (Araque et al., 2017) proposed a classifier ensemble model that combines surface-level features and generic word vectors for the sentiment classification. However, our work differs from these systems in the following ways: **a)** we perform aspect level sentiment analysis for six different languages (belong to different language family); **b)** we propose four different architectures to successfully combine the neural network learned representations and the handcrafted features; **c)** the proposed architectures handle both aspect extraction (a sequence labelling task) and aspect sentiment classification (a classification task); and **d)** we achieve better performance for most of the problem/language pairs.

3   Proposed Method

Overall, aspect based sentiment analysis can be thought of as a two-step process, i.e. aspect term extraction and aspect sentiment classification. Aspect term extraction is a sequence labelling task where each token of a sentence needs to be classified as either inside the boundary of an aspect term or outside. We adopted *BIO* notation to mark each token as either *Begin, Intermediate* or *Outside* of an aspect term. A '*B*' signifies the beginning of an aspect term and successive '*I*s' signify a multi-token aspect term (e.g. *spicy tuna rolls*). A single-token aspect term will be tagged as '*B*'. For the second problem, i.e. aspect sentiment classification, we define a context window of size ±5 around each aspect term and consider all the tokens within the window for an instance. The intuition behind such an approach is that the sentiment-bearing clue words often occur close to the aspect terms. An example scenario is depicting in Table 1.

Review:	*Rice*	was	good	but	the	main	attraction	was	*spicy*	*tuna*	*rolls*	.
BIO Notation:	**B**	O	O	O	O	O	O	O	**B**	**I**	**I**	O
Aspect Terms:						**Rice** and **Spicy tuna rolls**						

Context window (±5)	$Prev_5$	$Prev_4$	$Prev_3$	$Prev_2$	$Prev_1$	$Aspect_{term}$	$Next_1$	$Next_2$	$Next_3$	$Next_4$	$Next_5$
Rice	null	null	null	null	null	*Rice*	was	good	but	the	main
Spicy tune roll	but	the	main	attraction	was	*spicy tuna roll*	.	null	null	nulll	null
Aspect Sentiment:						*Positive* for Rice and *Positive* for Spicy tuna rolls.					

Table 1: An example review from restaurant domain and its respective processing for aspect term extraction (i.e. BIO notations) and aspect sentiment classification (i.e. contextual processing).

Our proposed neural network architecture employs a Bi-LSTM network for learning sentence embeddings, which are then fed to a fully-connected dense layer for classification. Given a sentence, we first compute the word embeddings of each word and feed them into the Bi-LSTM network at different time steps for the prediction. We refer to this architecture as A1. In addition, we inject extra hand-crafted manual features to assist the neural architecture. We design three architectures (i.e. A2, A3 & A4 in Figure 1) for the successful combination of word embeddings and the hand-crafted features. The basic difference among these three architectures are the way features are injected into the model. A high-level architecture of our proposed method is depicted in Figure 1.

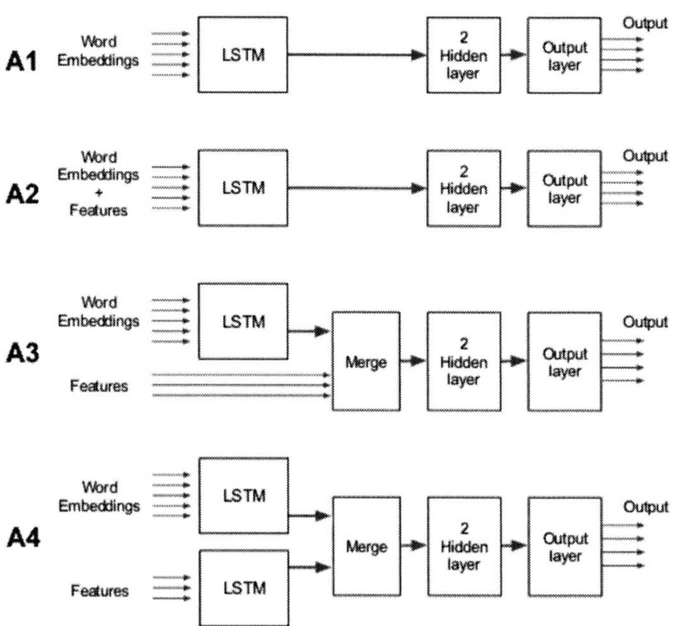

Figure 1: Proposed architectures for aspect identification and classification. **A1:** Only word embeddings are fed to Bi-LSTM network; **A2:** Word embeddings and extracted features are combined and fed into single Bi-LSTM network. **A3:** Extracted features are directly merged with Bi-LSTM output of word embedding. **A4:** One Bi-LSTM network each for word embeddings and extracted features. All the four architectures are language-agnostic in nature.

Architecture A1 makes use of word embeddings as the sole input for the network. In A2, we concatenate the word embeddings with the hand-crafted features at the input and then feed this combined input to the network for learning. In comparison, architecture A3 learns the sentence embedding through Bi-LSTM network on top of word embedding only, which is then merged with the hand-crafted features before feeding into the fully connected layers for prediction. In contrast, architecture A4 utilizes two separate Bi-LSTM networks for word embeddings and hand-crafted features, respectively. Subsequently, the learned sequences of each Bi-LSTM are concatenated and fed into the fully-connected layers for further prediction. The choice of separate Bi-LSTMs for the hand-crafted features in architecture A4 is driven by the fact that the dimension of a word embedding is usually very high as compared to its corresponding hand-crafted features. If trained together, as in architecture A2, extracted features of low dimension usually get overshadowed by the high-dimensional word embeddings. Thus making it non-trivial for the network to learn from the extracted features. Further, to exploit the sequence information of words in a sentence, we pass hand-crafted features of each word through a separate Bi-LSTM layer. E.g. in the following sentence there is one negative word (i.e. *horrible*) and one negation (i.e. *not*) but no positive words. However, in a model that takes into account only the simple polar word score, the sentence would have high relevance towards the negative sentiment. However, the sequence information of the phrase "*not any more*" dictates the positive sentiment of the sentence.

"It was used to be a horrible place to eat but not any more."

In contrast to A4, architecture A3 does not rely on the sequence information of the extracted features and allows the network to learn on its own. We use 300 dimension Word2Vec (Mikolov et al., 2013) word embeddings for the experiments. Each Bi-LSTM layer contains 100 neurons while two dense layers contain 100 and 50 neurons, respectively.

Features

As additional features, we extract the following information for each token in an instance.

– Aspect term extraction: Distributional thesaurus (DT)[1] (Biemann and Riedl, 2013) defines the lexicon expansion of a token based on a similar context. It is usually very effective for the handling of unseen text. If a token in the test set never appears in the training set, it becomes a non-trivial task for the classifier to make a correct prediction. By employing DT feature, the classifier can additionally utilize lexical expansion of the current token for mapping with the training set, thus minimize the chance of unseen text. For each token, we use its top 3 DT expansions as features.

Language	Train					Test				
	#sent.	#aspects	pos	neg	neu	#sent.	#aspects	pos	neg	neu
English	2,000	2,507	1,657	749	101	676	859	611	204	44
Spanish	2,070	2,720	1,925	674	120	881	1,072	750	274	48
French	1,733	2,530	1,164	1,212	154	696	954	441	434	79
Dutch	1,711	1,860	1,062	646	152	575	613	369	211	33
German	19,432	19,432	1,179	5,045	13,208	2,566	2,566	105	780	1,681
Hindi	5,417	4,469	1,986	569	1,914	10-fold cross validation				

Table 2: Dataset statistics

– Aspect sentiment classification: We employ publicly available lexicons of Chen and Skiena (2014) for extracting the polar information of each token. It contains a list of positive and negative words for 136 different languages. Additionally, we append the positive and negative words of 4 well-known

---

[1] http://ltmaggie.informatik.uni-hamburg.de/jobimtext/documentation/
calculate-a-distributional-thesaurus-dt/

Datasets	Aspect Extraction (F1-score)				Aspect Classification (Acc)			
	A1	A2	A3	A4	A1	A2	A3	A4
English	62.0	63.1	62.4	**64.9***	82.4	82.7	82.1	**83.4**
Spanish	72.0	71.8	72.4	**73.0***	86.4	86.3	86.1	**87.1***
French	67.1	**67.8***	63.6	64.9	75.0	**75.3***	75.2	74.3
Dutch	65.2	65.6	**65.7^{+}**	64.2	80.9	80.7	**81.9***	81.4
German	23.1	22.0	22.4	**24.0***	86.7	**87.2***	86.6	**87.2***
Hindi	50.0	49.3	50.4	**53.5***	64.5	66.3	65.8	**66.9***

Table 3: Comparison of various models for aspect extraction and aspect classification on test dataset. *A1, A2, A3 & A4* refers to four architectures depicted in Figure 1. *Statistically significant (*T*-test) *w.r.t.* other architectures (*p-values*< 0.05). $^{+}$Significant *w.r.t.* A4.

lexicons of English language (Bing Liu opinion lexicon, Ding et al. 2008; MPQA subjectivity lexicon, Wilson et al. 2005; SentiWordNet, Baccianella et al. 2010; and Vader sentiment, Hutto and Gilbert 2014) through the application of Google Translator. For German, we additionally use GermanPolarityClues lexical resource (Waltinger, 2010). The final list contains 2757, 2164, 3271, 1615, 17627 and 11874 positive words for *English*, *Spanish*, *Dutch*, *French*, *German* and *Hindi*, respectively. Similarly, there are 5112, 1735, 5834, 3038, 19962 and 2225 negative words in the list.

4 Experiments, Results and Analysis

4.1 Datasets

We evaluate our proposed approach on the benchmark datasets of SemEval-2016 shared task on aspect based sentiment analysis (Pontiki et al., 2016) (Task 5), which contain user reviews across multiple languages. The datasets of English, Spanish, French and Dutch are related to the reviews of consumer electronics and restaurants. We also evaluate our approach on the GermEval-2017 shared task on ABSA (Wojatzki et al., 2017), which comprises of reviews in the German language. The training datasets contain 2,070, 1,733, 1,711 & 19,432 reviews in Spanish, French, Dutch and German, respectively. Whereas, test datasets contain 881, 696, 575 & 2,566 reviews for the respective languages. For Hindi, we employed ABSA dataset developed by Akhtar et al. (Akhtar et al., 2016). There are total 4469 aspect terms in 5417 sentences across 12 domains. We perform 10-fold cross validation for the evaluation in this work. Table 2 lists the brief statistics of the various datasets for different languages.

4.2 Preprocessing

We extract each instance from the SemEval and the GermEval dataset to take into account only the relevant information and remove the XML tags. We use NLTK[2] (Shallow parser[3] for Hindi) to tokenize each sentence of the dataset. The aspect terms can span over multiple words in a sentence and hence, we use the BIO encoding scheme. In this notation, B, I and O denote the beginning, internal and outside tokens of aspect term respectively.

4.3 Results

We use Python based deep learning library Keras [4] with Tensorflow[5] for implementing the systems. The weight matrices were initialized randomly using numbers from a truncated normal distribution. Model is

---

[2]https://www.nltk.org/
[3]http://ltrc.iiit.ac.in/showfile.php?filename=downloads/shallow_parser.php
[4]https://keras.io/
[5]https://www.tensorflow.org/

trained with 32 batch size and 0.25 *Dropout* (Srivastava et al., 2014) with *Adam* (Kingma and Ba, 2014) optimizer. We employ *Relu* (Glorot et al., 2011) as activation function for the hidden layers, whereas for the output layer we use *softmax* classifier. Following the guidelines of SemEval-2016 (Pontiki et al., 2016) and GermEval-2017 (Wojatzki et al., 2017), we employ F1-score as the evaluation metric for aspect term extraction. For classification, we compute accuracy and F1-score for SemEval-2016 and GermEval-2017, respectively. Similarly, we adopt F1-score and accuracy for the aspect term extraction and aspect sentiment classification in Hindi. In Table 3, we present the results of all the four architectures

Systems	Aspect Extraction (F1-score)						Aspect Classification (Accuracy)					
	En	Es	Fr	Du	De	Hi	En	Es	Fr	Du	De*	Hi
State-of-the-art systems at SemEval-2016 (Pontiki et al., 2016)												
Baseline (Pontiki et al., 2016)	44.0	51.9	45.4	50.6	-	-	76.4	77.7	67.4	69.3	-	-
NLANGP (Toh and Su, 2016)	72.3†	-	-	-	-	-	-	-	-	-	-	-
GTI (Alvarez-López et al., 2016)	66.5	68.5†	-	-	-	-	69.9	-	-	-	-	-
IIT-TUDA (Kumar et al., 2016)	42.6	64.3	66.6†	56.9†	-	-	86.7	83.5†	72.2	76.9	-	-
XRCE (Brun et al., 2016)	61.98	-	65.3	-	-	-	88.1†	-	78.8†	-	-	-
TGB (Çetin et al., 2016)	55.0	55.7	-	51.7	-	-	80.9	82.0	-	77.8†	-	-
State-of-the-art systems at GermEval-2017 (Wojatzki et al., 2017)												
Baseline (Wojatzki et al., 2017)	-	-	-	-	17.0	-	-	-	-	-	48.1*	-
System (Mishra et al., 2017)	-	-	-	-	22.0	-	-	-	-	-	42.1*	-
System (Ji-Ung Lee and Gurevych, 2017)	-	-	-	-	20.3	-	-	-	-	-	48.2*	-
State-of-the-art systems for Hindi (Akhtar et al., 2016)												
System (Akhtar et al., 2016)	-	-	-	-	-	41.0	-	-	-	-	-	54.0
System (Akhtar et al., 2016)	-	-	-	-	-	-	-	-	-	-	-	65.9
Proposed Approach	**64.9**	**73.0**	**67.8**	**65.7**	**24.0**	**53.5**	**83.4**	**87.1**	**75.3**	**81.9**	**87.2***	**66.9**
Architecture	**A4**	**A4**	**A2**	**A3**	**A4**	**A4**	**A4**	**A4**	**A2**	**A3**	**A4**	**A4**

Table 4: Comparison with the state-of-the-art systems of SemEval-2016 and GermEval-2017. *F1-score. Official evaluation metric for aspect classification at GermEval-2017 was F1-score. †Best system for respective language-problem pair.

for each language/problem pair. In aspect extraction problem, architecture A4 yields the best F1-score for *Spanish* (73.0%), *German* (24.0%), *English* (64.9%) and *Hindi* (53.5%), whereas for *French* and *Dutch* we obtain the best F1-score with architectures A2 (67.8%) and A3 (65.7%), respectively. We observe similar trends for aspect classification as well with architecture A4 performing better for *Spanish* (87.2% accuracy), *German* (87.2% F1-score), *English* (83.4% accuracy) and *Hindi* (66.9% accuracy). Similar to aspect extraction, architectures A2 and A3 report better performance for *French* (75.34%) and *Dutch* (81.9%), respectively. Among all four architectures, architecture A1 has the least performance across all six languages for both the problems. It suggests that the hand-crafted features -when fused into the network- assist the system to learn in a better way than the system learnt with only word embeddings. We also perform statistical significance test (T-test) on the obtained results and observe that the performance of the architecture A4 is significant with 95% confidence for *English*, *Spanish*, *German* and *Hindi* for both the problems.

Further, we compare our proposed system with state-of-the-art systems as listed in Table 4. Our proposed system shows an improvement over the existing state-of-the-art for 9 out of 12 language/problem pairs. For aspect extraction, the system achieves an improvement of 4.5, 1.2, 8.8, 2 and 12.5 points for *Spanish*, *French*, *Dutch*, *German* and *Hindi*, respectively. Our system manages to improve the score of sentiment classification for *Spanish*, *Dutch*, *German*, and *Hindi* by 3.56, 4.17, 12.3 and 1 points, respectively. Improvement of the system performance across the language/problem pairs suggests about the generic nature of our proposed approach. Also, significance *T-test* shows that improvement of the proposed method over the state-of-the-art systems are statistically significant with p-values< 0.05.

From Table 3, we observe that architecture A4 performs the best for four languages, i.e., *Spanish*, *German*, *English* and *Hindi* irrespective of the problems. Similarly, the performance of the architectures

A2 & A3 is best for *French* and *Dutch*, respectively. Since architecture A4 is the clear winner in 8 out of 12 language/problem pairs and also reports comparable performance in other cases - with maximum 2.9 points below the best architecture as reported in Table 3 -, we recommend it as the default choice for all the languages and problems.

4.4 Error Analysis

We perform error analysis on the predicted outputs, using automatic translations (Google) for languages we are not proficient in. Following are the few cases where our proposed system often faces challenges.

Aspect term extraction: Aspect term extraction is a quite challenging task. The BIO notation is an effective solution for tagging an aspect term; however, it is highly skewed towards the O class, i.e., only a small percentage of tokens in the vocabulary qualify for the aspect term. Despite this limitation, BIO notations result in decent outputs with the few exceptions. In Table 5, we list a few common error patterns along with the examples. Our system faced difficulties when one or more terms can independently qualify as an aspect term. In the first two examples, our system misclassifies the multi-token aspect terms '*customer service*' and '*atencin del personal*' (attention of the staff) as single aspect terms. It predicts the first token of the aspect term (i.e., '*customer*' (first example) and '*atencin*' (attention) (second example)) as one aspect term and the last token (i.e., '*service*' and '*personal*' (staff)) as the other aspect term. Despite both the tokens of aspect term '*customer service*' is identified as aspect terms, it results in *recall=0* and *precision=0*.

Table 5: Common error pattern for aspect term extraction.

Language	Review	Gold Aspect Terms	Predicted Aspect Terms	Possible Reason
Source (EN)	*Best restaurant in the world, great decor, great customer service, friendly manager*	*restaurant, decor,* **customer service**, *manager*	*restaurant, decor,* **customer**, **service**, *manager, pizza*	Individual tokens in a multi-token
Source (ES)	*La atención del personal impecable.*	**atención del personal**	**atención, personal**	aspect term qualify
Translation (EN)	*Attention of the staff was impeccable.*	**Attention of the staff**	**Attention, staff**	for aspect terms .
Source (EN)	*I had yummy lamb korma, saag paneer, samosas, naan, etc.*	*lamb korma, saag paneer, samosas, naan*	*lamb korma*	Sequence of dishes (rare occurrence)
Source (FR)	*Ravioles et tartiflette correctes, crĺpe suzette passable.*	*Ravioles, tartiflette, crĺpe suzette*	*Ravioles*	
Translation (EN)	*Ravioles and tartiflette correct, crepe suzette passable.*	*Ravioles, tartiflette, crepe suzette*	*Ravioles*	
Source (FR)	*...le riz arborio aux truffes apparaissant dans le menu...*	**riz arborio aux truffes**	**riz arborio**	Presence of subordinating conjunction in between an aspect term.
Translation (EN)	*...the arborio rice with truffles appearing in the menu...*	**arborio rice with truffles**	**arborio rice**	
Source (EN)	*Great draft and bottle selection and the pizza rocks.*	**draft and bottle selection**, *pizza*	**bottle selection**, *pizza*	

In the third and fourth examples of Table 5, a number of dishes which are served in the restaurant are mentioned. For both examples, our system manages to identify only some dishes. A possible reason would be the rare occurrence of these dishes in the training set. The last two examples suffer from the presence of subordinating conjunctions (i.e. 'and', 'with' etc.) in the multi-token aspect terms (i.e. '*riz arborio aux truffes*' (arborio rice with truffles)). In general, 'and', 'with' or other conjunctions does not qualify for the aspect term except in the company of multi-token aspect terms. However, such occurrences are not very common, and the underlying system misclassifies them as outside aspect term, i.e., O. The second example (i.e. '*atención del personal*' (attention of the staff)) may also qualify for the similar reason.

Aspect sentiment classification: For aspect sentiment classification, we observed two most common sources of errors across languages, i.e., lack of polar information inside the defined context window (± 5 neighbouring words) and presence of the sarcastic or metaphoric phrase in the review. We list a few error cases in Table 6. The first example belongs to the Spanish language, which contains an aspect term '*calidad-precio*' (quality-price). The actual sentiment towards the aspect term is *positive*; however, in the absence of clue words (i.e. '*restaurantes de referencia de Zaragoza*' (*recommended restaurants of*

Table 6: Common error pattern for aspect sentiment classification.

Language	Review	Aspect Term	Actual Sentiment	Predicted Sentiment	Possible Reason
Source (ES)	*En lo referente a* **calidad-precio** *y dentro de su categora, desde mi punto de vista, debe ser uno de los restaurantes de referencia de Zaragoza.*	*calidad-precio*	*Positive*	*Neutral*	Lack of polar information inside context window
Translation (EN)	*Regarding* **quality-price** *and within its category, from my point of view, it must be one of the recommended restaurants of Zaragoza.*	*quality-price*			
Source (EN)	*Finally, my wife stood face to face in front of one of the* **staff** *and she asked, Are you waiting for a table?".*	*staff*	*Negative*	*Positive*	Sarcasm
Source (EN)	*The* **lemon chicken** *tasted like sticky sweet donuts.*	*lemon chicken*	*Negative*	*Positive*	Metaphor

Zaragoza)) inside the context window, our proposed system predicts its sentiment as *neutral*.

Predicting sentiment for the sarcastic and metaphoric text are usually challenging due to the difference in its *textual-meaning* and *actual-meaning* (i.e., what is said is not meant or vice-versa). Our system also finds it non-trivial to correctly classify an aspect term in the presence of sarcastic (second example of Table6) or metaphoric (third example) text. In the second example, the staff's unresponsiveness behaviour irked the writer, who had to ask for a table sarcastically. Similarly, in the third example writer was not amused by the quality of *lemon chicken* and compared it with the *sticky sweet donuts* as figure-of-speech.

5   Conclusion

In this paper, we have proposed a language-agnostic deep neural network approach for solving the problems of aspect-based sentiment analysis. Our system employs Bi-LSTM network for learning the sentence embeddings, which is assisted by a few handcrafted features. To show the effectiveness, we evaluated the proposed approach on six languages (i.e. *English, Spanish, French, Dutch, German* and *Hindi*) and two problems (i.e. *aspect term extraction* and *aspect sentiment classification*). We also evaluated different ensemble architectures to combine sentence embeddings and handcrafted features. Comparisons with the existing system suggest that our proposed approach attains the state-of-the-art performance for almost each of the language/problem pair.

6   Acknowledgement

Asif Ekbal acknowledges the Young Faculty Research Fellowship (YFRF), supported by Visvesvaraya PhD scheme for Electronics and IT, Ministry of Electronics and Information Technology (MeitY), Government of India, being implemented by Digital India Corporation (formerly Media Lab Asia).

References

Akhtar, M. S., A. Ekbal, and P. Bhattacharyya (2016). Aspect based Sentiment Analysis in Hindi: Resource Creation and Evaluation. In *Proceedings of the Tenth International Conference on Language Resources and Evaluation (LREC 2016), May 23-28, 2016*, Portoro, Slovenia, pp. 2703–2709. European Language Resources Association (ELRA).

Akhtar, M. S., A. Kumar, A. Ekbal, and P. Bhattacharyya (2016). A Hybrid Deep Learning Architecture for Sentiment Analysis. In *Proceedings of the 26th International Conference on Computational Linguistics (COLING 2016): Technical Papers, December 11-16, 2016*, Osaka, Japan, pp. 482–493.

Alvarez-López, T., J. Juncal-Martinez, M. Fernández-Gavilanes, E. Costa-Montenegro, and F. J. González-Castano (2016). GTI at SemEval-2016 Task 5: SVM and CRF for Aspect Detection and

Unsupervised Aspect-based Aentiment Analysis. In *Proceedings of the 10th International Workshop on Semantic Evaluation (SemEval-2016)*, San Diego, CA, USA, pp. 306–311.

Araque, O., I. Corcuera-Platas, J. F. Snchez-Rada, and C. A. Iglesias (2017, July). Enhancing Deep Learning Sentiment Analysis with Ensemble Techniques in Social Applications. *Expert Syst. Appl. 77*(C), 236–246.

Baccianella, S., A. Esuli, and F. Sebastiani (2010). SentiWordNet 3.0: An Enhanced Lexical Resource for Sentiment Analysis and Opinion Mining. In *Proceedings of the 7th International Conference on Language Resources and Evaluation (LREC)*, Valletta, Malta, pp. 2200–2204.

Balamurali, A. R., A. Joshi, and P. Bhattacharyya (2012). Cross-Lingual Sentiment Analysis for Indian Languages using Linked WordNets. In *COLING 2012, 24th International Conference on Computational Linguistics, Proceedings of the Conference: Posters, 8-15 December 2012, Mumbai, India*, pp. 73–82.

Biemann, C. and M. Riedl (2013). From Global to Local Similarities: A Graph-Based Contextualization Method using Distributional Thesauri. In *Proceedings of the 8th Workshop on TextGraphs in conjunction with Empirical Methods on Natural Language Processing*, Seattle, WA, USA, pp. 39–43.

Brun, C., J. Perez, and C. Roux (2016). XRCE at SemEval-2016 Task 5: Feedbacked Ensemble Modeling on Syntactico-Semantic Knowledge for Aspect Based Sentiment Analysis. In *Proceedings of the 10th International Workshop on Semantic Evaluation (SemEval-2016)*, San Diego, CA, USA, pp. 277–281.

Çetin, F. S., E. Yıldırım, C. Özbey, and G. Eryiğit (2016). TGB at SemEval-2016 Task 5: Multi-Lingual Constraint System for Aspect Based Sentiment Analysis. In *Proceedings of the 10th International Workshop on Semantic Evaluation (SemEval-2016)*, San Diego, CA, USA, pp. 337–341.

Chen, Y. and S. Skiena (2014). Building Sentiment Lexicons for All Major Languages. In *Proceedings of the 52nd Annual Meeting of the Association for Computational Linguistics (Volume 2: Short Papers)*, Baltimore, MD, USA, pp. 383–389.

Ding, X., B. Liu, and P. S. Yu (2008). A Holistic Lexicon-Based Approach to Opinion Mining. In *Proceedings of the 2008 International Conference on Web Search and Data Mining*, Stanford, CA, USA, pp. 231–240.

Ghosal, D., M. S. Akhtar, D. Chauhan, S. Poria, A. Ekbal, and P. Bhattacharyya (2018, October-November). Contextual inter-modal attention for multi-modal sentiment analysis. In *Proceedings of the 2018 Conference on Empirical Methods in Natural Language Processing*, Brussels, Belgium, pp. 3454–3466. Association for Computational Linguistics.

Ghosh, A., G. Li, T. Veale, P. Rosso, E. Shutova, J. Barnden, and A. Reyes (2015). Semeval-2015 task 11: Sentiment analysis of figurative language in twitter. In *In Proceedings of the 9th International Workshop on Semantic Evaluation (SemEval 2015)*, pp. 470–478.

Glorot, X., A. Bordes, and Y. Bengio (2011). Deep Sparse Rectifier Neural Networks. In *Proceedings of the 14th International Conference on Artificial Intelligence and Statistics (AISTATS-11)*, Ft. Lauderdale, FL, USA, pp. 315–323.

Graves, A., S. Fernández, and J. Schmidhuber (2005). Bidirectional LSTM Networks for Improved Phoneme Classification and Recognition. In *Proceedings of the 15th International Conference on Artificial Neural Networks: Formal Models and Their Applications - Volume Part II*, Warsaw, Poland, pp. 799–804.

Hutto, C. J. and E. Gilbert (2014). VADER: A Parsimonious Rule-Based Model for Sentiment Analysis of Social Media Text. In *Proceedings of the 8th International Conference on Weblogs and Social Media (ICWSM-14)*, Ann Arbor, MI, USA, pp. 216–225.

Jagtap, V. and K. Pawar (2013). Analysis of Different Approaches to Sentence-level Sentiment Classification. *International Journal of Scientific Engineering and Technology (ISSN: 2277-1581) Volume 2*, 164–170.

Ji-Ung Lee, Steffen Eger, J. D. and I. Gurevych (2017). UKP TU-DA at GermEval 2017: Deep Learning for Aspect Based Sentiment Detection. In *Proceedings of the GermEval 2017 Shared Task on Aspect-based Sentiment in Social Media Customer Feedback*, Berlin, Germany, pp. 22–29.

Kim, S. and E. Hovy (2006). Extracting opinions, opinion holders, and topics expressed in online news media text. In *Proceedings of the Workshop on Sentiment and Subjectivity in Text*, Sydney, Australia, pp. 1–8.

Kingma, D. and J. Ba (2014, 12). Adam: A Method for Stochastic Optimization. In *International Conference on Learning Representations*, Vancouver, BC, Canada.

Kiritchenko, S., X. Zhu, C. Cherry, and S. Mohammad (2014). NRC-Canada-2014: Detecting Aspects and Sentiment in Customer Reviews. In *Proceedings of the 8th International Workshop on Semantic Evaluation (SemEval 2014)*, Dublin, Ireland, pp. 437–442. Association for Computational Linguistics and Dublin City University.

Kumar, A., S. Kohail, A. Kumar, A. Ekbal, and C. Biemann (2016). IIT-TUDA at SemEval-2016 Task 5: Beyond Sentiment Lexicon: Combining Domain Dependency and Distributional Semantics Features for Aspect Based Sentiment Analysis. In *Proceedings of the 10th International Workshop on Semantic Evaluation (SemEval-2016)*, San Diego, CA, USA, pp. 1129–1135.

Mikolov, T., I. Sutskever, K. Chen, G. S. Corrado, and J. Dean (2013). Distributed Representations of Words and Phrases and their Compositionality. In *Advances in Neural Information Processing Systems*, Lake Tahoe, NV, USA, pp. 3111–3119.

Mishra, P., V. Mujadia, and S. Lanka (2017). GermEval 2017 : Sequence based Models for Customer Feedback Analysis. In *Proceedings of the GermEval 2017 Shared Task on Aspect-based Sentiment in Social Media Customer Feedback*, Berlin, Germany, pp. 36–42.

Mohammad, S. M., S. Kiritchenko, and X. Zhu (2013, June). NRC-Canada: Building the State-of-the-Art in Sentiment Analysis of Tweets. In *In Proceedings of the seventh international workshop on Semantic Evaluation Exercises (SemEval-2013)*, Atlanta, Georgia, USA.

Naderalvojoud, B., B. Qasemizadeh, and L. Kallmeyer (2017). HU-HHU at GermEval-2017 Sub-task B: Lexicon-Based Deep Learning for Contextual Sentiment Analysis. In *Proceedings of the GermEval 2017 Shared Task on Aspect-based Sentiment in Social Media Customer Feedback*, Berlin, Germany, pp. 18–21.

Pang, B., , and L. Lee (2005). Seeing stars: Exploiting class relationships for sentiment categorization with respect to rating scales. In *Proceedings of ACL*, pp. 115–124.

Pang, B. and L. Lee (2008). Opinion Mining and Sentiment Analysis. *Foundations and Trends in Information Retrieval 2*(1-2), 1–135.

Pang, B., L. Lee, and S. Vaithyanathan (2002). Thumbs up?: sentiment classification using machine learning techniques. In *Proceedings of the ACL-02 conference on Empirical methods in natural language processing-Volume 10*, pp. 79–86. Association for Computational Linguistics.

Pontiki, M., D. Galanis, H. Papageorgiou, I. Androutsopoulos, S. Manandhar, A.-S. Mohammad, M. Al-Ayyoub, Y. Zhao, B. Qin, O. De Clercq, et al. (2016). SemEval-2016 Task 5: Aspect Based Sentiment Analysis. In *Proceedings of the 10th International Workshop on Semantic Evaluation (SemEval-2016)*, San Diego, CA, USA, pp. 19–30.

Pontiki, M., D. Galanis, J. Pavlopoulos, H. Papageorgiou, I. Androutsopoulos, and S. Manandhar (2014, August). SemEval-2014 Task 4: Aspect Based Sentiment Analysis. In *Proceedings of the 8th International Workshop on Semantic Evaluation (SemEval 2014)*, Dublin, Ireland, pp. 27–35.

Poria, S., E. Cambria, D. Hazarika, N. Mazumder, A. Zadeh, and L.-P. Morency (2017). Multi-level multiple attentions for contextual multimodal sentiment analysis. In *Data Mining (ICDM), 2017 IEEE International Conference on*, pp. 1033–1038. IEEE.

Srivastava, N., G. Hinton, A. Krizhevsky, I. Sutskever, and R. Salakhutdinov (2014). Dropout: A Simple Way to Prevent Neural Networks from Overfitting. *Journal of Machine Learning Research 15*, 1929–1958.

Toh, Z. and J. Su (2016, June). Nlangp at semeval-2016 task 5: Improving aspect based sentiment analysis using neural network features. In *Proceedings of the 10th International Workshop on Semantic Evaluation (SemEval-2016)*, San Diego, California, pp. 282–288. Association for Computational Linguistics.

Turney, P. D. (2002). Thumbs up or thumbs down?: Semantic orientation applied to unsupervised classification of reviews. In *Proceedings of the 40th ACL*, pp. 417–424.

Waltinger, U. (2010, May). GermanPolarityClues: A Lexical Resource for German Sentiment Analysis. In *Proceedings of the 7th International Conference on Language Resources and Evaluation (LREC)*, Valletta, Malta, pp. 1638–1642.

Wilson, T., J. Wiebe, and P. Hoffmann (2005). Recognizing Contextual Polarity in Phrase-level Sentiment Analysis. In *Proceedings of the Conference on Human Language Technology and Empirical Methods in Natural Language Processing*, Vancouver, BC, Canada, pp. 347–354.

Wojatzki, M., E. Ruppert, S. Holschneider, T. Zesch, and C. Biemann (2017). GermEval 2017: Shared Task on Aspect-based Sentiment in Social Media Customer Feedback. In *Proceedings of the GermEval 2017 Shared Task on Aspect-based Sentiment in Social Media Customer Feedback*, Berlin, Germany, pp. 1–12.

Zadeh, A., P. P. Liang, S. Poria, E. Cambria, and L.-P. Morency (2018). Multimodal Language Analysis in the Wild: CMU-MOSEI Dataset and Interpretable Dynamic Fusion Graph. In *Proceedings of the 56th Annual Meeting of the Association for Computational Linguistics (Volume 1: Long Papers)*, Melbourne, Australia, pp. 2236–2246.

Predicting Metaphor Paraphrase Judgements in Context

Yuri Bizzoni
University of Gothenburg
yuri.bizzoni@gu.se

Shalom Lappin
University of Gothenburg
shalom.lappin@gu.se

Abstract

We conduct two experiments to study the effect of context on metaphor paraphrase aptness judgments. The first is an AMT crowd source task in which speakers rank metaphor-paraphrase candidate sentence pairs in short document contexts for paraphrase aptness. In the second we train a composite DNN to predict these human judgments, first in binary classifier mode, and then as gradient ratings. We found that for both mean human judgments and our DNN modeling, adding document context compresses the aptness scores towards the centre of the scale, raising low out of context ratings and decreasing high out of context scores. We briefly consider two possible explanations for this compression effect.

1 Introduction

A metaphor is a way of forcing the normal boundaries of words' meaning in order to better express an experience, a concept or an idea. At least to a native speaker's ear, some metaphors sound more conventional (like the usage of the words *ear* and *sound* in this sentence), others more original. This is not the only way to judge a metaphor. One of the most important qualities of a metaphor is its appropriateness, its *aptness*. This poses the question of how good a metaphor is for conveying a given experience or concept. While a metaphor's degree of conventionality can be measured through probabilistic methods, like language models, it is harder to model its aptness. Chiappe et al. (2003) define *aptness* as "the extent to which a comparison captures important features of the topic".

It is possible to express an opinion about some metaphors' and similes' aptness (at least to a degree) without previously knowing what they are trying to convey, or the context in which they appear[1]. For example, we don't need a particular context or frame of reference to construe the simile *She was screaming like a turtle* as strange, and less apt for expressing the quality of a scream, than *She was screaming like a banshee*. In this case, the reason why the simile in the second sentence works better is intuitive. A salient characteristic of a banshee is a powerful scream. Turtles are not known for screaming, and so it is harder to define the quality of a scream through such a comparison, except as a form of irony.[2] Other cases are more complicated. The simile *crying like a fire in the sun* (*It's All Over Now, Baby Blue*, Bob Dylan) is powerfully apt for many readers, but simply odd for others. Fire and sun do not cry in any way. But at the same time the simile can express the association we draw between something strong and intense in other sensory modes, such as vision and touch, on one hand and a loud cry on the other.

Nevertheless, most metaphors and similes need some kind of context, or external reference point to be interpreted. The sentence *The old lady had a heart of stone* is apt if the old lady is cruel or indifferent, but it is unreasonable as a description of a situation in which the old lady is kind and caring. We assume that, to an average reader's sensibility, the sentence models only the first situation appropriately.

---

[1] While it can be argued that metaphors and similes at some level work differently and cannot always be considered as variations of the same phenomenon (Sam and Catrinel, 2006; Glucksberg, 2008), for this study we treat them as belonging to the same category of figurative language.

[2] It is important not to confuse aptness with transparency. The latter measures how easy it is to understand a comparison. Chiappe et al. (2003) claim, for example, that many literary or poetic metaphors score high on aptness and low on transparency, in that they capture the nature of the topic very well, but it is not always clear why they work.

This is the view of metaphor aptness that we adopt in this paper. Following Bizzoni and Lappin (2018), we treat a metaphor as apt in relation to a literal expression that it paraphrases.[3] If the metaphor is judged to be a good paraphrase, then it closely "models" the core information of the literal sentence through its metaphorical shift. We refer to the prediction of readers' judgments on the aptness candidates for the literal paraphrase of a metaphor as the *metaphor paraphrase aptness task* (MPAT). Bizzoni and Lappin (2018) address the MPAT by using Amazon Mechanical Turk (AMT) to obtain crowd sourced annotations of metaphor-paraphrase candidate pairs. They train a composite Deep Neural Network (DNN) on a portion of their annotated corpus, and test it on the remaining part. Testing involves using the DNN as a binary classifier on paraphrase candidates. They derive predictions of gradient paraphrase aptness for their test set, and assess them by Pearson coefficient correlation to the mean judgments of their crowd sourced annotation of this set. Both training and testing are done independently of any document context for the metaphorical sentence and its literal paraphrase candidates.

In this paper we study the role of context on readers' judgments concerning the aptness of metaphor paraphrase candidates. We look at the accuracy of Bizzoni and Lappin (2018)'s DNN when trained and tested on contextually embedded metaphor-paraphrase pairs for the MPAT. In Section 2 we describe an AMT experiment in which annotators judge metaphors and paraphrases embedded in small document contexts, and in Section 3 we discuss the results of this experiment. In Section 4 we describe our MPAT modeling experiment, and in Section 5 we discuss the results of this experiment. Section 6 surveys some work on metaphor aptness and computational methods to deal with it. In Section 7 we draw conclusions from the studies presented in this paper, and we indicate directions for future work in this area.

2   Annotating Metaphor-Paraphrase Pairs in Contexts

Bizzoni and Lappin (2018) have recently produced a dataset of paraphrases containing metaphors designed to allow both supervised binary classification and gradient rankings. This dataset contains several pairs of sentences, where in each pair the first sentence contains a metaphor, and the second is a literal paraphrase candidate.

This corpus was constructed with a view to representing a large variety of syntactic structures and semantic phenomena in metaphorical sentences. Many of these structures and phenomena do not occur as metaphorical expressions, with any frequency, in natural text and were therefore introduced through hand crafted examples.

Each pair of sentences in the corpus has been rated by AMT annotators for paraphrase aptness on a scale of 1-4, with 4 being the highest degree of aptness. In Bizzoni and Lappin (2018)'s dataset, sentences come in groups of five, where the first element is the "reference element" with a metaphorical expression, and the remaining four sentences are "candidates" that stand in a degree of paraphrasehood to the reference.

Here is an example of a metaphor-paraphrase candidate pair.

1a. The crowd was a roaring river.

  b. The crowd was huge and noisy.

---

[3]Bizzoni and Lappin (2018) apply Bizzoni and Lappin (2017)'s modeling work on general paraphrase to metaphor.

The average AMT paraphrase score for this pair is 4.0, indicating a high degree of aptness.

We extracted 200 sentence pairs from Bizzoni and Lappin (2018)'s dataset and provided each pair with a document context consisting of a preceding and a following sentence,[4] as in the following example.

2a. They had arrived in the capital city. **The crowd was a roaring river**. It was glorious.

  b. They had arrived in the capital city. **The crowd was huge and noisy**. It was glorious.

One of the authors constructed most of these contexts by hand. In some cases, it was possible to locate the original metaphor in an existing document. This was the case for

(i) Literary metaphors extracted from poetry or novels, and

(ii) Short conventional metaphors (*The President brushed aside the accusations*, *Time flies*) that can be found, with small variations, in a number of texts.

For these cases, a variant of the existing context was added to both the metaphorical and the literal sentences. We introduced small modifications to keep the context short and clear, and to avoid copyright issues. We lightly modified the contexts of metaphors extracted from corpora when the original context was too long, ie. when the contextual sentences of the selected metaphor were longer than the maximum length we specified for our corpus. This was necessary due to the fact that the original, natural contexts can have an excessive length and include far-reaching references to previous content. In such cases we reduced the length of the sentence and we slightly simplified the text, while sustaining its meaning. We tried to sustain "naturalness" of the context. Since the same context is used for metaphors and their literal candidate paraphrases, we specified short contexts that make sense for both the figurative and the literal sentences, even when the pair had been judged as non-paraphrases. We kept the context as neutral as possible in order to avoid biasing effects on crowd source judgments.

For example, in the following pair of sentences, the literal sentence is *not* a good paraphrase of the figurative one (a simile).

3a. He is grinning like an ape.

  b. He is smiling in a charming way. (*average score:* 1.9)

We opted for a context that is natural for both sentences.

4a. Look at him. **He is grinning like an ape.** He feels so confident and self-assured.

  b. Look at him. **He is smiling in a charming way.** He feels so confident and self-assured.

We sought to avoid, whenever possible, an incongruous context for one of the sentences that could influence our annotators' ratings.

We collected a sub-corpus of 200 contextually embedded groups of two sentences. We tried to keep our data as balanced as possible, drawing from all four "classes" of paraphrase aptness ratings (between 1 to 4) that Bizzoni and Lappin (2018) obtained. We selected 44 pairs of *1* ratings, 51 pairs of *2*, 43 pairs of *3* and 62 pairs of *4*.

We then used AMT crowd sourcing to rate the contextualized paraphrase pairs, so that we could observe the effect of document context on assessments of metaphor paraphrase aptness.

To test the reproducibility of Bizzoni and Lappin (2018)'s ratings, we launched a pilot study for 10 original, non-contextually embedded pairs, selected from all four "categories" of aptness. We observed that the annotators provided mean ratings very similar to those reported in Bizzoni and Lappin (2018).

---

[4]Our annotated data set and the code for our model is available at
`https://github.com/yuri-bizzoni/Metaphor-Paraphrase`.

The Pearson coeffecent correlation between the mean judgments of our out-of-context pilot annotations and Bizzoni and Lappin (2018)'s annotations for the same pair was over 0.9.

We then conducted an AMT annotation task for the 200 contextualized pairs. On average, 20 different annotators rated each pair. We considered as "rogue" those annotators who rated the large majority of pairs with very high or very low scores, and those who responded inconsistently to two "trap" pairs. After filtering out the rogues, we had an average of 14 annotators per pair.

3   Annotation Results

We found a Pearson correlation of 0.81 between the in-context and out-of-context mean human paraphrase ratings for our two corpora. This correlation is virtually identical to the one that Bernardy et al. (2018) report for mean acceptability ratings of out-of-context to in-context sentences in their crowd source experiment. It is interesting that a relatively high level of ranking correspondence should occur in mean judgments for sentences presented out of and within document contexts, for two entirely distinct tasks.

Our main result concerns the effect of context on mean paraphrase judgment. We observed that it tends to flatten aptness ratings towards the centre of the rating scale.

Of the metaphors that had been considered highly apt (average rounded score of *4*) in the context-less pairs, 71.1% received a more moderate judgment (average rounded score of *3*). On the other hand, the reverse movement was rare: only 5% of pairs rated *3* out of context (2 pairs) was boosted to a mean rating of *4* in context.

At the other end of the scale, 68.2% of the metaphors judged at *1* category of aptness out of context were raised to a mean of *2* in context, while only the 3.9% of pairs rated *2* out of context were lowered to *1* in context.

Ratings at the middle of the scale - *2* (defined as semantically related non-paraphrases) and *3* (imperfect or loose paraphrases) - remained largely stable, with little movement in either direction. 9.8% of pairs rated *2* were re-ranked as *3* when presented in context, and 10% of pairs ranked at *3* changed to *2*.

It seems that context tends to "improve" metaphors with a low level of aptness, but lowers the judgments on metaphors with a high level of aptness.

The division between *2* and *3* separates paraphrases from non-paraphrases. Our results suggest that this binary rating of paraphrase aptness was not strongly affected by context. Context operates at the extremes of our scale, raising low aptness ratings and lowering high aptness ratings. This effect is clearly indicated in the regression chart in Fig 1.

This effect of context on human ratings is very similar to the one reported in Bernardy et al. (2018). They find that sentences rated as ill formed out of context are in part improved when they are presented in their document contexts. However the mean ratings for sentences judged to be highly acceptable out of context declined when assessed in context. Bernardy et al. (2018)'s linear regression chart for the correlation between out-of-context and in-context acceptability judgments as collected in their survey looks remarkably like our Fig 1. There is, then, a striking parallel in the compression pattern that context appears to exert on human judgments for two entirely different linguistic properties.

This pattern requires an explanation. Bernardy et al. (2018) suggest that adding context causes speakers to focus on broader semantic and pragmatic issues of discourse coherence, rather than simply judging syntactic well formedness (measured as naturalness) when a sentence is considered in isolation. On this view, compression of rating results from a pressure to construct a plausible interpretation for any sentence within its context. If this is the case, an analogous process may generate the same compression effect for metaphor aptness assessment of sentence pairs in context. Speakers may attempt to achieve broader discourse coherence when assessing the metaphor-paraphrase aptness relation in a document context. Out of context they focus more narrowly on the semantic relations between a metaphorical sentence and its paraphrase candidate. Therefore, this relation is the centre of a speaker's concern and receives more fine-grained assessment when considered out of context than in context.

However, a second possibility is that adding context to the aptness task increases the general cognitive

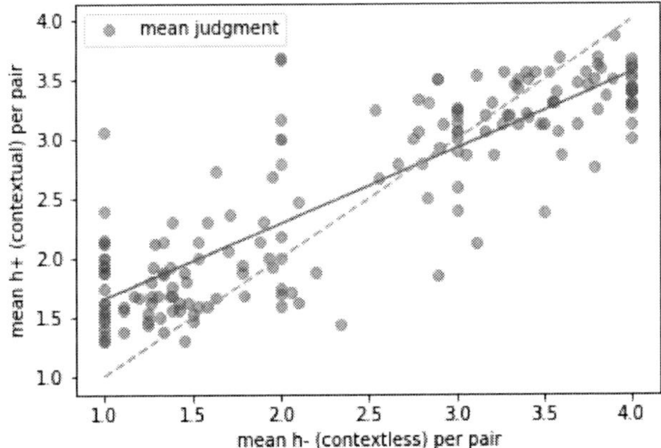

Figure 1: In-context and out-of-context mean ratings. Points above the broken diagonal line represent sentence pairs which received a higher rating when presented in context. The total least-square linear regression is shown as the second line.

load involved in processing the sentence. This effect may also cause hearers/readers to focus less on the properties of the sentences for which a judgment is solicited, and more on processing the entire discourse unit. Such a shift in focus might also produce the observed compression effect, but for different reasons than those that the pragmatic discourse coherence explanation proposes. This issue clearly requires further research. We discuss these two possible interpretations in more in detail in Section 7.

4 Modelling Paraphrase Judgments in Context

We use the DNN model described in Bizzoni and Lappin (2018) to predict aptness judgments for in context paraphrase pairs. It has three main components:

1. Two encoders that learn the representations of two sentences separately

2. A unified layer that merges the output of the encoders

3. A final set of fully connected layers that operate on the merged representation of the two sentences to generate a score. Our pairs are evaluated through this final score.

The encoder for each pair of sentences taken as input is composed of two parallel "Atrous" Convolutional Neural Networks (CNNs) and LSTM RNNs, feeding two sequenced fully connected layers.

The encoder is preloaded with the lexical embeddings from Word2vec Mikolov et al. (2013). The sequences of word embeddings that we use as input provides the model with dense word-level information, while the model tries to generalize over these embedding patterns.

The combination of a CNN and an LSTM allows us to capture both long-distance syntactic and semantic relations, best identified by a CNN, and the sequential nature of the input, most efficiently identified by an LSTM. Several existing studies, cited in Bizzoni and Lappin (2017), demonstrate the advantages of combining CNNs and LSTMs to process texts, and show that using these two architectures together has a positive effect on language processing.

The model produces a single classifier value between 0 and 1. We transform this score into a binary output of 0 or 1 by applying a threshold of 0.5 for assigning 1. In this way, we can use the model's output for two evaluation methodologies: classification and ranking.

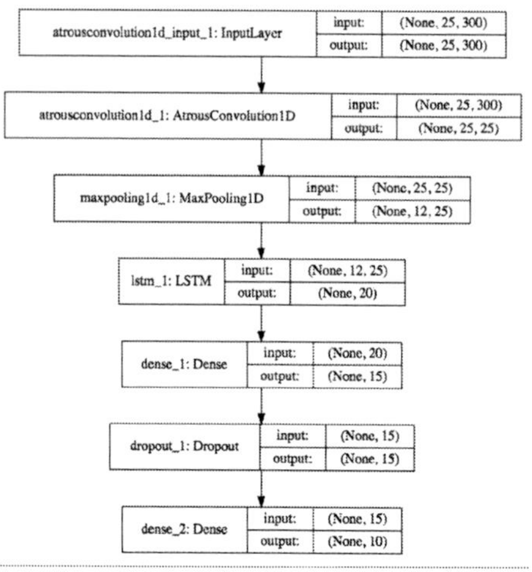

Figure 2: DNN encoder for predicting metaphorical paraphrase aptness from Bizzoni and Lappin (2018). Each encoder represents a sentence as a 10-dimensional vector. These vectors are concatenated to compute a single score for the pair of input sentences.

The architecture of the model is given in Fig 2.

We use the same general protocol as Bizzoni and Lappin (2018) for training with supervised learning, and testing the model.

Following the methodology applied in Bernardy et al. (2018), the input to the encoders is the concatenation of the word embeddings of the whole paragraph (context and focus sentence).

Using Bizzoni and Lappin (2018)'s out-of-context metaphor dataset and our contextualized extension of this set, we apply four variants of the training and testing protocol.

1. Training and testing on the in-context dataset.

2. Training on the out-of-context dataset, and testing on the in-context dataset.

3. Training on the in-context dataset, and testing on the out-of-context dataset.

4. Training and testing on the out-of-context dataset (Bizzoni and Lappin (2018)'s original experiment provides the results for out-of-context training and testing).

When we train or test the model on the out-of-context dataset, we use Bizzoni and Lappin (2018)'s original annotated corpus of 800 metaphor-paraphrase pairs. The in-context dataset contains 200 annotated pairs. As for the baseline, we rely on Bizzoni and Lappin (2018)'s earlier work on paraphrase, where, together with several alternative versions of the neural model, a baseline relying on vector cosine similarity between sentences is provided, and outperformed by the model.

5   MPAT Modelling Results

We use the model both to predict binary classification of a metaphor paraphrase candidate, and to generate gradient aptness ratings on the 4 category scale (see Bizzoni and Lappin (2018) for details). A positive binary classification is accurate if it is $\geq$ a 2.5 mean human rating. The gradient predictions are derived from the softmax distribution of the output layer of the model. The results of our modelling experiments are given in Table 1.

The main result that we obtain from these experiments is that the model learns binary classification to a reasonable extent on the *in-context* dataset, both when trained on the same kind of data (in-context

Training set	Test set	F-score	Correlation
With-context*	With-context*	0.68	-0.01
Without-context	With-context	**0.72**	**0.3**
With-context	Without-context	0.6	0.02
Without-context	Without-context	0.74	0.75

Table 1: F-score binary classification accuracy and Pearson correlation for three different regimens of supervised learning. The * indicates results for a set of 10-fold cross-validation runs. This was necessary in the first case, when training and testing are both on our small corpus of in-context pairs. In the second and third rows, since we are using the full out-of-context and in-context dataset, we report single-run results. The fourth row is Bizzoni and Lappin (2018)'s best run result. (Our single-run best result for the first row is an F-score of 0.8 and a Pearson correlation 0.16).

pairs), and when trained on Bizzoni and Lappin (2018)'s original dataset (out-of-context pairs). However, the model does not perform well in predicting gradient in-context judgments when trained on in-context pairs. It improves slightly for this task when trained on out-of-context pairs.

By contrast, it does well in predicting both binary and gradient ratings when trained and tested on out-of-context data sets.

Bernardy et al. (2018) also note a decline in Pearson correlation for their DNN models on the task of predicting human in-context acceptability judgments, but it is less drastic.

They attribute this decline to the fact that the compression effect renders the gradient judgments less separable, and thus harder to predict. A similar, but more pronounced version of this effect may account for the difficulty that our model encounters in predicting gradient in-context ratings. The binary classifier achieves greater success for these cases because its training tends to polarise the data in one direction or the other.

We also observe that the best combination seems to consist in training our model on the original out-of-context dataset and testing it on the in-context pairs. In this configuration we reach an F-score (0.72) only slightly lower than the one reported in Bizzoni and Lappin (2018) (0.74), and we record the highest Pearson correlation, 0.3 (which is still not strong, compared to Bizzoni and Lappin (2018)'s best run, 0.75[5]). This result may partly be an artifact of the the larger amount of training data provided by the out-of-context pairs.

We can use this variant (out-of-context training and in-context testing) to perform a fine-grained comparison of the model's predicted ratings for the same sentences in and out of context. When we do this, we observe that out of 200 sentence pairs, our model scores the majority (130 pairs) higher when processed in context than out of context. A smaller but significant group (70 pairs) receives a lower score when processed in context. The first group's average score *before adding context* (0.48) is consistently lower than that of the second group (0.68). Also, as Table 2 indicates, the pairs that our model rated, *out of context*, with a score lower than 0.5 (on the model's softmax distribution), received on average a higher rating *in context*, while the opposite is true for the pairs rated with a score higher than 0.5. In general, sentence pairs that were rated highly out of context receive a lower score in context, and vice versa. When we did linear regression on the DNNs in and out of context predicted scores, we observed substantially the same compression pattern exhibited by our AMT mean human judgments. Figure 3 plots this regression graph.

6 Related Cognitive Work on Metaphor Aptness

Tourangeau and Sternberg (1981) present ratings of aptness and comprehensibility for 64 metaphors from two groups of subjects. They note that metaphors were perceived as more apt and more comprehensible to the extent that their terms occupied similar positions within dissimilar domains. Interestingly,

---

[5]It is also important to consider that their ranking scheme is different from our design: the Pearson correlation reported there is the average of the correlations over all groups of 5 sentences present in the dataset.

OOC score	Number of elements	OOC Mean	OOC Std	IC Mean	IC Std
0.0-0.5	112	0.42	0.09	0.54	0.1
0.5-1.0	88	0.67	0.07	0.64	0.07

Table 2: We show the number of pairs that received a low score out of context (first row) and the number of pairs that received a high score out of context (second row). We report the mean score and standard deviation (Std) of the two groups when judged out of context (OOC) and when judged in context (IC) by our model. The model's scores range between 0 and 1. As can be seen, the mean of the low-scoring group rises in context, and the mean of the high-scoring group decreases in context.

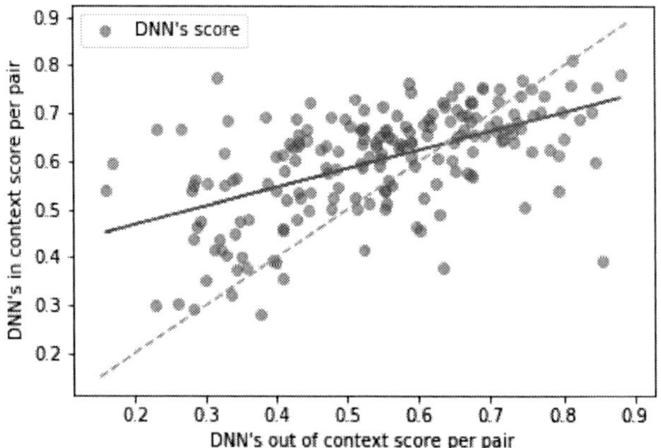

Figure 3: In-context and out-of-context ratings assigned by our trained model. Points above the broken diagonal line represent sentence pairs which received a higher rating when presented in context. The total least-square linear regression is shown as the second line.

Fainsilber and Kogan (1984) present experimental results in support of the claim that imagery does not clearly correlate with metaphor aptness. Aptness judgments are also subject to individual differences.

Blasko (1999) points to such individual differences in metaphor processing. She asked 27 participants to rate 37 metaphors for difficulty, aptness and familiarity, and to write one or more interpretations of the metaphor. Subjects with higher working memory span were able to give more detailed and elaborate interpretations of metaphors. Familiarity and aptness correlated with both high and low span subjects. For high span subjects aptness of metaphor positively correlated with number of interpretations, while for low span subjects the opposite was true.

McCabe (1983) analyses the aptness of metaphors with and without extended contexts. She finds that domain similarity correlates with aptness judgments in isolated metaphors, but not in *contextualized* metaphors. She also reports that there is no clear correlation between metaphor aptness ratings in isolated and in contextualized examples.

Chiappe et al. (2003) study the relation between aptness and comprehensibility in metaphors and similes. They provide experimental results indicating that aptness is a better predictor than comprehensibility for the "transformation" of a simile into a metaphor. Subjects tended to remember similes as metaphors (i.e. remember *the dancer's arms moved like startled rattlesnakes* as *the dancer's arms **were** startled rattlesnakes*) if they were judged to be particularly apt, rather than particularly comprehensible. They claim that context might play an important role in this process. They suggest that context should ease the transparency and increase the aptness of both metaphors and similes.

Tourangeau and Rips (1991) report a series of experiments indicating that metaphors tend to be interpreted through emergent features that were not rated as particularly relevant, either for the tenor or for the vehicle of the metaphor. The number of emergent features that subjects were able to draw from a metaphor seems to correlate with their aptness judgments.

Bambini et al. (2018) use Event-Related Brain Potentials (ERPs) to study the temporal dynamics of metaphor processing in reading literary texts. They emphasize the influence of context on the ability of a reader to smoothly interpret an unusual metaphor.

Bambini et al. (2016) use electrophysiological experiments to try to disentangle the effect of a metaphor from that of its context. They find that de-contextualized metaphors elicited two different brain responses, $N400$ and $P600$, while contextualized metaphors only produced the $P600$ effect. They attribute the $N400$ effect, often observed in neurological studies of metaphors, to expectations about upcoming words in the absence of a predictive context that "prepares" the reader for the metaphor. They suggest that the $P600$ effect reflects the actual interpretative processing of the metaphor.

This view is supported by several neurological studies showing that the $N400$ effect arises with unexpected elements. This happens, for example, when new presuppositions are introduced into a text in a way not implied by the context (Masia et al. (2017)). It can also occur because of unexpected associations with a noun-verb combination, not indicated by previous context, as when it is preceded by a neutral context (Cosentino et al. (2017)).

7   Conclusions and Future Work

We have observed that embedding metaphorical sentences and their paraphrase candidates in a document context generates a compression effect in human metaphor aptness ratings. Context seems to mitigate the perceived aptness of metaphors in two ways. Those metaphor-paraphrase pairs that were given a very low score out of context tend to receive an increased score in context, while those with very high scores out of context decline in rating when presented in context. At the same time, the demarcation line between paraphrase and non-paraphrase is not particularly blurred by the introduction of extended context around the expression.

As previously observed by McCabe (1983), we found that context has an influence on humans' aptness ratings for metaphors, although, unlike them, we did find a correlation between the two sets of ratings. Chiappe et al. (2003)'s expectation that context should facilitate a metaphor's aptness was supported only in one sense. Aptness increases for low-rated pairs. But it decreases for high-rated pairs.

We applied Bizzoni and Lappin (2018)'s DNN for the MPAT to an in-context test set, experimenting with both out-of-context and in-context training corpora. We obtained reasonable results for binary classification of paraphrase candidates for aptness, but the performance of the model declined sharply for the prediction of human gradient aptness judgments, relative to its performance on a corresponding out-of-context test set. This appears to be the result of the increased difficulty in separating rating categories introduced by the compression effect.

Strikingly, the linear regression analyses of human aptness judgments for in- and out-of-context paraphrase pairs, and of Bizzoni and Lappin (2018)'s DNN predictions for these pairs reveal similar compression patterns. These patterns produce ratings that cannot be clearly separated along a linear ranking scale.

To the best of our knowledge ours is the first study of the effect of context on metaphor aptness on a corpus of this dimension, using crowd sourced human judgments as the gold standard for assessing the predictions of a computational model of paraphrase. We also present the first comparative study of both human and model judgments of metaphor paraphrase for in-context and out-of-context variants of metaphorical sentences.

Finally, the compression effect that context induces on paraphrase judgments corresponds closely to the one observed independently in another task, which is reported in Bernardy et al. (2018). We regard this effect as a significant discovery that increases the plausibility and the interest of our results. The fact that it appears clearly with two tasks involving different sorts of DNNs and distinct learning regimes (unsupervised learning with neural network language models for the acceptability prediction task, as opposed to supervised learning with our composite DNN for paraphrase prediction) reduces the likelihood that this effect is an artefact of our experimental design.

It is important to note that this shift towards the centre of the scale, recorded both for humans and for our model, is *not* consistent with a simple homogenization effect for the compared items. If the addition of identical context to both sentences just made it harder for the network to see the differences between the two items, we would expect the shift in aptness judgment to go in one direction on the scale. All contextualized pairs should be rated as better paraphrases than their decontextualized equivalents. The same effect should hold for human annotators.

As we suggested earlier, two explanations for the compression effect come to mind. On the first compression is the result of a specifically linguistic phenomenon. In the presence of a larger textual context speakers concentrate on the pragmatic coherence of the discourse, and so they pay less attention to the properties of the sentence for which assessment is solicited. This is the approach that Bernardy et al. (2018) propose. On the second explanation compression is the result of the increase in cognitive load that processing the context imposes.

To distinguish between these accounts it would be interesting to experiment with two different kinds of contexts: a natural one for each sentence, and a random context that is unrelated in content to the sentence. If the cognitive load hypothesis is correct, the compression effect should be present with both types of context, as they each increase processing. However, if the effect appears only with natural contexts, then this result would lend support to the pragmatic coherence hypothesis. Random contexts do not generally facilitate coherent discourse interpretations, and so we would expect speakers to exhibit a tendency to focus on the naturalness of the test sentence in isolation. This should reduce or cancel the observed compression effect. One of our main concerns in future research will be to achieve a better understanding of the compression effect of context on human judgments and DNN models.

While our dataset is still small, we are presenting an initial investigation of a phenomenon which is, to date, little studied. We are working to enlarge the dataset. In future work we will expand both our in- and out-of-context annotated metaphor-paraphrase corpora. While the corpus we used contains a number of hand crafted examples, it would be preferable to find these example types in natural text, and we are working on this. We are seeking to expand the size of the data set. It will also be useful to conduct qualitative analyses on the kinds of metaphors and similes that are more prone to a context-induced rating switch. We intend to improve the reliability of our modelling experiments by using alternative DNN architectures for the MPAT.

Acknowledgments

We are grateful to our colleagues in the Centre for Linguistic Theory and Studies in Probability (CLASP), FLoV, at the University of Gothenburg for useful discussion of some of the ideas presented in this paper. We would also like to thank two anonymous reviewers and Matthew Purver for their insightful and detailed comments on an earlier draft. The research reported here was done at CLASP, which is supported by a 10 year research grant (grant 2014-39) from the Swedish Research Council.

References

Bambini, V., C. Bertini, W. Schaeken, A. Stella, and F. Di Russo (2016). Disentangling metaphor from context: an erp study. *Frontiers in psychology 7*, 559.

Bambini, V., P. Canal, D. Resta, and M. Grimaldi (2018). Time course and neurophysiological underpinnings of metaphor in literary context. *Discourse Processes*, 1–21.

Bernardy, J.-P., S. Lappin, and J. H. Lau (2018). The influence of context on sentence acceptability judgmements. *Proceedings of ACL 2018, Melbourne, Australia*, 456–461.

Bizzoni, Y. and S. Lappin (2017). Deep learning of binary and gradient judgements for semantic paraphrase. In *IWCS 2017 - 12th International Conference on Computational Semantics - Short papers, Montpellier, France, September 19 - 22, 2017.*

Bizzoni, Y. and S. Lappin (2018). Predicting human metaphor paraphrase judgments with deep neural networks. *Proceedings of The Workshop on Figurative Language Processing, NAACL 2018, New Orleans LA*, 45–55.

Blasko, D. G. (1999). Only the tip of the iceberg: Who understands what about metaphor? *Journal of Pragmatics 31*(12), 1675–1683.

Chiappe, D. L., J. M. Kennedy, and P. Chiappe (2003). Aptness is more important than comprehensibility in preference for metaphors and similes. *Poetics 31*(1), 51–68.

Cosentino, E., G. Baggio, J. Kontinen, and M. Werning (2017). The time-course of sentence meaning composition. n400 effects of the interaction between context-induced and lexically stored affordances. *Frontiers in psychology 8*, 813.

Fainsilber, L. and N. Kogan (1984). Does imagery contribute to metaphoric quality? *Journal of psycholinguistic research 13*(5), 383–391.

Glucksberg, S. (2008). How metaphors create categories–quickly. *The Cambridge handbook of metaphor and thought*, 67–83.

Masia, V., P. Canal, I. Ricci, E. L. Vallauri, and V. Bambini (2017). Presupposition of new information as a pragmatic garden path: Evidence from event-related brain potentials. *Journal of Neurolinguistics 42*, 31–48.

McCabe, A. (1983). Conceptual similarity and the quality of metaphor in isolated sentences versus extended contexts. *Journal of Psycholinguistic Research 12*(1), 41–68.

Mikolov, T., I. Sutskever, K. Chen, G. S. Corrado, and J. Dean (2013). Distributed representations of words and phrases and their compositionality. In C. J. C. Burges, L. Bottou, M. Welling, Z. Ghahramani, and K. Q. Weinberger (Eds.), *Advances in Neural Information Processing Systems 26*, pp. 3111–3119. Curran Associates, Inc.

Sam, G. and H. Catrinel (2006). On the relation between metaphor and simile: When comparison fails. *Mind & Language 21*(3), 360–378.

Tourangeau, R. and L. Rips (1991). Interpreting and evaluating metaphors. *Journal of Memory and Language 30*(4), 452–472.

Tourangeau, R. and R. J. Sternberg (1981). Aptness in metaphor. *Cognitive psychology 13*(1), 27–55.

Predicting Word Concreteness and Imagery

Jean Charbonnier
Hochschule Hannover
jean.charbonnier@hs-hannover.de

Christian Wartena
Hochschule Hannover
christian.wartena@hs-hannover.de

Abstract

Concreteness of words has been studied extensively in psycholinguistic literature. A number of datasets has been created with average values for perceived concreteness of words. We show that we can train a regression model on these data, using word embeddings and morphological features. We evaluate the model on 7 publicly available datasets and show that concreteness and imagery values can be predicted with high accuracy. Furthermore, we analyse typical contexts of abstract and concrete words and review the potentials of concreteness prediction for image annotation.

1 Motivation

Concreteness and imagery of words has been studied for several decades in the field of psycholinguistics and psychology. Values for concreteness and imagery of words are obtained by instructing and asking experimentees to score words on a numeric scale for these aspects.

We assume that concrete nouns occur in other contexts than abstract nouns do and that nouns with a high imagery value occur together with other words than nouns with a low imagery. This is not as simple as it might sound, since most words can be used in different senses: e.g., nouns with high imagery might be accompanied by colour adjectives, but colours also fit perfectly with political parties and ideas. Nevertheless, we expect that there are differences in the distribution of abstract and concrete words and words with high and low imagery. If these differences indeed exist, and if concreteness and imagery are important aspects of the meaning of a word, we would expect that the characteristics of the context of concrete words are present in learned distributional representations of word meanings. This finally, can be verified quite easily and is exactly what we will test in the following: it should be possible to read off the concreteness and imagery of a word from its distributional representation.

If it is possible to predict the concreteness and imagery of a word from its distributional representation, this also has a very practical aspect: Retrieving these values from experiments is an expensive and time consuming task. If these values are needed for a psycholinguistic experiment or for some application it would be an advantage if we could compute them instead.

A practical application, that in fact was our initial motivation for this research, is the annotation of images (Charbonnier et al., 2018). We need to find terms in the caption (and surrounding text) of an image that describe that image. We expect that nouns with high concreteness and imagery values are much more likely to refer to concepts depicted in the image than abstract words do. Our basic intuition is illustrated by the image caption pair shown in Fig. 1. Here the noun *robot* in the caption is very concrete, while the other nouns (*systems, platform, research, development*) are much more abstract. The most concrete noun in this example describes quite well what is shown by the image.

The remainder of the paper is organised as follows: Section 2 gives an overview of common definitions of concreteness and imagery. In section 3 we review the most relevant literature on this topic. Section 4 gives an overview of the available datasets with human judgements on

Image	Caption
	The iCub humanoid robot: an open-systems platform for research in cognitive development.
	Source
	Vernon, David, Michael Beetz, and Giulio Sandini. "Prospection in cognition: the case for joint episodic-procedural memory in cognitive robotics." *Frontiers in Robotics and AI 2 (2015)*.

Figure 1: Typical image and caption from a scientific publication.

concreteness and imagery of words. In section 5 we present our method for predicting concreteness. The results are given in section 6. The source code for all experiments is available on GitHub[1].

2 Concreteness and Imagery

Concreteness of words has received a lot of attention in psycholinguistic research. Here concreteness refers to the degree to which the concept denoted by a word refers to a perceptible entity (Brysbaert et al., 2014). Brysbaert et al. (2014) found that subjects largely rated the haptic and visual experiences, even if they were explicitly asked to take into account experiences involving any senses. Friendly et al. (1982) define concrete words as words that "refer to tangible objects, materials or persons which can be easily perceived with the senses". They define imagery[2] as the ease with which a word arouses a mental image. Many studies found that there is a high correlation between concreteness and imagery (Friendly et al., 1982; Algarabel et al., 1988; Clark and Paivio, 2004).

It is assumed that concreteness influences learning, recognition memory and the speed of visual recognition, reading and spelling (Spreen and Schulz, 1966). A recent overview of research in this area is e.g. given by Borghi et al. (2017).

3 Related Work

A few studies deal with the question whether values for concreteness can be predicted by machine learning techniques. Rabinovich et al. (2018) predict the concreteness of words indirectly by assigning a concreteness value to sentences in which a word occurs. The concreteness value of a sentence is based on the presence of seed words. The set of seed words is constructed by selecting words with derivational suffixes that are typical for highly abstract nouns. The correlation between manual assigned values from various subsets of the dataset from Brysbaert et al. (2014) (MT40k, see also Section 4.1) and the MRC database (see Section 4.2) and predicted values ranges from 0.66 to 0.74

Rothe et al. (2016) try to find low dimensional feature representations of words in which at least some dimensions correspond to interpretable properties of words. One of these dimensions is concreteness. For training and testing they use GoogleNews embeddings and two subsets of frequent words from the concreteness data by in MT40k. For their test set of 8,694 frequent words they found a moderate correlation with the human judgements and a value for Kendall's τ of 0,623.

Tanaka et al. (2013) use word concreteness to determine the reading difficulty of a text. Like we will do below, they train a regression model to predict concreteness values. As features they use a small number of manually constructed co-occurrence features, like co-occurrence with sense

---

[1] https://github.com/textmining-hsh/Concreteness

[2] Most authors seem to use the term *imagery*, while others also use *imageability* and *visualness*. We will use *imagery* throughout this paper, even when describing datasets using one of the other terms.

verbs. For training and evaluation they use a subset of 3,455 nouns from the Medical Research Council Psycholinguistic Database (see Section 4 for details). Pearson's correlation and Kendall's τ between the values from the database and their predictions are 0.675 and 0.502, respectively, for imagery, and 0.688 and 0.508, respectively, for concreteness.

Turney et al. (2011) proposed to use distributional vector representations as features to train a classifier that distinguishes abstract from concrete nouns. Turney constructed word embeddings for each word especially for this task. The recent work of Ljubešić et al. (2018) builds on this idea and tries to predict concreteness values instead of only considering two classes and uses standard word embeddings instead of training specialized word embeddings for the task. They found a Spearman correlation coefficient of 0.887 between the predicted concreteness values and the values form MT40k. The focus of their work is on transferring concreteness values form one to another language. In the current paper we will investigate this approach in more detail and evaluate on more datasets.

Hessel et al. (2018) use image captions to predict the likelihood of the occurrence of a word in the image and thus indirectly the concreteness or imagery of the word. In fact this exactly inverse method of our approach to annotating images: while Hessel et al. (2018) use likely descriptive terms to predict concreteness, we aim to find terms describing the image using concreteness.

4   Data

In order to support psycholinguistic research on differences of human processing of concrete and abstract words, for almost half a century researchers have collected concreteness values for words. The typical way to obtain these values is by averaging concreteness rates from several subjects in a controlled setting (Paivio et al., 1968). Recently, *Amazon Mechanical Turk* was used to get ratings for a large number of words (Brysbaert et al., 2014).

Despite the overlap between the available datasets we decided to evaluate our predictions on several, but not all collections, since all of them have their specific characteristics and have been used in other studies.

4.1   Datasets used for training and testing concreteness and imagery

We used four datasets for evaluation and one, the largest, for training. All datasets have values for concreteness, three of them also have values for imagery. To avoid confusion, we will treat the datasets with imagery and concreteness values as different datasets. Thus we have a total number of seven datasets. Table 1 gives an overview of the size of these datasets and their pairwise overlap. The table also shows for how many of the words in each of the datasets we find word embeddings in two common used resources of pretrained embeddings. Though we do not have enough imagery data to train a good model, we can, given the high correlation between imagery and concreteness values, also evaluate our concreteness model on imagery data. An overview of the correlation for words occurring in different data sets is provided in Table 2.

MT40k   The dataset provided by Brysbaert et al. (2014) consist of 37,058 words and 2,896 two-word phrases rated by over 4,000 persons located in the USA using the online crowd sourcing tool *Amazon Mechanical Turk* (therefore we call this dataset MT40k). Each word was rated by at least 20 people. In the experiment 60,099 single words and 2,940 two-word expressions were used. Words that did not receive enough valid ratings got discarded. The remaining set of almost 40,000 English lemmas were known by at least 85% of the participants.

The results were validated with the concreteness values from the database of Coltheart (1981). For 3,935 words that are found in both collections, the Pearson correlation of the concreteness scores is $r = 0.919$. Unlike the other datasets below that use a scale from 1 to 7, MT40k ranges from 1 to 5. This scale was used because it was shown that 5 is the maximum number of categories humans can work with reliably. The data is available as a CSV file[3] with all 60,099 words included. Words that did not receive enough valid ratings, are included in the file with a missing concreteness value.

PYM$_C$ The dataset created by Paivio et al. (1968) (PYM) consists of 925 nouns with ratings for concreteness, imagery and meaningfulness and was one of the first datasets for these values. Many other datasets are extension of this collection or used the same methodology to construct the dataset. In the following we denote words and concreteness values form this data set as PYM$_C$. The data for PYM and CP are available as a CSV file [4].

PYM$_I$ PYM$_I$ denotes the set all 925 nouns in PYM and their imagery values.

CP$_A$ Clark and Paivio (2004) collected and published various ratings and norms they could find for the 925 words from PYM. These ratings include also a previously unpublished set of imagery ratings (called IMG2 in their paper) that are different from the imagery values in PYM. We refer to this additional imagery ratings as CP$_A$.

CP$_E$ Clark and Paivio (2004) also extended the word pool of Paivio et al. (1968) with more words, also including words with other part of speech than noun. The total size of the word pool is 2,311. For the new words ratings were collected in the same way as for the original words, including imagery ratings for 2,111 words. We refer to this extended dataset as CP$_E$.

TWP$_I$ The Toronto Word Pool (TWP) by Friendly et al. (1982) consists of 1,080 common English words selected from the Thorndike-Lorge word count[5]. It includes not only nouns but also verbs, adjectives, adverbs and prepositions. Furthermore, the selected words all have a frequency of 20+ in Thorndike-Lorge and have a maximum of two syllables or eight letters. Only 20% of the words from PYM fulfil these restrictions. Hence the overlap between PYM and TWP is quite small. We refer to the TWP imagery ratings as TWP$_I$ The experiment was done by 400 volunteering (160 male, 240 female) undergraduate psychology participants between 1977 and 1978. Every participant got one of 4 different lists with 270 words to rate. The values from TWP were extracted by using OCR and parsing from the scanned original paper.

TWP$_C$ TWP$_C$ denotes the concreteness values for all 1,080 words from TWP.

Newcombe Newcombe et al. (2012) constructed a dataset of 200 abstract and 200 concrete nouns, handpicked from TWP and PYM. The selected words have a concreteness and imagery rating of 5.0 or higher, whereas the abstract nouns are rated below 3.9. These data do not include any words with unclear concreteness and thus are intended to be used for experiment in which concrete and abstract words have to be contrasted. The words where extracted from the appendix of the paper with OCR and are manually corrected.

Training Corpus We constructed a set for training from the MT40K data set by removing all words from MT40K that also occur in either TWP, CP, PYM or Newcombe. In this way, we make sure that the words for which we predict imagery and concreteness, are never included in the training data. Furthermore we removed all two-phrase words and all words that are not part of the two resources for pretrained embeddings.

Table 1: Size of datasets and the overlap with other data set.

	Size	$\cap$ Google	$\cap$ fastText	$\cap$ MT40k	$\cap$ TWP	$\cap$ PYM	$\cap$ CP_E
MT40k	39954	33975	37058				
TWP	1080	1080	1080	1077			
PYM	925	921	925	877	167		
CP_E	2111	2100	2111	1905	340	925	
Train	32783	31246	32783	32783	0	0	0

Table 2: Pearson correlation between the values for concreteness and imagery for the words in the intersection of two datasets.

	MT40k	TWP_C	PYM_C	TWP_I	PYM_I	CP_A
TWP_C	0.896					
PYM_C	0.936	0.899				
TWP_I	0.816	0.822	0.789			
PYM_I	0.857	0.836	0.831	0.929		
CP_A	0.717	0.731	0.596	0.897	0.803	
CP_E	0.834	0.851	0.831	0.917	1.000	0.803

4.2 Further sources for concreteness

Besides the used datasets described above there are a number of further data sets that are aggregations of other datasets, very small, specialized or similar to newer data sets.

Spreen and Schulz (1966) determined concreteness ratings for 329 nouns. Gilhooly and Hay (1977) selected 205 five letter words with single-solution anagram with imagery and concreteness to analyse their effect on anagram solving. The Handbook of Semantic Word Norms (Toglia and Battig, 1978) gives concreteness values for 2,854 words. Gilhooly and Logie (1980) selected 1,944 nouns from Thorndike-Lorge word count and tried to have an even distribution over word length and frequency. Coltheart (1981) collected data from different publications to construct the Medical Research Council Psycholinguistic Database (MRCDB), a database with 98,538 words, 8,288 of which have values for imagery and concreteness originating from PYM, Toglia & Batting and Gilhooly & Logie. The Colorado Meaning Norms (Nickerson and Cartwright, 1984) contain 90 nouns from PYM and Toglia & Batting put into three concreteness groups (Low, Medium, High).

4.3 Embeddings

As distributional models for the words we use precomputed word embeddings from GoogleNews and fastText. The regression model will use the latent feature valures from these embeddings to predict the concreteness values. GoogleNews embeddings were trained on a part of the GoogleNews dataset, which is about 100 billion words. The model contains 300-dimensional vectors for 3 million words and phrases (Mikolov et al., 2013).

The fastText embeddings (Mikolov et al., 2018) are available in four versions. Two versions (with and without subword information) with 1 million word vectors are trained on Wikipedia 2017, UMBC webbase and statmt.org news with 16 billion tokens available. The other two version (also available with and without subword information) with 2 million word vectors trained on the Common Crawl with 600B tokens. In our experiments we used the version trained on Common Crawl without subword information, as it yields the best results.

5 Determining Word Concreteness

Given the availability of labelled data, the obvious way to predict concreteness is to train a regression model.

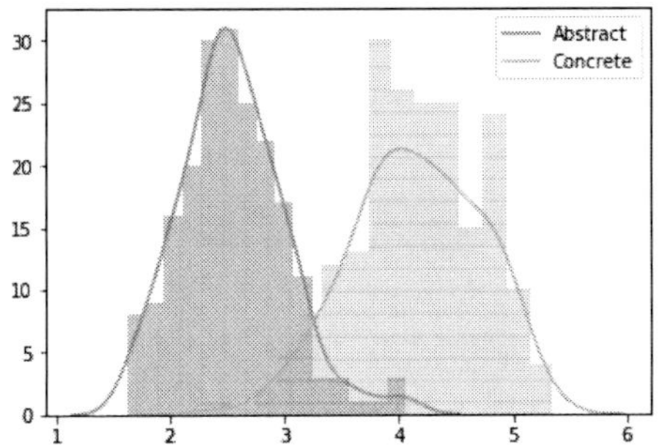

(a) Predictions by the classifier trained with GoogleNews word embeddings

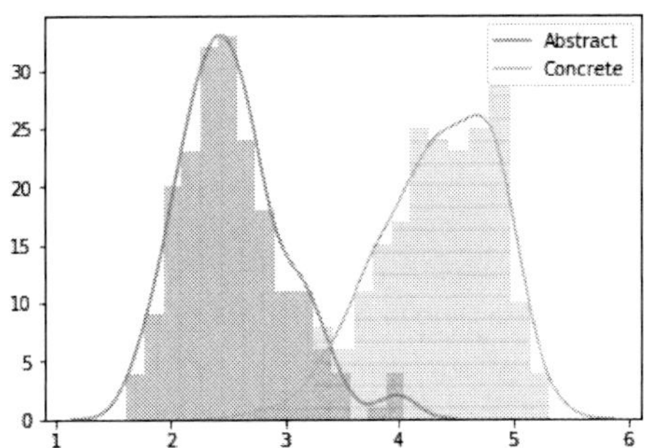

(b) Predictions by the classifier trained with fastText word embeddings

Figure 2: Relative number of predicted concreteness values for abstract words (green) and concrete words (orange) from the Newcombe data.

5.1 Feature Selection

We identified three types of features, that could be useful for this task. In the first place, concrete words might occur in specific contexts, e.g. as object of *to see* or with adjectives like *green* or *wet*, etc. This fact was already used by Tanaka et al. (2013). Since the best context information for words currently available are word embeddings, we use word embeddings as features.

Furthermore, as noted by Rabinovich et al. (2018), certain suffixes can be important for determining concreteness. E.g. the suffix *-ness*, used to form a noun from an adjective, often refers to abstract concepts. Thus we take every possible suffix from within our training data with at least 1 character and at most 4 characters. We use the 200 most frequent suffixes as features.

Finally, the part of speech (POS) of a word might give a cue. Proper nouns, e.g., might more often refer to something concrete than verbs. Each word gets for each POS a value that is the relative frequency of all its lemmata for that POS found in WordNet.

5.2 Experimental setup

We trained a SVM to build a regression model. For the training we used $\gamma = 0.01$, $C = 1.0$ and an rbf kernel as parameters, found by grid search. We use the training corpus described above to train the regression model.

We evaluated the classifier using different sets of features with tenfold cross validation on the training data. Using all available features we evaluated the classifier on other datasets as well. In most datasets used for evaluation, there are a small number of words for which there are no pretrained word embeddings (see Table 1). For these words the SVM cannot predict a value. Hence, we will predict the value 3 (neutral, neither concrete nor abstract) for these words in the evaluation.

For the evaluation of all datasets with concreteness values we use Pearson's r and Kendall's τ to measure the correlation between the true values and the model's predictions. We took the output of our regression model as is, even if its prediction is outside of the target interval $[1, 5]$ of our training data.

The dataset from Newcombe contains only binary data. Here we can order the words according to the predicted concreteness value and use the Area under the ROC Curve (AUC) as evaluation measure.

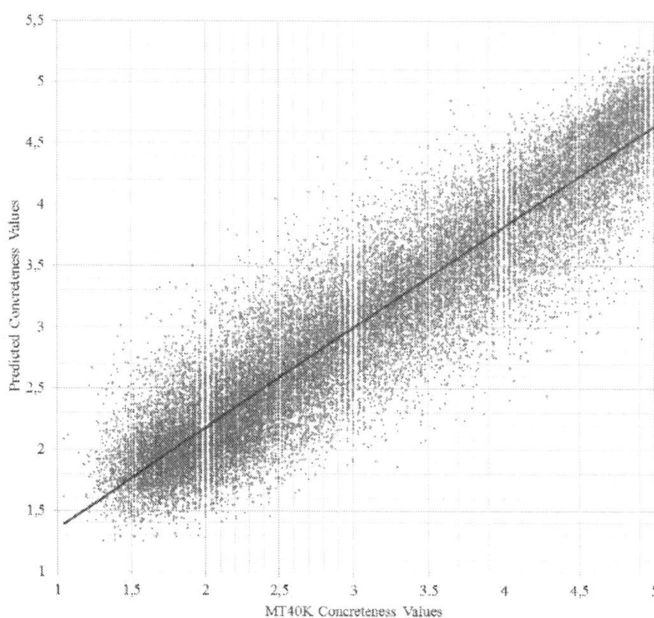

Figure 3: Original and predicted values (using 10 fold cross validation) for MT40K data using SVM with FastText word embeddings.

6 Results

Fig. 2 gives the distribution of predicted concreteness values for the concrete and abstract words from Newcombe and shows that the predicted values can distinguish quite well between concrete and abstract words. The AUC for this binary classification is 0.990 using fastText embeddings, POS and suffixes and 0.981 using GoogNews embeddings, POS and suffixes.

The correlation between the original and predicted MT40k concreteness values (aggregated from cross validation) is visualized in Fig. 3, and clearly shows the strong linear correlation. The corresponding correlation strength is given in Table 3. We see that the model trained with fastText gives consistently higher correlations that using GoogleNews embeddings. Adding the suffix or POS helps increasing the correlation for GoogleNews. Combining suffix and POS increases the performance also slightly, even for the already well performing fastText embeddings. Using only GoogeNews embeddings for cross validation on MT40k data, the (average) value for Kendall's τ is only 0.652, which is still in the same order of magnitude as the correlation found by Rothe et al. (2016) using the same features and a subset of frequent words from the MT40k data. Furthermore we see that the correlations found are much higher that those found by Tanaka et al. (2013) and Rabinovich et al. (2018). The result is comparable and just slightly higher than the correlation found by Ljubešić et al. (2018), who found a Spearman coefficient of 0.887. The Spearman coefficient for our best feature combination using fastText vectors is 0.900 with 10 fold cross validation.

The correlation of the predicted concreteness with the data from the other data sets is given in Table 4. Table 5 gives the correlation with the imagery datasets. Since the model was trained with concreteness values the smaller correlation for imagery scores is as expected. In fact, we see that the correlation values we found are consistently slightly below the correlation values for the overlapping parts of each dataset with MT40k, which shows that we are very close to the highest reasonably possible result. Note, that we excluded all words in the intersection of the datasets from the training data.

Finally, Table 6 gives some examples of predicted and original values for some abstract and

Table 3: Pearson (r) and Kendall (τ) correlation results using our training corpus with cross-validation and different features.

Embedding	fastText		GoogleNews	
Correlation	r	τ	r	τ
pos + suffix	0.604	0.428	(0.604)	(0.428)
emb	0.905	0.711	0.856	0.652
emb + suffix	0.908	0.716	0.872	0.671
emb + pos	0.908	0.717	0.870	0.671
emb + pos + suffix	0.911	0.721	0.879	0.680

Table 4: Pearson (r) and Kendall (τ) correlation between our concreteness estimations on the concreteness values of the TWP and PYM datasets using fastText and GoogleNews embeddings.

Embedding	fastText		GoogleNews	
Correlation	r	τ	r	τ
TWP_C	0.881	0.698	0.852	0.656
PYM_C	0.902	0.741	0.877	0.703

concrete words from the MT40k dataset in order to get an impression of involved words and values. We could not detect any pattern in the words for which the predictions differ a lot from the experimental values. We expected that the predictions might make many mistakes for those words where the experimentees disagreed a lot. In the MT40k the variance of all concreteness values is given, so this can be checked easily. We found that there is no correlation (Pearson correlation coefficient is 0.132) between the variance in the original data and the prediction error.

Table 5: Pearson (r) and Kendall (τ) correlation between our imagery estimations on the imagery values of the TWP, PYM and CP datasets using fastText and GoogleNews embeddings.

Embedding	fastText		GoogleNews	
Correlation	r	τ	r	τ
TWP_I	0.774	0.559	0.731	0.514
PYM_I	0.813	0.618	0.770	0.568
CP_A	0.676	0.499	0.619	0.453
CP_E	0.796	0.569	0.745	0.521

7 Discussion and Future Work

We have shown that concreteness of words as perceived by a subject of a rating experiment can be predicted on the base of word embeddings. Besides contextual information, morphological cues turn out to help somewhat.

Word embeddings essentially encode information about the contexts a word appears in. Thus we can conclude that concrete words appear in different contexts than abstract words. Tanaka et al. (2013) e.g. assume that concrete words occur often in the context of sense verbs. In order to get an impression of the words that are typical for the context of abstract and concrete words we computed the concreteness values for a random selection of 5,000 words from ukWaC (Ferraresi et al., 2008) and selected the 200 most abstract and 200 most concrete words. For each of these 400 words we computed the positive pointwise mutual information (ppmi) with a set of 17,400 mid-frequency words for co-occurrence within a window of 2 words. For each word of this set of 17,400 words we compute the average ppmi with the abstract and concrete words, respectively. The words with high average ppmi values for concrete or abstract words are typical for the context of these 200 words. The words with the highest ppmi value are given in Table 7. As one can see, we found mainly material properties for very concrete words. For abstract words we

Table 6: Overview of high, medium and low concreteness for words from MT40K with their original and our predicted values.

rank	word	MT40k	predicted
1	watermelon	4.89	5.3246
2	hamburger	5.00	5.3123
3	postbox	4.54	5.2518
4	surfboard	4.57	5.2468
5	typewriter	4.88	5.2311
17711	magnetically	2.96	2.7366
17712	evenness	2.43	2.7364
17713	undrafted	2.63	2.7364
17714	distorted	2.57	2.7363
17715	amusement	2.07	2.7361
32779	inconceivable	1.38	1.2549
32780	irrelative	1.81	1.2532
32781	transcendental	1.48	1.2449
32782	notwithstanding	1.38	1.2225
32783	behooves	1.58	1.1129

Table 7: 30 words with highest pointwise mutual information in ukWaC with prototype of abstract and concrete words, resp.

Concrete			Abstract		
stuffed	plastic	dried	notions	purely	notion
wooden	lined	underneath	conceptions	theories	reasoning
giant	topped	coated	interpretation	manner	theory
black	leather	shaped	manifestations	concepts	rationality
underside	coloured	rubber	understanding	profound	nature
metal	bamboo	glass	rational	philosophical	expression
homemade	blue	washed	conception	analysis	utterly
bowl	red	mounted	discourses	manifestation	linguistic
decorated	yellow	steel	significance	aspects	aesthetic
white	bag	powder	expressions	psychological	discourse

found words such as *philosophical, conception, linguistic, discourse* and *theories.*

One of the goals of our project is to find good keywords for images from scientific publications. These images often have very long captions (see Sohmen et al., 2018). Thus, the captions and eventually the sentences explicitly referring to an image usually will provide enough text for extracting words describing the image (Josi et al., 2018).

To get a first impression of the potential of concreteness for finding words describing scientific images we consider the image that was also used by Josi et al. (2018), here shown in Fig. 4. Initially, 53 words and phrases (noun phrases that are titles of Wikipedia articles) were selected from the caption and referring context. Table 8 shows 10 terms with the highest idf values (in the complete collection of 2,9 million image captions) and the highest predicted concreteness values, resp. For two word phrases we used the maximum of the (predicted) concreteness values of the parts as the concreteness of the phrase. The idf values were computed directly for the phrases. In this example we clearly see the different aspects of both weighting schemes: idf favours specific terms that do not describe the image, like *Griffith university* and *Queensland*. Most words selected by high concreteness, describe quite well what can bee seen on the image (except the most concrete word, *wood*), but are not specific enough: an arm and a rib are clearly present in the image, *deep* fascia is nevertheless a more adequate key word. Thus we expect that we will need to combine concreteness with other relevance measures for this application.

Image	Caption
	Schematic drawing of the left thorax and upper limb, demonstrating the chondroepitrochlearis muscle (CEM) inserting into the deep brachial fascia (bf) and the fibrous band (tuberoepicondylar band, tb) (PM: pectoralis major; fs: fascial sling; cj: costochondral junction; and Me: medial epicondyle).
	Source
	Sujeewa P. W. Palagama, Raymond A. Tedman, Matthew J. Barton, and Mark R. Forwood, "Bilateral Chondroepitrochlearis Muscle: Case Report, Phylogenetic Analysis, and Clinical Significance," *Anatomy Research International*, vol. 2016, Article ID 5402081, 2016.

Figure 4: Image and caption from a scientific publication used in Josi et al. (2018) to illustrate keyword extraction form image captions.

Acknowledgements

This research was part of the NOA project and funded by the DFG under grant no. 315976924 We would like to thank the anonymous reviewers for their valuable feedback.

Table 8: Ranking of potential keywords selected from the caption and referring context of the images shown in Fig. 4 based on idf concreteness.

(a) Terms ranked by idf (in a collection of 2,9 Million image captions).

rank	term	idf
1	axillary fascia	20.0
2	griffith university	18.1
3	brachial fascia	17.5
4	quartus	15.7
5	medical literature	14.4
6	common name	13.9
7	deep fascia	13.9
8	epicodyle	12.7
9	joint capsule	12.4
10	queensland	12.2

(b) Terms with predicted concreteness and concreteness values from MT40k.

rank	term	pred. concr.	MT40k
1	wood	4.93	4.85
2	arm	4.80	4.96
3	biceps	4.68	4.93
4	rib	4.65	4.90
5	cartilage	4.43	4.71
6	thorax	4.43	4.56
7	tendon	4.40	4.47
8	cadaver	4.39	4.48
9	joint capsule	4.32	4.52
10	septum	4.26	4.48

References

Algarabel, S., J. C. Ruiz, and J. Sanmartin (1988). The University of Valencia's computerized word pool. *Behavior Research Methods, Instruments, & Computers 20*(4), 398–403.

Borghi, A. M., F. Binkofski, C. Castelfranchi, F. Cimatti, C. Scorolli, and L. Tummolini (2017). The challenge of abstract concepts. *Psychological Bulletin 143*(3), 263.

Brysbaert, M., A. B. Warriner, and V. Kuperman (2014, September). Concreteness ratings for 40 thousand generally known English word lemmas. *Behavior Research Methods 46*(3), 904–911.

Charbonnier, J., L. Sohmen, J. Rothman, B. Rohden, and C. Wartena (2018). Noa: A search engine for reusable scientific images beyond the life sciences. In G. Pasi, B. Piwowarski,

L. Azzopardi, and A. Hanbury (Eds.), *Advances in Information Retrieval*, Cham, pp. 797–800. Springer International Publishing.

Clark, J. M. and A. Paivio (2004, Aug). Extensions of the Paivio, Yuille, and Madigan (1968) norms. *Behavior Research Methods, Instruments, & Computers 36*(3), 371–383.

Coltheart, M. (1981, November). The MRC Psycholinguistic Database. *The Quarterly Journal of Experimental Psychology Section A 33*(4), 497–505.

Ferraresi, A., E. Zanchetta, M. Baroni, and S. Bernardini (2008). Introducing and evaluating ukwac, a very large web-derived corpus of english. In *Proceedings of the 4th Web as Corpus Workshop (WAC-4) Can we beat Google*, pp. 47–54.

Friendly, M., P. E. Franklin, D. Hoffman, and D. C. Rubin (1982, September). The Toronto Word Pool: Norms for imagery, concreteness, orthographic variables, and grammatical usage for 1,080 words. *Behavior Research Methods & Instrumentation 14*(4), 375–399.

Gilhooly, K. J. and D. Hay (1977, January). Imagery, concreteness, age-of-acquisition, familiarity, and meaningfulness values for 205 five-letter words having single-solution anagrams. *Behavior Research Methods & Instrumentation 9*(1), 12–17.

Gilhooly, K. J. and R. H. Logie (1980, July). Age-of-acquisition, imagery, concreteness, familiarity, and ambiguity measures for 1,944 words. *Behavior Research Methods & Instrumentation 12*(4), 395–427.

Hessel, J., D. Mimno, and L. Lee (2018). Quantifying the visual concreteness of words and topics in multimodal datasets. In *Proceedings of the 2018 Conference of the North American Chapter of the Association for Computational Linguistics: Human Language Technologies, Volume 1 (Long Papers)*, pp. 2194–2205. Association for Computational Linguistics.

Josi, F., C. Wartena, and J. Charbonnier (2018). Text-based annotation of scientific images using wikimedia categories. In M. Elloumi, M. Granitzer, A. Hameurlain, C. Seifert, B. Stein, A. M. Tjoa, and R. Wagner (Eds.), *Database and Expert Systems Applications*, Cham, pp. 243–253. Springer International Publishing.

Ljubešić, N., D. Fišer, and A. Peti-Stantić (2018, July). Predicting concreteness and imageability of words within and across languages via word embeddings. In *Proceedings of The Third Workshop on Representation Learning for NLP*, Melbourne, Australia, pp. 217–222. Association for Computational Linguistics.

Mikolov, T., K. Chen, G. Corrado, and J. Dean (2013). Efficient estimation of word representations in vector space. *arXiv preprint arXiv:1301.3781*.

Mikolov, T., E. Grave, P. Bojanowski, C. Puhrsch, and A. Joulin (2018). Advances in pre-training distributed word representations. In *Proceedings of the International Conference on Language Resources and Evaluation (LREC 2018)*.

Newcombe, P., C. Campbell, P. Siakaluk, and P. Pexman (2012). Effects of Emotional and Sensorimotor Knowledge in Semantic Processing of Concrete and Abstract Nouns. *Frontiers in Human Neuroscience 6*, 275.

Nickerson, C. A. and D. S. Cartwright (1984, July). The University Of Colorado Meaning Norms. *Behavior Research Methods, Instruments, & Computers 16*(4), 355–382.

Paivio, A., J. C. Yuille, and S. A. Madigan (1968). Concreteness, imagery, and meaningfulness values for 925 nouns. *Journal of Experimental Psychology 76*(1, Pt.2), 1–25.

Rabinovich, E., B. Sznajder, A. Spector, I. Shnayderman, R. Aharonov, D. Konopnicki, and N. Slonim (2018, September). Learning Concept Abstractness Using Weak Supervision. *ArXiv e-prints*.

Rothe, S., S. Ebert, and H. Schütze (2016). Ultradense word embeddings by orthogonal transformation. In *Proceedings of the 2016 Conference of the North American Chapter of the Association for Computational Linguistics: Human Language Technologies*, pp. 767–777. Association for Computational Linguistics.

Sohmen, L., J. Charbonnier, I. Blümel, C. Wartena, and L. Heller (2018). Figures in scientific open access publications. In E. Méndez, F. Crestani, C. Ribeiro, G. David, and J. C. Lopes (Eds.), *Digital Libraries for Open Knowledge*, Cham, pp. 220–226. Springer International Publishing.

Spreen, O. and R. W. Schulz (1966). Parameters of abstraction, meaningfulness, and pronunciability for 329 nouns. *Journal of Verbal Learning & Verbal Behavior 5*(5), 459–468.

Tanaka, S., A. Jatowt, M. P. Kato, and K. Tanaka (2013). Estimating content concreteness for finding comprehensible documents. In *Proceedings of the Sixth ACM International Conference on Web Search and Data Mining*, WSDM '13, New York, NY, USA, pp. 475–484. ACM.

Toglia, M. P. and W. F. Battig (1978). *Handbook of Semantic Word Norms*. Oxford, England: Lawrence Erlbaum.

Turney, P. D., Y. Neuman, D. Assaf, and Y. Cohen (2011). Literal and metaphorical sense identification through concrete and abstract context. In *Proceedings of the Conference on Empirical Methods in Natural Language Processing*, EMNLP '11, Stroudsburg, PA, USA, pp. 680–690. Association for Computational Linguistics.

Learning to Explicitate Connectives with Seq2Seq Network for Implicit Discourse Relation Classification

Wei Shi[†] and Vera Demberg[†,‡]
[†]Dept. of Language Science and Technology
[‡]Dept. of Mathematics and Computer Science, Saarland University
Saarland Informatics Campus, 66123 Saarbrücken, Germany
{w.shi, vera}@coli.uni-saarland.de

Abstract

Implicit discourse relation classification is one of the most difficult steps in discourse parsing. The difficulty stems from the fact that the coherence relation must be inferred based on the content of the discourse relational arguments. Therefore, an effective encoding of the relational arguments is of crucial importance. We here propose a new model for implicit discourse relation classification, which consists of a classifier, and a sequence-to-sequence model which is trained to generate a representation of the discourse relational arguments by trying to predict the relational arguments including a suitable implicit connective. Training is possible because such implicit connectives have been annotated as part of the PDTB corpus. Along with a memory network, our model could generate more refined representations for the task. And on the now standard 11-way classification, our method outperforms the previous state of the art systems on the PDTB benchmark on multiple settings including cross validation.

1 Introduction

Discourse relations describe the logical relation between two sentences/clauses. When understanding a text, humans infer discourse relation between text segmentations. They reveal the structural organization of text, and allow for additional inferences. Many natural language processing tasks, such as machine translation, question-answering, automatic summarization, sentiment analysis, and sentence embedding learning, can also profit from having access to discourse relation information. Recent years have seen more and more works on this topic, including two CoNNL shared tasks (Xue et al., 2015, 2016).

Penn Discourse Tree Bank (Prasad et al., 2008, PDTB) provides lexically-grounded annotations of discourse relations and their two discourse relational arguments (i.e., two text spans). Discourse relations are sometimes signaled by explicit discourse markers (e.g., *because, but*). Example 1 shows an explicit discourse relation marked by "because"; the presence of the connective makes it possible to classify the discourse relation with high reliability: Miltsakaki et al. (2005) reported an accuracy of 93.09% for 4-way classification of explicits.

Discourse relations are however not always marked by an explicit connective. In fact, implicit discourse relations (i.e. relations not marked by an explicit discourse cue) outnumber explicit discourse relations in naturally occurring text. Readers can still infer these implicit relations, but automatic classification becomes a lot more difficult in these cases, and represents the main bottleneck in discourse parsing today. Example 2 shows an implicit contrastive relation which can be inferred from the two text spans that have been marked *Arg1* and *Arg2*. When annotating implicit relations in the PDTB, annotators were asked to first insert a connective which expresses the relation, and then annotate the relation label. This procedure was introduced to achieve higher inter-annotator agreement for implicit relations between human annotators. In the approach taken in this paper, our model mimics this procedure by being trained to explicitate the discouse relation, i.e. to insert a connective as a secondary task.

1. *[I refused to pay the cobbler the full $95]$_{Arg1}$ **because** [He did poor work.]$_{Arg2}$*

— *Explicit, Contingency.Cause*

2. *[In the energy mix of the future, bio-energy will also have a key role to play in boosting rural employment and the rural economy in Europe .]$_{Arg1}$ (**Implicit = However**) [At the same time , the promotion of bio-energy must not lead to distortions of competition.]$_{Arg2}$*

— *Implicit, Comparison.Contrast*

The key in implicit discourse relation classification lies in extracting relevant information for the relation label from (the combination of) the discourse relational arguments. Informative signals can consist of surface cues, as well as the semantics of the relational arguments. Statistical approaches have typically relied on linguistically informed features which capture both of these aspects, like temporal markers, polarity tags, Levin verb classes and sentiment lexicons, as well as the Cartesian products of the word tokens in the two arguments (Lin et al., 2009). More recent efforts use distributed representations with neural network architectures (Qin et al., 2016a).

The main question in designing neural networks for discourse relation classification is how to get the neural networks to effectively encode the discourse relational arguments such that all of the aspects relevant to the classification of the relation are represented, in particular in the face of very limited amounts of annotated training data, see e.g. Rutherford et al. (2017). The crucial intuition in the present paper is to make use of the annotated implicit connectives in the PDTB: in addition to the typical relation label classification task, we also train the model to encode and decode the discourse relational arguments, and at the same time predict the implicit connective. This novel secondary task forces the internal representation to more completely encode the semantics of the relational arguments (in order to allow the model to decode later), and to make a more fine-grained classification (predicting the implicit connective) than is necessary for the overall task. This more fine-grained task thus aims to force the model to represent the discourse relational arguments in a way that allows the model to also predict a suitable connective. Our overall discourse relation classifier combines representations from the relational arguments as well as the hidden representations generated as part of the encoder-decoder architecture to predict relation labels. What's more, with an explicit memory network, the network also has access to history representations and acquire more explicit context knowledge. We show that our method outperforms previous approaches on the 11-way classification on the PDTB 2.0 benchmark.

The remaining of the paper is organized as follows: Section 2 discusses related work; Section 3 describes our proposed method; Section 4 gives the training details and experimental results, which is followed by conclusion and future work in section 5.

2   Related Work

2.1   Implicit Discourse Relation Classification

Implicit discourse relation recognition is one of the most important components in discourse parsing. With the release of PDTB (Prasad et al., 2008), the largest available corpus which annotates implicit examples with discourse relation labels and implicit connectives, a lot of previous works focused on typical statistical machine learning solutions with manually crafted sparse features (Rutherford and Xue, 2014).

Recently, neural networks have shown an advantage of dealing with data sparsity problem, and many deep learning methods have been proposed for discourse parsing, including convolutional (Zhang et al., 2015), recurrent (Ji et al., 2016), character-based (Qin et al., 2016a), adversarial (Qin et al., 2017) neural networks, and pair-aware neural sentence modeling (Cai and Zhao, 2017). Multi-task learning has also been shown to be beneficial on this task (Lan et al., 2017).

However, most neural based methods suffer from insufficient annotated data.Wu et al. (2016) extracted bilingual-constrained synthetic implicit data from a sentence-aligned English-Chinese corpus. Shi et al. (2017, 2018) proposed to acquire additional training data by exploiting *explicitation* of connectives during translation. Explicitation refers to the fact that translators sometimes add connectives into

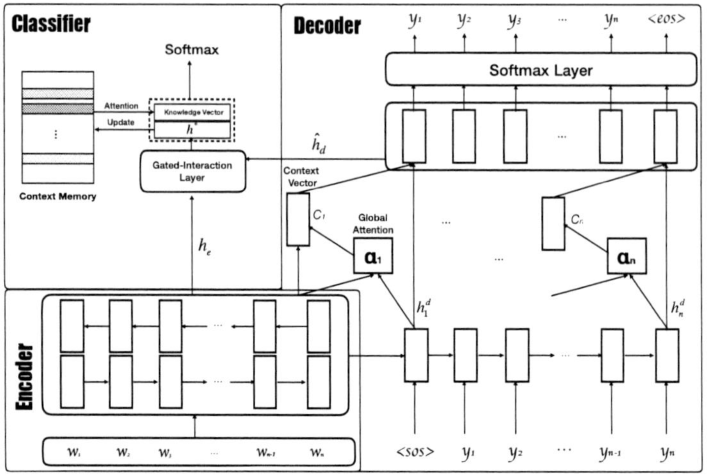

Figure 1: The Architecture of Proposed Model.

the text in the target language which were not originally present in the source language. They used explicitated connectives as a source of weak supervision to obtain additional labeled instances, and showed that this extension of the training data leads to substantial performance improvements.

The huge gap between explicit and implicit relation recognition (namely, 50% vs. 90% in 4-way classification) also motivates to incorporate connective information to guide the reasoning process. Zhou et al. (2010) used a language model to automatically insert discourse connectives and leverage the information of these predicted connectives. The approach which is most similar in spirit to ours, Qin et al. (2017), proposed a neural method that incorporates implicit connectives in an adversarial framework to make the representation as similar as connective-augmented one and showed that the inclusion of implicit connectives could help to improve classifier performance.

2.2 Sequence-to-sequence Neural Networks

Sequence to sequence model is a general end-to-end approach to sequence learning that makes minimal assumptions on the sequence structure, and firstly proposed by Sutskever et al. (2014). It uses multi-layered Long Short-Term Memory (LSTM) or Gated Recurrent Units (GRU) to map the input sequence to a vector with a fixed dimensionality, and then decode the target sequence from the vector with another LSTM / GRU layer.

Sequence to sequence models allow for flexible input/output dynamics and have enjoyed great success in machine translation and have been broadly used in variety of sequence related tasks such as Question Answering, named entity recognition (NER) / part of speech (POS) tagging and so on.

If the source and target of a sequence-to-sequence model are exactly the same, it is also called Auto-encoder, Dai and Le (2015) used a sequence auto-encoder to better represent sentence in an unsupervised way and showed impressive performances on different tasks. The main difference between our model and this one is that we have different input and output (the output contains a connective while the input doesn't). In this way, the model is forced to explicitate implicit relation and try to learn the latent pattern and discourse relation between implicit arguments and connectives and then generate more discriminative representations.

3   Methodology

Our model is based on the sequence-to-sequence model used for machine translation (Luong et al., 2015), an adaptation of an LSTM (Hochreiter and Schmidhuber, 1997) that encodes a variable length input as a fix-length vector, then decodes it into a variable length of outputs. As illustrated in Figure 1, our model consists of three components: Encoder, Decoder and Discourse Relation Classifier. We here use different LSTMs for the encoding and decoding tasks to help keep the independence between those two parts.

The task of implicit discourse relation recognition is to recognize the senses of the implicit relations, given the two arguments. For each discourse relation instance, The Penn Discourse Tree Bank (PDTB) provides two arguments (Arg_1, Arg_2) along with the discourse relation (*Rel*) and manually inserted implicit discourse connective ($Conn_i$). Here is an implicit example from section 0 in PDTB:

3. **Arg$_1$**: This is an old story.
   Arg$_2$: We're talking about years ago before anyone heard of asbestos having any questionable properties.
   Conn$_i$: in fact
   Rel: Expansion.Restatement

During training, the input and target sentences for sequence-to-sequence neural network are $[Arg_1; Arg_2]$ and $[Arg_1; Conn_i; Arg_2]$ respectively, where ";" denotes concatenation.

3.1 Model Architecture

3.1.1 Encoder

Given a sequence of words, an encoder computes a joint representation of the whole sequence.

After mapping tokens to Word2Vec embedding vectors (Mikolov et al., 2013), a LSTM recurrent neural network processes a variable-length sequence $x = (x_1, x_2, ..., x_n)$. At time step t, the state of memory cell c_t and hidden h_t are calculated with the Equations 1:

$$\begin{bmatrix} i_t \\ f_t \\ o_t \\ \hat{c}_t \end{bmatrix} = \begin{bmatrix} \sigma \\ \sigma \\ \sigma \\ \tanh \end{bmatrix} W \cdot [h_{t-1}, x_t]$$

$$c_t = f_t \odot c_{t-1} + i_t \odot \hat{c}_t$$
$$h_t = o_t \odot \tanh(c_t)$$

(1)

where x_t is the input at time step t, i, f and o are the input, forget and output gate activation respectively. $\hat{c}_t$ denotes the current cell state, σ is the logistic sigmoid function and $\odot$ denotes element-wise multiplication. The LSTM separates the memory c from the hidden state h, which allows for more flexibility incombining new inputs and previous context.

For the sequence modeling tasks, it is beneficial to have access to the past context as well as the future context. Therefore, we chose a bidirectional LSTM as the encoder and the output of the word at time-step t is shown in the Equation 2. Here, element-wise sum is used to combine the forward and backward pass outputs.

$$h_t = \left[\overrightarrow{h_t} \oplus \overleftarrow{h_t} \right]$$

(2)

Thus we get the output of encoder:

$$h_e = [h_1^e, h_2^e, ..., h_n^e]$$

(3)

3.1.2 Decoder

With the representation from the encoder, the decoder tries to map it back to the targets space and predicts the next words.

Here we used a separate LSTM recurrent network to predict the target words. During training, target words are fed into the LSTM incrementally and we get the outputs from decoder LSTM:

$$h_d = \left[h_1^d, h_2^d, ..., h_n^d \right]$$

(4)

Global Attention

In each time-step in decoding, it's better to consider all the hidden states of the encoder to give the decoder a full view of the source context. So we adopted the global attention mechanism proposed in Luong et al. (2015). For time step t in decoding, context vector c_t is the weighted average of h_e, the weights for each time-step are calculated with h_t^d and h_e as illustrated below:

$$\alpha_t = \frac{\exp(h_t^{d^\top} \mathbf{W}_\alpha h_e)}{\sum\limits_{t=1}^{n} \exp(h_t^{d^\top} \mathbf{W}_\alpha h_e)} \tag{5}$$

$$c_t = \alpha h_e \tag{6}$$

Word Prediction

Context vector c_t captured the relevant source side information to help predict the current target word y_t. We employ a concatenate layer with activation function tanh to combine context vector c_t and hidden state of decoder h_t^d at time-step t as follows:

$$\hat{h_t^d} = \tanh(\mathbf{W_c} \left[c_t ; h_t^d \right]) \tag{7}$$

Then the predictive vector is fed into the softmax layer to get the predicted distribution $\hat{p}(y_t|s)$ of the current target word.

$$\hat{p}(y_t|s) = softmax(\mathbf{W}_s \hat{h_d} + \mathbf{b}_s)$$
$$\hat{y}_t = \arg\max_{y} \hat{p}(y_t|s) \tag{8}$$

After decoding, we obtain the predictive vectors for the whole target sequence $\hat{h_d} = \left[h_1^d, h_2^d, ..., h_n^d \right]$. Ideally, it contains the information of exposed implicit connectives.

Gated Interaction

In order to predict the coherent discourse relation of the input sequence, we take both the $h_{encoder}$ and the predictive word vectors h_d into account. K-max pooling can "draw together" features that are most discriminative and among many positions apart in the sentences, especially on both the two relational arguments in our task here; this method has been proved to be effective in choosing active features in sentence modeling (Kalchbrenner et al., 2014). We employ an average k-max pooling layer which takes average of the top k-max values among the whole time-steps as in Equation 9 and 10:

$$\bar{h}_e = \frac{1}{k} \sum_{i=1}^{k} topk(h_e) \tag{9}$$

$$\bar{h}_d = \frac{1}{k} \sum_{i=1}^{k} topk(\hat{h}^d) \tag{10}$$

$\bar{h}_e$ and $\bar{h}_d$ are then combined using a linear layer (Lan et al., 2017). As illustrated in Equation 11, the linear layer acts as a gate to determine how much information from the sequence-to-sequence network should be mixed into the original sentence's representations from the encoder. Compared with bilinear layer, it also has less parameters and allows us to use high dimensional word vectors.

$$h^* = \bar{h}_e \oplus \sigma(\mathbf{W}_i \bar{h}_d + \mathbf{b}_i) \tag{11}$$

Explicit Context Knowledge

To further capture common knowledge in contexts, we here employ a memory network proposed in Liu et al. (2018), to get explicit context representations of contexts training examples. We use a memory matrix $M \in R^{K \times N}$, where K, N denote hidden size and number of training instances respectively. During training, the memory matrix remembers the information of training examples and then retrieves them when predicting labels.

Given a representation h^* from the interaction layer, we generate a **knowledge vector** by weighted memory reading:

$$k = M \, softmax(M^T h^*) \tag{12}$$

We here use dot product attention, which is faster and space-efficient than additive attention, to calculate the scores for each training instances. The scores are normalized with a softmax layer and the final knowledge vector is a weighted sum of the columns in memory matrix M.

Afterwards, the model predicts the discourse relation using a softmax layer.

$$\hat{p}(r|s) = softmax(\mathbf{W}_r[k; h^*] + \mathbf{b}_r)$$
$$\hat{r} = \arg\max_y \hat{p}(r|s) \tag{13}$$

3.2 Multi-objectives

In our model, the decoder and the discourse relation classifier have different objectives. For the decoder, the objective consists of predicting the target word at each time-step. The loss function is calculated with masked cross entropy with L2 regularization, as follows:

$$Loss_{de} = -\frac{1}{n} \sum_{t=1}^{n} y_t \log(\hat{p_y}) + \frac{\lambda}{2} \parallel \theta_{de} \parallel_2^2 \tag{14}$$

where y_t is one-hot represented ground truth of target words, $\hat{p_y}$ is the estimated probabilities for each words in vocabulary by softmax layer, n denotes the length of target sentence. λ is a hyper-parameter of $L2$ regularization and θ is the parameter set.

The objective of the discourse relation classifier consists of predicting the discourse relations. A reasonable training objective for multiple classes is the categorical cross-entropy loss. The loss is formulated as:

$$Loss_{cl} = -\frac{1}{m} \sum_{i=1}^{m} r_i \log(\hat{p_r}) + \frac{\lambda}{2} \parallel \theta_{cl} \parallel_2^2 \tag{15}$$

where r_i is one-hot represented ground truth of discourse relation labels, $\hat{p_r}$ denotes the predicted probabilities for each relation class by softmax layer, m is the number of target classes. Just like above, λ is a hyper-parameter of $L2$ regularization.

For the overall loss of the whole model, we set another hyper-parameter w to give these two objective functions different weights. Larger w means that more importance is placed on the decoder task.

$$Loss = w \cdot Loss_{de} + (1 - w) \cdot Loss_{cl} \tag{16}$$

3.3 Model Training

To train our model, the training objective is defined by the loss function we introduced above. We use Adaptive Moment Estimation (Adam) (Kingma and Ba, 2014) with different learning rate for different parts of the model as our optimizer. Dropout layers are applied after the embedding layer and also on the top feature vector before the softmax layer in the classifier. We also employ L_2 regularization with small λ in our objective functions for preventing over-fitting. The values of the hyper-parameters, are provided in Table 2. The model is trained firstly to minimize the loss in Equation 14 until convergence, we use scheduled sampling (Bengio et al., 2015) during training to avoid "teacher-forcing problem". And then to minimize the joint loss in Equation 16 to train the implicit discourse relation classifier.

4 Experiments and Results

4.1 Experimental Setup

We evaluate our model on the PDTB. While early work only evaluated classification performance between the four main PDTB relation classes, more recent work including the CoNLL 2015 and 2016 shared tasks on Shallow Discourse Parsing (Xue et al., 2015, 2016) have set the standard to second-level classification. The second-level classification is more useful for most downstream tasks. Following other

Settings	Train	Dev	Test
PDTB-Lin	13351	515	766
PDTB-Ji	12826	1165	1039
Cross valid. per fold avg.	12085	1486	1486[1]

Table 1: Numbers of train, development and test set on different settings for 11-way classification task. Instances annotated with two labels are double-counted and some relations with few instances have been removed.

works we directly compare to in our evaluation, we here use the setting where AltLex, EntRel and NoRel tags are ignored. About 2.2% of the implicit relation instances in PDTB have been annotated with two relations, these are considered as two training instances.

To allow for full comparability to earlier work, we here report results for three different settings. The first one is denoted as PDTB-Lin (Lin et al., 2009); it uses sections 2-21 for training, 22 as dev and section 23 as test set. The second one is labeled PDTB-Ji (Ji and Eisenstein, 2015), and uses sections 2-20 for training, 0-1 as dev and evaluates on sections 21-22. Our third setting follows the recommendations of Shi and Demberg (2017), and performs 10-fold cross validation on the whole corpus (sections 0-23). Table 1 shows the number of instances in train, development and test set in different settings.

The advantage of the cross validation approach is that it addresses problems related to the small corpus size, as it reports model performance across all folds. This is important, because the most frequently used test set (PDTB-Lin) contains less than 800 instances; taken together with a lack in the community to report mean and standard deviations from multiple runs of neural networks (Reimers and Gurevych, 2018), the small size of the test set makes reported results potentially unreliable.

Preprocessing

We first convert tokens in PDTB to lowercase and normalize strings, which removes special characters. The word embeddings used for initializing the word representations are trained with the CBOW architecture in *Word2Vec*[2] (Mikolov et al., 2013) on PDTB training set. All the weights in the model are initialized with uniform random.

To better locate the connective positions in the target side, we use two position indicators ($\langle conn \rangle$, $\langle /conn \rangle$) which specify the starting and ending of the connectives (Zhou et al., 2016), which also indicate the spans of discourse arguments.

Since our main task here is not generating arguments, it is better to have representations generated by correct words rather than by wrongly predicted ones. So at test time, instead of using the predicted word from previous time step as current input, we use the source sentence as the decoder's input and target. As the implicit connective is not available at test time, we use a random vector, which we used as "impl_conn" in Figure 2, as a placeholder to inform the sequence that the upcoming word should be a connective.

Hyper-parameters

There are several hyper-parameters in our model, including dimension of word vectors d, two dropout rates after embedding layer q_1 and before softmax layer q_2, two learning rates for encoder-decoder lr_1 and for classifier lr_2, top k for k-max pooling layer, different weights w for losses in Equation (16) and λ denotes the coefficient of regularizer, which controls the importance of the regularization term, as shown in Table 2.

---

[1]Cross-validation allows us to test on all 15057 instances.

[2]`https://code.google.com/archive/p/word2vec/`

d	q_1	q_2	lr_1	lr_2	k	w	λ
100	0.5	0.2	$2.5e^{-3}$	$5e^{-3}$	5	0.2	$5e^{-4}$

Table 2: Hyper-parameter settings.

Methods	PDTB-Lin	PDTB-Ji	Cross Validation
Majority class	26.11	26.18	25.59
Lin et al. (2009)	40.20	-	-
Qin et al. (2016a)	43.81	45.04	-
Cai and Zhao (2017)	-	45.81	-
Qin et al. (2017)	44.65	**46.23**	-
Shi et al. (2017) (with extra data)	**45.50**	-	**37.84**
Encoder only (Bi-LSTM) (Shi et al., 2017)	34.32	-	30.01
Auto-Encoder	43.86	45.43	39.50
Seq2Seq w/o Mem Net	45.75	47.05	40.29
Proposed Method	**45.82**	**47.83**	**41.29**

Table 3: Accuracy (%) of implicit discourse relations on PDTB-Lin, PDTB-Ji and Cross Validation Settings for multi-class classification.

4.2 Experimental Results

We compare our models with six previous methods, as shown in Table 3. The baselines contain feature-based methods (Lin et al., 2009), state-of-the-art neural networks (Qin et al., 2016a; Cai and Zhao, 2017), including the adversarial neural network that also exploits the annotated implicit connectives (Qin et al., 2017), as well as the data extension method based on using explicitated connectives from translation to other languages (Shi et al., 2017).

Additionally, we ablate our model by taking out the prediction of the implicit connective in the sequence to sequence model. The resulting model is labeled Auto-Encoder in Table 3. And seq2seq network without knowledge memory, which means we use the output of gated interaction layer to predict the label directly, as denoted as Seq2Seq w/o Mem Net.

Our proposed model outperforms the other models in each of the settings. Compared with performances in Qin et al. (2017), although we share the similar idea of extracting highly discriminative features by generating connective-augmented representations for implicit discourse relations, our method improves about 1.2% on setting PDTB-Lin and 1.6% on the PDTB-Ji setting. The importance of the implicit connective is also illustrated by the fact that the "Auto-Encoder" model, which is identical to our model except it does not predict the implicit connective, performs worse than the model which does. This confirms our initial hypothesis that training with implicit connectives helps to expose the latent discriminative features in the relational arguments, and generates more refined semantic representation. It also means that, to some extent, purely increasing the size of tunable parameters is not always helpful in this task and trying to predict implicit connectives in the decoder does indeed help the model extract more discriminative features for this task. What's more, we can also see that without the memory network, the performances are also worse, it shows that with the concatenation of knowledge vector, the training instance may be capable of finding related instances to get common knowledge for predicting implicit relations. As Shi and Demberg (2017) argued that it is risky to conclude with testing on such small test set, we also run cross-validation on the whole PDTB. From Table 3, we have the same conclusion with the effectiveness of our method, which outperformed the baseline (Bi-LSTM) with more than 11% points and 3% compared with Shi et al. (2017) even though they have used a very large extra corpus.

For the sake of obtaining a better intuition on how the global attention works in our model, Figure 2 demonstrates the weights of different time-steps in attention layer from the decoder. The weights show how much importance the word attached to the source words while predicting target words. We can see that without the connective in the target side of test, the word filler still works as a connective to help predict the upcoming words. For instance, the true discourse relation for the right-hand example is *Expansion.Alternative*, at the word filler's time-step, it attached more importance on the negation "don't" and "tastefully appointed". It means the current representation could grasp the key information and try to focus on the important words to help with the task. Here we see plenty room for adapting this model to discourse connective prediction task, we would like to leave this to the future work.

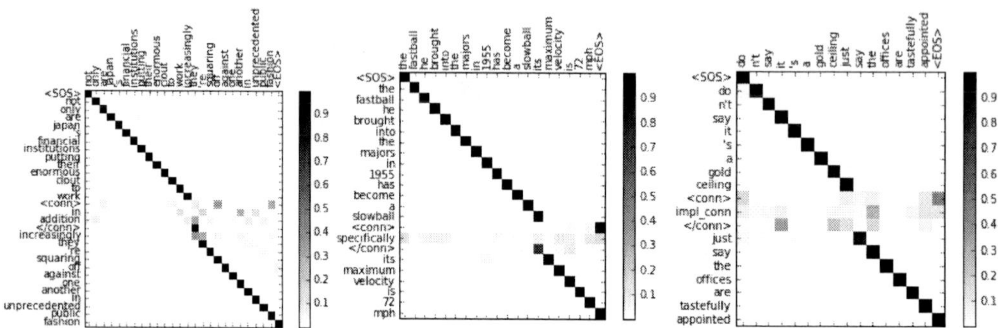

Figure 2: Visualization of attention weights during predicting target sentence in train and test, x-axis denotes the source sentence and the y-axis is the targets. First two figures are examples from training set with implicit connectives inside, while the following one, in which the implicit connective has been replaced by the word filler "impl_conn", is from test.

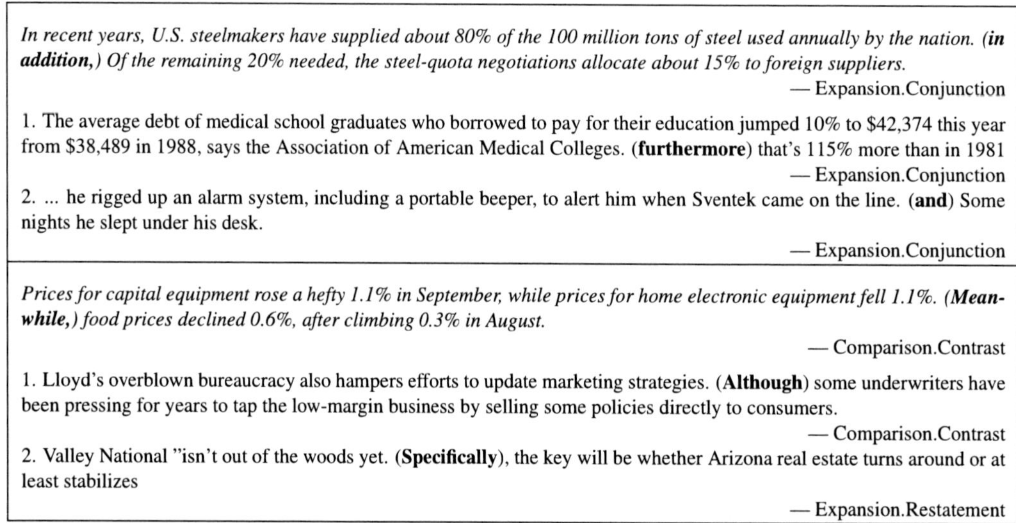

*In recent years, U.S. steelmakers have supplied about 80% of the 100 million tons of steel used annually by the nation. (**in addition**,) Of the remaining 20% needed, the steel-quota negotiations allocate about 15% to foreign suppliers.*

— Expansion.Conjunction

1. The average debt of medical school graduates who borrowed to pay for their education jumped 10% to $42,374 this year from $38,489 in 1988, says the Association of American Medical Colleges. (**furthermore**) that's 115% more than in 1981

— Expansion.Conjunction

2. ... he rigged up an alarm system, including a portable beeper, to alert him when Sventek came on the line. (**and**) Some nights he slept under his desk.

— Expansion.Conjunction

*Prices for capital equipment rose a hefty 1.1% in September, while prices for home electronic equipment fell 1.1%. (**Meanwhile**,) food prices declined 0.6%, after climbing 0.3% in August.*

— Comparison.Contrast

1. Lloyd's overblown bureaucracy also hampers efforts to update marketing strategies. (**Although**) some underwriters have been pressing for years to tap the low-margin business by selling some policies directly to consumers.

— Comparison.Contrast

2. Valley National "isn't out of the woods yet. (**Specifically**), the key will be whether Arizona real estate turns around or at least stabilizes

— Expansion.Restatement

Table 4: Example of attention in Context Knowledge Memory. The sentences in italic are from PDTB test set and following 2 instances are the ones with top 2 attention weights from training set.

Relation	Train	Dev	Test
Comparison	1855	189	145
Contingency	3235	281	273
Expansion	6673	638	538
Temporal	582	48	55
Total	12345	1156	1011

Table 5: Distribution of top-level implicit discourse relations in the PDTB.

We also try to figure out which instances' representations have been chosen from the memory matrix while predicting. Table 4 shows two examples and their context instances with top 2 memory attentions among the whole training set. We can see that both examples show that the memory attention attached more importance on the same relations. This means that with the Context Memory, the model could facilitate the discourse relation prediction by choosing examples that share similar semantic representation and discourse relation during prediction.

Methods	Four-ways		One-Versus-all Binary (F_1)			
	F_1	Acc.	Comp.	Cont.	Expa.	Temp.
Rutherford and Xue (2014)	38.40	55.50	39.70	54.42	70.23	28.69
Qin et al. (2016b)	-	-	**41.55**	57.32	71.50	35.43
Liu et al. (2016)	44.98	57.27	37.91	55.88	69.97	37.17
Ji et al. (2016)	42.30	**59.50**	-	-	-	-
Liu and Li (2016)	46.29	57.17	36.70	54.48	70.43	**38.84**
Qin et al. (2017)	-	-	40.87	54.46	72.38	36.20
Lan et al. (2017)	**47.80**	57.39	40.73	**58.96**	**72.47**	38.50
Our method	46.40	**61.42**	**41.83**	**62.07**	69.58	35.72

Table 6: Comparison of F_1 scores (%) and Accuracy (%) with the State-of-the-art Approaches for four-ways and one-versus-all binary classification on PDTB. Comp., Cont., Expa. and Temp. stand for Comparison, Contingency, Expansion and Temporal respectively.

4.2.1 Top-level Binary and 4-way Classification

A lot of the recent works in PDTB relation recognition have focused on first level relations, both on binary and 4-ways classification. We also report the performance on level-one relation classification for more comparison to prior works. As described above, we followed the conventional experimental settings (Rutherford and Xue, 2015; Liu and Li, 2016) as closely as possible. Table 5 shows the distribution of top-level implicit discourse relation in PDTB, it's worth noticing that there are only 55 instances for Temporal Relation in the test set.

To make the results comparable with previous work, we report the F_1 score for four binary classifications and both F_1 and Accuracy for 4-way classification, which can be found in Table 6. We can see that our method outperforms all alternatives on COMPARISON and CONTINGENCY, and obtain comparable scores with the state-of-the-art in others. For 4-way classification, we got the best accuracy and second-best F_1 with around 2% better than in Ji et al. (2016).

5   Conclusion and Future Work

We present in this paper a novel neural method trying to integrate implicit connectives into the representation of implicit discourse relations with a joint learning framework of sequence-to-sequence network. We conduct experiments with different settings on PDTB benchmark, the results show that our proposed method can achieve state-of-the-art performance on recognizing the implicit discourse relations and the improvements are not only brought by the increasing number of parameters. The model also has great potential abilities in implicit connective prediction in the future.

Our proposed method shares similar spirit with previous work in Zhou et al. (2010), who also tried to leverage implicit connectives to help extract discriminative features from implicit discourse instances. Comparing with the adversarial method proposed by Qin et al. (2017), our proposed model more closely mimics humans' annotation process of implicit discourse relations and is trained to directly explicitate the implicit relations before classification. With the representation of the original implicit sentence and the explicitated one from decoder, and the help of the explicit knowledge vector from memory network, the implicit relation could be classified with higher accuracy.

Although our method has not been trained as a generative model in our experiments, we can see potential for applying it to generative tasks. With more annotated data, minor modification and fine-tuned training, we believe our proposed method could also be applied to tasks like implicit discourse connective prediction, or argument generation in the future.

6   Acknowledgments

This work was supported by German Research Foundation (DFG) as part of SFB 1102 "Information Density and Linguistic Encoding". We would like to thank the anonymous reviewers for their careful reading and insightful comments.

References

Bengio, S., O. Vinyals, N. Jaitly, and N. Shazeer (2015). Scheduled sampling for sequence prediction with recurrent neural networks. In *Proceeding of NIPS*, pp. 1171–1179.

Cai, D. and H. Zhao (2017). Pair-aware neural sentence modeling for implicit discourse relation classification. In *IEA-AIE*, pp. 458–466. Springer.

Dai, A. M. and Q. V. Le (2015). Semi-supervised sequence learning. In *Proceedings of NIPS*, pp. 3079–3087.

Hochreiter, S. and J. Schmidhuber (1997). Long short-term memory. *Neural computation 9*(8), 1735–1780.

Ji, Y. and J. Eisenstein (2015). One vector is not enough: Entity-augmented distributional semantics for discourse relations. *TACL 3*, 329–344.

Ji, Y., G. Haffari, and J. Eisenstein (2016). A latent variable recurrent neural network for discourse relation language models. In *Proceedings of NAACL*, pp. 332–342.

Kalchbrenner, N., E. Grefenstette, and P. Blunsom (2014). A convolutional neural network for modelling sentences. In *Proceedings of ACL*.

Kingma, D. and J. Ba (2014). Adam: A method for stochastic optimization. *arXiv preprint arXiv:1412.6980*.

Lan, M., J. Wang, Y. Wu, Z.-Y. Niu, and H. Wang (2017). Multi-task attention-based neural networks for implicit discourse relationship representation and identification. In *Proceedings of EMNLP*, pp. 1299–1308.

Lin, Z., M.-Y. Kan, and H. T. Ng (2009). Recognizing implicit discourse relations in the penn discourse treebank. In *Proceedings of EMNLP*, pp. 343–351.

Liu, Q., Y. Zhang, and J. Liu (2018). Learning domain representation for multi-domain sentiment classification. In *Proceedings of NAACL*, pp. 541–550.

Liu, Y. and S. Li (2016). Recognizing implicit discourse relations via repeated reading: Neural networks with multi-level attention. In *Proceedings of EMNLP*, pp. 1224–1233.

Liu, Y., S. Li, X. Zhang, and Z. Sui (2016). Implicit discourse relation classification via multi-task neural networks. In *Proceedings of AAAI*, pp. 2750–2756.

Luong, M.-T., H. Pham, and C. D. Manning (2015). Effective approaches to attention-based neural machine translation. In *Proceedings of EMNLP*, pp. 1412–1421.

Mikolov, T., I. Sutskever, K. Chen, G. S. Corrado, and J. Dean (2013). Distributed representations of words and phrases and their compositionality. In *Proceedings of NIPS*, pp. 3111–3119.

Miltsakaki, E., N. Dinesh, R. Prasad, A. Joshi, and B. Webber (2005). Experiments on sense annotations and sense disambiguation of discourse connectives. In *Proceedings of the Fourth Workshop TLT-2005*.

Prasad, R., N. Dinesh, A. Lee, E. Miltsakaki, L. Robaldo, A. Joshi, and B. Webber (2008). The penn discourse treebank 2.0. In *Proceedings of LREC*.

Qin, L., Z. Zhang, and H. Zhao (2016a). Implicit discourse relation recognition with context-aware character-enhanced embeddings. In *Proceedings of COLING*.

Qin, L., Z. Zhang, and H. Zhao (2016b). A stacking gated neural architecture for implicit discourse relation classification. In *Proceedings of EMNLP*, pp. 2263–2270.

Qin, L., Z. Zhang, H. Zhao, Z. Hu, and E. Xing (2017). Adversarial connective-exploiting networks for implicit discourse relation classification. In *Proceedings of ACL*, pp. 1006–1017.

Reimers, N. and I. Gurevych (2018). Why comparing single performance scores does not allow to draw conclusions about machine learning approaches. *arXiv preprint arXiv:1803.09578*.

Rutherford, A., V. Demberg, and N. Xue (2017). A systematic study of neural discourse models for implicit discourse relation. In *Proceedings of EACL*, pp. 281–291.

Rutherford, A. and N. Xue (2014). Discovering implicit discourse relations through brown cluster pair representation and coreference patterns. In *Proceedings of EACL*, pp. 645–654.

Rutherford, A. and N. Xue (2015). Improving the inference of implicit discourse relations via classifying explicit discourse connectives. In *Proceedings of NAACL*, pp. 799–808.

Shi, W. and V. Demberg (2017). On the need of cross validation for discourse relation classification. In *Proceedings of EACL*, pp. 150–156.

Shi, W., F. Yung, and V. Demberg (2018). Acquiring annotated data with cross-lingual explicitation for implicit discourse relation classification. *arXiv preprint arXiv:1808.10290*.

Shi, W., F. Yung, R. Rubino, and V. Demberg (2017). Using explicit discourse connectives in translation for implicit discourse relation classification. In *Proceedings of IJCNLP*, pp. 484–495.

Sutskever, I., O. Vinyals, and Q. V. Le (2014). Sequence to sequence learning with neural networks. In *Proceedings of NIPS*, pp. 3104–3112.

Wu, C., X. Shi, Y. Chen, Y. Huang, and J. Su (2016). Bilingually-constrained synthetic data for implicit discourse relation recognition. In *Proceedings of EMNLP*, pp. 2306–2312.

Xue, N., H. T. Ng, S. Pradhan, R. Prasad, C. Bryant, and A. Rutherford (2015). The conll-2015 shared task on shallow discourse parsing. In *Proceedings of CoNLL-15 Shared Task*, pp. 1–16.

Xue, N., H. T. Ng, A. Rutherford, B. Webber, C. Wang, and H. Wang (2016). Conll 2016 shared task on multilingual shallow discourse parsing. In *Proceedings of CoNLL-16 shared task*, pp. 1–19.

Zhang, B., J. Su, D. Xiong, Y. Lu, H. Duan, and J. Yao (2015). Shallow convolutional neural network for implicit discourse relation recognition. In *Proceedings of EMNLP*, pp. 2230–2235.

Zhou, P., W. Shi, J. Tian, Z. Qi, B. Li, H. Hao, and B. Xu (2016). Attention-based bidirectional long short-term memory networks for relation classification. In *Proceedings of ACL*, pp. 207–212.

Zhou, Z.-M., Y. Xu, Z.-Y. Niu, M. Lan, J. Su, and C. L. Tan (2010). Predicting discourse connectives for implicit discourse relation recognition. In *Proceedings of COLING*, pp. 1507–1514.

Cross-Lingual Transfer of Semantic Roles: From Raw Text to Semantic Roles

Maryam Aminian[1], Mohammad Sadegh Rasooli[2], Mona Diab[1,3]
[1]The George Washington University, Washington
[2]Facebook AI, Menlo Park, CA
[3]AWS, Amazon AI
{aminian,mtdiab}@gwu.edu, rasooli@fb.com

Abstract

We describe a transfer method based on annotation projection to develop a dependency-based semantic role labeling system for languages for which no supervised linguistic information other than parallel data is available. Unlike previous work that presumes the availability of supervised features such as lemmas, part-of-speech tags, and dependency parse trees, we only make use of word and character features. Our deep model considers using character-based representations as well as unsupervised stem embeddings to alleviate the need for supervised features. Our experiments outperform a state-of-the-art method that uses supervised lexico-syntactic features on 6 out of 7 languages in the Universal Proposition Bank.

1 Introduction

Despite considerable efforts on developing semantically annotated resources for semantic role labeling (SRL) (Palmer et al., 2005; Erk et al., 2003; Zaghouani et al., 2010), majority of languages do not have such annotated resources. The lack of annotated resources for SRL has led to a growing interest in transfer methods for developing semantic role labeling systems. The ultimate goal of transfer methods is to transfer supervised linguistic information from a rich-resource language to a target language of interest. Amongst transfer methods, annotation projection is a method that projects supervised annotation from a rich-resource language to a low-resource language through automatic word alignments in parallel data (Hwa et al., 2002; Padó and Lapata, 2009). Recent work on annotation projection for SRL (Kozhevnikov and Titov, 2013a; van der Plas et al., 2014; Akbik et al., 2015; Aminian et al., 2017) presumes the availability of accurate supervised features such as lemmas, part-of-speech (POS) tags and syntactic parse trees. However, this is not a realistic assumption for truly low-resource languages, for which (accurate) supervised features are hardly available.

This paper considers the problem of annotation projection of *dependency-based* SRL in a scenario for which *only* parallel data is available for the target language. Recent state-of-the-art SRL systems have shown a significant reliance on the predicate lemma information while in a low-resource language, a lemmatizer might not be available. We first demonstrate that unsupervised stems can be used as an alternative to supervised lemma features. We further show that we can obtain a robust and simple SRL model for the target language without relying on *any* explicit linguistic feature (including lemmas), either supervised or unsupervised. We achieve this goal by changing the structure of a state-of-the-art deep SRL system (Marcheggiani et al., 2017) to make it independent of supervised features. Our model solely rely on word and character level features in the target language.

The main contribution of this work is on applying annotation projection without relying on supervised features in the target language of interest. To the best of our knowledge, this is the first study that builds a cross-lingual SRL transfer model in the absence of any explicit linguistic information in the target language. We make use of the recently released Universal Proposition Banks (Akbik et al., 2016)[1],

---

[1]https://github.com/System-T/UniversalPropositions

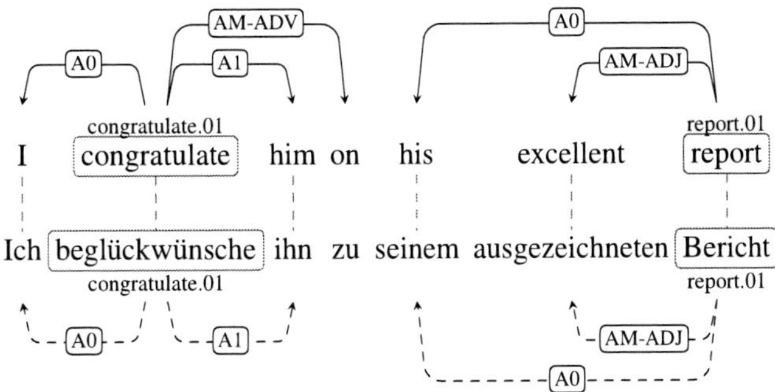

Figure 1: An example of annotation projection for an English-German sentence pair from the Europarl corpus (Koehn, 2005). Supervised predicate-argument structure of the English sentence (edges on top) is generated using our supervised SRL system trained on PropBank 3 (Palmer et al., 2005). Dashed lines in the middle show intersected word alignments from Giza++ (Och and Ney, 2003). Dashed edges at the bottom show the projected predicate-arguments.

a semi-automatically annotated data that unifies the annotation scheme for all languages. We show the effectiveness of our method on a range of languages, namely German, Spanish, Finnish, French, Italian, Portuguese, and Chinese. We compare our model to a state-of-the-art baseline that uses a rich set of supervised features and show that our model outperforms on six out of seven languages in the Universal Proposition Banks. Furthermore, for Finnish, a morphologically rich language, our model with unsupervised features improves over the model that relies on a supervised lemmatizer.

This paper is structured as the following: §2 briefly overviews the dependency-based SRL task and annotation projection, §3 describes our approach, §4 shows the experimental results and analysis, §5 gives overviews about the related work, and §6 concludes the paper and proposes suggestions for future work.

2   Background

In this section, we provide a brief overview of dependency-based SRL and annotation projection.

Dependency-based SRL   In dependency-based SRL, the goal is to find arguments along with their roles for each predicate in a sentence. Formally, in a sentence $x = [x_i]_{i=1}^n$ with n words, and m predicates $\mathbb{P} = [(p_i, \psi_i); 1 \le p_i \le n]_{i=1}^m$ where ψ_i is the *sense* of the predicate with index p_i in the sentence, we find the semantic dependencies between each word in the sentence with respect to each predicate:

$$\mathbb{L}_x = [(p_i \xrightarrow{r} j|\psi_i); 1 \le j \le n, p_i \in \mathbb{P}]$$

where r is the role of the jth word as an argument for the predicate word x_{p_i}. In case that a word is not an argument, r is NULL. Evaluation of the system output is conducted on semantic dependencies $(p_i \xrightarrow{r} j|\psi_i)$; thus the SRL system should find predicate senses as well as argument roles. During training, these dependencies are used as training instances for a machine learning algorithm. Previous work (Björkelund et al., 2009; Roth and Lapata, 2016; Marcheggiani et al., 2017) factorized this task into predicate sense disambiguation, argument identification, and argument classification.

Annotation Projection   In annotation projection, we assume that we have a parallel data $\mathcal{P} = [(s^{(1)}, t^{(1)}), \cdots, (s^{(k)}, t^{(k)})]$ such that each sentence $s^{(i)}$ is a translation of sentence $t^{(i)}$. Here, we assume that $s^{(i)}$ belongs to a rich-resource language in which annotated resources are available. In contrast, $t^{(i)}$ belongs to a low-resource target language where annotated data and tools such as semantic roles, dependency trees, part-of-speech tags, word senses, and lemmas might not be available.

For every sentence $s^{(i)}$, we run a supervised SRL system to obtain its supervised argument structure $\mathbb{L}_{s^{(i)}}$. Assuming that $s^{(i)} = [s_1^{(i)}, \cdots, s_{l_i}^{(i)}]$ and $t^{(i)} = [t_1^{(i)}, \cdots, t_{l_i'}^{(i)}]$, we use an automatic word alignment system to obtain *one-to-one* word alignments. We define $0 \le a_j^{(i)} \le l_i$ as the index of the source word that is aligned to the jth word in the ith target sentence, where $a_j^{(i)} = 0$ indicates a missing alignment. We use the following conditions to project a semantic dependency from a source sentence to a target sentence:

$$(a_p^{(i)} \xrightarrow{r} a_m^{(i)}|y) \in \mathbb{L}_{s^{(i)}} \Rightarrow \text{add } (p \xrightarrow{r} m|y) \text{ to } \mathbb{L}_{t^{(i)}}$$

where $\mathbb{L}_{s^{(i)}}$ is the supervised argument structure and $\mathbb{L}_{t^{(i)}}$ is the projected argument structure for the ith sentence. We assume that there is a universal predicate sense that is common across languages (this is the case in the Universal Propositon Banks). Figure 1 shows an example for an English-German translation pair. We use the projected data as training data in a supervised learning system to train a SRL system in the target language. In practice, many words do not receive any projected label mainly due to missing alignments. Thus, $\mathbb{L}_{t^{(i)}}$ usually contains sentences with partially projected semantic dependencies.

3   Our Model

Our goal is to train a SRL system on the projected predicate-argument structures without having supervised features such as supervised lemmas, dependency parse trees, and part-of-speech tags. Our model has two main components: 1) joint argument identification and classification which we simply refer to as argument classifier , and 2) predicate sense disambiguation. Our argument classifier is inspired by the model of Marcheggiani et al. (2017): we use predicate-specific BiLSTM encoders, and a role+predicate-specific decoder. However, unlike the model of Marcheggiani et al. (2017), which relies heavily on POS tags and predicate lemmas, we do not use a supervised lemmatizer and POS tagger in any layer. Instead, we benefit from character representations and unsupervised stems to bring in unsupervised features to our model.

3.1   Joint Argument Identification and Classification

Given a sentence $s = [s_i]_{i=1}^n$ that contains n tokens with m predicates in the predicate set $\mathbb{P}$, we run m *separate* predicate-specific deep BiLSTM encoders $[\mathbb{E}_j]_{j=1}^m$ to extract contextualized representations for each token given a predicate index p_j.

Input Representation   For each encoder $[\mathbb{E}_j]_{j=1}^m$, we represent each token s_i as the concatenation of its word embedding (x_i^{re} and x_i^{pe}), character embedding (x_i^{char}) and predicate lemma embedding ($x_{i,j}^{lem}$):[2]

$$x_{i,j} = [x_i^{re}; x_i^{pe}; x_i^{char}; x_{i,j}^{le}]$$
$$\forall i \in [1, \cdots, n]; j \in [1, \cdots, m]$$

where:

- $x_i^{re} \in \mathbb{R}^{d_w}$ is a randomly initialized word embedding vector;

- $x_i^{pe} \in \mathbb{R}^{d_w}$ is an external pre-trained word embedding that is fixed during training;

- $x_i^{char} \in \mathbb{R}^{d_{ch}}$ is character representation of each token s_i. For every token, we obtain x_i^{char} by running a deep bidirectional LSTM (Hochreiter and Schmidhuber, 1997) on top of each word. We use the concatenation of the final backward representation of the first character, and final forward representation of the last character to represent each token:

$$x_i^{char} = \texttt{BiLSTM}(x_i^c[1 : |s_i|]; |s_i|)$$

---

[2] We use [;] notation to show vector concatenation.

where $x_i^c \in \mathbb{R}^{d_c}$ is a randomly initialized character embedding and $|s_i|$ is the number of characters in token s_i;

- $x_{i,j}^{le} \in \mathbb{R}^{d_{le}}$ is a lemma vector for each word s_i with respect to the predicate that is targeted in $\mathbb{E}_j$. $x_{i,j}^{le}$ is active if s_i is the predicate word, otherwise, a zero vector is used to represent the lemma embedding:

$$x_{i,j}^{le} = \begin{cases} [x_i^{le}; 1] & \texttt{if i = p_j} \\ [\overrightarrow{0}; 0] & \texttt{otherwise} \end{cases}$$

where the concatenated zero/one value is a flag to indicate if the current token is the targeted lemma. In our model, we use one of the following options to represent predicate lemma:

- Represent each lemma by a deep character BiLSTM. This BiLSTM is different from the character BiLSTM in x^{char}.

- Use an unsupervised morphological analyzer to give the surface-form stem of each word. This way, we can use a lemma embedding dictionary without requiring a lemmatizer.

Predicate-Specific Encoder   A deep BiLSTM is used to get the final representation for each token in a sentence. In the following notation, $h_{i,j}$ is the final hidden state from the deep BiLSTM model for the ith token with respect to the jth predicate:

$$h_{i,j} = \texttt{BiLSTM}(s_{1:n,j}; i) \in \mathbb{R}^{d_h}$$

Role+Predicate-Specific Decoder   Given the BiLSTM representations, we perform an affine transformation on the concatenation of $h_{p_j,j}$ (predicate representation) and $h_{i,j}$ (argument representation) to find the probability of having the ith token as the argument of predicate p_j with role r (including the NULL role):

$$p(r|h_{p_j,j}, h_{i,j}) = \texttt{softmax}_{\texttt{r}}(W_{j,r}[h_{p_j,j}; h_{i,j}])$$

where $x_{j,r}$ is a parameter matrix that encodes the information of role r and the jth predicate. This matrix is calculated as follows:

$$W_{j,r} = \texttt{RELU}(U[u_j^l, v_r])$$

where $u_j^l \in \mathbb{R}^{d_l'}$ is another predicate lemma embedding parameter which is specifically used for the decoder layer, $v_r \in \mathbb{R}^{d_r}$ is a randomly initialized role embedding, U is a parameter matrix, and RELU is the rectified linear units activation function (Nair and Hinton, 2010). Similar to the input layer, we represent u_j^l by 1) a different deep character BiLSTM, *or* 2) a surface-form stem obtained from an unsupervised morphological analyzer.

A graphical depiction of the network in a case for which lemmas are represented by character BiLSTMs is shown in figure 2. As shown in the figure, we use two different character BiLSTMs in order to represent lemmas: one for the input representation and the other for the decoder representation.

4   Experiments

Datasets and Tools   We use English as the source language and project SRL annotations to the following languages: German, Spanish, Finnish, French, Italian, Portuguese, and Chinese. We use the Europarl parallel corpus (Koehn, 2005) for the European languages and a random sample of 2 million sentence pairs from the MultiUN corpus (Eisele and Chen, 2010) for Chinese. We use the Giza++ tool (Och and Ney, 2003) with its default setting for word alignment. We run Giza++ in source-to-target and the reverse

Figure 2: A graphical depiction of our joint argument identification and classification model without using part-of-speech tags, lemmas, and syntax. In this example, the predicate-specific encoder considers word *eats* as the sentence predicate and the goal is to score the assignment of argument *apple* with label A_0. Our model contains three *different* character BiLSTMs; at the bottom, a character BiLSTM is run to acquire a character-based representation for all the words in the sentence in the absence of POS tags. There are two character BiLSTMs for predicate lemma: one in the encoder level (next to the second word) to model predicate lemma in the input layer and the other in the decoder level (top left). In this example, we just show one layer of BiLSTM but we use a deep BiLSTM in our experiments.

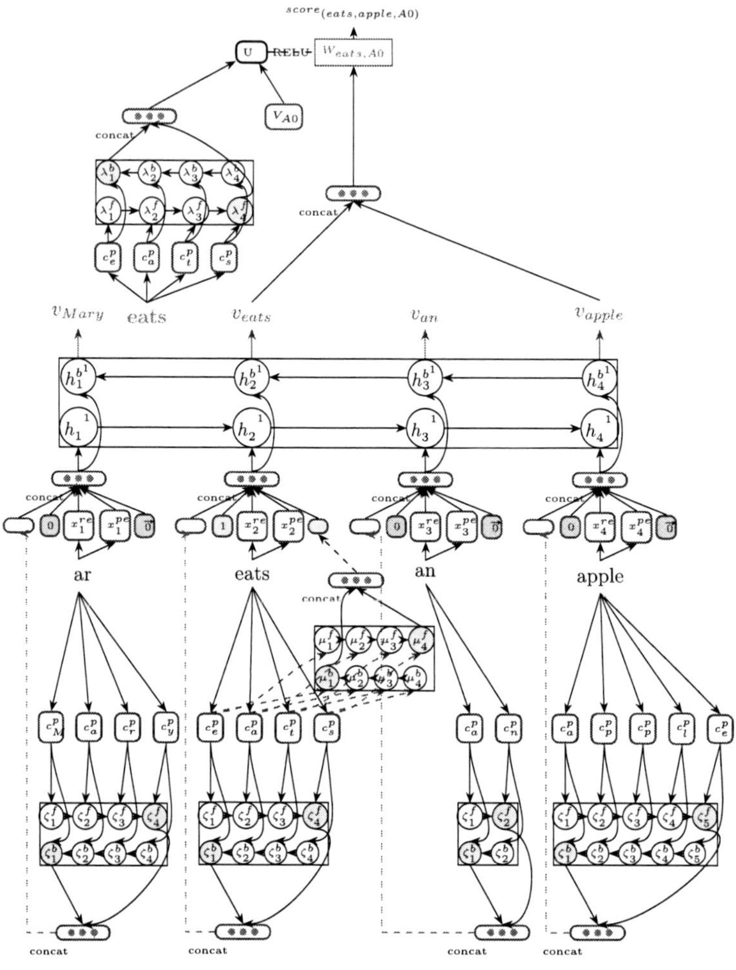

direction and get the intersection of alignment links. For English, we use the pre-trained embedding vectors generated using the structured skip-gram model of Ling et al. (2015). For the target languages, we train Word2vec (Mikolov et al., 2013) on Wikipedia data to generate embedding vectors.

We implement our deep network using the Dynet library (Neubig et al., 2017). We use the dimension of 100 for word embeddings, 50 for characters, 512 for LSTM encoders, 128 for role and lemma embeddings in the decoder, and 100 for decoder lemma embedding. We pick random minibatches of size 1000 with a fixed learning rate of 0.001 for learning the parameter values with the Adam optimizer (Kingma and Ba, 2014). The depth of BiLSTM network is set to one for character representation (x^{char}) and three for predicate-specific representations (x^{le}, u^l).

Predicate Disambiguation Our model is agnostic to predicate senses but since our automatic evaluation relies on automatic predicate senses, we need a disambiguation module. Predicate disambiguation systems typically contains separate classifiers for each predicate lemma (Björkelund et al., 2009). Since we do not have a reliable lemmatizer in the target language, we train a single classifier for all predicates. We encode a sentence with a three-layer deep BiLSTM and run a softmax layer on top of each predicate to disambiguate the predicate sense of each predicate.

Predicate identification on the source side For projection experiments, first of all we need to identify predicates in the source language. Input to our predicate identifier is the concatenation of word embed-

Lang.	#Sent.	#Tokens	#Types	#Pred.
de	332K	6M	90K	867K
es	903K	25M	120K	3M
fi	558K	8M	243K	1M
fr	924K	26M	93K	3M
it	617K	17M	88K	2M
pt	632K	17M	98K	2M
zh	821K	21M	183K	1M

Table 1: Sizes of the projected data.

ding, pre-trained fixed word embedding, POS embedding[3], and character representation (obtained from a character BiLSTM) for every token in the sentence. We use a deep BiLSTM to get the final representation for each token. The ultimate predictions are made by performing an affine transform on the BiLSTM hidden output.

4.1 Projection Experiments

Our supervised SRL system is a reimplementation of the model of Marcheggiani et al. (2017). We generate automatic English predicate senses using a system similar to the predicate disambiguation module of Björkelund et al. (2009) except that we replace the logistic regression classifier with the averaged Perceptron algorithm (Collins, 2002). In order to comply with the Universal Proposition Bank annotation scheme, we convert the argument spans in the English PropBank v3 (Palmer et al., 2005) to dependency-based arguments by labeling the syntactic head of each span.

For annotation projection, we define density of alignments to find sentences with relatively-dense alignments:

$$\texttt{density}^{(i)} = \frac{\sum_{j=1}^{l'_j} \mathbb{I}(a_j^{(i)} > 0)}{l'_i}$$

where l'_i is the length of the ith target sentence in parallel data, $a_j^{(i)}$ is the alignment index for the jth word in the target sentence, and $\mathbb{I}(a_j^{(i)} > 0)$ is an indicator for a non-NULL alignment. We prune the target sentence pairs with density less than 80% for all European languages. We set this threshold to 60% for Chinese in order to obtain a comparable number of sentences to the European languages. Table 1 summarizes the sizes of projected datasets after applying the density filter. We set the number of training epochs to 2 for all languages based on development results obtained from the English to German projections.

Since the original model of Marcheggiani et al. (2017) heavily relies on the predicate lemma information for making robust prediction, we further assess the influence of using explicit linguistic features in our model by using a) supervised lemma from the UDPipe pre-trained models (Straka and Straková, 2017), and b) unsupervised stems obtained from unsupervised morphological analyzer. We use the unsupervised morphological analyzer of Virpioja et al. (2013), and obtain morpheme classes by running Morfessor FlatCat (Grönroos et al., 2014) on the output of the analyzer. We run the *fixed-affix* finite-state machine of (Rasooli et al., 2014) to obtain a single stem for all words including the out-of-vocabularies.

Results We compare our character-based approach (*CModel*) with three different models: 1) The cross-lingual model of Aminian et al. (2017) (*Bootstrap*) that uses a rich set of supervised features including supervised lemmas, POS tags, and dependency parse information, 2) a variant of our model that uses supervised lemmas (*SLem*) generated by a lemmatizer to represent predicate lemmas in the input and the decode layers, and 3) a model similar to the second model but using unsupervised stems (*UStem*) generated by an unsupervised morphological analyzer to represent predicate lemmas. Here, we aim to asses

---

[3]Since this is only used for a supervised setting, we are able to use POS features.

System	de	es	fi	fr	it	pt	zh
Bootstrap	59.8 (55.0)	60.6 (52.2)	59.0 (53.1)	71.0 (63.4)	59.2 (52.3)	61.2 (53.9)	50.3 (42.5)
SLem	61.7 (57.0)	62.4 (55.7)	62.5 (59.2)	65.0 (58.9)	61.8 (56.4)	63.0 (56.8)	52.1 (43.7)
UStem	62.0 (57.4)	63.0 (56.0)	64.5 (58.8)	65.3 (59.2)	61.3 (55.4)	62.8 (56.8)	52.6 (43.2)
CModel	61.0 (57.0)	62.5 (56.0)	64.6 (58.9)	65.1 (58.5)	61.0 (55.5)	62.9 (56.5)	52.7 (42.7)
Supervised	74.5 (72.0)	77.8 (75.2)	74.0 (69.6)	88.9 (87.5)	77.9 (75.9)	66.6 (62.4)	68.8 (68.6)

Table 2: Results of projection experiments using our character based model (*CModel*) on the Universal PropBank test sets compared to different baselines: the SRL system of *Aminian et al. (2017)* (*Bootstrap*), *SLem* that shows the results of our model when supervised lemma is used and *UStem* that show the results of our model with unsupervised stem. Numbers in parenthesis show results with automatic predicate senses.

the effects of using different levels of explicit linguistic features ranging from fully specified supervised features to unsupervised features in our model. The *Bootstrap* model uses an iterative bootstrapping approach by utilizing a special cost function and benefiting from a rich set of supervised lexico-syntactic features, thereby, it is considered a hard baseline. Since *Bootstrap* has a large number of features, the model is not memory-wise scalable to our projection data sizes. Therefore we train the *Bootstrap* model on a random sample of 20K sentences. This number is similar to the number of sentences used in the original experiments (Aminian et al., 2017).

Table 2 shows labeled F-scores using both gold and automatic predicate senses on the test portion of the Universal Proposition Banks. The last raw in the table shows results from the supervised SRL systems trained on the training portion of the Universal Proposition Banks for each language, thereby can servr as an upper bound for our model. As shown in Table 2, our model (*CModel*) outperforms the *Bootstrap* model for all languages except French. Additionally, our model performs on par to the supervised lemma and unsupervised stem models. This demonstrates the power of our approach even though our model has access to fewer linguistic features in the target language. Using unsupervised stems outperforms supervised lemma on all languages except Portuguese and Italian. This further highlights the reliance of the model on the accuracy of lemmatizer.

Analysis　As shown in Table 2, using automatic predicate senses leads to a significant reduction in accuracy. This degradation is caused by two reasons. First, training a single classifier for all predicates in the absence of explicit predicate lemma information, and second, using unified predicate senses for all languages leads to lower precision for out-of-vocabulary words. This happens due to the fact that we cannot make use of the default sense of predicate (`lemma.01`). Among all the languages in our experiments, French is the only language that our model underperforms the *Bootstrap* model. Our analysis on French shows that our model has not been able to correctly predict A0 and A1 arguments in 20% and 30% of cases, and labeled them as `NULL`.

5　Related Work

There has been a great deal of interest in using transfer methods for SRL by different techniques such as enhancing the quality of projections (Padó and Lapata, 2005, 2009), joint learning of syntax and semantics (van der Plas et al., 2011; Kozhevnikov and Titov, 2013b), and iterative bootstrapping to learn a robust model from erroneous projections (Akbik et al., 2015; Aminian et al., 2017). Previous work presumes availability of a wide range of supervised lexico-syntactic features for the target language. Consequently, their performance heavily relies on accuracy of the available tagging tools (Akbik et al., 2015). For instance, Akbik et al. (2015) reports lower argument precision for languages that do not have accurate syntactic parsers such as Arabic and Hindi. In contrary to the previous studies, our work builds a cross-lingual SRL system without having any supervised features for the target language.

One obstacle for developing transfer models is the absence of a unified annotation scheme for all languages. There has been a great deal of work in developing universal annotation schemes for a variety of tasks such as POS tagging (Petrov et al., 2011), dependency parsing (Nivre et al., 2017), morphology (Kirov et al., 2018), and SRL (Kozhevnikov and Titov, 2013a; Wang et al., 2017). Our work makes use of the recently released Universal Proposition Bank (Akbik et al., 2016). This dataset maps every predicate lemma in every language to its corresponding English lemma following the frame and role label schemes of the English Proposition Bank 3.0 (Palmer et al., 2005)

In the realm of *supervised* SRL methods, however, there have been several efforts to build SRL models that do not need a wide range of linguistic features (specifically syntactic features) (Marcheggiani et al., 2017; Zhou and Xu, 2015; He et al., 2017, 2018; Cai et al., 2018; Mulcaire et al., 2018). In a more recent study, Mulcaire et al. (2018) proposed a polyglot SRL system that benefits from the similarities between the semantic structures of different languages to improve monolingual SRL. All those studies, however, assume the availability of semantically annotated datasets for the target language, thus making them non-applicable to low-resource languages.

6   Conclusion

We have described a method for cross-lingual transfer of dependency-based SRL systems via annotation projection. Our model is agnostic to linguistic features leading to a robust model that can be trained on projected text on a target language without annotated data. We have shown that our model achieves comparable performance in annotation projection and also supervised SRL. In addition to improving the performance of our model with the current setting, future work should study more effective ways to apply the transfer methods; e.g. combining with the direct transfer method in the absence of large parallel corpora.

Acknowledgments

The first and third authors have been partly funded by the DARPA LORELEI grant and generous support by Leidos Corp.. We would like to acknowledge the useful comments by three anonymous reviewers who helped in making this publication more concise and better presented.

References

Akbik, A., l. chiticariu, M. Danilevsky, Y. Li, S. Vaithyanathan, and H. Zhu (2015). Generating high quality proposition banks for multilingual semantic role labeling. In *Proceedings of the 53rd Annual Meeting of the Association for Computational Linguistics and the 7th International Joint Conference on Natural Language Processing (Volume 1: Long Papers)*, pp. 397–407. Association for Computational Linguistics.

Akbik, A., v. kumar, and Y. Li (2016). Towards semi-automatic generation of proposition banks for low-resource languages. In *Proceedings of the 2016 Conference on Empirical Methods in Natural Language Processing*, pp. 993–998. Association for Computational Linguistics.

Aminian, M., M. S. Rasooli, and M. Diab (2017, November). Transferring semantic roles using translation and syntactic information. In *Proceedings of the Eighth International Joint Conference on Natural Language Processing (Volume 2: Short Papers)*, Taipei, Taiwan, pp. 13–19. Asian Federation of Natural Language Processing.

Björkelund, A., L. Hafdell, and P. Nugues (2009). *Proceedings of the Thirteenth Conference on Computational Natural Language Learning (CoNLL 2009): Shared Task*, Chapter Multilingual Semantic Role Labeling, pp. 43–48. Association for Computational Linguistics.

Cai, J., S. He, Z. Li, and H. Zhao (2018). A full end-to-end semantic role labeler, syntactic-agnostic over syntactic-aware? In *Proceedings of the 27th International Conference on Computational Linguistics*, pp. 2753–2765. Association for Computational Linguistics.

Collins, M. (2002, July). Discriminative training methods for hidden Markov models: Theory and experiments with perceptron algorithms. In *Proceedings of the 2002 Conference on Empirical Methods in Natural Language Processing*, pp. 1–8. Association for Computational Linguistics.

Eisele, A. and Y. Chen (2010, may). Multiun: A multilingual corpus from united nation documents. In N. C. C. Chair), K. Choukri, B. Maegaard, J. Mariani, J. Odijk, S. Piperidis, M. Rosner, and D. Tapias (Eds.), *Proceedings of the Seventh conference on International Language Resources and Evaluation (LREC'10)*, Valletta, Malta. European Language Resources Association (ELRA).

Erk, K., A. Kowalski, S. Padó, and M. Pinkal (2003, July). Towards a resource for lexical semantics: A large german corpus with extensive semantic annotation. In *Proceedings of the 41st Annual Meeting of the Association for Computational Linguistics*, Sapporo, Japan, pp. 537–544. Association for Computational Linguistics.

Grönroos, S.-A., S. Virpioja, P. Smit, and M. Kurimo (2014, August). Morfessor flatcat: An hmm-based method for unsupervised and semi-supervised learning of morphology. In *Proceedings of COLING 2014, the 25th International Conference on Computational Linguistics: Technical Papers*, Dublin, Ireland, pp. 1177–1185. Dublin City University and Association for Computational Linguistics.

He, L., K. Lee, M. Lewis, and L. Zettlemoyer (2017). Deep semantic role labeling: What works and what's next. In *Proceedings of the 55th Annual Meeting of the Association for Computational Linguistics (Volume 1: Long Papers)*, pp. 473–483. Association for Computational Linguistics.

He, S., Z. Li, H. Zhao, and H. Bai (2018). Syntax for semantic role labeling, to be, or not to be. In *Proceedings of the 56th Annual Meeting of the Association for Computational Linguistics (Volume 1: Long Papers)*, pp. 2061–2071. Association for Computational Linguistics.

Hochreiter, S. and J. Schmidhuber (1997). Long short-term memory. *Neural computation 9*(8), 1735–1780.

Hwa, R., P. Resnik, A. Weinberg, and O. Kolak (2002). Evaluating translational correspondence using annotation projection. In *Proceedings of the 40th Annual Meeting on Association for Computational Linguistics*, pp. 392–399. Association for Computational Linguistics.

Kingma, D. P. and J. Ba (2014). Adam: A method for stochastic optimization. *arXiv preprint arXiv:1412.6980*.

Kirov, C., R. Cotterell, J. Sylak-Glassman, G. Walther, E. Vylomova, P. Xia, M. Faruqui, S. Mielke, A. D. McCarthy, S. Kübler, et al. (2018). Unimorph 2.0: Universal morphology. *arXiv preprint arXiv:1810.11101*.

Koehn, P. (2005). Europarl: A parallel corpus for statistical machine translation. In *MT summit*, Volume 5, pp. 79–86.

Kozhevnikov, M. and I. Titov (2013a). Bootstrapping semantic role labelers from parallel data. In *Second Joint Conference on Lexical and Computational Semantics (*SEM), Volume 1: Proceedings of the Main Conference and the Shared Task: Semantic Textual Similarity*, pp. 317–327. Association for Computational Linguistics.

Kozhevnikov, M. and I. Titov (2013b). Cross-lingual transfer of semantic role labeling models. In *Proceedings of the 51st Annual Meeting of the Association for Computational Linguistics (Volume 1: Long Papers)*, pp. 1190–1200. Association for Computational Linguistics.

Ling, W., C. Dyer, A. W. Black, and I. Trancoso (2015, May–June). Two/too simple adaptations of word2vec for syntax problems. In *Proceedings of the 2015 Conference of the North American Chapter of the Association for Computational Linguistics: Human Language Technologies*, Denver, Colorado, pp. 1299–1304. Association for Computational Linguistics.

Marcheggiani, D., A. Frolov, and I. Titov (2017, August). A simple and accurate syntax-agnostic neural model for dependency-based semantic role labeling. In *Proceedings of the 21st Conference on Computational Natural Language Learning (CoNLL 2017)*, Vancouver, Canada, pp. 411–420. Association for Computational Linguistics.

Mikolov, T., I. Sutskever, K. Chen, G. S. Corrado, and J. Dean (2013). Distributed representations of words and phrases and their compositionality. In *Advances in neural information processing systems*, pp. 3111–3119.

Mulcaire, P., S. Swayamdipta, and N. A. Smith (2018). Polyglot semantic role labeling. In *Proceedings of the 56th Annual Meeting of the Association for Computational Linguistics (Volume 2: Short Papers)*, pp. 667–672. Association for Computational Linguistics.

Nair, V. and G. E. Hinton (2010). Rectified linear units improve restricted boltzmann machines. In *Proceedings of the 27th international conference on machine learning (ICML-10)*, pp. 807–814.

Neubig, G., C. Dyer, Y. Goldberg, A. Matthews, W. Ammar, A. Anastasopoulos, M. Ballesteros, D. Chiang, D. Clothiaux, T. Cohn, et al. (2017). Dynet: The dynamic neural network toolkit. *arXiv preprint arXiv:1701.03980*.

Nivre, J., Ž. Agić, L. Ahrenberg, M. J. Aranzabe, M. Asahara, et al. (2017). Universal Dependencies 2. LINDAT/CLARIN digital library at Institute of Formal and Applied Linguistics, Charles University in Prague.

Och, F. J. and H. Ney (2003). A systematic comparison of various statistical alignment models. *Computational Linguistics 29*(1), 19–51.

Padó, S. and M. Lapata (2005). Cross-linguistic projection of role-semantic information. In *Proceedings of Human Language Technology Conference and Conference on Empirical Methods in Natural Language Processing*.

Padó, S. and M. Lapata (2009). Cross-lingual annotation projection for semantic roles. *Journal of Artificial Intelligence Research 36*(1), 307–340.

Palmer, M., D. Gildea, and P. Kingsbury (2005). The proposition bank: An annotated corpus of semantic roles. *Computational Linguistics, Volume 31, Number 1, March 2005*.

Petrov, S., D. Das, and R. McDonald (2011). A universal part-of-speech tagset. *arXiv preprint arXiv:1104.2086*.

Rasooli, M. S., T. Lippincott, N. Habash, and O. Rambow (2014, June). Unsupervised morphology-based vocabulary expansion. In *Proceedings of the 52nd Annual Meeting of the Association for Computational Linguistics (Volume 1: Long Papers)*, Baltimore, Maryland, pp. 1349–1359. Association for Computational Linguistics.

Roth, M. and M. Lapata (2016). Neural semantic role labeling with dependency path embeddings. In *Proceedings of the 54th Annual Meeting of the Association for Computational Linguistics (Volume 1: Long Papers)*, pp. 1192–1202. Association for Computational Linguistics.

Straka, M. and J. Straková (2017, August). Tokenizing, pos tagging, lemmatizing and parsing ud 2.0 with udpipe. In *Proceedings of the CoNLL 2017 Shared Task: Multilingual Parsing from Raw Text to Universal Dependencies*, Vancouver, Canada, pp. 88–99. Association for Computational Linguistics.

van der Plas, L., M. Apidianaki, and C. Chen (2014). Global methods for cross-lingual semantic role and predicate labelling. In *Proceedings of COLING 2014, the 25th International Conference on Computational Linguistics: Technical Papers*, pp. 1279–1290. Dublin City University and Association for Computational Linguistics.

van der Plas, L., P. Merlo, and J. Henderson (2011). Scaling up automatic cross-lingual semantic role annotation. In *Proceedings of the 49th Annual Meeting of the Association for Computational Linguistics: Human Language Technologies*, pp. 299–304. Association for Computational Linguistics.

Virpioja, S., P. Smit, S.-A. Grönroos, M. Kurimo, et al. (2013). Morfessor 2.0: Python implementation and extensions for morfessor baseline. Technical report, Aalto University.

Wang, C., A. Akbik, l. chiticariu, Y. Li, F. Xia, and A. Xu (2017, September). Crowd-in-the-loop: A hybrid approach for annotating semantic roles. In *Proceedings of the 2017 Conference on Empirical Methods in Natural Language Processing*, Copenhagen, Denmark, pp. 1913–1922. Association for Computational Linguistics.

Zaghouani, W., M. Diab, A. Mansouri, S. Pradhan, and M. Palmer (2010, July). The revised arabic propbank. In *Proceedings of the Fourth Linguistic Annotation Workshop*, Uppsala, Sweden, pp. 222–226. Association for Computational Linguistics.

Zhou, J. and W. Xu (2015). End-to-end learning of semantic role labeling using recurrent neural networks. In *Proceedings of the 53rd Annual Meeting of the Association for Computational Linguistics and the 7th International Joint Conference on Natural Language Processing (Volume 1: Long Papers)*, pp. 1127–1137. Association for Computational Linguistics.

Evaluating the Representational Hub
of Language and Vision Models

Ravi Shekhar[†], Ece Takmaz[*], Raquel Fernández[*] and Raffaella Bernardi[†]
[†]University of Trento, [*]University of Amsterdam
`raffaella.bernardi@unitn.it` `raquel.fernandez@uva.nl`

Abstract

The multimodal models used in the emerging field at the intersection of computational linguistics and computer vision implement the bottom-up processing of the "Hub and Spoke" architecture proposed in cognitive science to represent how the brain processes and combines multi-sensory inputs. In particular, the Hub is implemented as a neural network encoder. We investigate the effect on this encoder of various vision-and-language tasks proposed in the literature: visual question answering, visual reference resolution, and visually grounded dialogue. To measure the quality of the representations learned by the encoder, we use two kinds of analyses. First, we evaluate the encoder pre-trained on the different vision-and-language tasks on an existing *diagnostic task* designed to assess multimodal semantic understanding. Second, we carry out a battery of analyses aimed at studying how the encoder merges and exploits the two modalities.

1   Introduction

In recent years, a lot of progress has been made within the emerging field at the intersection of computational linguistics and computer vision thanks to the use of deep neural networks. The most common strategy to move the field forward has been to propose different multimodal tasks—such as visual question answering (Antol et al., 2015), visual question generation (Mostafazadeh et al., 2016), visual reference resolution (Kazemzadeh et al., 2014), and visual dialogue (Das et al., 2017)—and to develop task-specific models.

The benchmarks developed so far have put forward complex and distinct neural architectures, but in general they all share a common backbone consisting of an encoder which learns to merge the two types of representation to perform a certain task. This resembles the bottom-up processing in the 'Hub and Spoke' model proposed in Cognitive Science to represent how the brain processes and combines multi-sensory inputs (Patterson and Ralph, 2015). In this model, a 'hub' module merges the input processed by the sensor-specific 'spokes' into a joint representation. We focus our attention on the encoder implementing the 'hub' in artificial multimodal systems, with the goal of assessing its ability to compute multimodal representations that are useful beyond specific tasks.

While current visually grounded models perform remarkably well on the task they have been trained for, it is unclear whether they are able to learn representations that truly merge the two modalities and whether the skill they have acquired is stable enough to be transferred to other tasks. In this paper, we investigate these questions in detail. To do so, we evaluate an encoder trained on different multimodal tasks on an existing *diagnostic task*—FOIL (Shekhar et al., 2017)—designed to assess multimodal semantic understanding and carry out an in-depth analysis to study how the encoder merges and exploits the two modalities. We also exploit two techniques to investigate the structure of the learned semantic spaces: Representation Similarity Analysis (RSA) (Kriegeskorte et al., 2008) and Nearest Neighbour overlap (NN). We use RSA to compare the outcome of the various encoders given the same vision-and-language input and NN to compare the multimodal space produced by an encoder with the ones built with the input visual and language embeddings, respectively, which allows us to measure the relative weight an encoder gives to the two modalities.

In particular, we consider three visually grounded tasks: visual question answering (VQA) (Antol et al., 2015), where the encoder is trained to answer a question about an image; visual resolution of referring expressions (ReferIt) (Kazemzadeh et al., 2014), where the model has to pick up the referent object of a description in an image; and GuessWhat (de Vries et al., 2017), where the model has to identify the object in an image that is the target of a goal-oriented question-answer dialogue. We make sure the datasets used in the pre-training phase are as similar as possible in terms of size and image complexity, and use the same model architecture for the three pre-training tasks. This guarantees fair comparisons and the reliability of the results we obtain.[1]

We show that the multimodal encoding skills learned by pre-training the model on GuessWhat and ReferIt are more stable and transferable than the ones learned through VQA. This is reflected in the lower number of epochs and the smaller training data size they need to reach their best performance on the FOIL task. We also observe that the semantic spaces learned by the encoders trained on the ReferIt and GuessWhat tasks are closer to each other than to the semantic space learned by the VQA encoder. Despite these asymmetries among tasks, we find that all encoders give more weight to the visual input than the linguistic one.

2 Related Work

Our work is part of a recent research trend that aims at analyzing, interpreting, and evaluating neural models by means of auxiliary tasks besides the task they have been trained for (Adi et al., 2017; Linzen et al., 2016; Alishahi et al., 2017; Zhang and Bowman, 2018; Conneau et al., 2018). Within language and vision research, the growing interest in having a better understanding of what neural models really learn has led to the creation of several diagnostic datasets (Johnson et al., 2017; Shekhar et al., 2017; Suhr et al., 2017).

Another research direction which is relevant to our work is transfer learning, a machine learning area that studies how the skills learned by a model trained on a particular task can be transferred to learn a new task better, faster, or with less data. Transfer learning has proved successful in computer vision (e.g. Razavian et al. (2014)) as well as in computational linguistics (e.g., Conneau et al. (2017)). However, little has been done in this respect for visually grounded natural language processing models.

In this work, we combine these different research lines and explore transfer learning techniques in the domain of language and vision tasks. In particular, we use the FOIL diagnostic dataset (Shekhar et al., 2017) and investigate to what extent skills learned through different multimodal tasks transfer.

While transfering the knowledge learned by a pre-trained model can be useful in principle, Conneau et al. (2018) found that randomly initialized models provide strong baselines that can even outperfom pre-trained classifiers (see also Wieting and Kiela (2019)). However, it has also been shown that these untrained, randomly initialized models can be more sensitive to the size of the training set than pre-trained models are (Zhang and Bowman, 2018). We will investigate these issues in our experiments.

3 Visually Grounded Tasks and Diagnostic Task

We study three visually grounded tasks: visual question answering (VQA), visual resolution of referring expressions (ReferIt), and goal-oriented dialogue for visual target identification (GuessWhat). While ReferIt was originally formulated as an object detection task (Kazemzadeh et al., 2014), VQA (Antol et al., 2015) and GuessWhat (de Vries et al., 2017) were defined as classification tasks. Here we operationalize the three tasks as retrieval tasks, which makes comparability easier.

- **VQA:** Given an image and a natural language question about it, the model is trained to retrieve the correct natural language answer out of a list of possible answers.

---

[1]The datasets are available at https://foilunitn.github.io/.

Figure 1: Illustrations of the three visually-grounded tasks (left) and the diagnostic task (right).

- **ReferIt:** Given an image and a natural language description of an entity in the image, the model is asked to retrieve the bounding box of the corresponding entity out of a list of candidate bounding boxes.

- **GuessWhat:** Given an image and a natural language question-answer dialogue about a target entity in the image, the model is asked to retrieve the bounding box of the target among a list of candidate bounding boxes. The GuessWhat game also involves asking questions before guessing. Here we focus on the guessing task that takes place after the question generation step.

Figure 1 (left) exemplifies the similarities and differences among the three tasks. All three tasks require merging and encoding visual and linguistic input. In VQA, the system is trained to make a language-related prediction, while in ReferIt it is trained to make visual predictions. GuessWhat includes elements of both VQA and ReferIt, as well as specific properties: The system is trained to make a visual prediction (as in ReferIt) and it is exposed to questions (as in VQA); but in this case the linguistic input is a coherent sequence of visually grounded questions and answers that follow a goal-oriented strategy and that have been produced in an interactive setting.

To evaluate the multimodal representations learned by the encoders of the models trained on each of the three tasks above, we leverage the FOIL task (concretely, task 1 introduced by Shekhar et al. (2017)), a binary classification task designed to detect semantic incongruence in visually grounded language.

- **FOIL (diagnostic task):** Given an image and a natural language caption describing it, the model is asked to decide whether the caption faithfully describes the image or not, i.e., whether it contains a foiled word that is incompatible with the image (foil caption) or not (original caption). Figure 1 (right) shows an example in which the foiled word is "dog". Solving this task requires some degree of compositional alignment between modalities, which is key for fine-grained visually grounded semantics.

4 Model Architecture and Training

In cognitive science, the hub module of Patterson and Ralph (2015) receives representations processed by sensory-specific spokes and computes a multimodal representation out of them. All our models have a common core that resembles this architecture, while incorporating some task-specific components. This allows us to investigate the impact of specific tasks on the multimodal representations computed by the representational hub, which is implemented as an encoder. Figure 2 shows a diagram of the shared model components, which we explain in detail below.

4.1 Shared components

To facilitate the comparison of the representations learned via the different tasks we consider, we use pre-trained visual and linguistic features to process the input given to the encoders. This provides a

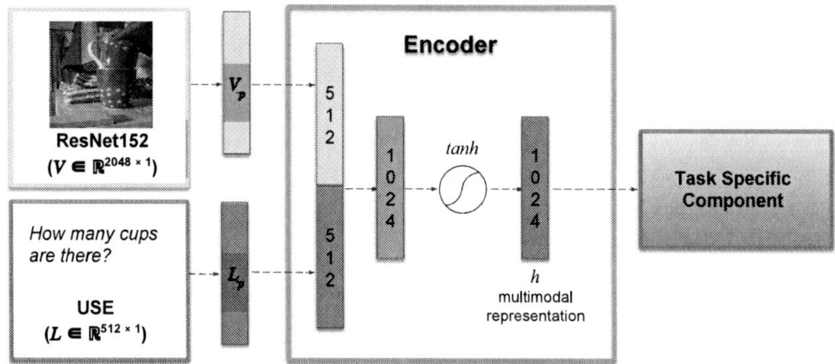

Figure 2: General model architecture, with an example from VQA as input. The encoder receives as input visual (ResNet152) and linguistic (USE) embeddings and merges them into a multimodal representation (h). This is passed on to a task-specific component: an MLP in the case of the pre-training retrieval tasks and a fully connected layer in the case of the FOIL classification task.

common initial base across models and diminishes the effects of using different datasets for each specific task (the datasets are described in Section 5).

Visual and language embeddings To represent visual data, we use ResNet152 features (He et al., 2016), which yield state of the art performance in image classification tasks and can be computed efficiently. To represent linguistic data, we use Universal Sentence Encoder (USE) vectors (Cer et al., 2018) since they yield near state-of-the-art results on several NLP tasks and are suitable both for short texts (such as the descriptions in ReferIt) and longer ones (such as the dialogues in GuessWhat).[2]

In order to gain some insight into the semantic spaces that emerge from these visual and linguistic representations, we consider a sample of 5K datapoints sharing the images across the three tasks and use average cosine similarity as a measure of space density. We find that the semantic space of the input images is denser (0.57 average cosine similarity) than the semantic space of the linguistic input across all tasks (average cosine similarity of 0.26 among VQA questions, 0.35 among ReferIt descriptions, and 0.49 among GuessWhat dialogues). However, when we consider the retrieval candidates rather than the input data, we find a different pattern: The linguistic semantic space of the candidate answers in VQA is much denser than the visual space of the candidate bounding boxes in ReferIt and GuessWhat (0.93 vs. 0.64 average cosine similarity, respectively). This suggests that the VQA task is harder, since the candidate answers are all highly similar.

Encoder As shown in Figure 2, ResNet152 visual features ($V \in \mathbb{R}^{2048 \times 1}$) and USE linguistic features ($L \in \mathbb{R}^{512 \times 1}$) are input in the model and passed through fully connected layers that project them onto spaces of the same dimensionality. The projected representations (V_p and L_p) are concatenated, passed through a linear layer, and then through a *tanh* activation function, which produces the final encoder representation h:

$$h = \tanh\left(W \cdot [V_p; L_p]\right) \tag{1}$$

where $W \in \mathbb{R}^{1024 \times 1024}$, $V_p \in \mathbb{R}^{512 \times 1}$, $L_p \in \mathbb{R}^{512 \times 1}$, and $[\cdot; \cdot]$ represents concatenation.

4.2 Task-specific components

The architecture described above is shared by all the models we experiment with, which thus differ only with respect to their task-specific component.

---

[2]The dialogues in the GuessWhat?! dataset consist of 4.93 question-answer pairs on average (de Vries et al., 2017).

Pre-training task component For the three tasks we consider, the final encoder representation h is given to a Multi-Layer Perceptron (MLP), which generates either a language embedding (VQA model) or a visual embedding (ReferIt and GuessWhat models). The three task-specific models are trained with a cosine similarity loss, which aims to get the generated embedding closer to the ground truth embedding and farther away from any other embeddings in the list of candidates. Details of how, for each datapoint, the list of candidates is selected are provided in Section 5. The embeddings of such candidates are obtained with USE (for VQA) and ResNet (for ReferIt and GuessWhat). As mentioned above, the high density of the VQA candidate answers' space makes the task rather hard.

FOIL task component To evaluate the encoder representations learned by the pre-trained models, the task-specific MLPs are replaced by a fully connected layer, which is trained on the FOIL task using a cross-entropy loss. We train the FOIL task component using the following settings:

- **Random$_2$** The encoder weights are randomly initialized and the FOIL classifier layer is untrained. This provides a lower-bound baseline with random performance.

- **Random** The encoder weights are randomly initialized and then frozen while the FOIL classifier layer is trained on the FOIL task. This provides a strong baseline that is directly comparable to the task-specific setting explained next.

- **Pre-trained (VQA, ReferIt, GuessWhat)** The encoder weights are initialized with the Random setting's seeds and the model is trained on each of the tasks. The weights of the task-specific encoders are then frozen and the FOIL classifier layer is trained on the FOIL task. With this setting, we are able to diagnose the transfer and encoding properties of the pre-trained tasks.

- **Fully trained on FOIL** The encoder weights are initialized with the Radom setting's seeds. Then the full model is trained on the FOIL task, updating the weights of the projected vision and language layers, the encoder, and the FOIL layer. This provides the upper bound on the FOIL classification performance, as the entire model is optimized for this task from the start.

5 Experimental Setup

We provide details on the data sets and the implementation settings we use in our experiments.

Pre-training datasets For the three visually grounded tasks, we use the VQA.v1 dataset by Antol et al. (2015), the RefCOCO dataset by Yu et al. (2016), and the GuessWhat?! dataset by de Vries et al. (2017) as our starting point. All these datasets have been developed with images from MS-COCO (Lin et al., 2014). We construct *common image* datasets for by taking the intersection of the images in the three original datasets. This results in a total of 14,458 images. An image can be part of several data points, i.e, it can be paired with more than one linguistic input. Indeed, the 14,458 common images correspond to 43,374 questions for the VQA task, 104,227 descriptions for the ReferIt task, and 35,467 dialogues for the GuessWhat task.

To obtain datasets of equal size per task that are as similar as possible, we filter the resulting data points according to the following procedure:

1. For each image, we check how many linguistic items are present in the three datasets and fix the minimum number (k) to be our target number of linguistic items paired with that image.

2. We select n data points where the descriptions in ReferIt and dialogues in GuessWhat concern the same target object (with $n \leq k$).

3. Among the n data points selected in the previous step, we select the m data points in VQA where the question or the answer mention the same target object (computed by string matching).

4. We make sure all the images in each task-specific dataset are paired with exactly k linguistic items; if not, we select additional ones randomly until this holds.

	common image datasets		FOIL dataset		
	training	validation	training	validation	testing
# images	13,058	1,400	63,240	13,485	20,105
# language	27,374	2,942	358,182	37,394	126,232

Table 1: Statistics of the datasets used for the pre-training tasks and the FOIL task.

This results in a total of 30,316 data points per dataset: 14,458 images shared across datasets, paired with 30,313 linguistic items. We randomly divided this *common image* dataset into training and validation sets at the image level. The training set consists of 13,058 images (paired with 27,374 linguistic items) and the validation set of 1,400 images (paired with 2,942 linguistic items). Table 1 provides an overview of the datasets.

As mentioned in Section 3, we operationalize the three tasks as retrieval tasks where the goal is to retrieve the correct item out of a set of candidates. In the VQA.v1 dataset (multiple choice version), there are 18 candidate answers per question. In GuessWhat?! there are on average 18.71 candidate objects per dialogue, all of them appearing in the image. We take the same list of candidate objects per image for the ReferIt task.

FOIL dataset   The FOIL dataset consists of image-caption pairs from MS-COCO and pairs where the caption has been modified by replacing a noun in the original caption with a foiled noun, such that the foiled caption is incongruent with the image—see Figure 1 for an example and Shekhar et al. (2017) for further details on the construction of the dataset.[3] The dataset contains 521,808 captions (358,182 in training, 37,394 in validation and 126,232 in test set) and 96,830 images (63,240, 13,485 and 20,105, in training, validation and test set, respectively) – see Table 1. All the images in the test set do not occur either in the FOIL training and validation set, nor in the common image dataset described above and used to pre-train the models.

Implementation details   All models are trained using supervised learning with ground truth data. We use the same parameters for all models: batch size of 256 and Adam optimizer (Kingma and Ba, 2014) with learning rate 0.0001. All the parameters are tuned on the validation set. Early stopping is used while training, i.e., training is stopped when there is no improvement on the validation loss for 10 consecutive epochs or a maximum of 100 epochs, and the best model is taken based on the validation loss.

6   Results and Analysis

We carry out two main blocks of analyses: one exploiting FOIL as diagnostic task and the other one investigating the structure of the semantic spaces produced by the pre-trained encoders when receiving the same multimodal inputs.

Before diving into the results of these analyses, we evaluate the three task-specific models on the tasks they have been trained for. Since these are retrieval tasks, we compute precision at rank 1 (P@1) on the validation sets and compare the results to chance performance. Given the number of candidate answers and objects per task in our datasets, chance P@1 is 0.055 for VQA and 0.05 for ReferIt and GuessWhat. Our task-specific models obtain P@1 values of 0.14 for VQA (mean rank 2.84), 0.12 for ReferIt (mean rank 3.32), and 0.08 for GuessWhat (mean rank 4.14). Not surprisingly given the challenging nature of these tasks, the results are not high. Nevertheless, the representations learned by the models allow them to perform above chance level and thus provide a reasonable basis for further investigation.

---

[3]Madhysastha et al. (2018) found that an earlier version of the FOIL dataset was biased. We have used the latest version of the dataset available at `https://foilunitn.github.io/`, which does not have this problem.

6.1 Analysis via diagnostic task

In this first analysis, we assess the quality of the multimodal representations learned by the three multimodal tasks considered in terms of their potential to perform the FOIL task, i.e., to spot semantic (in)congruence between an image and a caption. Besides comparing the models with respect to task accuracy, we also investigate how they learn to adapt to the FOIL task over training epochs, how much data they need to reach their best performance, and how confident they are about the decisions they make.

FOIL accuracy Table 2 shows accuracy results on the FOIL task for the different training settings described in Section 4.2. We report accuracy for the task overall, as well as accuracy on detecting original and foiled captions. As expected, the $Random_2$ setting yields chance performance ($\approx$50% overall, with a surprisingly strong preference for classifying captions as foiled). The model fully trained on FOIL achieves an accuracy of 67.59%. This confirms that the FOIL task is challenging, as shown by Shekhar et al. (2017), even for models that are optimized to solve it. The Random setting, where a randomly initialized encoder is trained on the FOIL task, yields 53.79% accuracy overall – higher than the chance lower bound by $Random_2$, but well below the upper bound set by the fully trained model.

The key results of interest for our purposes in this paper are those achieved by the models where the encoder has been pre-trained on each of the three multimodal tasks we study. We observe that, like the Random encoder, the pre-trained encoders achieve results well below the upper bound. The VQA encoder yields results comparable to Random, while ReferIt and GuessWhat achieve slightly higher results: 54.02% and 54.18%, respectively. This trend is much more noticeable when we zoom into the accuracy results on original vs. foiled captions. All models (except $Random_2$) achieve lower accuracy on the foil class than on the original class. However, the GuessWhat encoder performs substantially better than the rest: Its foil accuracy is not only well above the Random encoder, but also around 2% points over the fully trained model (49.34% vs. 47.52%). The ReferIt encoder also performs reasonably well (on a par with the fully trained model), while the VQA encoder is closer to Random.

This suggests that the ReferIt and the GuessWhat encoders do learn a small degree of multimodal understanding skills that can transfer to new tasks. The VQA encoder, in contrast, seems to lack this ability by and large.

	overall	original	foiled
$Random_2$	49.99	0.282	99.71
Random	53.79	65.33	42.25
VQA	53.78	66.09	41.48
ReferIt	54.02	60.39	47.66
GuessWhat	54.18	59.02	49.34
Fully FOIL	67.59	87.66	47.52

Table 2: Accuracy on the FOIL task for the best model of each training setting.

Learning over time In order to better understand the effect of the representations learned by the pre-trained encoders, we trace the evolution of the FOIL classification accuracy over time, i.e., over the first 50 training epochs. As shown in Figure 3a, all the pre-trained models start with higher accuracy than the Random model. This shows that the encoder is able to transfer knowledge from the pre-trained tasks to some extent. The Random model takes around 10 epochs to catch up and after that it does not manage to improve much. The evolution of the accuracy achieved by the ReferIt and GuessWhat encoders is relatively smooth, i.e., it increases progressively with further training epochs. The one by the VQA model, in contrast, is far less stable.

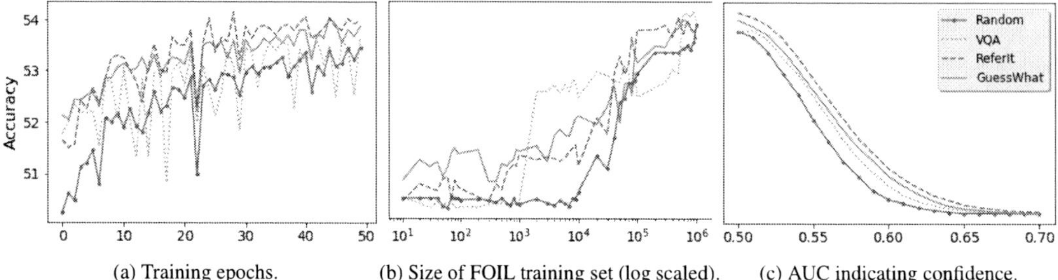

(a) Training epochs.   (b) Size of FOIL training set (log scaled).   (c) AUC indicating confidence.

Figure 3: Comparisons among the pre-trained encoders and the randomly initialized encoder, regarding their accuracy over training epochs, with varying data size, and across different decision thresholds.

Size of FOIL training data   Next, we evaluate how the accuracy achieved by the models changes when varying the size of the FOIL training set. By controlling the amount of training data, we can better tease apart whether the performance of the pre-trained models is due to the quality of the encoder representations or simply to the amount of training the models undergo on the FOIL task itself. Figure 3b gives an overview. The GuessWhat encoder has a clear advantage when very little training data is available, while the other encoders start at chance level. Both GuessWhat and ReferIt increase their accuracy relatively smoothly as more data is provided, while for the VQA model there is a big jump in accuracy once enough FOIL data is available. Again, this suggests that the representations learned by the GuessWhat encoder are of somewhat higher quality, with more transferable potential.

Confidence   Finally, we analyse the confidence of the models by measuring their Area Under the Curve (AUC). We gradually increase the classification threshold from 0.5 to 0.7 by an interval of 0.01. This measures the confidence of the classifier in making a prediction. As shown in Figure 3c, all models have rather low confidence (when the threshold is 0.7 they are all at chance level). The Random model exhibits the lowest confidence, while the ReferIt model is slightly more confident in its decisions than the rest, followed by the GuessWhat model.

6.2 Analysis of the multimodal semantic spaces learned by the encoders

In this section, we analyse the encoders by comparing the similarity of the multimodal spaces they learn and by comparing the learned multimodal spaces to the visual and linguistic representations they receive as input in terms on nearest neighbours.

Representation similarity analysis   Representation Similarity Analysis (RSA) is a technique from neuroscience (Kriegeskorte et al., 2008) that has been recently leveraged in computational linguistics, for example to compare the semantic spaces learned by artificial communicating agents (Bouchacourt and Baroni, 2018). It compares different semantic spaces by comparing their internal similarity relations, given a common set N of input data points. Each input $k \in N$ is processed by an encoder for a given task Ti, producing vector h_{Ti}^{k}. Let H_{Ti}^{N} be the set of vector representations created by the encoder of Ti for all the items in N; and let H_{Tj}^{N} be the corresponding set of representations by the encoder of task Tj. These two semantic spaces, H_{Ti}^{N} and H_{Tj}^{N}, are not directly comparable as they have been produced independently. RSA remedies this by instead comparing their structure in terms of internal similarity relations. By computing cosine similarity between all pairs of vectors within each semantic space, we obtain a vector of cosine similarities per space, which captures its internal structure. These similarity vectors have identical dimensionality, namely $N(N-1)/2$ values, and hence can be directly compared by computing Spearman correlation between them. The resulting RSA scores (corresponding to the aforementioned Spearman correlation coefficients) tell us the extent to which the two sets of representations are structurally similar.

218

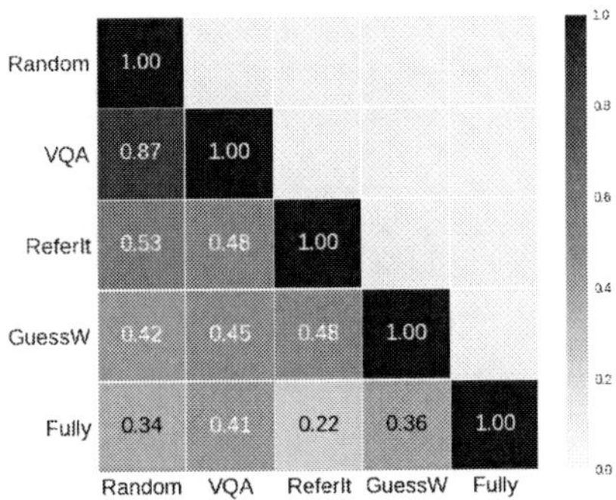

Figure 4: RSA scores indicating degree of structural similarity between the multimodal semantic spaces produced by the various encoders when receiving 5,000 data points from the FOIL test set consisting of unique images paired with their original captions.

The outputs of the encoders are compared when the same set of inputs is given. We give as input 5,000 data points from the FOIL test set, randomly sampled from only the ones with original captions and containing unique images, and compare the representations produced by the encoders under investigation. Figure 4 shows that the semantic space produced by the encoder fully trained on FOIL is rather different from all the other models, and that the VQA semantic space is very similar to the one produced by the randomly initialized encoder.

Nearest neighbour overlap   We analyse the encoder representations using nearest neighbour overlap. Collell and Moens (2018) proposed this measure to compare the structure of functions that map concepts from an input to a target space. It is defined as the number of k nearest neighbours that two paired vectors share in their respective semantic space. For instance, if $k = 3$ and the 3 nearest neighbours of the vector for 'cat' v_{cat} in space V are $\{v_{dog}, v_{tiger}, v_{lion}\}$, and those of the vector of 'cat' z_{cat} in space Z are $\{v_{mouse}, v_{tiger}, v_{lion}\}$, the nearest neighbour overlap (NN) is 2. The value is then normalized with respect to the number of data points and the number of k nearest neighbours.

	$k = 1$		$k = 10$	
	ResNet152	USE	ResNet152	USE
Random	0.829	0.363	0.876	0.365
VQA	0.638	0.350	0.703	0.386
ReferIt	0.754	0.346	0.780	0.366
GuessWhat	0.658	0.329	0.689	0.359
Fully FOIL	0.171	0.254	0.246	0.291

Table 3: Average nearest neighbour overlap between the encoder multimodal representations and the ResNet152 and USE embeddings, respectively.

We take the encoder to be a mapping function from each of the modality-specific representations to the multimodal space, and we use the NN measure to investigate whether the structure of the multimodal space produced by the encoder is closer to the visual ResNet152 embeddings or to the linguistic USE embeddings given as input. We use simple visual and language inputs, namely, objects and the word corresponding to their object category. We consider the 80 object categories of MS-COCO (e.g., dog, car, etc.) and obtain their USE representations. We build their visual ResNet152 embedding by selecting 100 images for each category from MS-COCO, and then compute their average. We compute the NN by setting $k = 1$ and $k = 10$. The results, given in Table 3, show that the multimodal spaces learned by all the models (except the model with the encoder fully trained on the FOIL task) are much closer to the visual input space than to the linguistic one. This behaviour could be related to the different density of the visual and linguistic semantic spaces of the input data we pointed out in Section 4.1, where we observed that input images have higher average cosine similarity than input questions, descriptions, and dialogues, respectively.

7 Conclusion

Our goal in this paper has been to evaluate the quality of the multimodal representations learned by an encoder—the core module of all the multimodal models used currently within the language and vision community—which resembles the cognitive representational hub described by Patterson and Ralph (2015). Furthermore, we investigated the transfer potential of the encoded skills, taking into account the amount of time (learning epochs) and training data the models need to adapt to a new task and with how much confidence they make their decisions. We studied three multimodal tasks, where the encoder is trained to answer a question about an image (VQA), pick up the object in an image referred to by a description (ReferIt), and identify the object in an image that is the target of a goal-oriented question-answer dialogue (GuessWhat). To carry out this analysis, we have evaluated how the pre-trained models perform on a diagnostic task, FOIL (Shekhar et al., 2017), designed to check the model's ability to detect semantic incongruence in visually grounded language.

Overall, we found that none of the three tasks under investigation leads to learning fine-grained multimodal understanding skills that can solve the FOIL task, although there are differences among tasks. Our analysis shows that the VQA task is easier to learn (the model achieves a rather high mean rank precision). However the multimodal encoding skills it learns are less stable and transferable than the ones learned through the ReferIt and GuessWhat tasks. This can be seen by the large amount of data the model has to be exposed to in order to learn the FOIL classification task and by the unstable results over training epochs. None of the models transfers their encoding skills with high confidence, but again the VQA model does it to a lower extent.

The RSA analysis confirms the higher similarity of the multimodal spaces generated by the ReferIt and GuessWhat encoders and the high similarity between the VQA space and the space produced by the randomly initialized encoder. From the NN analysis, it appears that for all models (except for the one fully trained on the FOIL task) the visual modality has higher weight than the linguistic one in the construction of the multimodal representations.

These differences among tasks could be due to subtle parallelisms with the diagnostic task: ReferIt and GuessWhat may resemble some aspects of FOIL, since these three tasks revolve around objects (the foiled word is always a noun), while arguably the VQA task is more diverse as it contains questions about, e.g., actions, attributes, or scene configurations. In future work, it would be interesting to evaluate the models on different diagnostic datasets that prioritise skills other than object identification.

Acknowledgements

We kindly acknowledge the Leibniz-Zentrum für Informatik, Dagstuhl Seminar 19021 on *Joint Processing of Language and Visual Data for Better Automated Understanding*. The Amsterdam team was partially funded by the Netherlands Organisation for Scientific Research (NWO) under VIDI grant nr. 276-89-008, *Asymmetry in Conversation*. We gratefully acknowledge the support of NVIDIA Corporation with the donation to the University of Trento of the GPUs used in our research.

References

Adi, Y., E. Kermany, Y. Belinkov, O. Lavi, and Y. Goldberg (2017). Fine-grained Analysis of Sentence Embeddings Using Auxiliary Prediction Tasks. In *International Conference on Learning Representations (ICLR)*.

Alishahi, A., M. Barking, and G. Chrupała (2017). Encoding of phonology in a recurrent neural model of grounded speech. In *Proceedings of the 21st Conference on Computational Natural Language Learning (CoNLL 2017)*, pp. 368–378. Association for Computational Linguistics.

Antol, S., A. Agrawal, J. Lu, M. Mitchell, D. Batra, C. L. Zitnick, and D. Parikh (2015). VQA: Visual question answering. In *International Conference on Computer Vision (ICCV)*.

Barrault, L., F. Bougares, L. Specia, C. Lala, D. Elliott, and S. Frank (2018). Findings of the third shared task on multimodal machine translation. In *Proceedings of the Third Conference on Machine Translation (WMT)*, Volume 2, pp. 304323. Association for Computational Linguistics.

Bouchacourt, D. and M. Baroni (2018). How agents see things: On visual representations in an emergent language game. In *Proceedings of the 2018 Conference on Empirical Methods in Natural Language Processing*, pp. 981–985. Association for Computational Linguistics.

Cer, D., Y. Yang, S.-y. Kong, N. Hua, N. Limtiaco, R. S. John, N. Constant, M. Guajardo-Cespedes, S. Yuan, C. Tar, et al. (2018). Universal sentence encoder. *arXiv preprint arXiv:1803.11175*.

Collell, G. and M.-F. Moens (2018). Do neural network cross-modal mappings really bridge modalities? *arXiv preprint arXiv:1805.07616*.

Conneau, A., D. Kiela, H. Schwenk, L. Barrault, and A. Bordes (2017). Supervised learning of universal sentence representations from natural language inference data. In *Proceedings of the 2017 Conference on Empirical Methods in Natural Language Processing*, pp. 670–680.

Conneau, A., G. Kruszewski, G. Lampl, L. Barrault, and M. Baroni (2018). What you can cram into a single \\$&!#* vector: Probing sentence embeddings for linguistic properties. In *Proceedings of ACL*.

Das, A., S. Kottur, K. Gupta, A. Singh, D. Yadav, J. M. Moura, D. Parikh, and D. Batra (2017). Visual Dialog. In *Proceedings of the IEEE Conference on Computer Vision and Pattern Recognition*.

de Vries, H., F. Strub, S. Chandar, O. Pietquin, H. Larochelle, and A. C. Courville (2017). Guesswhat?! Visual object discovery through multi-modal dialogue. In *Conference on Computer Vision and Pattern Recognition (CVPR)*.

Dobnik, S., M. Ghanimifard, and J. D. Kelleher (2018). Exploring the functional and geometric bias of spatial relations using neural language models. In *Proceedings of the First International Workshop on Spatial Language Understanding (SpLu)*, pp. 1–11.

He, K., X. Zhang, S. Ren, and J. Sun (2016). Deep residual learning for image recognition. In *Proceedings of the IEEE conference on computer vision and pattern recognition*, pp. 770–778.

Johnson, J., B. Hariharan, L. van der Maaten, L. Fei-Fei, C. L. Zitnick, and R. Girshick (2017). Clevr: A diagnostic dataset for compositional language and elementary visual reasoning. In *Proceedings of CVPR 2017*.

Kazemzadeh, S., V. Ordonez, M. Matten, and T. L. Berg (2014). Referit game: Referring to objects in photographs of natural scenes. In *EMNLP*.

Kingma, D. P. and J. Ba (2014). Adam: A method for stochastic optimization. *arXiv preprint arXiv:1412.6980*.

Kriegeskorte, N., M. Mur, and P. A. Bandettini (2008). Representational similarity analysis-connecting the branches of systems neuroscience. *Frontiers in systems neuroscience 2*, 4.

Lin, T.-Y., M. Maire, S. Belongie, J. Hays, P. Perona, D. Ramanan, Dollar, P., and C. L. Zitnick (2014). Microsoft COCO: Common objects in context. In *Proceedings of ECCV (European Conference on Computer Vision)*.

Linzen, T., E. Dupoux, and Y. Goldberg (2016). Assessing the Ability of LSTMs to Learn Syntax-Sensitive Dependencies. *Transactions of the Association for Computational Linguistics 4*, 521–535.

Madhysastha, P., J. Wang, and L. Specia (2018). Defoiling foiled image captions. In *Conference of the North American Chapter of the Association for Computational Linguistics: Human Language Technologies*, New Orleans, LA.

Mostafazadeh, N., I. Misra, J. Devlin, M. Mitchell, X. He, and L. Vanderwende (2016, August). Generating natural questions about an image. In *Proceedings of the 54th Annual Meeting of the Association for Computational Linguistics (Volume 1: Long Papers)*, Berlin, Germany, pp. 1802–1813. Association for Computational Linguistics.

Patterson, K. and M. A. L. Ralph (2015). *Neurobiology of Language*, Chapter The Hub-and-Spoke Hypothesis of Semantic Memory. Elsevier.

Razavian, A. S., H. Azizpour, J. Sullivan, and S. Carlsson (2014). CNN features off-the-shelf: an astounding baseline for recognition. In *Proceedings of the IEEE Conference on Computer Vision and Pattern Recognition Workshops*, pp. 806–813.

Shekhar, R., S. Pezzelle, Y. Klimovich, A. Herbelot, M. Nabi, E. Sangineto, and R. Bernardi (2017). "foil it! find one mismatch between image and language caption". In *Proceedings of the 55th Annual Meeting of the Association for Computational Linguistics (ACL) (Volume 1: Long Papers)*, pp. 255–265.

Suhr, A., M. Lewis, J. Yeh, and Y. Artzi (2017, July). A corpus of natural language for visual reasoning. In *Proceedings of the Annual Meeting of the Association for Computational Linguistics*, Vancouver, Canada, pp. 217–223. Association for Computational Linguistics.

Wieting, J. and D. Kiela (2019). No training required: Exploring random encoders for sentence classification. In *ICLR (accepted)*.

Yu, L., P. Poirson, S. Yang, A. C. Berg, and T. L. Berg (2016). Modeling context in referring expressions. In *European Conference on Computer Vision*, pp. 69–85. Springer.

Zhang, K. W. and S. R. Bowman (2018). Language modeling teaches you more syntax than translation does: Lessons learned through auxiliary task analysis. In *Proceedings of the 2018 EMNLP Workshop BlackboxNLP: Analyzing and Interpreting Neural Networks for NLP*, pp. 359–361. Association for Computational Linguistics.

The Fast and the Flexible: Training Neural Networks to Learn to Follow Instructions from Small Data

Rezka Leonandya
University of Amsterdam
rezka.aufar@gmail.com

Dieuwke Hupkes
University of Amsterdam
d.hupkes@uva.nl

Elia Bruni
University of Amsterdam
elia.bruni@gmail.com

Germán Kruszewski
Facebook AI
germank@gmail.com

Abstract

Learning to follow human instructions is a long-pursued goal in artificial intelligence. The task becomes particularly challenging if no prior knowledge of the employed language is assumed while relying only on a handful of examples to learn from. Work in the past has relied on hand-coded components or manually engineered features to provide strong inductive biases that make learning in such situations possible. In contrast, here we seek to establish whether this knowledge can be acquired automatically by a neural network system through a two phase training procedure: A (slow) offline learning stage where the network learns about the general structure of the task and a (fast) online adaptation phase where the network learns the language of a new given speaker. Controlled experiments show that when the network is exposed to familiar instructions but containing novel words, the model adapts very efficiently to the new vocabulary. Moreover, even for human speakers whose language usage can depart significantly from our artificial training language, our network can still make use of its automatically acquired inductive bias to learn to follow instructions more effectively.

1 Introduction

Learning to follow instructions from human speakers is a long-pursued goal in artificial intelligence, tracing back at least to Terry Winograd's work on SHRDLU (Winograd, 1972). This system was capable of interpreting and following natural language instructions about a world composed of geometric figures. While this first system relied on a set of hand-coded rules to process natural language, most of recent work aimed at using machine learning to map linguistic utterances into their semantic interpretations (Chen and Mooney, 2011; Artzi and Zettlemoyer, 2013; Andreas and Klein, 2015). Predominantly, they assumed that users speak all in the same natural language, and thus the systems could be trained offline once and for all. However, recently Wang et al. (2016) departed from this assumption by proposing SHRDLURN, a coloured-blocks manipulation language game. There, users could issue instructions in any arbitrary language to a system that must incrementally learn to interpret it (see Figure 1 for an example). This learning problem is particularly challenging because human users typically provide only a handful of examples for the system to learn from. Therefore, the learning algorithms must incorporate strong inductive biases in order to learn effectively. That is, they need to complement the scarce input with priors that would help the model make the right inferences even in the absence of positive data. A way of giving the models a powerful inductive bias is by hand-coding features or operations that are specific to the given domain where the instructions must be interpreted. For example, Wang et al. (2016) propose a log-linear semantic parser which crucially relies on a set of hand-coded functional primitives. While effective, this strategy severely curtails the portability of a system: For every new domain, human technical expertise is required to adapt the system. Instead, we would like these inductive biases to be learned automatically without human intervention. That is, humans should be free from the burden of

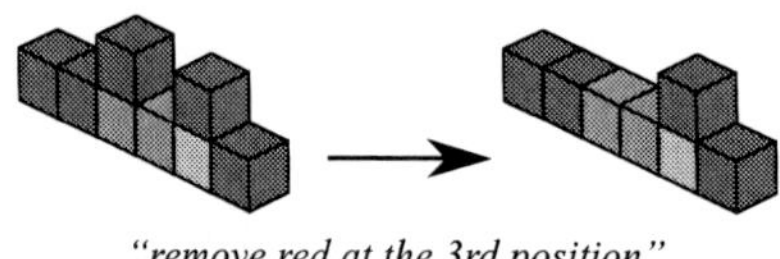

Figure 1: Illustration of the SHRDLURN task of Wang et al. (2016)

thinking what are useful primitives for a given domain, but still obtain systems that can learn fast from little data.

In this paper, we introduce a neural network system that learns domain-specific priors directly from data. This system can then be used to quickly learn the language of new users online. It uses a two phase regime: First, the network is trained *offline* on easy-to-produce artificial data to learn the mechanics of a given task. Next, the network is deployed to real human users who will train it *online* with just a handful of examples. While this implies that some of the manual effort needed to design useful primitive functions would go in developing the artificial data, we envision that in many real-world situations it could be easier to provide examples of expected interactions than thinking of what could be useful primitives involved in them. On controlled experiments we show that our system can recover the meaning of sentences where some words where scrambled, even though it does not display evidence of compositional learning. On the other hand, we show that the offline training phase allows it to learn faster from limited data, compared to a neural network system that did not go through this pre-training phase. We hypothesize that this system learns useful inductive biases, such as the types of operations that are likely to be requested. In this direction, we show that the performance of our best-performing system correlates with that of Wang et al., where these operations were encoded by hand.

The work in this paper is organized as follows: We first start by creating a large artificially generated dataset to train the systems in the offline phase. We then experiment with different neural network architectures to find which general learning system adapts best for this task. Then, we propose how to adapt this network by training it online and confirm its effectiveness on recovering the meaning of scrambled words and on learning to process the language from human users, using the dataset introduced by Wang et al. (2016).

2 Related Work

Learning to follow human natural language instructions has a long tradition in NLP, dating at least back to the work of Terry Winograd Winograd (1972), who developed a rule-based system for this endeavour. Subsequent work centered around automatically learning the rules to process language (Shimizu and Haas, 2009; Chen and Mooney, 2011; Artzi and Zettlemoyer, 2013; Vogel and Jurafsky, 2010; Andreas and Klein, 2015). This line of work assumes that users speak all in the same language, and thus a system can be trained on a set of dialogs pertaining to some of those speakers and then generalize to new ones. Instead, Wang et al. (2016) describe a block manipulation game in which a system needs to learn to follow natural language instructions produced by human users using the correct outcome of the instruction as feedback. What distinguishes this from other work is that every user can speak in their own –natural or invented– language. For the game to remain engaging, the system needs to quickly adapt to the user's language, thus requiring a system that can learn much faster from small data. The system they propose is composed of a set of hand-coded primitives (e.g., `remove`, `red`, `with`) that can manipulate the state of the block piles and a log-linear learning model that learns to map n-gram features from the linguistic instructions (like, for instance, '*remove red*') to expressions in this programming language (e.g., `remove(with(red))`). Our work departs from this base in that we provide no hand-coded primitives to solve this task, but aim at learning an end-to-end system that follows natural language instructions from human feedback. Another line of research that is closely related to ours, is that of *fast mapping* (Lake et al., 2011; Trueswell et al., 2013; Herbelot and Baroni, 2017), where the goal is to acquire a new concept from a single example of its usage in context. While we don't aim at learning

```
S      →      VERB COLOR at POS tile
VERB   →             add | remove
COLOR  →      red | cyan | brown | orange
POS    →      1st | 2nd | 3rd | 4th |
              5th | 6th | even | odd |
          leftmost | rightmost | every
```

(a) Grammar of our artificially generated language

```
Instruction     remove red at 3rd tile
Initial Config.  BROWN X X # RED X X # ORANGE RED X
Target Config.   BROWN X X # RED X X # ORANGE X X
```

(b) Example of an entry in our dataset. We show three rather than six columns for conciseness.

Figure 2: Artificially generated data

new concepts here, we do want to learn from few examples to draw an analogy between a new term and a previously acquired concept. Finally, our work can be seen as an instance of the transfer learning paradigm (Pan and Yang, 2010), which has been successful in both linguistic (Mikolov et al., 2013; Peters et al., 2018) and visual processing (Oquab et al., 2014). Rather than transferring knowledge from one task to another, we are transferring between artificial and natural data.

3   Method

A model aimed at following natural language instructions must master at least two skills. First, it needs to process the language of the human user. Second, it must act on the target domain in sensible ways (and not trying actions that a human user would probably never ask for). Whereas the first aspect is dependent on each specific user's language, the second requirement is not related to a specific user, and could – as illustrated by the successes of Wang et al.'s log-linear model – be learned beforehand. To allow a system to acquire these skills automatically from data, we introduce a two-step training regime. First, we train the neural network model offline on a dataset that mimics the target task. Next, we allow this model to independently adapt to the language of each particular human user by training it online with the examples that each user provides.

3.1   Offline learning phase

The task at hand is, given a list of piles of coloured blocks and a natural language instruction, to produce a new list of piles that matches the request. The first step of our method involves training a neural network model to perform this task. We used supervised learning to train the system on a dataset that we constructed by simulating a user playing the game. In this way, we did not require any real data to kick-start our model. Below we describe, first, the procedure used to generate the dataset and, second, the neural network models that were explored in this phase.

Data   The data for SHRDLURN task takes the form of triples: a start configuration of colored blocks grouped into piles, a natural language instruction given by a user and the resulting configuration of colored blocks that comply with the given instruction[1] (Figure 1). We generated 88 natural language instructions following the grammar in Figure 2a. The language of the grammar was kept as minimal as possible, with just enough variation to capture the simplest possible actions in this game. Furthermore, we sampled as many as needed initial block configurations by building 6 piles containing a maximum of 3 randomly sampled colored blocks each. The piles in the dataset were serialized into a sequence by encoding them into 6 lists delimited by a special symbol, each of them containing a sequence of color tokens or a special `empty` symbol. We then computed the resulting target configuration using a rule-based interpretation of our grammar. An example of our generated data is depicted in Figure 2b.

---

[1] The original paper produces a rank of candidate configurations to give to a human annotator. Since here we focus on pre-annotated data where only the expected target configuration is given, we will restrict our evaluation to top-1 accuracy.

Model   To model this task we used an encoder-decoder (Sutskever et al., 2014) architecture: The encoder reads the natural language utterance $\mathbf{w} = w_1, \ldots, w_m$ and transforms it into a sequence of feature vectors $\mathbf{h_1}, \ldots, \mathbf{h_m}$, which are then read by the decoder through an attention layer. This latter module reads the sequence describing the input block configurations $\mathbf{x} = x_1, \ldots, x_n$ and produces a new sequence $\hat{\mathbf{y}} = \hat{y}_1, \ldots, \hat{y}_n$ that is construed as the resulting block configuration. To pass information from the encoder to the decoder, we equipped the decoder with an attention mechanism (Bahdanau et al., 2014; Luong et al., 2015). This allows the decoder, at every timestep, to extract a convex combination of the hidden vectors $\mathbf{h}$. We trained the system parameters $\theta = (\theta_{\text{enc}}, \theta_{\text{dec}})$ so that the output matches the target block configuration $\mathbf{y} = y_1, \ldots, y_n$ (represented as 1-hot vectors) using a cross-entropy loss:

$$\mathbf{h} = \text{encoder}_{\theta_{\text{enc}}}(\mathbf{w})$$

$$\hat{\mathbf{y}} = \text{decoder}_{\theta_{\text{dec}}}(\mathbf{x}|\mathbf{h})$$

$$\mathcal{L}(\mathbf{y}, \hat{\mathbf{y}}) = \sum_{i=1}^{n} y_i \log \hat{y}_i$$

Both the encoder and decoder modules are sequence models, meaning that they read a sequence of inputs and compute, in turn, a sequence of outputs, and that can be trained end-to-end. We experimented with two state-of-the-art sequence models: A standard recurrent LSTM (Hochreiter and Schmidhuber, 1997) and a convolutional sequence model (Gehring et al., 2016, 2017), which has been shown to outperform the former on a range of different tasks (Bai et al., 2018). For the convolutional model we used kernel size $k = 3$ and padding to make the size of the output match the size of the input sequence. Because of the invariant structure of the block configuration that is organized into lists of columns, we expected the convolutional model (as a decoder) to be particularly well-fit to process them. We explored all possible combinations of architectures for the encoder and decoder components. Furthermore, as a simple baseline, we also considered a bag-of-words encoder that computes the average of trainable word embeddings.

3.2   Online learning phase

Once the model has been trained to follow a specific set of instructions given by a simulated user, we want it to serve a new, real user, who does not know anything about how the model was trained and is encouraged to communicate with the system using her own language. To do so, the model will have to adapt to follow instructions given in a potentially very different language from the one it has seen during offline training. One of the first challenges it will encounter is to quickly master the meaning of new words. This challenge of inferring the meaning of a word from a single exposure goes by the name of 'fast-mapping' (Lake et al., 2011; Trueswell et al., 2013). Here, we take inspiration from the method proposed by Herbelot and Baroni (2017), who learn the embeddings for new words with gradient descent, freezing all the other network weights. We further develop it by experimenting with different variations of this method: Like them, we try learning only *new* word embeddings, but also learning the full embedding layer (thus allowing words seen during offline training to shift their meaning). Additionally, we test what happens when the full encoder weights are unfrozen, allowing to adapt not only the embeddings but also how they are processed sequentially. In the latter two cases, we incorporate L_2 regularization over the embeddings and the model weights.

Human users interact with the system by asking it in their own language to perform transformations on the colored block piles, providing immediate feedback on what was the intended target configuration.[2] In our system, each new example that the model observes is added to a buffer B. Then, the model is further trained with a fixed number of gradient descent steps S on predicting the correct output using examples randomly drawn from a subset $B_{\text{TR}} \subseteq B$ of this buffer.

In order to reduce the impact of local minima that the model could encounter when learning from just a handful of examples, we train k different copies (rather than training a single model) each with

---

[2]In our experiments, we use pre-recorded data from Wang et al. (2016).

a set of differently initialized embeddings for new words. In this way, we can pick the best model to make a future prediction, not only based on how well it has fitted previously seen data, but also by how well it generalizes to other examples. For choosing which model to use, we use a different (not necessarily disjoint) subset of examples called $B_{\text{VA}} \subseteq B$. We experimented with two model selection strategies: **greedy**, by which we pick the model with the lowest loss computed over the full training buffer examples ($B_{\text{VA}} = B_{\text{TR}} = B$); and **1-out**, where we save the last example for validation and pick the model that has the lowest loss on that example ($B_{\text{VA}} = B[\text{LAST}]$, $B_{\text{TR}} = B[0 : \text{LAST} - 1]$)[3]. Algorithm 1 summarizes our approach.

Algorithm 1 Online Training

1: Initialize models $m_1, \ldots, m_k$
2: Let B be an empty training buffer
3: **for** $t = 1,2,...,T$ **do**
4:     Observe the input utterance $\mathbf{w}_t$ and block configuration $\mathbf{x}_t$
5:     SELECT best model m_i using data B_{VA}
6:     Predict $\hat{\mathbf{y}}_t = m_i(\mathbf{w}_t, \mathbf{x}_t)$
7:     Observe feedback $\mathbf{y}_t$.
8:     Record prediction accuracy ($\mathbf{y}_t == \hat{\mathbf{y}}_t$)
9:     Add ($\mathbf{w}_t, \mathbf{x}_t, \mathbf{y}_t$) to B
10:     TRAIN $m_1, \ldots, m_k$ on data B_{TR}
11: **procedure** SELECT($m_1, \ldots, m_k, B_{\text{VA}}$)
12:     Let $C_i \leftarrow \sum_{(\mathbf{w},\mathbf{x},\mathbf{y}) \in B_{\text{VA}}} \mathcal{L}(\mathbf{y}, m_i(\mathbf{w}, \mathbf{x}))$
13:     **return** m_i having minimal C_i
14: **procedure** TRAIN($m_1, \ldots, m_k, B_{\text{TR}}$)
15:     **for** $i = 1, \ldots, k, s = 1, \ldots, S$ **do**
16:         Draw $\mathbf{w}, \mathbf{x}, \mathbf{y} \sim B_{\text{TR}}$
17:         Predict $\hat{\mathbf{y}}_t = m_i(\mathbf{w}_t, \mathbf{x}_t)$
18:         Compute $\nabla_{\theta_i} \mathcal{L}(\mathbf{y}, \hat{\mathbf{y}}_t)$
19:         Update m_i by a gradient step on θ_i

---

4 Experiments

We seek to establish whether we can train a neural network system to learn the rules and structure of a task while communicating with a scripted teacher and then having it adapt to the particular nuances of each human user. We tackled this question incrementally. First, we explored what is the best architectural choice for solving the SHRDLURN task on our large artificially-constructed dataset. Next, we ran multiple controlled experiments to investigate the adaptation skills of our online learning system. In particular, we first tested whether the model was able to recover the original meaning of a word that had been replaced with a new arbitrary symbol – e.g. *"red"* becomes *"roze"*– on an online training regime. Finally, we proceeded to learn from real human utterances using the dataset collected by Wang et al. (2016).

4.1 Offline training

We used the data generation method described in the previous section to construct a dataset to train our neural network systems. To evaluate the models in a challenging compositional setting, rather than producing a random split of the data, we create validation and test sets that have no overlap with training instructions or block configurations. To this end, we split all the 88 possible utterances that can be generated from our grammar into 66 utterances for training, 11 for validation and 11 for testing. Similarly, we split all possible 85 combinations that make a valid column of blocks into 69 combinations for training,

---

[3]Other than these, there is wealth of methods in the literature for model selection (see, e.g. Claeskens et al., 2008). To limit the scope of this work, we leave this exploration for future work.

Model	Val. Accuracy	Test Accuracy
seq2seq	78	79
seq2conv	**99**	**100**
conv2seq	73	67
conv2conv	64	74
bow2seq	57	63

Table 1: Model's accuracies (in percentages) evaluated on block configurations and utterances that were completely unseen during offline training. Results expressed in percentages.

8 for validation and 8 for testing, sampling input block configurations using combinations of 6 columns pertaining only to the relevant set. In this way, we generated 42000 instances for training, 4000 for validation and 4000 for testing.

We explored all possible combinations of encoder and decoder models: LSTM encoder and LSTM decoder (**seq2seq**), LSTM encoder and convolutional decoder (**seq2conv**), convolutional encoder and LSTM decoder (**conv2seq**), and both convolutional encoder and decoder (**conv2conv**). Furthermore, we explored a bag of words encoder with an LSTM decoder (**bow2seq**). We trained 5 models with our generated dataset and use the best performing for the following experiments. We conducted a hyperparameter search for all these models, exploring the number of layers (1 or 2 for LSTMs, 4 or 5 for the convolutional network), the size of the hidden layer (32, 64, 128, 256) and dropout rate (0, 0.2, 0.5). For each model, we picked the hyperparameters that maximized accuracy on our validation set and report validation and test accuracy in Table 1.

As it can be noticed, seq2conv is the best model for this task by a large margin, performing perfectly or almost perfectly on this challenging test split featuring only unseen utterances and block configurations. Furthermore, this validates our hypothesis that the convolutional decoder is better fitted to process the structure of the block piles.

4.2 Recovering corrupted words

Next, we ask whether our system could adapt quickly to controlled variations in the language. To test this, we presented the model with a simulated user producing utterances drawn from the same grammar as before, but where some words have been systematically corrupted so the model cannot recognize them anymore. We then evaluated the model on whether it can recover the meaning of these words during online training. For this experiment, we combined the validation and test sections of our dataset, containing in all 22 different utterances, to make sure that the presented utterances were completely unseen during training time. We then split the vocabulary in two disjoint sets of words that we want to corrupt, one for validation and one for testing. For validation, we take one verb ("add"), 2 colors ("orange" and "red"), and 4 positions ("1st", "3rd; ; "5th" and "even"), keeping the remaining alternatives for testing. We then extracted a set of 15 utterances containing these words and corrupted each occurrence of them by replacing them with a new token (consistently keeping the same new token for each occurrence of the word). In this way, we obtained a validation set where we can calibrate hyper-parameters for all the test conditions that we describe below. We further extracted, for each of these utterances, 3 block configurations to pair them with, resulting in a simulated session with 45 instruction examples. For testing, we created controlled sessions where we corrupted: one single word, two words of different type (e.g. verb and color), three words of different types and finally, all words from the test set vocabulary[45]. Each condition allows for different a number of sessions because of the number of ways one can chose words from these sets. By keeping the two vocabularies disjoint we make sure that by optimizing the hyperparameters of our online training scheme, we don't happen to be good at recovering words from a particular subset.

We use the validation set to calibrate the hyperparameters of the online training routine. In particular,

---

[4]We also experimented with different types of corrupted words (verbs, colors or position numerals) but we found no obvious differences between them.

[5]The dataset is available with the supplementary materials at `https://github.com/rezkaaufar/fast-and-flexible`.

we vary the optimization algorithm to use (Adam or SGD), the number of training steps (100, 200 or 500), the regularization weight $(0, 10^{-2}, 10^{-3}, 10^{-4})$, the learning rate $(10^{-1}, 10^{-2}, 10^{-3})$, and the model selection strategy (greedy or 1-out), while keeping the number of model parameters that are trained in parallel fixed to $k = 7$. For this particular experiment, we considered learning only the embeddings for the new words, leaving all the remaining weights frozen (model **1**). To assess the relative merits of this model, we compared it with ablated versions where the encoder has been randomly initialized but the decoder is kept fixed (model **2**) and a fully randomly initialized model (model **3**). Furthermore, we evaluated the impact of having multiple ($k = 7$) concurrently trained model parameters by comparing it with just having a single set of parameters trained (model **4**). We report the best hyperparameters for each model in the supplementary materials. We use online accuracy as our figure of merit, computed as $\frac{1}{T} \sum_{t=1}^{T} \mathbb{I}[\hat{\mathbf{y}}_t == \mathbf{y}_t]$, where T is the length of the session. We report the results in Table 2.

	Transfer	Adapt	N. of corrupted words			
			1	2	3	all
	$k = 7$					
1.	Enc+Dec	Emb.	90.9	**88.1**	**86.1**	**73.3**
2.	Dec.	Enc.	**93.8**	85.9	82.4	55.5
3.	∅	Enc + Dec	43.3	35.5	36.1	36.7
	$k = 1$					
4.	Enc+Dec	Emb.	86.1	84.3	81.8	55

Table 2: Online accuracies (in percentages) for the word recovery task averaged over 7 sessions for 1 word, 17 for 2 words, 10 for 3 words and a single interaction for the all words condition, having 45 instructions each. "Transfer" stands for the components whose weights were saved (and not reinitialized) from the offline training. "Adapt" stands for the components whose weights get updated during the online training.

First, we can see that –perhaps not too surprisingly– the model that adapts only the word embeddings performs best overall. Notably, it can reach 73% accuracy even when all words have been corrupted (whereas, for example, the model of Wang et al. (2016) obtains 55% on the same task). The only exception comes in the single corrupted word condition, where re-learning the full encoder seems to be performing even better. A possible explanation is given by the discrepancy between this condition and the validation set, which was more akin to the "all" condition, resulting in suboptimal hyperparameters for the condition with a single word changed. Nevertheless, it is encouraging to see that the model can quickly learn to perform the instructions even in the most challenging setting where all words have been changed. In addition, we can observe the usefulness of having multiple sets of parameters trained, by comparing the "Embeddings" models by default trained with $k = 7$ models and when $k = 1$, noting that the former is consistently better.

4.3 Adapting to human speakers

Having established our model's ability to recover the meaning of masked known concepts, albeit in similar contexts as those seen seen during training, we moved to the more challenging setting where the model needs to adapt to real human speakers. In this case, the language can significantly depart from the one seen during the offline learning phase, both in surface form and in their underlying semantics. For these experiments we used the dataset made available by Wang et al. (2016), collected from turkers playing SHRDLURN in collaboration with their log-linear/symbolic model. The dataset contains 100 sessions with nearly 8k instruction examples. We first selected three sessions in this dataset to produce a validation set to tune the online learning hyperparameters. All the remaining 97 sessions were left for testing. In order to assess the relative importance of our pre-training procedure on each of our model's components, we explored 6 different variants of our model. On one hand, we varied which set of pre-trained weights were kept without reinitializing them: **(a)** All the weights in the encoder plus all the weights of the decoder; **(b)** only the decoder weights while randomly initializing the encoder; or **(c)** no weights and thus, resetting them all (this taking the role of a baseline for our method). On the other hand, we explored which subset of weights we adapt, leaving all the rest frozen: **(1)** Only the word embeddings[6], **(2)** the full weights of the encoder or **(3)** the full network (both encoder and decoder). Among the 9 possible combinations, we restricted to the 6 that wouldn't result on random components not being updated (for example (c-2) would result in a model with a randomly initialized decoder that is never trained), thus leaving out (c-1), (c-2) and (b-1). For each of the remaining 6 valid training regimes, we ran an independent hyperparameter search choosing from the same pool of candidate values as in the word recovery task (see Section 4.2). We picked the hyperparameter configuration that maximized the average online accuracy on the three validation sessions. The best hyperparameters are reported on the supplementary materials.

| | | **Adapt** | | | | | |
| | | (1) Embeddings | | (2) Encoder | | (3) Encoder+Decoder | |
		acc.	r	acc.	r	acc.	r
Reuse	(c) Nothing (Random)	-	-	-	-	13.5	0.58
	(b) Decoder (Random Encoder)	-	-	**23**	0.83	21	0.7
	(a) Encoder + Decoder	18.2	0.74	22.6	**0.84**	21.3	0.72

Table 3: For each (valid) combination of set of weights to re-use and weights to adapt online, we report average online accuracy on Wang et al. (2016) dataset and pearson-r correlation between online accuracies obtained by our model and those reported by the author. Results obtained on 220 sessions, with about 39 ± 31 interactions each.

We then evaluated each of the model variants on the 97 interactions in our test set using average online accuracy as figure of merit. Furthermore, we also computed the correlation between the online accuracy obtained by our model on every single session and that obtained by Wang et al.'s system which was endowed with hand-coded functions. The higher the correlation, the more our model behaves in a similar fashion to theirs, learning or failing to do so on the same sessions.

The results of these experiments are displayed in Table 3.

In the first place, we observe that models using knowledge acquired in the offline training phase (rows a and b) perform (in terms of accuracy) better than a randomly initialized model (c-3), confirming the effectiveness of our offline training phase. Second, a randomly initialized encoder with a fixed decoder (b-2) performs slightly better than the pre-trained one (a-2). This result suggests that the model is better off ignoring the specifics of our artificial grammar[7] and learning the language from scratch, even from very few examples. Therefore, no manual effort is required to reflect the specific surface form of a user's language when training the system offline on artificial data. Finally, we observe that the models that perform the best are those in column (2) which adapt the encoder weights and freeze the decoder ones. This is congruent to what would be expected if the decoder is implementing task-specific knowledge because the task has remained invariant between the two phases and thus, the components presumedly related to solving it should not need to change. Interestingly, variants in these column also correlate the most with the symbolic system. Moreover, performance scores seem to be strongly aligned with the correlation coefficients. As a matter of fact the 7 entries of online accuracy and pearson r are themselves correlated with $r = 0.99$, which is highly significant even for these few data points. This result is compatible with our hypothesis that the symbolic system carries learning biases which, the better our models are at capturing, the better they will perform in the end task. Still, evidence for our hypothesis, based both on the effectiveness of the pre-training step and on the fact that similar systems should succeed and fail on similar situations, is still indirect. We leave for future work the interesting

---

[6]Here we report adapting the full embedding layer, which for this particular experiment performed better than just adapting the embeddings for new words.

[7]Recall that the encoder is the component that reads and interprets the user language, while the decoder processes the block configurations conditioned on the information extracted by the encoder.

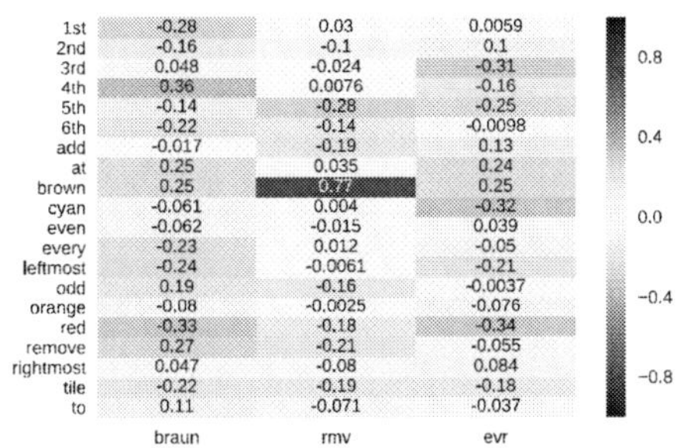

	braun	rmv	evr
1st	-0.28	0.03	0.0059
2nd	-0.16	-0.1	0.1
3rd	0.048	-0.024	-0.31
4th	0.36	0.0076	-0.16
5th	-0.14	-0.28	-0.25
6th	-0.22	-0.14	-0.0098
add	-0.017	-0.19	0.13
at	0.25	0.035	0.24
brown	0.25	0.77	0.25
cyan	-0.061	0.004	-0.32
even	-0.062	-0.015	0.039
every	-0.23	0.012	-0.05
leftmost	-0.24	-0.0061	-0.21
odd	0.19	-0.16	-0.0037
orange	-0.08	-0.0025	-0.076
red	-0.33	-0.18	-0.34
remove	0.27	-0.21	-0.055
rightmost	0.047	-0.08	0.084
tile	-0.22	-0.19	-0.18
to	0.11	-0.071	-0.037

(3a) Cosine similarities of the newly learned word embedding for the corrupted version of the words "brown", "remove" and "every" with the rest of the vocabulary.

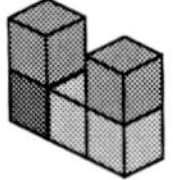

(3b) Example of failing case for our system. During offline training it had not seen other colored blocks to be used as referring expressions for locations.

question of through which mechanisms the decoder is implementing useful task-specific information, and whether they mimic the functions that are implemented in Wang et al.'s system, or whether they are of a different nature.

Furthermore, to test whether the model was harnessing similarities between our artificial and the human-produced data, we re-trained our model on our artificial dataset after scrambling all words and shuffling word order in all sentences in an arbitrary but consistent way, thus destroying any existing similarity at lexical or syntactic levels. Then, we repeated the online training procedure keeping the decoder weights, obtaining 20.7% mean online accuracy, which is much closer to the results of the models trained on the original grammar than it is to the randomly initialized model. With this, we conclude that a large part of the knowledge that the model exploits comes from the tasks mechanics than from specifics of the language used.

Finally, we note that the symbolic model attains a higher average online accuracy of 33% in this dataset, showing that there is still room for improvement in this task. Yet, it is important to remark that since this model features hand-coded domain knowledge it is expected to have an advantage over a model that has to learn these rules from data alone, and thus the results are not directly comparable but rather serve as a reference point.

5 Analysis

Word recovery To gain some further understanding of what our model learns, we examined the word embeddings learned by our model in the word recovery task. In particular, we wanted to see whether the embedding that the model had re-learned for the corrupted word was similar to the embedding of the original word. We analyzed a session in which 3 words had been corrupted: "brown", "remove" and "every". Recall from Section 4.2 that these sessions are 45-interactions-long with 15 different utterances issued on 3 different inputs each. We then evaluated how close each of the corrupted versions of these words (called "braun", "rmv" and "evr") were to their original counterparts in terms of cosine similarity. Interestingly, the model performs very well, with an online accuracy of about 80%, with 50% of the errors concentrated on a single utterance that contains all corrupted words together: "rmv braun at evr tile". However, as shown on Figure 3a, the system seems to be assigning most of the semantics associated to "brown" to the embedding for "rmv" ("brown" has much higher cosine similarity to "rmv" than to "braun"), implying that the system is confounding these two words. This is consistent with previous findings on machine learning systems (Sturm, 2014), showing that systems can easily learn some spurious correlation that fits the training data rather than the ground-truth generative process. Similar observations were brought forward on a linguistic context by Lake and Baroni (2017), where the authors show that, after a system has learned to perform a series of different instructions (e.g., "run", "run twice", "run left"), a new verb is taught to it ("jump"), but then it fails to generalize its usage to previously known contexts ("jump twice", "jump left"). While our system seems to be capable of compositional *process-*

ing, as suggested by the high accuracy on our compositional split shown in Section 4.1, it is not able to harness this structure during learning from few examples, as evidenced by this analysis. In other words, it is not capable of compositional *learning*. One possible route to alleviate this problem could include separating syntax and semantics as is customary on formal semantic methods (Partee et al., 1990) and, as recently suggested in the context of latent tree learning (Havrylov et al., 2019), so that syntax can guide semantics both in processing and learning.

Human data   On the previous section we have shown that the performance of our system correlates strongly with the symbolic system of Wang et al. Yet, this correlation is not perfect, and thus, there are sessions in which our system performs comparatively better or worse on a normalized scale. We looked for examples of such sessions in the dataset. Figure 3b shows a particular case that our system fails to learn. Notably it is using other blocks as referring expressions to indicate positions, a mechanism that the model had not seen during offline training, and thus it struggled to quickly assign a meaning to it.

On more realistic settings, language learning does not take the form of our idealized two-phase learning process, but it is an ongoing learning cycle where new communicative strategies can be proposed or discovered on the fly, as this example of using colors as referring expressions teaches us. Tackling this learning process requires advances that are well out of the scope of this work [8]. However, we see these challenges as exciting problems to pursue in the future.

6   Conclusions

Learning to follow human instructions is a challenging task because humans typically (and rightfully so) provide very few examples to learn from. For learning from this data to be possible, it is necessary to make use of some inductive bias. Whereas work in the past has relied on hand-coded components or manually engineered features, here we sought to establish whether this knowledge can be acquired automatically by a neural network system through a two phase training procedure: A (slow) offline learning stage where the network learns about the general structure of the task and a (fast) online adaptation phase where the network needs to learn the language of a new specific speaker. Controlled experiments demonstrate that when the network is exposed to a language which is very similar to the one it has been trained on except for some new synonymous words, the model adapts very efficiently to the new vocabulary, albeit making non-compositional inferences. Moreover, even for human speakers whose language usage can considerably depart from our artificial language, our network can still make use of the inductive bias that has been automatically learned from the data to learn more efficiently. Interestingly, using a randomly initialized encoder on this task performs equally well or better than the pre-trained encoder, hinting that the knowledge that the network learns to re-use is more specific to the task rather than discovering language universals. This is not too surprising given the minimalism of our grammar.

To the best of our knowledge we are the first to present a neural model to play the SHRDLURN task without any hand-coded components. We believe that an interesting direction to explore in the future is adopting meta-learning techniques (Finn et al., 2017; Ravi and Larochelle, 2017), to tune the network parameters having in mind that they should serve for adaptation, or adopting syntax-aware models, which may improve sample efficiency for learning instructions. We hope that bringing together these techniques with the presented here, we can move closer to having fast and flexible human assistants.

Acknowledgments

We would like to thank Marco Baroni, Willem Zuidema, Efstratios Gavves, the i-machine-think group and all the anonymous reviewers for their useful comments. We also gratefully acknowledge the support of Facebook AI Research to make this collaboration possible.

---

[8] An easy fix would have been adding instances of this mechanism to our dataset, possibly improving our final performance. Yet, this bypasses the core issue that we attempt to illustrate here. Namely, that humans can creatively come up with a potentially infinite number of strategies to communicate and our systems should be able to cope with that.

References

Andreas, J. and D. Klein (2015). Alignment-based compositional semantics for instruction following. In *Proceedings of the 2015 Conference on Empirical Methods in Natural Language Processing (EMNLP)*, pp. 1165–1174.

Artzi, Y. and L. Zettlemoyer (2013). Weakly supervised learning of semantic parsers for mapping instructions to actions. *Transactions of the Association of Computational Linguistics 1*, 49–62.

Bahdanau, D., K. Cho, and Y. Bengio (2014). Neural machine translation by jointly learning to align and translate. In *Proceedings of the 3rd International Conference on Learning Representations (ICLR2015)*.

Bai, S., J. Z. Kolter, and V. Koltun (2018). An empirical evaluation of generic convolutional and recurrent networks for sequence modeling. *CoRR abs/1803.01271*.

Chen, D. L. and R. J. Mooney (2011). Learning to interpret natural language navigation instructions from observations. In *AAAI*, Volume 2, pp. 1–2.

Claeskens, G., N. L. Hjort, et al. (2008). Model selection and model averaging. *Cambridge Books*.

Finn, C., P. Abbeel, and S. Levine (2017). Model-agnostic meta-learning for fast adaptation of deep networks. In *International Conference on Machine Learning*, pp. 1126–1135.

Gehring, J., M. Auli, D. Grangier, and Y. N. Dauphin (2016). A convolutional encoder model for neural machine translation. In *Proceedings of the 55th Annual Meeting of the Association for Computational Linguistics (ACL)*, pp. 123–135.

Gehring, J., M. Auli, D. Grangier, D. Yarats, and Y. N. Dauphin (2017, 06–11 Aug). Convolutional sequence to sequence learning. In D. Precup and Y. W. Teh (Eds.), *Proceedings of the 34th International Conference on Machine Learning*, Volume 70 of *Proceedings of Machine Learning Research*, International Convention Centre, Sydney, Australia, pp. 1243–1252. PMLR.

Havrylov, S., G. Kruszewski, and A. Joulin (2019). Cooperative learning of disjoint syntax and semantics. *Proceedings of NAACL 2019*.

Herbelot, A. and M. Baroni (2017). High-risk learning: acquiring new word vectors from tiny data. In *Proceedings of the 2017 Conference on Empirical Methods in Natural Language Processing*, pp. 304–309.

Hochreiter, S. and J. Schmidhuber (1997, November). Long short-term memory. *Neural Computation 9*(8), 1735–1780.

Lake, B., R. Salakhutdinov, J. Gross, and J. Tenenbaum (2011). One shot learning of simple visual concepts. In *Proceedings of the Annual Meeting of the Cognitive Science Society*, Volume 33.

Lake, B. M. and M. Baroni (2017). Still not systematic after all these years: On the compositional skills of sequence-to-sequence recurrent networks. *CoRR abs/1711.00350*.

Luong, M., H. Pham, and C. D. Manning (2015, September). Effective approaches to attention-based neural machine translation. In *Proceedings of the 2015 Conference on Empirical Methods in Natural Language Processing*, Lisbon, Portugal, pp. 1412–1421. Association for Computational Linguistics.

Mikolov, T., I. Sutskever, K. Chen, G. S. Corrado, and J. Dean (2013). Distributed representations of words and phrases and their compositionality. In *Advances in neural information processing systems (NIPS)*, pp. 3111–3119.

Oquab, M., L. Bottou, I. Laptev, and J. Sivic (2014). Learning and transferring mid-level image representations using convolutional neural networks. In *Computer Vision and Pattern Recognition (CVPR), 2014 IEEE Conference on*, pp. 1717–1724. IEEE.

Pan, S. J. and Q. Yang (2010). A survey on transfer learning. *IEEE Transactions on knowledge and data engineering 22*(10), 1345–1359.

Partee, B. B., A. G. ter Meulen, and R. Wall (1990). *Mathematical methods in linguistics*, Volume 30. Springer Science & Business Media.

Peters, M. E., M. Neumann, M. Iyyer, M. Gardner, C. Clark, K. Lee, and L. Zettlemoyer (2018). Deep contextualized word representations. *Proceedings of NAACL 2018*.

Ravi, S. and H. Larochelle (2017). Optimization as a model for few-shot learning. In *Proceedings of the International Conference of Learning Representations(ICLR)*.

Shimizu, N. and A. R. Haas (2009). Learning to follow navigational route instructions. In *IJCAI*, Volume 9, pp. 1488–1493.

Sturm, B. L. (2014). A simple method to determine if a music information retrieval system is a "horse". *IEEE Transactions on Multimedia 16*(6), 1636–1644.

Sutskever, I., O. Vinyals, and Q. V. Le (2014). Sequence to sequence learning with neural networks. In *Advances in neural information processing systems (NIPS)*, pp. 3104–3112.

Trueswell, J. C., T. N. Medina, A. Hafri, and L. R. Gleitman (2013). Propose but verify: Fast mapping meets cross-situational word learning. *Cognitive psychology 66*(1), 126–156.

Vogel, A. and D. Jurafsky (2010). Learning to follow navigational directions. In *Proceedings of the 48th Annual Meeting of the Association for Computational Linguistics*, pp. 806–814. Association for Computational Linguistics.

Wang, S. I., P. Liang, and C. D. Manning (2016). Learning language games through interaction. In *Proceedings of the 54th Annual Meeting of the Association for Computational Linguistics (ACL)*, pp. 2368–2378.

Winograd, T. (1972). Understanding natural language. *Cognitive psychology 3*(1), 1–191.

Fast and Discriminative Semantic Embedding

Rob Koopman
OCLC Research
rob.koopman@oclc.org

Shenghui Wang
OCLC Research
shenghui.wang@oclc.org

Gwenn Englebienne
University of Twente
g.englebienne@utwente.nl

Abstract

The embedding of words and documents in compact, semantically meaningful vector spaces is a crucial part of modern information systems. Deep Learning models are powerful but their hyperparameter selection is often complex and they are expensive to train, and while pre-trained models are available, embeddings trained on general corpora are not necessarily well-suited to domain specific tasks. We propose a novel embedding method which extends random projection by weighting and projecting raw term embeddings orthogonally to an average language vector, thus improving the discriminating power of resulting term embeddings, and build more meaningful document embeddings by assigning appropriate weights to individual terms. We describe how updating the term embeddings online as we process the training data results in an extremely efficient method, in terms of both computational and memory requirements. Our experiments show highly competitive results with various state-of-the-art embedding methods on different tasks, including the standard STS benchmark and a subject prediction task, at a fraction of the computational cost.

1 Introduction

Modern information systems rely extensively on the embedding of words and documents in compact, semantically meaningful vector spaces, where semantic similarity/relatedness can be computed and used efficiently. Various embedding methods are essentially all based on the *Distributional Hypothesis* (Harris, 1954; Sahlgren, 2008), and rely on co-occurrence evidence found in a corpus — whether computed globally or in a local context.

The recent success of local context predictive models such as Word2Vec (Mikolov et al., 2013) have initiated the development of more complex and powerful deep learning models (Bojanowski et al., 2016; Peters et al., 2018). The resulting embeddings combine compactness and discriminating ability, but the associated computational requirements are substantial and the optimal hyperparameter settings are not easy to find. It is, therefore, more common that embeddings are pre-trained on large corpora and plugged into a variety of downstream tasks (sentiment analysis, classification, translation, etc.). However, such transfer learning might fail to capture crucial domain-specific semantics.

Revisiting the methods based on global co-occurrence counts, high dimensional spaces built from the raw global co-occurrence counts are normally mapped to a more compact, lower-dimensional space of embeddings, using dimensionality reduction methods such as Principal Component Analysis (Pearson, 1901), Locally Linear Embeddings (Roweis and Saul, 2000), and Random Projection (Achlioptas, 2003; Johnson and Lindenstrauss, 1984). The latter has the unique advantage of being computationally cheap in the creation of the low-dimensional space, while being a linear projection method for which no optimisation is required at test time. On the flip side, the lack of optimisation means separation of datapoints is obtained by a comparatively larger increase of the dimensionality, and the linearity of the method further limits how compact the low-dimensional representation can be. However, thanks to the simplicity of the model, very efficient optimisations can be made to the algorithms and the resulting embeddings can be made to be effective even in high-dimensional spaces.

In our approach, we use a two-step process where we first reduce the dimensionality of the term vectors by an extremely efficient implementation of random projection. We then project the term vectors on the hyperplane orthogonal to the average language vector, which improves how discriminative the vector representations are, and assign appropriate weights for building document embeddings.

The main contributions of this papers are:

- a method that computes the Random Projection of terms as expressed in terms of their co-occurrences in documents without storing the matrix of term co-occurrences,

- a method to compensate for uninformative language elements by projection on the hyperplane orthogonal to the average language vector,

- an effective weighing, adaptable to the domain and empirically verified, of the resulting vectors which optimises the discriminative power of terms, and

- on the whole, a practical method which requires no iterative parameter optimisation and computes embeddings and associated weights in a single pass through the documents of the training corpus.

As we show in our experiment section, the resulting method is highly competitive with the state-of-the-art, in terms of sentence similarity computation and downstream classification task, and has much lower computational space and time requirements.

2 Related work

Term embedding Much research has adopted the notion of *Statistical Semantics* (Furnas et al., 1983; Weaver, 1955) or in Linguistics the *Distributional Hypothesis* (Harris, 1954; Sahlgren, 2008). Various distributional semantic models have been proposed to represent (embed) words in a continuous vector space where semantically similar words are mapped to nearby points ('are embedded nearby each other'). The approaches fall into two main categories (Baroni et al., 2014). First, methods based on global co-occurrence counts (e.g., Latent Semantic Analysis (Dumais, 2005)) which compute statistics of how often some word co-occurs with its neighbour words in a large text corpus, and then use dimensionality-reduction methods (e.g., Singular-Value Decomposition (Trefethen and Bau III, 1997), Random Projection (Achlioptas, 2003; Johnson and Lindenstrauss, 1984; QasemiZadeh et al., 2017)) to map the co-occurrence statistics of each word to a small, dense vector. Second, local context predictive methods (e.g. neural probabilistic language models) which directly try to predict a word from its neighbours or vice versa in terms of learned small, dense embedding vectors. The recent successes in the latter models, e.g. Word2Vec (Mikolov et al., 2013; Baroni et al., 2014) have initiated the development of more complex models with deep learning, such as FastText (Bojanowski et al., 2016), ElMO (Peters et al., 2018). However, that also brings high computational cost and complex parameters to optimise.

Document embedding There are currently many competing deep learning schemes for learning sentence/document embeddings, such as Doc2Vec (Le and Mikolov, 2014), lda2vec (Moody, 2016), FastText (Bojanowski et al., 2016), Sent2Vec (Pagliardini et al., 2018), InferSent (Conneau et al., 2017), etc. These are generally powerful, but are comparatively computationally very expensive. A simple baseline such as averaged word embeddings is fast and still gives strong results in the annual Semantic Textual Similarity task, as reported by Cer et al. (2017). However, assigning the proper weights to words when calculating the sentence/document embedding is non-trivial. Arora et al. (2017) proposed to remove a common component (remove the projection of the vectors on the first principal component of the test set's representation) after sentences are embedded as the weighted average of word embeddings. This is a relatively cheap but effective improvement, but 1) it requires re-adapting the term vectors to each new set of sentences, 2) it requires performing Singular-Value Decomposition, which is $O(n^3)$ and therefore still quite challenging in the case of large datasets, and 3) the subtraction of the first principal component does not reduce the rank of the model: it improves the discriminative power in practice, but does not combat over-fitting.

We propose a model that addresses these three issues: it is only trained on the training set; it does not require any optimisation (its computational time is linear in the size of the training set and can be implemented extremely efficiently); it uses linear projection to reduce the rank of the model. With only two straightforward parameters to tune — the term vectors' dimensionality and the minimum threshold below which rare words are discarded — the simplicity of our model is also a desirable feature in practice.

3   Algorithm

Let a document be a set of words for which co-occurance is relevant,[1] and n_D be the total number of documents and n_V the number of *frequent* terms.[2] A term is frequent when it occurs in more than K documents in the corpus, where K is flexible depending on the size of the corpus. As we show in Section 5.1.2, however, with the weightings we propose in our approach, K can be very low. D is the chosen dimensionality of the embedding vectors.

Further, let v_a be the D-dimensional *average vector* of the training documents. For each frequent term $t \in V$, we have the following parameters: $c_t(d)$, The number of occurrences of term t in document d; d_t the number of documents that term t occurs in; $\vec{v}_t$ the raw embedding vector of term t; $\vec{r}_t$ a D-dimensional "random vector" for term t, *i.e.*, $\vec{r}_t$ is a row of $\mathbf{R}$ (In our approach, this vector is binary and contains an equal number of +1 and -1); w_t the weight assigned to term t for document embedding.

Algorithm 1 Computing term embeddings

1: **procedure** COMPUTING TERM EMBEDDINGS
2:     $\forall t : \vec{v}_t \leftarrow \vec{0}$ ▷ Initialise a D-dimensional zero vector for each term t
3:     $\forall t : w_t \leftarrow 0$ ▷ Initial weight for each term is 0
4:     $\vec{v}_a \leftarrow \vec{0}$ ▷ Initialise a D-dimensional zero vector as the average vector
5:     **for all** documents d **do**
6:         $\vec{v} \leftarrow \vec{0}$ ▷ Initialise a D-dimensional zero vector
7:         **for all** terms t in document d **do**
8:             $\delta \leftarrow \frac{1 + \log(c_t(d))}{\sqrt{d_t}}$ ▷ Section 3.2
9:             $\vec{v} \leftarrow \vec{v} + \delta\, \vec{r}_t$ ▷ Section 3.1 and Section 3.2
10:        **for all** terms t in document d **do**
11:            $\vec{v}_t \leftarrow \vec{v}_t + \vec{v}$ ▷ Section 3.1
12:        $\vec{v}_a \leftarrow \vec{v}_a + \vec{v}$ ▷ Section 3.3
13:    **for all** terms t **do**
14:        $w_t \leftarrow 1 - \cos(\vec{v}_t, \vec{v}_a)$ ▷ Section 3.4
15:        $\vec{v}_t \leftarrow \vec{v}_t - (\vec{v}_t \cdot \vec{v}_a)\, \vec{v}_a$ ▷ Section 3.3
16:        $\vec{v}_t^* \leftarrow \vec{v}_t / ||\vec{v}_t||^2$

3.1   Fast Random Projection

Traditional random projection starts by computing a matrix of (weighted) term co-occurrences $\mathbf{C}$ of size $n_V \times n_V$, where n_V is the total number of terms. This matrix contains, for each pair of terms t_i and t_j, the number of documents (or paragraphs, or sentences) of the corpus in which both t_i and t_j occur. Using a matrix of random projection vectors $\mathbf{R}$ of size $n_V \times D$, we can then project our n_V-dimensional representation of each term to a lower D-dimensional space:

$$\mathbf{C}'_{[n_V \times D]} = \mathbf{C}_{[n_V \times n_V]}\mathbf{R}_{[n_V \times D]} \tag{1}$$

---

[1]In this context, a document could therefore be a sentence, a paragraph, a fixed-size window, a bibliographic record, *etc.*

[2]Terms could be words or phrases. Common phrases are automatically detected using a method similar to that described by Mikolov et al. (2013).

However, computing $\mathbf{C}'$ requires us to store both $\mathbf{C}$ and $\mathbf{R}$, which can be challenging in terms of storage space and unacceptably expensive for large vocabularies. Instead, we propose a method to compute $\mathbf{C}'$ without ever explicitly representing $\mathbf{C}$, simply by leveraging the linear nature of the projection (Eq. 1), updating $\mathbf{C}'$ directly as we go through the corpus.

Algorithm 1 does this by decomposing $\mathbf{C}$ in Eq. 1 into the sum of individual documents' co-occurrence matrices, $\mathbf{C} = \sum_d \mathbf{C}_d$, so that

$$\mathbf{C}' = \sum_d \mathbf{C}_d \mathbf{R} \tag{2}$$

where $\mathbf{C}_d$ is a matrix of zeros and ones indicating whether two terms co-occurred in the document. Importantly, we can further decompose the matrix multiplication by relying on the properties of $\mathbf{C}_d$: every term in the document co-occurs equally with every other term in the document, so that all of the document's terms contribute equally to the projection. We can, therefore, sum all the relevant rows of $\mathbf{R}$ and add the result to the relevant rows of $\mathbf{C}'$, making the time complexity linear in the size of the corpus, and the space complexity linear in the vocabulary size and constant in the number of documents .

3.2 Weighted counts

To improve the robustness of the approach, we weight the co-occurrence matrix $\mathbf{C}$ to reduce the effect of terms that are extremely common in certain documents and of terms that occur in the vast majority of documents. We use the term's average modified TF.IDF score in the training documents. Experimentally, we verified that the traditional IDF term of $\log \frac{N}{d_t}$ suppresses frequent terms too much, and replace it by a factor of $\sqrt{N/d_t}$, which has a similar effect but a longer tail and can also be seen as the normalisation constant of the t-test statistic (Manning and Schütze, 1999). For the TF term, we use a factor of $1 + \log c_t(d)$ and ignore the constant N which cancels out in the subsequent normalisation. Each row of $\mathbf{R}$ is therefore weighted accordingly in the decomposition outlined above.

3.3 Orthogonal projection

Traditional models discard both very infrequent words (because they are too rare for the model to be able to capture their semantics from the training data) and very frequent words (so-called "stop words" because they do not provide any semantically useful information). In our approach, we give a continuous weight to terms based on how frequently they occur and compute the average "language vector" of the corpus, $\vec{v}_a$. Unsurprisingly, this vector is very similar to the average vector of stop words. Intuitively, words are increasingly more informative as they differ more from the average vector. By this reasoning, we project word vectors on the orthogonal hyperplane to $\vec{v}_a$ (Algorithm 1 line 15),[3] resulting in a representation where the uninformative component of terms is eliminated, and normalise the vectors to have unit length. When computing document vectors, we down-weight terms according to their similarity to $\vec{v}_a$ (see Section 3.4). This step is crucial to get distinctive document embeddings.

As a nice side effect, projection makes it possible to handle multilingual corpora. The vocabulary of one language tends to be largely orthogonal to that of other languages (since words of one language tend to co-occur almost exclusively with words of the same language), so that projection using one language's average vector does not have much effect on the terms in other languages. This makes it possible to handle different languages effectively, within the same vector space.

3.4 Term weight assignment

Using the projection described above, the component that differentiates a term from the average vector is kept as its final embedding. Similarly, how different a term is from $\vec{v}_a$ also indicates how much that term contributes to the semantics of a document it is part of. In fact, we can interpret the cosine similarity as

---

[3] We use projection rather than subtracting $\vec{v}_a$ to prevent orthogonal vectors from gaining undue importance.

a lower bound on the mutual information (MI) between the two vectors (Foster and Grassberger, 2011). In order to give a higher weight to the most informative terms, we assign a higher weight to words with lower MI by setting the final weight of each term to be $w_t = 1 - \cos(\vec{v}_t, \vec{v}_a)$.

3.5 Text embedding

With the frequent terms' embedding vectors and their proper weights, we can compute text embedding as the weighted average of its component term embeddings. For a text $\mathcal{T}$, we obtain a set of vectors $\mathcal{V} = \{\vec{v}_{t_1}^*, \ldots, \vec{v}_{t_n}^*\}$, where n is the number of terms in text $\mathcal{T}$ and $\vec{v}_{t_i}^*$ is the final embedding vector for term t_i. The embedding of text $\mathcal{T}$ is calculated as follows:

$$\vec{v}_d = \frac{\sum_{i=1}^{n} w_{t_i} \cdot \vec{v}_{t_i}^*}{\sum_{i=1}^{n} w_{t_i}}. \tag{3}$$

where w_{t_i} is the weight for term t_i and out-of-vocabulary words are ignored. Note how term and document vectors all have unit length, making similarity computations elegant and effective.

4 Experimental methodology

We performed three experimental evaluations: in Experiment 1, we compare our method to the state-of-the-art on the standard STS benchmark; in Experiment 2, we qualitatively evaluate the weights assigned to terms; in Experiment 3, we evaluate our embedding method in terms of subject prediction. For our experiments, we implemented a parallelised version of the algorithm in C. All experiments were carried out on the same server with 2 Intel Xeon Silver 4109T 8-core processors and 384GB memory.

For meaningful evaluation, we trained all methods on the same two datasets using publicly available code for the state-of-the-art methods, and compared the resulting models on the standard STS benchmark. One dataset is the generic Simple English Wikipedia.[4] The other domain-specific one is a subset of the MEDLINE database that consists of 10^6 MEDLINE articles, randomly selected from `WorldCat.org`. In the latter dataset, each article is written in English and has a title and an abstract, to ensure sufficient textual information for computing the word embeddings. This dataset is of interest to our research and provides an interesting use case, as it consists of scientific articles and contains an above-average proportion of technical terms and jargon. Very rare terms carry critical meaning and make the task of word embedding particularly challenging.

5 Experimental results

5.1 Experiment I: STS Benchmark and Computational efficiency

The Semantic Textual Similarity (STS) Benchmark[5] is a SemEval task organized between 2012 and 2017. It consists of 8628 pairs of English sentences, selected from image captions, news headlines and user forums. The similarity between these sentence pairs was annotated using a five point scale via crowdsourcing (Agirre et al., 2016). Participating systems calculate the similarity between these sentence pairs and are evaluated based on their Pearson correlation with the gold standard STS annotations.

We trained our method on the September 2018 datadump of Simple English Wikipedia, where we applied a sliding window of 80 terms, with 50% overlap. This resulted in 628,382 windows, each being considered as a separate document for co-occurrence counting. A total of 199,430 unique 256-dimensional term vectors were obtained, their weights were calculated (Section 3.4), and used to embed the sentences in the STS benchmark (Section 3.5). The results are listed in Table 1, together with several state-of-the-art methods on the STS benchmark as published by Cer et al. (2017).

---

[4]`https://dumps.wikimedia.org/other/cirrussearch/20180910/`
[5]`http://ixa2.si.ehu.es/stswiki/index.php/STSbenchmark`

Table 1: STS scores and train times of different methods and different settings.

Method	Dev	Test	Dataset used	Train time
Doc2Vec (PV-DBOW)	72.2	64.9	AP-NEWS	Unknown
	31.0	27.0	S.E. Wikipedia	23m
	53.7	49.8	MEDLINE	2h3m
FastText	65.3	53.6	Wikipedia	Unknown
	48.6	38.9	S.E. Wikipedia	51m
	52.8	41.1	MEDLINE	3h4m
Sent2Vec	78.7	75.5	Twitter	Unknown
	68.8	62.2	S.E. Wikipedia	18m
	65.4	55.0	MEDLINE	3h10m
Our method	75.1	64.6	S.E. Wikipedia	17s
	73.6	58.9	MEDLINE	43s
Effect of projection and weighting in our method				
No projection, no weighting	31.4	34.2	MEDLINE	43s
No projection, TFIDF weighting	45.3	46.3	MEDLINE	43s
With projection, no weighting	57.3	45.2	MEDLINE	43s
With projection, TFIDF weighting	68.4	55.8	MEDLINE	43s
With projection, our weighting	73.6	58.9	MEDLINE	43s

We then ran the publicly available implementations of Word2Vec (Mikolov et al., 2013), Doc2Vec (Le and Mikolov, 2014), GloVe (Pennington et al., 2014), FastText (Bojanowski et al., 2016) and Sent2Vec (Pagliardini et al., 2018) and trained them on the two datasets using the same machine. The common hyperparameters were chosen to generally maximise the different methods' performance for this task, and are: a vector size of 256, a minimal number of word occurrences of 10, number of negative samples of 10, window size of 10, using hierarchical softmax, a learning rate of 1.0 and a number of threads of 16. All the other parameters were kept to their default values. When trained on the MEDLINE dataset, for word embedding only, it took Word2Vec and GloVe 29 and 35 minutes, respectively. As sentence-level embedding methods, Doc2Vec cost more than 2 hours to train. FastText and Sent2Vec also required more than 3 hours. In contrast, our combined term and document embedding — which includes the 10^6 Medline articles and 340×10^3 unique terms — requires only 43 s.

In analysing the STS benchmark results (Table 1), it is apparent that our method substantially outperforms all baseline methods when trained on the same dataset. Also notice how the training dataset has a clear impact on each method's performance, and even though the Simple English Wikipedia dataset is more limited, both in vocabulary and in size, than the datasets used for publication by the other methods, our method still outperforms the published results of the other baselines in terms of STS scores, and is very competitive with Sent2Vec. All methods suffer a drop of performance on the generic STS benchmark when trained on the MEDLINE dataset, as a consequence of the domain-specific nature of the dataset, but this drop is least pronounced in the case of our method. This suggests that a careful search for a more appropriate training set would improve the method's performance even further.

Finally, we should emphasise how low the train times are for our method. Since we do not require any iterative optimisation of the model parameters, our method's results are deterministically determined by the training data, they do not depend on parameter initialisation, and training is orders of magnitudes faster than the other methods.

5.1.1 Effect of projection and weighting

We here report the effects of projection on the hyperplane orthogonal to $\vec{v}_a$ (see Section 3.3) and weighting (see Section 3.4) in our method. As shown in Table 1, the projection greatly improves our method

Table 2: STS scores and train times w.r.t. K

K	Dev	Test	Train time(s)	#terms
5	73.9	60.5	55s	753,422
10	73.6	58.9	43s	339,729
20	71.5	57.8	37s	183,058
40	69.0	55.2	35s	109,662
80	65.7	52.1	32s	68,461

in terms of STS scores. Our weighting also substantially outperforms TFIDF weighting (both with and without projection), which itself outperforms no weighting. The difference in train time is negligible.

5.1.2 Effect of K

Decreasing the threshold K below which terms are ignored, results in a disproportionate increase of the number of terms that are included, with the computed vectors for those added terms being increasingly noisy. Because of the added computational burden and the noisiness of the estimation, traditionally a comparatively large cutoff value for K is chosen. With our proposed method, however, very small values for K are practical and the runtime does not grow much when a smaller K is chosen.

Table 2 reports the effect of K on the STS benchmark and the corresponding runtime, when training with the 10^6 MEDLINE articles. With a K as small as 5, the runtime stays reasonable, while it brings real benefits in terms of the STS benchmark, beyond those reported in Table 1 (where all methods use $K = 10$), because more infrequent terms get embedded.

5.2 Experiment II: Qualitative evaluation of weights for individual terms

Table 3 gives examples of terms with their raw document counts and final weights. As expected, *traditional* stop words such as "for" and "also" have extremely low weights. Frequent terms such as "treatment," "analysis," "system," and "subsequent" are to some extent *domain-specific* stop words which have low semantic value and therefore low weights too. However, more meaningful or *discriminative* terms such as "inflammatory," "mRNA," "antibodies" and "immune" have much higher weights even when they are also used very frequently.

At the other end of the spectrum, less frequent terms are likely to carry discriminative information for representing the semantics of the whole documents; however not all equally infrequent words have equally high weights. For example, "comprised" and "clarify" have much lower weights than "cytometry," "spleen," "cox" and "embryos" which are expected to be key topics for documents which contain them. The orthogonal projection and weighting help to give discriminative terms a boost when calculating the document embedding, no matter how frequently these terms are used.

In addition, we observed that the average cosine similarity between all documents is smaller by orders of magnitude when orthogonal projection and weighting is performed compared to when it is not, suggesting the documents are distributed in more compact clusters. That being said, without a proper evaluation with domain experts, it is not easy to evaluate the genuine validity of such operation. Our future work will include conducting such user-in-the-loop evaluation.

5.3 Experiment III: Subject prediction

In most digital library catalogs, bibliographic records are indexed using controlled vocabularies or thesauri to improve the discoverability of the content. These vocabularies are either generic, such as Library of Congress Subject Headings (LCSH),[6] or domain-specific, such as Medical Subject Headings (MeSH)[7] which is used for indexing articles in the MEDLINE database. Traditionally, assigning a most relevant

---

[6] http://id.loc.gov/authorities/subjects.html

[7] https://www.nlm.nih.gov/mesh/

Table 3: Examples of term counts and their adjusted weights

t	d_t	w_t		t	d_t	w_t
for	720,776	0.003322		comprised	6099	0.293460
also	230,896	0.024318		timing	6098	0.336269
treatment	171,984	0.079871		artificial	6093	0.465012
analysis	170,669	0.042365		cytometry	6086	0.776044
system	99,582	0.077036		adjuvant	6085	0.501349
inflammatory	27,743	0.356823		spleen	6080	0.523253
mRNA	27,681	0.318550		mucosal	6080	0.505713
achieved	27,382	0.114748		cox	6072	0.608585
antibodies	27,379	0.433778		embryos	6055	0.724599
subsequent	27,289	0.060512		clarify	6053	0.298637

subset of subject headings to describe a record is done manually by professional taxonomists. However, such manual assignment is very time-consuming and can no longer keep up with the speed at which new records are produced. Therefore automatically assigning a set of relevant subjects to articles becomes increasingly important.

We evaluated our embedding method on the use case of subject prediction. This remains a difficult problem and is a form of Extreme Multi-label Text Classification (XMTC) (Prabhu and Varma, 2014; Bhatia et al., 2015; Liu et al., 2017), where the prediction space normally consists of hundreds of thousands to millions of labels and data sparsity and scalability are the major challenges. In our MEDLINE dataset, there are more than 324,619 MeSH headings indexing 896,300 articles (the other articles do not have any subjects) with on average 16 headings per article. However, only 102,484 MeSH headings are used to index more than 10 articles.

We propose to treat the MeSH headings as terms in the documents they are associated with, so that terms, documents and MeSH headings are all embedded in the same D-dimensional semantic space. Our assumption is that an article would be indexed by its most related subject headings, *i.e.*, the MeSH headings with the highest cosine similarities to the document itself. To evaluate this, we computed embeddings for term and MeSH headings using the training dataset (previously selected 10^6 MEDLINE articles). We then prepared a separate testing dataset which contains 10^4 articles randomly selected from `WorldCat.org`. The articles in the testing dataset all have an abstract and are indexed by at least one MeSH heading. For each of these articles, we computed the document embedding using the terms in its title and abstract, following Eq. 3. We then computed their most similar MeSH headings and compared them with the actual ones. Notice how this method is, therefore, not biased towards predicting the more common (and often less informative) subjects.

For FastText and Sent2Vec, we did the same, *i.e.*, using the document-subject similarities to select the potential candidates. Since FastText and Sent2Vec can be used to train a supervised text classifier (Joulin et al., 2017), we additionally trained a classifier where each article's title and abstract were concatenated as a text, and their actual MeSH subject headings were used as the labels to predict. We trained a separate FastText and Sent2Vec text classifier, which we used to predict the most likely subjects for the documents in the testing dataset, based on their title and abstract. The parameters for training a classifier were exactly the same as those for generating word embeddings, but the train time was dramatically shorter, less than 5 minutes with the same machine.

All candidate subjects were ranked, by their similarities to the document or by the probabilities according to the corresponding classifiers, as appropriate. Figure 1 shows the precision@n and recall@n for different methods/settings. Both FastText and Sent2Vec perform much worse than our method if using document-subject similarities for subject prediction. As multi-label classifiers, their performance are nearly identical to each other and the quality of the predicted subjects are comparable with our similarity-based prediction. Their precision@n is higher than our method for low values of n while it

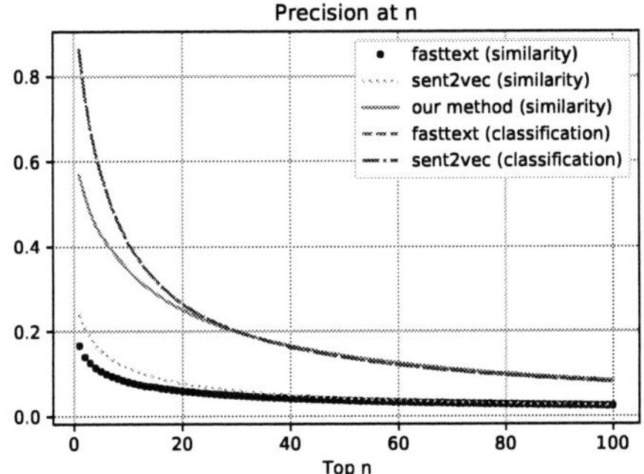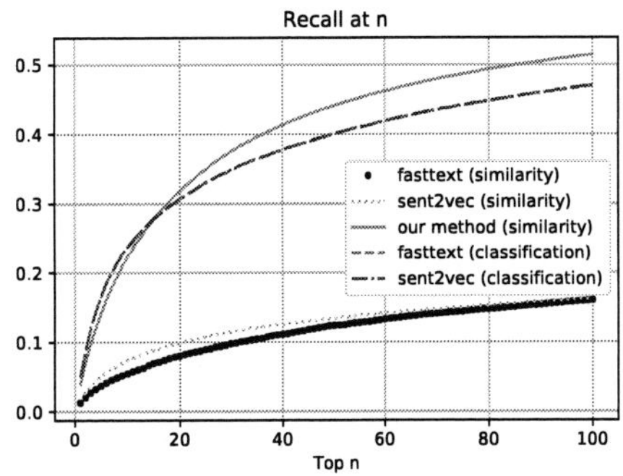

Figure 1: The performance comparison when predicting subjects

quickly decreases to be almost the same as ours. Up to top 20 candidates, the recall for three methods are more or less the same, but our method is able to predict more actual subjects at lower ranks, where the recall outperforms FastText and Sent2Vec.

Table 4 lists the 23 actual MeSH headings of an example article.[8] The MeSH terms that reflect the major points of this article are marked with an asterisk (*). The 25 most relevant MeSH headings predicted by three methods are also listed. It is not surprising that subjects such as "Humans" and "Female" are predicted first by FastText and Sent2Vec, because they are the most frequent ones used in the training dataset. In fact, many of the subjects predicted by these two classifiers are very common (see their document counts in Table 4). These classifiers have trouble finding subjects which describe the articles more precisely, while our method ranks specific subjects such as "Lens Capsule, Crystalline/Surgery" high in the list, even though fewer than 100 articles in the training set are indexed by this subject.

We realise that this evaluation has its limitations. As shown in Table 4, highly related MeSH headings such as "Lenses Intraocular" and "Phacoemulsification Methods" are predicted as good candidates for this article, both of which are reasonable and potentially useful. But since they are not the subject headings that the professional taxonomists have chosen, their value cannot be easily assessed. This illustrates how precision/recall may not be a very meaningful evaluation metric in this application. It also shows how this method could provide good recommendations to cataloguers.

6   Conclusion

We have described a novel, simple, effective and efficient method for term and document embeddings. As we have shown, our method has important practical benefits: 1) it is fast and has low hardware requirements, having linear time complexity and constant space complexity in function of the number of documents, resulting in very short run-times in practice. 2) Since no iterative optimisation is needed, the resulting embeddings are not affected by parameter initialisation and there is no uncertainty about the quality of the results of a run. 3) It computes semantically discriminative term embeddings and weightings with a single pass through the training data, and has the capacity to effectively include very rare words. Our experiments show it outperforms state-of-the-art methods in terms of the STS benchmark and subject prediction when trained on the same datasets, while at the same time being computationally cheaper by orders of magnitude.

In the future, we will integrate sub-word information into the embedding process and evaluate how effectively previously unseen words can be embedded. We will consider a wider variety of evaluation methods, especially getting domain experts involved.

---

[8] https://www.ncbi.nlm.nih.gov/pubmed/14670424

Table 4: An example of actual MeSH headings versus the top 25 predicted ones by our method, FastText and Sent2Vec, where the ones in bold match the actual headings. The raw document counts of the actual MeSH terms and those predicted by Sent2Vec are also given.

d_t	Actual headings (alphabetical order)	Our method	FastText	Sent2Vec	d_t
920	Acrylic Resins	**Lens Implantation, Intraocular**	**Humans**	**Humans**	579975
118655	Aged	Lenses Intraocular	**Female**	**Female**	328885
40642	Aged, 80 and over	**Phacoemulsification***	**Middle Aged**	**Aged**	118655
24	Capsulorhexis	**Lens Capsule, Crystalline/Surgery***	**Aged**	**Middle Aged**	168714
328885	Female	**Aged**	**Risk Factors**	Adult	194200
579975	Humans	**Visual Acuity**	**Male**	**Risk Factors**	34538
847	Laser therapy*	**Middle Aged**	Adult	**Male**	336647
65	Lens Capsule, Crystalline/Pathology	**Retrospective Studies**	**Aged, 80 and over**	**Aged, 80 and over**	40642
79	Lens Capsule, Crystalline/Surgery*	**Lens Capsule, Crystalline/Pathology**	Prospective Studies	**Retrospective Studies**	32642
317	Lens Implantation, Intraocular	**Risk Factors**	Follow-Up Studies	Follow-Up Studies	27911
336647	Male	Cataract Complications	**Retrospective Studies**	Prospective Studies	25714
168714	Middle Aged	Phacoemulsification Methods	Cohort Studies	**Visual Acuity**	2026
225	Phacoemulsification*	Prospective Studies	Risk Assessment	Incidence	11468
392	Polymethyl Methacrylate	Follow-Up Studies	Prognosis	Cohort Studies	12275
351	Postoperative Complications/Pathology	Cataract Extraction Methods	Logistic Models	Adolescent	75361
823	Postoperative Complications/Surgery*	**Aged, 80 and over**	Case Control Studies	Risk Assessment	9271
2914	Probability	**Female**	**Visual Acuity**	Logistic Models	7258
32642	Retrospective Studies	Cataract Extraction Adverse Effects	Adolescent	Time Factors	50339
34538	Risk Factors	**Male**	Time Factors	Prognosis	17160
10203	Sex Factors	Visual Acuity Physiology	Treatment Outcome	Postoperative Period	1720
294	Silicone Elastomers	Pseudophakia Physiopathology	Incidence	Postoperative Complications	3961
7046	Survival Analysis	Cataract Extraction	Postoperative Period	Treatment Outcome	40496
2026	Visual Acuity	Adult	Proportional Hazards Models	Case Control Studies	13306
		Humans	Young Adult	Visual Acuity Physiology	949
		Cohort Studies	Postoperative Complications	Age Factors	16319

References

Achlioptas, D. (2003). Database-friendly random projections: Johnson-Lindenstrauss with binary coins. *Journal of Computer and System Sciences 66*(4), 671–687.

Agirre, E., C. Banea, D. Cer, M. Diab, A. Gonzalez-Agirre, R. Mihalcea, G. Rigau, and J. Wieb (2016). Semeval-2016 task 1: Semantic textual similarity, monolingual and cross-lingual evaluation. In *Proceedings of the SemEval-2016.*

Arora, S., Y. Liang, and T. Ma (2017). A simple but tough-to-beat baseline for sentence embeddings. In *Proceedings of 6th International Conference on Learning Representations.* Poster.

Baroni, M., G. Dinu, and G. Kruszewski (2014). Don't count , predict ! A systematic comparison of context-counting vs . context-predicting semantic vectors. *Proceedings of the 52nd Annual Meeting of the Association for Computational Linguistics.*, 238–247.

Bhatia, K., H. Jain, P. Kar, M. Varma, and P. Jain (2015). Sparse local embeddings for extreme multi-label classification. In C. Cortes, N. D. Lawrence, D. D. Lee, M. Sugiyama, and R. Garnett (Eds.), *Advances in Neural Information Processing Systems 28*, pp. 730–738. Curran Associates, Inc.

Bojanowski, P., E. Grave, A. Joulin, and T. Mikolov (2016). Enriching word vectors with subword information. *arXiv preprint arXiv:1607.04606.*

Cer, D., M. Diab, E. Agirre, I. Lopez-Gazpio, and L. Specia (2017). Semeval-2017 task 1: Semantic textual similarity multilingual and crosslingual focused evaluation. In *Proceedings of the 11th International Workshop on Semantic Evaluation (SemEval-2017)*, Vancouver, Canada, pp. 1–14.

Conneau, A., D. Kiela, H. Schwenk, L. Barrault, and A. Bordes (2017). Supervised learning of universal sentence representations from natural language inference data. In *Proceedings of the 2017 Conference on Empirical Methods in Natural Language Processing*, pp. 670–680. Association for Computational Linguistics.

Dumais, S. T. (2005). Latent semantic analysis. *Annual Review of Information Science and Technology 38*, 188–230.

Foster, D. V. and P. Grassberger (2011, Jan). Lower bounds on mutual information. *Phys. Rev. E 83*, 010101.

Furnas, G. W., T. K. Landauer, L. M. Gomez, and S. T. Dumais (1983). Statistical semantics: Analysis of the potential performance of keyword information systems. *Bell System Technical Journal 62*(6), 17531806.

Harris, Z. (1954). Distributional structure. *Word 10*(23), 146162.

Johnson, W. and J. Lindenstrauss (1984). Extensions of Lipschitz mappings into a Hilbert space. *Contemporary Math. 26*, 189–206.

Joulin, A., E. Grave, P. Bojanowski, and T. Mikolov (2017). Bag of tricks for efficient text classification. In *Proceedings of the 15th Conference of the European Chapter of the Association for Computational Linguistics: Volume 2, Short Papers*, pp. 427–431. Association for Computational Linguistics.

Le, Q. V. and T. Mikolov (2014, 5). Distributed Representations of Sentences and Documents. *International Conference on Machine Learning - ICML 2014 32*, 11881196.

Liu, J., W.-C. Chang, Y. Wu, and Y. Yang (2017). Deep learning for extreme multi-label text classification. In *Proceedings of the 40th International ACM SIGIR Conference on Research and Development in Information Retrieval*, SIGIR '17, New York, NY, USA, pp. 115–124. ACM.

Manning, C. D. and H. Schütze (1999). *Foundations of Statistical Natural Language Processing*. Cambridge, MA, USA: MIT Press.

Mikolov, T., I. Sutskever, K. Chen, G. Corrado, and J. Dean (2013). Distributed representations of words and phrases and their compositionality. In *Proceedings of the 26th International Conference on Neural Information Processing Systems - Volume 2*, NIPS'13, USA, pp. 3111–3119. Curran Associates Inc.

Moody, C. E. (2016, May). Mixing Dirichlet Topic Models and Word Embeddings to Make lda2vec. *arXiv e-prints*, arXiv:1605.02019.

Pagliardini, M., P. Gupta, and M. Jaggi (2018). Unsupervised learning of sentence embeddings using compositional n-gram features. In *Proceedings of the 2018 Conference of the North American Chapter of the Association for Computational Linguistics: Human Language Technologies, Volume 1 (Long Papers)*, pp. 528–540. Association for Computational Linguistics.

Pearson, K. (1901). Liii. on lines and planes of closest fit to systems of points in space. *The London, Edinburgh, and Dublin Philosophical Magazine and Journal of Science 2*(11), 559–572.

Pennington, J., R. Socher, and C. D. Manning (2014). GloVe: Global vectors for word representation. In *Empirical Methods in Natural Language Processing (EMNLP)*, pp. 1532–1543.

Peters, M. E., M. Neumann, M. Iyyer, M. Gardner, C. Clark, K. Lee, and L. Zettlemoyer (2018). Deep contextualized word representations. In *Proceedings of the 16th Annual Conference of the North American Chapter of the Association for Computational Linguistics: Human Language Technologies*.

Prabhu, Y. and M. Varma (2014). Fastxml: A fast, accurate and stable tree-classifier for extreme multi-label learning. In *Proceedings of the 20th ACM SIGKDD International Conference on Knowledge Discovery and Data Mining*, KDD '14, New York, NY, USA, pp. 263–272. ACM.

QasemiZadeh, B., L. Kallmeyer, and A. Herbelot (2017). Non-negative randomized word embeddings. In *Proceedings of Traitement automatique des langues naturelles (TALN2017)*.

Roweis, S. T. and L. K. Saul (2000). Nonlinear dimensionality reduction by locally linear embedding. *science 290*(5500), 2323–2326.

Sahlgren, M. (2008). The distributional hypothesis. *Rivista di Linguistica 20*(1), 3353.

Trefethen, L. N. and D. Bau III (1997). *Numerical linear algebra*. Philadelphia: Society for Industrial and Applied Mathematics.

Weaver, W. (1955). Translation. In W. Locke and D. Booth (Eds.), *Machine Translation of Languages*, pp. 15–23. Cambridge, Massachusetts: MIT Press.

Using Multi-Sense Vector Embeddings for Reverse Dictionaries

Michael A. Hedderich[1], Andrew Yates[2], Dietrich Klakow[1] and Gerard de Melo[3]

[1]Spoken Language Systems (LSV), Saarland Informatics Campus, Saarbrücken, Germany
[2]Max Planck Institute for Informatics, Saarland Informatics Campus, Germany
[3]Rutgers University, New Brunswick, NJ, USA
{mhedderich, dietrich.klakow}@lsv.uni-saarland.de,
ayates@mpi-inf.mpg.de, gdm@demelo.org

Abstract

Popular word embedding methods such as word2vec and GloVe assign a single vector representation to each word, even if a word has multiple distinct meanings. Multi-sense embeddings instead provide different vectors for each sense of a word. However, they typically cannot serve as a drop-in replacement for conventional single-sense embeddings, because the correct sense vector needs to be selected for each word. In this work, we study the effect of multi-sense embeddings on the task of reverse dictionaries. We propose a technique to easily integrate them into an existing neural network architecture using an attention mechanism. Our experiments demonstrate that large improvements can be obtained when employing multi-sense embeddings both in the input sequence as well as for the target representation. An analysis of the sense distributions and of the learned attention is provided as well.

1 Introduction

One problem with popular word embedding methods such as word2vec (Mikolov et al., 2013) and GloVe (Pennington et al., 2014) is that they assign polysemic or homonymic words the same vector representation, i.e., words that share the same spelling but have different meanings obtain the same representation. For example, the word *"kiwi"* can signify either a green fruit, a bird or, in informal contexts, the New Zealand dollar, which are three semantically distinct concepts. If only a single vector representation is used, then this representation is likely to primarily reflect the word's most prominent sense, while neglecting other meanings (see Figure 1). More generally, a word vector may be a linear superposition of features of multiple unrelated meanings (Arora et al., 2018), resulting in incoherent vector spaces.

In recent years, several ideas have been proposed to overcome this problem. They have in common that they obtain different vector representations for the different meanings of polysemes or homonyms. Most prior work only evaluates these multi-sense vectors on single word benchmarks, however, and there is comparably little evidence for the benefits of using these embeddings in other applications.

One multi-word task that suffers from the presence of polysemy and homonymy is the building of a reverse dictionary that can take definitions of words as input and infers the corresponding words. In this work, we present the following contributions: (1) We show that multi-sense vectors are a better representation for the target words in this task. (2) We propose a technique to select multi-sense vector embeddings for the words in the input sequence. It is based on an attention mechanism and can be incorporated into an existing end-to-end neural network architecture outperforming single-sense vector representations. (3) We provide a comparison between pre-trained and task-specific multi-sense embeddings as well as contextual word embeddings. (4) We analyze the distribution of multi-sense words in the data and the attention the network learns.

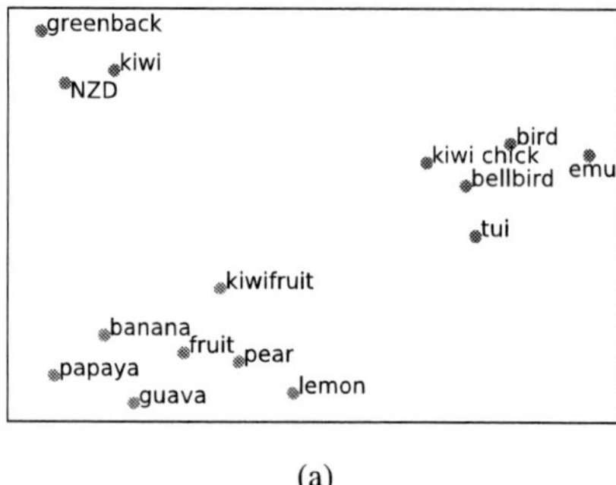
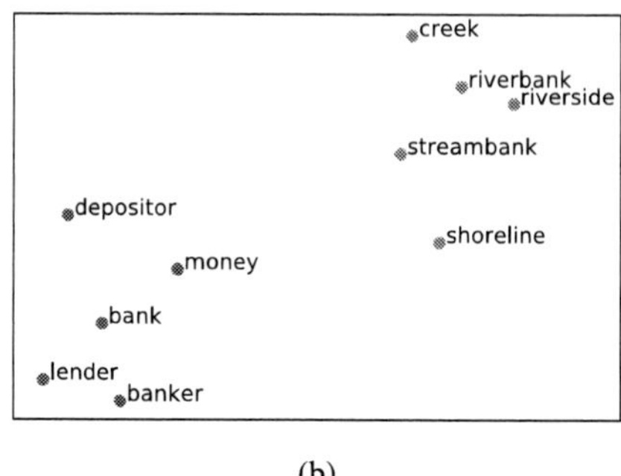

(a)   (b)

Figure 1: 2D projections of Google News word2vec vectors using t-SNE (Maaten and Hinton, 2008). The vector for the word *kiwi* is located near the embedding for the New Zealand dollar (violet) and not near other birds (blue) or fruits (green). For *bank*, the vector lies in a neighborhood of financial terms (blue), further apart from other river related terms (green).

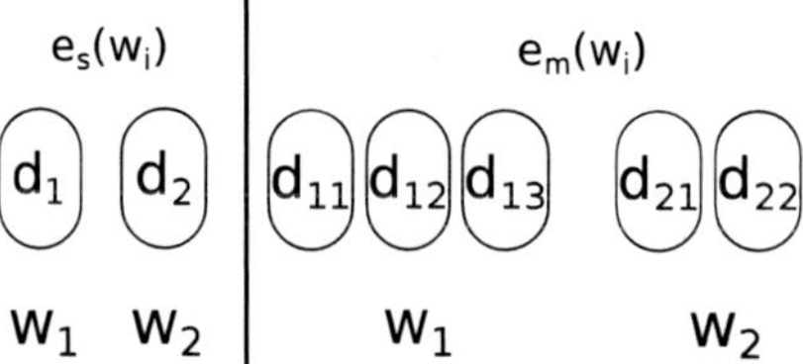

Figure 2: Single-sense embedding e_s compared to multi-sense embedding e_m for a sequence of input words w_1, w_2.

2   Task and Architecture

In this section, we give further details on the different embeddings, the reverse dictionary task and the corresponding architecture. We also motivate the use of multi-sense embeddings for the target and input vectors with qualitative examples and a quantitative analysis.

2.1   Single- and Multi-Sense Word Embeddings

A single-sense word embedding e_s maps a word or token to an l-dimensional vector representation, i.e. $e_s(w_i) = \mathbf{d}_i \in \mathbb{R}^l$ for a word w_i. They are often pre-trained on large amounts of unlabeled text and serve as a fundamental building block in many neural NLP models. Popular word embeddings include word2vec, GloVe and fastText (Bojanowski et al., 2017). If a word has several meanings, these are still mapped to just a single vector representation.

Multi-sense word embeddings e_m overcome this limitation by mapping each word w_i to a list of sense vectors $e_m(w_i) = (\mathbf{d}_{i1}, ..., \mathbf{d}_{ik})$, where k is the number of senses that one considers w_i to have. The vector $\mathbf{d}_{ij}$ then represents one sense of the given word. This difference is visualized in Figure 2. Often, these embeddings can also be pre-trained on unlabeled text. A discussion of different multi-sense word embeddings is given in Section 5.

2.2   Reverse Dictionaries

A reverse dictionary is a tool for authors and writers seeking a word that is *on the tip of their tongue*. Given a user-provided definition or description, a reverse dictionary attempts to return the corresponding

248

word (Zock and Bilac, 2004). We create a dataset for this task using the WordNet resource (Miller, 1995). For each word sense in this lexical database, we consider the provided gloss description as the input, and the word as the target.

the size of something as given by the distance around it → circumference

More details about the dataset are given in Section 4.1. Hill et al. (2016) presented a neural network approach for this task and also set it in the wider context of sequence embeddings. Each instance consists of a description, i.e. a sequence of words $(w_1, ..., w_n)$, and a target vector $\mathbf{t}$. Each word of the input sequence w_i is mapped with a single-sense word embedding function e_s (e.g. word2vec) to a vector representation $e_s(w_i)$. This sequence of vectors is then transformed into a single vector

$$\hat{\mathbf{t}} = f(e_s(w_1), ..., e_s(w_n)). \tag{1}$$

For f, the authors use—among others—a combination of an LSTM (Hochreiter and Schmidhuber, 1997) and a dense layer. The network is trained with the cosine loss between $\mathbf{t}$ and $\hat{\mathbf{t}}$. During testing or when employed by a user, the model produces a ranking of the vocabulary words $(\alpha_1, ..., \alpha_{|V|})$ by comparing the vector representation $e_s(\alpha_i)$ of each vocabulary word α_i with the prediction $\hat{\mathbf{t}}$ in terms of the cosine similarity measure. The k most similar words are returned to the user. We choose this task and architecture to show which benefits multi-sense vectors can bring to a downstream application and how they can easily be incorporated into an existing architecture. Two major limitations of single-sense vectors in this approach are presented in the following two subsections.

2.3 Target Vectors

The first limitation is that of the target vector, as exposed in Figure 1b. For the single-sense embedding, the vector for *bank* lies in a neighborhood consisting of financial terms with words such as *banker*, *lender* and *money*. Given a description of a river *bank* as input (*the slope beside a body of water*), a model trained on single-sense vectors as targets would have to produce a vector $\mathbf{t}$ (red point) that resides in a region of the semantic space that relates to financial institutions (blue points), rather than to nature and rivers (green points) with terms such as *riverside* or *streambank*.

In Figure 3a, we observe that 68% of the target words in our training data have more than one possible sense in WordNet. While the sense distinctions in WordNet tend to be rather fine-grained, this shows that in general the phenomenon of encountering multiple senses for a target word is not limited to only a few instances but affects a large portion of the data.

To cope with this, we propose to rely on multi-sense vectors for the target $\mathbf{t}$. Using these, we can assign the vector corresponding to the correct sense to each target in the training data. During testing, the correct target sense should obviously not be known to the model. We hence use for the ranking a vocabulary that consists of all sense vectors of all words.

2.4 Input Vectors

The second limitation of the existing architecture is the fact that it uses single-sense vectors for the input sequence. For example, within the definition of a *bluff, a high steep bank usually formed by river erosion*, the word *bank* refers to the phenomenon in nature. Therefore, the vector embedding for *bank* should also semantically reflect this and should not reside in a semantic region relating to the dominating, financial meaning.

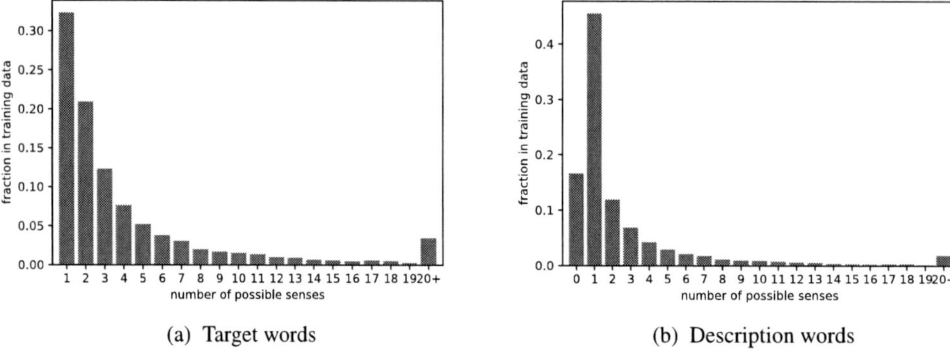

(a) Target words

(b) Description words

Figure 3: Number of possible senses, according to WordNet (see Section 4.2), of the target words (left) and input words (rights) in the training data. Out-of-vocabulary words are listed as having 0 senses.

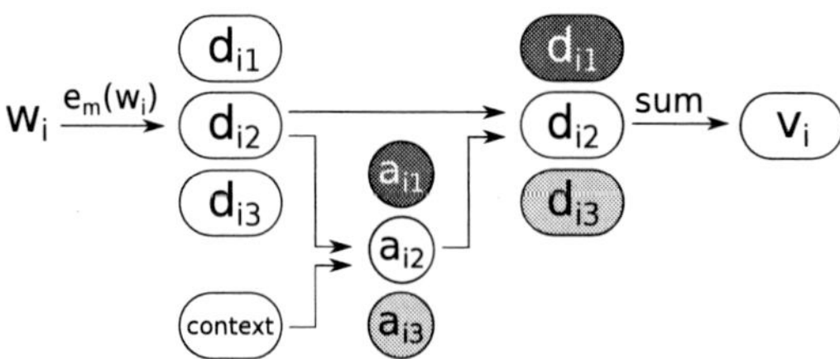

Figure 4: Visualization of the multi-sense vector selection using attention.

The analysis in Figure 3b shows that 38% of the words in the input sequence have more than one possible sense. This is a smaller percentage than in the case of target vectors, mostly due to out-of-vocabulary words and frequently occurring single-sense words such as stopwords. Nevertheless, this shows that multi-sense considerations are relevant for over a third of the words in the input definitions.

In contrast to the target vectors, we cannot directly link each input word to the correct sense vector because annotating every description word with the corresponding sense would be very expensive. Instead, we propose to provide the model with all possible sense vectors for each description input word and to perform the selection directly within the neural network architecture in an end-to-end fashion. Our approach to achieve this in a differentiable way, employing an attention mechanism, is given in the next section.

3 Multi-Sense Vector Selection

The process of selecting multi-sense vectors is visualized in Figure 4. For an input sequence of words $(w_1, ..., w_n)$, first a representation of the context is computed. For this, a single-sense word embedding function e_s is used and an LSTM transforms this sequence into a context vector $\mathbf{c}$:

$$\mathbf{c} = \mathrm{LSTM}(e_\mathrm{s}(w_1), ..., e_\mathrm{s}(w_n))$$

For each word w_i, the multi-sense embedding function e_m provides one or more sense vectors $e_\mathrm{m}(w_i) = (\mathbf{d}_{i1}, ..., \mathbf{d}_{ik})$. Each sense vector $\mathbf{d}_{ij}$ is compared to the context by computing the raw attention

$$r_{ij} = f(\sigma(\mathbf{c}, \mathbf{d}_{ij})), \tag{2}$$

where σ is a similarity function (dot product or cosine similarity in our case) and f is a non-linear function (ReLU in our experiments). The raw attention is normalized to yield attention weights

$$a_{ij} = \frac{\exp(r_{ij})}{\sum_h \exp(r_{ih})}, \tag{3}$$

and we obtain a new representation

$$\mathbf{v}_i = \sum_{j=1}^{k} a_{ij} \mathbf{d}_{ij}. \tag{4}$$

For each input word, instead of $e_s(w_i)$, the vector $\mathbf{v}_i$ is used in the task architecture. Equation 1 then becomes

$$\hat{\mathbf{t}} = f(\mathbf{v}_1, ..., \mathbf{v}_n). \tag{5}$$

4 Experimental Evaluation

In the following, we will detail our experiments to evaluate the effect of multi-sense embeddings both for the input description and for the target words.

4.1 Data

The dataset was created by extracting all single word lemmas from WordNet version 3.0[1]. Each instance consists of a lemma as the target word and its corresponding definition as the description. We make this dataset publicly available[2]. When creating the data, we used an 80%/10%/10% train/dev/test split of the WordNet synsets. The data was split along synsets and not words to avoid any leakage of information from the test to the training data. For a fairer comparison with the single-sense baseline, we only used instances where the target word was in the vocabulary of the single-sense embedding. This resulted in 85,136 train, 10,521 development and 10,502 test instances. The descriptions were tokenized using SpaCy version 2.0.11 (Honnibal and Montani, 2017). The distribution of the part-of-speech tags of the target words is given in Table 1.

---

[1] We do not use the original dataset by Hill et al. (2016) as it contains a flaw where a substantial part of the "unseen" test instances are also part of the training data.

[2] https://github.com/uds-lsv/Multi-Sense-Embeddings-Reverse-Dictionaries

	noun	verb	adj	adv
target words by POS	59%	17%	20%	4%
target word with 1 sense	38%	6%	34%	54%
target word with 2 senses	21%	13%	26%	21%
target word with 3+ senses	41%	81%	40%	25%

Table 1: The first row shows the distribution of the part-of-speech tags (POS) of the target words in the dataset. The rest of the table contains the distribution of the number of senses, according to WordNet, given a specific POS.

4.2 Embeddings

In this work, we consider as our single-sense embedding e_s the popular 300-dimensional word2vec vectors trained on the Google News corpus[3]. For the multi-sense embedding e_m, we chose the DeConf embeddings by Pilehvar and Collier (2016), which reside in the same space as the word2vec embeddings. It should be noted that DeConf uses the WordNet *graph structure* for the pre-training of the embeddings, while for our reverse dictionary data we only use the WordNet *glosses* as definitions.

4.3 Baselines

We compare our **multi-sense** approach that we introduced in the previous sections to the following baselines:

- For the **single-sense** baseline, we use the reverse dictionary architecture proposed by Hill et al. (2016), which also serves as the foundation of all the multi-sense models.

- In **first multi-sense**, we experiment with using the first multi-sense vector for every word as a single-sense vector, i.e. $\mathbf{v}_i = \mathbf{d}_{i1}$. This is motivated by the fact that the WordNet-based multi-sense vectors tend to be roughly ordered by frequency of occurrence (see analysis in Section 4.7).

- **Random multi-sense** evaluates using a randomly selected multi-sense vector.

- The model **not-pretrained** is based on the approach of Kartsaklis et al. (2018). They recently proposed a method to obtain single-sense and multi-sense vector embeddings during training (in contrast to our use of pre-trained embeddings for both). While one of their experiments also evaluates on a reverse-dictionary setting, their results are unfortunately not directly comparable, as their targets are WordNet synsets and not words. We, therefore, integrate their proposed technique into our architecture in two ways: For the model *not pre-trained*, we use their equivalent version of $\mathbf{v}_i$. This means that we use their code for the training of the single and multi-sense embeddings as well as for the creation of $\mathbf{v}_i$ based on the context and the multi-sense embedding. The model **only e_s pre-trained** differs from this in that we use the pre-trained single-sense embedding instead of training it from scratch.

- The **BERT** model belongs to the class of contextual word embeddings. This approach has been rapidly become popular with works by Peters et al. (2018), Radford et al. (2018), Peters et al. (2018b) and Devlin et al. (2018). Instead of using a direct mapping of words to vector representations, these approaches pre-train a neural language model on a large amount of text. The language model's internal state for each input word is then used as a corresponding word vector representation for a different task. They can be viewed as inducing word vector representations that are specific to the surrounding context. We compare against the current state-of-the-art model BERT (Devlin et al., 2018). For this, the output of BERT's last Transformer layer is used as the sequence $(\mathbf{v}_1, ..., \mathbf{v}_n)$.

---

[3] https://code.google.com/archive/p/word2vec/

Input Vectors	Target Vector	MR ↓	Acc@10 ↑	Acc@100 ↑	MRR ↑
single-sense	single-sense	535.5	0.115	0.301	0.067
single-sense	multi-sense	**135**	**0.203**	**0.458**	**0.131**
multi-sense	single-sense	481	0.121	0.315	0.069
multi-sense	multi-sense	**107**	**0.224**	**0.490**	**0.144**

Table 2: Median rank, accuracy @10 and @100 and mean reciprocal rank of single- compared to multi-sense target vectors. The first row is the model architecture proposed by Hill et al. (2016).

4.4 Hyperparameters

We follow the choices of Hill et al. (2016) with an LSTM layer size of 512, a linear dense layer that maps to the size of the target vector and a batch size of 16. The input descriptions are clipped to a maximum length of 20 words and the number of senses per word is limited to 20. If a word does not exist in the multi-sense embedding, we fall back to the single-sense embedding. The pre-trained single and multi-sense word embeddings have a dimensionality of 300 and are fixed during training. For the embeddings created during training with the method of Kartsaklis et al., we experiment with the same dimensionality of 300 as well as with an embedding size of 150 (as suggested in their work). Apart from this, we follow the configuration of Kartsaklis et al. for their components. For the contextual BERT embeddings, the authors' pre-trained, uncased model is used in the "base" and "large" variation and the pre-trained embeddings are again fixed. Since the BERT embeddings have a higher dimensionality (768 and 1024 respectively), the model architecture might underfit. We, therefore, experiment with different LSTM layer sizes up to 5,120, as well as with 2 LSTM layers and with adding a layer that transforms the embeddings to the same dimensionality of 300. For optimization, Adam (Kinga and Adam, 2015) is used for all models except for *only e_s pre-trained*, which achieved better results using stochastic gradient descent with a fixed learning rate of 0.01.

4.5 Metrics

For evaluation, the vocabulary is ranked according to the cosine similarity of the produced vector $\hat{t}$ as explained in Section 2.2. As the vocabulary, we use the union of all target words of the training, development, and test sets. Following Hill et al. (2016), we report the median rank as well as the mean accuracy @10 and @100. We also computed the mean reciprocal rank, which is a common metric in information retrieval.

4.6 Results

Table 2 shows the difference in performance between using single-sense and using multi-sense vectors as targets t, as detailed in Section 2.3. Although the number of candidates is larger when every target word has multiple candidate target vectors, the separation of the representation of the target words into different vectors according to their senses clearly helps the model to produce a reasonable representation of the input sequence. This effect is independent of whether the input is encoded using single- or multi-sense vectors. It should be noted again that the model does not have access to the true sense during testing and that instead all possible sense vectors are used for ranking. The pre-trained, contextual BERT vectors perform very poorly as target vectors. This might be due to the larger vector size, the more complex representation or the missing or uncommon context. In fact, we found that BERT obtains only 0.009 mean reciprocal rank even if we provide it with the ground truth definitions as contexts to generate the target representations.

Input Vectors	MR ↓	Acc@10 ↑	Acc@100 ↑	MRR ↑
single-sense (Hill et al., 2016)	135	0.203	0.458	0.131
first multi-sense	126	0.216	0.470	0.139
random multi-sense	137.5	0.208	0.457	0.136
not pre-trained 150 dim (Kartsaklis et al., 2018)	818	0.060	0.208	0.037
not pre-trained 300 dim (Kartsaklis et al., 2018)	574	0.087	0.260	0.053
only e_s pre-trained	162	0.198	0.439	0.128
BERT base LSTM 512 (Devlin et al., 2018)	253.5	0.151	0.373	0.091
BERT base LSTM 4096 (Devlin et al., 2018)	183	0.181	0.423	0.109
BERT large LSTM 512 (Devlin et al., 2018)	249	0.156	0.375	0.093
BERT large LSTM 2048 (Devlin et al., 2018)	220	0.159	0.391	0.098
multi-sense (cosine similarity)	117	0.221	0.480	0.143
multi-sense (dot product similarity)	**107**	**0.224**	**0.490**	**0.144**

Table 3: Median rank, accuracy @10 and @100 and mean reciprocal rank for the experiments with different input vectors. The multi-sense vectors are used as target vectors.

In Table 3, we report the results for different approaches of handling the input vectors, as introduced in Sections 2.4 and 3. As target vectors, we use multi-sense vectors. Picking a random sense vector tends to perform slightly worse than using the single-sense vector embedding and both are outperformed by picking the first multi-sense vector of every word. This might be due to the fact that the first sense-vector tends to correspond to the most frequently occurring sense and that the representation of this sense is better in the multi-sense setting because it can focus on this meaning.

Using the same LSTM size of 512, the contextual BERT embeddings do not perform well. Adding a learnable linear or ReLU layer to transform them to a lower dimensionality or adding a second LSTM layer does not help either. Increasing the size of the LSTM improves performance until a certain point before it drops again. This might be due to a trade-off between the model underfitting and the learnability of the additional parameters. In the table, we report the best configuration for the "base" and "large" variation. In future work, it might also be interesting to experiment with fine-tuning the language model component of this architecture.

The model that uses the embedding training and multi-sense vector selection of Kartsaklis et al. seems to struggle with building good embeddings in this setting with the 300-dimensional embeddings performing somewhat better but still not well. Providing pre-trained single-sense embeddings improves the performance considerably. Although they are not trained task-specifically, the pre-training of the single-sense embeddings on large amounts of unlabeled data seems to result in a very useful embedding space. This is consistent with other works in the literature, e.g. Qi et al. (2018).

Our attention based multi-sense vector approach using pre-trained single- and multi-sense embeddings obtains the best results with respect to all four metrics, with the dot product similarity function performing somewhat better than cosine similarity. This shows that using pre-trained multi-sense vectors and selecting the right sense vectors can be beneficial in sequence embedding tasks.

4.7   Study of Senses and Attention

In this section, we present a small study to gain more insight into the different senses occurring in the input sequences as well as into the learned attention. This is also intended as guidance for future work. For a subset of the input definitions from the training data, we manually labeled to which sense from the

Model	L
random multi-sense	0.25
first multi-sense	0.53
attention	0.31
attention-argmax	0.39

Table 4: Result of the analysis of the probability assigned to the true sense of multi-sense words for different models.

multi-sense embedding each word belongs. This data is made publicly available. Out of 275 words, 157 (57%) only had one vector representation, 18 words (7%) had a sense that was not covered by the corresponding multi-sense embedding entry, and 100 (37%) had one sense of the multiple possible meanings provided by the multi-sense embedding. On the latter, we calculated similarly to data likelihood the sum of the probabilities that different models assign to the correct sense:

$$L(m) = \sum_w p_m(\tau(w) \mid w),$$ (6)

where m is the model, w is a word and $\tau(w)$ is the true sense of the word. For *random multi-sense*, the probability was the reciprocal of the number of senses of a word. For *first multi-sense*, the probability was 1 if it was the first sense of a word in the multi-sense embedding and 0 otherwise. For *attention*, we used the normalized attention a of the true sense. For *attention-argmax*, probability 1 was assigned to the sense that had the maximum attention. The results are given in Table 4.

As mentioned earlier, the first sense of the multi-sense embedding often reflects the dominant usage, being correct in about half of the cases. The attention approach suffers from the dilution that a soft attention entails. Due to the use of the soft-max function, all senses get at least a small amount of the probability mass. An attention mechanism that uses a more skewed probability distribution might be beneficial here. From *attention-argmax*, we see that the attention method also does not always assign the largest amount of attention to the correct sense. The fact that this architecture still outperforms the others can be explained by the compositional nature of the attention mechanism. Also, some of the senses in the DeConf multi-sense embeddings tend to be very fine-grained. This means that even if not the exact sense is given the most attention, a similar sense might be. For future work, it would be interesting to improve on the context creation and sense selection component, explore options to fine-tune the embeddings as well as experiment with other multi-sense embeddings that might have a smaller number of different senses per word.

5   Related Work

Hill et al. (2016) proposed to map dictionary definitions to vectors both for the practical application of reverse dictionaries as well as to study representations of phrases and sequences. In this setting, Bastos (2018) experimented with recursive neural networks and additional part-of-speech information. Independently of Hill et al., Scheepers et al. (2018) also used dictionary definitions to evaluate ways to compose sequences of words. They studied different single-sense word embeddings and composition methods such as vector addition and recurrent neural networks. The work by Bosc and Vincent (2018) improves word embeddings with an auto-encoder structure that goes from the target word embedding back to the definition. We consider these three works complementary to ours, as they study different single-sense architectures.

In recent years, several approaches to creating multi-sense vector embeddings have been proposed. Rothe and Schütze (2015), Pilehvar and Collier (2016) and Dasigi et al. (2017) use an existing single-sense word embedding and a lexical resource to induce vectors representing different senses of a word. The latter also employ an attention-based approach for creating vectors based on the context for predicting prepositional phrase attachments. Pilehvar et al. (2017) use the same DeConf multi-sense embedding for integrating them in a downstream application. In contrast to our work, they require, however, a semantic network to do the disambiguation. In Sense2Vec (Trask et al., 2015), the authors create embeddings that distinguish between different meanings given the corresponding part-of-speech or named entity tag. They obtain an embedding that distinguishes e.g. between the location Washington and the person with the same name. The method requires the input data to be tagged with POS or NE tags. Athiwaratkun and Wilson (2017) represent multiple meanings as a mixture of Gaussian distributions. The number of senses per word is fixed globally to the number of Gaussian components. Raganato et al. (2017) and Pesaranghader et al. (2018) use bidirectional LSTMs to learn a mapping between words and multiple senses (not sense vectors) as a supervised sequence prediction task requiring sense-tagged text. An extensive survey on further ideas and work regarding vector representations of meaning is given by Camacho-Collados and Pilehvar (2018).

Tang et al. (2018) analyzed different attention mechanisms in the specific context of ambiguous words in machine translation. They limit their approach, however, to single-sense vectors and the established method of using attention over other parts of the sentence to improve the translation process.

6   Conclusion

In this work, we study the use of multi-sense vector embeddings for the reverse dictionary task. We show that single-sense embeddings such as word2vec do not adequately reflect all meanings of polysemes and homonyms and that improvements can be obtained by using multi-sense embeddings both for the target words and for the words in the input description. For the latter, we proposed a method based on attention that automatically selects the correct sense from a set of pre-trained multi-sense vectors depending on the context in an end-to-end fashion. It outperforms single-sense vectors, multi-sense embeddings trained in a task-specific way as well as pre-trained contextual embeddings. Our analysis of the sense selection process shows avenues for interesting future work.

Acknowledgment

The authors would like to thank the reviewers for their helpful comments. Michael Hedderich thankfully acknowledges the support by the obtained fellowship within the FITweltweit program of the German Academic Exchange Service (DAAD). Gerard de Melo's research is in part supported by the Defense Advanced Research Projects Agency (DARPA) and the Army Research Office (ARO) under Contract No. W911NF-17-C-0098. Any opinions, findings and conclusions, or recommendations expressed in this material are those of the authors and do not necessarily reflect the views of the funding agencies.

References

Arora, S., Y. Li, Y. Liang, T. Ma, and A. Risteski (2018). Linear algebraic structure of word senses, with applications to polysemy. *Transactions of the Association for Computational Linguistics 6*, 483–495.

Athiwaratkun, B. and A. G. Wilson (2017). Multimodal word distributions. In *Proceedings of the 55th Annual Meeting of the Association for Computational Linguistics (ACL)*.

Bastos, A. (2018). Learning sentence embeddings using recursive networks. *arXiv preprint arXiv:1810.04805*.

Bojanowski, P., E. Grave, A. Joulin, and T. Mikolov (2017). Enriching word vectors with subword information. *Transactions of the Association for Computational Linguistics 5*, 135–146.

Bosc, T. and P. Vincent (2018). Auto-encoding dictionary definitions into consistent word embeddings. In *Proceedings of the 2018 Conference on Empirical Methods in Natural Language Processing (EMNLP)*.

Camacho-Collados, J. and M. T. Pilehvar (2018). From word to sense embeddings: A survey on vector representations of meaning. *Journal of Artificial Intelligence Research*.

Dasigi, P., W. Ammar, C. Dyer, and E. Hovy (2017). Ontology-aware token embeddings for prepositional phrase attachment. In *Proceedings of the 55th Annual Meeting of the Association for Computational Linguistics (ACL)*.

Devlin, J., M.-W. Chang, K. Lee, and K. Toutanova (2018). Bert: Pre-training of deep bidirectional transformers for language understanding. *arXiv preprint arXiv:1810.04805*.

Hill, F., K. Cho, A. Korhonen, and Y. Bengio (2016). Learning to understand phrases by embedding the dictionary. *Transactions of the Association for Computational Linguistics 4*, 17–30.

Hochreiter, S. and J. Schmidhuber (1997). Long short-term memory. *Neural computation 9*(8), 1735–1780.

Honnibal, M. and I. Montani (2017). spacy 2: Natural language understanding with bloom embeddings, convolutional neural networks and incremental parsing.

Kartsaklis, D., M. T. Pilehvar, and N. Collier (2018). Mapping text to knowledge graph entities using multi-sense lstms. In *Proceedings of the 2018 Conference on Empirical Methods in Natural Language Processing (EMNLP)*.

Kinga, D. and J. B. Adam (2015). Adam: A method for stochastic optimization. In *International Conference on Learning Representations (ICLR)*, Volume 5.

Maaten, L. v. d. and G. Hinton (2008). Visualizing data using t-sne. *Journal of machine learning research 9*(Nov), 2579–2605.

Mikolov, T., K. Chen, G. Corrado, and J. Dean (2013). Efficient estimation of word representations in vector space. *arXiv preprint arXiv:1301.3781*.

Miller, G. A. (1995). Wordnet: a lexical database for english. *Communications of the ACM 38*(11), 39–41.

Pennington, J., R. Socher, and C. D. Manning (2014). Glove: Global vectors for word representation. In *Proceedings of the 2014 Conference on Empirical Methods in Natural Language Processing (EMNLP)*.

Pesaranghader, A., A. Pesaranghader, S. Matwin, and M. Sokolova (2018). One single deep bidirectional lstm network for word sense disambiguation of text data. In E. Bagheri and J. C. Cheung (Eds.), *Advances in Artificial Intelligence*, Cham, pp. 96–107. Springer International Publishing.

Peters, M., M. Neumann, M. Iyyer, M. Gardner, C. Clark, K. Lee, and L. Zettlemoyer (2018). Deep contextualized word representations. In *Proceedings of the 2018 Conference of the North American Chapter of the Association for Computational Linguistics: Human Language Technologies (NAACL-HLT)*.

Peters, M., M. Neumann, L. Zettlemoyer, and W.-t. Yih (2018b). Dissecting contextual word embeddings: Architecture and representation. In *Proceedings of the 2018 Conference on Empirical Methods in Natural Language Processing (EMNLP)*.

Pilehvar, M. T., J. Camacho-Collados, R. Navigli, and N. Collier (2017). Towards a seamless integration of word senses into downstream nlp applications. In *Proceedings of the 55th Annual Meeting of the Association for Computational Linguistics (ACL)*.

Pilehvar, M. T. and N. Collier (2016). De-conflated semantic representations. In *Proceedings of the 2016 Conference on Empirical Methods in Natural Language Processing (EMNLP)*.

Qi, Y., D. Sachan, M. Felix, S. Padmanabhan, and G. Neubig (2018). When and why are pre-trained word embeddings useful for neural machine translation? In *Proceedings of the 2018 Conference of the North American Chapter of the Association for Computational Linguistics: Human Language Technologies (NAACL-HLT)*.

Radford, A., K. Narasimhan, T. Salimans, and I. Sutskever (2018). Improving language understanding by generative pre-training. Technical report, OpenAI.

Raganato, A., C. Delli Bovi, and R. Navigli (2017). Neural sequence learning models for word sense disambiguation. In *Proceedings of the 2017 Conference on Empirical Methods in Natural Language Processing (EMNLP)*.

Rothe, S. and H. Schütze (2015). Autoextend: Extending word embeddings to embeddings for synsets and lexemes. In *Proceedings of the 53rd Annual Meeting of the Association for Computational Linguistics (ACL)*.

Scheepers, T., E. Kanoulas, and E. Gavves (2018). Improving word embedding compositionality using lexicographic definitions. In *Proceedings of the 2018 World Wide Web Conference (WWW)*.

Tang, G., M. Müller, A. Rios, and R. Sennrich (2018). Why self-attention? a targeted evaluation of neural machine translation architectures. In *Proceedings of the 2018 Conference on Empirical Methods in Natural Language Processing (EMNLP)*.

Trask, A., P. Michalak, and J. Liu (2015). sense2vec-a fast and accurate method for word sense disambiguation in neural word embeddings. *arXiv preprint arXiv:1511.06388*.

Zock, M. and S. Bilac (2004). Word lookup on the basis of associations: From an idea to a roadmap. In *Proceedings of the Workshop on Enhancing and Using Electronic Dictionaries*. Association for Computational Linguistics.

Using Wiktionary as a Resource for WSD : The Case of French Verbs

Vincent Segonne[1], Marie Candito[1], Benoît Crabbé[1]

[1]Université Paris Diderot
[1]Laboratoire de Linguistique Formelle
vincent.segonne@linguist.univ-paris-diderot.fr
marie.candito@linguist.univ-paris-diderot.fr
benoit.crabbe@linguist.univ-paris-diderot.fr

Abstract

As opposed to word sense induction, word sense disambiguation (WSD), whether supervised or semi-supervised, has the advantage of using interpretable senses, but requires annotated data, which are quite rare for most languages except English (Miller et al., 1993). In this paper, we investigate which strategy to adopt to achieve WSD for languages lacking data that was annotated specifically for the task, focusing on the particular case of verb disambiguation in French. We first study the usability of Eurosense (Bovi et al. 2017), a multilingual corpus extracted from Europarl (Kohen, 2005) and automatically annotated with BabelNet (Navigli and Ponzetto, 2010) senses. Such a resource opened up the way to supervised and semi-supervised WSD for resourceless languages like French. While this perspective looked promising, our evaluation showed the annotated senses' quality was not sufficient for supervised WSD on French verbs. Instead, we propose to use Wiktionary, a collaboratively edited, multilingual online dictionary, as a new resource for WSD. Wiktionary provides both sense inventory and manually sense tagged examples which can be used to train supervised and semi-supervised WSD systems. Yet, because senses' distribution differ in lexicographic examples as found in Wiktionary with respect to natural text, we then focus on studying the impact on WSD of the training data size and senses' distribution. Using state-of-the art semi-supervised systems, we report experiments of wiktionary-based WSD for French verbs, evaluated on FrenchSemEval (FSE), a new dataset of French verbs manually annotated with wiktionary senses.

1 Introduction

Word Sense Disambiguation (WSD) is a NLP task aiming at identifying the sense of a word occurrence from its context, given a predefined sense inventory. Although the task emerged almost 70 years ago with the first work on Automatic Machine Translation (Weaver, 1955), it remains unresolved. The recent breakthrough in neural net models allowed a better representation of the context and thus improved the quality of supervised disambiguation systems (Melamud et al., 2016; Yuan et al., 2016; Peters et al., 2018). Nevertheless, although WSD has the advantage of providing interpretable senses (as opposed to the unsupervised task of word sense induction), it also has the drawback of heavily relying on the availability and quality of sense-annotated data, even in the semi-supervised setting.

Now, such data is available in English, essentially with SemCor (Miller et al., 1993), a corpus manually sense-annotated with Wordnet (Miller, 1995) senses. But for most languages, sense disambiguated data are very rare or simply don't exist. This is mainly due to the fact that manual semantic annotation is very costly in time and resources (Navigli, 2009). Nevertheless, Bovi et al. (2017) recently presented Eurosense, a multilingual automatically sense-disambiguated corpus extracted from Europarl (Koehn, 2005) and annotated with BabelNet (Navigli and Ponzetto, 2012) senses.

In this article, we focus on supervised WSD for French verbs and investigate a way to perform the task when no manually sense-annotated training data specifically designed for the task are available.We focus on verbs because they are known to be central to understanding tasks, but also known to lead to lower WSD performance (Raganato et al., 2017). In section 2 we report a study on the suitability of using Eurosense as training data for our task. Because the results of our evaluation were inconclusive, we decided to explore Wiktionary, a free collaboratively edited multilingual online dictionary which provides a sense inventory and manually sense tagged examples, as resource for WSD. We give a general description of Wiktionary in section 3. In section 4, we present FrenchSemEval, a new manually sense annotated dataset for French verbs, to serve as evaluation data for WSD experiments using Wiktionary as sense inventory and training examples. Because senses' distribution differ in the lexicographic examples found in Wiktionary with respect to natural text, we provide in section 5 a descriptive statistical comparison of the wiktionary example corpus and SemCor. The WSD first experiments are reported in section 6 and we provide an analysis of the results in section 7. We finally conclude and give insights of future work in section 8.

2   Eurosense

In this section we present our investigation on the suitability of using Eurosense as training data for supervised WSD on French verbs. We first present Eurosense and then describe our manual evaluation of the resource regarding French verbs.

Eurosense   is a multilingual Europarl-based corpus that was automatically sense-annotated using the BabelNet (Navigli and Ponzetto, 2012) multilingual sense inventory. This sense inventory was originally built by merging the English Wordnet and the English Wikipedia. Subsequent releases integrate senses (mapped or added) from other resources, as listed in BabelNet statistics page[1]. Two versions of Eurosense are available: the "high coverage" corpus and the "high precision" corpus. Both result from jointly disambiguating the parallel Europarl corpus using the Babelfy (Moro et al., 2014) WSD system. A further refinement step was then performed to obtain the high precision version. The refinement aims at enforcing the intra-sentence coherence of annotated senses, in terms of similarity of their corresponding Nasari distributional vectors (Camacho-Collados et al., 2016). The resource was evaluated both intrinsically and extrinsincally.

The intrinsic evaluation was carried out through a manual evaluation of the annotation on four languages (English, French, German and Spanish). Fifty sentences present in all four languages were randomly sampled and manually evaluated both before and after the refinement step. The results showed a good inter-annotator agreement the judges agreed 85% of the time, and the average Kappa score (Cohen, 1968) was 67.7 %) and an improvement of the precision of the annotation after refinement at the expense of a lower coverage. For English, the high-precision Eurosense annotations cover 75% of the content words and have a 81.5% precision[2]. As For French results are lower though: coverage is 71.8% and precision is 63.5%.

Closer to our WSD objective, Bovi et al. (2017) report an extrinsic evaluation of Eurosense that uses it as additional training data for all-words WSD, evaluated on two standard datasets for English, the SemEval 2013 task 12 (Navigli et al., 2013) and the SemEval 2015 task 13 (Moro and Navigli, 2015). The authors compared results of the *It Make Sense* (IMS) system (Zhong and Ng, 2010) when trained on SemCor alone versus SemCor augmented with examples sampled from the high precision Eurosense corpus (up to 500 additional training examples per sense). They report a slight improvement in the latter case, the Fscore rising from 65.3 to 66.4 on SemEval-2013, and from 69.3 to 69.5 on SemEval-2015.

These results give a contrasted picture of the usability of Eurosense as training data for WSD for French: the extrinsic evaluation concerns English, and a setting that uses Eurosense as additional data (picking examples from Eurosense annotated with senses present in SemCor only). For French, the situation is necessarily worse, given that (i) the intrinsic evaluation of Eurosense is lower for French, (ii) we focus on verbs, whose disambiguation is known to be more difficult (Raganato et al., 2017), and (iii),

---

[1]`https://babelnet.org/stats`
[2]Note the precision is computed as an average between the two annotators, and not with respect to an adjudicated version.

most importantly, Eurosense would be used as sole training data and not as additional data. This poses extra constraints on the quality of the annotations, hence in order to further investigate the usability of Eurosense for our purpose, we decided to first perform another evaluation of the Eurosense annotations, focused on French verbs.

Evaluation of Eurosense on French verbs   We randomly selected 50 sentences from the French version of Eurosense's high coverage corpus, and for all the non-auxiliary verbs (160 occurrences), we manually judged whether the Eurosense automatic sense tag was correct : we split the 160 occurrences in three sets, each set being independently annotated by two judges and adjudicated by a third one. The judges were asked to answer "correct" if the Eurosense tag seemed correct, even if some other tag in the BabelNet inventory[3] was possible or even more precise. The agreement between the two judges was 0.72, and the kappa was 0.67, a level described as good in the literature. Note this is a binary task only, which is different from asking the judges to annotate the correct tag as Bovi et al. (2017) did for all parts-of-speech. Yet our agreement score is even lower, shedding light on an overall greater difficulty of judging the annotated sense of verbs. Indeed, we were then able to measure that the proportion of Eurosense automatic annotations that we judged correct after our adjudication is 44% only. Moreover, during this annotation task we could notice that because BabelNet aggregates several data sources (including Wordnet, Verbnet, FrameNet, Wiktionary among others), the BabelNet sense inventory exhibits a high number of senses per verb. To better quantify this observation, we sampled 150 sentences, and measured that the average number of BabelNet senses per verb type occurring in these sentences is 15,5. More importantly, we could notice that the frontiers of the various senses sometimes appeared difficult to judge, making it difficult to grasp the exact perimeter of a sense.These mixed results led us to investigate other sources of sense-annotated data for French.

3   Wiktionary as data for WSD

Wiktionary is a collaboratively edited, open-source multilingual online dictionary, hosted by the Wikimedia Foundation. It provides an interesting open-source resource and several studies already showed its usefulness for various NLP tasks (e.g. lemmatization (Liebeck and Conrad, 2015)), especially in the lexical semantic field, for extracting or improving thesauri (Navarro et al., 2009; Henrich et al., 2011; Miller and Gurevych, 2014). In this section we briefly present Wiktionary's most interesting features along with our motivations to investigate the use of this resource for WSD on French verbs.

Wiktionary's main advantages is that it is entirely open-source, multilingual and has a good coverage for a substantial number of languages (according to wiktionary statistics[4], 22 languages have more than $50,000$ wiktionary entries each). Each entry consists of a definition and one or several examples, either attested or created, each example being a potential sense-annotated example for the lemma at hand. Definitions and examples point to other wiktionary pages, which can be useful, although not as useful as if links to wiktionary senses (not pages) would be provided. The structured nature of wiktionary makes it possible to extract wordnets rather easily (as was done for English, German and French by Sérasset (2012), in the RDF format). On the qualitative level, our interest for wiktionary rose after studying random verbal entries for French: we could observe that in general the granularity level is "natural" and that the sense distinctions are easy to grasp. On the quantitative level, we report in table 1 several statistics for the French wiktionary[5], in which it can be seen that the resource is large (we will see in the next section that the coverage in corpus is good indeed).

---

[3]The sense inventory had been previously extracted via the HTTP API see `https://babelnet.org/guide`

[4]`https://en.wiktionary.org/wiki/Wiktionary:Statistics`

[5]In all the following, all the statistics and work on the French wiktionary corresponds to the 04-20-2018 dump available via Dbnary (Sérasset, 2012).

POS	Nb of entries	Nb of senses	Mean nb of senses per entry	Nb of examples
Noun	81099	112428	1.39	1511517
Verb	27271	41207	1.51	55206
Adj	25865	33732	1.30	46212
Adv	5904	6012	1.29	5904

Table 1: Statistics from French Wiktionary of the 04-20-2018 dump available via the tool of Sérasset (2012)

These advantages come at the cost of Wiktionary's main potential drawback, namely its crowd-sourced nature. Firstly, this means that it is constantly evolving, since any user can edit pages at any time (unless pages that users with more editing rights might have protected). Indeed, new pages are created every day while already existing pages are deleted, modified, merged (note though that every change occurring in the resource is kept in track). Secondly, this means that the resource is not curated by skilled lexicographers only, and the "guidelines" are themselves collaboratively built.

Despite this potential disadvantage, several features of Wiktionary seemed particularly suitable for the task of WSD and this, combined with the fact that sense-annotated data for French verbs are quasi-inexistent[6], makes it a serious candidate for a new resource of WSD. To investigate this opportunity for our objective of French verb WSD, we present FrenchSemEval, a new dataset manually annotated for WSD of French verbs which we used to carry out several evaluations, we describe the new resource in the next section.

4 FrenchSemEval : An evaluation corpus for French verb disambiguation

Since the first Senseval evaluation serie in 1998 (Kilgarrif, 1998), a various number of evaluation frameworks were proposed to evaluate different WSD tasks, but only a few include French test datasets (Lefever and Hoste, 2010; Navigli et al., 2013) and unfortunately these only focus on nouns[7]. In this section we present FrenchSemEval[8] a new French dataset in which verb occurrences were manually annotated with Wiktionary senses. Our objective was to evaluate whether Wiktionary's sense inventory is operational for humans to sense-annotate a corpus, and if so, to use it as evaluation data for WSD experiments. We describe the annotation process along with several statistics about the resulting dataset and the quality of the annotations.

4.1 Data selection

To build FrenchSemEval, we chose to focus on moderately frequent and moderately ambiguous verbs. Rare verbs are often monosemous, and very frequent verbs tend to be very polysemous and extremely difficult to disambiguate (we thus left these for future work). FrenchSemEval was built using the following steps: we first selected a vocabulary of verbs based on their frequency in corpus. We selected verbs appearing between 50 and 1000 times in the French Wikipedia (dumped on 2016-12-12 hereafter fr-Wikipedia). Secondly, from this pre-selected list of verbs we extracted those having a number of senses comprised between two and ten in Wiktionary's sense inventory. For these verbs, we chose to extract 50 occurrences primarily from corpora comprising other annotations (the French TreeBank (FTB) (Abeillé

---

[6]Verbs are annotated with frames in the French FrameNet data (Djemaa et al., 2016), but in such data, only some notional domains were considered, and verb occurrences not pertaining to such domains were not disambiguated.

[7]Except for SensEval1 but only the English dataset was given to public domain.

[8]The dataset is available here http://www.llf.cnrs.fr/dataset/fse/

Number of sentences	3121
Number of annotated verb tokens	3199
Number of annotated verb types	66
Mean number of annotations per verb type	48.47
Mean number of senses per verb type	3.83

Table 2: Statistics for the FrenchSemEval corpus (FSE).

and Barrier, 2004) and the Sequoia (Candito and Seddah, 2012) treebank[9]), supplementing the corpus when necessary by occurrences sampled from fr-Wikipedia, in order to reach 50 occurrences per verb.

4.2 Annotation process

The annotation has been performed by three students[10] for nearly a month. We used WebAnno (Yimam et al., 2014; de Castilho et al., 2016) an open-source adaptable annotation tool. Sentences had already been pre-processed into CoNLL format (Nivre et al., 2007) with the *Mind The Gap* (MTG) parser (Coavoux and Crabbé, 2017) and were plugged in WebAnno. We were thus able to provide files (one file per verb) containing sentences in which occurrences of the specific verb were marked for annotation. The annotators were asked to annotate only the marked occurrences. We integrated in WebAnno the sense inventory from Wiktionary, including definitions and examples of senses, and added two extra tags: "OTHER_POS" and "MISSING_SENSE". The former was to use when an occurrence was wrongly tagged as verb, and the latter was to use when the sense of an occurrence didn't exist in the sense inventory. As Wiktionary is constantly evolving through time, we used the 04-20-2018 dump available via Dbnary (Sérasset, 2012). The annotation was performed in double annotation and adjudication.

4.3 Resulting resource

Table 2 reports various statistics about the resulting dataset. It contains 3199 occurrences for 66 different verbs, which means nearly 50 annotated instances per verb (about 100 OTHER_POS occurrences were discarded). The annotators agreed more than 70% of the time and obtained a Kappa score of 0.68 which is good according to the literature. We believe that these metrics indicate an annotation quality which may not be extremely high but still sufficient to validate the coherence of the Wiktionary sense inventory, definitions and examples, despite its non-expert crowd-sourced nature.

5 Descriptive statistical study of the datasets

The best-suited data for training a supervised WSD system is a corpus with sense tags for all content words. Training on such a corpus benefits from basic frequency information found in the corpus. This is particularly striking for WSD, as the "most frequent sense" baseline is known to be very high. In the case of French, as for the majority of languages, we lack such a corpus, and turn to the Wiktionary examples to serve as training examples for a significant portion of the lexicon. Yet, because senses' distribution differ in the lexicographic examples found in Wiktionary with respect to natural text, we first provide some statistics for a running text sense-annotated corpus such as SemCor (for English) versus a lexicographic training set such as Wiktionary examples (for French).

---

[9]The FTB contains 18500 sentences, from articles from Le Monde newspaper, and Sequoia contains 3099 sentences from Europarl, the European Medicine Agency, a regional newspaper (L'Est Républicain) and fr-Wikipedia.

[10]None of them had previous experience in annotation.

Language	Corpus (# annotations)	AMBIG_trainSI		AMBIG_fullSI	
		type	token	type	token
English	SemCor (88334)	1.97	7.91	3.24	10.94
	SenseEval2 (517)	4.90	6.7	7.58	10.28
	SemEval 2007 (296)	5.15	6.89	7.78	10.17
	SenseEval 2015 (251)	5.69	6.25	8.48	9.16
French	Wiktionary (55206)	1.66	5.49	1.74	5.68
	FSE (3199)	6.02	6.74	6.15	6.91

Table 3: Ambiguity rates for verbs, in the English usual training set (SemCor) and usual evaluation sets, and in the French training set (Wiktionary) and evaluation set (FSE). **AMBIG_trainSI** corresponds to using for the number of senses the sense inventory in the corresponding training corpus, whereas **AMBIG_fullSI** corresponds to using the full sense inventory.

5.1 Comparison of the sense distribution in training examples

We study here the distribution of the annotated senses in training data. When looking at the number of training examples per sense, we obtain an average of 9.6 and a mean absolute deviation of 11.9 for SemCor, whereas the average is only 2.0 for FR-Wiktionary, and the mean absolute deviation is 0.9. It is clear that using wiktionary examples will lack the genre-dependent but nonetheless very informative information of sense frequency in corpus.

5.2 Evaluation of the task difficulty: comparison of ambiguity rates

We now turn to comparing the difficulty of the WSD task, when tested on English SenseEval datasets versus on FrenchSemEval. Note that performance of WSD systems cannot be used for that purpose, given that it is not comparable across languages and datasets. For a corpus consisting in a sequence of tokens $t_1 \ldots t_N$, we rather compute the average ambiguity rate that a WSD system has to face, in two settings:

- **token_AMBIG_fullSI**: the ambiguity rate per token, using the full sense inventory:

$$\frac{1}{N} \sum_{i=1}^{N} \text{n\_senses}(t_i)$$

- **token_AMBIG_trainSI**: the ambiguity rate per token, using the sense inventory found in the training corpus

$$\frac{1}{N} \sum_{i=1}^{N} \text{attested\_n\_senses}(t_i)$$

For further information, although not directly measuring corpus WSD difficulty, we also provide the ambiguity rate per verb type, both using the full inventory or that attested in the training set (shown in the "type" columns in Table 3).

We report these metrics in Table 3. When studying the difference between the "fullSI" versus "trainSI" modes, namely when using the full sense inventory versus that found in the training set, we have a different trend for the English corpora (containing natural text) and the French ones: for SemCor and the English evaluation sets, there is a drop of ambiguity in trainSI mode. This illustrates the usual difficulty to cover rare senses in a corpus of natural text. Note though that for the French corpora, based on the wiktionary inventory, there is almost no difference between the two modes of computation, illustrating that almost all senses have examples in wiktionary.

When comparing, for each language, the figures for the training corpora (SemCor and Wiktionary examples) and for the evaluation datasets, it can be noted that the average ambiguity per token is similar for training and evaluation datasets, but the average ambiguity per type is much smaller for the training corpora (3.24 for SemCor, and 1.74 for Wiktionary). This is because the lexicon covered in the training corpora is much larger, and contains many more monosemic verbs. .

As far as training corpora are concerned, it can be seen that the overall average ambiguity is higher for SemCor than for Wiktionary (e.g. in fullSI mode, 10.94 per token ambiguity for SemCor, versus 5.68 for Wiktionary). It shows that the sense inventory for Wiktionary is slightly less ambiguous than Wordnet's (both for the senses found in SemCor, and overall).

6 Experiments on supervised WSD

To investigate the suitability of using Wiktionary for supervised WSD on French verbs, we evaluated state-of-the-art supervised WSD systems on FrenchSemEval, using the examples of Wiktionary's senses as training data. As for the representation of the instances we used two different models that we describe below. We then applied a supervised disambiguation method to evaluate the performance of the models. We first describe the models we used to obtain vector representations of the instances and the disambiguation algorithm we used for evaluation. Then we propose several experiments based on FSE and finally we evaluate the models using Wiktionary as input for disambiguation.

6.1 Models for context representations

AWE   We implemented a simple model that we use as baseline. We first train a word2vec (Mikolov et al., 2013) model on fr-Wikipedia[11] to obtain non contextual word vectors. We then represent the context of an occurrence by averaging the vectors of the words found in its context window, which we defined as the 5 words on the left and 5 words on the right of the target word. This is a common model often referred in the literature as averaged-word-embeddings (AWE).

C2V   Context2vec (Melamud et al., 2016) is a recurrent neural model that learns a function mapping the context around a target word to a vectorial representation. The context2vec model represents the context using a bi-directional recurrent neural network (Hochreiter and Schmidhuber, 1997) that allow us to take the context of the sentence into account, thus contrasting with AWE. All codes and implementations are available publicly so we only adapted it and trained the model on the whole French Wikipedia. We then applied the learnt model to obtain vectorial representations of our target verb occurrences.

6.2 Supervised disambiguation algorithm

We replicated the supervised WSD method used in (Yuan et al., 2016): a sense representation is computed from annotated data by averaging the context vector representation of its instances, in our case the Wiktionary examples or instances from FSE. Then each test instance is sense tagged with the sense whose representation is the closest, based on cosine similarity.

6.3 Protocol

Wiktionary experiment   We did a first experiment simply using the examples of the senses in the Wiktionary sense inventory as training data and then we performed disambiguation on FSE.

In domain experiments   In order to better identify the potential error sources, we also performed experiments with "in-domain" training instances, namely instances directly taken from FSE. To evaluate the impact of the number of training examples per sense, a property that is quite different for a lexicographic training set as opposed to a corpus-based training set, we performed experiments on different sets, using N_{max} a varying maximum number of examples per sense. More precisely, for each verb we

---

[11]We used the fr-Wikipedia dump of 10-20-2017

selected respectively 1, 2, 5 and 10 maximum training examples per sense from the dataset and evaluated the disambiguation on the remaining examples.

6.4 Results and Analysis

The results of our experiments on Wiktionary are presented in table 4. Although both automatic systems perform better than the Most Frequent Sense baseline (MFS), using only the literary Wiktionary examples to build a classifier for newspaper and Wikipedia test instances remains a rather adversarial setup[12]. We thus investigated two potential ways to leverage the hardness of this initial setup: domain adaptation and the amount of training examples.

Models	score
MFS	0.30
AWE	0.40
C2V	**0.43**

Table 4: WSD accuracies when training on Wiktionary examples, and testing on FSE.

To study the effect of the amount of training instances, since Wiktionary is limited in terms of number of examples per sense, we switched to using FSE both for training and testing. We used a variable number of maximum training examples per sense from $N_{max} = 1$ to $N_{max} = 10$ and we used the remaining examples as test set[13]. The results of these experiments are summarized in Table 5 and illustrated in Figure 1.

Let us observe first the impact the amount of training data. The mean number of examples in Wiktionary for the verbs occurring in FSE is $N_{avg} = 3.1$ and the results show that all classifiers dramatically improve when the available training examples per verb grows up to $N_{max} = 10$. This means that if we were able to expand with absolute certainty the small amount of examples in Wiktionary, we could get a much higher disambiguation performance.

Second, using the same setup we can compare the behaviour of the classifiers when predicting out of domain (Table 4) with in domain predictions (Table 5). Recall that Wiktionary examples are often long literary sentences whereas the test instances are sampled from newspaper or Wikipedia. Again as Wiktionary has $N_{avg} \approx 3$ training examples per sense we can see that the domain adaptation effect is worth roughly 20 points in accuracy.

Models	$N_{max} = 1$	$N_{max} = 2$	$N_{max} = 3$	$N_{max} = 5$	$N_{max} = 10$
MFS	0.32	0.38	0.45	0.52	0.70
AWE	0.44	0.53	0.58	0.64	0.70
C2V	0.5	0.57	0.62	0.68	**0.74**
Mean number of training ex. per sense	1	1.81	2.61	3.86	6.30
Mean size training data per verb	3.83	6.95	9.81	14.8	24.15
Mean size test data per verb	44.63	41.51	38.65	33.66	24.31

Table 5: Training on FSE examples, with varying maximum number of examples per sense (N_{max}). Top: WSD accuracies. Bottom: training / test sets statistics.

Third, we can observe that the 3 classifiers (MFS, AWE,C2V) do behave consistently in the different configurations. To understand why MFS is a rather weak predictor in our setup, we have to recall that

---

[12] As a comparison, results for supervised WSD for English verbs are around 0.55 in the benchmark of Raganato et al. (2017).

[13] We say that we use N_{max} as a maximum number of training examples because some senses may have only $K < N_{max}$ annotated instances in the whole data set.

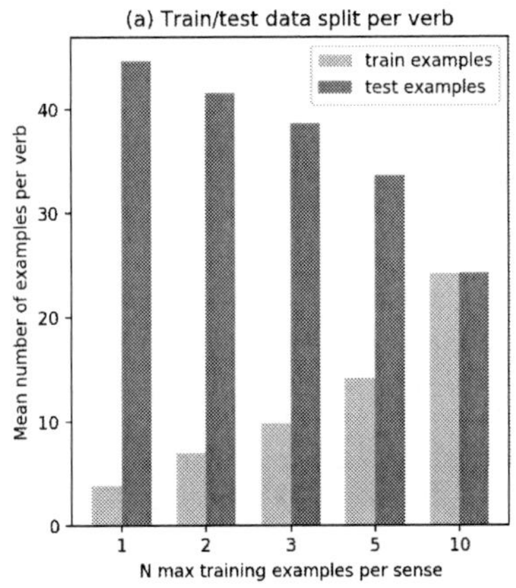
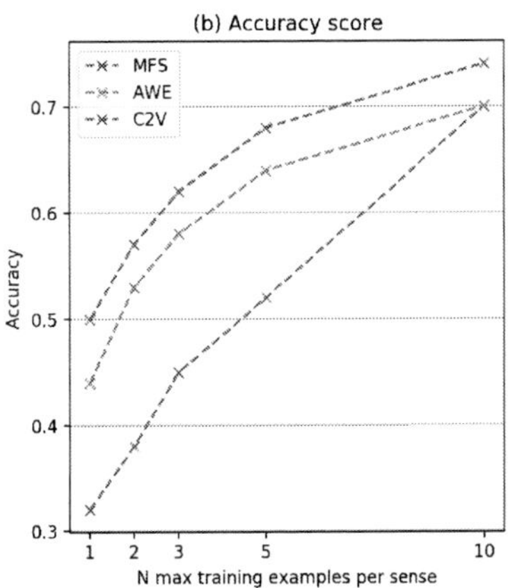

Figure 1: Illustration of results reported in table 5.

contrary to Semcor and Senseval, FSE is built following a lexicographic perspective: the sentences are sampled in a non natural way (e.g. monosemic words are excluded). We observe (table 5) that in these conditions the MFS is a weaker (although still strong) baseline and that standard sequential neural models are able to outperform it, especially when there are few training examples. Among the neural models C2V performs consistently better than AWE but we believe that these models or some extensions of these models to be designed in the future might well still show significant improvements.

Lastly, we can observe that among all models, C2V performs best on every test setup. It supports (Melamud et al., 2016)'s results, especially regarding the fact that Context2vec succeeds better in capturing context information than the common averaging of word vector representations.

7 Conclusions and future work

Word Sense Disambiguation is a task rarely seen for languages other than English. One obvious reason to explain that is the lack of costly sense annotated resources for those languages. In this paper we provide some elements seeking to set up a methodology to perform word sense disambiguation for other languages than English, such as French, without requiring the cost of annotating sense disambiguated corpora.

For this purpose we considered using Eurosense and Wiktionary as training data for Verb Sense Disambiguation. As our first experiments with Eurosense turned out to be inconclusive, we then turned our attention to Wiktionary. We studied how to use it as a resource for Word Sense Disambiguation and we develop FrenchSemEval, a new French WSD evaluation dataset, thanks to which we were able to extract preliminary evaluation results. Our current results showed that the Wiktionary sense inventory has an appropriate granularity for a good quality sense annotation, and that training on Wiktionary examples only leads to encouraging WSD results for verbs. But we could also quantify the gain in performance that could be obtained by adding a moderate number of seed instances. Hence automating the selection and annotation of additional instances might pay off to improve verb sense disambiguation.

References

Abeillé, A. and N. Barrier (2004). Enriching a french treebank. In *Proceedings of LREC 2004, Lisbon, Portugal*.

Bovi, C. D., J. Camacho-Collados, A. Raganato, and R. Navigli (2017). Eurosense: Automatic harvesting of multilingual sense annotations from parallel text. *Proceedings of the 55th Annual Meeting of the Association for Computational Linguistics (Volume 2: Short Papers) 2*, 594–600.

Camacho-Collados, J., M. T. Pilehvar, and R. Navigli (2016). Nasari: Integrating explicit knowledge and corpus statistics for a multilingual representation of concepts and entities. *Artificial Intelligence 240*, 36–64.

Candito, M. and D. Seddah (2012). Le corpus sequoia: annotation syntaxique et exploitation pour l'adaptation d'analyseur par pont lexical. In *TALN 2012-19e conférence sur le Traitement Automatique des Langues Naturelles*.

Coavoux, M. and B. Crabbé (2017, April). Incremental discontinuous phrase structure parsing with the gap transition. In *Proceedings of the 15th Conference of the European Chapter of the Association for Computational Linguistics: Volume 1, Long Papers*, Valencia, Spain, pp. 1259–1270. Association for Computational Linguistics.

Cohen, J. (1968). Weighted kappa: Nominal scale agreement provision for scaled disagreement or partial credit. *Psychological bulletin 70*(4), 213.

de Castilho, R. E., E. Mujdricza-Maydt, S. M. Yimam, S. Hartmann, I. Gurevych, A. Frank, and C. Biemann (2016). A web-based tool for the integrated annotation of semantic and syntactic structures. In *Proceedings of the Workshop on Language Technology Resources and Tools for Digital Humanities (LT4DH)*, pp. 76–84.

Djemaa, M., M. Candito, P. Muller, and L. Vieu (2016, May). Corpus Annotation within the French FrameNet: a Domain-by-domain Methodology (regular paper). In Calzolari, Choukri, Declerck, Goggi, and Grobelnik (Eds.), *LREC 2016), Portoroz, Slovenia*, pp. 3794–3801.

Henrich, V., E. Hinrichs, and T. Vodolazova (2011). Semi-automatic extension of germanet with sense definitions from wiktionary. In *Proceedings of the 5th Language and Technology Conference (LTC 2011)*, pp. 126–130.

Hochreiter, S. and J. Schmidhuber (1997). Long short-term memory. *Neural computation 9*(8), 1735–1780.

Kilgarrif, A. (1998). Senseval: An exercise in evaluating word sense disambiguation programs. In *Proceedings of the first international conference on language resources and evaluation (LREC 1998), Granada, Spain*, pp. 581–588.

Lefever, E. and V. Hoste (2010). Semeval-2010 task 3: Cross-lingual word sense disambiguation. In *Proceedings of the 5th International Workshop on Semantic Evaluation*, pp. 15–20. Association for Computational Linguistics.

Liebeck, M. and S. Conrad (2015, July). Iwnlp: Inverse wiktionary for natural language processing. In *Proceedings of the 53rd Annual Meeting of the Association for Computational Linguistics and the 7th International Joint Conference on Natural Language Processing (Volume 2: Short Papers)*, Beijing, China, pp. 414–418. Association for Computational Linguistics.

Melamud, O., J. Goldberger, and I. Dagan (2016). context2vec: Learning generic context embedding with bidirectional lstm. In *Proceedings of The 20th SIGNLL Conference on Computational Natural Language Learning*, pp. 51–61.

Mikolov, T., I. Sutskever, K. Chen, G. S. Corrado, and J. Dean (2013). Distributed representations of words and phrases and their compositionality. In *Advances in neural information processing systems*, pp. 3111–3119.

Miller, G. A. (1995). Wordnet: a lexical database for english. *Communications of the ACM 38*(11), 39–41.

Miller, G. A., C. Leacock, R. Tengi, and R. T. Bunker (1993). A semantic concordance. In *Proceedings of the workshop on Human Language Technology*, pp. 303–308. Association for Computational Linguistics.

Miller, T. and I. Gurevych (2014). Wordnet—wikipedia—wiktionary: Construction of a three-way alignment. In *LREC*, pp. 2094–2100.

Moro, A. and R. Navigli (2015). Semeval-2015 task 13: Multilingual all-words sense disambiguation and entity linking. In *Proceedings of the 9th international workshop on semantic evaluation (SemEval 2015)*, pp. 288–297.

Moro, A., A. Raganato, and R. Navigli (2014). Entity linking meets word sense disambiguation: a unified approach. *Transactions of the Association for Computational Linguistics 2*, 231–244.

Navarro, E., F. Sajous, B. Gaume, L. Prévot, H. ShuKai, K. Tzu-Yi, P. Magistry, and H. Chu-Ren (2009). Wiktionary and nlp: Improving synonymy networks. In *Proceedings of the 2009 Workshop on The People's Web Meets NLP: Collaboratively Constructed Semantic Resources*, pp. 19–27. Association for Computational Linguistics.

Navigli, R. (2009). Word sense disambiguation: A survey. *ACM Computing Surveys (CSUR) 41*(2), 10.

Navigli, R., D. Jurgens, and D. Vannella (2013). Semeval-2013 task 12: Multilingual word sense disambiguation. In *Second Joint Conference on Lexical and Computational Semantics (* SEM), Volume 2: Proceedings of the Seventh International Workshop on Semantic Evaluation (SemEval 2013)*, Volume 2, pp. 222–231.

Navigli, R. and S. P. Ponzetto (2012). Babelnet: The automatic construction, evaluation and application of a wide-coverage multilingual semantic network. *Artificial Intelligence 193*, 217–250.

Nivre, J., J. Hall, S. Kübler, R. McDonald, J. Nilsson, S. Riedel, and D. Yuret (2007). The conll 2007 shared task on dependency parsing. In *Proceedings of the 2007 Joint Conference on Empirical Methods in Natural Language Processing and Computational Natural Language Learning (EMNLP-CoNLL)*.

Peters, M. E., M. Neumann, M. Iyyer, M. Gardner, C. Clark, K. Lee, and L. Zettlemoyer (2018). Deep contextualized word representations. *arXiv preprint arXiv:1802.05365*.

Raganato, A., J. Camacho-Collados, and R. Navigli (2017). Word sense disambiguation: A unified evaluation framework and empirical comparison. In *Proceedings of the 15th Conference of the European Chapter of the Association for Computational Linguistics: Volume 1, Long Papers*, Volume 1, pp. 99–110.

Sérasset, G. (2012). Dbnary: Wiktionary as a lmf based multilingual rdf network. In *Language Resources and Evaluation Conference, LREC 2012*.

Weaver, W. (1955). Translation. *Machine translation of languages 14*, 15–23.

Yimam, S. M., C. Biemann, R. E. de Castilho, and I. Gurevych (2014). Automatic annotation suggestions and custom annotation layers in webanno. In *Proceedings of 52nd Annual Meeting of the Association for Computational Linguistics: System Demonstrations*, pp. 91–96.

Yuan, D., J. Richardson, R. Doherty, C. Evans, and E. Altendorf (2016). Semi-supervised word sense disambiguation with neural models. *arXiv preprint arXiv:1603.07012*.

Zhong, Z. and H. T. Ng (2010). It makes sense: A wide-coverage word sense disambiguation system for free text. In *Proceedings of the ACL 2010 System Demonstrations*, pp. 78–83. Association for Computational Linguistics.

A Comparison of Context-sensitive Models
for Lexical Substitution

Aina Garí Soler[1], Anne Cocos[2], Marianna Apidianaki[1,3], Chris Callison-Burch[2]

[1]LIMSI, CNRS, Univ. Paris Sud, Université Paris Saclay, F-91405 Orsay, France
[2]Department of Computer and Information Science, University of Pennsylvania
[3]LLF, CNRS, Univ. Paris Diderot
`aina.gari@limsi.fr, acocos@seas.upenn.edu,`
`marianna@limsi.fr, ccb@seas.upenn.edu`

Abstract

Word embedding representations provide good estimates of word meaning and give state-of-the art performance in semantic tasks. Embedding approaches differ as to whether and how they account for the context surrounding a word. We present a comparison of different word and context representations on the task of proposing substitutes for a target word in context (lexical substitution). We also experiment with tuning contextualized word embeddings on a dataset of sense-specific instances for each target word. We show that powerful contextualized word representations, which give high performance in several semantics-related tasks, deal less well with the subtle in-context similarity relationships needed for substitution. This is better handled by models trained with this objective in mind, where the inter-dependence between word and context representations is explicitly modeled during training.

1 Introduction

Contextualized word representations model complex characteristics of word usage, and give state-of-the-art performance in a variety of NLP tasks involving syntactic and semantic processing. Each proposed model accounts for context in a different way depending on the underlying architecture, and might account for local or long-distance phenomena. In this work, we compare different word representations on the lexical substitution (LexSub) task, which involves proposing meaning-preserving substitutes for words in specific contexts (McCarthy and Navigli, 2007). The importance of context in defining the meaning of word instances, and selecting the substitutes that best fit specific sentences, makes of the LexSub task an ideal testbed for a direct comparison of the contextualized representations built by different models.

We compare representations that model context in different ways: they exploit context embeddings generated within the skip-gram model (Melamud et al., 2015), learn a generic context embedding function using a bidirectional Long Short-Term Memory (LSTM) network (Melamud et al., 2016), or use vectors that are learned functions of the internal states of a deep bidirectional language model (biLM) (Peters et al., 2018a). Additionally, we experiment with a way to tune these state-of-the-art context-sensitive representations to sense-specific contexts of use, using a dataset of sentences containing each LexSub target word that are carefully chosen to reflect the senses of their potential substitutes. We explore the impact of this tuning on the LexSub task. Finally, we compare the performance of contextualized models to baseline models that exploit standard word embedding representations for measuring semantic similarity without directly accounting for context, such as Glove (Pennington et al., 2014) and FastText (Mikolov et al., 2018).

The results of this study highlight the importance of the architecture used for model training in capturing information relevant for lexical substitution. We show that contextualized representations that

Substitutes	Sentences
shoot (5)	The panther **fired** at the bridge and hit a truck.
sack (5), dismiss (1)	While both he and the White House deny he was **fired**, Frum is so insistent on the fact that he quit on his own that it really makes you wonder.
trainer (3), teacher (2), instructor (1), tutor (1)	As a **coach**, we speak and listen with the intent of helping people surface, question and reframe assumptions.
bus (5), carriage (1)	We hopped back onto the **coach** - now for the boulangerie!

Table 1: Examples of manually proposed substitutes for the verb *fire* and the noun *coach* in the SemEval-2007 Lexical Substitution dataset (McCarthy and Navigli, 2007). Numbers in brackets indicate the number of annotators who proposed each substitute.

have been shown to be very powerful in other semantics-related tasks perform less well in the LexSub task, while others that explicitly model the inter-dependence of words and their context manage to propose the best substitutes as measured by comparing their choices to human annotations in a gold standard dataset.

2 Related Work

The lexical substitution task consists in selecting meaning-preserving substitutes for words in context. Initially proposed as a testbed for word sense disambiguation systems (McCarthy and Navigli, 2007), in recent works it is mainly seen as a way of evaluating the in-context lexical inference capacity of vector-space models without explicitly accounting for sense (Kremer et al., 2014; Melamud et al., 2015). Examples of substitutes of words in context proposed by annotators in the SemEval-2007 Lexical Substitution dataset are presented in Table 1. The main idea behind these sense-unaware models is that the basic (out-of-context) representation of a word is adapted to each specific context of use. This is done by combining the basic vector of the word with the vectors of words found in its immediate context, or having a specific syntactic relation. Appropriate substitutes are synonyms or paraphrases of the word that are similar to this contextualized representation.

Melamud et al. (2015) use word embeddings generated using the word2vec skip-gram model (Mikolov et al., 2013). word2vec learns for every word type two distinct representations, one as a target and another as a context, both embedded in the same space. The context representations are generally discarded after training, considered internal to the model, and the output word embeddings represent context-insensitive target word types. Melamud et al. use the context embeddings in conjunction with the target word embeddings to model word instances in context, identify appropriate substitutes by measuring their similarity to the target and the context, and obtain state-of-the-art results on the LexSub task.

In later work, Melamud et al. (2016) propose *context2vec*, a model that uses a neural network architecture based on word2vec CBOW (Mikolov et al., 2013). context2vec replaces CBOW's representation of a word's surrounding context as a simple average of the embeddings of the context words in a fixed window, with a full sentence neural representation of context obtained using a bidirectional LSTM. Sentential contexts and target words are embedded in the same low-dimensional space, which is optimized to reflect inter-dependencies between them. This rich representation gives context2vec high performance in tasks involving context, such as lexical substitution, word sense disambiguation and sentence completion.

Peters et al. (2018a) propose a new type of deep contextualized word representations called *ELMo* (Embeddings from Language Models), where each token is assigned a representation that is a function of the entire input sentence. Vectors are derived from a bidirectional LSTM that is trained with a coupled language model (LM) objective on a large test corpus. ELMo representations are deep in the sense that they are a function of all of the internal layers of the biLM, which improves performance in several syntax and semantics-related tasks compared to using the top LSTM layer. The best combination of layers is learnt jointly with a supervised NLP task. An analysis on different tasks shows that lower layers efficiently encode syntactic information, while higher layers capture semantics (Peters et al., 2018b). The gains observed in syntactic tasks outweigh those on semantic-related tasks, such as coreference resolution, Semantic Role Labeling and word sense disambiguation. In this work, we apply the ELMo vectors for the first time to the lexical substitution task and compare their performance to the context-sensitive models of Melamud et al. (2015) and Melamud et al. (2016). We also propose a way to tune the ELMo representations to the LexSub task, by using a dataset containing a high number of sentences for words in context that represent meanings close to that of their possible substitutes.

3 Substitute-focused Contexts

Contextualized word embeddings for a given target word vary based on the sense of a target word instance. Unlike the variation in discrete sense-level embeddings (e.g. Iacobacci et al. (2015); Rothe and Schütze (2015); Flekova and Gurevych (2016), and others), this variation is continuous. One of our experiments aims to see whether incorporating discrete fine-grained sense information into our LexSub models, where senses are defined at the level of substitute paraphrases, can improve performance. For this purpose, we generate a dataset of "focused contexts" (hereafter abbreviated FC) for each target word which are specifically chosen to represent the specific sense that target word shares with each of its potential substitutes.

The starting point for our focused contexts dataset is the Paraphrase Database (PPDB) (Ganitkevitch et al., 2013; Pavlick et al., 2015), a collection of over 80M English paraphrase pairs. PPDB was automatically built using the pivot method (Bannard and Callison-Burch, 2005), which discovers same-language paraphrases by 'pivoting' over bilingual parallel corpora. Specifically, if two English phrases such as "*under control*" and "*in check*" are each translated to the same German phrase "*unter kontrolle*" in some contexts, then this is taken as evidence that "*under control*" and "*in check*" have approximately similar meaning. Because PPDB was constructed using the pivot method, it follows that each paraphrase pair $x \leftrightarrow y$ in PPDB has a set of shared foreign translations. This idea is core to the method for extracting substitute-focused sentences.

The sentences for paraphrase pair $x \leftrightarrow y$ are extracted from the English side of English-to-foreign bitext corpora as follows. We assume there exists some set F^{xy} of foreign phrases to which x and y have both been independently translated. To find sentences containing x that correspond to its sense as a paraphrase of y, we simply enumerate English sentences containing x from the parallel corpora where x is aligned to some $f \in F^{xy}$. Sentences for y are extracted symmetrically. We refer to the set of English sentences containing x as $S^{\dot{x}y}$, and the set of English sentences containing y as $S^{x\dot{y}}$. Note that for some other paraphrase pair involving x, say $x \leftrightarrow z$, there may be sentences that appear in both $S^{\dot{x}y}$ and $S^{\dot{x}z}$ if their sets of shared translations, F^{xy} and F^{xz}, overlap.

Intuitively, we would like the sentences containing x in $S^{\dot{x}y}$ to be "highly characteristic" of the meaning of y, and vice versa. However, not all pivot translations $f \in F^{xy}$ produce equally characteristic sentences. For example, consider the paraphrase pair *bug $\leftrightarrow$ worm*. Their shared translation set, $F^{bug,worm}$, includes the French terms *ver* (*worm*) and *espèce* (*species*), and the Chinese term 虫 (*bug*). In selecting sentences for $S^{bug,worm}$, the FC dataset should prioritize English sentences where *bug* has been translated to the most characteristic translation for *worm* – *ver* – over the more general 虫 or *espèce*.

The degree to which a foreign translation is "characteristic" of an English term can be quantified by the pointwise mutual information (PMI) of the English term with the foreign term. To avoid unwanted biases that might arise from the uneven distribution of languages present in our bitext corpora, we treat PMI as language-specific. Given language l containing foreign words $f \in l$, we use shorthand notation f_l to indicate that f comes from language l. The PMI of English term e with foreign word f_l can be computed as:

$$\mathrm{PMI}(e, f_l) = \frac{p(e, f_l)}{p(e) \cdot p(f_l)} = \frac{p(f_l|e)}{p(f_l)}$$

Substitutes	Substitute-focused sentences
sack	Yet what are proclamations on employment rights worth, when company bosses have a 'divine right' to hire and **fire**?
dismiss	They chose to **fire** a lot of people; to throw people out who weren't needed.
shoot	We hope that the generals and civilian oligarchs will not **fire** on the honduran people.
launch	A security source said electrical wiring found at the site suggested plans to **fire** the rockets by remote control.

Table 2: Examples of substitute-focused sentences for the verb *fire* corresponding to its substitutes.

The term in the numerator is the translation probability $p(f_l|e)$, which indicates the likelihood that English word e is translated to foreign term f_l in an English-l parallel corpus. Maximizing this term promotes the most frequent foreign translations for e. It is calculated as:

$$p(f_l|e) = \frac{\text{count}(e \rightarrow f_l)}{\sum_{f' \in l} \text{count}(e \rightarrow f')}$$

where $(e \rightarrow f_l)$ indicates the event that e is aligned to f_l in a bitext sentence pair. The term in the denominator is the likelihood of the foreign word, $p(f_l)$. Dividing by this term down-weights the emphasis on frequent foreign words. This is especially helpful for mitigating errors due to mis-alignments of English words with foreign stop words. The foreign word probability is calculated as:

$$p(f_l) = \frac{\text{count}(f_l)}{\sum_{f' \in l} \text{count}(f')}$$

To extract $S^{\dot{x}y}$, the set of English sentences containing x for paraphrase pair $x \leftrightarrow y$, we first order their shared translations, $f \in F^{xy}$, by decreasing $PMI(y, f)$. Then, for each translation f in order, we extract up to 2500 sentences from the bitext corpora where x is translated to f. This process continues until a maximum of 10k sentences containing x are generated. As a result of selecting sentences containing x in decreasing order of $PMI(y, f)$, the dataset includes contexts where the sense of x is most closely related to its paraphrase y.

To compile our dataset, we select sentences pertaining to all paraphrases of each target word in the LexSub datset. We extract sentences from the same English-to-foreign bitext corpora used to generate English PPDB (Ganitkevitch et al., 2013).

3.1 Deriving contextualized vectors from focused contexts

The focused context dataset groups sentences where a target word appears with a specific meaning, that of one of its paraphrases (possible substitutes) in PPDB. This makes the resource useful for lexical substitution, as it provides numerous examples of sentences for each target-substitute pair. In Table 2, we give examples of sentences for the word *fire* and its candidate substitutes (*sack, dismiss, shoot, launch*).

We use the sets of sentences available for each target-substitute pair to create contextualized representations for the candidate substitutes, using the approach proposed by Peters et al. (2018a) for applying the biLM representations to a supervised word sense disambiguation task. More precisely, we tune pretrained contextualized (ELMo) embeddings to the LexSub task using contexts from the FC dataset. A representation for a substitute of a target word is the average of the ELMo vectors obtained from the FC sentences corresponding to that substitute. For each substitute, we use the 100 sentences with the highest PMI, avoiding sentences with a high overlap in words.[1] The ELMo language model contains three layers, so each token in text has three different representations, one per layer. It is important to note that we do not train a neural model on this dataset, so we do not learn a linear combination of the biLM layers in the way ELMo is typically used. Instead, we experiment with the top layer (*FC-ELMo-top*) and

---

[1] We use an overlap threshold of 60%. This cleaning serves to discard highly similar sentences and ensure a varied vocabulary in the retained dataset. If for some substitutes less than 100 sentences are available after this filtering, we keep them all.

an average of the three layers (*FC-ELMo-avg*) of the biLM (5.5B) released by Peters et al. (2018a)[2]. We also use FC to tune context2vec embeddings released by Melamud et al. (2016) and pre-trained on the UkWac corpus[3] (*FC-c2v*). We create context representations from the high quality sentences retained for a target-substitute pair by replacing the target word with a blank slot. A representation for the substitute is then created by taking the average of all generated context representations. The obtained candidate vectors are used in the lexical substitution methods described in Section 4.

4   Lexical Substitution Methods

We present a head-to-head comparison of different context representations on the LexSub task. We evaluate all models on the SemEval Lexical Substitution task test set (McCarthy and Navigli, 2007). Given an instance of a target word t and a set of candidate substitutes ($S = \{s_1, s_2, ..., s_n\}$), each model provides a ranking of the substitutes depending on how well they describe the meaning of t in each specific sentence. Higher ranked substitutes are both good paraphrases of the target and a good fit in the context. In our experiments, candidate substitutes $S = \{s_1, s_2, ..., s_n\}$ for a target word t are its paraphrases in the Paraphrase Database (PPDB) XXL package (Pavlick et al., 2015)[4] that are also present in the gold standard annotations. This is a ranking variant of the LexSub task where systems are not expected to identify substitutes from the whole vocabulary, but rather to estimate the suitability of items in a specific pool of substitutes and rank them accordingly (Kremer et al., 2014). In what follows, we describe how the different methods represent words and contexts, and perform substitute ranking for new instances. An illustration of the different methods can be found in Figure 1.

4.1   Target-to-substitute similarity

ELMo representations are contextualized, in the sense that the embedding of a token is a function of the full sentence in which it appears. We propose a substitute ranking method that uses target-to-substitute (*tTs*) similarity, as measured by the cosine similarity of the corresponding ELMo representations. We use the top layer (*ELMo-top*) and the average of the three layers (*ELMo-avg*) of the biLM (5.5B) (Peters et al., 2018a) in the following way.

Given a new sentence C with an instance of the target word to be substituted, we first obtain an ELMo representation from this context corresponding to the target word. Then, we replace the target with all its potential substitutes, one at a time, and obtain the ELMo vector for each substitute in the context of C by feeding the new sentence as input to the biLM. Substitutes are then ranked by the cosine similarity of the target word's ELMo vector in C with that of the ELMo vector of each substitute in the same context.

We use this method with FC-ELMo as well. For each sentence, possible substitutes are ranked according to the similarity of their FC-ELMo embedding to the ELMo embedding of the target word in the sentence. We expect context to be indirectly taken into account by using such contextualized representations.

4.2   *AddCos*: *skip-gram* word and context embeddings

Melamud et al. (2015)'s method for lexical substitution is based on the skip-gram word embedding model. The novelty of the approach is that it explicitly leverages the context embeddings generated within skip-gram, generally considered as internal and discarded at the end of the learning process. The proposed context-sensitive substitutability measures for potential substitutes reflect a combination of two types of similarity: a) *target-to-substitute*, showing how similar a potential substitute is to the target word, and b) *target-to-context*, reflecting the substitute's compatibility with a given sentential context. Similarities are estimated using the vector Cosine distance between the respective skip-gram word and

---

[2]https://allennlp.org/elmo
[3]http://u.cs.biu.ac.il/ nlp/resources/downloads/context2vec/
[4]http://paraphrase.org

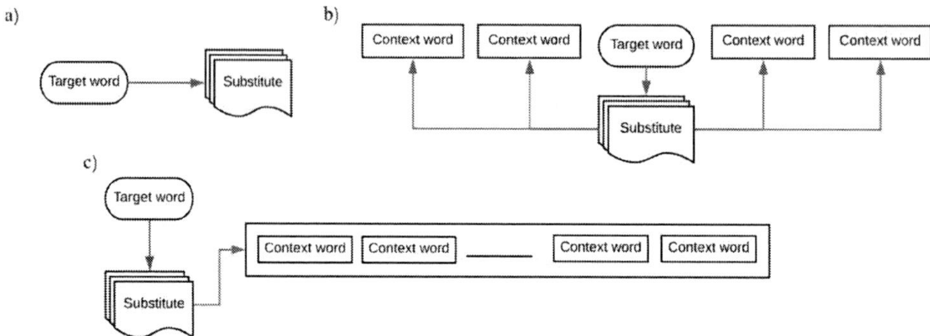

Figure 1: Illustration of the type of context information the different methods use: a) *tTs* uses target to substitute similarity only (Section 4.1); b) *AddCos* also uses similarities between a candidate and each of the words in the surrounding context (Section 4.2); c) *c2vf* makes use instead of a unique embedding representing the whole sentential context (Section 4.3).

context embeddings. The proposed measures differ in the way they combine the score elements together, using either an arithmetic or geometrical mean. We choose the more flexible additive approach which, contrary to the multiplicative variants, does not require high similarities in all elements of the product to highly rank a substitute, but can yield a high score even if one of the elements in the sum is zero. The *Add* measure (equation (1), hereafter called *AddCos* because of the Cosine function applied to the vector representations of words and contexts) estimates the substitutability of a candidate substitute s of the target word t in context C, where C corresponds to the set of the target word's context elements in the sentence, and c corresponds to an individual context element.

$$AddCos(t, s, C) = \frac{cos(s, t) + \sum_{c \in C} cos(s, c)}{|C| + 1}$$ (1)

The vectors used by the original method are syntax-based embeddings created with *word2vecf* (Levy and Goldberg, 2014). We use the lighter adaptation proposed by Apidianaki et al. (2018) which circumvents the need for syntactic analysis, and use 300-dimensional skip-gram word and context embeddings trained on the 4B words of the Annotated Gigaword corpus (Napoles et al., 2012).

We apply the AddCos method to ELMo as well as to FC-ELMo embeddings. When using standard ELMo embeddings, the target and context word representations of a sentence are their corresponding ELMo vector, and the vector of a candidate substitute is obtained by substituting the target word by the candidate in the sentence, as described in Section 4.1. To adapt this to FC-ELMo embeddings, substitute representations are replaced by their corresponding FC-ELMo vectors.

4.3 The *context2vec*-based model

The *context2vec* (*c2v*) model jointly learns context and word embeddings using bidirectional LSTM (Melamud et al., 2016). The proposed neural network is based on word2vec's CBOW architecture (Mikolov et al., 2013), but replaces its naive context modeling of averaged word embeddings in a fixed window with a full-sentence neural representation of context obtained using bidirectional LSTM. Words and contexts are embedded in the same space, which allows for calculating target-to-context (*t2c*), context-to-context (*c2c*) and target-to-target (*t2t*) similarities. A score for a candidate substitute is computed using the following formula:

$$c2v\_score = \frac{cos(s, t) + 1}{2} \times \frac{cos(s, C) + 1}{2}$$ (2)

where t and s are the word embeddings of the target and the substitute, and C is the *c2v* context vector of the sentence with an empty slot at the target's position. We use the 600-dimensional c2v embeddings released by Melamud et al. (2016).

We also use Equation (2) (hereafter called *c2vf*) with standard ELMo and FC-ELMo vectors. As with the AddCos method, we represent the target word in context by its ELMo embedding, and the substitute vectors are obtained with the in-place substitution approach described above (cf. Sections 4.1, 4.2). The context vector (C) is the average of the ELMo embeddings of all words in the context. To test FC-ELMo embeddings in this setting, each substitute is represented by its FC-ELMo embedding.

Finally, we experiment with FC-c2v embeddings, i.e. standard context2vec embeddings (Melamud et al., 2016) tuned on the FC dataset. Target and context are represented with standard c2v embeddings, and substitutes are represented with FC-c2v embeddings.

4.4 Baselines

We compare our models to two context-insensitive baselines that solely rely on the target-to-substitute similarity of standard, pre-trained word embeddings: 300-dimensional GloVe vectors (Pennington et al., 2014)[5] and 300-dimensional FastText vectors, both trained on Common Crawl (Mikolov et al., 2018).[6] Similar to tTs (Section 4.1), this approach only considers target-to-substitute similarity. With these uncontextualized embeddings the ranking proposed for each target word is always the same regardless of context.

We also propose an enriched version of the two baseline models by adding a simple representation of context consisting of the average of the embeddings of words in a sentence. We then compare target and substitute vectors to the generated context vector using the context2vec formula (Equation 2).

5 Evaluation

We compare the performance of the proposed models on a ranking task, where models assign scores to all candidate substitutes for a target word ($S = \{s_1, s_2, ..., s_n\}$) according to their suitability in new contexts. For evaluation, we use the dataset from the SemEval-2007 Lexical Substitution task (McCarthy and Navigli, 2007). The full dataset consists of 2,010 sentences, 10 for each of 201 target words (nouns, verbs, adjectives and adverbs), extracted from the English Internet Corpus (Sharoff, 2006), and annotated by five native English speakers. Words in this lexical sample were selected to ensure variety of senses. We filter the test set to preserve target words and substitutes present in PPDB 2.0 (XXL) and having a vector available in all tested models, to ensure all methods use exactly the same substitute pool per target word. Target words for which none or only one substitute was left were removed. The filtered test set used in our experiments includes 158 target words and 1,584 sentences.

The ranking performed by each model is compared to the gold ranking by means of Generalized Average Precision (GAP) (Kishida, 2005). GAP measures the quality of a ranking by comparing the resulting ranked list with the gold standard annotation, using substitution frequency as weights (i.e. number of annotators that suggested each substitute). GAP scores range between 0 and 1. A score of 1 indicates a perfect ranking where all correct substitutes precede all incorrect ones, and high-weight substitutes precede low-weight ones (Thater et al., 2010). We use the GAP implementation in Melamud et al. (2015)[7].

6 Results

The results of the proposed methods in the substitute ranking task are given in Table 3. The standard context2vec (c2v) model (Melamud et al., 2016) outperforms other methods, including those based on

---

[5]https://nlp.stanford.edu/projects/glove

[6]https://fasttext.cc/docs/en/english-vectors.html

[7]https://github.com/orenmel/lexsub

Method	Vectors	GAP
	Skip-gram (Apidianaki et al., 2018)	0.527
	ELMo-avg	0.527
AddCos (c=1)	ELMo-top	0.513
	FC-ELMo-avg	0.494
	FC-ELMo-top	0.491
	Skip-gram (Apidianaki et al., 2018)	0.520
	ELMo-avg	0.498
AddCos (c=4)	ELMo-top	0.476
	FC-ELMo-avg	0.481
	FC-ELMo-top	0.478
	UkWac c2v (Melamud et al., 2016)	**0.587**
	FC-c2v	0.492
c2vf	ELMo-avg	0.529
	ELMo-top	0.516
	FC-ELMo-avg	0.490
	FC-ELMo-top	0.480
	ELMo-avg (Peters et al., 2018a)	0.534
tTs	ELMo-top (Peters et al., 2018a)	0.531
	FC-ELMo-avg	0.493
	FC-ELMo-top	0.488
Glove + context	Glove (Pennington et al., 2014)	0.467
Fasttext + context	Fasttext (Mikolov et al., 2018)	0.491
Baselines	Glove (Pennington et al., 2014)	0.465
	Fasttext (Mikolov et al., 2018)	0.485

Table 3: Results of the substitute ranking experiment with all methods and embedding types. For AddCos models, c refers to the size of the window.

ELMo vectors. The superiority of context2vec is due to its training objective: context2vec is explicitly trained with pairs of target words and sentential contexts, optimizing the similarity of context vectors and potential fillers. This training objective makes the model highly suited for the LexSub task. In contrast, ELMo representations are trained as a general language model that predicts the immediate next tokens, while other types of similarity (e.g. target-to-substitute and substitute-to-context) used by the other methods are not explicitly accounted for. The underlying assumption of the AddCos and context2vec models that these similarities need to be high for good substitutes, does not thus apply in the case of ELMo embeddings.

The ELMo-avg and ELMo-top configurations – which use the top layer or an average of the three layers of the biLM – give comparable results, with ELMo-avg performing slightly better in all settings. Peters et al. (2018b) present a thorough analysis of the performance of different layers of the biLM models in different tasks, which shows that top layers are better suited for semantic-related tasks than lower layers. In the supervised word sense disambiguation (WSD) evaluation presented in Peters et al. (2018a) results obtained using the top layer were also slightly better than those of the middle layer. We believe the slight advantage of the ELMo-avg models, compared to ELMo-top, in LexSub, highlights an important difference between the two tasks. In LexSub, the selected substitute needs to correctly describe the meaning of the target word instance and to be a good fit in the context, producing a natural-sounding sentence. Substitute candidates for a word are often near-synonyms that would be preferred in different contexts. On the contrary, selection in WSD mainly relies on semantic adequacy. For example, when selecting one among available senses of a word in a resource like WordNet, the synonyms found in the selected synset might not all be good in-context substitutes. We believe the ELMo representation obtained by averaging the three layers to contain information regarding both the semantic and the syntactic

Sentence	*on the **way** out of the parking lot johnny felt a thump*
Candidate substitutes for *way.n*	sense, means, aspect, technique, passage, respect, direction, characteristic, journey, method, route, practice, fashion, manner
Gold ranking	route (3), passage (1), journey (1)

Table 4: A new instance of the target noun *way* (*way.n*) from the SemEval-2007 test set, the candidate substitutes extracted for the word from the PPDB XXL package, and the gold substitute ranking used for evaluation.

Method	Vectors	Ranked substitutes
c2vf	UkWac c2v (Melamud et al., 2016)	**route**, **journey**, manner, **passage**, direction, means, sense, aspect, method, fashion, respect, technique, characteristic, practice
tTs	ELMo-avg (Peters et al., 2018a)	**route, journey**, manner, direction, **passage**, method, means, respect, technique, sense, practice, aspect, fashion, characteristic
Baseline	Glove (Pennington et al., 2014)	sense, means, manner, **journey, route,** direction, respect, aspect, practice, method, technique, fashion, **passage**, characteristic
Baseline + ctxt	Glove (Pennington et al., 2014)	sense, means, manner, direction, respect, **journey**, aspect, **route**, practice, method, **passage**, technique, fashion, characteristic

Table 5: Examples of substitute rankings for the instance of the noun *"way"* given in Table 4 of the two best-performing methods (c2vf with standard c2v embeddings and tTs with ELMo-av embeddings) and the two methods with lowest GAP (baseline and baseline + context with Glove embeddings). Correct substitutes are marked in boldface to highlight their position in the ranking proposed by each model.

adequacy of a word. This does not contradict previous findings, since the semantics tasks in which the top ELMo layer was found to perform best were tasks that involve longer range dependencies and a more general notion of semantic similarity (e.g. coreference resolution).

The results obtained for FC-ELMO-* configurations show that ELMo representations do not benefit from the addition of discretized sense representations, rather the contrary. Whereas it looks like FC is introducing confusion to an already good model, we believe this could be due to the small amount of FC sentences used for tuning (100), which biases the model toward those sentences. Another reason could be that FC sentences selected using the PMI metric for a target-substitute pair are not always high quality, i.e. they might not contain, or not be representative enough, of the sense being expressed. In future work, we intend to experiment with a larger number of sentences for tuning, and with different ways for measuring the quality of sentences to be included in the FC resource.

The baseline methods that use uncontextualized word embeddings are not very far behind most FC-ELMo-* models. However, they do seem to slightly benefit from adding context. FastText vectors are trained with word2vec's CBOW architecture using position-dependent weighting, which results in richer context representations and is, we believe, the main reason of its advantage over Glove on this task.

Finally, we observe that, for the AddCos method, a smaller context window around the target word (c=1) is consistently slightly more effective than a bigger one (c=4). This suggests that the most relevant context clues for lexical substitution are found in the close vicinity of a target word.

In Tables 4 and 5, we give an example of a new target word instance and the substitute ranking proposed by some of the models. In Table 4, we also provide the candidate substitutes considered for the target word *way*, which are its paraphrases in PPDB XXL that are also present among the gold standard annotations for this word. Numbers in parentheses denote the number of annotators that proposed each substitute. We observe that the stronger models which use the c2v formula with the standard context2vec vectors (trained on UkWac) or the tTs method with ELMo-avg rank substitutes better than the baseline models.

7 Conclusion

We analyzed the behavior of different word and context representations in an in-context substitute ranking task. The compared methods differ as to the type of similarity they consider between words (target-to-substitute) and contexts (substitute-to-context). We experiment with the standard representations released for each approach, and fine-tune them to the LexSub task using an automatically compiled collection of sentences representing target-substitute pairs. Our results show that models trained with a slot-filling objective that optimizes the inter-dependencies between candidate substitutes and context, like context2vec, are a better fit for the LexSub task than purely context-based models, like ELMo. This is because they encode target-to-substitute similarity and local context appropriately for this task, which ensures the semantic and syntactic adequacy of the selected substitutes. The importance of these two parameters is also highlighted in our experiments by the performance of different combinations of ELMo layers, which shows that the substitute ranking task involves both semantic (top-layer) and syntactic (lower-layer) information.

In its current form, tuning on the sentences of the FC dataset does not seem to help the models. In future work, we plan to improve the quality of the substitute-focused contexts, to ensure a better representation of the meaning of target-substitute pairs that would be beneficial for this task. A large-scale resource of this type will be highly useful for training neural models for lexical substitution.

8 Acknowledgements

We would like to thank the anonymous reviewers for their thoughtful and constructive comments. This work has been supported by the French National Research Agency under project ANR-16-CE33-0013; the Allen AI Key Scientific Challenges program; the Google PhD Fellowship; and DARPA under grant numbers FA8750-13-2-0017 (the DEFT program) and HR0011-15-C-0115 (the LORELEI program).

References

Apidianaki, M., G. Wisniewski, A. Cocos, and C. Callison-Burch (2018). Automated paraphrase lattice creation for HyTER machine translation evaluation. In *Proceedings of the 2018 Conference of the North American Chapter of the Association for Computational Linguistics: Human Language Technologies, Volume 2 (Short Papers)*, New Orleans, Louisiana, pp. 480–485.

Bannard, C. and C. Callison-Burch (2005). Paraphrasing with bilingual parallel corpora. In *Proceedings of the 43rd Annual Meeting on Association for Computational Linguistics*, pp. 597–604.

Flekova, L. and I. Gurevych (2016). Supersense embeddings: A unified model for supersense interpretation, prediction, and utilization. In *Proceedings of the 54th Annual Meeting of the Association for Computational Linguistics (Volume 1: Long Papers)*, Volume 1, pp. 2029–2041.

Ganitkevitch, J., B. Van Durme, and C. Callison-Burch (2013). PPDB: The Paraphrase Database. In *Proceedings of the 2013 Conference of the North American Chapter of the Association for Computational Linguistics: Human Language Technologies*, Atlanta, Georgia, pp. 758–764.

Iacobacci, I., M. T. Pilehvar, and R. Navigli (2015). Sensembed: Learning sense embeddings for word and relational similarity. In *Proceedings of the 53rd Annual Meeting of the Association for Computational Linguistics and the 7th International Joint Conference on Natural Language Processing (Volume 1: Long Papers)*, Volume 1, pp. 95–105.

Kishida, K. (2005). *Property of average precision and its generalization: An examination of evaluation indicator for information retrieval experiments.* Technical Report NII-2005-014E, National Institute of Informatics Tokyo, Japan.

Kremer, G., K. Erk, S. Padó, and S. Thater (2014). What Substitutes Tell Us - Analysis of an "All-Words" Lexical Substitution Corpus. In *Proceedings of EACL*, Gothenburg, Sweden, pp. 540–549.

Levy, O. and Y. Goldberg (2014). Dependency-based word embeddings. In *Proceedings of the 52nd Annual Meeting of the Association for Computational Linguistics (Volume 2: Short Papers)*, Volume 2, pp. 302–308.

McCarthy, D. and R. Navigli (2007). Semeval-2007 task 10: English lexical substitution task. In *Proceedings of the 4th International Workshop on Semantic Evaluations (SemEval-2007)*, Prague, Czech Republic, pp. 48–53.

Melamud, O., J. Goldberger, and I. Dagan (2016). context2vec: Learning generic context embedding with bidirectional LSTM. In *Proceedings of The 20th SIGNLL Conference on Computational Natural Language Learning*, Berlin, Germany, pp. 51–61.

Melamud, O., O. Levy, and I. Dagan (2015). A simple word embedding model for lexical substitution. In *Proceedings of the 1st Workshop on Vector Space Modeling for Natural Language Processing*, Denver, Colorado, pp. 1–7.

Mikolov, T., K. Chen, G. Corrado, and J. Dean (2013). Efficient estimation of word representations in vector space. In *Proceedings of the International Conference on Learning Representations*, Scottsdale, Arizona.

Mikolov, T., E. Grave, P. Bojanowski, C. Puhrsch, and A. Joulin (2018). Advances in pre-training distributed word representations. In *Proceedings of the International Conference on Language Resources and Evaluation (LREC 2018)*, Miyazaki, Japan, pp. 52–55.

Napoles, C., M. Gormley, and B. Van Durme (2012). Annotated Gigaword. In *Proceedings of the Joint Workshop on Automatic Knowledge Base Construction and Web-scale Knowledge Extraction*, pp. 95–100.

Pavlick, E., P. Rastogi, J. Ganitkevitch, B. Van Durme, and C. Callison-Burch (2015). PPDB 2.0: Better paraphrase ranking, fine-grained entailment relations, word embeddings, and style classification. In *Proceedings of ACL/IJCNLP*, Beijing, China, pp. 425–430.

Pennington, J., R. Socher, and C. Manning (2014). Glove: Global vectors for word representation. In *Proceedings of the 2014 conference on empirical methods in natural language processing (EMNLP)*, Doha, Qatar, pp. 1532–1543.

Peters, M. E., M. Neumann, M. Iyyer, M. Gardner, C. Clark, K. Lee, and L. Zettlemoyer (2018a). Deep contextualized word representations. In *Proceedings of the 2018 Conference of the North American Chapter of the Association for Computational Linguistics: Human Language Technologies, Volume 1 (Long Papers)*, New Orleans, Louisiana, pp. 2227–2237.

Peters, M. E., M. Neumann, L. Zettlemoyer, and W.-t. Yih (2018b). Dissecting contextual word embeddings: Architecture and representation. In *Proceedings of the 2018 Conference on Empirical Methods in Natural Language Processing*, Brussels, Belgium, pp. 1499–1509.

Rothe, S. and H. Schütze (2015). Autoextend: Extending word embeddings to embeddings for synsets and lexemes. In *Proceedings of the 53rd Annual Meeting of the Association for Computational Linguistics and the 7th International Joint Conference on Natural Language Processing (Volume 1: Long Papers)*, Volume 1, pp. 1793–1803.

Sharoff, S. (2006). Open-source corpora: Using the net to fish for linguistic data. *International Journal of Corpus Linguistics 11*(4), 435–462.

Thater, S., H. Fürstenau, and M. Pinkal (2010). Contextualizing semantic representations using syntactically enriched vector models. In *Proceedings of the 48th Annual Meeting of the Association for Computational Linguistics*, Uppsala, Sweden, pp. 948–957.

Natural Language Semantics With Pictures: Some Language & Vision Datasets and Potential Uses for Computational Semantics

David Schlangen
Department of Linguistics, University of Potsdam, Germany[*]
david.schlangen@uni-potsdam.de

Abstract

Propelling, and propelled by, the "deep learning revolution", recent years have seen the introduction of ever larger corpora of images annotated with natural language expressions. We survey some of these corpora, taking a perspective that reverses the usual directionality, as it were, by viewing the *images* as semantic annotation of the natural language expressions. We discuss datasets that can be derived from the corpora, and tasks of potential interest for computational semanticists that can be defined on those. In this, we make use of relations provided by the corpora (namely, the link between expression and image, and that between two expressions linked to the same image) and relations that we can add (similarity relations between expressions, or between images). Specifically, we show that in this way we can create data that can be used to learn and evaluate lexical and compositional grounded semantics, and we show that the "linked to same image" relation tracks a semantic implicature relation that is recognisable to annotators even in the absence of the linking image as evidence. Finally, as an example of possible benefits of this approach, we show that an exemplar-model-based approach to implicature beats a (simple) distributional space-based one on some derived datasets, while lending itself to *explainability*.

1 Introduction

In model-theoretic formal semantics, the central semantic notion "truth" is explicated as a relation between a sentence and a mathematical structure, its *model*. Semantics textbooks are surprisingly evasive about what exactly this structure is meant to be, other than hinting at that it in some way represents the general "situation", or "world", that the sentence is taken to be talking about. In any case, what the model as a mathematical structure does is to provide a collection of *individuals* about which the sentence could be talking, and an *interpretation* of the non-logical lexical items occurring in the sentence, in terms of sets of individuals (or tuples of individuals). The collection of individuals is typically called the *domain* D, and the set of interpretations I, so that a model $M = \langle D, I \rangle$.

It is this intended relation with the world that allows us to see an analogy between these structures and photographic images. A photograph is a frozen moment in time, a representation of how the world was (or looked like) at a certain moment, at a certain place and from a certain perspective. And just as a sentence in formal semantics is evaluated relative to a model, a sentence describing a situation can be seen as true *relative to an image* — if (and only if) the image *depicts* a situation of the described type. Hence, in a slight reversal of our usual way of talking, we can say that a given *image* does (or does not) make a given sentence true (instead of saying that the sentence is a true description of the image), and we can see the image as a model of the sentence.[1]

What does this sleight of hand buy us? A very large amount of data to play with! The field of computer vision has as one of its central aims to find meaning in pixels – see e.g., Davies (2012), Marr

---

[*]Work done while author was at Bielefeld University.

[1]There are interesting subtleties here. In our everyday language, we are quite good at ignoring the image layer, and say things like "the woman is using a computer", instead of "the image shows a woman using a computer", or "this is a computer", instead of "this is an image of a computer". This also seems to carry over to tense, where we can say "is using", instead of "was using at the time when the picture was taken". There are however contexts in which talk about the image *as* image is relevant, and this can happen in large corpora such as discussed here. So this is something to keep in mind.

(1982) – and a convenient way of representing meaning is with natural language. It is also a field that has been data-driven for a long time, and so there is a large number of data sets available that in some way pair images with natural language expressions.[2] Recent years have specifically seen the creation of large scale corpora where images are paired with ever more detailed language (e.g., single sentence or even full paragraph captions describing the image content; facts about the image spread over question and answer; detailed descriptions of parts of the image in terms of agents and patients; see references below).[3] Given the understanding that all these expressions are meant to "fit" to the images that they are paired with, and using the slight conceptual inversion of treating the images as "truthmakers" (Fine, 2017) for the sentences, this gives us an unprecedentedly large set of language expressions that are "semantically annotated."[4,5] As we will show, this gives us material to learn about the lexical and compositional semantics that underlies the use of the expressions.

The **contributions of this paper** are as follows: 1.) To make explicit a perspective that so far has been taken only implictly in the literature, which is to view images as *models* of natural language expressions; 2.) to show by example that taking this perspective opens up interesting data sets for computational semantics questions; 3.) specifically, to look at how grounded interpretation functions could be learned from and tested on this data, and; 4.) how data can be derived that expresses various implicature relationships; and 5.) to show how exemplar-based model building can be used to predict some of those relations. Our code for working with the corpora mentioned here (and some others) is available at `http://purl.com/cl-potsdam/sempix`.

2 Background

2.1 The Approach: Learning Semantics From Relations in Corpora

Our general approach will be to look at relations that are expressed in the data or can be added using computational methods, and then to ask what these can tell us about *semantic* relations like truth and entailment, and in turn what these tell us about the meanings of expressions. Figure 1 illustrates the idea. The corpora provide us with an "annotates" relation between images and expressions; in the Figure, holding between I_1 and e_1 and e_2, and I_2 and e_3, where the expressions for example could be captions. Implicitly, there is also an "annotates same image" relation that holds between expressions; here, e_1 and e_2, as alternative captions of the same image. Standard natural language processing and computer vision techniques (see below) allow us to compute similarity relations between pairs of images (e.g., I_1 and I_2) and between pairs of expressions (e_1, e_3). The question then is whether these relations can tell us something about *satisfaction / denotation* ($\models$, $\llbracket \cdot \rrbracket$) and *entailment* ($\models$, $\vdash$).

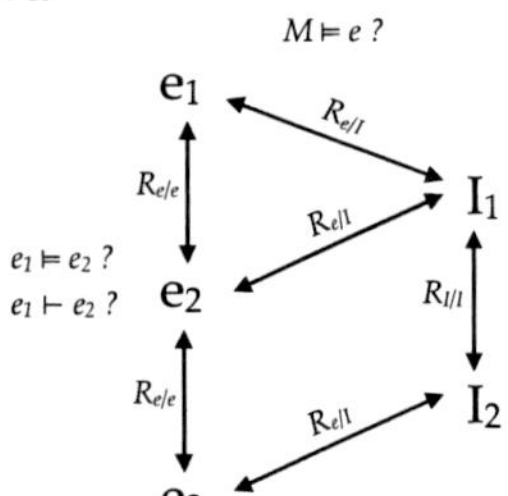

Figure 1: Relations in corpora & to be derived

2.2 Corpora Used Here

We make use of data from the following corpora:

    • **MSCOCO / RefCoco / GoogleREX:** The "Microsoft Common Objects in Context (COCO)" collection (Lin et al., 2014) contains over 300k images with object segmentations (of objects from 80 pre-specified categories), object labels, and nearly 400,000 image captions. It was augmented with 280,000

---

[2]See for example the (incomplete) lists at `http://www.cvpapers.com/datasets.html` and `https://riemenschneider.hayko.at/vision/dataset/`.

[3]While there are by now some non-English or even multi-lingual corpora, the majority provide *English* language annotations, including all of those that we discuss here.

[4]The corpora we discuss here provide almost 8 million distinct natural language expressions (with many more that can be derived from them). In comparison, the largest "classical" semantics resource, the Groningen Meaning Bank (Bos et al., 2017), provides some 10,000 annotated sentences, and the Parallel Meaning Bank (Abzianidze et al., 2017) another 15,000. There is no competition here, though: the Meaning Bank annotations are obviously much deeper and much more detailed; the proposal in this paper is to view the image corpora discussed here as complementary.

[5]The relation between images and models is implicit in (Young et al., 2014), from where we took inspiration, but not further developed there in the way that we are attempting here. Hürlimann and Bos (2016) make an explicit connection between image and models, but only look at denotations; as do Schlangen et al. (2016).

referring expressions by Yu et al. (2016), using the ReferitGame where one player needs to get another to identify a predetermined object in the image, with the players getting feedback on their success. Mao et al. (2016) also provide expressions for COCO objects, but collected monologically with the instructions to provide an expression that uniquely describes the target object.

- **Flickr30k / Flickr30kEntities:** Flickr30k (Young et al., 2014) is a collection of 30,000 images from a public image website which were augmented with 160,000 captions; Plummer et al. (2015) annotated these captions with positions of the objects in the images that they mention (Flickr30kEntities).

- **Visual Genome:** This dataset by Krishna et al. (2016) combines images from COCO and another data set (yielding around 100k images), and augments them with 2 million "region descriptions", which are statements true about a part of an image, and resolved for the entities mentioned and their relations. These descriptions are parsed into object names and attributes, and normalised by reference to the Word-Net ontology (Fellbaum, 1998). Krause et al. (2017) added 20,000 image description paragraphs (i.e., extended, multi-sentence captions) for some of the images.

All these data sets give us images paired with natural language expressions; in most of them, the relation between image and expression is annotated more fine-grainedly by linking regions within the image to (parts of) the expressions.[6] Also, some corpora provide an additional layer that could be seen as corresponding to the logical form of the expression, for example by normalising nouns to a resource like WordNet (Fellbaum, 1998) or by annotating the predicate / argument structure.

3 Expressions and Denotations

3.1 Images as Semantic Models: An Example

Above, we have introduced our analogy between semantic models and images. An example shall make it clearer. Figure 2 shows an image (from COCO) with *object segmentations* (rectangular patches indicating the position of an object in the image) and identifiers, as provided by the corpus. We can directly treat this as the *domain* provided by the model, so that here $D = \{o_{92839}, o_{93793}, o_{387589}, o_{387727}, o_{505664}, o_{510191}, o_{660005}, o_{1168354}, o_{1587273}, o_{1716887}, o_{1863940}, o_{1864058}, o_{1864291}\}$.

The corpus also provides natural language annotations for these objects, for example "the

Figure 2: A Segmented Image from COCO

woman in white" and "the woman in black" (for o_{505664}, o_{510191}, respectively). We can use this to "reverse engineer" the interpretation functions covering these words, and in particular derive that $I(woman) \subseteq \{o_{505664}, o_{510191}\}$. If we make an additional *exhaustivity* assumption over the set of annotations, we can strengthen this to $I(woman) = \{o_{505664}, o_{510191}\}$; that is, make the assumption that these are the *only* objects (in this image / the set of segmented objects from that image) to which this term can be applied. We will need to make this assumption when we want to generate *negative instances* used in machine learning, but need to keep in mind that in general, this assumption is unwarranted, as exhaustivity was not a goal when creating the corpora.

Continuing with the discussion, we can think more about what this view on the corpora offers for doing semantics. Our domain D is now populated not just with identifiers or symbols from a vocabulary, but rather with objects that have an internal structure. In the example above we were able simply to read off the interpretation function for the word from the annotation. But we can try to use

$o_{505664} =$

Figure 3: Invidual

---

[6]This makes working with the images easier, as it allows us to assume that the task of *object recognition* (detecting contiguous regions of pixels that belong to the same object) has already been successfully performed. This is not a strict requirement for working with images these days, however, as high-performing models are available that do this job (Redmon and Farhadi, 2018), (He et al., 2017), but these still add noise from which one might want to abstract for the purposes discussed here.

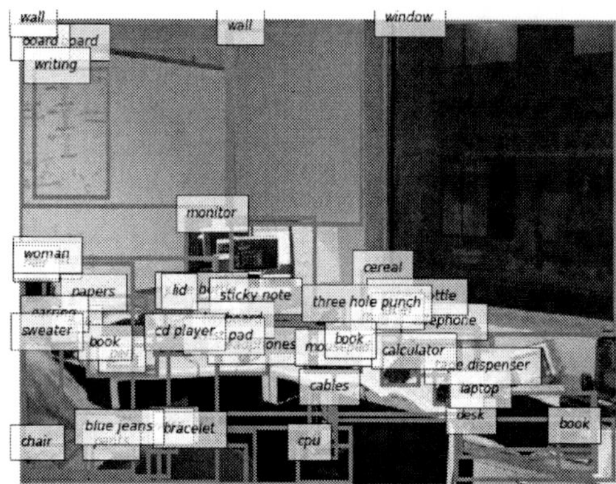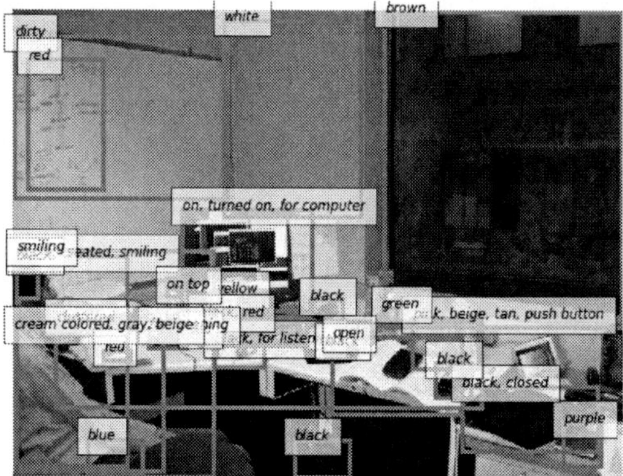

Figure 4: Object "names" (left) and "attributes" (right) from Visual Genome, for an example image

instances like this to *generalise* this function. That is, we can try to turn I into a "constructive" function that not just records a fact ("object o is in the denotation of predicate ϕ"), but rather produces a *judgement*, given a (structured, visually represented) object; we may write $I_{woman}(D)$ to make this explicit.[7]

With this in hand, we can now explore how the available data could help us learn and evaluate lexical interpretation functions and their composition. We will look at the available expression types in order of increasing syntactic complexity. The relation that we will make use of first is the "annotates" relation between expressions e and (parts of) images I. This relation gives us the value of $[\![e]\!]^{\langle D,I \rangle}$ (which is an entity or a truth value); the interest is in learning about $[\![\cdot]\!]^{\langle \cdot,I \rangle}$ as it covers the constituents of e and their composition.

3.2 Expression Types Found in Corpora

3.2.1 Sub-Sentential Expressions

Of the corpora discussed here, only Visual Genome provides open-class **single word** annotations. Objects in the corpus are associated with "names" (typically **nouns**), and "attributes" (typically **adjectives**), which were semi-automatically segmented out of larger expressions provided by annotators (to be discussed below). Figure 4 shows this for one image from the set. (It illustrates at the same time how fine-grainedly the corpus is segmented—on average it provides 36 object bounding boxes per image.)

The Visual Genome annotation provides over 105,000 word form types, of which about 10,500 have at least 10 instances. Using the normalisation to WordNet synsets in the corpus, this reduces to roughly 8,000 types, of which 3,500 occur at least 10 times. The distribution (not shown here) is roughly Zipfian—and reveals a certain bias in the data, with "man" occuring twice as often as "woman", for example. This is a sizeable vocabulary for which interpretation functions can be learned from this data.

We have briefly mentioned the problem of getting *negative instances* of word denotations, as required by typical machine learning methods. One method is to sample from the set of objects in a given image that are *not* annotated with a word; but this requires making the aforementioned (non-warranted) exhaustivity assumption. Schlangen et al. (2016) have shown this to be unproblematic for the data that they used; establishing to what degree it would be here we leave to future work. It is likely to be more of a problem for adjectives, where the choice of what to mention is governed much more by the context than the choice of which name to use for an object.

This data can be assembled into simple nominal phrases (ADJ + N; e.g. "brown window" for top right of Figure 4). Semantically, these would be **indefinite noun phrases**, as all that is guaranteed is that they are appropriate for the object that they apply to (but there may be others of that type in a given image). With the denotation being known, this can be used to evaluate the semantic composition.

---

[7]This perspective has previously been taken by Schlangen et al. (2016) and developed for simple expressions; the present section builds on that work.

More interesting and complex are the noun phrases found in the **referring expression** corpora (the ReferIt variants; see above). These expressions were produced in the form that they are recorded in the corpora (unlike the single word expressions discussed above), and in an actual context of use, namely with the aim to single out an object to a present interlocutor. This makes this data set also interesting from a pragmatic point of view, as one can ask how the context (in the image, but also in the production situation) may have influenced the linguistic choices. The following shows the referring expressions available for the tennis player on the right in the image from Figure 2 above; also shown is the annotation from the GoogleREX corpus:

(1) a. RefCoco: lady in black on right | girl in black | woman in black
     b. RefCoco+: black shirt | girl in black | player in black
     c. GoogleREX: woman in black tank top and shorts holding tennis racket | woman in black outfit shaking other tennis player hand

Contrasting the GoogleREX expressions illustrates the influence of the context of use on the shape of the expressions. The GoogleREX annotators did not have interlocutors and were just tasked with producing expressions that describe the object uniquely. The ReferIt expressions do this as well, but additionally, they do this in the most efficient and effective way, as the players had an incentive to be as fast as possible, while ensuring referential success. This shows: The average length of RefCOCO expressions is 3.5 token, that of GoogleREX 8.3.[8]

We also find **relational expressions** like the following in these corpora, which identify the *target* object by relating it to another one (the *landmark*):

(2) woman under suitcase | laptop above cellphone right | black van in front of cab

To learn the interpretation of such relational items (here, "under", "above", "in front of"), it would be good to have grounding information also about the landmark. The corpora mentioned so far do not give us this,[9] and so we turn to Visual Genome, and away from referring expressions.

Visual Genome was collected with the explicit purpose of providing material for learning "interactions and relationships between objects in an image" (Krishna et al., 2016). The starting point of the annotation was the marking of a region of interest in the image, and the annotation of that region with a "region description", ie. an expression that is true of that region. Note the difference to referring expressions: no stipulation is made about whether it is or is not true of *other* objects in the image. Annotators were encouraged to provide region descriptions that are relational, and these then form the basis of an abstracted representation of that relation. Figure 5 shows an example of such a region description; the corresponding annotation is shown in (3), slightly re-arranged to make clearer its similarity to classical logical forms (LFs).[10]

Figure 5: A region description from Visual Genome

(3) `"next to a":be.v.01(1060704:puzzle.n.01, 1060699:computer_monitor.n.01)`

---

[8]These corpora have been used by Kazemzadeh et al. (2014), Yu et al. (2016), Mao et al. (2016), Schlangen et al. (2016), Cirik et al. (2018) to train and test models of referring expression resolution.

[9]For a portion of GoogleREX, this was added by Cirik et al. (2018).

[10]What this also illustrates is that the normalisation decisions made in the corpus can occasionally be somewhat questionable. Here, the part "next to a" is normalised to the verb "be"; presumably, the annotator added the elided copula here and rather ignored the spatial relation.

Figure 7: "A man standing in the snow with skis on." (left), and distractors (visual similarity, middle; semantic similarity, right)

There are over 5 million region descriptions in Visual Genome, of which almost 2 million are parsed into this logical form. There are around 37,000 different relational terms in this set, of which around 3,100 occur more than 10 times. From this, a sizable number of relational interpretation functions could be learned.

Before we move on, we note that in about 6.8% of the region descriptions there is more than one object associated with an expression; as in the example in Figure 6, where "desktop computers" is resolved to four different bounding boxes. Such configurations could be used to learn the function of the plural morpheme. Looking at the expressions, there are also more than 1,000 instances each of quantifiers and numerals such as "several", "two", "many", which provides opportunity to learn their meaning.

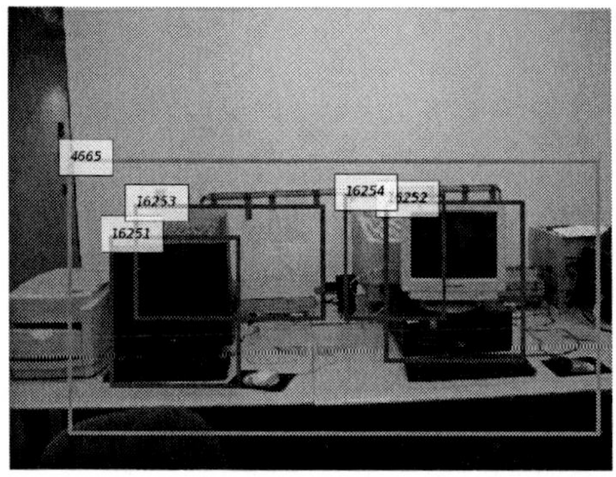

Figure 6: "there are desktop computers on the desk"

3.2.2 Sentences

We now turn to expressions that need to be evaluated relative to the image as a whole. Such expressions can be *constructed* for example by plugging the nominal phrases from above into the sentence frame "there is NP_{indef}" (e.g., "there is a brown window" for Figure 4), to yield **existential assertions**. Negative examples (where the constructed sentence is false) can be selected by sampling an image that is not annotated as containing an object of that type, again making use of an exhaustivity assumption.

Constructing examples in this way gives us control over the complexity of the expression, at the cost of a loss in naturalness. Some of the corpora, however, also come with *attested* examples of expressions that are meant to describe the image as a whole; COCO for example provides over 400,000 of such **captions**. Figure 7 (left) gives an example of an image/caption pair.

How can we sample negative instances, where the image is *not* described by the caption? One method is to simply sample an arbitrary image from the corpus: there will be a good chance that it does not fit the caption. Too good a chance, perhaps, in that we are likely to hit an image that does not even contain any of the entity types mentioned in the expression. To make the task harder, we can now make use of one of the derived relations described above, namely a simiarity relation between images.

We looked at two ways of defining such a relation. *Visual* similarity ($sim_{I/I}^{vis}$) is the inverse of the cosine distance in image representation space, using a pre-trained convolutional neural network (we used VGG-19, Simonyan and Zisserman (2014), pre-trained on ImageNet Russakovsky et al. (2015)). We compute *content-based* or *semantic* similarity ($sim_{I/I}^{sem}$) by vectorising the image annotation (in a many-hot representation with the object types as dimensions), using SVD to project the resulting matrix into a lower-dimensional space. Given our analogy between semantic models and images, with this we then have a similarity relation between models, and we can select distractor images / models that are more challenging to refute. Figure 7 shows distractors selected via visual (middle) and semantic (right)

Figure 8: Image described by paragraph (see text; left), and distractors (visual similarity, middle; semantic similarity, right)

similarity. As this illustrates, quite fine-grained resolution abilities are required to recognise these as not fitting the caption. (Man, but skis not on; man with skis on, but not standing.)

Captions from COCO are not finely grounded (no links between objects in the image and parts of the expression). Flickr30kEntities provides this; for reasons of space, we do not show an example here. We also skip over the *wh*-questions (with answers) that are available for COCO and Visual Genome, noting only that they add an interesting generation challenge (if set up as open answer task; if set up as multiple-choice task, this reduces to making a decision for a proposition).

3.2.3 Discourses

Finally, example (4) shows an **image description paragraph** for a Visual Genome image. The associated image and two distractors are shown in Figure 8. The semantic challenge here when evaluating such a paragraph relative to an image, at least when a probabilistic approach is taken, is that a decision must be made on how to combine the uncertain judgements from each constituent sentence.

(4)   The baseball player is swinging the bat. The ball is in the air. The dirt on the ground is light brown. The baseball player is wearing blue pants. The other baseball players are watching from The Dugout. The baseball player swinging the bat is wearing a dark-colored baseball hat. He's also wearing a bright red belt.

As this survey has shown, there is plenty of data available for learning grounded interpretation functions for individual words (nouns, adjectives, prepositions), and for evaluating (or even learning) how these functions must be put together to yield interpretations for larger expressions (NPs, sentences, and even discourses).

4   Expressions and Implications

4.1   Images as Implicit Link between Expressions

Besides the question of whether a statement is true of a given situation, an interesting question often is whether a statement *follows* from another one. There are various ways of tying down what exactly "follows" may mean. A very general one is given by Chierchia and McConnell-Ginet (1990), who use "A implies B" for cases where (the statement and acceptance of) A *provides reason* to also accept B.[11] This covers cases where a *proof* can be given that connects B to A (where the relation would be *syntactic consequence*, $\vdash$), cases where an argument can be made that any model that makes A true will also make B true (*semantic consequence*, $\models$), but also cases where A may just make B very plausible, given common sense knowledge (which we might call *common sense implicature*, and denote with $\models_{cs}$).

Here, we look at relations that we can take from the corpora and ask whether these can help us get at these semantic implicature relations. We make use of the fact that for most of the image objects in

---

[11]This is also how later the influential "recognising textual entailment" challenge (Dagan et al., 2006) would describe the relation, however also starting the tradition in natural language processing to overload the term "entailment" to cover all of what could more generally be called "implication". Young et al. (2014) call their task, defined via images as well and our inspiration for the work described here, with a qualifier as *"approximate* entailment".

the corpora, we have available more than one expression of the same type, e.g., more than one referring expression, or more than one caption. In the following, we take a look at some examples, sorting the discussion by the type of expressions that we pair.[12] We will argue that to predict the presence (or not) of an implicature relation, a different, complementary kind of lexical knowledge is required than for evaluation relative to an image (or situation); cf. Marconi (1997).

4.2 Types of Relations

4.2.1 Same Level / Rephrasing

Example (5) shows referring expressions from RefCOCO (left) paired with another expression referring to the same object (middle) and with one referring to a randomly sampled other object from the corpus. The prediction task is to identify the left/middle pair as standing in an implicature relation, and the left/right pair as not standing in this relation. (To put a practical spin on it, this could be seen as detecting whether the second pair part could be a *reformulation* of the first, perhaps as response to a clarification request.)

(5)   a.   right girl on floor || lady sitting on right | guy on right
            b.   woman || left person | pizza on bottom right
            c.   man trying to help with suitcase || man in jacket | very top zebra

Despite the brevity of the expressions, as this example indicates, this task seems to require quite detailed lexical knowledge, for example detecting incompatiblity between "guy" and "girl" in (5-a), but compatiblity between "lady" and "girl". (If this knowledge were available, perhaps a *natural logic*-type (Moss, 2015) approach could then be taken.) Creating this dataset only requires that several referring expressions are available for the same object, and indeed RefCOCO for example provides on average 7.1 per object, for a total of over 140,000 referring expressions.

We randomly sampled 60 instances of such pairings (balanced pos/neg) and presented each to three workers on Amazon Mechanical Turk, asking for a semantic relatedness judgement (on a 4 step Likert-scale). Using the majority label and binning at the middle of the scale, the accuracy is 0.68. This indicates that while noisy, this method creates a recognisable semantic relation between these expressions.[13]

Example (6) shows similar pairings of captions, with the negative instance (the final part of each sub-example) taken from a distractor image selected for semantic image similarity. As this illustrates, the task only becomes harder, with the caption that is intended to be non-matching occasionally accidentally even intuitively being compatible after all. (Crowd accuracy, henceforth AMT, with same setup as described above: 0.63.)

(6)   a.   A woman with a painted face riding a skateboard indoors. || A woman with face paint on standing on a skateboard. | There are men who are skateboarding down the trail.
            b.   Man and woman standing while others are seated looking at a monitor. || A man and woman play a video game while others watch. | Two people standing in a living room with Wii remotes in their hands.

4.2.2 More Specific / Entailment

Since some of the corpora overlap in their base image data, we can intersect the annotation and create derived data sets. (7) shows examples of a caption from COCO (left) paired with an object from Visual Genome (slotted into a "there is (a) _" frame for presentation) taken from the same image (middle), and a randomly sampled object (right) in (7-a) and (7-b), and with region descriptions (also from Visual Genome) in the other examples.

---

[12]Our inspiration for this approach comes from two sources. As mentioned, Young et al. (2014) used image captions to create their "approximate entailment" data sets; our proposals here can be seen as a generalisation of this to other pairings. Further, the original "natural language inference" dataset by Bowman et al. (2015) used captions as seeds, but had the entailments and contradictions manually generated and not derived via image relations, as we do here.

[13]Note that the task was to judge pairs, not to decide between two hypotheses, which would presumably be a simpler task.

(7)   a.   A man wearing a black cap leaning against a fence getting ready to play baseball. || there is (a) man | there is (a) cow

      b.   Rice, broccoli, and other food items sitting beside each other || there is (a) health foods | there is (a) granite

      c.   A man playing Wii in a room || there is/are (a) a plant that sits on a desk | there is/are (a) field covered in green grass

      d.   A woman is riding a wave on a surfboard. || there is/are (a) Woman with the surfboard. | there is/are (a) Students sitting at their desks

Judging from these examples, quite detailed knowledge about situations and possible participants seems to be required to predict these relations. (AMT accuracy caption/object: 0.58, caption/region: 0.6.)

4.2.3 More Detailed / Elaboration

Finally, (8) shows examples of a caption (from COCO) paired with a paragraph (from Visual Genome-paragraphs) describing the same (middle) or another, but similar image. The task here is to detect whether the extended description fits with the short description or not, which again seems to require quite detailed knowledge about situations and likely sub-events. (AMT: 0.6.)

(8)   two people lying in a bunk bed in a bedroom.

       A boy and girl are sitting on bunk beds in a room. The boy is wearing a red shirt and dark pants. The girl is wearing a gray shirt and blue jean pants. There is a green and pink blanket behind the boy on the top bunk. The girl is sitting on a rolled up blanket. She is wearing red glasses on her eyes.

       A woman is sitting on a bed beside a little girl. She is wearing a sweater and black bottoms. The woman has eyeglasses on her eyes. The girl is wearing a colorful jacket. The girl is looking at a book that is opened on her lap. The bed is sitting against a white painted wall. There is a red blanket on the bed.

Using this general recipe, further datasets can be created with other combinations, for example pairing sets of region descriptions with further descriptions either from the same or from a different scene, or for the task of predicting the number of distinct entities introduced by a sequence of region descriptions. For reasons of space, we do not show examples here.

5   A Case Study: Model-Building for Predicting Entailment

Entailment tasks, triggered by the aforementioned "natural language inference" dataset (Bowman et al., 2015) have in recent years become a staple NLP task. They are typically tackled with very high-capacity machine learning models that classify distributed representations of the candidate relata, e.g., as in (Devlin et al., 2018). With the perspective developed here, we can liken such approaches to the *syntactic* way of defining entailment ($\vdash$), in that these approaches only take the surface form into account (and implicitly learn and use the required common sense knowledge).

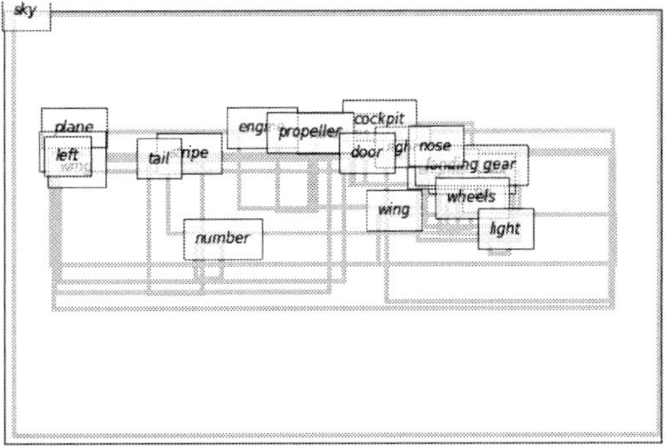

Figure 9: A Retrieved Abstract Exemplar Situation

A *semantic* approach seems possible as well, however. In its brute force form, it would implement the typical way in which *semantic consequence* is defined, by quantification over all models. Here, this would mean testing, along the lines developed in Section 3, whether all images (in a sub-corpus held for that purpose) that make the premise true also make the hypothesis true. We try something else here, which is more like model-building (Bos, 2003), for data of the type illustrated in (7) above.

The idea is as follows. Given the premise (in our case, always a caption), we retrieve a set of images (other than that from which the caption was taken), via captions that are nearest neighbours in a text embedding space (for which we used the "universal sentence encoder" by Cer et al. (2018)). That is, we make use of a derived expression/expression relation, to create a relation between an expression and a set of retrieved models. (One can think of these as situation exemplars stored in memory and retrieved via their short descriptions.) Figure 9 shows such a retrieved model (abstracted away from the actual image content, which is not used), for the trigger caption "An airplane flying through the sky on a cloudy day." and retrieved via its most similar caption "White and blue airplane flying in a grey sky.".

We then test the candidate expressions (or rather, their "logical forms", as given by Visual Genome) against this set of models. For objects (as in (7-a) and (7-b) above), this checks whether an object of the appropriate type is in the retrieved models; for relations, this additionally checks whether the relation is also present. If the required types are present in all models, this would yield a score of 1. We set a threshold (in our experiments, at 0.2), above which a positive decision is made. As baseline, we use token overlap between premise and hypothesis for objects and intersection over union for the longer region descriptions, and distance in the embedding space. We created 10,000 triples each for the caption/object and the caption/region task.

The results in Table 1 indicate that this rather simple model captures cases that the baselines do not. An example where this is the case is shown in (9); here the retrieved models seem to have provided the entities ("umpire" and "jacket") which are likely to be present in a baseball scene, but aren't literally mentioned in the premise.

Task	Model	Strg.Bsln	Embd.Bsln		Task	Model	Strg.Bsln	Embd.Bsln
Captions / Objects	0.67	0.58	0.64		Captions / Regions	0.65	0.54	0.50

Table 1: Results for Predicting Entailment via model retrieval (and baselines)

(9)   Baseball batter hitting ball while other players prepare to try and catch it. || jacket worn by umpire | silverware on a napkin

This is clearly not more than a first proof-of-concept. We've included it here to motivate our tentative conclusion that the perspective introduced in this paper might have value not only for deriving interesting data sets, but also for tackling some of the tasks. In future work, we will explore methods that directly predict image layouts [e.g., (Tan et al., 2018)], comparing them to direct prediction approaches and evaluating whether the former methods offer a plus in interpretability through the step of predicting abstract models.

6   Conclusions

Our goal with this paper was to show, with detailed examples and descriptive statistics, that language / vision corpora can be a fertile hunting ground for semanticists interested in grounded lexical semantics. There is data pairing various, ever more complex, kinds of expressions with image objects (either parts of images, or images as a whole). Moreover, using these corpora, data sets can be derived that pair expressions, where a semantic relation holds between the parts that is recognisable to naive annotators (if not alway very clearly). As an example, we've used the perspective of treating images as models to retrieve exemplar models via language descriptions (captions), and probe those for the likely presence of entities and relations in a mentioned situation. It is our hope that this perspective might be useful to other researchers, and with the code released with this paper, we invite everyone to ask their own questions of the data, and to implement ideas on how to learn grounded interpretation.

Acknowledgements   This work was done while I was at Bielefeld University and supported by the Cluster of Excellence Cognitive Interaction Technology "CITEC" (EXC 277), which is funded by the German Research Foundation (DFG). I thank Sina Zarrieß and the anonymous reviewers for comments.

References

Abzianidze, L., J. Bjerva, K. Evang, H. Haagsma, R. van Noord, P. Ludmann, D.-D. Nguyen, and J. Bos (2017, April). The parallel meaning bank: Towards a multilingual corpus of translations annotated with compositional meaning representations. In *Proceedings of the 15th Conference of the European Chapter of the Association for Computational Linguistics: Volume 2, Short Papers*, Valencia, Spain, pp. 242–247. Association for Computational Linguistics.

Bos, J. (2003). Exploring model building for natural language understanding. In *Workshop on Inference in Computational Semantics (ICoS)*.

Bos, J., V. Basile, K. Evang, N. Venhuizen, and J. Bjerva (2017). The groningen meaning bank. In N. Ide and J. Pustejovsky (Eds.), *Handbook of Linguistic Annotation*, Volume 2, pp. 463–496. Springer.

Bowman, S. R., G. Angeli, C. Potts, and C. D. Manning (2015). A large annotated corpus for learning natural language inference. In *Proceedings of the 2015 Conference on Empirical Methods in Natural Language Processing (EMNLP)*. Association for Computational Linguistics.

Cer, D., Y. Yang, S.-y. Kong, N. Hua, N. Limtiaco, R. S. John, N. Constant, M. Guajardo-Cespedes, S. Yuan, C. Tar, Y.-H. Sung, B. Strope, and R. Kurzweil (2018). Universal Sentence Encoder. *ArXiv*.

Chierchia, G. and S. McConnell-Ginet (1990). *Meaning and Grammar: An Introduction to Semantics*. Cambridge, MA, USA: MIT Press.

Cirik, V., T. Berg-kirkpatrick, and L.-p. Morency (2018). Using Syntax to Ground Referring Expressions in Natural Images. In *AAAI 2018*.

Dagan, I., O. Glickman, and B. Magnini (2006). The pascal recognising textual entailment challenge. In *Proceedings of the First International Conference on Machine Learning Challenges: Evaluating Predictive Uncertainty Visual Object Classification, and Recognizing Textual Entailment*, MLCW'05, Berlin, Heidelberg, pp. 177–190. Springer-Verlag.

Davies, E. R. (2012). *Computer and Machine Vision: Theory, Algorithms, Practicalities* (4th ed.). Amsterdam, Boston, Heidelberg, London: Elsevier.

Devlin, J., M.-W. Chang, K. Lee, and K. Toutanova (2018). BERT: Pre-training of Deep Bidirectional Transformers for Language Understanding. *ArXiv*.

Fellbaum, C. (Ed.) (1998). *WordNet: An Electronic Lexical Database*. Cambridge, USA: MIT Press.

Fine, K. (2017). A Theory of Truthmaker Content I: Conjunction, Disjunction and Negation. *Journal of Philosophical Logic 46*(6), 625–674.

He, K., G. Gkioxari, P. Dollár, and R. Girshick (2017). Mask R-CNN. In *2017 IEEE International Conference on Computer Vision (ICCV)*.

Hürlimann, M. and J. Bos (2016). Combining Lexical and Spatial Knowledge to Predict Spatial Relations between Objects in Images. In *5th Workshop on Vision and Language*, Berlin, Germany, pp. 10–18.

Kazemzadeh, S., V. Ordonez, M. Matten, and T. L. Berg (2014). ReferItGame: Referring to Objects in Photographs of Natural Scenes. In *Proceedings of the Conference on Empirical Methods in Natural Language Processing (EMNLP 2014)*, Doha, Qatar, pp. 787–798.

Krause, J., J. Johnson, R. Krishna, and L. Fei-Fei (2017, January). A hierarchical approach for generating descriptive image paragraphs. In *Proceedings - 30th IEEE Conference on Computer Vision and Pattern Recognition*.

Krishna, R., Y. Zhu, O. Groth, J. Johnson, K. Hata, J. Kravitz, S. Chen, Y. Kalantidis, L.-J. Li, D. A. Shamma, M. Bernstein, and L. Fei-Fei (2016). Visual genome: Connecting language and vision using crowdsourced dense image annotations.

Lin, T.-Y., M. Maire, S. Belongie, J. Hays, P. Perona, D. Ramanan, P. Dollr, and C. Zitnick (2014). Microsoft coco: Common objects in context. In *Computer Vision ECCV 2014*, Volume 8693, pp. 740–755. Springer International Publishing.

Mao, J., J. Huang, A. Toshev, O. Camburu, A. L. Yuille, and K. Murphy (2016, June). Generation and comprehension of unambiguous object descriptions. In *Proceedings of CVPR 2016*, Las Vegas, USA.

Marconi, D. (1997). *Lexical Competence*. Cambridge, Mass., USA: MIT Press.

Marr, D. (1982). *Vision: A Computational Investigation into the Human Representation and Processing of Visual Information*. San Francisco, USA: W.H. Freeman.

Moss, L. (2015). Natural logic. In S. Lappin and C. Fox (Eds.), *Handbook of Contemporary Semantic Theory 2nd edition*. Wiley-Blackwell.

Plummer, B. A., L. Wang, C. M. Cervantes, J. C. Caicedo, J. Hockenmaier, and S. Lazebnik (2015). Flickr30k entities: Collecting region-to-phrase correspondences for richer image-to-sentence models. In *Proceedings of ICCV*.

Redmon, J. and A. Farhadi (2018). Yolov3: An incremental improvement. *arXiv*.

Russakovsky, O., J. Deng, H. Su, J. Krause, S. Satheesh, S. Ma, Z. Huang, A. Karpathy, A. Khosla, M. Bernstein, A. C. Berg, and L. Fei-Fei (2015). ImageNet Large Scale Visual Recognition Challenge. *International Journal of Computer Vision 115*(3), 211–252.

Schlangen, D., S. Zarrieß, and C. Kennington (2016, August). Resolving references to objects in photographs using the words-as-classifiers model. In *Proceedings of ACL 2016*, Berlin, Germany.

Simonyan, K. and A. Zisserman (2014). Very deep convolutional networks for large-scale image recognition. *CoRR abs/1409.1556*.

Tan, F., S. Feng, and V. Ordonez (2018). Text2Scene: Generating Abstract Scenes from Textual Descriptions. *ArXiv*.

Young, P., A. Lai, M. Hodosh, and J. Hockenmaier (2014). From image descriptions to visual denotations: New similarity metrics for semantic inference over event descriptions. *Transactions of the Association for Computational Linguistics 2*.

Yu, L., P. Poirson, S. Yang, A. Berg, and B. T.L. (2016). Modeling context in referring expressions. In *Computer Vision ECCV 2016*, Volume 9906 of *Lecture Notes in Computer Science*. Springer.

Frame Identification as Categorization:
Exemplars vs Prototypes in Embeddingland

Jennifer Sikos
IMS, University of Stuttgart
Stuttgart, Germany
jen.sikos@ims.uni-stuttgart.de

Sebastian Padó
IMS, University of Stuttgart
Stuttgart, Germany
pado@ims.uni-stuttgart.de

Abstract

Categorization is a central capability of human cognition, and a number of theories have been developed to account for properties of categorization. Despite the fact that many semantic tasks involve categorization, theories of categorization do not play a major role in contemporary research in computational linguistics. This paper follows the idea that embedding-based models of semantics lend themselves well to being formulated in terms of classical categorization theories. The benefit is a group of models that enables (a) the formulation of hypotheses about the impact of major design decisions, and (b) a transparent assessment of these decisions.

We instantiate this idea on the frame-semantic frame identification task. We define four models that cross two design variables: (a) the choice of prototype vs. exemplar categorization, corresponding to different degrees of *generalization* applied to the input, and (b) the presence vs. absence of a fine-tuning step, corresponding to generic vs. task-adaptive categorization. We find that for frame identification, generalization and task-adaptive categorization both yield substantial benefits. Our prototype-based, fine-tuned model, which combines the best choices over these variables, establishes a new state-of-the-art in frame identification.

1 Introduction

Categorization is the process of forming categories and assigning objects to them, and is a central capability of human cognition (Murphy, 2002). Not surprisingly, cognitive psychology has shown substantial interest in theories of categorization. Two such prominent theories are *prototype* and *exemplar* models. In prototype theory, categories are characterized in terms of a single representation, the prototype, which is an abstraction over individual objects and captures the 'essence' of the category (Posner and Keele, 1968; Rosch, 1975). In computational models, the prototype is often computed as the centroid of the objects of a category, and new objects are classified by their similarity to different categories' prototypes. As a result, the decision boundary between every pair of categories is linear. In contrast, exemplar theories represent categories in terms of the potentially large set of objects, called exemplars, that instantiate the category (Nosofsky, 1986; Hintzman, 1986). New objects are classified by similarity to nearby exemplars, so in a computational model this becomes similar to a nearest-neighbor classification. In exemplar models, the decision boundary between categories can become non-linear, enabling more complex behavior to be captured, but at the cost of higher training data requirements.

Prototype and exemplar theories are typically not at the center of attention in contemporary computational linguistics. One reason is arguably that, due to their origin in psychology, they tend to restrict themselves to cognitively plausible parameters and learning mechanisms (Nosofsky and Zaki, 2002; Lieto et al., 2017), whereas the focus of computational linguistics is very much on the use of novel machine learning techniques for applications. We nevertheless believe that categorization theory is still relevant for computational linguistics, and lexical semantics in particular. In fact, the emergence of distributed representations (embeddings) as a dominant representational paradigm has had a unifying effect on work in lexical semantics. The properties of high-dimensional embeddings provide a good match with the assumption behind much of categorization theory – namely, that categories arise naturally from the similarity structure of individual objects (Erk, 2009).

Given this context, the exemplar–prototype dichotomy is a useful dimension on which models can be situated in terms of how much they generalize over objects: low for exemplar-inspired, but high for prototype-inspired models. Regarding the representation of word meaning in context, for example, the additive models first considered by Mitchell and Lapata (2008) fall into the prototype camp, while Erk and Padó (2010) propose exemplar-based models, and Reisinger and Mooney (2010) explore dynamic generalization in what they called 'multi-prototype' categorization models. However, for many tasks, such comparisons – on a level playing field – are missing.

An interesting recent development in the embedding literature is the emergence of the distinction between *pre-training* and *fine-tuning* (e.g., in BERT (Devlin et al., 2018), OpenAI's GPT (Radford et al., 2018), or ULM (Howard and Ruder, 2018)): pre-training constructs embeddings that are supposedly general and are robust across many tasks. Fine-tuning can then further optimize embeddings for one particular task, at the cost of robustness. Importantly, pre-training takes advantage of massive amounts of unlabeled data, while fine-tuning can leverage small amounts of task-specific labeled data. This distinction ties in nicely with open questions in the categorization literature concerning the respective roles of "bottom-up" similarity information and "top-down" theory information (Smith and Sloman, 1996): task-independent pre-training embeddings, and their similarities which shape the categorization process, can be understood as "bottom-up" information, while the transformations that fine-tuning introduces to optimize these embeddings for a specific task, arguably represent "top-down" information. Notably, such transformations can be understood equivalently as learning task-specific similarity metrics (Bellet et al., 2013). By learning general representations in a bottom-up pre-training phase and then comparing performance with additional top-down fine-tuning, we can discriminate how much general semantic knowledge is necessary to perform a categorization task and how much task-specific learning is required.

In this paper, we investigate a lexical semantic task, specifically the identification of frame-semantic frames (Baker et al., 1998) in running text, from this categorization perspective. Frames can be understood as semantic classes that are sensitive both to the topic of the context and to specific properties of the predicate-argument structure. We present four categorization models for the task, all of which are based on the state-of-the-art BERT model (Devlin et al., 2018) but which differ in how they use its embeddings. Two models are prototype-based (i.e., compute a representation for each frame), and two are exemplar-based (i.e., represent a frame solely in terms of its instances). Within each group, we compare the use of embeddings without fine-tuning ("bottom-up") and with fine-tuning ("top-down").

Contributions and Findings. This setup enables us to gauge, on a lexical semantic analysis task, (a) whether generalization helps, and what the size of the effect is; (b) whether there are benefits of top-down task adaptation; (c) whether there is an interaction between generalization and adaptation. We find that generalization indeed helps, as does top-down adaptation. Overall, our best model establishes a new state-of-the-art in frame identification.

Structure of the paper. In Section 2, we provide details on frame semantics and frame identification, as well as the current work in distributed semantic representations. We additionally outline the architecture of BERT its pre-training and fine-tuning steps. Section 3 defines the four models that we experiment with, and Section 4 describes the experimental setup. Finally, we describe and discuss results and analysis in Sections 5 and 6.

2 Background

2.1 Frame Semantics and Frame Identification

Frame Semantics is a theory of semantics that groups predicates in terms of the situations that they describe and their relevant participants (Fillmore, 1982). These situations, or scenarios, are formalized in terms of *frames*, conceptual categories which have a set of *lexical units* that evoke the situation, and a set of *frame elements* that categorize the participants and that are expected to be realized linguistically. For instance, *tell*, *explain*, and *say* are all capable of expressing the STATEMENT frame which describes the situation where SPEAKER communicates a MESSAGE to a RECIPIENT.

Frame Semantics has been implemented in a number of NLP applications thanks to the Berkeley FrameNet resource (Baker et al., 1998). The latest FrameNet lexicon release provides definitions for over 1.2k frames, and 13,640 lexical units (i.e., predicate–frame pairs), where there are approximately 12 lexical units per frame. FrameNet also provides sentence annotations that mark, for each lexical unit, the frame that is evoked as well as its frame elements in running text. This annotated corpus has sparked a lot of interest in computational linguistics, and the prediction of frame-semantic structures (frames and frame elements) has become known as *(frame-)semantic parsing* (Gildea and Jurafsky, 2002; Das et al., 2014).

2.1.1 Frame Identification

In this paper, we focus on the first step of frame-semantic parsing called *frame identification* or *frame assignment*, where an occurrence of a predicate in context is labeled with its FrameNet frame. This is a categorization task that presents two main challenges:

Ambiguity Most predicates in FrameNet are ambiguous, that is, they can evoke different frames depending on the context that they occur in. For example, *treat* has a medical sense (*treat a disease*) that evokes the MEDICAL_INTERVENTION frame and a social sense (*treat a person in some manner*) that evokes the TREATING_AND_MISTREATING frame. These distinctions can be relatively subtle: *say* can evoke (among others) the frames STATEMENT and TEXT_CREATION which differ mainly in the modality of the communicative act (*said to his friend* vs. *said in his book*).

Generalization As conceptual categories, frames are clearly open classes. No resource can exhaustively list all frames or the predicates that can evoke them.

Frame identification was first modeled as a supervised classification task, based on linguistic features (Das et al., 2010). While such systems address the ambiguity problem to some degree, they tend to struggle with generalization. An alternative approach investigated the use of other machine-readable dictionaries (Green et al., 2004), but was not able to fundamentally overcome the generalization problem.

Recent progress in supervised frame identification has come out of neural networks and distributed word representations (Peng et al., 2018; Hartmann et al., 2017). In these studies, frame-labeled corpora are used to learn embeddings for the frames as a side product of representation learning with different objective functions. Hermann et al. (2014) learned embeddings jointly for frames and the sentential contexts in which they were evoked. The current state-of-the-art in frame identification performs full-fledged semantic role labeling, i.e., it jointly assigns frames as well as frame elements, using a bi-directional LSTM architecture (Peng et al., 2018).

2.2 Distributed Representations of Word Meaning

Distributed representations of word meanings (embeddings) have become a standard representation format in semantics. These models are grounded in the distributional hypothesis (Harris, 1954), according to which similar words are expected to appear in similar contexts. Based on this hypothesis, word (and phrase) meaning is represented as vectors (embeddings) in a semantic space whose dimensions correlate with properties of the context, and in which closeness between two vectors indicates semantic relatedness.

Traditionally, "count" vectors were created by simply counting co-occurring context features, with the option of additional weighting and compression over those count vectors. Neural network-based "predict" vectors are learned by treating contextual features as parameters of an objective function that is optimized on a corpus. One of the first, and still popular, "predict" models is the word2vec Skipgram model (Mikolov et al., 2013). It optimizes a word embedding using a context bag of words. This model, however, learns representations only at the lexical level, so that occurrences of a word in different contexts (cf. *treat* in Section 2.1.1) are represented equally. This has changed with the latest generation of embedding models, such as AllenNLP's ELMo (Gardner et al., 2018) and Google's BERT (Devlin et al., 2018), which build *contextualized embeddings* for occurrences of words based on the context as well as their relative positions.

A second important recent development concerns the objective(s) used to learn the embedding. While traditional count vectors and early embedding models like Skipgram assume that embeddings are general, and trained in an *task-agnostic* fashion, there is an alternative thread of research that sees the training of embeddings as a side product of training *task-specific* neural network models on tasks like sentiment analysis or machine translation (Socher et al., 2013; Hill et al., 2017). The most recent models reconcile these two directions with a two-phase transfer learning setup. The first phase is *pre-training*, where task-agnostic embeddings are learned from large, unlabeled corpora. The second phase is *fine-tuning*, which adapts the pre-trained embeddings to a specific task using comparatively small amounts of task-specific labeled corpora.

2.2.1 Bidirectional Encoder Representations from Transformers (BERT)

BERT (Devlin et al., 2018) is a state-of-the-art embedding model that provides contextualized embeddings in a pre-training/fine-tuning setup. BERT is essentially a deep network of Transformer blocks (Vaswani et al., 2017) which use stacked self-attention mechanisms to capture relationships across different positions in a sequence. The two tasks that are used for pre-training are language modeling and recognition of discourse continuation. Representations from the pre-training step are then pooled and fed to the fine-tuning stage for classification. Fine-tuning proceeds by adding an additional, task-specific layer on top of the pre-trained BERT embeddings that maps embeddings onto the desired task output. In addition to learning weights for this final, task-specific classification layer, this procedure also updates the pooled, pre-trained embedding through backpropagation.

3   Categorization Approaches to Frame Identification

This section defines our four embedding-based models for frame identification. As motivated in Section 1, we based our model space on two well-known dichotomies from categorization research: exemplar vs. prototype theory, and pure bottom-up processing vs. a combined bottom-up plus top-down processing. This setup results in a 2x2 matrix and a total of four models, as sketched in Figure 1. To focus solely on the problem of frame identification as a categorization task, we assume that the frame-evoking predicates have already been identified in the texts of interest.

The first dimension distinguishes prototype vs exemplar models, shown in the figure as columns. We consider models to be exemplar-based when they only use representations for individual instances for their predictions (here, predicates in context), but do not compute aggregate embeddings at the category level (here, frames). One of the most straightforward implementations of this approach is nearest-neighbor classification (Daelemans and van den Bosch, 2005). In contrast, prototype-models do not use instance representations at prediction time, but instead aggregate them into category-level representations. The standard softmax classification, for example, is a clear prototype approach by virtue of learning a weight vector for each class whose dot product with an input represents the probability of that class. The geometric interpretation of this computation is a distance between the prototype vector and the input, using dot product.

The second dimension, shown in the figure as rows, distinguishes pure bottom-up from bottom-up plus top-down models. In categorization research, bottom-up models assume that general similarity information "as given" is sufficient to perform the classification. In an embedding-based setup, this corresponds to models where embeddings are (pre-)trained in a task-independent fashion and applied to the task as-is. Thus, the bottom-up models form categories purely from contextual features that have been learned in a generalized, unsupervised fashion. In contrast, combined bottom-up plus top-down models assume that top-down information, such as a preconceived notion of a category or similarity

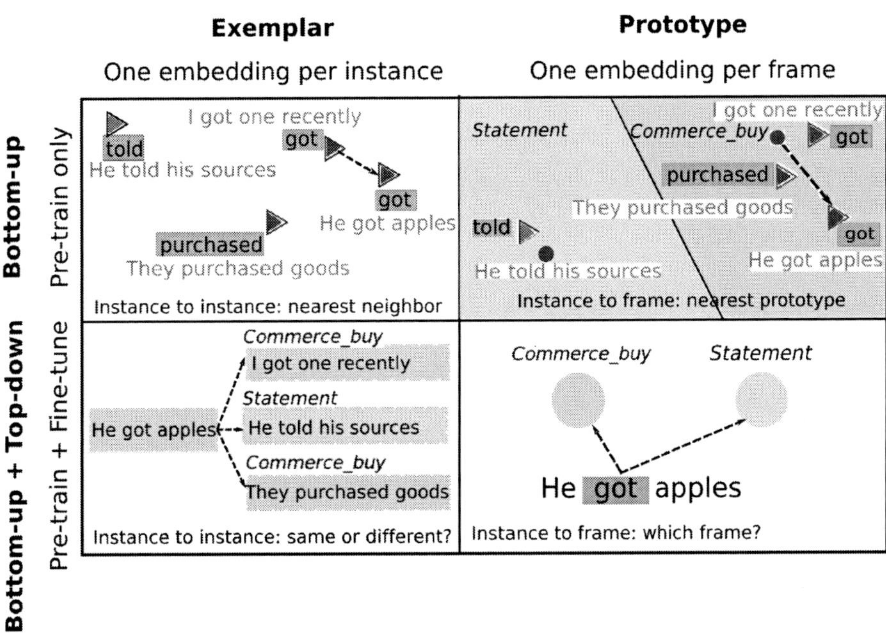

Figure 1: Four categorization models for frame identification, showing processing of the same predicate in context (*He got apples*) across model architectures. Blue stands for frame COMMERCE_BUY, light red for frame STATEMENT. Triangles are instances, dots are prototypes.

metric, influences processing for this task. In the context of current embedding-based models, we treat the fine-tuning procedure in BERT (cf. Section 2.2.1), where representations are fine-tuned using a small amount of task-specific data as an approximate top-down effect on categorization.

3.1 Bottom-up (Pre-trained Embeddings)

Bottom-up frame identification models use only the pre-trained embeddings to predict the frame of a lexical unit in context. The classification performed by these models shows how well frame classification can be carried out by relying on general lexical semantic relatedness, without explicit knowledge about frame-semantic grouping.

Bottom-up Exemplar. In exemplar theories, categorization proceeds by comparing a target instance to prior seen instances, and the target is assigned the same class as its closest seen instance. To classify a predicate in context, we perform single nearest neighbor classification: we compare its pre-trained, contextualized embedding to all pre-trained, contextualized embeddings of predicates in the training set, and assign the frame label of the closest training predicate. We use the standard embedding similarity metric, cosine similarity. In the example in Figure 1 (top left), the nearest neighbor to the test instance *He got apples* is *I got one recently*, which leads to the assignment of the COMMERCE_BUY frame.

Bottom-up Prototype. In the prototype model, the frame categories are formed by building a summary representation of all known instances in a category. We take advantage of the general effectiveness of averaged representations and compute frame prototypes as the unweighted centroid of all pre-trained, contextualized predicate embeddings for the frame's training instances. Frame classification then assigns a novel instance to the category of its most similar prototype. We again use cosine similarity, which is identical (modulo normalization) to softmax classification. The example in Figure 1 (top right) shows the prototypes of the two frames as dots, the "regions" of the two frames by background color, as well as the (linear) decision boundary between prototypes. The test instance *He got apples* is assigned to the COMMERCE_BUY frame because it is closest to the prototype of that frame.

3.2 Combined Bottom-up plus Top-down (Pre-trained and Fine-tuned Embeddings)

Bottom-up plus top-down frame identification models optimize the embeddings according to task-specific data and a loss function during a fine-tuning phase. Prediction then uses the fine-tuned embeddings instead of pre-trained ones.

Bottom-up plus Top-down Exemplar. For our exemplar-based model, we apply fine-tuning to make the embeddings for predicates that evoke the same frame more similar, and embeddings evoking different frames less similar. We frame the fine-tuning step as a binary classification task that decides, for a pair of predicates in sentence context, whether they evoke the same or different frames. The input consists of the concatenated contextualized embeddings of the two predicates. An example of the training input is below, where the BERT model adds a special [SEP] token between the text pair. The *treated* predicate from the first sentence evokes the MEDICAL_INTERVENTION frame, whereas the *got* predicate in the second sentence evokes COMMERCE_BUY.

Input Sequence	The doctor treated the patient [SEP] He got apples
Label	different

Formally, for each predicate in context i with frame $f(i)$, we define $P^+(i)$ as a set of (positive) instances with the same frame, $P^-(i)$ as a set of (negative) instances with different frames, and $same(i, i')$ as the binary prediction of the model. We then define the objective function as a cross-entropy loss between the gold label (same / different) and $same(i, i')$.

$$L_{ex} = -\sum_i [\sum_{i' \in P^+(i)} \log p(same(i, i')) + \sum_{i' \in P^-(i)} \log(1 - p(same(i, i')))] \tag{1}$$

We select $P^-(i)$ from the set of frame candidates for a given lexical unit. For predicates with only a single frame, we randomly select a negative instance from the entire frame class inventory. For each predicate in the training data, we use two positive and negative instances, which we obtain by random sampling.

At prediction time, we pair the target predicate with all instances of all frame candidates for this predicate and run them through the trained classification model, as shown in the bottom-left corner of Figure 1. For Unseen predicates (see Section 4), we pair target predicates with one randomly selected example from each frame in the entire frame inventory. We then label the target predicate with the frame of the instance with the highest same-frame probability. In this model, the top-down knowledge that is passed to the network corresponds to the similarity metric between frame-evoking predicates.

Bottom-up plus Top-down Prototype. For the prototype model, we fine-tune the embeddings specifically to learn frame classes (cf. the bottom right hand example in Figure 1). Since we will train on full-text annotation (described in further detail in Section 4), frame identification proceeds as a token sequence classification, where each token is assigned a frame prediction. An example of the training data is shown below, where the input to the model is the sequence of plain text tokens, and the gold class labels are the sequence of correct frame assignments. In the gold label sequence, non-predicates are assigned an outside (O) label.

Input Sequence	The	doctor	treated	the	patient
Label	O	MEDICAL_ PROFESSIONALS	MEDICAL_ INTERVENTION	O	MEDICAL_ INTERACTION_SCENARIO

The loss function is a straightforward multi-class cross-entropy loss averaged over each class for every token. Here, the set of labels are the entire set of frames in the FrameNet lexicon, plus the added 'outside' class label – resulting in a large set of possible classes (1,021 classes). At prediction time, the model predicts a frame label for each token in the input sequence independently. As is the case in the bottom-up prototype model, no global optimization takes place. We only consider predictions for predicates (according to the gold standard) for the purposes of evaluation.

4 Experiments

4.1 Dataset

We work with the dataset sampled by Das et al. (2014) from the FrameNet Release 1.5 full-text annotations. This dataset contains a total of 78 documents with frame-annotated sentences drawn from the British National Corpus. In total, 39 documents were selected for training and 16 for development with a total of 19,582 target predicates, and 23 documents for testing with 4,458 target predicate annotations. This is the standard dataset used for evaluation of frame identification systems.

4.2 Model Setup and Hyperparameters

BERT provides several pre-trained models for English that were trained on the concatenation of the BooksCorpus (Zhu et al., 2015) and Wikipedia. We use the pre-trained BERT-large, cased model, trained with the highest number of layers (L=24), hidden units (H=1024), and self-attention heads (A=16). The final layer of the BERT transformer provides embeddings for each token in the sentence that can be interpreted as contextualized meaning representations. According to the authors of the BERT model, performance is shown to improve when the n final layers for each token are concatenated. We use n=4.

For the fine-tuned models, we re-used the hyperparameters of the pre-trained model. Since both of our fine-tuning tasks are classification tasks, we add a standard softmax classification layer with cross-entropy loss on top of BERT (described earlier in Section 3.2). Due to the computational cost of attention mechanisms, the fine-tuned models require a limit on the maximum sequence length. We set the sequence length to 180 in the prototype model, which in this case means that even long sentences can be fed to the model. The exemplar model, on the other hand, takes two text sequences as input (see Section 3.1) which doubles the overall size of the input sequence. We increased the maximum sequence length to 200 for this model to keep as many tokens as possible in training while also being computationally feasible.

We note that our prototype model required a significant number of epochs to converge. Most tasks in the BERT paper achieve near-optimal accuracy with 3–4 training epochs, while our model required about 30 epochs. We attribute this to the number of classes (at most 4 classes in the BERT paper, more than 1000 classes for frame identification). The exemplar model follows more closely with other BERT tasks, and we perform 5 training epochs for the exemplar model.

4.3 Evaluation Metrics

The general evaluation metric for frame identification is accuracy: the relative frequency of correct assignments to predicates. Since the task of frame identification is moot for single-frame lexical units, frame identification systems standardly (Das et al., 2014; Peng et al., 2018; Hermann et al., 2014) report accuracy on two different subsets of the data: (1) all instances from the test set, called "Full Lexicon", because it includes lexical units that are unambiguous; and (2) only instances of predicates from the test set that can evoke multiple frames, called "Ambiguous". In the data set we use, the test partition contains 2,029 ambiguous predicates out of a total of 4,458 predicate instances.

In addition, some prior work reports specific metrics on infrequent predicates, for which prediction is particularly challenging. "Unseen" reports accuracy for predicates that are completely unseen in the training data and their predictions over all possible frames – meaning the frame lexicon is not used for evaluation at test time[1]. "Rare" reports accuracy on predicates that occur less than 11 times in the training

---

[1](Das et al., 2014) improve their Unseen results with a graph that was constructed over a large corpus of sentences in combination with the FrameNet lexical unit example sentences. We only report Unseen results which where produced over the

	Model	Full Lexicon	Ambiguous	Rare	Unseen
Results from literature	Das et al. (2014)	83.60	69.19	82.31	23.08
	Hermann et al. (2014)	88.41	73.10	85.04	44.67
	Hartmann et al. (2017)	87.63	73.8	NA	NA
	Yang and Mitchell (2017)	88.2	75.7	NA	NA
	Peng et al. (2018)	90.0	78.0	NA	NA
	Model	**Full Lexicon**	**Ambiguous**	**Rare**	**Unseen**
Our Work	Bottom-up Exemplar	82.52	64.44	81.09	11.07
	Bottom-up Prototype	84.67	69.18	83.68	09.59
	Bottom-up + Top-down Exemplar	84.09	65.06	84.18	18.89
	Bottom-up + Top-down Prototype	**91.26**	**80.77**	**91.85**	30.20

Table 1: Accuracy results for Frame Identification on Das et al. (2014) benchmark dataset (test partition) data. The test set contains 144 unseen and 2,555 rare predicates.

5 Results

Table 1 shows the performance of the four models as well as prior results from recent literature. Regarding the impact of the exemplar and prototype dimensions that we introduced in Section 3, we find that the exemplar model does worse overall than the prototype model in both configurations (overall "Full Lexicon" accuracy: 2% for bottom-up, 7% for bottom-up plus top-down). This indicates that the prototype setup appears better suited to the task than the exemplar one, at least on the data we experimented with. Second, we see a substantial effect of top-down processing (fine-tuning): 1.5% for exemplars, over 6% for prototypes. The clear winner is the bottom-up plus top-down (fine-tuned) prototype model: with an accuracy of 91.26%, it outperforms the previous state of the art (Peng et al., 2018). This shows that frame categorization can indeed profit from task-based optimization. That being said, it is worth noting that even the bottom-up prototype model with only generic pre-training performs at or above the level of the supervised SEMAFOR model (Das et al., 2014) which incorporated linguistic and ontological features in a log-linear model. Thus, the bottom-up vector space models do have a claim to robust performance.

Accuracy on "Ambiguous" predicates largely mirrors the patterns we find on "Full Lexicon" accuracy. They bolster the interpretation that both prototype representation and fine-tuning lead to clear gains. Results on "Rare" and "Unseen" predicates are more difficult to compare due to lack of reported results (marked as NA). The numbers for "Rare", again, seem to follow the "Full Lexicon" trend, and outperform the state of the art. The results for the "Unseen" category do so too, but are below the previously reported results. The reason is that Das et al. (2014) employ additional processing to unseen predicates based on a context similarity graph. For simple supervised classification without the extra component, comparable to our 30.20% setting, they report an Accuracy of 23.08%.

5.1 Sentence Length

Next, we aim to determine how much the sentence length affects predictions of classes in the bottom-up versus the bottom-up plus top-down models. Results are shown in Figure 2. We find that the performance of the bottom-up models declines as sentence length increases, and the opposite is seen in the top-down prototype model.

The most natural explanation for this pattern starts from the realization that the BERT model incorporates long-range dependencies via its self-attention mechanisms. That is, these long-range dependencies, coupled with the bidirectionality in the BERT model, introduces a rich notion of context. However, in the

---

full-text annotations for fair comparison.

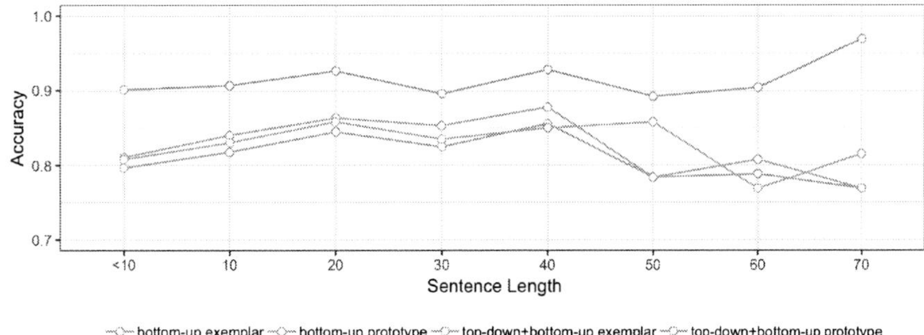

Figure 2: Impact of sentence length on accuracy

Frame	BU+TD Prototype	BU+TD Exemplar	BU Prototype	BU Exemplar
CAPABILITY	1.00	0.73	0.48	0.73
POSSESSION	1.00	0.94	0.92	0.81
WEAPON	1.00	0.97	0.98	1.00
LOCATIVE_RELATION	0.97	0.84	0.89	0.79
TEMPORAL_COLLOCATION	0.89	0.76	0.76	0.71

Table 2: Accuracies for top 5 frames from Bottom-up+Top-down Prototype model across all four model

bottom-up models these self-attention weights have the potential to introduce noise for long sentences, which is exactly what we observe. In contrast, fine-tuning of the self-attention weights can apparently turn long sentences into an asset by providing rich context hints for improved frame classification.

The outlier in this analysis is the fine-tuned bottom-up plus top-down exemplar model whose performance fluctuates between the fine-tuned prototype model and the bottom-up models. Given the analysis of the previous paragraph, this may not be surprising: the supervision provided to the fine-tuned exemplar model is less informative than that for the prototype model (cf. Section 3.2): the exemplar supervision does not name the frame(s) involved, and only provides information for one predicate pair in a potentially long sequence. Arguably, this makes it much more difficult for BERT to properly adapt its self-attention weights.

5.2 Frame-level and Predicate-level Analysis

We now look at the most accurate frames and predicates from our best model and compare the accuracies for these inputs across our four models. This analysis gives us insight regarding what types of semantic information are already learned by the bottom-up models versus the knowledge that is gained by learning frame-specific semantics in the top-down setting.

Table 2 shows the analysis at the frame level. The best model assigns three frames perfectly. For one of them, CAPABILITY, there is a dramatic performance gap, where the other models show accuracies of 0.73 and less. This frame includes lexical units such as *can.v* and *able.a*, which are both frequent and unspecific and therefore somewhat difficult to learn without frame-specific tuning. The same is true for three other frames, POSSESSION, and TEMPORAL_COLLOCATION, and LOCATIVE_RELATION, which also have a high number of frequent, ambiguous predicates including modals and prepositions (*have.v, in.prep, on.prep*). The final frame, WEAPON, behaves rather differently in that the models perform almost equally well. Since the predicates in this frame form a coherent topic and tend to be low in ambiguity (*bomb.n, missile.n, shotgun.n*), they are quite easily learned with only generalized embeddings.

The analysis at the predicate level is shown in Table 3. We see a distinction very similar to the frame

Predicate	**BU+TD** **Prototype**	BU+TD Exemplar	BU Prototype	BU Exemplar
people.n	1.00	1.00	0.97	0.97
know.v	0.96	0.89	0.90	0.87
have.v	0.92	0.85	0.85	0.74
in.prep	0.91	0.69	0.80	0.59
can.v	0.91	0.59	0.29	0.62

Table 3: Accuracies for top 5 predicates from Bottom-up+Top-down Prototype model across four model

level between high-ambiguity and low-ambiguity predicates. Highly frequent, ambiguous predicates such as *have.v*, *know.v*, *can.v*, and *in.prep* profit hugely from frame-specific fine-tuning since their pre-trained, contextualized embeddings are presumably more widely spread out. In contrast, the *people.n* predicate performs well in all models including the bottom-up ones.

6 Discussion and Conclusions

In this paper, we have taken up an old strand of research in cognitive psychology, categorization, and demonstrated how such research contributes to computational lexical semantics. We have argued that theories of categorization have something valuable to offer to neural embedding-based models of natural language semantics, namely a framework in which to ground model design and understand their consequences. We have considered two dimensions: (a) the distinction between prototype and exemplar categorization, where prototype models produce a summary representation of its categories, while exemplar models represent the input objects themselves; and (b) the decision between pure similarity-driven "bottom-up" categorization, and task-specific "top-down" categorization, which finds its direct counterpart in current embedding models in the distinction between pre-trained and fine-tuned embeddings.

Along these two dimensions, we have defined four models for frame-semantic frame identification with BERT embeddings. Empirically, we found that for this task it worked best (a) to learn category representations via a prototype, and (b) to fine-tune the representations with a small amount of frame-labeled data. Further analysis showed that the benefit of the fine-tuning was in particular to improve model performance in the face of *abstractness* and *ambiguity*: while all models work well on frames describing coherent, concrete topics and containing concrete predicates drawn from their topics (WEAPONS), only fine-tuned models perform well on frames that capture abstract semantic generalizations that do not correspond to coherent regions in embedding space (LOCATIVE_RELATION) or ambiguous predicates such as the predicate *can.v*, which is able to evoke five frames: PRESERVING, CAPABILITY, LIKELIHOOD, and POSSIBILITY.

While the benefit of fine-tuning is expected based on previous work, the relative performance of prototype and exemplar models was less predictable. Our analysis indicates that the outcome of our study – a win for prototypes – is presumably tied to the studies' use of full-text frame annotation, which can be exploited straightforwardly in a prototype setting to tune the long-distance dependencies captured by BERT's self-attention mechanisms.

References

Baker, C. F., C. J. Fillmore, and J. B. Lowe (1998). The Berkeley FrameNet project. In *Proceedings of ACL/COLING*, Montreal, QC, pp. 86–90.

Bellet, A., A. Habrard, and M. Sebban (2013). A survey on metric learning for feature vectors and structured data. *CoRR abs/1306.6709*.

Daelemans, W. and A. van den Bosch (2005). *Memory-based Language Processing*. Studies in natural language processing. Cambridge University Press.

Das, D., D. Chen, A. F. Martins, N. Schneider, and N. A. Smith (2014). Frame-semantic parsing. *Computational Linguistics 40*(1), 9–56.

Das, D., N. Schneider, D. Chen, and N. A. Smith (2010). Probabilistic frame-semantic parsing. In *Proceedings of NAACL/HLT*, Los Angeles, California, pp. 948–956.

Devlin, J., M.-W. Chang, K. Lee, and K. Toutanova (2018). BERT: Pre-training of deep bidirectional transformers for language understanding. *arXiv preprint arXiv:1810.04805*.

Erk, K. (2009). Representing words as regions in vector space. In *Proceedings of CoNLL-2009*, Boulder, CO, pp. 57–65.

Erk, K. and S. Padó (2010). Exemplar-based models for word meaning in context. In *Proceedings of ACL*, Uppsala, Sweden, pp. 92–97.

Fillmore, C. J. (1982). Frame Semantics. In *Linguistics in the Morning Calm*, pp. 111–138. Seoul, Korea: Hanshin.

Gardner, M., J. Grus, M. Neumann, O. Tafjord, P. Dasigi, N. F. Liu, M. Peters, M. Schmitz, and L. Zettlemoyer (2018). Allennlp: A deep semantic natural language processing platform. In *Proceedings of Workshop for NLP Open Source Software (NLP-OSS)*, pp. 1–6. Association for Computational Linguistics.

Gildea, D. and D. Jurafsky (2002). Automatic labeling of semantic roles. *Computational Linguistics 28*(3), 245–288.

Green, R., B. J. Dorr, and P. Resnik (2004). Inducing frame semantic verb classes from WordNet and LDOCE. In *Proceedings of ACL*, Barcelona, Spain, pp. 375–382.

Harris, Z. S. (1954). Distributional structure. *Word 10*(2-3), 146–162.

Hartmann, S., I. Kuznetsov, T. Martin, and I. Gurevych (2017). Out-of-domain framenet semantic role labeling. In *Proceedings of EACL*, Valencia, Spain, pp. 471–482.

Hermann, K. M., D. Das, J. Weston, and K. Ganchev (2014). Semantic frame identification with distributed word representations. In *Proceedings of ACL*, Baltimore, MD, pp. 1448–1458.

Hill, F., K. Cho, S. Jean, and Y. Bengio (2017). The representational geometry of word meanings acquired by neural machine translation models. *Machine Translation 31*(1–2), 3–18.

Hintzman, D. L. (1986). "Schema abstraction" in a multiple-trace memory model. *Psychological review 93*(4), 411.

Howard, J. and S. Ruder (2018). Universal language model fine-tuning for text classification. In *Proceedings of ACL*, Melbourne, Australia, pp. 328–339.

Lieto, A., D. P. Radicioni, and V. Rho (2017). Dual peccs: a cognitive system for conceptual representation and categorization. *Journal of Experimental & Theoretical Artificial Intelligence 29*(2), 433–452.

Mikolov, T., I. Sutskever, K. Chen, G. S. Corrado, and J. Dean (2013). Distributed representations of words and phrases and their compositionality. In *Proceedings of NIPS*, Lake Tahoe, NV, pp. 3111–3119.

Mitchell, J. and M. Lapata (2008). Vector-based models of semantic composition. In *Proceedings of ACL*, Columbus, OH, pp. 236–244.

Murphy, G. L. (2002). *The Big Book of Concepts*. Boston, MA: MIT Press.

Nosofsky, R. M. (1986). Attention, similarity, and the identification–categorization relationship. *Journal of Experimental Psychology: General 115*(1), 39–61.

Nosofsky, R. M. and S. R. Zaki (2002). Exemplar and prototype models revisited: Response strategies, selective attention, and stimulus generalization. *Journal of Experimental Psychology: Learning, Memory, and Cognition 28*(5), 924–940.

Peng, H., S. Thomson, S. Swayamdipta, and N. A. Smith (2018). Learning joint semantic parsers from disjoint data. In *Proceedings of NAACL*, pp. 1492–1502.

Posner, M. I. and S. W. Keele (1968). On the genesis of abstract ideas. *Journal of Experimental Psychology 77*(3), 353–363.

Radford, A., K. Narasimhan, T. Salimans, and I. Sutskever (2018). Improving language understanding with unsupervised learning. Technical report, OpenAI.

Reisinger, J. and R. J. Mooney (2010). Multi-prototype vector-space models of word meaning. In *Proceedings of HLT/NAACL*, Los Angeles, CA, pp. 109–117.

Rosch, E. (1975). Cognitive representations of semantic categories. *Journal of Experimental Psychology: General 104*, 192–233.

Smith, E. and S. A. Sloman (1996). Similarity- versus rule-based categorization. *Memory & Cognition 22*(4), 377–386.

Socher, R., A. Perelygin, J. Wu, J. Chuang, C. D. Manning, A. Ng, and C. Potts (2013). Recursive deep models for semantic compositionality over a sentiment treebank. In *Proceedings of the 2013 Conference on Empirical Methods in Natural Language Processing*, pp. 1631–1642. Association for Computational Linguistics.

Vaswani, A., N. Shazeer, N. Parmar, J. Uszkoreit, L. Jones, A. N. Gomez, Ł. Kaiser, and I. Polosukhin (2017). Attention is all you need. In *Proceedings of NIPS*, Long Beach, CA, pp. 5998–6008.

Yang, B. and T. Mitchell (2017). A joint sequential and relational model for frame-semantic parsing. In *Proceedings of EMNLP*, Copenhagen, Denmark, pp. 1247–1256.

Zhu, Y., R. Kiros, R. Zemel, R. Salakhutdinov, R. Urtasun, A. Torralba, and S. Fidler (2015). Aligning books and movies: Towards story-like visual explanations by watching movies and reading books. In *Proceedings of the IEEE international conference on computer vision*, Santiago, Chile, pp. 19–27.

Association for Computational Linguistics
209 N. Eighth Street
Stroudsburg, Pennsylvania 18360

ISBN 978-1-5108-8760-2